THE BOOK OF HEAVEN

A Story of Hope for the Outcasts, the Broken,
and Those Who Lost Faith

K. & H. Asher

Unless otherwise indicated, all scripture quotations are from The ESV® Bible (The Holy Bible, English Standard Version®), copyright © 2001 by Crossway, a publishing ministry of Good News Publishers. Used by permission. All rights reserved.

Excerpt from "*Science of the Heart, Exploring the Role of the Heart in Human Performance Volume 2*, by Rollin McCraty. Reprinted by permission.

Disclaimers:
I have changed some names to protect individuals' privacy.
This book does not replace the advice of a medical professional.
Consult your physician before making any changes to your diet or regular health plan.
To maintain the anonymity of the individuals involved, I have changed some details.
The information in this book was correct at the time of publication, but the Author does not assume any liability for loss or damage caused by errors or omissions.
These are my memories, from my perspective, and I have tried to represent events as faithfully as possible.
I have made every effort to contact all copyright holders.

Printed in U.S.A.

Table of Contents

PART TWO

To Ruth and Esther

How many deaths did I die
Before I was awakened to new life again?
And how many half-truths did I bear witness to
'Til the proof was disproved in the end?
And how long? How far?
What was meant to illuminate, shadowed me still
And all You ever wanted
Only me, on my knees
Singing, holy, holy
And somehow all that matters now is
You are holy, holy
And all I have is gratitude to offer You. [1]

Acknowledgments

The events recorded in this book are detailed to the best of our ability. It is our intention to share an important story that brings hope to many, not to harm anyone. If there is one thing we have learned, it's that God loves us, all of us, and wants each to repent and receive Jesus as their Savior and Lord. Despite how much it hurts, the truth is still the truth and demands to be told. Countless documents, emails, texts and other documentation have been reviewed to ensure the most accurate account of our story. Some parts of the story happened before I was born and very young, so I have done my best to corroborate my own memory and the recollections of others for those details. We recognize others may feel differently than we do about the events recorded in this book, but these events still happened and even more. In order to protect confidentiality, many of the names and places in this book have been changed.

To our family and friends who have walked this journey with us and given generously to make this book a reality, I cannot begin to tell you what your love and support has meant to us. Because of you we are rich beyond measure.

To my children, I know it's been the hardest life. I love you. Hold tight. God is good.

To J- and J-'s parents, you will always be our heroes, the moment when hope became real.

To Soma, like a stone thrown to the water with ripples never ceasing, you changed our lives.

To Sarah who loves me in the darkness as much as in the light, your friendship is one of my deepest treasures. In everything you seek Jesus, which is why I will always love you.

To Carol for sharing in my joy and sorrow, for listening and loving through it all.

To Shana who poured over every page meticulously and edited with wisdom, excellence, and love, your insights proved to be immeasurable. You took on this task simply out of love without knowing the depths you would go with me. I am forever grateful.

To Steve for your expertise, belief in a book that had barely begun to be written, and friendship. You are proof of how good-hearted men can be.

To Aaron Green for your relentless efforts to obtain print licenses and to the artists and publishing companies who granted me permission to print your work.

To HearthMath Institute and the executive committee for your support, and for granting me permission to use your research.

To Austin for your countless hours with Houston, for your dedication, inspiration, patience, and your endless dictation. You are a rock for Houston and so many others.

To Jen for your Herculean efforts and advocacy in working with our kids, doing what many of us can't.

To Suzanne and Grace for showing me the unseen and for loving Jesus.

To Melissa for being my defender, you were the first person who ever stood up for me against the strongholds. You were my shield. You give attorneys a good name.

To Dr. Noel for believing that anything is possible and proving it with your actions.

To Steve Brown for caring, for reading, for being honest, for praying for me, and for teaching truth and love. You will always be my favorite pastor.

xii

To Matt for listening to my shattered heart and just loving me with God's love.

To Mark and Kari for the gift of your hearts, for your incredible faith, devotion, and love, for your generosity and investment in our family, for your friendship that is immeasurable. I thank God for you for so many reasons. Your kindness fills my heart with gratitude.

To Tahni, Chrissy, Carole, Leigh, Sabra and the many other women in our group who contributed to this book, made a safe place for those of us who have nowhere to share our hearts, who know how hard this journey is and still praise our Savior.

To Carol for the gift of your heart. It is my prayer that our miracles are just beginning.

To Andrea, Kristie, Wynn, and Nancy who read this book and delved into the vastness of our hearts, thank you for loving us.

To Libby for being the other half of my heart in more ways than I may ever know. Where have you been all my life? You are joy, love, and goodness down to your very core.

To all Houston's teachers, coaches, and therapists who love him like he's your own. Thank you for the years of love and effort to reach him, teach him, to be his friend. This is *our* victory.

To Houston's many voiceless friends for their courage and faith despite adversity that is beyond comprehension. You are beautiful and brilliant and wonderfully made. Heroes, every one.

I especially want to mention how grateful we are to Josiah Cullen and our friend Jordyn; you are both prophets, called by God and obedient to His calling.

Ido Kedar, you are a brilliant hero and your words have rescued more people than you know.

To the parents who live life never getting to live life because they choose to love their child, God sees us.

To the elder at my church who believes that God heals and answers the impossible prayers.

To Him, to LOVE. For *better is one day in your courts than a thousand elsewhere.* [2]

[2] Psalm 84:10

Introduction

"When we try to pick out anything by itself,
we find it hitched to everything else in the Universe."
— John Muir, 1911

This is the story of a miracle - more accurately, more miracles than I may ever know. John Muir was right. Everything, every action, being and breath is connected in the most beautiful labyrinth of wild wrong and beautiful good. Our Maker is Life and Love itself and the author of this reckless ride. In complete honesty, I never believed I would see a real miracle like water turning into wine or the lame walking or the mute speaking. I thought those miracles were just in Biblical times. I was convinced good would never come in this life. After a long life of struggles, I was granted a glimpse, one minute of miraculous. In that moment I was given a choice. I could accept reality or believe in the miracle I longed for. I decided to believe in the impossible. It was a fundamental shift and it changed everything. For almost five years while being bombarded with reasons to give up on my little seed of faith, I kept believing with absolutely nothing else to cling to except my one glimpse at what could be and the faith it sparked. Then, I got it - the impossible, the unexplainable, the unbelievable. It changed everything. To tell this miracle I have to tell the hard part. I really don't want to, but it's necessary for many reasons, most importantly to show how God loves to show His power by turning mourning into dancing, like He turned mud into man.

"Truth is like poetry. And most people don't f...ing like poetry." [3] And there we have it. That is exactly how I feel about my truth. After all, "Woe is me is not an attractive narrative." [4] Anytime I would try to insist on justice, the biggest perpetrator of injustice in my life would mock me and tell me I had a victim mentality. That one statement alone kept me silent and conflicted. I could not deny the damage done to my life and heart but somehow, I was supposed to feel great about it, unaffected, oblivious to who was responsible and do nothing about it. Somehow, I was supposed to be as hard hearted and cruel as those who find joy in crushing others. I'm from the *grin and bear it* generation, which considered the discussion of any abuse or trauma experienced to be bad manners and in poor taste. How convenient for those doling out the wrongdoing or too self-absorbed to care. The world loves to put the weight of wrong on the recipients and tell the wrong makers they should feel no shame, all is forgiven. This is the paradox of a world that has no stomach for holding the guilty responsible and no heart for weeping with and for the brokenhearted. Bootstraps and a *might makes right* philosophy are our governors. Yet, those who have been worn down or find themselves living under the sole of someone's boot can't stay there, even if no one is there to help, even if there is no justice.

Over the years as the story was happening, I lost count of how many people in astonishment would exclaim, "You have to write a book!" I would always shrug it off. Who wanted to read that? My kids needed me. I didn't have time to write another book. I didn't want to relive the pain. I used to avoid support groups because I had enough just carrying the weight of my own journey. I preferred pretending like I was coping well enough under the circumstances. I hid my truth behind my smile. That's all people wanted to see anyway.

---

[3] Adam McKay; The Big Short
[4] Maureen Dowd

When the miracle began, there was even more insistence. I would respond that it was an easy statement to make by those who had never gone through the process of writing a book. There was also safety in privacy. Eventually, their persistence worked. I decided to start persuading Houston that we needed to tell our story. I had a specific direction and message that would avoid some of the more difficult parts of our lives. We would bring awareness to one of the most life altering and misunderstood challenges of our time, non-speaking and unreliably speaking autism. In my mind it was settled. But Houston was resolute. His focus was intent on something much more grand, important, and eternal. He only wanted to talk about one thing. God. We did not agree. I knew the risks. But he had seen the truth and refused to write if he couldn't write what he had witnessed and knew to be true. "I am God's herald. I am going to tell about God's love for us," he told me. We were at an impasse. And so the book idea was pushed to the bottom of our endless sea of projects and therapies.

My daughter gave me empty journals and told me I was a writer and needed to start writing again. Like an obstinate child I shut her kind encouragement in a drawer so I wouldn't be reminded. I focused on work and my son's endless therapeutic efforts. NO. That was my defiant and resolute answer. Even though our story was true, the risks of telling it were too great. It was my job to protect my son. In His infinite wisdom and pursuit of *His* purposes, not mine, God decided to send me to Nineveh, or someplace like it, after I had already been living in the wilderness most of my life. It was uprooting and filled with so much that made me want to hide forever.

And that's when Houston joyfully declared it was time to write. And like someone who's been spit out of a whale's belly, I complied, begrudgingly. God removed any distractions that prevented me from writing, first my job and then a global pandemic so I couldn't job hunt. He surrounded me with loving people who would ask fun questions every time we talked, such as, "How's the book coming?" "How many pages have you written?" and "What's your writing schedule?" FINE! Alright, already! People who love you can really be annoying trying to encourage you to do what's necessary.

There was discouragement too. "Everyone has sad stories. Why would anyone want to read yours?" I didn't know how to respond when my friend said that to me after I had started this process, probably because I agreed. It was easy for me to give into those voices and thoughts because it meant I could keep hiding. True, some stories are worth telling because the ending is so great or because the person's endurance or heroism inspires us to our own greatness. I wasn't feeling those hallmarks. The safety of smallness seemed wise actually. Then Houston told me, "Jesus told me to tell you - I love your story. That is what I want to use to work good." *Ugh* was my heart's response. The message was straightforward and in direct opposition to my hesitancy. But could I trust Him to protect me if I shared the stories I had been hiding in my heart all these years? Could I trust Him after everything? Well, no. Not the way I wanted to define protection. "Safe? Who said anything about safe? 'Course he isn't safe. But he's good. He's the King, I tell you."[5] So, even though I am scared, I am telling this story for Him. After all, the story is true, and He is the author.

"Writing about yourself seems to be a lot like
sticking a branch into clear river-water and rolling up the muddy bottom." [6]

I still struggle with internal resistance. So much of this story is difficult to share. I know there are pieces, painful, private pieces, I will keep to myself and sweet secrets too. Yet I still hope to share enough that the reader will understand the thoughts, failures, wanderings, and prayers I have traversed. I have told portions of my story before, usually with a focus on one aspect of my life, but never as I actually lived it, all woven and tangled together, with yearnings and struggles fighting for domination. When you get to the place where you feel like you have been drinking from the fire hydrant that is my life, please keep reading and remember you were warned. I promise the end is worth it. As I think about it, wrestling has always characterized my life - a battle with grit, long endured and intertwined, so

---

[5] The Lion the Witch and the Wardrobe; C.S. Lewis
[6] Shawshank Redemption

much so that the two opponents appear as one being, seem as one flesh, with no end, no final triumphant arm ever raised. I must admit, an end is what I have longed for. It's just gone on too long. People with no real trouble think that sounds weak, but they don't know. Rest is wonderful to the weary. I promise I'm not being melodramatic.

Houston scolded me that I must stop that thought. I am not to think how much I long for the end of the race. I am to put all my energy and effort into the belief that in the faith and effort, everything will one day be made new. He's right. So I take another breath. I pause. I gulp. I keep fighting. I don't concede, no matter how big the adversities, no matter how strong the enemies. To the outside it might appear I am fighting a losing battle. It often feels that way on the inside too. But from the outside and the inside it can't be seen what God is doing from above. He looks at my struggle knowing the wonder He is weaving through my fight, knowing losing only happens when I quit seeking Him. For this reason, for His good and His love which has never left me, I cannot quit. I've tried. No one will let me. Though my enemies will not relent, though my friends and even those who love me forsake me, though everything has been used up or stolen, I will continue this fight. *"Though the wrong seems oft so strong, God is the ruler yet. This is my Father's world. The battle is not done. That Jesus who died will be satisfied. Oh earth and heaven will be one."* [7] And one day, I will be home and there will be peace.

"Security is mostly a superstition.
It does not exist in nature, nor do the children of men as a whole experience it.
Avoiding danger is no safer in the long run than outright exposure.
The fearful are caught as often as the bold. Faith alone defends.
Life is either a daring adventure, or nothing."
— Helen Keller

[7] This is My Father's World; Maltbie D. Babcock

PART ONE

Before there was time
There were visions in Your mind
There was death in the fall of mankind
But there was life in salvation's design

Before there were days
There were nights I could not see Your face
But the night couldn't keep me from grace
When You came and You took my place

Before there was time
You counted the hairs on my head
You knew all the words that I've said
You purchased me back from the dead

Before I was made
You searched me and knew my ways
You numbered all of my days
And You set forth the steps I would take

So I cry holy only
Begotten Son of God
Ancient of days
Cry holy only
Begotten Son of God
And sing the praises
Of the One who saved me
And the promises He made [8]

---

[8] *Before There Was Time*; By Aaron Senseman. Copyright Msi Music admin. o/b/o Stuntman Music

1

Before There Was Me

*Know therefore that the LORD your God is God, the faithful God
who keeps covenant and steadfast love with those who love Him
and keep His commandments, to a thousand generations.*
—Deuteronomy 7:9

My dad grew up in Des Moines, Iowa, the oldest of four children who took seriously his responsibility to help his mother. She needed him. He mentioned how grown up it made him feel to be put in charge and how his mother always told him how much he helped her and how important it was. His dad was a quiet man. Severe epileptic seizures had resulted in the loss of his factory job. The daily dose of lithium and a severe hearing loss resulted in a father who sat quietly on the couch in front of the television, not engaging much with anyone. This put all the burden of providing on my grandmother Ruth, a hardworking, God fearing schoolteacher. Ruth always felt like she had been disobedient to God's calling to be a missionary. Her identical twin sister, Esther, answered that call. Esther never married and was dearly loved by her many nieces and nephews. Ruth and Esther were two of six children raised in the depression in the rural Midwest. Their youngest brother David, in his old age, sent my dad a gift and a letter reminiscing about his sister Ruth. He told my dad that Ruth was one of the most loving and remarkable people he had ever known. He wanted to make sure my dad knew how special his mother was.

From what I know, Ruth loved Jesus and had a faith that got people talking, sometimes good, and sometimes not. I only have a few distinct stories of my grandmother. She would fall asleep writing letters of faith and encouragement at the kitchen table to the many people in her life, the pen trailing off into ineligible scribble. She saw it as her duty to love everyone God introduced to her and make sure they knew about Jesus Christ and His amazing grace. But she was a wife and mother and her scope of influence seemed quite limited from her perspective. She prayed. A lot. She was never idle. Every moment of her life had purpose. At dinner every night she would triumphantly announce the total cost of that particular meal, daily trying to outdo her own frugality. She said prayers of gratitude for the big wheel of government cheese. She ran late for everything. I got the impression she was running a race to fit as much life and love into her days as possible. Maybe she knew there was a countdown. Maybe that's how we should all live.

My grandfather didn't have the same sense of urgency about anything. He would wait in the car for her to get everyone ready for church and be annoyed at her tardiness yet unwilling to assist. She was a horrible driver. Once on an ice-covered road the car started spinning out of control. She threw her hands up in the air and screamed repeatedly, "Jesus help me! Jesus help me!" as the car spun out of control until it finally landed in a ditch with a backseat full of wide-eyed children and no seatbelts. In true Jesus take the wheel fashion, this was answered prayer. To her children, I got the impression they would have rather her faith was sustained with her hands on the wheel in silent prayer. She would have my dad read her daily Bible reading to her as she drove him around town. He was not fooled. He knew this was her trying to put God's word in his heart. There is a story about once, when she was worshipping, that had a lasting impression on my dad and definitely on Ruth's in-laws. This particular Sunday she was caught up with the Holy Spirit and began dancing up the aisle. My dad stood watching from a pew, frozen and abashed, 'That's - - my - - mom.' This was just not something that was done in front of this side of the family. Apparently, my German great grandparents were angry and mortified by their daughter-in-law's Sunday worship scene. They were strong, steady, serious farmers where there still remained a good amount of Mennonite influence. Lancaster, Pennsylvania was deep in their roots. Besides being virtuous and humble, they valued discretion in every manner of life. All the fences on their farm and all seven gables on their farmhouse were always whitewashed. The cows even knew better than to escape their pastures. The china was turned upside down at each setting for each meal until grace had been offered. They sat on their pew every Sunday. Everyone and everything knew its place. There was never an excuse for spectacle. They were iconic *American Gothic*. Good, responsible, and honorable to their core. In their old age when I knew them, I think they had softened or maybe they were just happy to have family visiting. I imagine Ruth must have struggled with that judgment of her worship or maybe of her. But I also know at that time, the expectations were different. She was different. Her faith had power. It had joy.

Certainly, she made mistakes too. I know of some that my aunt told me. When I heard one of those mistakes, it didn't seem like it was about her, but I understood how someone like her ended up being pulled by a thousand different familial pressures, making choices that likely burdened her heart of love and wearied her spirit. At some point, Ruth cut off her long. beautiful braid that my grandfather loved and gave it to him. With the weight of life, she needed one less thing holding her back. Heaven was beckoning. When she finally went to the doctor regarding the grapefruit sized lump in her chest, there was not much time left. She had just been too busy taking care of others to take care of herself. Maybe there were other reasons too, but that would be speculation on my part. She saw any adversity she experienced as a consequence for not following God to the mission field, even the cancer. In these last days a minister tried to console her self-doubt and condemnation. I can only hope that she found peace here before she found peace in His arms. The loss of Ruth changed everything. The love and faith she was so determined to impart was suddenly cut short.

At the funeral for blocks and blocks, there were cars and people lined up outside because the church could not fit all of the people that wanted to honor my grandmother. My dad said he has never seen so many people at a funeral before or since. He thought to himself, 'How does she know all these people??' But that was Ruth, spreading the story of Jesus and living His love with her every breath. My dad was 17 when she died. I believe that pain is still in his heart. He left for college a few months later and the whole family scattered. My uncle left to play college ball and then went to the west coast where he found love. My aunt doubled up on work and school, moving out to find a life and family of her own as quickly as she could. Her goal was always to have a family to love well. She did just that. My youngest aunt was left alone with a father who did not talk much, and she ran her brilliant mind to a university as fast as her determined self could. The world doesn't have enough degrees to prove how much her mind is capable of. Ruth was the spirited, selfless rock that rooted them all. And she was gone.

After a few years at a small Midwestern evangelical college my dad met my mother. Virginia was several years younger. This was the late sixties, and while they were shielded from the drug culture, they were not shielded from the shift that had taken place across the generational lines or from the ghosts in their past. My mother had a beautiful voice and was strangely brilliant. I always thought she looked like a sad Elizabeth Taylor without all the heavy makeup. I never saw her smile. My dad was captivated, thrilled at the match. I think she saw my dad as an escape from her father. My dad saw her as the new start to a family he wanted so much to replace. Of course, he should have known better. The signs of instability were everywhere, but, thinking like a girl, he believed he could fix her.

She was from a Pentecostal family in South Georgia. Southern Baptist is the norm in that part of the state, so I always had the feeling her family was a little outside of typical. It wasn't until later that I knew how much outside. My dad, who grew up in a tidy home with a tidy budget in a tidy town, went to meet his new finance's parents. He drove up to a scanty trailer, unprepared for his introduction to what can only be described as a freakish mixture of brilliance, insanity, good, evil, and hoarding he had not even known was possible. Although I don't have an image, I have seen subsequent decor in some of these dwellings, so I have an idea of what assaulted my dad's senses. As his eyes began to adjust his mind was racing to determine why, how (or anything really) to explain what he saw. There, centered in a corner, was a large wooden monster of an archaic television, upon top of which was placed a second television, then a third, and finally a fourth teetering, towering and buzzing its technicolor 1969 glamour. Apparently, when one television died, it was not replaced per se, just repurposed as a TV stand or tower as it had become over the years.

The trailer seeped with heaviness, darkness, and hidden cruelty. My dad knew nothing of this realm to recognize when to run. My grandmother was a scared woman, focused on her ailments and the eggshells she tip-toed through. Her faith was a simple one. She loved her children, but she had no power. Then there were the men of the family. My great grandfather was called the walking Bible. With his photographic memory, it was rumored he had memorized the entire Bible. He was brilliant but ruled his family with terror and violence. He would take his son along with him to share the Lord and leave him to wait outside the homes of the women he would visit. Obviously, the gospel he preached was not for children's eyes and ears. The base carnality, draped with Scripture, could not be masked no matter how swiftly and sharply he spoke the Word of God. He had a mind that could out manipulate anyone stupidly daring enough to contradict or confront him. His son, my grandfather, had the same brilliant, maniacal mind. He was an inventor, a man whose mind never stopped moving, a musician, who instilled music in both of his children, an abuser who twisted and used people for his own power and control, and a molester.

I only saw my grandfather a few times in my entire life, the last was at my mother's funeral. From the little I know, this moment does suitable justice to depict his character. I remember him laughing a queer laugh, one that bordered on bizarre, particularly while his daughter's ashes stood nearby. I watched in astonished silence as this old, skinny, creepy man poked, tickled, and teased a 17-year-old Filipino girl who I quickly discovered was his daughter, his *other* daughter. I, his granddaughter, was 36. I remember hearing when I was 18 that my grandfather had taken an 18-year-old bride from the Philippines. And here was the child from that child bride. I had no words.

Except for my grandmother, none of her family seemed able to grasp the solemnity of the moment or offer any love, respect, or remembrance of my mother. I had only a handful of memories and they weren't happy. These men shed no tears. It resembled a potluck church basement barbeque rather than a wake. My uncle had met with me earlier and, with gleeful voyeurism, asked if I wanted to see my mother before she was cremated. "Without her wig!" he whispered excitedly and half-chuckled and choked to stop the laugh that came from somewhere deep inside him. My skin crawled and I felt myself trembling in the Memphis heat and humidity of August. I shook my head silently, my tacit reply, biting my lip so I wouldn't cry and so my jaw would not drop in shocked horror. When I changed into a black dress for my mother's memorial service and stepped into the living area of my grandmother's dark, dated nursing home for the poor, my uncle and grandfather gawked at me, and uttered what I can only describe as a catcall. They looked at me with lust and chuckled. Under their gaze I felt shame. My stomach groaned with nausea as I sat there, trapped with these people that disgusted me. I sat down quickly in a chair and put my hands under my legs, hunching over to hide any part of me they could stare at. My head began spinning with thoughts of what my mother had likely endured. I had brought pictures of my mother and me as a little girl to have something with which to connect to these strangers. They flipped through them indifferently, making jokes about other things, and tossed the pictures aside. I was repulsed that I shared any genetic relation to them. I remember not wanting to sit back in the chair, as if I might catch their particular strain of disturbed obscenity.

There were several other moments over the years that made me cringe and exposed the depravity in their hearts, even though they spoke freely of God. When my uncle died, I spoke to my aunt (long remarried) about how deeply uncomfortable he had made me feel. She told me there were no excuses and she could only imagine the details, but she could tell me that my mother and uncle were so badly abused that there was no way they could have ever lived a normal life with normal relationships. I share that so my mother's actions have some sense of explanation in her world of pain and madness.

When my mother met my dad in college, it was because she had moved across the country to live with my uncle and aunt who attended there as well. After she had divulged the molestation by my grandfather, they had taken her into their home. During this time, she invited unknown men to her brother's couch. Despite being caught, it kept happening. She was only 18 to 19 years old during this time period. This became a recurring and understandably unacceptable issue for my aunt and uncle in this evangelical community. Being young themselves and unaware of the depth of emotional and psychological effects from molestation, they likely viewed her behavior as inconsiderate to their offer of shelter, rebellious, maybe immoral, and shameful. I'm making assumptions based on statements made over the years. There was one much older man in particular, that my mother met during this period. She connected to him like a tether. No matter what other choices she made, that's where or to whom she was hooked. Then there was my dad. He came in as my mother's savior and was likely viewed quite heroically by the entire group. Sometimes I look back at all these old Baby Boomers and try to imagine them as the barely twenty-year-olds that they were, making enormous life decisions while blind, and unaware of all the future held. But of course, like all twenty-year-olds, they already knew everything. It was 1969. Love was the answer. What could possibly go wrong?

In short succession, life began happening. My dad graduated. My parents married. He was sent to Vietnam. As a graduate with a psychology degree, my dad had been assigned to a particular unit in the Army that had been given the harrowing task of tackling the heroin epidemic among the soldiers in Vietnam. His unit was charged with caring for soldiers while they went through withdrawal before they were sent back home. He lost all interest in psychology as a career after that experience. He came back home eager to start a family with his young wife. She had no problem conceiving, and they had a baby girl. This should have been a joyous occasion and a new start for two young people who wanted and needed a new beginning so much. But this little girl, my older sister, did not survive more than a few hours. She had anencephaly and did not fully develop enough to survive outside the womb. The details were the kind that break people's belief in happy endings and plant seeds of fear in its place. There was another miscarriage after that small life was lost. My mother, already a mess, became terrified of loss, terrified to love. Then I guess some force of nature came upon her and everything stuck whether she wanted it to or not, and she had me. She wasn't happy about it.

2

After I Arrived

For you formed my inward parts; you knitted me together in my mother's womb. I praise you,
for I am fearfully and wonderfully made. Wonderful are your works; my soul knows it very well.
My frame was not hidden from you when I was made in the secret place,
when I was woven together in the depths of the earth. Your eyes saw my unformed body;
all the days ordained for me were written in your book before one of them came to be.
How precious to me are your thoughts, God! How vast is the sum of them!
Were I to count them, they would outnumber the grains of sand—
when I awake, I am still with you.
— Psalm 139:13-18

My dad gave me the name Zoë Nicole after a character in a novel back when absolutely no one had that name. "Zoë means life, abundant life. I named you right," he would tell me over the years. Zoë is Greek, meaning a life real, genuine, active, vigorous, blessed and devoted to God. It is mentioned one hundred thirty times in the New Testament. Due to the relentless teasing I received from the name as a little girl, I was unimpressed with his choice. As an adult the name soared in popularity, to which I just shook my head. My timing has always been off. When I was a few months old, my young parents moved from the Midwest to a small South Georgia town to start life. There were no real roots there, so the decision seemed to be a strange one, perpetuated by the indiscriminate life forces that move people through life, like employment for a young person with no real direction still trying to figure out what he wanted to do when he grew up, and the rest of the family followed in tow. That's how Georgia became home. After all, if you don't know where you want to go, here is as good a place as any to call home. He probably wondered "Why Georgia Why?" long before John Mayer ever did.

My Mommy was not prepared to be a wife and mother. I'm certain she was still dealing with all the damage done in her childhood home. The lover she had met still had her heart. But life doesn't often pause to let you heal. Babies expect to be loved. Husbands who work expect there to be dinner. As I was busy being a baby and a toddler, there were other pregnancies that ended in miscarriage. The loss of my sister and the other miscarriages rooted in my mother's broken heart, turning the tender shoots and dreams of family into shards of glass piercing every part of her spirit. There is literally not one single photograph of her smiling, just beauty bathed in darkness. In every image she has a far-off look of deep overwhelming sadness, even with her baby girl giggling on her lap. The easiest way to explain what happened in the next few years is to say that this life just didn't suit my mother, the way broken glass doesn't suit an unquenched thirst. Maybe she read the <u>Feminine Mystique</u>. Maybe she saw other women leave. Maybe the pain of her past made being a mother too difficult. Maybe the lost children made the grief inescapable. Maybe she knew she made a mistake. Maybe I was too much.

While this was still not commonplace in the seventies, it was increasing in frequency as women began to grapple with the gender roles society defined for them, the reality of their relationships, and their own desires. But whatever her reasoning or feelings, the bottom line was this: She did not want to be a housewife or a mother and have a simple suburban life. She wanted a grand story and was still very young. She began having an affair and dreamed of becoming an actress. I remember her flair for the dramatic. After she left my dad, she would take me to her belly dancing class, and I would stare wide-eyed at all the bangles, bells, and belly buttons swirling like a dervish all around me while I stood rooted on that gymnasium floor in my little black and white saddle oxford shoes. Clearly, I had a heavy helping of those solid, unwavering German genes. How odd I must have seemed in that scene, like I was a lost child and had wandered into her life, uninvited. Maybe this was just some of the seventies and the permissiveness of the times rubbing off on her, but there was sadness and searching in her I recognized even as a little girl. Actually, it was more like a relentless chase, as if she was both being chased and chasing the unreachable.

Wanting to find a purpose beyond laundry and childcare, my mother became involved in community theater. For the time, it became her world. She had an affair with a married man and became pregnant. He was uninterested in more than a quick adulterous high and didn't even consider leaving his wife. Although she grieved the miscarriages, the fear of having someone else's child and the possible consequences overtook her. She had an abortion, a quick fix to circumstances spinning out of control. A hole she couldn't fill marked its place. There was a letter in her purse my dad found. When he confronted her, she announced she didn't love him and wanted a divorce. I was told there was almost no discussion by both of them. Despite the grief and anger of the moment my dad announced with a certain resoluteness that did not allow for debate - he was keeping me. That was that. She breathed a sigh of relief. Those were her words to me when I was 18 after I went searching for her. She told me how happy leaving him and leaving me had made her. She was free, she thought.

I remember that day. It was my first distinct memory that I could place on a timeline. As most children remember the past, the hall was probably not so ominously long, quiet and dark. After all, it was probably a standard 1200 sq ft ranch. And yet, even as a very little girl, I knew something serious was about to happen. When my dad called my name there was a knowing and soberness that made me not want to walk down the hall. I remember walking slowly and quietly, looking up at the walls and feeling so small. Eventually, they both sat on the couch facing me, probably trying to make eye contact and reassure me. My mother told me she was going to leave. They waited for my response. I understood. She wouldn't be there anymore. What's strange is how much I must have already sensed her not being present. Even that young, I knew. I asked with all the seriousness and consternation of a three-and-a-half-year-old in the midst of a life defining moment if I could visit her and what color was her kitchen. She told me years later that I had always been a daddy's girl which made her both resentful and relieved. It was part of her self-justification that she wasn't needed or wanted. She knew I would be just fine. And with that she was gone.

The rarity of her visits enhanced the vividness of those memories. One evening she took me to watch her perform. I knew it was a very adult thing to do, which made me feel special. But the places she took me never felt safe. I watched her pretend to be someone else and the oddity of the scene made an impression on me. I realized no one else's mommy was on stage and no other children were present. At some point I fell asleep in my seat and the stage and auditorium cleared. My mother left me sleeping in the dark theater and joined the cast party. I'm sure there was no ill intent. Motherhood was simply a vague afterthought made more dim after several cocktails. I don't remember many details except a feeling of darkness, terror and abandonment. Maybe that's when fear began. Maybe later. After that incident I saw my mother less frequently. My father was infuriated by her carelessness and indifference to my wellbeing. The attitude my dad had toward my mother shifted dramatically. If I was going to see her, my dad was angry, very angry, the kind you sense and tiptoe about without a word being spoken. At first, I saw her on the weekends, then every other weekend, then once a month, then once a year, then never again in my childhood. The decline in visitations was rapid, especially after they both remarried. I would be so eager when I knew she was coming and would wait expectantly but silently by the door. This was before the days of more rigorous child visitation enforcement by the courts, so as the parent with primary custody, he had all the power. There were some Friday afternoons when she didn't come. I restrained all the natural eagerness to see my mom so my dad wouldn't see it. I hated to see him angry. I held in my sadness and disappointment tightly in my little heart and pretended I was just fine. Although I had little data to interpret, my impression was straight forward. She didn't come get me because she didn't want to see me. It wasn't so much a head scratcher as it was a heart hurter. The environment was such that I knew I couldn't ask my dad why or tell him I missed her. It was the way things were and you were to keep quiet about it and move along. Even though I was young, I knew missing her was perceived as betrayal. My little heart grew heavy with all the things it couldn't say and wasn't allowed to feel.

Both of my parents remarried quickly it seemed to me. When my mother moved to Atlanta, five hours away, she had a totally new life. In her little apartment, she would make me an eagle's nest on the mornings I stayed with her. I thought it was absolutely magical. I had fantasies of living with her and what our life would be like. She bought me a doll and a Bad News Bear which she kept at her place for me to play with when I was there. A playbill, from one of her performances that she had framed, hung by the front door, and a gawdy 70's macrame owl seemed to stare at me over the couch. Thank goodness she didn't let the acid go to her head and go overboard with orange and pea green like the rest of that generation. It makes me chuckle recalling how the color of her kitchen and the details of her home mattered to me. Apparently, I wanted to decorate even before first grade. I was a very sweet, loving, and compliant little girl because I wanted my parents to spend time with me. Motherhood was just not the priority for this generation as it had been in generations past. It took a backseat to feminine self-discovery and careers. After all, isn't work how you show your worth? We were the latch key generation. Like most of us who grew up in the seventies and eighties, you entertained and even raised yourself. Attention was reserved for injuries, chores, lectures, and punishment.

When I heard my mother was getting married, there was anticipation in my little heart. I thought maybe this meant I would see her more and be part of her new family. I imagined all sorts of wonderful scenes in my future, each more idealistic, and in reality, ludicrous, given the facts of the situation. My mother married a man who was the epitome of the song Macho Man, popular at the time. He had bushy hair, a huge mustache, wore silky shirts unbuttoned to expose as much chest hair as possible and layers of necklaces. He walked with a 70's strut. I wondered incredulously to myself when I met him, "Men wear jewelry?? This is who she likes?" He was nothing, absolutely nothing like my daddy. Like everything else, I kept my disgust quiet. My mother's new husband came with two boys. As I watched these boys, strangers to me, playing wildly and loudly in my mother's new home, I couldn't see how this new arrangement would ever work and wondered how I would fit into this new family. How would my mother, who didn't want to parent a quiet little girl who liked to color and draw, ever parent two rambunctious boys, even if it was every other weekend? It was the oddest mismatch of personalities and relationships. 'This will never last,' I thought to myself, and shook my little head.

One night I lay under some covers on a make-shift bed in a sterile home office trying to calm my uneasiness at the strangeness of this new place so I could drift off to sleep. Then *he* suddenly appeared in the doorway and came and sat down uncomfortably close to me, the Macho Man. His hips were next to my head. The smell of his cologne was dense and thick. I waited in vain for my mother to appear, thinking maybe she was coming to tuck me in, but she never appeared. He kept trying to find things to talk to me about in the dark but barely spoke above a whisper. I nodded meekly to his questions and shrunk deeper into the covers to pull away from him. He rubbed his hairy hand on my back and my shoulders and petted my head. I squeezed my doll to my chest, frozen, hardly breathing. After a while he left. I couldn't shake the fear. I knew something about him wasn't right and didn't want to be alone with him. I never mentioned it to anyone because I never mentioned anything to anyone. After that night I visited my mother twice before my dad ended all the visitation. The last visit we celebrated my 8th birthday. My mother gave me the Broadway album of Annie for my birthday. It was the last gift I ever received from her. She had no idea it became my childhood anthem.

When it was just me and my dad, it was easy to see he was floundering, trying to figure it all out. Single parenthood was not what he had signed up for. Before my mother had left there had been steady bedtime stories and other moments of play that gave me a sense of belonging and peace. After she left, the eggshells were everywhere. The stress of his new life with me in tow rattled him. He had no mother or father to help and no ex-wife willing to do her share. I never wanted him to be upset with me. I remember wetting the bed and taking every single towel I could reach in the closet to cover the wet mattress and take care of it myself. Life was quiet and lonely. The best moments were each night after work when he would take me to Shoney's, and I would order the cheeseburger with an American flag. I loved Shoney's. Those simple meals with my daddy were the absolute happiest of my childhood. I was loved. I was safe. There was meat, cheese and fried potatoes with ketchup. Life was good.

My dad saw it differently. He was fixated on one thing, recasting the role my mother vacated and making sure everything looked like he thought it should. He tried all he could with his limited means to make a life for me. There was a glorious trip to Disney World and a trip to Washington state to be a flower girl in my uncle's wedding. My uncle was such a kind man. He had dated a girl he worked with in the mountains, and they hiked and lived life so joyfully. She sang songs and was silly and joyful. She loved me and I loved her. Her mother had made my flower girl dress and doted on me like I was her own. My new aunt was what love looked like. I played with my baby cousins and felt so grown up when I put my baby cousin on my hip. My other aunt found safety pins to hold my pants up that were far too large for me. There were hikes in the woods and dinners. There was love and I was happy. I saw in my dad's siblings what he didn't have. More than anything else, my dad wanted his own family with all the appropriate pieces. I realized that because the family was spread out all over the country, they couldn't be a part of my life. I was sad when everyone departed for their own homes, and it was just the two of us again. I could see my dad's sadness too.

One of the strangest trips was when he sent me to visit my mother's family in Virginia. I don't have any framework for how or why this arrangement was necessary, but for whatever the reason when I was five my dad put me on a plane by myself headed for Virginia. I was frightened but thrilled. The stewardess let me see the cockpit and gave me wings and checked on me often. I don't know how to describe the feeling other than to say it felt like adventure, like the unknown, terrifying and yet so very good. I felt independent and quite grown up for a little girl who still didn't know how to tie her shoes. For what seemed like a whole summer to my five-year-old recollection, but was probably only a week or two, I played with my cousins. My cousin Kristie and I were inseparable. She loved my curly hair and my saddle oxfords. We made lemonade stands and held garage sales and played every single moment we were awake. I loved my Aunt Francine. She was so good to me. Finally, there was family. I kept wondering if my mother would visit me there with her family. She never came. Then my dad arrived, there was a day by the water, and we visited D.C where I felt tiny and overwhelmed at the meaning behind the monuments. My spirit, although young, understood them. The visit was soon over, and I went back home. I missed my cousins. I missed my Aunt Francine. I missed my Mommy.

Christmas Eve that year my life was changed forever. I found out God loved me. I'm amazed now by His timing. He knew what was about to happen. He knew how much I would need to cling to Him. At the service with all the candles, wreaths, and robes, the pastor called all the children down to the front of the sanctuary to tell us a Christmas story. I still remember looking up at him in his robe and listening as he asked if anyone wanted a present. We all raised our hands. Kindly and carefully, he handed out little ornaments. Oh, how I bless that man without even knowing his name. He could never have known what He was about to do. He was just a man who had determined to be faithful to tell the good news of God's love, never knowing which seed he cast would root and grow beyond any gardener's dream. I took the little plastic red geometric ornament he handed me that encased a white flower with a red bead at its center and held it gently. The pastor then told us about how God wanted to give us a gift and that gift was far more precious than the one we held in our hands. It was His son, the Messiah, Jesus, the Christ. All we had to do to receive this most precious gift from God Himself was tell Him we were sorry for disobeying, believe He was the only way to be forgiven, and love Him when we received Him. I looked at my little red ornament that was mine now and something simple but extraordinary happened. I realized the gift was for me. Jesus was for me. I was for Him. And from that day on I belonged to Him. That little red ornament still hangs on my Christmas tree every year on the highest branch. A few years later I heard in a service that I needed to walk to the front of the church and say a certain prayer. At first, I was puzzled. I thought God was already in my heart. But not wanting to miss a step, I marched down there and did it again for others to see, just to be sure. 'You're with me God, *right?*'

After a short time in our home, my dad moved us into an apartment. Everything was changing. I wanted to be with my dad all the time, which was just not possible. He first took me to the Jack and Jill nursery. I remember most that while I was there my hair finally grew long enough for pigtails like the other girls. It was, in my short little life, the greatest thing that had happened. Finally, I didn't look quite as muc.75

h like a boy. The pigtails were so short and curly they curled into themselves and resembled tiny horns. Although not the long, straight hair I so wished to have, it was better than no pigtails at all. Many of my thoughts at that time were hoping not to be mistaken for a boy. Without knowing better, too often my dad dressed me like a boy. With my Shirley Temple hair, striped crew necks, and strange name, I was often mistaken for one. Adults and children would squint their faces as I said my name and ask with puzzlement in a thick South Georgia accent, "*Whud* you say your name wuz? *Joey??*" to see if they had misunderstood. Adults would chuckle with a fat belly laugh. "That's not a real name." "*Whud* did you name her that fur?" and my personal favorite, "Are you a boy or a girl?" Kids thought my name was weird and enjoyed making fun of it. The teasing was routine, and I did what I always did, took it in and never said a word. I felt very much alone.

After my mother had left, my dad found a woman, Pat, who watched children during the workday, mostly boys. It was a dark, hot home with dogs everywhere. She seemed a bit gruff and indifferent to the kids she watched, doing her due diligence to make certain we ate lunch, took naps, and stayed in the yard. Most of the time we were sent outside to play and there was not much to do. Hot wheel ramps were scattered everywhere in the house and there was always something boiling in the kitchen. There were no books. We were often kept busy shucking corn and snapping beans. The best moment was when the puppies were born. I stood in awe at their tiny bodies all overlapping and nestled together as they nursed. It was as if the mess of them had merged into one wiggly, warm, wonderful oneness. The mother looked at them with pride and exhaustion, examining us and then resting her head on her leg. After a long wait, I was allowed to hold one of the puppies and I thought I had never held anything so wonderful before that moment. Life, love… I went home so perfectly happy, as if I had discovered the secret to life. Then, in what only seemed to me to be a few days later, there were horrific tiny yelps in the yard. I went closer to see what the commotion was. I think I shrieked. Pat and another woman who we saw frequently were sitting at the picnic bench in the middle of the yard cutting off the puppies' tails and sewing them shut. One boy chased me with a puppy tail, laughing. I ran with a shriek and wouldn't go anywhere near. I didn't understand because there seemed to be no explanation. *Why?! It's babies!* It wasn't a cruel place, but it wasn't a kind place. There was nothing to do if you didn't like frogs, snails and puppy dog tails. The trauma of seeing her cut off the puppies' tails and sew them shut never left my thoughts. I hated what they did. I hated that place.

On my fifth birthday I lay sweating quietly on a bed next to a window, unable to take the required nap in the South Georgia summer heat with no air conditioning and a fan blowing hot sticky air. I saw my dad drive up and walk up to the house. My heart leapt and I sat straight up in bed. Excitedly I slipped my shoes on. I was going home early. My dad loved me and was rescuing me. Then in absolute shock and sadness I saw him get back in his car and drive off without me. I didn't understand and I lay there alone, crying silently. The critical part of this small moment is that the feeling struck something deep within me that stayed. Later that day we were all taken to the park and there was my dad with a cake and a party to surprise me. All I wanted in that moment was for my daddy to never leave me. That birthday was so different than the year before when my mom had been there serving and cutting cake with all my playmates. My relatives had called to talk to me, and I was given the most beautiful gift a girly girl could get, an umbrella to twirl. What a difference a year makes. My daddy was trying so hard to make my new life without a mother, happy and good, but it was like making a cake without sugar, it fell flat and was missing something essential.

One day at Pat's house, a new girl my age started coming on a somewhat regular schedule. I was thrilled to have a girl to play with in that very boy world. I didn't feel quite so alone while she was there. Pat, seeing our little friendship, decided to play matchmaker with my dad and my friend's mother. She was a young single mother and I guess Pat thought that was all my dad needed, and life would be all patched up perfectly. My dad had only dated a few women during his short life as a single father. He only dated this new woman a few (six) short weeks before they decided to marry and in a brief ceremony it was done. I was thrilled my friend would be my sister. That seemed like an answer to the loneliness.

Before he had met her my dad had asked me what she looked like, I took his arm and looked all over until I found a freckle. Pointing at the freckle I told him, "She has these ALLLLL over her. And her hair is orange." He laughed. Soon after, I visited my new friend's home, and I met her mother's roommate and her child. The roommate was bossy and unkind. She laughed gruffly without smiling and smoked constantly. I remember there was some reason we had to change clothes in one room, and I was quite modest. I had never undressed in front of a stranger and never seen a grown woman without clothes, even my mother. She saw my hesitancy and crudely said, "No one wants to look at you. We all have the same parts, just different sizes. Now change!" Everyone was poor, scrambling to make an existence and children were mostly in the way. They were quickly and crudely put in their place. It wasn't at all like my dad's home where there was peace and love even though something was missing. During my dad's brief courtship with his future wife, my little friend was finishing up hospital treatments. I remember once we drove to the parking lot of the hospital, and he pointed to her room so I could wave. That's all I remember of their dating. I don't remember any impression I had of this woman he proposed to before they were married. My dad told me later that his best friend and best man, who was a wise and good man, warned my dad not to marry her. "She is just a single mother looking for someone to support her and her child. Don't do it. She will ruin Zoë's life." How he knew or what he saw I don't know. He was right.

What I didn't know was there were other women in my life who loved me and wanted to take me when my dad was struggling and even more so when he remarried. He was warned. He didn't listen. Later in life they told me how precious I was and that there had never been a sweeter, kinder little girl. They said I lit up every room I entered with how much love I tried to show people. This is the opposite of what I heard growing up. Of course, no one helped me. What was meant to happen did.

In the beginning I thought the addition to our family of two was wonderful. I shared a room with my new stepsister, and we played every day. We would play songs on the jukebox at the community center and swim. It seemed like it took forever for me to learn to swim after throwing up in the pool the summer before and being shamed out of swim lessons. I doubt that helped my dad's stress level during his life as a single dad. After the wedding my dad seemed distracted with work and his new wife. Our lives evolved rapidly as she changed our lives to make it the way she wanted. Suddenly there was this stranger in my home giving me chores and orders. I was very compliant but there was no teaching and definitely no love. If you didn't do something her way, a monster was unleashed, a fury I had never witnessed, a fury that never lost its edge nor its ability to rattle me with its hate. Wide eyed and alone, fear took hold in my heart.

The first fundamental thing that changed was she didn't allow my dad to spend any time with me. As a child you don't have any awareness that isolation is the first thing an abuser will do to take control. Although I didn't know it, when she moved in, my dad moved out of my life. Immediately his new wife made it clear to him he needed to make more money. He was only allowed to spend time with her. I was five and was put to work doing the dishes after each meal and shortly after that, the list of chores included every household chore except cooking. I remember dragging a chair into the galley apartment kitchen so I could climb on the chair and reach the sink. I started washing dishes. I remember she started laughing and took a picture of me washing dishes. I didn't understand what was funny. My dad was rather incredulous at the scene, kind of like, "Oh, *this* is how you're supposed to raise kids??" I remember looking at him, questioning him with my eyes, waiting for him to step in, and him intentionally never looking at me and then nervously joining in her laughter. I think I knew right then it was going to be bad. It's not that I don't appreciate the benefit of chores and teaching children responsibility, but there was something deeply wrong about how this played itself out. I'll explain in time. I sensed it immediately. From that moment, I knew my dad was not in charge. I knew with the same certainty that he would also not interject to object. I was on my own.

After that, things were never the same. There was never another bedtime story. If I tried to talk to my dad or spend time with him, his wife would unleash a verbal onslaught of profanity and wicked accusations that never lasted less than an hour and usually went on well after we went to bed. I learned quickly to leave my dad alone so I wouldn't be the cause of her vicious attacks that would, in an instant, turn their fury on me. Usually, she would scream at him about how worthless he was because he was such a failure as a provider. I would lay in bed listening to her shrieking as my lullaby. My dad shut down completely. There were also wild accusations regarding any attention he showed me, so he stopped acknowledging me at all except to enforce her punishments. He was ordered, not asked, to give my new stepsister all his parental focus and attention. I remember looking around to see if my stepmother was near before I ever approached my dad. His blankness at my quiet attempts to connect pulsated my fear that I was alone. I was right. Fear, and more often fright, fueled the air like gasoline. The eggshells turned into land mines, and I did what I could not to lose a limb.

Decades later I asked my dad if he had any idea what she was really like before he married her. He told me his first mistake was not dating her longer because her true nature would certainly have exposed itself. Loathing, wild rage has little desire to restrain its appetite for destruction. In that short courtship there was only one incident that had disturbed him. They had been playing checkers and he was winning. He had gotten up to go to the bathroom and when he returned the pieces had been moved. My dad loved checkers and chess and planned every move strategically, weighing each piece with every possible play and consequence. He looked at the board and asked, somewhat confused and incredulous, "Did you *move* the pieces?" And the monster's eyes flashed with hate before they roared with a vehemence and violence and twisted blame that had my dad apologizing profusely for asking the obvious truthful question. When he told me that story, he added, "I didn't know that was the real person. I thought it was a fleeting moment. I had never seen someone lie that way. I'm sorry. I know I should have known better." His head bowed remorsefully at a past he couldn't change and damage he couldn't undo. I always thought at that moment in his life he must have been so determined to put pieces together even if they didn't fit. The wordsmiths and logophiles have yet to come up with a word for her particular brand of violence, cruelty, and lies. To me she is a destroyer, a thief.

Within a few months of their quick nuptials we had moved to a North Georgia town. I started a new school and the brightness I had as a child shriveled to hide within the safety of my shell. I certainly intended to be happy. It is who I was and still am. I had a Raggedy Anne alarm clock that joyfully introduced me to each new day, cheering me on with these sweet words, "Wake up - Wake up! It's time to start your happy day!" I would bounce out of bed with a smile, immediately make my bed and carefully pick something pretty to wear from a sad collection of hand me downs. That is the joyful heart I was born with, the one I know is still deep within me and calls to me under the heaps of burdens and baggage. For decades the scars sealed off the joy within me and whispered the lie that it was dead in the embers. The mocking, laughing lies assured me I would never get it back. My heart kept fighting. I thought God made me to be happy and love people. I did not understand why it didn't seem to work in reverse. Reciprocity is something all humans innately expect until the world jades them, and even then, their hearts still crave the return of their energies. I think it's because we were made in the image of God. He pours out His infinite love to us in more ways than we can comprehend, and all He wants is to be loved in return.

Over this first year in our new town, I became intensely fearful and timid in every aspect of my life. I was afraid to speak to other students and adults, afraid to make any mistake, afraid of making myself heard, afraid of anything that would put me in the line of fire. It was at this home that I would wait by the door for my mother, now only 90 minutes away, but she would never come. I was trapped. My first-grade teacher was not warm and fuzzy and expressed her annoyance to my new parental unit at finding all my assignments completed but shoved into the desk bag tied to the side of my desk that was reserved for crayons and scissors. "Why is she afraid of turning in her assignments?" she demanded. I don't remember the consequences, but it taught me I had better never miss an assignment and, if it wasn't perfect, I would pay dearly. The teasing ramped up around my name and my teacher would incorrectly correct the spelling and punctuation in my name in bright red ink. She never did figure out how to spell my name correctly or understand what a dieresis is. So, I kept to myself. At recess I would busy myself by braiding pine straw and collecting rocks. I hid the beautiful rocks in my pillowcase until they were found, and I was scolded for basically being weird. My collection was thrown out. One afternoon I fell asleep on the bus and missed my bus stop. When I woke there were older kids on the bus. I huddled down on the bus seat, frozen in fear, unable to ask for help. My little mind raced with all the trouble I would surely be in when I was found. Hours went by before the bus driver found me, and I was returned. There was a badgering and another scream fest, demanding to know why I didn't tell the bus driver. The truth stuck in my throat like glue. At this point my dad knew something was wrong, but he chose fear. He chose her.

She told him this proved who I was, and he let that narrative sink deep into his psyche. His wife used the incident to beat home the point that I was a liar and a troublemaker and needed more discipline. It's hard to explain how a little heart breaks when you see your only parent poisoned against you and listen to him believe lies about you. This is what she would scream at me in disgust nearly every day of my childhood, except that it was peppered with profanity the way pepper falls out of a jar when someone doesn't screw the lid on. My dad would always follow her lead and look at me in disgust and repeat her labels. Eventually I did start lying to save myself. My flickering hope gasped its last breath, and the heaviness of loneliness blanketed me. At six years old, I knew I had no one.

I hate this part. As I said, there were chores. I was six and scrubbing bathtubs and toilets. I literally, not once, in the 13 years I ever lived with that woman, ever saw her scrub a floor, a toilet, or a tub. That was for kids, more specifically, for me. I remember often she and her friends, with drinks in hands, would laugh about housework, sneering with hilarity, "That's what kids are for!!" and the peels of drunken laughter would follow. Baby Boomers are just awesome, aren't they? It's so great we children could help alleviate the burdens of parenthood for them, after all, someone has to make sure they get to do everything their heart desires. My generation is still picking up the pieces our parents didn't want to be bothered with. Anyway, once, when I was six, I didn't scrub the bathtub to her satisfaction. I was brought in and the soap scum with the scrub marks through it was laid out as evidence of my incompetence - no - intentional disobedience and laziness. A beating was necessary. Believe me, I scrub a mean tub now. Then there was the vacuuming and dusting. There's a proper order, as I'm sure you know. My stepsister and I were given these tasks and whatever was more difficult was given to me. I chuckle because my stepsister's idea of dusting was spraying Pledge around a room, so the scent hung in the air and swiping one path on one random piece of furniture in each room.

On this particular afternoon we were in the master bedroom where I was vacuuming, and she was doing her usual casual stroll around the perimeter of the room with the dust rag. I was held accountable for making sure there were perfect tracks in the carpet from the vacuum cleaner. This required detail was actually quite satisfying. I felt some sense of accomplishment in creating order and beauty. I had this sense that if you do a job, then you might as well do a job well. No matter what you do, enjoy it. I would sing to myself and no one would say anything because they only heard the noisy hum of the vacuum cleaner. That night my stepsister and I were called into the master bedroom where both parents sat on the bed. Their faces were stern. We stood in front of them, and the inquisition began. "Who?" it was asked, "Who knocked the push pin out of the wall holding the curtain tie back?" I looked at the window and there it was, the curtain tie was wrapped around the ruffled curtain and it hung in the middle of the window instead of pulled to the side. The pin had been left in the carpet in my perfect parallel tracks and the curtain hung disheveled. I knew it was my stepsister, and I knew she had done it when she was doing her version of dusting. She was a slob. Her side of the room was a disaster. She would never comb her hair. She never did her share of anything, and I can't remember anything she did well. My friendship and the accompanying excitement of having a sister had waned significantly in that first year, but on this particular day, any true friendship ended.

In response to their questioning, I immediately and confidently replied it wasn't me. In shock I heard my stepsister deny it. I turned and looked at her in shock. We were ordered to go into the bathroom and discuss it until the guilty party confessed. Once behind the door, I angrily said in a hushed voice, "You know you did it." She had a smirk on her face and said, "No I didn't." I continued to tell her I knew it was her because she had been dancing around the room with the dust rag and I was not near the wall because I was vacuuming and you could see the vacuum tracks and they went away from the window, not beside it. She very smugly refused to change her story. When we went back in the room, we both still denied the crime. Without another question my stepsister and stepmother left the room.

In that moment my level of fear escalated. My dad had never treated me this way before. He stared at me and with contempt said, "I know it was you. You're a liar. I'm going to spank you and you're going to keep getting a spanking every five minutes until you confess." With that, the belt came off and he began beating me in a rage that I had never experienced. I couldn't scream loud enough or catch my breath. I fell on the ground rolling and holding my ass and sobbing hysterically. He yelled over me demanding to know if I was ready to confess. I could see in his face and hear in his voice, there was no love, there was no mercy. *Who was he? Where was my daddy?* I couldn't even breathe. In that moment of terror, I had to make a choice. Would I lie and admit to something I didn't do to save myself? I was six and I didn't think I could take another beating like that with so much hate and fury. So, I looked up at my dad and told him I did it. He nodded knowingly and my heart shattered. How was this happening? My dad knew me. He marched me out to the kitchen, and I was forced to falsely confess and apologize to my stepmother and my stepsister. My stepmother and stepsister smiled the same smug smile. Her mother had served her a bowl of ice cream while I was wailing under a belt. I found out what kind of person she was, someone who eats ice cream while her friend is being beaten for something she did. From that moment on I knew several things about how my upbringing would go, I would always be blamed, the truth didn't work, I had to say and do whatever would protect me, there would be no rescue, and the only thing I could do was survive. The fact that I was alone was deeply imprinted on my heart.

Apples don't fall far from the trees that bear them and a tree is known by its fruit. It should be no surprise that my stepsister's character was that of her mother's. She treated me just like her mother did and there were never consequences. Quite the opposite. I was to blame, no matter the situation. All of this made me want to never make a mistake. Fear, not pride, was my motivation. Once I was on a seesaw with my stepsister that my dad had made. My dad loved being handy. I think so much of my desire to create and build comes from him. There is satisfaction in it. In simple projects like the seesaw, the tire swing, the gardens, and the table he built, he found pride in himself which he desperately needed to combat her daily shrills of worthlessness. On that bright yellow seesaw out under the beautiful Georgia skies, I was quite unsuspecting of intentional cruelty. Some switch flipped in my stepsister's head, and she got an idea. As I went up in the air, she stayed down, and an evil smile crept on her face. I started to get scared. I begged her to let me down and her smile got bigger. Then she jumped off and I crashed to the ground. The force knocked the wind right out of me like a violent punch. I thrashed and rolled on the ground unable to take a breath. My lungs wouldn't work. Panic... Breathe... Breathe... Oh please give me a breath. It seemed like forever before I could breathe again. And finally, that first knifelike breath. I wept and with tears pouring down my face found my dad and told him she had done it on purpose. When he looked down at me, I saw what seemed to be love and belief, but he also understood the consequences of defending me. Nothing happened. I got a hug. I learned to keep my distance and never trust my stepsister. Living with the enemy is no easy task at any age.

Earlier that year, my stepmother gave birth to a baby boy. Immediately the environment went from really bad to much worse. When he was brought home, my stepsister, just eight months older than me, was encouraged to hold him. I was afraid to ask for the same privilege. When I did, there was resistance. I remember defending myself in my mind, "I'm so careful. I'm so kind." But I said nothing. Whining or questioning was never allowed. I had learned quickly to keep quiet about any and all decisions they made. Decisions were always final and absent of any generosity of spirit. Finally, I got to hold my baby brother.

This... I breathed slower and softer as I held his little hand and touched his tiny fingers. This was good. My thoughts drifted to those precious little puppies, perfectly safe in the tenderness of their mother's watchful eye. Then the moment was over. Although I asked often, I was rarely allowed to hold my brother. It was obvious he belonged to my stepmother. I was not in the inner circle, but I did notice, oddly, my daddy wasn't either. My dad was always trying to pacify and please his wife to gain some momentary reprieve from her vicious verbal onslaughts. It was a strange dichotomy, one that a six-year-old can only sense and feel, not explain. When I see the photos of us smiling or all those awful road trips, I remember how I had to fake so many smiles and the multiple efforts I made to ingratiate myself to her so she would relent her attacks. I told her I loved her so many times. My stomach turned violently every time I said the words. I gave her poems and pictures all trying to save myself from her hateful violent rage. There was not a genuine moment of safety or kindness or joy. Every smile of mine was made to order and every moment of spontaneity of spirit was regretted.

There was one other incident during that period that I think is important. My dad's new wife was violent. She would back my dad into a corner and scream two inches from his face and hit him repeatedly while she was screaming vulgarity at him. One time, as she hit him over and over, he lost control and hit her back on the side of her head. It busted her eardrum. She went to the hospital, and we were taken to visit her. She had a huge bandage on her head and that smug smile on her face. I remember thinking, 'She's enjoying this. What a fake. I hope he will leave her now.' That didn't happen. She used this incident over and over and over to tell people she was abused and to remind my dad he was a wife beater. No one knew the truth about her. He was trapped. He knew he was abandoning me. He wept for certain, but he made a choice. He hardened his heart to me and did everything to please her. Fear was his keeper.

My father's wife prided herself on being a storyteller. I have to admit, she really could weave a tale. Facts were fiction to twist to her suiting. She would lie and never break eye contact, straight into your eyes. I would learn that the most talented liars practice this skill like an artist who hones their craft. When I was young, I would try to find truth in her lies. I never could find any and it felt like I was looking for missing puzzle pieces. It was as if she didn't know how to tell the truth. Her constant lies made me uncomfortable, and I didn't want to be anywhere near her. I found it baffling why she found so many lies necessary. She would tell lies when the truth would do just fine. The worst lie was her smile. I was always astonished how she could be screaming with such uncontrolled hate and the phone would ring and she would scream one last wretched word with her hand on the receiver and then answer in the most syrupy, sweet voice, "Hello? Well, *hey*! How *arrre* you?" and that lie of a smile would appear in a blink along with the loud, phony laugh. She would smile to everyone and then scowl at us with hate. It's hard to even remember all the lies. It was as if she had to lie and scream in order to breathe.

Car rides were unbearable, an instructional manual in verbal assault and a how-to for any foul mouth who wanted to learn the art of blasphemy and imprecation. There were the ones in the beginning when the back windows didn't roll down more than a few inches and there was no A/C, and your legs would stick and be scorched by the seats. My stepsister, no longer a friend, would try to harass and antagonize me to keep herself amused. I would sometimes squeal for her to stop, and, if it happened more than once, there would be stops on the roadside to pick out a switch. If there was any sound from the backseat, there was a screeching threat. The heat and humidity aggravated her hostility like summer thunder clouds flickering with lightning flashes that leave ground dwellers scattering for protection from imminent strikes. But the worst were the car rides with my dad. My dad is one of those people who remembers at the last minute that he needs to pack a special tool, water a plant, check the pilot light and several other things at the exact time that was set to leave. This cute, slightly annoying idiosyncrasy enraged his wife. We would sit in a hot car waiting, listening to her anger gearing up like practice for a pregame tongue lashing. When he would finally get in the car, it would start. Before the car was out of the driveway, the high-pitched carpet bombing of profanity would begin. After we moved, most car rides were five hours, and usually to her parents' home. Her mercurial anger would rise like the hell I knew I was living in. The screaming would usually subside after four hours, replaced with icy, merciful silence. It was always the same chorus of themes. He was worthless. He was a horrible husband and father. He couldn't do anything right. He couldn't make money. He was a blankety blank blank, m… f… stupid blank blank who couldn't blank blank. When she had worn that one out, she would start in on me. I would listen as the liar screamed lies about me to my dad that resembled the lies she had just said about him. He never defended himself. He never defended me. The hate thickened the air. To feel joy and be a child was much like being a daisy growing under the weight of a hot brick.

Before third grade, we moved to another home on the other side of town. I was thrilled about the move. I saw this as a chance to make my life a little better. In second grade I had become a diligent student not wanting to make any mistakes. I was so scared of getting in trouble like I had the year before when I didn't turn in my work. One day I went to tear the worksheet out of my workbook, and the page ripped in half. I was terrified. This was back in the day when teachers paddled students. Every afternoon after recess, the boys that had been fighting would line up at the teacher's desk and she would bend them over her knee one at a time and paddle them. I stared at the torn worksheet and my mind raced trying to figure out what to do. I felt my pulse pounding in my head and was certain everyone could hear the jack hammer beating of my heart. I was certain the teacher would be angry. I nervously slid my workbook back and hid the torn sheet. When she asked me for my work, I could barely get the lie out of my throat. I told her I couldn't find it. She had me look for it. I pretended to look in all sorts of different spots around the room and in the cubby under my desk. It seemed like I looked for hours but was probably only twenty minutes. I'm not sure what I thought would happen next. I was just afraid. Finally, I showed her the torn sheet. She decided to make an example of me. She told the class, "This is what you get for lying." And with that she bent me over her knee and paddled me in front of the class. No girl had ever been paddled. The shame was almost unbearable. When she was done, she stood in front of the class and told them not to tell anyone. Looking back, I think she knew it was wrong, but it was done. She couldn't take it back, just try to cover it up. I went to my desk and wept the rest of the day. No one spoke to me. Between this incident and the day I was sick and forced to go to school where I promptly vomited all over the milk in the cafeteria - I was ready for a new school.

When we moved to the home across town with giant oak trees and Victorian homes, I begged my dad to start letting me go by my middle name, Nicole. To me, it seemed a perfect solution to stop the teasing. New school, new name. My dad consulted with his wife. I was told that children aren't allowed to pick their own name - that is a right reserved for parents. He let me choose a middle name but told me my first name would be my stepmother's, the name of my abuser. There was hate, sadness, and relief all twisted together in the new name. The middle name I chose was Kathleen. In later years both my mother, her family, and other people who knew me told me, with absolute certainty, that there had been no reason to change my name and that my stepmother had manipulated and plotted to use this opportunity to gain further control and to prevent my mother from finding me. Somehow, in forcing her name on me, she stole my identity, my mother's rights, and gained almost total power over me. At the age of eight, all I knew was that I hated my name, hated my life. My consolation was simple- at least I wouldn't be teased for my name.

On my birthday that year I received packages from my grandmother and my Aunt Francine. My mother's mother was a simple country woman who had lived through her own personal hell with my grandfather. She had found the courage to get out and after that, lived a simple, but timid life. The one thing she tried to do well was let people know she loved them and send them gifts. We called her Marn. Marn's heart was beautiful. Marn didn't have the best taste, but you knew her gifts were sent with love, and you loved them because of that. When the gifts arrived that year, my stepmother packaged up all the gifts and sent them back to my family. She told them it was not fair for me to get gifts if her daughter didn't and that all gifts would be returned to the sender. The fact that it wasn't her daughter's birthday was irrelevant. I wouldn't be allowed to keep or even open a single gift. She also instructed them and me that all communication with that side of the family was no longer allowed. My dad supported her. They were creating a new family and the past wasn't welcome in it. I was now made to act as if my stepmother's family was my own and robbed of all the people who loved me. It was a brazen act of isolation and alienation, and no one stopped her.

When my dad's siblings came to visit one Christmas, I was ecstatic. I clamored for their love and attention. In my mind, I imagined it would be like it was when I was a flower girl or when I would play with my uncle who loved being young and silly. But it was different now. My stepmother saw me trying to engage, trying to draw with my aunt, trying to be loved. She and my dad took me into a room alone to redefine my relationship with them. She couldn't launch into one of her fits with all the people in the house, so she drew a stick figure picture of me with arrows to all of my family. She glared at me and, with a venomous voice, told me I was trying to harass everyone, but they had an iron plate over them to protect them. She pointed to the old iron fireplace cover and then drew lines over each stick figure's head. "All your efforts are useless. Everyone sees you for who you are. For the rest of their visit, you are to STAY AWAY from them." Her eyes and her voice gleamed in power. My dad just nodded. I knew that wasn't who I was. I knew I just wanted to be loved, but at that point, I wasn't writing the story. I stayed away. It was during this time that my Aunt Esther died of breast cancer as well. I remember going into her hospital room and not understanding how she could possibly be gone soon. She was my grandmother's twin and so, to me, she was the embodiment of both of them. When I was very small, she had brought me back China dolls with soft bodies and porcelain faces, hands and feet and a Native American doll with an exquisite headdress that held real feathers and the tiniest beadwork. In every room I ever had, those dolls sat in the place of honor on my dresser as if to constantly remind me who I was and that I was loved. After she was gone, those dolls were all I had of her and my grandmother.

My stepmother's parents were deeply Southern. The man who raised her was actually her stepfather. Her biological father was a fiery, red headed mystery man from West Virginia. At the risk of being stereotypical, the few stories I had heard made sense. At her parents' home, there was an endless parade of soap operas, golf, and the most jaw dropping concoction of diabetes inducing sweet tea ever made. I would watch it being made. Sugar would be poured in until the pitcher was at least a third full, followed by a wooden spoon and then the hot tea. She would stir and stir until it was dissolved and then test. Quite often more sugar was added.

Her mother collected figurines of black children and called them the same word that Paula Deen used in her thick Southern drawl. Every time I looked at them, my stomach turned in disgust. It was like a little collection in memoriam of segregation, a tribute to the supremacy they felt entitled to because it was draped in Southern sweetness. I didn't know the word at the time, but it was paternalism. Paternalism is racism draped in condescension and pity, covered with civility. No matter how unintentional the offenses might be, when one group views another as anything other than equal this is how injustice takes hold. In South Georgia in the 1980s, racism was ever present. I don't know if it has changed. I hope it has. Some towns were worse than others. What was weird was how you could just sense it. That was the one great thing my stepmother gave me. Because she was so racist, I despised racism in every form. I lacked the indifference that was so common among my peers. I would be nothing like her. She made it easy to recognize condescension, superiority, and hate and bolt the other way. As a child you couldn't say anything. That would be disrespectful, and you would pay dearly. But I saw. I thought for myself. I decided what was black and what was right.

For us kids, there was nothing to do when we visited. Her mother took care of teachers' children who were too young for school, which meant there were preschool toys everywhere. We visited them at least once a month. The routine was set - listen to hours of screaming for the duration of the car ride, then do the chores at her parents' house, bury yourself in a book for two days, attend a Southern Baptist worship service with hellfire, brimstone and a shocking number of bad toupees, and then another car ride back full of screaming, profanity, and threats. This was my new family. I never could connect.

That same year I was called into the kitchen. My stepmother scowled at my dad as he had a very serious and heated discussion with my mother over the phone. My mother had heard about the new edict and insisted that she still had parental rights. My dad told her she had abandoned me and that I didn't want anything to do with her. She demanded to speak to me. My dad covered the receiver with his hand. With anger and authority, he told me I was to tell my mother I didn't want her in my life. My heart gripped in stifling fear, and I couldn't get my feet to move. It took some time for me to move. I walked slowly to the phone and held it in both hands. My dad towered over me and told me what words to say. I could feel the words choking me and I could hardly get them out. I knew I couldn't cry in front of them. I knew what would happen if I said no. The fear and sorrow of never seeing my mother again, the fear of what would happen to me if I didn't say these words *and* if I did, gripped me as the final door to my childhood cage slammed shut. My dad held his shoulders up in satisfaction and the evil, satisfied smile smugly spread across my stepmother's face. I walked out of the kitchen with my head down and then ran to my room to cry in silence. I felt like my desire to survive had made me betray my mother and myself. From that day on I started dreaming of how to rescue myself. I had a Holly Hobby diary that held all my secrets. Dear Diary became the sweetest relief of whispers, the truth of my heart poured out on those pages so I could have the strength to keep up the lie I was told was required of me. That meant I said I love you and sometimes even had to offer a kiss to the person who took my mother, my father, my family, my joy and any hope of stability, security or a happy childhood. I struggled so much to make the lie true in my heart. I tried with everything in me to love my enemy and do good to those who persecuted me. I tried, I tried, I tried. Those little pages told the truth. One day I would wish they didn't.

My faith was something extraordinary as a child. It pierced everything. It was a very Calvinist doctrine that I was taught - conservatism, the authority of Scripture, the omnipotence of God, radical depravity matched only by radical grace, the rigid doctrines of authority, submission, and suffering. But I also knew in my heart, God was LOVE. I remember being in that beautiful old sanctuary after a church service as the congregation voted on which denomination to be a part of as the Presbyterian church split. One was painted as being obedient to Scripture, the other as being obedient to Love. As a child I watched perplexed. I thought those were the same.

I put a great deal of Scripture to memory during those years. *I have hidden Your word in my heart that I might not sin against You* [9] The verses I held in my heart were to fight real enemies, there was nothing abstract about it. When I found my old Children's Bible with the picture of Jesus on the cover, lovingly holding a lamb, I was astonished to see what I had written. I am so grateful to the men and women who taught and still teach Sunday School and Vacation Bible School. You never know who you are going to impact and what is going to sink deeply and root itself in a child's heart. Clearly, I reaped the benefits of their efforts to share their faith and walk uprightly. In that old Bible, I saw the framework of a mature faith and an extensive knowledge and application of Scripture. I saw a little girl who loved Jesus and wanted so desperately to please Him and walk by His side. I read my prayers and my notes on how to interpret and apply the lives of the patriarchal fathers, the story of Egypt and the Promised Land, the Ten Commandments, the Prophets and their battles, the stories in Esther and Daniel, the undeniable divinity and miracles of Christ, the attributes and names of God, the Lord's Prayer, the Parables, the Golden Rule, the Trinity, the Fruit of the Spirit, the letters of Paul and the apostles, how to live a life in Christ, the Armor of God, and the Beatitudes.

The Beatitudes, the Fruit of the Spirit, I Corinthians 13, and the Golden Rule, more than any other passages, shaped how I perceived all of life and how I responded to my circumstances. I had a little thought

[9] Psalm 119:11

process I would go through to check to see if I was honoring God by staying true to these values. Are you being humble? Are you being meek? Are you seeking peace? Are you seeking righteousness? Are you being merciful? Do you have a pure heart? Are you loving? Are you forgiving? Are you patient? Are you kind? Are you faithful? Are you trusting? Are you gentle? Are you controlling yourself? And most importantly, Are you considering others more important than yourself? By no means did I live up to it perfectly, but these scriptures became my filter and barometer to judge my own mindset and behavior. He was the Potter. I was the clay. He was my Lord and I just wanted to follow what He taught me and become more like Him. I became quite content to live a meek and humble life centered on loving others, being and doing good, trusting God to work it all out when I got to heaven. If I suffered or had to endure wrong, it was okay because - And we know that all things work together for the good of those who love God, to them who are called according to His purpose.[10] *My rule was this - I would love my enemies and do good to those who persecuted me. I thought this would eventually - what's the word - work. Kill with kindness they say. As an adult I found the rate of effectiveness for this particular method had less than satisfactory results and understood it was a requirement, like an offering of obedience, that offered uncertain satisfaction and definitely no guarantee of success or reciprocity.*

The other teaching came from Girl Scouts. It was simple but it touched everything in life. Always leave a place better than you found it. As a child, my interpretation was very literal. I would scan rooms I walked into to see what I could do to help make a place cleaner or more beautiful. My heart kept my mind constantly seeking beauty, love, and the cross of my Savior, Jesus Christ. The older I got, I realized this translated to people too. Whatever would help them and give them more life, love, and hope than when I found them was what I intended to do. It was this heart that kept me looking for good in people. Although I never disavowed either of these teachings, I discovered just how hard true change in the world and in people really is. I might be called to live His gospel, but it was the Holy Spirit who changed hearts. I chose to keep living this way because something in me told me anything else was darkness. But there was an ocean of disappointment and hurt along the journey. There was my Bible and there was my diary. One held all the reasons to believe, love, and persevere, and the other all the pieces of my broken heart.

What I wrote in that diary was how much I missed my mother and how much I longed for her to come rescue me. I wrote the truth about how I was treated and how it made me feel. I wrote about the father I missed so much, even though he was right in front of me. I wrote about my stepmother's rages, the cruelty, and the oppression, even though I didn't know that word yet. I wrote about all the things I longed for that I would make certain my children had. It wasn't pretty, but it was true.

Life continued in the same downward spiral and my stepmother gained more control every day. I remember being puzzled by exactly what she spent her time doing during the day, as the only thing I could identify was taking care of my brother and making dinner. I was responsible for vacuuming and dusting each morning before school, all the dishes at each meal, the laundry, the ironing, and each day after school there was a list of chores that included all inside and outside cleaning. I remember being so excited about the portable dishwasher that I could roll to the sink after the dishes were rinsed and then attach the hose as tightly as possible to the faucet and make sure the other hose was in the drain. If a piece of laundry came out smaller than it went in or with a stain, I had to pay for it to be replaced, usually with my birthday money or money from odd jobs. At times my dad would give us an allowance for extra chores. It wasn't much but he tried to help in a constructive way. When she did finally get a part time job at a photoshop, I was thrilled. I wanted to be a latch key kid. As soon as my chores and homework were done, I could watch Little House on the Prairie, old reruns from the 60's and 70's, and on rare, wonderful occasions, the After School Special in total uninterrupted peace.

[10] Romans 8:28

The best antidote for a child in this environment was staying out of the line of fire. My escapes from my stepmother were attempting to be as perfect as possible, staying outside, riding my bike, climbing the tall crape myrtle in the backyard, swinging in the tire swing. Inside the house it was my books and records that kept me out of sight. Our new home didn't look like much from the street. My dad planted rose bushes next to the fire hydrant. I loved trying to balance on top of the bright yellow hydrant. One of the chores would be to weed the bed, but that also meant smelling the roses. There was something satisfying about getting dirty while taking care of those roses. I loved the dandelions and white clover too. They were everywhere. One summer, I decided to make a flower chain with all the white clover. I knotted each one so carefully, making sure it was tight but didn't break. It was just me and God and that flower chain. We had long, quiet endless hours of summer to talk. This went on for a while. At some point, the flower chain was so long I thought maybe I should find a way to enter it in the Guinness Book of World Records. It ran from the furthest point in the backyard all the way up two flights of stairs, around the corner, and up to the front porch swing. Unfortunately, the stems had grown so brittle over the summer that they broke with any movement. I spent so much time repairing the chain that I finally abandoned the project. I've never heard of or seen a longer chain and still wish I had a picture of it. But the point of that flower chain wasn't the length of it, it was the sweetness of the time I spent being a child talking to God and doing something great.

The house was quaint, old and needed a lot of repairs. It had a horrible roach problem. When you turned the lights on in the kitchen, the roaches would scatter. But kind of like a little sister with peanut butter and jelly on her face among grown up debutantes, the house didn't know it didn't fit in the neighborhood. At some point, it had been turned into apartments so there was an unused kitchen downstairs. All the renovations and repurposes created so many places to hide. Across the street was a magnificent Victorian home. When two young girls moved in, we got the opportunity to climb the magnolia tree in the front yard almost daily and explore the grand mansion. We created Marylou Retton floor routines with our humble round-offs on that wide porch and used a picnic bench for the balance beam routines. There were lots of splinters that summer. Being surrounded by so many grand homes started my love affair with old houses. That neighborhood held homes gated regally with iron fences, beautiful churches with stained glass windows, grand homes that escaped Sherman's March through Georgia, and a Main Street with a newsstand, deli, an old theater and a library that Carnegie had funded just past the Romulus and Remus statue. One of my favorite things to do was walk to the library and get lost in the basement surrounded by the smell of old books. Except for the scent of babies, honeysuckles, and roses, the only other scent that makes me lose myself is the smell of old books. There was also a hill with an abandoned school that we would play chase on and roll down. There were sweet old ladies who served tea and cookies and crazy old cat ladies that lived in spooky run-down mansions. I have yet to find anything modern or suburban that had as much character and substance as one of those old homes on that street with broken sidewalks, English gardens, and hills that required downshifting.

At our home, on the poor end of the street, one side of the front porch held a front porch swing and at the opposite end were rotten boards that you stepped on precariously to look out over a one and a half story drop to the backyard down below. The metal rail rattled if you touched it, just barely remaining attached. As a child it seemed like a terrifying distance. In that corner of the yard down below was a fence covered with honeysuckles that I learned to suck the dew out with expert precision. The backyard sloped down even further, and from the back of the yard, you could see all three stories of our home. The basement had one outside entrance to a dark, dingy, dirt floor basement. Inside there was one light bulb. Precariously, over the unfinished basement was a loft perched above that backyard basement door. The loft was as hot and dingy as the basement, but it had two things that made it my favorite spot in the whole house - a window overlooking my favorite climbing trees and a place to hide from my stepmother and get lost in a world of words. I can't begin to know how many books I read by that window, but they let me live a different life. They gave me hope that life would not always be this way and that I had what it took to withstand anything. I wanted to be like the heroes and heroines I read about. I wanted a life and a story that deserved to be told. It still amazes me how hope ignites the strongest spark in the darkest places.

One winter while we lived there, it snowed, and all the kids ran to the clock tower hill to sled. The clock tower stood 104 feet tall on the tallest hill and could be seen across the whole town. It rang every hour and served as the neighborhood alarm and dinner bell for children. Since it rarely snowed, there were not a lot of actual sleds. Kids were sliding down the scarily steep hill on flattened cardboard boxes and makeshift plastic sleds. I'm surprised no one had lugged a plastic kiddie pool to the scene. After watching the fun and waiting patiently a long time, I was finally invited to join one of the neighborhood girls on a plastic sled. With no way to steer the sled, we were at the mercy of ice, gravity, and physics, never a safe combination. Unseen to us, a large chunk of ice had been upturned on the hill. When we hit the ice, the sled flipped around backwards and slid diagonally and at tremendous speed into a telephone pole where I took the full impact. I remember rolling around on the ice unable to breathe, people screaming and sliding trying to get me. I remember someone pumping on my chest and sirens. Not surprisingly, I felt like I had hit a telephone pole headfirst.

My survival seemed to be irrelevant. On the way home from the hospital, I was lectured about all the money they had to waste on me and how it was my fault because I hadn't asked permission to go to the hill. So, I was grounded indefinitely. That became the favored term of imprisonment. There was no end. It was just a life sentence that would start and stop arbitrarily. The new punishing procedures, as well as having to ask permission to play outside, were new for me. Before, I had been told to go play outside-period. Suddenly, the rules were different. I was supposed to ask permission to go anywhere or do anything. The sweet freedom of that neighborhood and all its beauty was cut short. Almost two weeks after the accident, my father talked my stepmother into cutting my restriction short since I had been so sweet and obedient. Exhilarated and literally jumping for joy, I rushed outside and started plucking icicles off the side of the house. I ran up the stairs to the front yard and was stopped short and ordered back inside. I was informed I would be grounded again because I didn't ask and receive permission to go outside. My heart sunk. It seemed that no matter what, all the little joys would be taken from me. I watched out the window as everyone played and went back to my books.

At school, there were some wonderful teachers and students and the typical troublemakers. My greatest discovery during this time was that I excelled at school. I loved learning. Third grade was incredible. In fourth grade, eager to find out what I was capable of, I learned hard truths about education. Being in a classroom with a desire to be educated doesn't guarantee learning anything. It helps when someone lights the way. My school had a specific way of handling the more unruly boys. Some of the teachers were hired to teach children and others were hired to control them. They put all the behavior problems in one classroom and sprinkled a few girls in there for good measure. I was in one of those classes.

Mrs. Shropshire ruled like I had never seen a teacher rule before. In her deep, thundering voice she would shout - no - boom at the boys to be quiet for almost any disruption. Her threats were never vague or empty. Then the next second, the lights would be turned off. She would walk around the room slowly, slapping her hand with her ruler and then the desk - sometimes hand - of anyone who didn't have their head down. We would stay in that position, head on our desks, for entire classes. There was almost no learning and not one single smile that I can remember. Mrs. Blanton was the other fourth grade teacher.

Her classroom was separated by a folding partition from Mrs. Shropshire's. The light and laughter from her room spilled through the cracks and around the edges, contrasting starkly against our silent school cell. When we would change classes for two hours each day to Mrs. Blanton's room, there would be projects, teaching, learning, and even lights. NO ONE was saying or even thinking, "Stay away from the light!" The light was all we longed for.

One day for a vocabulary assignment we were told to write a sentence for each word on our list. With all the long spells of silence in the adjacent room, I was so eager to create that I quite lost control of myself. In my best script I poured out long elaborate sentences with clauses and multiple prepositional phrases, each sentence a story unto itself. The words seemed to have a rhythm and beauty that danced out of my pen. It was sheer delight! With pride, I turned in my work and enjoyed the simple happiness that is a byproduct of creativity. In a different, yet somehow similar way, I had the same happiness I had from my flower chain. I was happy to make ideas real on paper, happy to make something pretty that was ordinary, happy to do more than what was expected of me. Although I wanted to please, it was really just for me and who made me. Then Mrs. Blanton graded our papers. She did not scold my run-on sentences. Instead, she hunted me down in the smelly cafeteria to show me my paper. She was so excited as she held it up and told me she gave me an A+++ and that if she could give me more, she would. Then she told me I needed to consider writing more, that I had a gift. I was stunned. I'm sure she was too. She had no idea that the little girl who didn't say a word had a head and heart full of wonder. In that moment, I found out I was good at something that was important. My gifts, even me, had value. I shyly thanked her and smiled, but in my heart, I was leaping. It was a great encouragement to know not everyone thought about me the way my stepmother and father did. The marks on my report card were full of good grades and praise, and I began to see myself the way they saw me, by my scores, and by teachers whom I could impress. That year created a great distinction in my mind. I clearly and literally associated love and learning with light; anger, fear, and stagnancy with darkness. The light's better - way, way better.

My stepsister was a bad student. My good grades accentuated her poor ones. Her and her mother's hate lurked constantly, waiting for opportunities to pounce. I rarely spoke. One of the great blessings of that home was that our bedrooms were downstairs, while the master and my brother's bedroom were upstairs at street level. I did my best to stay hidden downstairs. My stepsister could be vicious too, but I had learned to stay out of her way for the most part. She would leave her chores undone, I would tell her she needed to help, and she would give that same smug smile, shrug and say, "NO!" I did them for her because I had learned what happened if there was anything left undone. By this point, I had gotten into a routine that seemed to keep them both at bay, but it was exhausting.

During this time, one of the strangest things began to happen. My little brother refused to say my name anymore. It went on for months and months. He would ignore me and would abruptly run away from me toward his mother and other sister. I didn't understand why. I tried to play with him and entertain him to no avail. I had this sense that he was being told bad things about me. For once, my dad decided to do something about a situation. I am almost certain he suspected my stepmother was manipulating my little brother. He sat him down at the kitchen table and wouldn't let him get up until he said my name. It was very strange and made me feel, well, like crap. It took a few hours of preschool stubbornness before he finally, obstinately, muttered my name and in the same moment slunk off the chair and ran away. It was a hollow victory in my opinion. The damage had already been done.

In the adult world, other forces were moving. Unbeknownst to me, my stepmother had been engaged in some type of escapade that stirred rumors about her. I just remember that the storyline that she screamed at my dad had changed. Now, it was not only how worthless he was and horrible I was, but it was also what a stupid, small minded, gossiping town we lived in. Now, of course, I realize that the rumors were in all likelihood very, very true. From my perspective, the town was perfect. I had joined Girl Scouts, was getting great grades, attended Sunday School, and had made quite a few friends. I wasn't sure what was wrong with our town at all. Mostly I ignored what she said. So complete were her lies that if she said it, I knew it wasn't true. But the constant badgering on my dad did what it was intended to do, and we moved again. Aww… upward mobility.

This move was the fifth move in six years. We stayed in Central Florida for my middle school years with two moves and two schools in those three and a half years. That summer before the move, my stepmother took me to get my hair cut and had all my hair cut off. I was in shock. It took everything in me not to burst out crying. It was shaved on the sides and in the back. I was told it looked better on me than the way I wore my hair, curly and in long layers. I knew she did it to make me look ugly. Once again, I looked like a boy. I was made to keep it short for years. To add insult to injury, she never cut her daughter's hair, and it was longer and curlier than mine. She would never brush it, and it would get matted. My stepmother and my dad would spend hours untangling her hair with her screaming at the kitchen sink. I remember reaching my hand to the back of my neck, feeling the short hairs and weeping inside.

At my new school, I tried hard to fit in and make new friends. Sixth grade is such a precipice. Madonna, Cindy Lauper, Pat Benatar - these were the stars of the day. I didn't have the resources and clothes to put together that kind of a wardrobe, but I did have a sleeveless jean jacket that I wore often. One day in the lunch line, this boy behind me got my attention. I was excited but tried to be cool about it. When I looked at him, he said, "Hey, so are you a boy or a girl?" I was crushed. Other fun memories involved the bus. The bus stops were actually fun. We would play Chinese jump rope while waiting for the bus. The bus rides were a different story. One day, I deliberately made the mistake of sitting on the outside as opposed to the inside of a bus seat. I was aware there was an internal order to the seating arrangement, but, for whatever reason, that day I decided it wasn't fair and I was going to take a stand (or a seat, more accurately). The cool kids began harassing me for not knowing my place. At first, I tried to reason with them, and they quickly ganged up on me. The things that happened next were vile. Someone told the principal what happened, and the next day I was both lauded by the principal and rebuked by the bus driver for not telling her. For my protection, I was placed on the seat directly behind the driver. I never made eye contact with anyone on the bus again.

The school itself was not a great one. It had a real inner-city vibe with barbed wire and cubicles as far as you could see. There were fights and promiscuities I had never seen before, and not enough oversight in my parents' opinion. I was given 25 cents for milk each day. I remember the first day when I was given back a nickel in change. To my wonderful surprise the milk was only 20 cents. The extra daily change plus Friday's milk money afforded me the exact amount to buy myself a milkshake at the end of each week. It was the one splurge I had ever been able to allow myself and no one knew. When my stepmother discovered I had misappropriated the funds, there was an ugly, ugly reckoning. It was proof I was a liar and a thief and headed for trouble in that sorry excuse for a school.

After almost two thirds of the school year had gone by, one Sunday night my dad and his wife called us both into the living room to let us know that they were putting us in a private Christian school that was part of the church we had been attending. We would not be allowed to return even one day or say goodbye to our friends. We were just gone. The next morning we were driven to the new school. It was tiny. There were less than twenty kids in the whole sixth grade. To help pay for the tuition, we were sent to the office after school to clean, file papers, and do whatever other tasks needed to be done. My dad told me it was good to invest, to have to put some labor towards my education. The school was largely wealthy Christian families. We most assuredly did not fit in. There was one cute boy in the whole of sixth grade and he knew it. The class was too small to have cliques. There was just a pecking order. The main thing I remember from sixth grade was learning how to conjugate verbs and there was a thorough emphasis on Scripture memory and Biblical studies.

Seventh grade is rarely good at any school, but this class has to be pretty high on the list of how not to educate eleven- and twelve-year-olds. We were put in one classroom with one tiny window for the entire day with one teacher who clearly hated her job. If she thought anyone was a disruption, she would put them in the closet in the back of the room to do their work. She would send several kids into the closet at a time. All sorts of mischief happened in that dark room. She must have considered herself a creative disciplinarian. Once we watched in horror as the most awkward boy in the class was forced to eat paper for something he said and then threw up. I hurt for him as he sat with his hands over his head ashamed to look at anyone. I knew that feeling well. I remember the day we entered the class to find our teacher had brought in two refrigerator boxes and the two most rambunctious boys' desks were placed inside them so they could hear, but not see or participate. In her mercy, she had cut a panel so they could enter and exit. They would often yell out ridiculous things from inside their cardboard cells. A few times, I caught a glimpse inside both of those boxes and was astonished to see them covered in the most remarkable graffiti and drawings. It's funny how often cages don't do their intended damage. Caged birds still sing. Jailed people still draw. Bound people still hope and believe. What is it about human beings that refuse to be crushed?

One day, to gain some sort of order and curtail the ugly way the cooler students treated their classmates, our teacher decided to bring a student to the front of the room where everyone was to give them a compliment. Oh, how she overestimated these good Christian youth. I was the first one chosen. I sat on the stool in the front of the class, and everyone took turns saying something kind and writing it on a piece of construction paper taped to the chalkboard. I remember the cool kid and his best friend, whispering and snickering as they looked at me. Whatever they were saying was obviously hilarious. The teacher noticed and called them to come forward to offer a compliment. The best friend kept giggling as he wrote, and I noticed with growing dread that the cool kid could hardly stop his laughter or his winning smile. My stomach tightened. Then he turned and announced to the class, "I really like the white sweater you wear every other day." With that, the cool kid in his plaid Ralph Lauren button down and his cool friend busted out laughing and the exercise in kindness was over. Youth are both particularly sensitive and particularly cruel. Needless to say, the cool kids had pointed out the excruciatingly obvious truth - we did not have money for nice clothes or even a variety of average ones. The shaming had worked. Humiliated, I sat down.

How I dressed hadn't even been a consideration since I didn't have many clothes. I began to get creative. To help improve my style, status and expand my wardrobe, I asked to wear one of my dad's button downs. I had seen all kinds of cute ways to wear men's clothes. The way I styled it was apparently quite fitting, and I got compliments from a lot of my classmates. For the first time, I felt like I was in control of how my peers treated me. I realized that was the power of appearance. It didn't have to be true, it just had to impress people. My stepsister heard the compliments and saw the shift. She demanded to wear the shirt the next day. I begged her and then pleaded with my dad not to let her wear it the next day because the kids would make fun of us. My dad didn't see a problem and said yes. I cringed for what I knew would come next. The howls of laughter didn't stop the entire day, nor did the comments about how we were dirty people who wore dirty clothes, and what else did we share and other creative middle school ways of humiliation.

After that it was brutal. We became a daily pastime to find something to make fun of. I hated being paired with my enemy, as if we had some sort of connection or shared any blood. I had grown used to smiling and playing the part, but it's so hard to keep trying to feel love for someone you don't trust. Our simple PBJ sandwich with nothing else in our lunches even became a target. I stopped eating lunch completely and ate my PBJ when I got home. We were the only ones at the school that had to walk home, and we would wait until everyone else was gone before we started the mile and half trek in the hot Florida midday sun. I remember the pastor of the church once stopped and offered us a ride. It had to have been close to 100 degrees that day, and the humidity made it hard to take a breath. It was like heaven had pulled up and opened the door while we were sweating with our tongues hanging out in Florida hell. Immediately I remembered the story of the Good Samaritan and smiled, thanking him. We climbed inside. The pastor laughed and told dad jokes as he drove along. I'm sure it was nothing for him. I already respected him because even with a spinal injury that significantly impaired his mobility, he spent his life loving people and telling them about God's love, one wonderful story at a time. But to me, his kindness was everything. As the ice-cold A/C blew on my swollen face, it was Jesus telling me He was still with me. He was by my side, even in the sweltering sun. And one other thing… As I sat in that car, I heard Him whispering to me, "Don't you see? The people who love Me love others and they show it." I saw.

Eventually the year ended. Eventually, the stories about our teacher's discipline style got back to the administration and she was only allowed to teach P.E and coach. I guess they didn't think coaching would provide many opportunities for refrigerator box incarceration or forced paper snacking. During that year, there had been one brilliant, bright spot. Once a day, another teacher would come to our class to teach us History and Bible. Even to those who didn't hear his teaching, he was still the only light in our days. It was from this man that I was first exposed to remarkable stories of faith and heroism, as well as the injustices of the Third Reich and Uganda, and how to find God in the midst of these things. He thought if we were going to learn the truth of God, we should learn the truth about evil too. I soaked up these words and stories like a sponge. I saw there were so many unbearable, awful wrongs, and yet God was still capable of working good through them. Good impressed me. I was in awe of it. It never ceased, even when it was in agony, alone, exhausted and defeated. It just couldn't stop itself. It seemed to spring from some eternal source that found a way through every manner to clog it up. Good was trampled, set fire, mocked, imprisoned, tortured, betrayed - and in the end good rose again and again and won. It was just the sort of truth and belief I could cling to, and I was searching for a rung to hold on.

One of the things my dad did during this time was take me to get sewing lessons so I could make my own clothes. This proved to be a wonderful gift. My favorite part was him driving me there and back. It was the only time since he had been married when it was just the two of us. I loved every minute. I nervously went to my new class, completely unsure of what to expect. It was me and a room of middle-aged women at a long table in the back of a small fabric store. I sat quietly and began to learn and quickly realized that grown women don't raise their hand when they have a question. By the end of the course, we would have our very own piece of clothing. That seemed incredible, that something would exist that currently wasn't even a thought. What I discovered is that sewing takes vision, the ability to put something together backwards and in pieces, meticulous attention to details, and, above all, patience. No one can really prepare you for how many mechanical and measuring difficulties there are in this craft. It's an art meant for engineers. Excitedly, I took it all in. As the instructor began teaching us how to read a pattern and the importance of sizing, she called me up to demonstrate. "The perfect figure on a woman is 34-24-34, with a 10-inch difference between breast, hips and waist creating a perfect hourglass," And added chuckling, "but don't worry, no one has a perfect figure."

She turned to me and said, "Honey, hold your arms up a bit," and began measuring. She finished and paused, then asked me to hold me arms up to measure me again with a puzzled look on her face. "Well," and she turned to face the group. "This young thing has a perfect figure. I've never seen that before in my life. 34-24-34." In my head, I wondered in puzzlement, 'Am I pretty? I thought I looked like a boy.' Then she asked me, "So hon, what are you making?" "A jacket," I said quietly. I wanted something bright and beautiful to wear to stop some of the comments from my classmates.

It took me two months, eight two-hour Saturday sessions. I was so proud of every buttonhole, the cuffs, the collar, the waist. Eagerly, I wore it to our end of the year party that year at the home of one of the cool boys. As a group of us hung out in the yard, he suddenly blurted out with a Coke in hand and mocking in his voice, "Did you *make* that? HAHAHAHA!" And all the kids joined in, because that's what kids do. Shame swallowed me whole. That was that. I never wore the jacket again.

When summer arrived, we were without a home. The first part of the summer, we house sat. The largest part of the job was to care for the dogs who would have massive panic attacks during thunderstorms, which was every single day in Central Florida. One of the dogs, a large Labrador Retriever, busted holes through doors during some of the storms. I had never seen anxiety have that much control over any living creature. One storm came on so suddenly that we weren't able to get back to the house before she had busted through the outside door and was running in a harried, panicked frenzy through the neighborhood. I felt the same intense panic, terrified something would happen to her before we found her. It was a fear I would learn well.

One night, I was watching tv in the living room alone while my dad had taken his wife out to be entertained. She demanded that. It was not optional. My stepsister was gone, and my brother was asleep. Who knows what my stepmother had said or done at dinner, but suddenly my dad stormed in and sat on the couch and tried to talk to me to distract himself from his obvious anger. Since he almost never talked to me, I was surprised and excited. I heard doors slamming and heels clacking angrily on the tile floor. She loomed over him, screaming. Then she went too far. "Why are you in here talking to her?! What, are you trying to have sex with her?!" and pointed accusingly at me. I jumped off the couch and ran to the boy's bedroom I had been sleeping in. As I ran out of the room my dad's voice boomed, "HOW DARE YOU! YOU BETTER LEAVE HER OUT OF THIS!" while she screamed some of the most repulsive things I had ever heard. Surrounded by Little League paraphernalia and curled tightly under the covers, I shuddered as the war waged in the other room. My dad actually stood up TO her and FOR me, but it was all so wicked and made me feel dirty to even have those things said about me.

Shortly after that, we left and spent the rest of the summer in a condo at the beach. I was never sure if it was because of that fight or the dogs. My dad was rarely there. On the first or second day there, my stepmother had an eye injury and spent the whole summer in bed. It was heaven. All I had to do was cook pretty basic meals, clean the small condo, do the laundry and watch my brother at the pool or the beach. The two of us looked like we could have been in Coppertone ads by the end of the summer. He realized I was fun. I loved spending time with him. Unbeknownst to me, there was a concern. Overnight, it seemed, I had developed a figure. I had my white two piece and a Hawaiian Tropic tan. Halfway through the summer, right after my thirteenth birthday, I was told I was only allowed to wear a one-piece from that day forward. I was told I was getting too much attention. My stepsister laughed in my face and kept wearing her two-piece. The next day, I was given a one-piece with wide straps and what I thought was a juvenile print. It seemed there was really no end to the things my stepmother could think of to try to discourage me. I tried so hard to not let it bother me, but it did. I was literally the only person not in elementary school wearing a one-piece. But she couldn't control everything. At the end of summer after several fun filled days with some cute boys by the pool, I was taken by complete surprise by my first kiss. OHHHH… I liked that a lot. Maybe, just maybe, I was not ugly or the liar or the problem I was told I was. Maybe, I was smart and beautiful, fun and kind. Maybe I was even good. I began to think I could decide who I was.

The next year included another move to a split-level home that had a pool and a giant tree that went straight through the middle of the screened in porch on the back of the house. The new neighborhood was near a lake and there were neighbors to babysit for and earn extra money. Although it was half of minimum wage, that $2 an hour felt like freedom. I took every job I could to get away from that home. My dad worked long hours to meet his wife's financial demands and to stay away from the storm. But it was always there, pacing and lurking for him. Dinner and a storm siege every night, that makes it hard to come home.

I discovered boys too. In the neighborhood, it was very different from the environment at school. A group of us would pal around, pathetically shoot baskets, swim in each other's pools, laugh and be young. One of the neighborhood girls had us meet some of her guy friends from a nearby neighborhood at the library. We sat outside of the library and talked. One boy in particular took no time at all to give me all his attention. My interest was piqued. Like the boy at the beach, it felt AMAZING to have someone interested in me. Although we had only been sitting there less than ten minutes, somehow my stepmother drove by and saw us there in the park talking behind the library. It took me about one/tenth of a second to figure out how she miraculously knew where I was. Watching me be attacked was deeply satisfying for my stepsister. The brakes screeched right on the railroad tracks and the minivan rocked at the violent abrupt stop. She rolled down the window and shrieked from the minivan, "GET IN THE CAR!!!" Trembling, I stood and walked toward the car, hurrying my pace. Hate shot out of her eyes like a laser, fierier than her flaming red hair. I don't begin to remember everything she called me. My stomach tumbled over and over, and I just said quietly, "yes ma'am," on repeat for hours. What else could I say? Long term, I was grounded, of course. No phone, outdoors, or music, and no end to the sentence. With little else to do, I poured into books, schoolwork, and drawing. Drawing had a meditative quality to it that made me forget where I was. It was a skill I hadn't realized I had that kept bringing me little moments of joy. But even with all the distractions I tried to give myself, the youthful desire for social connection and belonging was ever present. It is astonishing to me, even now, how many mistakes would spring from this one longing. My stupid didn't stop for years.

When the adults left, they would take the phones with them. This was standard parental procedure for the serious disciplinarians. My next-door neighbor smuggled notes to me from the boy who had shown so much interest. We would write back and forth, and he asked to see me. Like a stupid kid who has been shut up from everything, I jumped at the chance to see him. I kept all the notes too, another sign of my youthful sentimentality, or dimwittedness as it turned out. And then it happened. My parents had taken everyone except me for some outing, and I told my neighbor that I was alone and to let the boy know. Within twenty minutes he was there. We made out on my bed. I felt so weird. I didn't know what I was doing. I was beyond terrified of getting caught and couldn't enjoy the moment. The best part was the relief when he left.

Shortly after that, my stepmother began to rage about me to my dad again. I always wondered if my neighbor had said something to my stepsister who had then told my stepmother what she had heard. But that's just speculation on my part. To shut her up, he went through my room, tossing my mattress upside down, throwing all my clothes out onto the floor, and upending every possible hiding place. Then he found it - the truth - the notes from the boy and my Holly Hobby diary. I hadn't seen him like that ever before. He lost control. It was anger, desperation, deep, deep sorrow and rage all firing at the same time. He showed my stepmother everything and it fueled her in a way that is difficult to explain. She knew I hated her. She knew I wanted my mother. It got much, much worse. Every type of punishment was used. There was no teaching. The goal was pain. Ingeniously, my stepmother outlawed makeup as well, and would show up at school to make sure I wasn't wearing it at school and then washing it off before I got home. On the weekends, my dad would stand guard over me and in pent up anger, mock me while I did all sorts of outdoor labor. They reminded me daily I was getting what I deserved. My stepmother declared I was listening to devil music and took all my mixtapes of U2 and OMD that friends had made for me, pulled all the tape out in front of me, and threw them away. U2's Joshua Tree is still to this day my favorite album. The band's faith and fight against injustice inspired me. There was one particular song by OMD, beyond the Pretty in Pink If you Leave hit that everyone loved, that I had played over and over before she destroyed it. Above the 80's electronic pop music played the speech Martin Luther King Jr. gave the night before his assassination, as well as some of his other words. Quite simply, the song gave me hope and direction for what I wanted my life to be about. The promised land, where justice and freedom had been fought for and won, it called to me.

His words rooted in my heart. After everything that would give me any hope or independence was taken, I developed a very patient resignation. The situation could not be remedied. The only hope was to accept it for what it was until the day I could do something to change it. There was nothing I could do but cry at night in bed and tell God I was sorry. And I was. I was really, really sorry I had been that dumb. Even now I wonder if it's dumb to write down everything that happened, even if it is true.

My dad's idea to fix the situation was to have my stepmother adopt me. He thought love could be demanded and signed into existence. I cringed at the thought. This was not an environment where I could object. It's extraordinarily difficult to sign legal documents and give away your identity and all your power over to your abuser. Nor was it the last time I would bind myself to someone I didn't love. In my effort to minimize the tension and the restrictions, I nodded obligingly. I tried my best to show her affection, despite the constant, tightening knot and grip in my stomach. One day at her parents' home, with nothing to do, I drew a picture of us walking to the courthouse and gave it to her as a gift, hoping it would ease her cruelty. It didn't. When I signed those papers, it was for survival. It's a horrible thing to betray yourself to save yourself, but people do it all the time.

From that point, there seemed to be no end to the ways she would unleash her violent tempest. Anything was a reason for a manic explosion. The speed at which she would switch from syrupy sweet to raging demon was dizzying. Once when I was doing the dishes after dinner, I had the radio set on a station and my stepsister kept changing it. I kept changing it back. I didn't think much of it and just finished up cleaning. Afterall, I was the one doing the work. Afterward I went to my room. Without warning, my stepmother busted into my room with my stepsister right behind her. She had a belt in her hand. Without saying a word, she just started beating me over and over all over my body and started screaming obscenities. I crouched in a heap and wept. My dad wasn't even home to see it. The next day there were horrible black stripes on my arms, and I wore a shirt that showed them. It was my cry for help. I feel stupid for doing that. The same boy that mocked my homemade jacket accused me of trying to get attention, which of course was true, but it wasn't his attention I wanted. One of the boys who had been banished to the refrigerator box the year before was the only one who reached out to me with compassion. Although I can't recall what he said, I remember how he made me feel. He was kind. And when he lifted his shirt up and showed me his black and blue stomach, I knew I wasn't alone. He had a stepdad. I now had a friend.

The tempestuous wild hate in our home began to get beyond my ability to manage with tiptoeing. My stepmother would unleash so much venom on my dad and never get any satisfaction unless he attacked me. The oddest part was watching her instantly become calm when my dad was finally incited to turn his anger against me. As both an observer and a receiver of her tirades, I realized she was trying to provoke a reaction that could feed and escalate the monstrous spewing of hate, lies, and violence that needed to erupt out of her over and over again. This was who she was at her very core. One morning, over some infraction I can't recall, probably lunches being made or my stepsister's lies, my dad whipped me so hard with a board that my tailbone broke. When I would fall on the ground, he would scream at me to get up and if I didn't immediately, something in him would take over. For over three months I was in excruciating pain every time I had to sit, which as a student was often. Then on another occasion, during some tirade where I just stood there taking it, my stepmother hit me so hard that my eardrum ruptured and for several days I couldn't hear out of my right ear. I was crying in the sanctuary of the church and the principal of the Christian school was notified. I bawled and told him I couldn't hear. "I can't hear! I can't hear!!! I could tell by his face he didn't know what to do. A week later my ear began to heal, I thought, and I got in the pool. The next second this piercing pain in my ear made me jump out of the pool and run inside to cry. It was months before I regained full hearing in that ear. But the good news is I did. I kept healing. I kept getting stronger. The Corey Hart song *Never Surrender* was written on the inside of all my notebooks. Something had happened inside me. I just knew this wasn't the end of the story. I knew I would never give up.

Although I don't know the reason, halfway through my freshman year we had to move back to the first small South Georgia town I had lived in as a child. Another move. To my surprise, I loved it. Public school was big and scary, but also large enough that I was not immediately identified with my stepsister. There were still plenty of things that forced us to be together, but I could finally make my own identity. I fumbled for a bit but eventually found a group of friends that were good hearted, humble, wicked smart and loved God. Almost everyone was just getting by so the rich kid element was inconsequential. For the most part people treated you the way they wanted to be treated. There were kids there that pushed me and teachers that inspired me. Before long I was third in my class. The tiny church we went to had an even tinier youth group with a youth pastor who wanted to teach us to sing. Suddenly, we were making music. Suddenly, choir practice was the best hour of the entire week. I never knew music could be so exhilarating, so soul lifting. Suddenly, I knew what it felt like to lift my voice and sing praises to my King.

In that small South Georgia town, life began again. Some kids would complain about how there was nothing to do or how everybody just got pregnant and never made anything of themselves. There was some truth to that. But to me, small towns held all the values the Bible taught. All those words about the last being first and the meek inheriting the earth and loving your neighbor, well… people actually did try, with all their imperfections, to actually personify and live those values. There were still boot wearin, cow tippin, dip spittin, gun totin, Confederate flag carryin' rednecks all over the place, but there were also mamas and daddies that called out bad behavior and made them hang their heads and apologize and then go serve people they had disrespected. The general idea was - *Honey, we are all a mess, but Jesus loves us anyway. Don't you worry about it. God has never abandoned us in spite of us. What can I do to help? Oh, and gosh darnit, can I borrow a cup of sugar? I think one of the kids has been eating right out of the jar. You need to come over in the mornin' for coffee so we can catch up. You have got to help me figure out what to do with these wild boys, tomatoes, (insert any number of things here). It's going to be alright. Don't fret one more minute. Go get yourself a bucket of KFC for dinner and don't forget to say grace. And my favorite - If you lay a hand on her YOU are going to answer to ME!* I just saw flawed people who tried to love in spite of their shortcomings, in spite of how much money they had, in spite of any number of obstacles. Their hope wasn't here. It was in heaven. It was in someone who had been perfect *for* them.

The normal benchmarks of adolescence began to approach. Each one brought me closer to a life of my own, but it was a fight. In my heart I knew who I was, and I wasn't going to allow her false declarations about me change what I believed about myself. Every attempt she made to crush, control, and destroy just made me more resolute. I kept how I felt lodged deep inside me and smiled and said yes ma'am and no ma'am, whatever was required to stay safe. I longed for the day when I could tell the truth and not fear for my life. If there was one thing I knew I would never be, it was to be like her.

Learning to drive was as awful as you might assume it would be. The first excursion was on a rare family trip to Iowa to visit my dad's family. My gruff uncle (my aunt's husband) who had been in a chronic bad mood since the 1970's, decided at fifteen I needed to learn to drive, and the country roads of the Amana colonies were just the place to learn. I was terrified. We climbed into his giant sedan and started driving on an old gravel road. I could barely see over the wheel. Dust flew as we took off toward the corn fields. Apparently, I had gotten the driving skills of my father's mother. As I drove around a bend going too fast, I slammed on the brakes. I could feel the backend begin to fishtail and, in a panic, I swerved the other way. It took literally one to two seconds before I started skidding into a cornfield at full speed and took out a huge path of corn before my uncle pulled the emergency break and slammed his head into the windshield. The first person to drive by was the farmer. With his cigarette stuck to his bottom lip, and his cap pulled down low just above his eyes, he just stared in shock and horror.

When we got back to the hotel, I laid down on the bed, frightened into an anxious, nauseous heap of nerves. I knew what was coming. The door flew open and bashed against the wall as she, in less than a second, stood screaming and spitting into my face with furious wild hate. This time, I deserved it, I thought to myself. That night at dinner with the entire family I was the butt of the joke. As my stepmother mocked me, my family - the aunts and uncles I loved - joined in the teasing. They had no idea how much that hurt. They had no idea how much it bolstered my stepmother. To me, it seemed she had won. She had convinced them I was this awful child. I was so so sorry for hurting my uncle, and there was nothing I could do to fix it. The incident set me up for massive driving anxiety. It was almost a year before I was allowed to try to drive again. I couldn't seem to get the brake and gas right anytime someone was yelling at me. This led to some seriously close encounters with some bushes and a mailbox. My dad would remind me constantly how I drove like his mother. I wish I had known to take a comparison to her as a massive compliment, despite the bad driver label.

Now in high school, my drive went into overdrive. Good grades were my escape out of my present prison. I had the whole thing planned out. I loaded up on Gifted and the new AP class that was offered, earned the absolute best grades I could attain, and was involved in multiple extracurricular activities. I was focused on anything that could boost my scholarship eligibility. My stepmother did her best to sabotage this as well. After my debate coach told my stepmother how well I had done on the debate team, she told my dad it was giving me a big head. And just like that, my days of debate were over. When I was chosen to speak at a Christian youth retreat about my faith, she accused me of being arrogant and self-righteous and, just a few weeks before the retreat, told my youth group leader I wasn't allowed to speak. When I was chosen for the Governor's Honors Program after multiple interviews, essays, and exams, she was in absolute shock and told me there was no way they would pay for me to go. I remember my heart dropping until I kept reading the letter and excitedly told them that it was paid for - food, lodging, everything! Then she said the only reason I had gotten in was because she had helped edit my answers on the application. I guess she was also responsible for the essays, papers, interviews, and examinations I took in order to be chosen as well. My dad was proud. It felt amazing to see him proud of me. For once, that was the end of the matter. I was going - one entire summer away from the madness. It was my first taste of what life could be like. It was the most wonderful summer of my childhood.

I had two boyfriends while I lived in South Georgia. Both were good boys from good families. Even though they had grown up in the South where parents have historically been stricter, they were shocked at the restrictions I was living with. I was always reminded that my stepsister's freedom was because she had proved she could be trusted. Oh, what they didn't know… My dating life was heavily monitored. My first boyfriend, Samuel, who was a few years older, finally ended our relationship because he wasn't going to have a girlfriend that he could rarely take on dates. I remember going into an absolute panic in his car because he was not getting me home in time. Even two minutes past my curfew would have serious implications. I can't imagine that was enjoyable for him. My second boyfriend, Andrew, was actually a few months younger than me and so a grade behind me. I had helped him with algebra, and we became friends quite effortlessly. Good grief he was a happy kid, and fun. His dad taught him to work harder than anyone and his mom taught him to serve others. His "yes ma'ams" and "no ma'ams" got me more leniency than I had previously had. His positivity and kindness mixed with his boyish exuberance and energy resulted in a young man who just couldn't seem to ever have a bad day or be in a bad mood. I absolutely loved everything about him. He would take me boggin' in his giant 4-wheel drive truck that didn't seem to have any mufflers. He taught me to dip my fries in a Wendy's frosty. I would watch Andrew play baseball and Friday night football, and we would meet friends afterwards to have pizza. He showed me the backroads through the woods where we hung out with the mosquitos and made memories. Andrew didn't have a relationship with God, but thought it was great that I did. When I talked to him about my faith, he was kind and attentive, but uninterested. It was the sweetest, "No thanks. I'm good," I think I've heard of all the times I ever shared my faith. If I asked him to stop, he always would and then he would kiss me sweetly. It was like being in young love with your best friend. We could pick weeds and wash cars and have one hell of good time just laughing.

One day Andrew had dropped by to see me and was standing in our foyer. No one knew he was there. In shock, he heard one of my stepmother's screaming fits that would make a sailor blush and take notes. To me, it had included no violence, wasn't terribly long in duration, and therefore, wasn't too bad. I walked down the stairs and saw his mouth hanging open in shock. He grabbed my arm and walked outside. "You said it was bad, but that's BAD! Is she always like that? I've never heard anyone talk like that. What are you going to do? You can't keep living like this!" I fell into his arms at the sheer kindness, concern, and validation of his words. At that moment, I just knew if I stayed with him, everything was going to be alright.

My stepsister and I were complete opposites. Although we were forced to do things together due to sheer proximity, that was the absolute end of our connection or similarities. We had very different ideas on how to do high school and how to treat people. I tried hard to distance myself. I will keep what happened, what she did to me, and what I saw to myself. I turned to God to make it right. He is El Roi - The God who sees. He knows. He saw. From His Word, I called on His promises. I prayed for my enemies. I tried to love despite my hurt, reminding myself that I was a sinner as well. In the worst moments I would always recall the messages of turning cheeks and submitting to authorities. It seemed everywhere were messages of submission and suffering. Endure - Endure - Endure. I beat it into my heart with every injustice. Right or wrong - this is how I was taught, and I learned the lesson well.

Lessons are funny things. They are everywhere and we are always learning, carefully cultivating and curating our own personal vignette of experiences and beliefs. An event that inspires one person is the same that defeats another. Most of my childhood the world seemed to have been in an East vs West / Wrong vs Right battle. I long for the days when the world wasn't clouded in ambiguity. There was oppression and there was freedom. It all spoke to me on a personal level. But it didn't seem that anything would ever change. That's just how things were. My English and History teachers that year were by far the greatest teachers I ever had. They were passionate and thoughtful and encouraged me to believe far beyond the confines of my circumstances. The struggle for freedom behind the Iron Curtain had fascinated me. Most of the essays I wrote that year were on this topic and one had compelled my teachers to nominate me for the Governor's Honors Program. There was a growing unrest from the years of conflict that Reagan had been able to rally even more intensely. Somehow in the midst of all the decades of poverty and oppression, hope had taken root.

I was sixteen and it was almost seven a.m. That morning, I was in a bit of a rush, wanting to hurry inside and meet my friends for breakfast before school started. We met once a week to keep us all connected and focused on our faith. I loved those friends. But that morning, as I passed by the newsstand outside the restaurant, a headline caught my eye and without thought my legs stopped. I stood frozen at what I saw. The wall, the Berlin Wall, the wall that had divided and defined the world as I always knew it, was gone. The world's current oppressive reality was finally history. I realized in that moment that all the good I believed in for the world and for myself was truly possible. It wasn't just an ideal, it was something that could actually happen. The more I thought about it, the more I stared at that crumbling, graffitied wall, the more I realized why the wall had died. It was a lie, a lie that crushed and killed. And good, although it took so long, had to prevail because it was true. Right there in that moment outside a breakfast buffet in South Georgia, I saw what hope can conquer when people don't give up. That message sunk deep down into my soul and became an anchor I would hold on to for a very long time. Every time something happened to rip the roots of hope away, that one truth would start weaving hope all over again. It just refused to die.

The end of my junior year I began planning what was going to be the greatest senior year I could imagine. I found I had many talents. I had gotten over the former mocking of handmade clothes and made dresses and jumpers in floral patterns that looked just as good if not better than all the Laura Ashley clothing of the day. I could draw, write, speak, sew, and sing. Because of the drama I lived with, I prided myself on self-control and logic. My studies in English and History and the ridiculous number of papers I wrote over those years shaped how I processed events and behavior. I was always looking for the logic, the consequence being that it made me see people and things from multiple angles. This is a skill that served me well throughout life. Although I was quiet and still timid due to years of crushing, I had begun to bud. I had made cheerleading and worked hard to be ranked third in my class. I was president of a prestigious organization and had been chosen to attend Governor's Honors for the summer. I had wonderful friends at church and school and a best friend for a boyfriend. My teachers were helping me work on scholarships to attend the University of Georgia. Freedom was one year away. The light at the end of the tunnel was bright and beckoning me.

That same year, my stepmother had started another campaign to move out of this "stupid hick town". We were in our second home since we had moved back to that town, and my dad had found us a wonderful Colonial home in a good neighborhood. I was so distracted by my own life I didn't even pay attention to her rantings. One day as she complained viciously about our small town, I chimed in that I loved it and didn't want to leave. She launched into me again. Her favorite tactic was to back me into a corner and terrorize me. She did the same thing to my dad. It could last for hours. This particular day was in the dining room. I never said anything except the appropriate "yes ma'am" or "no ma'am" that was expected to answer her crazy accusations. Usually, she would just slap me or hit me in the head when I was in this position. This day, for whatever reason, maybe she thought me speaking my mind absolutely could not be allowed, she punched me in the nose. My dad came in soon after that and I was crying and holding my face. For a moment, he defended me. I could hear him yelling at her, "I SAW HER FACE!" as I ran out the house and down a few blocks to my friend, Brittany's house. I stayed there for a few hours. When I felt like it might be safe, I walked back home.

My dad was waiting for me. It had turned. She had lied, twisted, and spun the whole thing and now I was in trouble. I sat there silent, stunned, even though the evidence of the truth was on my face.

With less than two weeks until my senior year began my dad made the announcement that we were moving back to Central Florida. Everything I had worked so hard for, all my friendships, my academic standing, the dreams of going to Georgia, all of it was snatched away, gone, just like that. My stepmother practically pranced triumphantly as my heart broke. It was awful breaking up with my best friend. That loving boy took me in his arms and held me. Andrew put his forehead on mine and told me we were going to write and talk as much as we could. He believed we could make it. Then he gave me a sweet name and said it was only for him. My faith in the goodness of men was wrapped in that one strong, loving, happy heart.

On the drive to Florida, my stepmother didn't scream at my dad; she was that excited. When I look back at my dad's choices over all those years, I feel he must have thought if he could just make her happy, life would get better. Happy wife, happy life so they say. The formula was deeply flawed. Someone was rotten to the core. We arrived in Florida three days before my senior year. I was a complete stranger - again. I pulled myself together and listened to music as I set up my new room. I didn't know what to do. I didn't know how to recraft my dreams at that point. I hated the never-ending heat and humidity, the flatness, the dirty sand that was everywhere, the low, ugly buildings, and the oppressiveness that seemed to be everywhere. I didn't understand why there seemed to be so many people on drugs. I knew I still had to graduate and get out as quickly as possible. But where? I didn't want to be stuck in Florida. With no way to afford out-of-state tuition, I didn't know what to do. All I could do was see what scholarships I qualified for right where I was. It was like being moved to a new prison days before I would have been released.

When we went to register, the registrar attempted to schedule me in a number of gifted classes after reviewing my course load and my grades. My stepmother wouldn't allow it and told her, "No, those give her a big head." She knew those classes gave me hope. I hung my head in shame. I couldn't get over all the wealth at that school. The vast majority of the kids had expensive sports cars. The teachers' parking lot looked like a typical student parking lot. There were no trucks with mud on them. There were no dip cans. There were no muscle cars that a sixteen-year-old had rebuilt with his dad. There was money and heroin. I didn't even begin to know how to fit in. I had a Southern accent that kids thought was amusing. I sulked and did schoolwork. I stopped eating. My stepmother would scream at me for missing my old life. I was not allowed to feel. "Stop f...ing feeling sorry for yourself!" … And another round would start again. It was dizzying how the rage would take over her. To have so much hate poured out five inches from your face day after day takes a toll. I don't think, unless you experience it, that you can ever truly understand that level of evil. It is never satisfied. She got it in her head I needed to be forced to integrate into my new school. She instructed my stepsister to find me a date to the dance and whoever she chose I would have to take. My stepsister was not kind. She found the most socially awkward student she could find. When the other kids heard who I was taking to the dance, they laughed out loud and one of them literally fell on the floor laughing so hard. That just upset me more. Now I felt bad for this kid and myself. I tried so hard to fake a smile. I was good at it by then. But inside I just wanted to crawl away and hide.

Eventually I found someone to date. He was not like Andrew, but it took the edge off the loneliness and sadness to have someone to be with. I still wrote and talked to my old love as much as I could. Getting his letters lit up my heart for days. This new boyfriend, Nathan, hated my parents and had no problem letting them see his disdain. To say that caused problems would be a massive understatement. I begged him not to show it. He saw through my stepmother's phoniness and constantly pressured me not to put up with it. I looked at him incredulously. Did he want me to *die*?? Clearly, he didn't understand how dangerous that was.

Nathan also spent every moment together pressuring me for sex. He just wouldn't stop - at all. One night he snuck in my bedroom window. I heard every sound in the house and thought any moment my life would be over. All I could think was how scared and stupid I was. He talked me into skipping school one day and I didn't have enough practice breaking rules to feel the thrill of it. My anxiety and fret over getting caught was, I was reminded, "a total buzzkill." So I did things I didn't want to do and faked smiles so the buzz stayed right where he wanted it to be. Like I said, my stupid didn't stop for years.

One night Nathan came to see me at my friend's house. We went for a drive and stopped at a park in front of a lake. We sat on the bank in the hot, humid night air. It started sprinkling and he ran and got some blankets that we crawled under. He kept pushing and pushing. Finally I gave in. I was just so tired of the nagging, so tired of the whole conversation. I gave in and it hurt so badly. He didn't notice my tears. I was so angry with myself after that. Ashamed. There was this awful pit deep in my gut. Why couldn't I keep saying no and just be done? I didn't want to sleep with this guy. I didn't want to pray. I'd let Him down. Where was God anyway? He had taken everything. When hope was finally within my grasp, He allowed it to be ripped away. He had allowed me to be abused for years. At the precise moment I most needed to, I just couldn't talk to Him, couldn't trust Him. I stopped taking communion. I put a wall up. I knew I had brokenness in my heart. I desperately wanted to be done with school so I could run away from the hurt and the hate. I thought I should run from my Savior too. The need to run from everything I knew began burning deep within me. It was almost all I thought about.

Halfway through my senior year we moved again. My stepmother wanted to live in a certain part of town where we had lived before. Since my parents had divorced when I was four, I had moved nine times in thirteen years. The rental home we moved into was an old cinder block home that soaked up all the humidity and dampness and wreaked of mold. It was only three bedrooms, so our beds were given away and I slept on a mattress on the floor in the same room with my stepsister. To get out of the house and earn money for my escape, I got a job at Baskin Robbins. I started decorating cakes and working every chance I could. My boss loved me and quickly gave me a raise. I kept scratching my head, thinking, "Other people like me, why am I so hated at home?"

I had saved several hundred dollars from babysitting and my part-time job. It was my freedom fund. One day when I came home, I realized all my money was gone. In a panic, I asked where it was and was told that it wasn't my money. My stepmother told me she had put a roof over my head, and it was time I should be contributing. I understood the logic of everyone contributing but my heart was devastated, destroyed. The thief just took it. She didn't even ask. I had to get out.

I did notice something peculiar during those last few months before I left. My stepmother had started doing some freelance writing. It started out with brochures and then progressed to courses. She had one client in particular she kept talking about. She had known him from church. I knew the family only slightly. But the whole thing struck me as odd. I remember hearing her on the phone with him and that same phony, sickeningly sweet voice. I couldn't figure out what she was doing and if this is just how she was going to be with clients, but it seemed off for a business relationship. There was too much familiarity. My dad seemed to be clueless.

After I had finished the dishes one evening, my old boyfriend, Andrew called. I was so excited to hear his voice. I sat on the laundry room floor in the dark with the phone cord stretched across the kitchen and just talked and smiled at the ease and openness between us. Suddenly and viciously, there was a violent and abrupt pull on the cord, and the phone was ripped out of my hand and went crashing through the kitchen. I stood up, stunned, and walked into the kitchen to see my stepmother standing there with the cord in her hand and savage rage on her face. She wanted blood. She was ready to pounce. I looked around the kitchen thinking to myself, *'Did I forget to clean something?'* The kitchen was in perfect order. My mind raced to think of what I had done to set her off. It didn't take long to find out. It was me talking on the phone to my old boyfriend, not moving on or something. She went on a venomous spew. At some point, I rolled my eyes and was hit violently in the face faster than I can explain. That generation loved to slap their kids, but this was no slap. It came from uncontrollable hate. Immediately, I grabbed my face as the hot stinging pulsed on my cheek and eye. And from somewhere deep within me came the fateful words, "I can't stand you!" As soon as I said it, I wished I could take it back. After all the years of harassment and abuse, she had finally been able to provoke me to talk back. In that moment she felt free to do anything. My dad heard the chaos and came running into the room, not to defend me but to defend her. The things that happened next were so god awful violent that I simply can't bear to put them on paper. It went on for hours. They were going to force an apology out of me, and I refused. No matter what they did I kept refusing. It was as if the strength that I had used to endure had been switched to a different channel and now it was the reservoir to not give in. At one point, I thought I wouldn't survive the night. Somehow some measure of sanity came over my dad and he backed down, telling me all he had done is restrain a disobedient, rebellious child. There was no remorse. "Clean yourself up and go to bed."

The next morning, we were late to school. When I saw my boyfriend, he took one look at me and turned and walked the other way. I kept my head down and spoke to no one that day. During my last class of the day, I saw an administrator walking towards me. She pointed at me and said, "Come with me now." It was an order. I went to the office. There were child welfare agents there. They took pictures. I was trembling. I begged them not to do anything. I told them I was terrified, terrified of what they would do now. Please just let it pass. They tried to be compassionate but clearly had absolutely no idea of what they had just unleashed. That afternoon both my dad and stepmother were in the car to pick us up from school. I trembled uncontrollably and the sick nausea took over. I couldn't hear the screaming and threats because my ears were buzzing so furiously. I had never more wanted the earth to open up and swallow me whole. I remember them repeating over and over again what I had better say. There were more agents that came to the house and interviewed us. I was interviewed in the living room with them standing by and watching. How I was supposed to feel safe to tell the truth is beyond me. I remember realizing very quickly, oh this system doesn't work at all. It just puts kids in more danger. From that moment on, my dad hated me more than she did. The next few months were a blur of loathing dirty looks and dirty words. Oh, they made sure not to touch me and would get right up in my face to remind me of that. And that is the environment I graduated high school in. I hated taking those pictures after graduation with the forced fake smiles. But it was over. I was almost out.

3

Independence

And I feel like I'm naked in front of the crowd
Cause these words are my diary, screaming out loud
And I know that you'll use them, however you want to
But you can't jump the track, we're like cars on a cable,
And life's like an hourglass, glued to the table
No one can find the rewind button now...
— Anna Nalick [11]

Eleven days after I turned 18, on a Saturday morning, something triggered another tirade and just like that I called a coworker from Baskin Robbins. She pulled up in her car and I took what I could. My stepmother started screaming that everything I had belonged to them and nothing that I thought was mine was mine at all. They grabbed belongings out of my hands as I tried to leave. Finally, I left.

Because I had no money and no car, my choices were quite limited. After losing my Georgia residency in the move, I needed to go to a Florida school since I qualified for their state scholarships. The obvious choice was the local university so I spent that summer working every single hour they would allow me to work so I could save up money again. When school started, I found a room to share. The one splurge I allowed myself was to rush and join a sorority. Why I chose a sorority over groceries is beyond me. I guess my hunger to belong and be loved was far greater. I thought this was my chance to fit in and have the life everyone else seemed to have. I budgeted so carefully and realized there was almost no money left. I found a job within walking distance and took the bus or walked everywhere I needed to go. I didn't eat much at all.

That first year, I was still that same good high school girl, naive, kind, feeling the need to be perfect to be accepted. I dated a young man way too old for me that could not be considered a boy. Brian would pick me up after classes and we would go to his home near campus where he lived with his family. His sister was my age. She was so many things I wasn't - a rough, witty tomboy and wickedly smart. She was sarcastic and moody but loved her family. Their parents were some of the kindest people I have ever known in my life. Immediately they accepted me into their family.

I had decided that first semester to find my real mother and meet her. It didn't take that long which surprised me. She was living in Alabama with her third husband. After classes ended, I purchased a bus ticket and headed off to rekindle this relationship. I was so naive. I didn't recognize her, but from her dramatic approach I knew it must have been her. I had already explained that my name had been changed. The awkwardness was almost unbearable, but I was determined to find a way to love this stranger standing before me. She brought me to a rundown trailer that wreaked of cigarette smoke. The heaviness of their home was

[11] *Breath (2 a.m.)*; Words & Music by Anna Nalick, © 2004 AnniBonna Music (ASCAP) All Rights Adminstered by Concord Sounds c/o Concord Music Publishing, All Rights Reserved Used by Permission; *Reprinted by Permission Hal Leonard LLC*

suffocating. My mother showed me letters she had written to me that were returned and her attempt to find me with the postmaster. I could tell, based on the letters, that at some point after we had moved to Florida, she had given up. It was an effort, but a small one. I poured over her pictures of me as a child. She told me bits and pieces of her life since then that seemed avoidably tragic. I kept my thoughts to myself and looked on this stranger with the compassion I had held for my mother all those years. I tried to explain to her how bad it had been, but the oddest part was it didn't seem to resonate with her at all. She began talking about her new husband and the Vietnam War and their marches to Washington. Her husband had no warmth and had barely spoken to me. He was abrupt and rude to her. The little I saw of him was angry and quick tempered, and yet my mother seemed to idolize him. She oozed dramatic acts of adoration that almost seemed worshipful. Not knowing her well, I studied her trying to determine if it was sincere.

We went on a hike to the DeSoto Falls, trying awkwardly to connect. I had jumped at the chance to get out of the dark heavy trailer. There was something intensely evil about the place. On our hike, I told her what I knew of her father and how he had brought a girl my age to the states from the Philippines and married her. It was the one sincere moment I had with my mom. She got quiet and the drama in her voice vanished for a moment. She began to speak softly and almost logically. She stared out over the falls lost in some other moment for a long time. As I watched her silently, I knew the stories were true. When she did begin speaking, she talked about a horrific crime that had happened at those falls. I was stunned. It was the kind of awful evil that no one has a response for. It was almost as if she told that story to get me to stop talking and stop asking questions. I did. The second day I was there, I began to get violently ill. The suddenness with which I got sick was very suspicious. It was if the trailer itself was attacking me. Being a logical person and knowing that didn't make sense, I tried to brush it off, but deep inside me I knew this was from some different kind of evil that I had never experienced. I knew I needed to go back to Florida. I had to get out of that place. With a fever of 104° I got on the bus, shaking. Brian picked me up and took me straight to his parents' house. His mother began to care for me the way no one ever had in my life. My fever got dangerously worse. My feverish brain tried to sort through the strange mix of people, emotions, events and my thoughts on the whole matter. Something was not right, and my spirit seemed to be under attack. I definitely had not found home when I found my mom.

When I started to feel better, Brian's mother wanted to hear how it went. She had bought me Christmas presents, nicer than I had ever received. I just looked at her in wonder. *Who are you? Why are you being nice to me?* It was if God had knelt down and kissed my forehead. From that moment on, she took up a place in my heart. It's remarkable how powerful love is, especially when offered to someone who's only known what it's like to be alone. I soaked it up. A few weeks later when her son broke up with me because he was dating a girl closer to his age, I was crushed. His family decided that he could break up with me, but they weren't going to. I couldn't believe what I was hearing. Did they really love me? After such a short time? Both his sister and his mother became like family.

My second semester I moved into an apartment with four girls from my sorority. I was so excited when I heard there was a bottom bunk available. I was still timid and shy and wanted so much to please everyone. I had no idea I had moved in with the mean girl of the sorority. The only person I had ever met like her was my stepmother. She would be syrupy sweet to you and you would tell her all your secrets. Then one side of her face would curl up, raised eyebrow and raised lip, as if she was calculating the most intoxicating cruelty she could devise. The first time I saw that face, I knew who she was. I laughed to myself how strikingly similar she looked to the Grinch. Cruelty certainly wears a few favorite masks. After I had moved in, another sister took me aside to warn me that they had harassed the poor girl before me and she had moved out. I listened but naively thought to myself, 'I'll just win her over with kindness,' and sought about doing just that.

By spring break there had been a complete shift. One day I was sitting on the couch and the mean girl stormed in and accused me of stealing her jewelry. I was shocked and horrified, stunned into silence. She spewed profanity and got down close in my face in an all too eerily familiar posture. I told her she could look through my things and that I would never take anything. She shot back that she was sure I had pawned them. I looked at her dumbfounded, incredulous at the thought. "That's crazy. At what pawn shop? With what car? The university bus doesn't travel out of the area. You can look through anything I have. I'll show you my bank account." She literally put her hands on her hips and stuck her nose in the air. Then she told me I wasn't on the lease and ordered me to get out. I told her I had given up my other place to live with them because she had needed another roommate. She didn't care. I later found out she had wanted another girl to move in and this was her way to get me out. Her next tactic was to gossip cruelly about me to the other sisters. Fortunately, she already had a mean girl rep, so no one took her seriously, but it still hurt. It took me a while to make arrangements. Those few weeks were hell. I ran out of toilet paper one day and went to get some out of the other bathroom. That night, they screamed for almost an hour about how they had proof I was in their room so that proved I was a thief. No amount of rational thinking was allowed. The other girls were terrified of her. I was frantic trying to find a place. I tried to convince my mother to come visit for the mother daughter brunch that spring as some kind of kindling to my hope that I wasn't alone. She declined and went on for almost an hour about how critical it was for her to join her husband at the Vietnam Memorial and the injustices they were fighting and on and on. I stopped listening after Vietnam. It seemed pretty clear she really wasn't that interested in me. Once, I was able to convince her to visit me. In that short visit, I realized she was beyond brilliant but deeply manipulative. My heart dropped. I didn't see myself in her at all. When I failed to invite her the next year, she called to let me know what an awful daughter I was. Try as I might, I couldn't see things her way.

No one was going to save me, so I had better save myself. I kept working. I rented a room and took classes all summer. I borrowed a bike from my summer roommate to get to campus until it was stolen. REALLY?? I worked even more to replace the bike. Discouraged, hungry, tired - it all rooted in me and I looked with bitterness at all the students who had it so easy. Father? Are you there? The arguments that there are always other people who have it worse didn't help. If He was my Abba, my Savior, my Lord, where was He? The silence broke something inside me. It was around this time that I decided to stop praying. In my limited view, He wasn't answering them anyway. What was the point? He obviously wasn't going to protect me or help me. I thought to myself, 'I've tried to live for you my whole life and look where it's gotten me. I think I'll do this on my own now. It's time I had fun like everyone else.' I held my breath waiting for the next semester. This time I would get it right.

That summer I reconnected with Andrew who had stopped writing and calling. In that year, he had changed. He was a new man. He had gone to the same retreat I had been a part of years before and had been transformed. His entire goal was to serve God's kingdom. Shortly after his transformation, he had a sudden onset of diabetes and was hospitalized for days. When he recovered, he was driven to share the good news of Christ to any who would listen and had a hunger to disciple others. He had led a walk-out at our school over some unethical way the administrators had treated a coach. He had basically become this 17-year-old giant of faith. I had lost mine, and he had gained his.

My sophomore year I took up residence in the sorority house. Everything about it seemed glamorous. My best friend was in the sorority house next to mine and at first it seemed there was a sweet girl behind every door. I was determined to make sure this year went perfectly. I got up early, went to class and then walked to work. After a lunch shift, I hit the books, went rollerblading and then got ready for the fun. My best friend would give her big political wide toothed smile to every phony we crossed paths with, which I noticed was increasingly my sorority sisters. She didn't suffer from the same debilitating disability that I had, always believing the best in people. She would constantly and lovingly tease me about it. "You know what your problem is? You keep trying to find good in people."

We laughed more than I had ever laughed in my life. I remember thinking, this is how life is supposed to be. Nights were the crescendo and never started before 10 pm. Drinking and laughter followed us from bar to frat house to crashing wherever we ended up, almost every night of the week. The thought of that lifestyle absolutely exhausts me now. The first semester was fun, more than I thought I would ever have. Very quickly though, it all started getting out of control. The girls in the house were vicious - snobbery, jealousy, backstabbing, boy stealing, friend abandonment, gossip - the entire realm of mean girl repertoire. There really are too many bad stories to tell. I had one great friend in another sorority who could fake a good girl image, wear designer shoes, call daddy in an emergency, be valedictorian, and at the same time, cuss like a sailor, drink like a sailor, and totally have my back like the very best sailors. She was authentic and, if you were her friend, you knew her good image was a front for her fun, loyal heart.

I was able to get another job at a bar where I could make more money because several of us from the sorority worked there. It was beer, wings, crab legs, oysters and short shorts. Quarter beer night was the worst. We would fill up buckets with tiny cups full of beer and hold them over our heads to get through the crowds without spilling it all. It would be so packed you would get groped the whole night by strangers as you walked through the crowds. And then there were the managers. One kept trying to pull me into the office with all kinds of excuses. I remember being relieved when I heard he was doing that to a number of the girls. I felt safe knowing everyone was rejecting him and stupidly thought the rejections would make him stop.

The Christmas party was held at The Edge on Christmas Eve in the afternoon. The Edge was where the Rave scene was peaking. I did not realize how quickly the drug scene in Central Florida was exploding. Knowing I was underage, the manager brought me a drink and told me to drink fast before anyone saw. I took a few big swallows and set the drink down. I was shocked when he grabbed me, groped me and pushed his leg up between my legs before I knew what was happening. "You know you want it," he yelled into my ear above the music. The rest of the night was scary. Almost immediately I began to lose consciousness. I didn't realize until months later, when my coworker told me all that happened, that I had been drugged. I thought my drink was just really strong and felt guilty for getting so wasted. Young, stupid and can't hold her liquor was the reason, I thought. I found out later one of the servers had pulled him away from me and taken my completely limp body home. I remember her yelling at me trying to keep me awake and seeing trees and electric poles out of the hatchback window where I was curled. Because the sorority house was closed, I had been spending the break with my adopted family. They were livid and rightly so. It was Christmas Eve, and we were supposed to go to a candlelight service. My drugged body couldn't move or even speak. I felt like I was going in and out of consciousness and my body was like a ragdoll. I was so ashamed. Here were these amazing people who treated me like a daughter and a sister, and I had acted so shamefully when they had invited me into their home. This was before anyone had really heard about roofies. I took all the guilt for being drugged. The good news was I never saw my manager again. He got fired for sexual harassment because enough of the girls complained. I kept working there because the money was good, and I needed it to survive. As for all the groping hands, you just grew numb to it and attempted to shrug it off. Part of the job. But there was always a part of me that winced and was repulsed every time a boy allowed himself to treat me like a thing, simply because he didn't have the capacity or desire to consider how his actions made another person feel. The same boys that could brawl over an accidental brush against someone in a crowded bar would intentionally grab a woman's most intimate body parts and laugh with no guilt. Women, I realized, were regarded as things, not people, not hearts, not minds, not souls. In disheartened disillusionment, I recognized and conceded that the economy of lust ruled men's hearts. There were no wrongs to account for if you didn't give a shit about anyone but yourself.

Perspective, wisdom, and even kindness can change how you view your past. A few months ago, on a random Sunday morning, a friend sent me a Ted Talk of this wise old woman, Caroline Myss. She said something I knew was true the second I heard it. I had already been studying the physiological effects of trauma so, when I heard her, it was like being handed a lost piece to our human puzzle. She said, "Choose to live an integritous life. That means I'm not going to put myself in a circumstance or force another person, when I know they're uncomfortable, to be in a circumstance where I know they're uncomfortable, in order to please me. I won't hold another person captive because that has no integrity. I will not do that. Now let me tell you something. Liars don't heal. So, you can eat all the wheatgrass you want. And you can do all this stuff with seeds and vegetables. (People laughed and she continued) But an honest person who eats cat food will go further than you. Dishonest people, people who lie, people who have moral crisis and do not get it, people who blame others for things they do and they know it, people who make choices and they know another person is going to pay for the consequences of that choice and they are conscious of it, they know for a fact that they are saying something that is not true and they know another person is going to be hurt by that, people who deliberately say things to hurt somebody - believe you me - your body knows you did that. Your mind knows you did that. Your heart and soul knows you did that… Make the decision to live an integrous life." I let the truth of that sink deep into my soul. And suddenly, the way people were, the way they are, the way they can't get better made sense. Sins stick - like superglue. And the sins of others to me, on me, those stuck too.

My whole college scene headed rapidly towards destruction. Boys' ability to use girls had ominous and unbridled opportunity at frat parties. There was a casual indifference to the usury. "Boys will be boys. And even that wouldn't matter if we could just prevent girls from being girls."[12] My heart seemed to retreat further and further inside me, as it was trying to hide from the ugly truth of the world. It didn't seem to occur to anyone that what happens at frat parties, should not stay at frat parties, it shouldn't happen at all.

It certainly didn't happen to just me. But after it happened once, I guess boys thought it was fine for it to happen again. What's *it* you ask? Well, *it* is any number of things that happen to girls after they have one too many drinks, someone slips something into your drink, the wrong kind of guy has his eye on you and doesn't take no for an answer, or better yet - the mob mentality of vulgarity and the uproarious shouts for flesh win over what a girl wants to happen to her. I think in light of the #metoo campaign, we have all heard stories. I still never wanted to tell mine. Those dark memories are rooted in the kind of shame that makes you want to leave town and change your name. I never could figure out why some of us were targets and our even drunker friends weren't. There was a night I woke up and when I stood up and tried to take a step, I tripped because my underwear had been pulled down around my ankles when I was asleep on a friends' couch. I sat up quickly trying to recall anything, anything at all. My body recorded what my mind didn't. My heart raced, pulsating shame to the places shame likes to root. For a front I tried to brush it off. My heart knew my brave face was a lie. The words I would use to describe myself at the time are scared, confused, groping.

Soon after, I started dating a guy in the fraternity. Let's call him Frat Boy. This is the groping, hoping for good from a snake. I thought if I was paired with one of them, the other frat brothers would know to stay away. One night, I was asleep with Frat Boy in his bed. There was no party, no alcohol, just two young adults and

² The Diary of a Young Girl; Anne Frank

one of them was asleep. In a moment of terror, I was shocked awake when the covers were ripped off and at least thirty guys were hooping and laughing in a crazed drunken frenzy. The covers were held three feet in the air while I curled tightly to cover myself and stayed curled up in a ball shaking. I caught a glimpse of him smiling victoriously and a hi-five. I wept silently while my body trembled uncontrollably. I never said another word to him. After a few hours, when I hoped they were all gone, I dressed and with my head hung down I walked back to the sorority house and crawled into bed. It was such a hilarious story. Aren't you laughing? Everyone on Greek Row wanted to retell it. I stopped going to class for a while. I couldn't face anyone.

After absorbing the shame, I tried just avoiding it. It was decided the best next thing to do was to change our go-to frat. My best friend and I decided to hang out with different sorority sisters who had guy friends at other houses. One guy in particular was a year younger, and I could tell he had a crush on me. I wasn't interested in anyone at that point, so we just spent a lot of time together. He let me use his computer to write papers, and I was his gal pal that helped him talk to girls. It went on for a while this way. One day, it was more than that. I tried pot with him. I hated it. I wasn't too impressed with myself either. Who was I?... God? Can you still hear me? I had this growing fear that all my mistakes were pushing God further and further away from me.

Then there was a fateful night. I wore this romper that crossed and buttoned in the back. HOW did these things ever come back into style??? Anyway, the next morning I woke up in my bed with the straps of the romper tied around my neck and a giant bruise on my forehead. I was confused. Because I woke up in my bed, I thought everything was fine. I had no memory beyond drinking more than I should. I was supposed to go skydiving that day. A group of us met and drove to the fields. One of the girls told me she couldn't believe I was there. Confused, I asked why. She began to tell me what she had heard. Even today, twenty-five years after it happened, I can hardly bear what others told me.

Apparently, with a line too long at the women's restrooms, I made my way upstairs to the resident bathrooms. In a stall, I couldn't get the damn buttons undone and ripped the straps off trying to get the romper off to go to the bathroom. Then, in glorious humiliation, I passed out on the toilet. At some point, some drunk boys saw a drunk girl under the stall. In Hulk style, they kicked the door in leaving a massive bruise on my forehead and found me, essentially naked on the toilet with my clothes around my ankles. This was some gift from the dark frat gods. Like some kind of crazed ritual, they carried me through the upstairs laughing in hideous victory before throwing me on my friend's bed. At that point, I don't have confirmation of anything, just what people told me they thought happened and the way no one would look at me or talk to me. There was the rumor my friend played some role, but this was never confirmed. I wasn't sure if my lack of memory was a gift or a curse. I couldn't defend myself because not even I knew what was true. A friend had found me, and she and her boyfriend had dressed me and carried me back to my bed. I was brought before a group of other sorority members and put on probation. I never really knew what for and I couldn't ask. I still don't want to know. This was justice - punish the girl for drinking too much, do nothing to the boys who took advantage of her. Later in life I would find that was still the basic formula for justice. I can see why. It's so much easier to blame the victim than hold the guilty responsible.

Sick, nauseous regret made it difficult to take a deep breath. I couldn't look anyone in the eyes. I was too young and too easily intimidated to realize that shaming and blaming a victim was how to avoid holding others responsible. If I had had a family to turn to, maybe something different would have happened. But I didn't. So, what was done *to* me became my responsibility. At the time, I had seen enough parties and drunk college students to know that I was definitely no worse than the average among them, and probably quite better. The shame debilitated me. That's the part about trauma that no one tells you about, that you lose the ability to be you anymore. Any ambition or interests - you don't feel worthy enough to have them, and in the aftermath, you just let everything go. Then you're adrift, no anchor, no direction. Very alone…. Jesus?... I was too ashamed to seek Him more than one prayer. I told myself I deserved the silence I received.

In the aftermath I decided to transfer to Georgia, even with out of state fees and everything else, I had to leave. One of my history professors had asked to publish my paper on George Washington, how he recruited former slaves and other people of color during the American Revolution, the influence their efforts had in the war, and on Washington himself. I knew it was an honor for an underclassman, but I wanted to dig a hole and never come out. I felt like I had no right to be honored for anything. Shame dirtied my heart. I was accepted to Georgia and breathed a sigh of relief. I worked every shift I could to earn enough money to move. I had to get away from the shame.

One day my friend Brittany from South Georgia called me, the same girl whose home I had run to years before. I was shocked and excited to hear she lived in Orlando. For a moment, it was as if a life raft had been extended to take me back to a place that was wholesome and good. When she walked into the sorority house, I hardly recognized her. She was emaciated. She had won our high school beauty pageant and Miss Congeniality as well. She was that awesome. This girl was talented, authentic, and wonderful. I couldn't believe what had happened to her. She told me about stripping and the great money she made. She tried persuading me into becoming a cocktail waitress where she worked. I adored this girl and it hurt my heart to see where she was. I wondered why she had reached out to me. I saw her shame and loneliness while I was living my own and realized how those feelings can bind you to people and drag you further down, as if you are carrying the weight of their demons too. Even then though, I saw her. I saw the incredible person that she was - *is* actually. I wanted to rescue her, rescue us both. But I was lost.

The next year was a time of great mistakes and uncertainty. I made choices that put me on this path that I have been walking since. At this point in the story, I have to remind the reader and myself that my stumblings and horrible wrong turns had always been part of God's plan. God always had my awful mess in mind. When I think of the great wonders of God, it is how He weaves good and bad together for His own purposes that impresses me more than all of His beautiful creation. If we wrote our stories, there would be no bad men and bad things wouldn't happen. We wouldn't have reason to overcome, to grow. We wouldn't seek Him or learn what it means to truly trust His will. Our dependence would be on ourselves. We wouldn't think we needed a savior. We wouldn't be in awe of how He can change us. We wouldn't know He answers prayers. We wouldn't know His mercies are new every morning. We wouldn't know how great, wide, deep, long, and high is His love and grace. We wouldn't know the only thing we need is Him. But God, in His infinite wisdom and mercy, wanted us to see just how wondrous He truly is. For what He is, is a miracle worker. The world likes to tell us the only thing we need is ourselves. It's not true. The only thing we need is Him.

The summer before I planned to move, I met a man while I was waiting tables who was way too old for me but showed a lot of interest. I'm sure, after what had happened, my self-esteem was almost non-existent. I had no interest in anyone from school and didn't feel like I deserved anything or anyone good. Sean was one of those people who teetered on the edge of brutality and sadism. I didn't see it at first, partly because of my own shame and partly because I was forever trying to see the good in people. He wasn't conniving, just rotten where good can't reach, where reaction, not rational thinking ruled him. He could be sweet but had a hair trigger temper and wayward appetites that he seemingly had no control over. He would help a friend move their couch, help a stranded motorist, and then do something so fiendish that it didn't seem possible that it was the same person. I was never sure how much of it was out of his control. As I was writing this, I had to remember why I had even gotten mixed up with Sean in the first place. Then I remembered. It was laundry.

Like I said, my stupid didn't stop for years. But if I hadn't dated Sean, I never would have met my children's father and the exact miracles I am writing about would never have happened. I would have met someone nice and had the socially appropriate number of children. There would have been barbecues, little league, swim lessons, some good vacations and a comfortable home. That would be it. But because of this guy, who probably belongs in jail or a psychiatric hospital, I get to tell the world about heaven. Go Figure…

After a few dates with Sean being above average in his ability to have a conversation and not become inebriated like most of the guys at school, I started spending more time with him. One day, at his invitation, I brought over my laundry and started a load, then went to work. When I got back, I stared in astonishment at a basket of clean, perfectly folded clothes - my clothes. I had been doing the laundry since I was eight so the idea of someone doing my laundry was an extraordinary gesture. Adding to that was the fact that I had never witnessed a guy do laundry before and certainly not anyone else's. Most of the girls I knew were always doing laundry for some guy they knew. He told me he just wanted to do something nice for me. I was stunned. So that is why I took the budding relationship a little more seriously and began seeing him - because of that one kind act. I can't remember any others. A few weeks later I went with Sean to Georgia. He was doing private investigating work and wanted someone to tag along. He promised to take me to Athens to check out the campus while we were there. I jumped at the opportunity. It was summer break, and I needed an escape, a summer fling before I left Florida for good.

While we were on that trip, something snapped inside him, and Sean began making wild, jealous accusations. The next thing I knew, I had broken ribs, a TV hurled at me, and a seriously messed up face. I was supposed to leave for Georgia. He sobbed about how sorry he was and that he was afraid of losing me, that he would never do that again. He did. I couldn't imagine going to Georgia in the condition I was in. Just like that my dreams of Georgia and escape were gone. Then a month later, I thought I was pregnant. Fear and shame won. I dug deeper into that hole I had made for myself and I stayed. I remember the lump in my throat when he sneered at the possibility of a baby and with a sinister gleam threatened, "That's nothing a few kicks in your gut won't take care of." I wasn't pregnant, but I didn't leave because I wasn't making enough money to get my own place. It took a few more nightmares before I left. I wasn't enrolled in school. I got a full-time job at minimum wage and lived with him and his brother, trying to piece my life back together.

That year, I learned about the underworld. I saw the dark places that evil has hold of and the people trapped there. It broke my heart. One day, Sean took me to a strip club at noon to run in to handle some business and get some money he was owed. It was so bright outside and so dark inside that it took my eyes some time to adjust to the light. The first image I saw is forever imprinted on my heart. I can never believe that strip clubs are the benign establishments where men blow off some steam because of that one moment. In the red, smoky, filthy air as my eyes adjusted to the darkness I saw a girl my age or younger. She was probably eight months pregnant with almost nothing on, and the disgusting, crusty old man she danced for had his hands all over her. I quickly looked at the ground and my eyes filled with tears while an enormous lump almost instantly stuck in my throat. I couldn't look up. In another moment a topless woman approached me and brazenly, in a way that was sexually aggressive, offered me a dance. She was almost touching me. I couldn't retreat into myself far enough. My arms were crossed and squeezed to my sides. I couldn't even look at her. I just shook my head and could feel all the blood rushing to my face. My heart pounded in my ears. She laughed at the remnants of my modesty. I just wanted to yank them all out of there. Then I was struck with the weight of my own sin and immediately thought, 'How did I get *here*?!' My next thought was of Jesus. 'You love them, don't you?' It was a statement of truth, not a question. I prayed for her, for myself. But there was more I had to see.

Sean's father was in his early sixties and looked eighty. He had never met a drink or a cigarette he hadn't consumed. His sons had tried to help him more than once. They got tired of everything that came with the addictions. At that point, his father was staying in a crumbling, pay by the week hotel in downtown Orlando where drug addicts, prostitutes, and people with AIDS went to die. He puffed away on his cigarettes with an oxygen tank by his side. It seemed as if he was smoking harder, trying to suck the last of his life out of the butt of a cigarette so it could be over. With the money from the strip club, Sean paid for another few weeks for his father to live there. My skin prickled and my stomach twisted and turned the whole time we were there. I tried to hold my breath. Dying has a smell and death was everywhere. I had never seen a place totally overtaken by sin and sorrow. There was no hope. Darkness and heaviness hung in the air. I was so shocked by the grief and the smell that I finally couldn't take it. I had to leave. I started walking fast and then running, shaking and in tears, wanting to vomit when I got to the car. For weeks, I would dream about the people already dead but still breathing. No one, no one should live like that. That year I saw what it's like to die without hope. I can't explain how horrible it is. Eventually his dad deteriorated enough to be admitted into hospice and then he died, his relationships in ruins. That was his legacy.

During this year, I focused on a few things I could control. I lifted weights and started running, amazed that I was good at both and how incredible it made me feel. I still didn't feel beautiful, but I did feel better. I was at least smart enough to realize I needed to find a way to fully support myself so I could get out of the mess I had allowed myself to get into. My best friends and my adopted family hated Sean. Low life thug was the term I heard most often. They made sure I knew I deserved better and wanted to know what was taking me so long. 'Money,' I would answer to myself, 'Isn't it obvious?' When you have people to support you financially, what you really have is better, easier choices. The night he and his brother brought home a prostitute when I was in the next bedroom was the final straw. They had even taken video. Sean's sister wanted a roommate, and I jumped at the chance. I didn't even say goodbye.

By the time I left, I had saved up $800 and bought a 1976 Ford Fairmont that cut off at every stoplight. A few months before I had moved out, Sean had taken me to watch a football practice. It was mid-day in Central Florida, and the football team was sweating madly in the heat and humidity. He pointed to a huge human being who was one of the assistant coaches and told me he had gone to high school with the Big Jock. I nodded and wondered if that guy was the same as my boyfriend. Then, in an attempt to be identified with something greater than himself, Sean talked about how his former classmate had played football for the university when they had won several impressive titles. At the time, these football players were treated like idols. They were the Bad Boys and they lived up to the title with pride. All the girls wanted to be *with* one of them and the boys wanted to *be* them. He was blond, athletic, good looking and took the drill sergeant role as an assistant coach to new heights of verbal harassment. The Big Jock had the whole offensive line doing a body crawl across the entire field with just their forearms while he made comments about their girth. The ribbing was so funny that the players were having to stop to let out belly laughs while they crawled in the suffocating Florida heat and humidity. When Sean introduced me to him, I noticed immediately he was interested in me. Besides continuing to direct comments to me to see if I would laugh, I caught him staring at me. I was shocked and flattered, but that was it. I chuckled at the ribbing and didn't think anything else about it. It would be months before I saw him again.

After quite a bit of the aforementioned hustling, I was able to get out of that relationship and landed a job bartending at a busy college bar. The skirt and top were short, and the tips absolutely saved me. By this point, I had seen a lot. I wasn't sheltered anymore, but I wasn't hardened either. Having money, for once, allowed me to not live in such a constant state of anxiety. I stopped partying because I would rather work and make money. I didn't have the stress of classes either. I actually felt free for the first time in my life. I started to feel slightly good about myself again. I couldn't even think about next steps, and I was ok with that. One day, one of the guys from the frat house of the night I didn't remember came into the bar and I served them. He saw me and busted out laughing. "This is her!! This is the girl I told you about!!" He almost choked on his beer from laughing so hard. I hung my head down fighting an urge to throw a beer in his face. Even a year later? Really? The old shame stirred in my belly, my throat clinched, and I quickly walked away so no one saw the tears. The rest of the night, I was blinking back the hot tears and couldn't talk to anyone.

My adopted family had been earnestly encouraging me to go back to church. And so, I began my attempt to tiptoe back to God. The very kind, gentle pastor gave me the verse, *You shall be holy because I the Lord your God am holy.*[13] I sighed when I read it and bit my lip so I wouldn't cry. All of the shame came rushing in like a dam had broken. Right… be holy… I really felt like he had handed me the most impossible verse. I wanted to cry and say, "But I've tried!" I felt the weight of it all. I wished the verse had said, *Persevere* or *Endure,* or *LOVE,* even *Turn the other cheek.* I was <u>really</u> good at that. The irony was that a few short weeks later at a Christmas gathering, this pastor's son, who was engaged at the time, suddenly and shockingly put his hand on my breast as we stood there talking and laughing in his father's backyard the second after my friend walked away to get a refill. He quietly whispered, "You know you want it." Actually, I didn't, and I stood there petrified. I couldn't think of a single word to say. Who would believe me? He was the pastor's son. There was nothing I could do but push his hand away and walk back to the party celebrating my Savior's birth, my heart pounding with humiliation, my stomach churning.

Then one night, as I stood behind the bar, this gorgeous man came walking in and started talking to me, never wandering far from the bar. Brad had the kindest smile I had ever seen. He was soft spoken and stationed at the Naval Nuclear Submarine program a few miles down the road. His friends were kind, he was kind. He got my number and asked me out the next night I didn't have to work. The following night was our big college night promotion, I can't remember if it was dollar beers or something else, but it was a promotion that attracted a lot of young, drunk, and dumb. Then the Big Jock came in, the man whose children I would have. He was a huge human being, broad chested and golden skinned, and walked in like he owned the place. He had a girl under each arm and the cockiest walk I had ever witnessed. I saw him walking in and recognized him immediately. He saw me and pointed right at me shouting, "I know you!!" He dropped his arms off both girls and came right up to the bar with the biggest bravado and gravitas. I was stunned. With his Cheshire cat smile, barrel chest, heavily sculpted blond hair, strong chin and massive arms staring right at me I had the urge to look behind me to see if it was someone else he was talking to. 'What on earth? *Me?'* He didn't so much ask as insist on getting my number. I was drawn into the whole scene and responded in some kind of hypnotic impulse at whatever he asked. Throughout the night, the Big Jock would leave his scene as king of the dance floor and come over to shoot his grin at me. And sure enough, he called and asked to take me out the afternoon before my other date. 'Cool,' I thought. 'An early and a late date.'

The day of my dates, I waited for a call from the Big Jock to confirm, for a knock at the door, for anything. The time came and went. Nothing. 'Wow. Stood up. Great guy. Fine by me,' I thought. 'I've got another date anyway.' Because Brad was living on base, I went to pick him up for our date. He was standing there waiting for me with the biggest, most beautiful smile. He was nervous, and it melted my heart. We went to a movie and dinner. He opened doors. He treated me tenderly. He asked what my dreams were and told me about his. As we got to know each other better, he kept telling me he could see these great things in me. I would shake my head. I had never had anyone see greatness in me, ever. He encouraged me to go back to school with the biggest smile on his face, like he believed in me or something. Every moment we spent

[13] Leviticus 19:2

together was lighthearted and loving. One day, we spent an entire Saturday on my back porch sipping beer and talking while we stripped and sanded a dresser and the rain poured for hours. We both knew it - love. It was undeniable. Every time we saw each other, we would embrace and kiss and laugh. We played. This is what it's like to be in love. Those few months were the happiest of my life. His friends were all hard working, good hearted, honorable people. They accepted me into their community immediately, and instantly I had a new set of friends. Where have you good people been all my life? It was like I had walked into a world of people who thought like I did, who treated others like they wanted to be treated.

There was only one thing we had ever disagreed about. Although I was certainly not living like I gave Him much thought, I loved God. I believed in and loved Jesus Christ. I belonged to Him. My distance was from shame and heartbreak and had nothing to do with love. Because we were both always talking and learning about each other, one day it came up - the existence of God. I realized there were people who were indifferent to God, but I had never known anyone close to me who outright stated as a fait accompli that there was no God. Sure, there were atheist professors, true to form, but I had taken for granted my faith, not realizing it was a gift that not everyone had been given. He felt he was proof that you could be a good person and not believe. He thought it was all an effort to control behavior through fear of some eternal judgment that didn't exist. A legend. A fable. A myth. Science was his god, but there was no intellectual snobbery. He was humble. He just didn't think it was true. He didn't think holiness or perfection was required, just a general conformity to the rules and ethical standards of the day. I was stunned. I felt foolish defending God when I was not exhibiting many outward signs of devotion or belief in Him. Yet, there I was, not talking to God, but defending Him.

One weekend, when I had a few days off, I went back to that South Georgia town I loved to see some old friends. I had worked hard and earned enough to trade in my old Ford Fairmont for a Ford Escort. I was excited to be in a car that I could trust beyond driving to work and back. In Georgia, everyone was moving on with life. Andrew had fallen in love with his college sweetheart, and I was absolutely thrilled for him. He deserved someone who had a heart as good as his. They were both innocent and good to their very cores. I looked at them and longed to be that good again. The next morning, I woke up early to drive back to Florida in the new-to-me used car I had saved up for. My thoughts were of how strange life is, how it moves us and directs us quite often in the directions we didn't intend to go, as if there was some other purpose other than the one we designed that was meant to be.

On that early morning while driving back to Florida, I dozed off at the wheel and woke suddenly starting to veer off the road. Inexperienced as I was, I overcorrected, just like on that gravel highway in Iowa, and the little bubble of a car flipped two and a half times across the highway like a tin can landing on the driver side. I only had the shoulder strap on. I went in and out of consciousness. I was taken to the hospital and there were some stitches and a lot of bruises, but I pretty much walked away. The first responders and the hospital staff couldn't believe it and kept telling me I had angels. I nodded respectfully. I was in shock. I wasn't ready to acknowledge angels or to thank my Savior for saving me. Angels? I'm Presbyterian. It was just the way things happened. What others called luck, was simply providence. I was only out a car and the eight months of wages it had taken to pay for it.

One night, after having another wonderful time, we came back to my place and Brad asked if he could call his parents back home in Arizona. His mom had been on him about checking in. Brad was the second of five and his mom adored him. You could tell it was mutual. This was back in the time of long-distance phone calls, so it was a big deal to talk for a long time. He went into my room for privacy and the door was closed for over an hour. When I went in my room he was sitting on the floor saying goodbye. His mood was somber. I asked how the call went. He was tight lipped which wasn't like him. Brad said his mom was telling him lots of stories about life. His answer was ambiguous and left me wondering if something was wrong. The next week I turned 21. He didn't call. I went out with my friends without feeling too excited. It was anti-climactic at best. I came home one day to find a birthday card and a flower. My heart ached as the silence could only be saying one thing. Without hardly a word he had pulled away. That weekend he heard I was at one of his friends' houses and met me there. Everyone left so we could talk. I couldn't handle hearing him say he didn't want me. With tears in my eyes, I told him that apparently this wasn't working out and asked for my key back. Brad sat silently for some time. It was like waiting for some hatchet to fall. He was resolute but when I looked in his eyes, I saw he didn't want this breakup, any of it. Finally, very quietly he spoke. "You're making this easy. Too easy." Very calmly, despite the tears I said, "I don't want to be with someone who doesn't want to be with me." He leaned over and kissed my forehead. It took everything in me not to grab him and hold him. Over the next few months, he would reach out again several times. But then it was too late. Later I found out his mom had encouraged him to end the relationship before it was too late. She didn't want him to fall in love with some bartender in Florida and screw his life up. 'Is that who I am?' I thought to myself. The label stung. I was more than that.

The day after the breakup my friends rallied. As I lay in a puddle crying, they threw clothes at me. "You're going out. No discussion." Reluctantly I pulled myself together and we went to Church Street Station's Howl at the Moon. I had been there so many times underage and this was my first time using my real ID. My friends got me drinks while I tried not to think about how much I missed Brad. After a few drinks, I could sing, and I did. Standing near the front we belted out song after song. Oh Mr. Piano Man, take it all away. The next moment is important because it changed the direction of my entire life. There was no reason for it. It was almost as if an unseen force had spun me in an abrupt about-face. With no reason to, I stopped singing in mid song and turned around. And that's when my life changed. Directly in front of me was the Big Jock who had stood me up, with, as usual, two drinks In his hands. He had an "oh shit" look on his face and stood frozen at the sight of me. I almost laughed out loud and shouted into the noise, "You stood me up!" He stumbled over his words trying to think of an excuse. "Let me guess, by the number of drinks you're carrying, you must be here on a date." He excused himself and came right back. The hilarity of the moment was priceless. He tried to make me laugh which I was eager to do, anything to forget my heart had been broken. He begged me to give him a chance to make it up to me. So, I gave him my number - again. He called the next morning and took me out to wine and dine me. I was so grateful for the distraction. I worked, went out with my friends, and the Big Jock kept calling. It wasn't long before it was a regular thing. I was not invested at all for a number of reasons. He had a serious drinking problem. He lied. And I knew I was not the only one.

One day while I was in his bed and he stood in a towel, he casually said, "So I've been seeing you and this other woman and well, she's got a good job and buys me things so I'm going to see her, not you." I don't think I've ever moved so fast in my life. It was a Road Runner moment. I was relieved. I hadn't figured out how to untangle myself and he had done it for me. It was also the one and only time I ever remember him being truthful. Weeks passed. I had started classes again. I wanted to become the woman Brad thought I was. One night while I was in my bedroom studying there were rocks hitting my second-floor window. When I went to look, there was the Big Jock, two stories below. "Why haven't you called me?" he yelled. Confused, I said, "You broke up with me. You don't call people who broke up with you." Then began the sales pitch. It is hard to explain why it worked, but it did. I let him in, and he proceeded to tell me how he didn't realize until after I left that he had fallen in love with me and to please give him another chance. Things were going to be so different. Blah, blah, blah... And I did. I gave him another chance. The second, no the third of too many to count. It was shortly after that I became pregnant. I just didn't know yet.

***

My roommate decided to move out with her boyfriend and ended our lease, only telling me after she had done it. I was homeless again. My good friend and I made plans for an apartment later that year. My adopted family insisted that I needed to settle down and stay in one place until I found another permanent living situation. Because of their huge, generous hearts, I moved in - and kept going to church - that was a must, an unwritten rider to the invitation. I hoped if I just went enough Sundays, I would be able to get past the shame. Intellectually I knew God still loved me, but I felt so far away from my Savior and Lord.

These wonderful people loved the Big Jock. Most people did. He was charming. He had the University of Bad Boys football player thing going for him. He knew how to sell himself. I felt like I was the only person who knew the truth and had to keep my skepticism to myself. All the men in my adopted family and a lot of my friends kept telling me how awesome he was, as if they all had a crush on him. Everyone was impressed. Except me.

At Thanksgiving, I responded to my dad's invitation to visit the family in Michigan where they had moved. For years he had told me he hated me and could never forgive me. After the police had called him when I was in the accident, he had decided he actually did love me. I still wanted a relationship with my dad and so, with fear in my heart, I flew to see them. It was all so foreign, the people, the place. It had been years since I had seen my brother. He was a teenager and preoccupied. I had brought my dad a book of all these incredible photographs of people who had been freed from communism in Eastern Europe. When I had seen the book, my heart had leapt. I wanted people to be free. It was what I wanted for myself, for those in communism or still suffering, for the countless people that are enslaved and oppressed by any number of things that work to crush and control. When I gave him that book, it was an introduction, albeit a very tentative one - *Hi, Dad. This is me. This is what I care about.* From the look on his face, I knew he didn't get it. He didn't get me. While I was there, I started feeling funny. I thought I was getting my period and it was a particularly painful one. I kept waiting. It never came. I couldn't wait to leave.

When I got back to Florida, the Big Jock and his new leaf were showing more interest in me. He kept asking if I had gotten my period. Finally, I took a test, and the line instantly popped into the small window. Truth literally stared at me in the face. I gasped. I decided there was no way that could be accurate. I took another three tests with the same instantaneous results. My good friend told me those home pregnancy tests were just home chemistry tests and to go see a real doctor. I went to the school clinic. The doctor asked what the problem was, and I told her. She told me, "You don't need to spend the money on another test. You're pregnant." I insisted. She obliged. It was true. I was pregnant, despite my concerted and consistent denial. Apparently, my not wanting something to be true didn't change the fact that it was. And somehow during that time, the person I was quietly vanished, and someone new began… I felt the truth of those words: "A single event can awaken within us a stranger totally unknown to us. To live is to slowly be born." [14]

I was as clueless and helpless as any child in a strange new world. What was I going to do? The thought sickened me. I knew my family wouldn't help. I knew the Big Jock's new leaf wouldn't last long as the possibility of a baby already had him heading for the door. And I knew there was no possible way to support myself, finish school, and raise a baby.

This part of the story hurts to tell, but it is true and important. My solution to a life spinning out of my control, to a life that would demand more shame and poverty was this. I decided I would just not eat. If I didn't

[14] Antoine de St. Exupery

eat, then the little blue line would surely go away. So, for about twenty-four hours I didn't. I don't think I can adequately describe the hunger that came over me during those hours. I know it doesn't seem like much, just one day, but that hunger consumed me. It was if my entire body, and maybe that little body inside me too, were battling my heart and my will. I didn't want to eat because eating meant accepting this, eating meant everything I was going to be would now be gone, eating meant becoming a mom when I didn't want to be. It was my last effort at denial, my last hope to make it all not true. But like I said, it was a force of hunger I have never experienced before or since. It occurred to me that this was not going to work, and this baby was not going anywhere. So, I gave up, or gave in, and ate, fearfully taking those first willful bites. I remember thinking at that moment, "I guess I'm going to have a baby," and yet another lump stuck in my throat. It stayed.

The next two months were spent hiding my secret and hiding myself. Only a few people knew, and I made myself as scarce as possible. I simply disappeared except for work and class. Even then, I kept my nose in a book or on the computer and only spoke when I was spoken to. I wore baggy shirts and baby-doll dresses. I hardly even made eye contact with anyone. My boyfriend dumped me for another girl after letting me know he just wanted us to raise this baby as friends. He did briefly try to persuade me to give the baby up for adoption, but I would not even entertain the idea. I knew enough about myself to know that once I had acknowledged the inevitable, that acknowledgement was the first moment I loved this little person inside me. Of course, it was not the first moment she was real or precious, she was always that, but it was the first moment I had shaken off selfishness and fear for the awesome envelopment of motherhood. My heart had not been baby proofed. Once that love opened my heart, I couldn't snuff it out or ignore it. I couldn't even conceive of the idea of giving my child away. This baby, for better or worse, had been given to me to love, and that was what I would do. I knew intensely that this little life deserved that and much, much more.

When I could not hide my secret any longer, I began to tell the adults in my life. I was twenty-one at the time. What should have been a chorus of joy for a new life had my circumstances been different or acceptable was instead an unrelenting echo of anger, blame, and shame. I was not allowed the privilege of expecting or experiencing joy. That was reserved for good girls. These were just some of the responses: "You have ruined your life! You are such a stupid idiot! If you don't give that baby up for adoption, we will NEVER lift a finger to help you! You'll never get a dime from us! (Although I never had received one of those dimes.) You and that baby can starve for all I care! How could you? You had better marry him!" As well as lots of screaming and quite a bit of profanity that I will spare you. "You'll have to find some other place to stay. You just can't stay here. I'm sorry." This particular statement was from the very generous family that had welcomed me into their home. My pregnancy was just too much for them. I knew they were so disappointed in me. My best friend said she just couldn't continue with our plans to share an apartment with me expecting a child. I really understood why she felt this way. Not only is a baby not the kind of housemate you want when you are twenty-one, but you don't even want to think about that future possibility.

My pregnancy had a plague-like effect on my life. The snickering and gossiping by other students and former friends were relentless, and the whispers were not so whispered. I just wanted the earth to open up and swallow me. I wanted to run away, to hide, to have never existed. Almost immediately after my humiliating condition became public knowledge, I found myself completely alone again — abandoned. There was also this mounting impatient pressure that made me feel I had no right to even show myself among decent folk, and I knew I had better come up with a plan soon. The fact that a pregnancy center never even crossed my mind shows just how few or unadvertised they were. A home for unwed mothers was synonymous with adoption in my mind, and I didn't know of one anyway. Besides, I couldn't leave school, as it was all I had. Even my doctor could not contain his annoyance at having to care for a stupid, foolish girl who got knocked up. My dad sent me a book by Dr. Laura Schlessinger, <u>Ten Stupid Things Women Do To Mess Up Their Lives.</u> The message was pretty clear. I highlighted everything in the book about not marrying drunks and men who couldn't be faithful, as well as other points and mailed the book back to him. I kept trying to be strong and stand up to everyone telling me to give up my baby or marry someone you don't love.

My options were almost nonexistent. I remember in desperation calling the Big Jock and telling him I had nowhere to live, and could we please just be roommates and nothing more until I could support myself and the baby. That time was like living through a fog so thick I couldn't even take a full breath. Every moment was just a gasp to get you to the next. I waited a few days for his answer. I wish I could have known how his response was going to change my life, but I didn't, and I was desperate. His proposal was this, his parents would help us get a place and get started, but only if we got married. I tried to explain to him why this was a bad idea for so many different reasons, but his parents had made up his mind for him. This was the only way he would help. And so, because I had decided this baby and I would eat, not just that one day but every day, and because I wanted this baby of mine to not be homeless and hungry, I agreed, and we got married. His official proposal was inside a drive through car wash in the dark. I looked at the floorboard and thought, 'This is it? This is the moment I'm going to remember forever?' I said yes very quietly. The shadows of lost dreams and grief darkened my heart. Others had determined my life. I was just some passenger on a journey who was given no choices but all the responsibility. He chuckled when I accepted and told me he did it in a car wash so he wouldn't have to get on one knee. I looked out the window so he wouldn't see the tears.

Two days before I got married, Brad called me and asked to see me. Even with my protruding belly that I couldn't hide anymore, I jumped at the chance. We rode around for a long time just talking and laughing. It felt so good to laugh and be in the presence of someone who loved me. It was one of the few kind moments where I saw someone just be a friend to someone who needed one. But that's what love is all about.

I remember having to force myself to walk up to that altar and forcing myself to smile. The dress I didn't care for and didn't want to be wearing, pulled tightly across my swelling abdomen. "At least I only have to wear this once," I thought and smiled meekly to myself. Even then I still looked for silver linings. I remember making vows I knew I would keep; vows I knew he wouldn't. I was so frightened, so terrified, and yet I forced myself against every rational thought, everything I had ever dreamed all for the sake of this little one inside me. I knew what I desired and what I was sacrificing. I was giving up all of me for this tiny person that needed me for a lifetime. I also remember wondering at the hypocrisy all around me. Everyone I knew was having sex and having it frequently, and the boys seemed to battle for the most partners. I knew I wasn't even the first to get pregnant, just the first in that circle to go through the humiliation of having the baby. I couldn't understand the punitive treatment I received, not for having sex, but for getting caught.

Apparently, pregnancy was the crime to be punished for, the scarlet letter to bear. And pregnancy was synonymous with stupidity. Smart girls were the ones who didn't get pregnant or didn't let anyone find out. Not bad grades, not laziness, not drunkenness or drug use, not deceit or theft, not even violence. Nothing seemed quite so heinous or deserving of social shunning and disgrace as a young girl pregnant and unmarried. I also marveled at the genius of men, not one of whom has ever been so stupid as to get themselves knocked up. What gene made them so responsible, so smart, so uniquely adept at removing themselves from this common but life wrecking quandary? As we stood there posing for our wedding-day picture, no one seemed to notice the very large bright red EXIT sign above our heads, captured forever in a three-by-five glossy. "How ironic," I think every time I see that photo. "That is exactly what we both wanted to do." He wasted no time getting right back into bed with the one girl and then many others. Two weeks after we were married my old roommate called me and asked, "How's your marriage?" I didn't know what to say. Then she proceeded, "I'm asking because I just saw your husband sitting at the TCBY holding hands and kissing some girl across the table. So, how's your marriage?" "Not good," I answered quietly. That night I told him I knew. He didn't speak to me for weeks and barely came back to the apartment.

The day I gave birth, the Big Jock disappeared. He showed up right before I started pushing. He had been eating and drinking all day. I guess he needed the strength. Then he ate the meal the hospital had prepared for me after I delivered. It's hard to explain all the feelings I was feeling that day. I knew I was alone. But then, just an hour later, that changed forever. I had a baby girl and fell in love.

4

After They Arrived

These are the days that must happen to you.
— Walt Whitman

No one can prepare you for that moment when you meet your first child. I just remember pushing and pushing and then opening my eyes to catch my breath, and there were the most beautiful sapphire eyes staring back at me from between my legs. I burst into tears. I had heard of people weeping for joy, but when it enveloped me it was like nothing I had ever known. How unearthly beautiful and wonderful and good! There, before me, was my baby girl, and nothing could be as sweet as that face at that moment. I remember being shocked because I hadn't thought or dreamed of what this baby would look like. I had been so busy being scared it hadn't occurred to me that anything so breathtaking and precious could come from me. Forgotten for that moment was all my shame and loneliness, forgotten was all my hurt and fear. All I could feel was love and joy and hope. As I nestled her close to me and kissed her soft cheek, she became my everything, and I couldn't help but think, "How could a baby be anything but a good thing?" So a mother and a daughter were born.

> *You're just too good to be true*
> *Can't take me eyes off of you*
> *You'd be like heaven to touch*
> *I wanna hold you so much*
> *At long last love has arrived*
> *And I thank God I'm alive*
> *You're just too good to be true*
> *Can't take my eyes off of you* [15]

After Morgan was born, I still worked hard to finish school, but it seemed so secondary, like a necessary afterthought. When I was with her, I wasn't that stupid girl who got herself pregnant, I was Mommy. I was love. I was warmth and a full belly. I was kisses and hugs and caresses. I was smiles and sweet lullabies. Everything was somehow going to be alright because she was in my arms. I loved holding her and watching her tiny hand wrap itself around my fingers. I loved her blue eyes and the sweet sounds she made. I loved watching for every new thing she would do. I loved the smell of her sweet soft skin; breathing it in was like taking a breath of happiness. She made me forget I was supposed to be ashamed. But of course, I could always count on others to remind me. I can't even begin to come up with a number to tell you just how many polite women, particularly at church, who would say, "What a beautiful baby," followed immediately by, "and how

---

[15] *Can't Take My Eyes Off Of You;* By Bob Gaudio and Bob Crewe. Copyright EMI Longitude Music Co. and Seasons Four Music © 1967 EMI Longitude Music, Songs of Universal, Inc., PW Ballads and Seasons Four Music Copyright Renewed All rights on behalf EMI Longitude Music, Admin by Sony Music Publishing. All rights on behalf PW Ballads and Seasons Four Music Admin by Songs of Universal, Inc. International Copyright Secured All Rights Reserved *Reprinted by Permission of Hal Leonard LLC*

long have you been married?" with a smile that could not hide the judgment they seemed too eager to bestow. Since I had obviously been stupid enough to get pregnant, I must have also been too stupid to deduce the intentions of their less than subtle but polite inquiries. Certainly, they must have felt a civic and even divine duty to squash any dignity or joy I had the audacity to show and to make certain I knew how much I didn't belong. Girls like me must be reminded of their place, the outline of the letter retraced on our chests lest we dare forget. I remember wondering if they realized other girls were watching how they treated me. Didn't they know boys would treat those girls the same way they treated me? Didn't they know those girls had the same fears, desires, and nature I did? Didn't they know their judgment meant other young girls would rid themselves of the same burden to avoid ridicule and a similar loss of dignity? Didn't they know that babies die because they insist unwed mothers wear shame for life?

Although I remained respectful and polite, there was something inside me that wouldn't let them take the joy that came from my baby girl. I guarded that joy like I guarded her. I had already given up my identity and put my dreams aside, and I just couldn't let anyone take away the one good thing I had gained through all of that loss. I also realized I was good at being her mommy. Although not always unspoken, I sensed that I was being watched and critiqued beyond what was reasonable; there was a scrutiny to every detail of my mothering. There was an eagerness to see me flounder and fail, a desire for me to give up on this idea of motherhood, an anxiousness to say, "I told you so." Before she was born, I knew they thought this baby would be better with someone else, but I knew there was nowhere better, nowhere she could possibly be loved and cared for more than with me, where inside she had first come to be. The reason was simple, she was part of me, lived inside of me, and belonged with me.

One woman told me how selfish she thought these young women were who dared to keep their own children when there were plenty of families who deserved these babies. Somehow the right to parent your own child had, in the minds of many, become an exclusive right only for those who were married. Married couples deserved babies, stupid girls did not. When I questioned this woman, she based her opinions on the idea that one parent was insufficient and that these young women drain their families' energies by keeping their children. I was stunned and couldn't speak for a moment. There were so many thoughts racing through my head and so many emotions racing through my heart that I was afraid to open my mouth for what might come out of it. So biased and antagonistic she was that I doubted if even logic might persuade her. I asked if she could ever conceive of giving one of her children away at birth. She was aghast at the thought. I asked why she thought these girls should feel differently about their own child that grew and moved within them. Their hearts were not exempt from love just because their finger was exempt a ring. Their bodies responded with the same overflow of devotion that awakens and erupts from any womb. I asked if she thought it was unreasonable to take a child away from a father if the mother died during childbirth. This too was an inconceivable thought for her.

The variables began to race through my mind, what about a widow, what about a woman abandoned? Would these women need to be stripped of their children too? It is just one parent, and one parent is insufficient, you said! Why, all of these people would drain their families and communities! Who, who and how few can both parent a child and support themselves solely on their own? Are children only a privilege for those with a middle-class income or more? Don't we eagerly help a new mother who is married? We bring gifts and food and drop by to give the new mother a rest. Why is this much needed helping hand a joy to offer if the new mother is married, but an unwelcome, unwanted, resented burden or duty if she is not? Why is one new life of more value or more reason to rejoice than another? Should we only rejoice over those children who are planned? Is this part of my punishment, the never-ending penalty for my fertile stupidity? Am I not entitled to my child? Am I to be robbed of the joy that she brings? Am I to be treated as if I am selfishly stealing someone else's child because I dare to do the insensible selfish thing, because I dare to love and care for my own baby? Forget my body! This is my BABY! My identity, my purpose became clearer than ever before. No matter what anyone else thought or said, or how I was treated, loving this sweet child of mine, while it was not all I wanted to do, it was what I wanted to do most.

During the first few months of her life, the Big Jock was very interested in our little baby girl and completely uninterested in me. He was gone as much as possible. I knew the other woman was still around. I had found nauseating love letters and receipts in his laundry when we didn't have enough money for diapers. Finally, one night I begged him to end our joke of a marriage. The ring wasn't even real. I felt stupid wearing it with people complimenting what I knew was a lie that I had to protect for the sake of his pride. I pleaded with him and told him that I knew he wasn't happy, that neither of us had wanted this and it was his parents' choice, not ours. At first, I thought he was seriously considering it. Then, he refused adamantly. He said the only way he would help is if we stayed married. My heart dropped. I knew I couldn't make it on my own. I did what I could to be a good wife in those circumstances. It seemed I was stuck in a new prison, so I might as well decorate. That December I quilted every day until I had stitched two quilts together by hand for Christmas - one for my husband and one for his family. I didn't have much to give, but I thought that my effort would say plenty. But if someone doesn't want you, they don't want your gifts either.

When my little Morgan was still very little, five and a half months old in fact, I stopped nursing so I could complete my internship. Education was still my way out, I thought. That one decision which seemed so practical set off a series of events that changed my life. Before I could schedule a doctor's appointment, I became pregnant again. I never even got my period. One day I was just sick, and it was very familiar. This time was so different though. I wasted not one moment in denial. I had so much joy from Morgan that I literally leaped in the air when I took that test. I couldn't wait to have another baby. The raised eyebrows, disapproving looks, and comments such as "Already?" and "Again?" were still thrown about plenty, and not surprisingly still stung. But I didn't care quite as much. I wanted to please these babies and make them smile. Although we never knew anything but broke during those years, I threw myself into making a simple, but happy home. I read all the books I could get my hands on and took classes taught by wise, God-fearing women. During this time, I also ran back to my God, who had never stopped loving me, never stopped beckoning me to Him, even when I ran from Him. It was so good to be close to Him and seek Him again. It was as if as soon as Morgan arrived, I had to be with someone who truly loved me. "It is no slight thing when those who are so fresh from God love us." [16]

Then one day as I blissfully played with Morgan, the phone rang, and the doctor's office was on the other line. Some memories are so clear you can relive them over and over, even if you don't want to. This was one of them. It was the one nurse who had never judged me, never given me a funny look, never acted as though my pregnancies were anything but a complete delight. I am grateful it was her that called and told me what no parent ever wants to hear, and really what no parent ever expects to hear—that something might be wrong and they're not sure what it is. "One of the blood tests showed something is not as it should be, and more tests are needed. It might be nothing you know. There are lots of false positives that turn out to be nothing. Oh honey, don't you worry…" She must have heard me stop breathing. I couldn't even think. My end was silent, stunned with fear. Something wrong… something wrong… had honestly never even crossed my mind. There was so much else wrong, how could more wrong be added? And I didn't even know what "this" was. It wasn't like fearing the unknown, it was knowing there was an unknown that you should and would fear. At that moment though, "this" was threatening my baby, and I could do absolutely nothing about it.

[16] Charles Dickens

As I hung up, I really couldn't catch my breath. Fear constricted my airwaves and that familiar lump rose in my throat. I don't remember answering the phone again, or how much time passed, but I must have because my next memory was me talking to my stepmother. This was before the days of caller ID. You just had to take your chances on answering phone calls or with the answering machine. My stepmother had divorced my father after having a long and protracted affair with that former client from church, leaving him penniless and with a suitcase of clothes. She had convinced him they needed to move back to Florida for her work. She had the house sold and the money in escrow while he finished tying up loose ends. Then she told him to meet her at a hotel where she delivered the news. She let him know she had moved into a gated neighborhood in Florida and put him on a list to refuse entry. Everything my dad had, including my brother, was in Florida. For months, my dad had been calling me weeping. He was lost. He had given up everything for that hellish marriage because he didn't want another divorce. He kept telling me how sorry he was and asking how could I ever forgive him. For years we hadn't spoken and the only words he said to me was that he despised me and would never forgive me for calling Child Services. The fact that I hadn't didn't matter. I was still responsible for what he had done. So, when he cried and called me every day and treated me with love, I was like a malnourished child in front of a buffet. He was crying over his divorce and I felt like doing an Irish jig. Finally, he was free. In the pit of his loss, he didn't see it that way. He felt she had stolen everything - me, my brother, everything he had worked for over the years. He was right about that. She was a thief and destroyed anything left behind.

That day on the phone she must have asked what was wrong. I could hardly speak. My panic sputtered out in short, breathless gasps to a woman I didn't care for at all. I still feared and distrusted her because of the countless cruel things she did to me and to my dad. "Why am I telling her?" I thought, as if my panic now had a voice all its own. Silence had always been my greatest defense, but before I could process my words or thoughts, she said words that evoked a power in me I didn't know I had. In one moment, she turned my fear into repulsed indignation, and my indignation into strength and purpose. What she said was this: "I would completely understand if you aborted this baby. After all, you need to consider your quality of life." For the second time that day my lungs seemed to stop taking in air. My what! My quality of life? My emotions raced to find words, but all I remember gasping was, "No, I can't." I was too stunned, too angry to be eloquent. Where were my words when I needed them? How often I have wished to go back and ask, and to defend my defenseless child.

So, if my child requires more help, more love, more patience, more money, more worry, and more of my time, I should simply get rid of this child? If my life were to be difficult, my dreams of normalcy or fairytale thwarted, then is it simply okay to kill my child? Shall I choose peaceful or pleasant over the life of my child? Shall I willfully choose to throw my own child in the trash, so I don't have to be bothered to care for a little life that requires so much more than most? Shall I choose me over you, little babe of mine? Shall I choose a pretty little life I can control and predict, full of glossy pictures and lovely vacation spots over a life that journeys through the shadows anys of hopelessness, just so this baby and I might reach a place of peace that is as vast as the sea and know the exuberance and gratitude that can come when only the tiniest of miraculous milestones is reached, the ones most people never even notice? Shall I choose "problem-free" and miss the unfathomable joy that comes simply from glimpsing the great, great good that has come as a direct result of this pain, this loss, this baby, this unwanted journey, that I DID NOT SIGN UP FOR! What is quality compared to life itself? Is quality more valuable than a life, than my own child's life? Without knowing what would happen, I knew this was my child, and that answered all the other questions. Just like Morgan and without my planning, a life had been given to me to love. His name is

Houston. He is the miracle I am living. At this moment, you are reading this book because of that one human being. How great is even one life.~

Then love arrived. When he was still quite little, I had him baptized. The moment they poured the holy water on his wobbly round head, I felt a flood of energy go completely through me. I was astonished by it but kept it to myself. I thought maybe it was just a rush of joy. He was so precious to me. Later the Big Jock asked me, "Did you feel something when Houston was baptized?" In shock I nodded my head. What *was* that?

5

The Vanishing

The world around you moves on as if your life was never shattered,
and all you want the world to know is that your baby mattered.
— AJ Clark-Coates

Before he was born, the doctors could not find "the something that was wrong" in the many tests and ultrasounds they poured over. Everything seemed perfect. So my fear quieted, and I waited. When he was born, I fell in love again, and everything seemed to be fine. He was so happy and full of life, all boy and all smiles. He was far beyond his developmental projections, smiling, crawling, climbing, playing with toys, playing with me and Morgan, laughing, tracking objects - that is until it all just stopped abruptly. It was such a short time like this, and I still want my baby back the way he was before he was taken from us. When I see his old smiles and his beautiful bright eyes, my stomach twists with all we lost.

When he was eight months old, he had a series of vaccines, including the DaTP. Five days later he broke out in a few little red freckles. I thought it was odd, but I didn't want to overreact. He didn't have a fever and his activity was normal. I was slowly introducing him to each new jarred baby food. The next day when I went to get him out of his crib, he stood holding on to the rail and I gasped. His sweet little body was covered in those strange freckles. I picked him up and cradled him against me as I went to call the doctor. My logical mind was quite certain the doctor would know what it was and would tell me not to worry, so I spoke very calmly and matter of fact about the freckles. He said to drop what I was doing and come in immediately. I did. When he examined Houston, he told me he had already admitted him to Arnold Palmer Hospital and asked if we wanted to have an ambulance take us there. "Tests," that is all I was told when I asked with growing fear, "Why?" When I arrived at the hospital the nurses took my beautiful, strong baby boy, and a hematologist stepped into the room. She spoke about the possibilities—leukemia, or immune thrombocytopenic purpura. I was numb. I felt like I was watching it all happen.

The old fear gnawed at my gut, but I somehow managed to drown out almost any feeling. Everyone said how strong and full of faith I was, but that wasn't true. I think when I handed Houston to those nurses, I handed over my heart too. I was just waiting to hear the diagnosis to know what to feel. It was ITP. Houston's body did not respond properly to his immunizations and had started killing off his own blood platelets. I was relieved it was not leukemia, and we followed the treatment protocol. But the nurse's phone call from when I was pregnant was never far from my mind. Was this the something that was wrong? How would it affect him long-term? Should I let him get more vaccines since his body obviously did not respond appropriately? Was there more to come? The old fear slowly, stealthily crept over my heart. I fought it with denial and a thousand reasons why not to fear. Hope and diversion became my shield from heartache and reality, though I used them more as blinders. Besides, I thought to myself, I didn't have time for worry, I had morning sickness.

I should pause here to talk about the Big Jock. He was less interested in Houston than Morgan. I guess the excitement had worn off. The day Houston was born, he was more interested in watching his old team play. They lost and he was pissed. Then our son was born. I don't think his mood changed. I was totally in love with these amazing little human beings. Not surprisingly, he had kept up the night life and the drinking got worse. It's not uncommon for men to take longer to settle into fatherhood and family life. I understood that. I wanted to believe it was just a matter of time, a maturing that would root and yield fruit. Once I had tried to talk to him about the way his family treated me, and his rage unleashed on me. The second time I tried to bring up the way his family treated me, we were driving. Before I knew what had happened, he had grabbed the back of my head and pounded it into the dashboard and ground it harder and harder while he raged on me. I was dizzy when he finally let go of me. I just turned my face so my tears wouldn't set him off again. The first time I had seen anything of his violent nature was when I tried to talk to him about his drinking. His response was to lunge at me and strangle me. Morgan shrieked at the sight and startled, he let go and ran out the door. He didn't come home for a long time. When he did, he refused to speak to me. I was afraid to bring it up. Although I didn't know it at the time, this would become the pattern.

At this point, the faith that sustained me had taken over my heart again like it had as a young girl, but it was a more mature faith. I decided the Big Jock could be whoever he wanted to be but I would still love. I was called to love those who persecuted me, to be an instrument of peace, to sow love, to shine light in the darkness. All we did without love meant nothing and this was where God had put me - to love this man and these babies. I would love even if I was unloved in return. It was my mini mission field. I focused on making new friends with other young mothers at church. My best friend from college had spent a year overseas and was going to law school, so I really needed to find new friends in the same stage of life. I cherished being with other women who wanted to grow in their faith and shape their families with the love and truth of Christ. I thought to myself, I can do this. I can love enough for the both of us. Making a good home, being a servant like Christ unto death, and duty were the messages drilled into every single Bible study - every-single-one. It wasn't a new lesson, just the adult version of the lessons I had been served as a child and youth. Obedience and submission were the foundational precepts drilled relentlessly from the pulpit and the small group studies. Always the good student, I did as I was taught.

With Houston I was happy because babies made me happy, but now it was a guarded happiness. The Big Jock's new focus was money, and he was determined to make a lot of it. I was doing the parenting of two. I needed to love them enough for the both of us. There was a shift inside me I couldn't explain. I just didn't trust the happiness. I thought it was the disheartenment of parenting alone. But there was something more. I couldn't allow my heart to be quite so deliciously happy as I had with Morgan. It was too risky. Now I knew something could go wrong. Happiness came in the same sweet package that fear did.

During that time the attempts at the pill had failed for medical reasons. I wasn't a fan of hormones in a pill at all. Imbalance is an understatement. I always think it's ironic how people talk about the pill like it's something magical with no side effects. It's so not. I had cysts and other complications. Blood clots were part of my family history and my doctor was concerned. It's extremely difficult to choose between doing what is expected as part of a marriage and preventing the biological consequences of that act because they come with judgment from society and a lifetime of responsibility. If you don't do one thing, you're called something. If you do that thing and a child is conceived, you're called something else, if you're overwhelmed, abused, or abandoned, well just suck it up, buttercup. I remember this one single guy at the pool saw me with my two beautiful babies and laughed at me. He said, "What are you, a breeder?" and laughed at his own joke. People are awesome, aren't they?

I became pregnant again. This time, like I did with Morgan, I waited as long as I could before I told anyone about this new baby. I knew what everyone would say, and of course, they said it. But this time I was angry. I had never asked for anyone's help. I had settled into a life of motherhood. Who were they to judge how many children I should have or what I should be doing with my life? What business was it of theirs? I had taken care of these babies without much help from my husband. He worked and went out with his friends most nights. There was never much money left over for us. Being a mommy was my life, my job. I loved these children and loved being their mother. The audacity of people's judgmental arrogance and their lack of kindness and compassion only served to make me more determined to exceed their efforts at parenthood. I worked harder than anyone I knew with only the smiles and kisses of my babies as compensation. I would show them.

That's when it started happening. The smiles and kisses of Houston became fewer and fewer, and very quietly he left us. I don't know exactly when it happened. I do remember asking our pediatrician if he was certain the vaccines were safe for Houston since he had an autoimmune disease. To me, you know, the stupid young mom who hadn't gone to medical school, it seemed dangerous to put more immunizations into a body that had responded self-destructively to past immunizations. He reassured me Houston would be fine. He literally - word for word - said to me, "That was a fluke. He'll be fine," right before he gave him three more shots. I was twenty-four. I still listened to my elders and doctors and did what they told me. Oh, how I wished I had instead listened to that gnawing resistance in my gut. But you do what the doctor says, especially when you are a young mother. And then you hope it will all be okay. But it wasn't. There wasn't one day that it happened, but it was if every day there was a little less of my perfectly precious baby boy. It was a long time before we got the diagnosis.

This is what I witnessed. My son wouldn't look at me anymore. He would squint his eyes all the time. One day I was trying to play patty cake with him, and I noticed he wouldn't clap his hands together. How does that suddenly stop? I didn't understand. Later, I rolled a ball to him and he wouldn't roll it back. I demonstrated for him repeatedly. Nothing. Again - How? How does a child suddenly lose simple abilities like this? He would cover his ears constantly. He would spin things. He would run from one end of the hall to the other. If I called him, he wouldn't respond, but if I turned on his favorite Winnie the Pooh video he would come running. When I took him outside, he would bolt for the pool which terrified me. I kept having to rescue him from the water. He would bend down and scoop up pebbles in his hands and run around everywhere with the rocks. He didn't want to be held anymore. The baby who loved to cuddle suddenly didn't want to be touched. He would arch his back trying to get down and not be touched. He didn't play anymore. He didn't engage with his sister, whom he adored, anymore. His bowel movements became unbearable. He developed bright red rashes on his cheeks, arms, and bottom. Our pediatrician was perplexed but had no answers.

We had moved into the third apartment since we had been married. It was a relic from the sixties that we had moved to in order to save money. I would put the kids in the wagon and walk them to the park every day. We only had one car so everything I did, I did walking, with kids in tow. Morgan played with other kids at the park and ran from the geese. Houston filled his hands with rocks and ran to the water. They were going in opposite directions. I didn't know Houston's behavior wasn't normal. Friends would tell me it's just the difference between boys and girls. I tried not to sound worried. I tried to believe they were right and settle the voice inside my heart that said something's not right.

I used to take the kids to the complex's laundromat with me, one basket at a time. Everything was a project. When the apartment washing machines broke down and wouldn't spin the laundry, I called the Big Jock's parents and then his sister to ask if I could please finish our laundry at their home. I still remember the silence and then the very cold - no. Just a no. No explanation. No help. No love. Just no. I cried. I took the babies and the sopping wet laundry that weighed a ton to a local laundromat and sat for hours with the babies until it was all done. If I had ever been unsure about where I stood with his family, at that point I knew. It took weeks before the machines were fixed.

In the ancient apartment, Morgan slept in the crib and Houston slept in the pack 'n' play that I had purchased from a woman I used to babysit for. I kept trying to find ways to reach my son. The movie *Mr. Holland's Opus* was out on video. There was a scene where the mother is banging a pot trying to get her son to acknowledge her without success. I panicked - 'Is Houston *deaf?*' The next day I tried it. He ignored me. He never looked in my direction but then put his hands over his ears. When I stopped banging, he took his hands off his ears. So, I tried something else. I put Winnie the Pooh on the lowest volume without being completely muted while he was at the other end of the apartment. He came sprinting down the hall. I didn't understand. *What the hell was going on?* He also developed an obsession for certain videos during this time. I thought it made him happy and I played them as often as I could. Flubber was his favorite. He would belly laugh and I played it repeatedly just to watch his joy and hear his laugh. Videos were the only thing he responded to. I would try to read to him, and he would squirm out of my lap and run away with his hands on his ears. I tried again and again and again and again and again. *Why??? What???* I just didn't understand. My belly kept getting bigger.

I felt like I was failing at every task I had been given. I couldn't get my husband or my son to respond to the love I was pouring out to them. In an effort to convince the Big Jock to come home at night, I decided to learn how to cook gourmet meals. He used to mock me about burning the taco shells the first meal I cooked for him. In that old kitchen, with babies at my feet, I scrubbed, cut, peeled, baked and sauteed. Night after night, I would make these elaborate meals. He would come home, shower and change clothes. Then, without taking a bite, he would look at his plate and tell me he wasn't hungry, didn't like that, had already eaten, was going to eat later, and countless other excuses. I never questioned him knowing it would lead to him exploding. I refused to give up. I would find a way to make this work.

He confessed to me that part of the problem was that he loved going out and being the guy everyone wanted to be with. Everyone knew him to be the party guy and he knew everyone, so it was hard to be someone different. He was very clear that he didn't want his pregnant wife going out with him. It was about this time that his college best friend and another friend came to live with us. The three of them were cast in a movie that needed football players. It's a famous movie. His extracurricular activities became particularly obvious. The after party included cocaine with the star of the movie. The Big Jock bragged and laughed about it. One of the last moments before the movie wrapped was a family day to watch a day of filming. The star of that film seemed distant from everyone. He followed Houston, who was 16 months old, around the football field as he ran around the enormous field in circles. There was a strange connection. I watched from a distance.

When the film wrapped, I felt this incredible drive to get out of Florida and begged the Big Jock to let us have a fresh start where he wasn't bombarded with old girlfriends and the ghosts of his heydays. He knew he couldn't say no to his appetites and agreed. For a moment, he truly wanted to be different. I thought to myself, if I do the work of love, it will work. I just have to keep trying. We sold everything we had and moved to Colorado. The weekend before I left, I went to my old church for the last time. I had spent so many years there. The preacher who had stopped to give me a ride all those years ago on a hot Florida afternoon had retired and they were inducting the new pastor. My old pastor taught that morning, and he was just as wonderful as ever. He was so obviously filled with God's love. There was a guest pastor from Atlanta as well. The guest pastor's message was profound because it was a message critical to the character of Christ, but rarely taught or implemented. It was the parable of the shepherd and the lost sheep. He taught how we are the sheep, and the sheep get fussy when Jesus leaves them to go after the one. But Jesus is going to keep going after that one lost sheep. That's where His heart is - saving the lost. It struck me on a deep spiritual level. That's right. Jesus loves saving those who are lost. It would be years before I realized that it wasn't just the lost who had not yet been found that Jesus loved. His heart was even more for His own who loved Him deeply and had gotten lost.

6

The Fall and the Flood

"I don't know how you do it," they say.
I didn't know I had a choice.
— Anonymous

I landed in Colorado with two babies and four weeks till my due date. The Big Jock had been working in the mortgage industry and was killing it. Three weeks later I had a beautiful baby girl, Reagan, who had the face of an angel, and the biggest blue eyes I have ever seen. I was in a great deal of pain, but the floodgates of love had come again to wash over me. As I tried to care for my newborn and play with Morgan and Houston, Houston wouldn't play with us. At this point we were in an empty apartment with no friends. We put a small TV/VCR on the box it came in and slept on the air mattress which also served as a couch. I did everything to connect with Houston during this time. No matter where we were, he was trying to run away. His hands were ALWAYS pressed tightly against the sides of his head as if he was trying to shut out the entire world. By this time, he started getting fast. If I let go of his hands, he would run. I remember running as fast as I could after my little boy with my newborn strapped to my chest and abandoning my not even three-year-old. I looked at every outing in terms of - where could he go, and could I catch him? I couldn't reach him - I couldn't teach him. It was as if he had slipped into a world all his own. As I wanted to fall deeply in love with this new baby, I felt myself chasing this huge piece of my heart that was trying to escape. All of his words stopped. All of them. All he did was run.

I thought, despite my pot banging and video experiments, that maybe he was deaf and took him for more tests, but he wasn't. They told me his hearing was perfect. Exceptional. I knew something was wrong, but I didn't know what it was. I knew he didn't look at me or at anyone else. He wasn't interested in people. I can't tell you what it is like to be rejected by your one-year-old, for your one-year-old to refuse to be held, refuse to look at you, and put his hands over his ears when you try to talk to him. I can't describe how it feels to have your one-year-old run from you at every possible opportunity and to not even let you hold him to read him a story. There just aren't words for that feeling. It resembles failure, but I could not for the life of me figure out how or why. So, I just carried the hurt and kept trying, simply because I didn't know what else to do. I remember telling my dad how Houston wouldn't let me hold him and he laughed and said, "That's just boys! They can't keep still."

Even though I was wrapped up with all of this, I had more than just this peculiar behavior of my baby to worry about. There was still a two-year-old, a newborn, and another move, this time to Atlanta. The Big Jock had done exceptionally well selling and was offered a management position in Atlanta, GA. There had been a few drunken nights with the new guys in Colorado, but he had actually tried to be a family so I thought the new job would be the next step toward adulthood and responsibility. It seemed like an adventure and he seemed ready to take on that roll and be part of a family. I took my role as a supportive wife and mother with the utmost seriousness. This young family needed him to be the very best version of himself, and I was going to be the biggest cheerleader he had ever had.

As an aside, at this point and at this vantage point in life, I need to say something important to young women. While we are all young at some point and trying to grow up, it's still not your responsibility to raise your husband. Stop that shit. It doesn't work.

I realized during this time that I was strong, and I was not a girl anymore. I was a woman who knew how to work hard and how to serve. I knew how to love, how to turn the other cheek, and how to be gracious and merciful. I knew the art of kindness and friendship. I knew how to be a good wife and mother, even when I wasn't treated like one. I knew how to put my trust in my Savior, who loved me and had promised that "all things work together for good for those who love God and are called according to His purpose." So, I set about making friends again and another place a home.

There wasn't much to pack. In an old minivan with a U-Haul in rear, two toddlers and a six-week-old baby in tow, we headed east and crossed the country. We stopped in Oklahoma to see the Big Jock's grandfather. He was such a good man, salt of the earth. I wondered what had happened through the generations. Somehow, something had been lost. The kids ran through his garden and Houston was obsessed with the bird bath. Water, rocks, sticks, food, pacifiers. Not people. It sounds like it might be typical unless you saw it. It wasn't. Since we were driving through Memphis, I decided to call my mother's mother who lived there. I had been sending her pictures and letters since I had reconnected with my mother, even though I had not talked to my mother in a few years. I had told my grandmother about my mother and all she could say was that her father, my grandmother's ex-husband, was a cruel man. That was the justification for everything. We made plans to meet at a Shoney's on the way. As we approached the entrance with the babies, both doors to the Shoney's burst open and in a dramatic scene she had certainly orchestrated in her mind, my mother came running toward me with both arms held up in the air and forced the most ridiculous dramatic hug ever. I have still never seen anything like it. I was angry. My grandmother hadn't even warned me. This visit was about visiting her, not my mother. I guess the decision was that I was going to do what they wanted, even if I didn't want to. Apparently, the Vietnam veteran had become severely abusive, and my mother had gone home to stay with her mother. My call was the reunification she had been praying for. The group of them just sat there and didn't eat while we ordered, ate, fed babies, and otherwise tried to fill the time with conversation that was inauthentic, while she made gushing hyperbolic compliments about my little ones. The Big Jock was pissed that the visit had turned into an ambush. I had no defense for them. I would only see my mother one more time before she died.

As soon as we were in Atlanta, I looked in the yellow pages for the church of the guest pastor I had heard on my last Sunday in Central Florida. I was thrilled to see it was relatively close to us. The Big Jock agreed to go and was pleasantly surprised that he liked it as much as he did. And it was settled, that is where we would go to church. I signed up for Bible studies to meet other young moms. I was fortunate to make wonderful friendships with women who had kids the same ages as mine. I didn't feel so weird for having three young children. We all did. We studied together and prayed for each other. We had playdates and the kids would all play together, that is, everyone except Houston.

Houston didn't seem to notice or care about anything except running and bodies of water. He would throw himself into streams, ponds, fountains, pools, and tubs. It seemed there was no safe place to play. Water, danger, and escape were everywhere. Every environment I took my children to for them to simply play and enjoy the delights of childhood offered two children joy and another child the opportunity to nearly kill himself. There I was with an infant on my hip dragging a three-year-old and chasing a two-year-old to prevent another water rescue. If we went to a friend's house for a playdate, he would climb into their tub fully clothed and turn the water on. I couldn't have a normal conversation with anyone because every second my eyes had to be focused on him and prepared to lurch forward to stop something. I was always listening for doors opening, faucets turning on, refrigerator doors, cabinets - everything. I had to be on guard every minute of every day. There was no rest. Eventually I realized I had to stay home, that going anywhere was just too dangerous. But at home all he did was eat, drink, and constantly run in circles. He couldn't stop, he was never satisfied. The noises he made all day were awful and ear piercing. I got to the point where I would never let go of him if we had to go anywhere, and he would strain and pull, trying to free himself to run his relentless pursuit toward whatever was most dangerous. I didn't know what to do and every day my heart broke. I felt more and more isolated.

One day at church during a Bible study, I looked up to the top of the enormous staircase and saw Houston at the top of it. I had just moments before checked him into the nursery. I sprinted to the top of the stairs and then brought him back to the nursery. No one could figure out how he had gotten out. A few weeks later he ran away from the group when they were on the playground and nearly made it to the busy street before they caught him. After picking him up after church one Sunday, the volunteer told me how he played with toys very differently. The look on her face was concerned. I didn't know how to respond. A few weeks later, he ran away from the rest of the group and threw himself in the lake. I became scared to even leave him in the nursery, but I so wanted to have this time with friends who loved God, where I could just be normal and find encouragement even if it was for only two hours a week. After this next event occurred, I knew it was over. He had gotten out of a fenced area where all the children were playing nicely and had thrown himself into the lake where they had to pull him out. The nursery worker very belligerently said to me, "Do you have something you want to tell us about him?!" I was shocked by her accusatory words and tone and responded, "He has a speech delay and..." She interrupted me and said accusingly and harshly, "I think he's autistic!" I felt like someone had punched me. I didn't say a word.

That afternoon as our kids played in the McDonald's play place, my friends wanted to know what was wrong. I still hadn't spoken. I couldn't eat. Thoughts and fears swirled in my heart and mind. I had positioned myself as usual where I could grab Houston if he bolted for the door and made sure I was close enough to protect anyone's food if he tried to grab it, which he always did. Then I told them what the nursery worker said. They were all quiet. I'm sure they had seen things too and hadn't known what or how to say something. Finally, with great compassion they said, "That was awful. She should never have said something like that. But maybe you could go to a doctor, just to find out if something is going on. That way, if someone says something like that to you, at least you'll be able to respond." I nodded. They had been kind. Their words were thoughtful, gentle, and loving. Like real friends, they led me to something constructive and didn't destroy my hope on the way there. It was a kindness I desperately needed. And that is how I started the process of diagnosis.

Before that moment, my only knowledge of autism was seeing the movie *Rain Man* when I was sixteen with Andrew. I had found the movie touching, frustrating, and so sad. We were both affected by the movie, but it was remote, as watching someone else's problems always is. The thought of someone living their life in an institution had made me physically sick to my stomach. Houston didn't speak at all, and I hadn't noticed any savant skills. When my dad came to visit us in Atlanta to meet these new babies, he was horrified. He told me with no concern about tempering the message that Houston was stimming. I didn't even know what the word meant but I knew it was bad. I went to my room, laid down on the bed and cried. How could this be happening? Didn't God see how hard I was trying? Didn't he see I was basically on my own? My hope was dwindling rapidly. This was before autism awareness. This was before the internet was commonplace or even home computers. This was before pediatricians had been educated. This was before there was hope. It would take me over a year and a half, and countless referrals to get a diagnosis. And then what?

To outsiders, it was somehow easy to label and have a moment of disgust or pity, depending on their nature and disposition. But I fought and struggled not to let my fear become reality. As crazy as it seems, there was somehow safety in denial. As long as I pretended the monster had not taken my son, I could hang on to my dreams, even if they were increasingly a fairy tale. As long as I pretended this was all normal, I could outrun grief and loss. As long as I closed my eyes, I could keep that pain at bay. I struggled with the idea of accepting yet another uncertain future. I didn't want to let go again, especially to a future that stole my joy, my hope, and my child. But no matter how long I kept my eyes tightly shut, the ugly monster was still there taking everything.

Today there are people who will take offense that I called autism a monster. The politics and messaging have changed significantly in the last two decades. Now you're supposed to celebrate autism and differences. Back then you were supposed to hide yourself and not bother the normal people. Whether autism was or wasn't a blessing is irrelevant because we were absolutely treated like it was a death sentence. I honestly don't have time to rewrite the past. I can only recount it. In time you will find out what Houston thinks about autism and what autism actually is. But this book is a book about the truth. And the truth is, as I saw my son disappear in front of my eyes and was unable to have any communication with him and reach him in any meaningful way, that separation from my own heart inside my son's body was a monster. I think anything that separates a child from their parent who loves them and from being known needs fixing.

When the official diagnosis was finally acquired the doctor hadn't even been able to get him to sit still for thirty seconds. It had taken us six months to get this appointment so we could get a diagnosis that would enable him to be approved for services. The developmental pediatrician literally chased him around a room for thirty minutes trying to do assessments. She finally sat down exhausted. Her face said everything I feared. Houston was unreachable to everyone. He was gone. SEVERE AUTISM… My heart had gone too. The unknown fear finally had a name, but the name was like death. It stole and ravaged everything. That is what makes loss so hard; you can't get back what you love. It's just gone. And you are left with a hole in your heart and in your life that won't stop aching.

It was during this time that Houston's bowel movements became grotesque. To call it chronic diarrhea doesn't come close to describing what came out of him. It was massive and smelled like something had died. It would go up his back and down to his knees five to eight times a day. It was so acidic it would make his bottom bleed. The pediatricians didn't care and didn't think any tests were necessary. "Just keep his bottom covered up with ointment," they suggested. And my baby would scream and reel in pain when I cleaned and covered his raw bottom. But the worst part about the poop was that Houston would smear this foul, filthy feces on everything. He smeared it in carpets, rugs, walls, toys, books, sheets, blankets, clothes, the TV, even the ceiling, and of course, all over himself. He would pee on everything. Every morning, every afternoon, every day, every night there was another awful poopy mess to clean. I can't remember how many times I ran to turn the alarm off in the middle of the night after Houston had set the motion detectors off; I would then run to find my little boy in the dark naked and would slip and fall or step in my son's feces or urine. He could scale any gate we put up to corral him, and he rarely slept for more than a few hours, if any.

The deeper the well Houston slipped into, the more I tried to find an answer, any reason to hope. All those years of reading and writing countless papers had made me extremely adept at research. I researched everything I could find because the doctors would not help me at all. They treated me and my children as if we had a communicable disease. Their apathy was palpable, arrogant, and infuriating. I once took my son to a specialist and showed him the bloody bottoms and grotesque feces. He looked down at me and said with a haughty tilt of his head, "Did you read something on the internet?" I told him I had been reading multiple medical journals but that *this* feces on *this* diaper was the reason I wanted tests performed. He responded with an annoyed and hubristic tone, "It's all sooo esoteric." When I asked him if he knew what that word meant, he couldn't tell me. He also couldn't or wouldn't help me. Houston began to have seizures and the neurologists couldn't keep him still long enough to get an effective reading from an EEG. I tried medication after medication to address the seizures and the rashes from the yeast overgrowth that were all over his body. His skin became sallow, and he developed dark circles under his eyes. I took all sugar, even fruit out of his diet. The screaming never seemed to stop. I had him in joint occupational and speech therapy as many times as possible. Nothing they did made any progress.

Then Houston got mumps. Mumps. He swelled up like a hot air balloon ready to burst. I didn't know a single soul who had mumps. NO ONE. How the hell does someone get mumps after an MMR booster? Isn't that what it's supposed to prevent? Do you people really think these things work? Doctors were indifferent. The little red freckles began to appear in small patches and disappear over time, recurring and disappearing for years with no explanation. Petechia is what I would learn the red freckles were called. Years later I discovered this was a marker of chronic ITP, chronic autoimmunity where the body continued attacking itself. The doctors did absolutely nothing. When I mentioned my concerns about vaccines, the physician's assistant had a nurse take my children out of the room and stood over me. The new policy was if you didn't get vaccines, they would refuse treatment of any kind, even well visits. I sat in the uncomfortable chair with pictures of animals painted on the walls while this woman I had met twice told me I was a horrible mother and that my child could get measles and DIE! I remember thinking, 'I prefer measles. Then we stand a fighting chance. Clearly, you've never lived with autism. Death, most days, would be preferred. Autism doesn't just take my child; it destroys me and all my other children along with it. I'm in my twenties and my future is already over. Just 60-80 more years of hell to go.' But I had to sit there in respectful silence and swallow every emotion, take the rebuke. I wasn't allowed to think for myself, even if I had blood tests to prove he had severe aluminum toxicity by age four with no other logical interaction with a toxic exposure to aluminum other than the vaccines. Policies trumped people. Don't they almost always?

> *"Now you are beginning to think for yourself instead of letting others think for you.*
> *that's the beginning of wisdom."* [17]

It's not the first time the medical community has been wrong, and definitely not the first time they have been wrong about autism. Mothers were originally to blame. Someone with a degree condemned mothers who were diagnosed as having no heart. The obtuse medical community didn't know how to recognize hearts that were broken. They still don't. Some doctors have tried to find other reasons for the aluminum toxicity and have conjectured mothers are to blame again, proposing that breastmilk is the source of the neurotoxicity. I did breastfeed Houston until he was eight months old. I had stopped right before the fateful DTaP vaccine with aluminum, formaldehyde, and thimerosal. I guess it's possible I ate an aluminum toxic diet for eight months and fed it to my baby without realizing it and somehow these substances passed through his intestines into his blood and into his brain. Certainly there have been infants affected by environmental toxins and I don't want to minimize those experiences. But I think the more likely scenario was that my son's immune system didn't work properly and wasn't fully developed. And when multiple genetically modified organisms were injected into his bloodstream, accompanied by nanoparticles of aluminum, formaldehyde and mercury, his body reacted with an

[17] Margaret Mitchell

autoimmune reaction and began attacking itself. And, despite the gamma globulin (IVIG) injections to boost his immune system, it is most likely the brain inflammation and oxidative stress from the aluminum and other chemicals had a catastrophic effect on his neurological development and his ability to metabolize nutrients for normal body and neurological functions. But who am I kidding? I'm just a mom. It's the breastmilk.

I think it's rather ironic that a society that now promotes and demands clean water, clean air, clean oceans, no preservatives, and organic and non-genetically modified food without the same barrage of scientific backed double blind placebo studies to PROVE the toxicity of our environment is A-OK with nanoparticles of aluminum and other preservatives that can bypass the blood brain barrier being injected into the bloodstreams of infants who don't have a fully developed immune system, even though aluminum is a known neurotoxin that inhibits more than 200 metabolic processes inside the body.[18] The problem with toxic heavy metals in the human body is the generation of free radicals and the chain reactions they cause. Aluminum in particular with "its free ion, Al(3+) (aq) is highly biologically reactive and uniquely equipped to do damage to essential cellular (neuronal) biochemistry."[19]

It is simply the nature of toxic metals, and it all comes down to the chemical and electrical activity of cells. To explain it in the simplest way, aluminum is a metal with free or loose electrons which is what contributes to its conductivity. Since electrons like to be in pairs, when these loose or free electrons are injected into the human body they steal electrons from other healthy cells, which then in turn become damaged and unable to function as designed. Then the cells that are damaged have loose electrons that steal other electrons from other cells and so on and so on. These free radicals are highly chemically reactive and attach to normal healthy cells, causing a chain reaction of oxidative stress to cells, proteins, and DNA. Neurologists are just beginning to investigate the effects of metal toxicity on developing minds as well as the elderly.

Autistic children and their families have been living with this reality for over two decades. I think it's ironic we are encouraged not to have aluminum or other metals in our drinking water and not to rub it on our armpits but it's ok to inject it directly into the bloodstreams of infants and toddlers. Maybe we really do need to vilify those awful breastfeeding mothers and make caricatures of anti-vax mothers who are putting the nation at risk. Certainly that's the cause. Let's ban breastmilk and nursing too. While we're at it, let's ban freedom of thought and speech. But clearly, I'm a horrible mother who wants to put every other child at risk of dying from measles, so don't listen to me. Pardon my sarcasm. I'm only two decades into living with the evidence of what vaccines did to my child. And I reserve the right to take that evidence and think for myself. I do not care if you do not come to the same conclusion I do. I am still telling the truth.

The truth is I am not a radical. I am against a medical mandate that treats all human beings as if they are biologically identical, that doesn't test for immune deficiencies before immunizing, that manufactures vaccines with known neurotoxins, and that vilifies parents for recognizing the obvious destruction that immunizations had on their child and giving them no legal recourse for justice. If we want to demand vaccines, why can't we demand organic, non-genetically modified, appropriately dosed, metal free vaccines spaced out instead of bombarding undeveloped immune systems with multiple diseases and neurotoxins at once? Is that reasonable? Or is that bad for business? Go ahead and think what you want about me. But does it really sound to you like I'm not thinking? Despite the ridicule of critics who apparently know everything, I knew I couldn't convince people who hadn't experienced it any more than I could change the atomic and cellular activity of a metal. Unfortunately, I never had the luxury of being politically correct and fitting in with what everyone believed or cared about. I was living with the truth. And my name is Katie, not Karen.

***

[18] https://www.ncbi.nlm.nih.gov/pmc/articles/PMC1474689/
https://pubmed.ncbi.nlm.nih.gov/1947146/
[19] https://pubmed.ncbi.nlm.nih.gov/24779346/

I wanted so much to just fit in and be normal. I tried to care about the things all young mothers care about - preschool, playdates, picture taking, playdough, and potty training. But we couldn't do anything normal. When I took my kids to the pool and was trying to put swimmies on the kids, Houston ran away and fell in on the opposite side of the enormous pool. I don't know what I did with Reagan who was a baby. I just dove in with my clothes and glasses and swam as fast as I could to get him. Another mom helped me pull him out. He hadn't lost consciousness but shrieked and trembled with fear. It took years to get him in a pool, but he was still obsessed with every other body of water. So almost every day, we had to stay home. We couldn't accept and rarely received invitations for playdates. Every day was filled with the horrors of my son being trapped in a world where I couldn't reach him and the stench of his feces. I spent nights researching articles, medical journals, anything I could find.

At that time, I knew of only one other child with autism. I've researched what the autism rates were in 1999 and 2000 when he was first diagnosed, and no matter which study you use, the rates are at a minimum three times greater today. However, based on the standard rates provided for these respective dates, the occurrence of autism is nine times greater today. (Before you question how broad the criteria is for diagnosis that I am referencing, I am referring to what is labeled as severe, low functioning, non-speaking autism on the autism spectrum. Detailed comparative analysis of the criteria and the autism studies over multiple decades is outlined by J.B. Handley.[20] The rates in 1999 were 1 in 500 and are now 1 in 54, which is a comparative ratio of 27:250. If we use the same percentage that is used today to designate the rates of acute symptoms, which is roughly one third, then the ratio between 1999 and 2020 is 9:83.)

I tried my hand navigating the bizarre world wide web which was nothing like it is today. This was pre-Google, pre - any organization of information. It was very similar to how I hunted down information like I had in the basement of my university library, where you would search massive journals that would refer you to articles found on another floor on microfiche that took hours to hunt down. Now I desperately searched though medical journals and studies for information, for a treatment, for a doctor that knew what to do, for a cure, for any word or hope to keep me believing there might be an end to this horror that had stolen my son. I just wanted him back. I tried diets restricting almost everything he wanted to eat for over a year and a half. I tried countless vitamins, supplements, and medications. There were blood tests, fecal tests which showed parasites, metal toxicity tests which showed extremely high levels of aluminum, hearing tests, EEGs which he could never sit still long enough for results, and developmental tests which were a joke because he couldn't stop moving to perform their tests. I lost count of all the tests that were administered and solutions I tried. Nothing was covered by insurance. The pediatricians at the children's medical group would literally roll their eyes. Their indifference was disheartening. It is a strange experience to beg doctors to help your child even as you show them tests that confirm something is medically wrong. I realized it was all up to me to figure out. There was an hour of daily audio therapy with special headphones that required holding him locked in my arms so he would stay still. The theory was that the different sound frequencies would retrain his brain. We were told the only real hope was ABA (Applied Behavioral Analysis) and you needed to do a minimum of forty hours a week if you had any hope of saving your child. If you didn't do enough by a certain age, then all hope was lost. I was racing against a clock. Whatever was left of me each day was spent scrubbing shit, crying, trying to reach my little boy, and giving my girls the mommy they needed. The one thing I did for myself during all of this was to start sewing and just trying to make something beautiful out of every broken thing I could. My life was a collection of broken pieces and remnants that I was trying to repurpose.

---

[20] How to End the Autism Epidemic; J.B. Handley

7

Drowning

A t some point, my old best friend-boyfriend, Andrew, called to catch up. Finally, someone I could tell the heartbreaking truth to who knew me. When I told him the line went completely silent. In the silence I heard all my fears confirmed and the death of all my dreams. I could hear him struggling to think of what to say. Finally, almost stuttering, he asked, "What does Morgan say?" I shook my head in disbelief. Morgan?? What does my four-year-old think?? What about me? Is anyone going to ask me what this has done to me??... No. No one. I don't think anyone could bear to hear the pain. No one had an answer to a grief and burden so great. I had noticed my friends inquired less and less. No one could bear to see my struggle when their lives were sweet and simple. It was just easier to forget me. Autism became like leprosy. The behaviors and demand for my attention resulted in almost complete isolation.

I needed a partner so badly. I put even more effort toward being a loving, serving wife to a man who was cold, drunk, cruel, and selfish, hoping the prayers and the love would work the miracle I needed. I prayed and begged my Savior to help me and heal my son and give me peace in this nightmare. I was so distracted and hurting. The Big Jock had started to have some success financially. The first thing he did was get a Corvette. This car was followed by a Porsche, and another Porsche, and a truck, and eventually I lost count. He bought a basement full of wood working equipment that he used a handful of times. He bought three sets of fishing gear and floats so he could take guests out to fish the Chattahoochee. And guns, more and more guns and ammunition. He had always had a collection of knives. I think he thought once he had all the things he always wanted, he would be happy. Houston's diagnosis had cemented something dark in his mind. He hated being home with us. He told me how he had made fun of kids with disabilities when he was young, and that Houston's autism was his punishment. I remember objecting, "I've never made fun of anyone. What about me? That can't be the reason." The dark spiral began. He began coming home late and eating expensive meals out. He would drink more and more until he would have some horrific episode and then swear to never drink again. We would see glimpses of an engaged father and then he would be gone. Maybe a month at most would go by before he would start again and round and round the crazy went. I was in shock at the amount of alcohol he could consume. He couldn't control his spending either, but his way to deal with it was to make more money. He bought the dog he had always wanted and left me with the untrained hound dog and little kids. My objections were ignored, more accurately they ignited one of his increasing rages, so I said nothing. It wasn't until he saw the dog jump on Houston, and he threw the dog at the window in a rage that he agreed to give the dog away to someone who had the time to train him.

It was in this nightmare with Houston not sleeping, scrubbing feces, taking care of babies, and tiptoeing through the land mines of growing alcoholism and abuse that I became pregnant again. I don't even know what I felt. I was almost in my second trimester before it occurred to me that I couldn't remember when I had last menstruated. I pulled back the pages of the calendar trying to remember. Everything was a blur. Every day was a struggle for hope, a struggle just to make it through. I spent most days crying and nauseous, trying not to be sick as I scrubbed that dead-smelling shit off every surface my son could think to smear it on. I had all these books in his room and many from my childhood. Books had been my life. I thought they would be some way to reach him. He would smear feces on the pages of the books or rip them out of the book. He smeared feces on everything. He obsessively had to have sticks in his hands and would rip things apart so he could hold anything that was a cylinder. This included curtain rods, stair spindles, pieces of chairs, toys, wooden or cardboard hangers. I couldn't keep up with the furious path of destruction. Like a little Tasmanian devil, he couldn't stop, couldn't slow down, couldn't sleep. I spent a lot of time finding or traveling to therapists. I set up a swing, a ball pit, a trampoline. I brushed his body to try to regulate his sensory system. Our favorite therapist would come to our home twice a week. It took her a year of ABA to get him to sit down for a full minute. She tried like I had for so long to get him to roll a ball back to her. It was all such a tearful blur. And then it was time to have a baby.

Very indicative of that period, I didn't have time to make it to the right hospital. The doctor had insisted I stop at his office first. After the ninety-second examination he put me in a wheelchair and had me wheeled me across the street. There was no discussion because there were no options. The urgency was everywhere. As soon as I stood up out the chair I bent over and started pushing. The nurse was shouting at me to stop. I couldn't. My body had taken over. There were people yelling everywhere, including me. It just happened so fast, and I got to experience natural childbirth, which is just awful. I am quite astonished more women don't die during childbirth. Still to this day, I am taken aback when women who have had natural childbirth and not almost died act arrogantly and self-righteously about their birth experiences, as if the millions of women who have died giving birth throughout generations where just weak, lazy, or lacked will power and stamina. Those people, those attitudes, leave me speechless. Childbirth is not a competition. It's more like a war. When my son was born, they took him away because they were working on me. I remember being surprised I was still alive and wondering why there was so much blood. I wept. I hurt so badly, and I couldn't stop shaking. I was in shock. They started doing all sorts of things to my body. Masks and gowns were moving fast, and people were shouting. They were sticking me, holding me, moving my body. It was a blur behind the pain that had taken over. I had no control over anything my body was doing. The Big Jock was in a big shock too. I vaguely have some memory of him almost fainting from all the blood and nurses shouting for him to sit down. He held his head in his hands. The next time the nurse came to check on me, he tried to sell her on refinancing her mortgage. She glanced at him and then looked at me with concern and pity. Even though I was trembling from shock and embarrassed I mouthed, "I'm so sorry." All I wanted to do was sleep. I felt sleep coming like a dark cloud that wanted to swallow me whole. I just wanted them to leave me there to sleep and sleep. Don't wake me. But there was a new baby to love, so I tried to be happy because that's what mommies are supposed to be.

Paul was the most loving, kind, beautiful boy. He had dimples that would put Brad Pitt's to shame. Those dimples - how much God must delight in showing His hand, making each human being uniquely wonderful. I think His joy in His children is greater than any natural wonder in this world. There was no reason for those delightful dimples, no evolutionary purpose, no gene I am aware of; yet every time he grinned, I couldn't help but fill with joy and smile at such a beautiful sight. I think Jesus knew how much I needed to see His love and to know His presence, so He gave me a beautiful baby with dimples to remind me there is goodness and joy beyond this monster called autism that ate up our lives.

When Paul was five weeks old, some of the Big Jock's friends from Florida came to visit. In all the commotion, he forgot to lock the front door as people and kids ran through the house. Houston slipped out the front door. Five minutes passed. Suddenly, my neighbor busted through the front door with terror on his face, screaming that Houston had been hit by a truck. I started running and before I could get to the door the neighbor who hit him ran in carrying him. There were blood curdling screams and blood everywhere. The Big Jock and I raced to the car with Houston in my lap screaming and thrashing. The Big Jock was roaring how he was going to kill that m…er f...er and I was crying, trying to calm Houston who was thrashing and shrieking. This wasn't crying. This was agony. The Big Jock pulled him from my arms and ran into the emergency room. I was left standing in the parking lot in shock. I started crying. I started hyperventilating. I was covered in my son's blood. I had no shoes on. I walked, sobbing, into the emergency room and cried with no shoes for a long time. A few hours later a friend brought my newborn and some flip-flops to the emergency room so I could breastfeed. No one said anything. I cried and nursed my baby. They transferred Houston to the hospital downtown. I followed. It was decided I needed to go home to be with the guests and our kids. I began to get a headache that was so piercing I couldn't hardly open my eyes. I purchased some ibuprofen from the vending machine. On the way home, I began to lose consciousness. I pulled over and tried to wake up. I barely made it home. My body was taking over. I took my baby who was crying to be fed into bed to nurse him. Then something happened to my body. Maybe it was the sheer exhaustion from the trauma and the shock. I woke in terror completely on top of my newborn. For the most terrifying moment I thought I had killed him. The weeping took over, maybe from fright, maybe from the trauma of eighteen hours before. It ignited a severe fright in me, but even more it ignited some horrific guilt I couldn't shake - at all. Houston was three and a half when he was struck by a truck. Miraculously, he lived and there were no internal injuries. He looked awful, almost like he had been burned. But he was alive. And my little baby was too.

The road rash on Houston left huge red patches on him as he healed. If he got excited and ran too much, which was all the time, the scars would inflame on his face and arms. One day, at his newest therapy, the two therapists brought him out to me and demanded an explanation for the red patches all over his face and arms. I just looked at them. Really? I don't know how to describe that emotion. I shook my head. I told them about the accident he had been in before we had started this latest therapy. I gave them the hospital and doctor information.

The Big Jock did what he could to not be too involved. He had a mortgage company he was growing, and he believed his greatness was just beginning the way the money flowed in. There were moments where I thought I might have seen a soft side. But any vulnerability was immediately overcompensated with his larger-than-life persona. To the world, he was a huge, barrel chested blond with a toothy, used car salesman smile, a firm handshake, and an enormous laugh who drank and told legendary football escapades that rarely involved football and made other men look at him in awe. He was the consummate charmer. He had learned a great deal in college in sociology and psychology and used every ounce of it to manipulate people. He very consciously would keep his eyes glued on people, boring into them. When it was necessary for him to be serious or humble, he would flip the switch and his somber mask would emerge instantaneously. He had practiced the body language so often that it was nothing for him, the soft voice, the bowed head, the penitent verbiage with the fingers laced together and ankles crossed. And people believed the lie he told with his lips and his demeanor. I knew better and fell for it more times than I can count. I was always searching for that trace of goodness in him to hold onto. But every time I thought I'd seen something worth grabbing hold of, it turned to a slithering snake and bit me. The more success he attained, the bigger the bravado grew. He would boast obnoxiously about his sales and use it as another reason to "celebrate" which meant gorging on food and alcohol.

When the Big Jock made a sale it was big laughs, dinner out and drinks - nothing could ever go wrong. He was the fun dad my kids adored. I never knew when the switch would flip, especially once the liquor started flowing. The money was his identity, the proof he had made it and become someone of significance. He wanted everything. He wanted all women to lust after him and all men to be jealous of him. If he didn't make the money, the darkness took over, deeper every time. I think he knew he was losing to the darkness. His attacks became more personal and frequent. One day I got a call from the police looking for him regarding a road rage incident. His brother-in-law had been in the car and witnessed it. I knew what the police and the witnesses said was true. It had been getting worse - frightening. There were other things that made me know there was more to be concerned about, but in all honesty, the only things I cared about were my children and my Savior. Around Christmas that year, he was sitting in the big, overstuffed chair saying one cruel thing to me after another with my baby sitting like a ball beside him, curled up and tucked under his arm. I finally went over to him and said, "Hand me the baby." He leapt out of the chair and grabbed me by the back of the head and threw me violently face first into the carpet with such force and friction over and over that I lost the skin on my forehead. He let me go and stormed off in his Porsche. I picked up my baby and cried. I told my friends I was a clutz and had fallen down the stairs. My life seemed hopelessly helpless, and I wanted to die, or just go to sleep and not wake up. But those babies needed me, and somehow, for them, I kept going. One thing I knew, though, I couldn't take any more. It was all too much.

When the Big Jock started to expand his new company while working from home, I had to leave with the kids to give him quiet. That was extremely difficult, but I wanted to be supportive since this is how we would pay the bills. I would go to parks and anywhere I could think of to keep them occupied. One day, I went to the mall with the kids to ride the merry go round and somewhere in that chaos one of the kids took my keys out of my purse and dropped them into someone else's bag. When I went to leave, I began to panic. I retraced my steps. I went to security. I talked to every store manager I could. Finally, I called the Big Jock and told him what happened, terrified at what he would say. I called on the mall security phone and asked if he would come get us. With an evil glee in his voice he said, "NO. I'm not f..king going to come get you. You figure it out." And hung up. Who was this? Who doesn't even help his wife and children? And so, it was in a food court of a mall that I realized for certain how much I really mattered. My mind and heart were so overwhelmed with the reality of being hated that I couldn't think of a next step. A stranger came up to me and told me he could tell something was wrong and asked if there was anything he could do. Tears welled up in my eyes and gravity won as they rolled down my face in streams. A locksmith who specialized in the new Chrysler coded lock entry was called. We waited for hours. Around seven p.m. I got home. Sarcastically the Big Jock sneered and said, "I knew you'd figure it out." Then he laughed. My face turned hot with hurt. His hate just kept coming. *Oh, how many ways can I hate you? Let me count the ways.*

8

Reality

Answer me quickly, O Lord! My spirit fails!
Hide not your face from me, lest I be like those who go down to the pit.
Let me hear in the morning of your steadfast love, for in you I trust.
Make me know the way I should go, for to you I lift up my soul.
— Psalm 143:7-8

One day I was nursing Paul on the couch and had fallen asleep sitting up. Houston's sleepless nights took a heavy toll. As I slept, I started dreaming of rain. The raindrops splattered loudly, too loudly, as if right next to me. Suddenly, I bolted upright realizing it was water pouring out of the ceiling behind me and hitting a cardboard box. I raced upstairs. I knew I was about to find my son drowned in the bathtub. I choked on a heaving wail and tears as my feet barely touched the stairs. I tried to breathe. There was water all the way out into the hallway carpet and pouring through the bathroom floor into the floor below. When I tore around the corner of the bathroom, there he was. His body bobbed back and forth in the water and his chin was covered. He just looked at me. I broke down crying and lifted him up out of the tub. The diaper exploded into millions of drenched pellets scattered all over the bathroom and hallway already soaked in water. I held him and cried ugly, ugly tears. From that moment I knew something had to be done. No one was going to help, and I couldn't keep going. I campaigned and cajoled and finally persuaded my husband to have a vasectomy. I was done having babies.

My husband's vasectomy was scheduled for a particular Wednesday. That weekend a familiar nausea came over me. Monday, I slipped out to the store and bought a pregnancy test. In my bathroom I held my breath, closed my eyes, and counted. When I opened my eyes, there it was, the little blue line. I cried. I couldn't do it, not another baby. I shrunk to the floor, cradled my knees and sobbed for what seemed like an hour. I wept because I knew what would happen. I would love this little one, and there would be nothing left of me. I would love this baby with the same fierce devotion I loved my other children. Loving these children and living with autism, domestic abuse, and infidelity was already too much. I was all used up, my youth and joy were gone, my heart was in pieces, my body exhausted and old. I also found myself consumed by a guilt I had known once before. The truth about my selfish, scared heart was this: I didn't want to be pregnant and to have another baby. I knew how the love of a child binds you and takes possession of your heart. I knew how vulnerable it makes you to love a child. I didn't want that hold on me again. I didn't know how I could love another baby like they need to be loved and survive myself. I was terrified. This one would most certainly kill me. The fear of another natural childbirth gripped me as well; the pain was still so vivid it made me cry. The Big Jock was delighted, and I was devastated. Triumphantly, he declared he didn't have to have a vasectomy. I remember thinking callously, "He must know this will kill me." I was so ashamed that I was not happy, and I was too rundown to fake it. 'Someone has to stop the madness,' I thought to myself.

Sometimes God uses the strangest things to get us out of the pits we find ourselves in. An old acquaintance had recently announced with great joy that she was expecting her first baby. I had kept my news quiet and did so for four months. But her husband visited, and my husband delightfully shared the news of our fifth baby. The congratulatory phone call came shortly thereafter. I didn't say too much, just answered her questions. Then I heard a familiar disdain and arrogance. "Well, you really need to find a better form of birth control! Ha! Ha! Ha!" Sometimes the audacity of people is truly astounding. I was too stunned and offended to respond. It took another phone call before I had climbed out of my depression enough to defend my motherhood and my child. Even with my heart filled with fear, I was able to ask, "Why do you think my child number five, or even more is not of just as much value and reason to rejoice as your first child?" Does a child's value decrease based on birth order or number of siblings? Does cost of living determine the value of a single life? While these thoughts did not take away my doubt, they sustained me through those months and the ones that followed.

The pregnancy was difficult. Morgan was in school and Houston was in a special needs preschool. I remember the teachers working so hard to get Houston to look them in the eyes. He wouldn't or couldn't. By the end of the year, they had pretty much corralled him in a corner with bookcases and a VCR because he kept running out of the classroom and down the hall. He would pull away from them like he pulled away from me. Morgan was a pistol. She was defiant and difficult with a sullen attitude. I was so tired. I would fall asleep driving them the two miles from school and jerk awake terrified. Another afternoon the school called me because I hadn't picked them up. I had collapsed exhausted and hadn't even remembered sitting down. Morgan was mad at me for forgetting her. I told her how sorry I was. I threw up on the side of the road, literally barefoot and pregnant. 'Really?' I thought to myself. 'Is this really my life?' Then Benjamin was born. Mercifully, he was a full breach, so as soon as I went into labor there was a cesarean, and I didn't die like I thought I might. My contractions started getting intense at the Big Jock's company Christmas party. I tried not to say anything for almost two hours. But then, afraid of trying to deliver a breech baby after what had happened the last time, I told him we had to go now. He was pissed. Can't you wait through *dessert*?! I shook my head no. I thought we might end up in an accident on the way to the hospital he was so drunk. They took me in immediately. My doctor didn't waste even one minute. I got sick from the anesthesia and the Big Jock complained how much that dinner I just puked had cost him. The medical staff rolled their eyes, and no one responded. Quickly the doctor delivered my baby boy. After they left with my baby the doctor looked at me earnestly and with kindness asked, "Are you *sure*? Are you *sure* you want your tubes tied? You're so young." I just wanted to cry when he asked me that. All I could move was my head. I looked up at him and said, "Yes. I'm sure." And my head collapsed to the bed.

I was still so tired and distraught over raising these babies with a cruel and indifferent husband and living with Houston's autism, but here was this baby, and he was not easy. He wanted to be held all the time. He would scream just to hear himself scream. He seemed to love the sound of his own screech. Yet he was so delightfully, willfully mischievous that you could never truly be upset with him. Breathtaking, he was that too. He would look at you with those big eyes and pout and my heart would melt. He had his sister's angelic face.

It was fear and grief that filled my days. Houston's autism created an intense loss, not just for him, not just for me, but for all my children. I loved him so much, but I hated what autism had taken, and I couldn't rescue my little boy. Nothing worked. At his therapy, I was told that he was being discharged effective immediately. I asked why. They told me that my time slot was very valuable, and they needed to reserve it for kids who they could actually help. Houston was using two therapists and had not made any progress in almost a year. That was that. They didn't even seem sorry. Even the experts had given up on my son. It was as if there was a death I couldn't mourn because my son was still here.

At some point I began to start wondering about what my life would have been like if all this hadn't happened. What would I have become? Where would my dreams have taken me? What had I given up? The old dreams I had laid aside stirred within me. I wanted to be more and do more than just be a mommy. I wanted to be mommy plus something else. I wanted my life to count for something beyond cleaning up poop. All those years of dying to self and sacrificing had left me dying to live. But I couldn't, I had to be a mommy and desperately wanted to stay being a mommy. I just needed being a mommy to not hurt so bad, take so much, and be so so hard. I needed more joy, more hope to make it through the many, many dark days. I needed the Occupation line on every form to be filled to not leave me searching for words, feeling like a failure with my insides nauseatingly empty, not because I thought what I did was nothing, but because I knew that is how others with better titles viewed me.

While I would tell myself not to care what others thought, I could see that none of us mothers, who only nurtured for a living, could escape the condescending looks or comments of the better employed. A battle raged within me that was so ugly and awful I didn't dare share my thoughts. I wanted to be free, to only have to think of me, and I hated myself for feeling that way. I knew it was wrong. I even thought maybe all I needed was a vacation. Maybe that would fix all that was wrong inside me. While all of this was going on in my heart, my husband couldn't have cared less. He was so cruel, so callous and uncaring, so unwilling to help me with the children, and so selfishly attendant to his own desires and whims that I began to break. I just couldn't handle the kids, the autism, and my husband's abuse anymore. This was just no way to live and no way to raise children. But the truth is the financial reality I lived in kept me trapped. All my dreams could do nothing to pay the bills or finance childcare. I was dreaming of two different lives, and only one was possible. There was no answer to my problem, just the knowledge that I had to persevere and make the best of a bad situation. It's like C.S. Lewis says, it's "very much like an honest man who pays his taxes. He pays them alright, but he does hope that there will be enough left over for him to live on."

My prayers were intense. I poured over the Bible for promises and pleaded with Jesus for relief. Once Houston and Morgan had started school I tried again to get involved in church. I wanted to help new believers begin to walk in faith. I took courses and read book after book for ecclesiastical leadership and theology, as well as doctrines essential to Calvinism. For those who haven't studied these doctrines they constitute specific fundamentals of Christian theology that define the filter to frame the things we don't understand about the nature of God and humankind, as well as God's interaction and intention with man. At the core, without diving into the nuances, the beliefs are thus: Total Depravity (some theologians have qualified that statement by renaming it Radical Depravity, Unconditional Election, Limited Atonement, Irresistible Grace, and the Preservation of the Saints.) What does this mean? God is holy and loves us. Man is most assuredly not holy but retains a knowledge of good and evil and a desire for good. Think of the scene in Full Metal Jacket standing before an open grave of dozens of Vietnamese.

Pogue Colonel : You write 'Born to kill' on your helmet and you wear a peace button. What's that supposed to be, some kind of sick joke?
Private Joker : No sir!
Pogue Colonel : What is it supposed to mean?
Private Joker : I don't know, sir.
Pogue Colonel : You don't know very much do you?
Private Joker : No sir!

Pogue Colonel : You'd better get your head and your ass wired together, or I will take a giant shit on you.

Private Joker : Yes, sir.

Pogue Colonel : Now answer my question or you'll be standing tall before the man.

Private Joker : I think I was trying to suggest something about the duality of man, sir!

And God, in response to our divided hearts which do the things we don't want to do and don't do the things we want to do,[21] offered His perfect son, Jesus Christ, as a sacrifice, the atonement for our sins so we can be children of God. God chooses us, those whom He has called respond to and receive His irresistible grace. Once we receive this grace through His son through the gift of faith, and not of our own merit, nothing can separate us from God's love. The deeper applications of these principles and the character of God are that everything is part of His perfect will, no matter how awful. He uses what He hates to accomplish what He loves. And so, in obedience, with a broken heart, I thanked God for His grace and prayed in thanksgiving for the good that would come from the things that tore my heart, the things I didn't understand. *Rejoice always, pray continually, give thanks in all circumstances; for this is God's will for you in Christ Jesus.*[22]

I sought His face very much on my knees. It wasn't like the posturing you might imagine. Let me paint the picture. Houston would leave water running everywhere. I lost count of how many collapsed ceilings and ruined carpets there were over the years. I would find shit smeared everywhere again and again and again. I would get all the rags and cleaners and get to work. My first offering to Him was thanksgiving. I would sing praise songs as I scrubbed and pray for a miracle. I would wake early in the morning before anyone to let His truth pour into my heart. I would get on the treadmill and run as fast as I could as long as I could, listening to the mighty choruses of worship and praise, offering those to Him on my headphones. It was a battle for my heart. That was all I knew to do. I just prayed it would actually DO something. All I could give Him was my praise. This was my way for a long time.

Then I had a thought. What if He couldn't work good from this? My songs of praise disappeared. I began crying as I cleaned. I would fight to hold back the vomit and hold my breath while I scrubbed. As the days became years it turned to wailing. I remember collapsing to my knees and screaming so loud that I lost my voice. Then my prayers of thanksgiving changed to "AND THIS ONE?! AND THIS ONE TOO?! Are you going to work good from this shit too, God?!!" Cleaning would leave me in a crumbled, tearful heap. I can't adequately explain how bad it smelled and how it would get into my nostrils and linger with me long after. *'Do You see? Do You hear my prayers? Are You even there?'* And then I would sob in shame wondering where my faith was. A very religious friend told me God wasn't concerned with those prayers. He may or may not answer them, but he was only concerned about spreading the Gospel and saving men's souls. I couldn't stomach those words. *'Who are You, God? Why so much pain? Why him? Do you have no mercy? Do You not hear his cries? Do You not hear mine? Where is the good You promised? Do I have no right to ask?'* I felt forgotten by my Savior. My friends didn't want to hear the stories I had to tell. Some actually had the audacity to tell me that. Some shared scriptures about suffering that were like knives in my heart and actually felt like they pierced my eardrums. I was told by people who had endured suffering that amounted to a broken nail to *consider it all pure joy, that tribulations brought*

---

[21] For I do not understand my own actions. For I do not do what I want, but I do the very thing I hate. Now if I do what I do not want, I agree with the law, that it is good. So now it is no longer I who do it, but sin that dwells within me. For I know that nothing good dwells in me, that is, in my flesh. For I have the desire to do what is right, but not the ability to carry it out. For I do not do the good I want, but the evil I do not want is what I keep on doing. Now if I do what I do not want, it is no longer I who do it, but sin that dwells within me. - Romans 7:15-20

[22] 1 Thessalonians 5:16-18

[23] James 1:2-3; Romans 5:3-4; Proverbs 3:12; 1 Corinthians 10:13

forth perseverance and perseverance, character, and that God disciplines those He loves, that He will never tempt us beyond what we can bear.[23] After all, what can the response possibly be when someone quotes scripture to you. Better bear it. That's what Christ did. Not my will, but thine. I wondered what was wrong with me that my son's torment and the abuse I endured didn't bring any joy at all, that loving my enemy and sleeping with him was shattering me into pieces. Clearly, I wasn't doing faith the right way. Self-righteous arrogance and haughtiness with a side of condescension emanated from those who shared these scriptures. The rebuke of their religious platitudes left me empty and lonely, feeling quite unloved. I couldn't determine what I wasn't believing or praying that could change how these circumstances affected me. Or maybe, the truths they preached just seemed untrue.

I learned after a few attempts at sharing the truth to keep my sad stories to myself. If I did share there would be uncomfortable silence, turned heads, cleared throats, or more opportunities for someone to give me a lesson in endurance or the consequences of sin on the world. It made me not want to say a word and just offer a meaningless, obligatory, polite grin. Obviously, church isn't a place for people with real problems. We are called to be Christ's ambassadors; we don't have time to take care of hurting people. We are called to be a blessing, not need one. Duh. There was not much love at church when your child was a serious problem.

On Sundays, he would run away from the new special needs classroom they opened (because of him) and grab every pacifier he could find. He would run to the bookstore for videos he was obsessed over. He would run to places where they couldn't find him. Dozens of people and security would be searching for him. I would leave my other kids with someone while searching with a giant pit in my stomach, choking back more tears and praying to find him. Once a volunteer told me she *knew* Houston knew what he was doing was wrong because he repeated "no" to her after she told him "no" while she put the videos, he had escaped to get in sight but out of reach while he screamed and cried, saying "no" over and over. He was a wreck. It was everything in me to explain to her what echolalia is. There was a complete, almost intentional ignorance, to accept and understand a condition that affected a child's behavior in a way that went beyond the normal definitions of intent and willful disobedience. If you didn't comply, the cause was disobedience or dimwittedness. I felt less and less welcome and more like a leper. God's people didn't want me there. I began to wonder about God. Over and over and over this song was my prayer, my posturing and pleading before my God. The words were the cries of my heart.

> *Oh, great God*
> *Be small enough to hear me now*
> *There were times when I was crying*
> *From the dark of Daniel's den*
> *And I had asked you once or twice*
> *If you would part the sea again*
> *Tonight I do not need a*
> *Fiery pillar in the sky*
> *Just want to know you're gonna*
> *Hold me if I start to cry*
>
> *Oh, great God*
> *Be small enough to hear me now*
> *Oh, great God*
> *Be close enough to feel me now*
> *Oh great God be close to me*

There have been moments when I could not face
Goliath on my own
And how could I forget we marched
Around our share of Jericho's
But I will not be setting out
A fleece for you tonight
Just wanna know if everything will be alright

Oh, great God be close enough to feel me now
Oh, praise and all the honor be
To the God of ancient mysteries
Whose every sign and wonder
Turn the pages of our history
But tonight my heart is heavy
And I cannot keep from whispering, whispering
Are you there?

And I know you could leave writing
On the wall that's just for me
Or send wisdom while I'm sleeping
Like in Solomon's sweet dreams
I don't need the strength of Samson
Or a chariot in the end
Just wanna know you still know how many
Hairs are on my head

Oh, great God
Are you small enough?
Be small enough to hear Me now [24]

9

Losing Hope

Give ear to my prayer, O God and hide not yourself from my plea for mercy!
Attend to me, and answer me; I am restless in my complaint and I moan,
because of the noise of the enemy, because of the oppression of the wicked.
For they drop trouble upon me, and in anger they bear a grudge against me.
— Psalm 55:1-3

The Big Jock wanted a house to match his new income. He picked out a massive estate home in a private five home development centered next to the eighth hole tee (if I remember correctly) on a private golf course. I begged over and over not to get that house. It was too big, too expensive, too bourgeois. It embarrassed me. He wanted to show off so badly. It controlled every purchase he made. There was an old farmhouse that was available, and I asked if we could move there instead. He laughed. No. Not his style. I asked (carefully) to see what he was signing. He erupted in rage. It was his f..king money! He could do whatever the f..k he wanted with it! I had no right to ever question him about money! He was the head of the household and I was to submit to him! The name calling went on and it was clear my job was to clean and take care of babies. Nothing else. At the same time, he would spend extravagant sums and yet demand to see the receipt every time I went to the grocery store. We were living where he wanted to live, and that was the end of the story. When I invited friends over there was a general, "Well, look at you…" attitude. Someone said, "Good grief, how much is the power bill on a place this size?" Another added that this wasn't being a wise steward of God's money. I heard it for the rebuke it was. Considering where they live now, I don't think they would repeat that statement today. Affluence, by the way, isn't necessarily a bad thing at all, as long as it doesn't change who you put your trust in or enlarge your view of yourself to be greater than anyone else. Affluence can do great good. It just has a way of changing one's perception of money management and removing the limitations of lack. But at that time, money was luxury most of us didn't have. My friends obviously hadn't gotten the memo, it was the Big Jock's money, not God's. What could I say? I just half smiled with deep embarrassment and shrugged my shoulders.

Because of his diagnosis Houston was enrolled in the special ed preschool for summer school. I drove him to the new school before we were even moved in to meet with the new teachers. They were kind and seemed to have a bigger program than the last school. I told them he wasn't potty trained. I told them he ran away. I told them he screamed. I told them they should never take their eyes off of him. They assured me he would be ok. That afternoon they brought him out to the car and talked to me almost like they wanted to get to know me. I laughed with them and for a moment just felt good about the new school, despite all the unknown. His teacher for upcoming kindergarten had called and told me she was determined to help me potty train him and to put him in regular underwear. No more pullups. I was astonished at her hope, at her help. At that point I had four children in diapers. I was dumbfounded. You're going to help me? You're going to help my son? I knew no pull ups meant more cleanups, but not having to do it all by myself was all I needed. I somehow knew this school, these teachers, weren't going to give up. I needed their hope. Years later that teacher from the first day of summer school told me that on his first day Houston had run away and been lost for hours. They hadn't wanted to tell me because they didn't know what kind of mom I was. When they told me, I laughed out loud. I'm the kind of mom who's chasing, who doesn't know what the hell she's doing. I just can't stop loving my son.

Soon after we moved into that home there was a massive thunderstorm. Benjamin was six months old. The house was so huge I was always running to find where Houston had gone. I was upstairs with Benjamin and heard what sounded like rain on the front porch. I raced down the stairs, holding the baby in my robe and my heart dropped as I saw the door standing wide open. In that one second I grappled with realizing he had figured out how to unlock the door, despite our best efforts, and that he was gone. Location totally unknown. He could be anywhere. Sheets of rain, lightning and thunder, wind that made the pine trees bough and bend left and right - a glorious sight of power except that my little boy was somewhere out in it and there was no way to know what direction to look. Panic took over and I ran in the wild storm with my baby and my robe whipping around me until it was stuck to me. He was nowhere to be seen. There were woods. There was another neighborhood with hills everywhere. There were roads. I ran back to the house, up the stairs, and put Benjamin in his crib. I didn't even check on the other kids. I threw clothes on and started running. The storm kept raging. Lightning cracked directly overhead. I cried so much I couldn't swallow, and I choked on the tears. *Please God. Please God. Please God. Please. Help me. Help me. Help me. Please.* Waves of sobs would stop me from being able to catch a breath. I kept running. I was soaked. I didn't even know where I was. I knew I needed to call the police and tried in the rain to remember what direction I had come. A car pulled up and rolled down the window. I knew what I must look like, desperate and hysterical. "Are you looking for your son?" the man asked me. And I fell to my knees, sobbing. He took me to his home where Houston had walked right through their open garage door, back door and into their family room and started fast forwarding and rewinding Disney videos. He didn't even acknowledge me as I clung to him and scooped him up. As the man drove us back, I couldn't believe how far my son had run. I thanked God. I kissed and held my boy. He squirmed to get away. At home I prayed, "Thank you, Lord." But I felt abandoned.

My dad brought my young cousin to visit on my birthday. The Big Jock hated when anyone who loved me was around. My kids loved this older cousin and clamored around the middle schooler. I could sense how annoyed my husband was that anyone he hadn't invited was staying in his home. I went to the bathroom to finish getting ready for my family birthday dinner. He followed me and started saying one insulting comment after another about my dad and young cousin. I couldn't take it anymore. Under my breath I whispered, "I hate you." He heard me. "What'd you say?!" He grabbed a towel and began snapping my head with the wet towel. "Do you hate me now? Do you hate me now? Do you hate me now? Do you hate me now?" And then this evil laugh came out of him. I stared at the floor, holding on to the sink, tears pouring down my face and my whole body trembling while the towel snapped in my face repeatedly. It took me quite a while to get myself to stop crying and cleaned up for my birthday dinner. At dinner, the kids were focused on their cousin and their pop. I sat in silence. I couldn't eat. The Big Jock leaned toward me and menacingly ordered, "I paid for that. You better eat it." Happy birthday to me.

I wondered where God was. Did He see the cruelty? Did a big house I didn't want make it ok? Did He care about my broken heart or just my sin? Would He ever answer any of my prayers? Was there any hope in this life? He had allowed so many things to make me cry, to make my heart break, to test my trust and faith. I was so tired. People with typical struggles don't understand that kind of exhaustion. It's a tired that goes down to your very bones and makes opening your eyes a battle in your heart as much as in your body. It makes smiling actually painful. It makes the sight of the easy, happy lives of others a repeated slap in your face. I resented the big house and all the empty space that was just for appearances. I resented the load He had put on me. Then I began to wonder if the only reason I believed all this stuff about God is because that is what I had been taught. Then I thought to myself, 'I've never questioned it. Maybe it's not even true.' I began in earnest to question my faith. Its scattered ruins surrounded me. I poured over arguments from atheists and arguments by atheists turned theists. It was a process. One tiny Lego of truth at a time until at last there was a reckoning in my shattered heart. I remember slamming C.S. Lewis shut and saying to myself, "CRAP! I believe it." My soul took a deep breath. I paused for a long momentous moment. "So now what?" The very air seemed to say, "Trust Me... Love."

Unsure of any next step beyond the chaos around me, I tried to find something to make beautiful, something to help heal. I looked at the edges of the woods and the patches of untilled, unsodden earth between our home and the golf path. Something nudged me there. So, while the babies napped every day I would go barefoot into the dirt and dig. I uprooted fallen trees and rocks and found dormant perennials at the garden center for almost nothing. They were just buckets of dirt with a marker. I thought how fun to plant something unseen and wait to see the gift. I learned about roses, camelias, and hydrangeas and dug up His earth with a growing admiration for the exquisite detail in every created thing. Something of my father's farming family had found its way into my heart. It was like the earth already knew me and welcomed me back every day. After noon there would be golf carts of drunk men that teed off about 10 yards from my patch of dirt who found the sight of me digging in the dirt in front of an estate home on a golf course a hilarious sight. I remember thinking, "Is that what men with money do? Drunk by 1:30? Is this their sum?" It was unimpressive. There were regulars that would question me about my progress and then turn to say something that would make them all laugh. By the time I had to leave, they had grown impressed with that little patch of dirt. I still wonder about my little plants. They were planted with love. They were planted with faith. Something good was put in the ground and it can't return void. It's just how He made His world work. My faith was stuck on me, even when I tried to reject it. Not because of me, because of Him. He wouldn't let me go.

10

The Letter

Hear my cry, O God, listen to my prayer, from the end of the earth
I call to you when my heart is faint. Lead me to the rock that is higher than I.
— Psalm 61:1-2

I t was about this time that at church it was announced our senior pastor would begin a series on faith. I heard it and all week I felt something bubbling inside me. I knew he didn't understand faith when there is no way to believe. I knew he didn't understand just how bad it can get. I knew he didn't know what it was like to lose the one thing you cherished and counted on to sustain you. The Holy Spirit pushed and prodded me until I said, "Fine." I got out a few pieces of paper and started writing. It was the first time I had written anything since college and the words came pouring out of me while teardrops fell on the letter. I sent it to him. He didn't know me, but he called and asked to read it for that service. I hadn't wanted my whole heart to be known like that but God did.

***

Dear Pastor,

Last Sunday it was announced you would begin a series on faith. Since I was a little girl I have always been so grateful for God's sovereignty. It was so wonderful to be able to trust that despite the awfulness around me God was still working in and through me. As one of my greatest comforts I clung to Romans 8:28 for my peace and security and even my happiness. "For all things work together for the good of those who love God who are called according to His purpose." Even though I didn't understand I trusted Him for a very long time. As I grew older, more awfulness came in different forms. But I knew I was loved so I was okay. I told myself I had the Lord and that was all I needed even if I desperately wanted more. I prayed for God to keep me focused on Him and His goodness and His love. Then my once happy, healthy baby boy vanished, and my son was diagnosed with autism amidst plenty of other very difficult circumstances. I could write a book on that alone, but I will try to spare you most of the details. I will say that one parent described it as if someone came in the night and stole your child and all you're left with is this bewildered body. Another parent commented that she always thought the worst thing that could happen to someone is to lose a child, but now, seeing what was happening to me, this was the most perverse way.

The thing is it is not just the autism. My son only slept a few hours a day. He ran in circles screaming and laughing hysterically, like he was hallucinating. He pushed his head on the ground, spun things for hours, made dolphin noises, bit himself hard - again and again, obsessed about bizarre things, put his hands on his ears and hummed, cried a heart wrenching cry, chewed holes in his clothes, chewed on everything, ran away over and over, caused several floods with his obsession with water, wouldn't look at me or acknowledge me sometimes, constantly removed his clothing - all of it, couldn't stop eating and drinking and running, couldn't sit even to let me read him a story, and he's just child number two out of five under the age of seven.

What got to me was the poop. I have calculated that I have scrubbed poop out of mattresses, walls, ceilings, carpet, furniture, TV's, rugs, and bedding over 500 times in the last three years. That does not include the diapers, the 6-8 daily diapers of chronic diarrhea and the bloody bottoms that came with them and that was just one child. They have a smell like something died, which is hard to handle when you're pregnant and smell sensitive and you're having to scrub it out of something. But I was so strong, so hopeful, so trusting. I remember the first time it happened. He had smeared poop all over the three-day old down comforter I had saved for. I remember thinking as I looked at the water-stained ceiling of our tiny apartment where the water heater from the apartment above us had emptied into ours, 'You want me to thank you for this, God?' And then praying, 'If you can bring good out of fleas in concentration camps for Corrie Ten Boom, you can bring good out of this. May Your will be done, not mine.'

When my son was three and half years old, five weeks after the birth of my fourth, he was hit by a truck. He looked awful, almost like he had been burned. But God's hand was on him and kept him from a life-threatening injury. I kept thanking God for his safety and kept trusting in God's will. But I was getting so tired and weary.

I guess that's when it started happening. Slowly at first, I started doubting. I was just too spent to trust in the face of my own reality, to believe that God would or could work all this poop for good. Then fear came soon after that. I remember your wife telling how you told her that this was just a season and it would pass. Yet I was drowning in the fear this would never pass, that I would spend the rest of my life surrounded by poop, but less and less able to cope with it. I begged God to cure Him, to give me peace and strength, to let me see His hand in this, to give me anything to get me through it. Then I was overcome with another fear. What if this was just preparation for an even bigger trial... I told God over and over that He was wrong - that I couldn't get through this. I told Him this yoke wasn't light at all but was taking my youth, my strength, my joy and my faith with it. There was nothing left in me. A dear friend told me I should be grateful that my circumstances forced me to cry out to Him and seek Him so desperately, to need Him so much. But I didn't want to be needy or helpless. After all I had been through growing up, I couldn't handle this. Now I knew I could handle nothing. My life seemed only to be misery ahead and misery behind.

The pastor stopped at that time and said what he thought for certain was coming. That this lady was going to say, "You're going to teach us about faith, but I want you to know it's not as easy as you say." But this was what I said...

That's when God showed me the greatest thing about faith. Him. When all my faith seemed to be gone there was only one thing left, Him, His grace. It was grace, God's unmerited favor on me when I doubted Him that had sustained me. It was grace that showed me I am loved when I have done nothing lovely. It is His gracious mercy that has forgiven me for all the awful things I have said and thought and done. It is His grace that has given me a kind word when I felt so utterly alone. It is His grace that has given my son a teacher determined to potty train him. It is His grace that awes me so much that I cannot help but love Him who first loved me. I have no idea what God's plan is, but I've learned that my only hope is in God's amazing grace.

The pastor said, "There's the answer. You want a faith walk? That walk gets stronger and stronger as we see He, and He alone is sufficient."

***

That day Benjamin had been baptized. We had invited guests for the baptism, and some stood near us. After the service, I ran to get the kids as usual. When I found the Big Jock, he couldn't make eye contact. He just stared at the fenced in plastic play area as Houston and Paul climbed around and Reagan played hide and seek and delighted every other child with her smile and giggles. He was holding back tears. He said, "That was the most incredible thing I've ever heard. I know it's been awful." Some of the guests joined us at our home afterward, and I went to the kitchen to begin getting dishes out to serve. The Big Jock began to give the tour that made him so proud. After less than ten minutes, he shouted up from the basement for me to come downstairs. I ran down and found Houston naked, covered in poop and poop smeared into the carpet. The guests looked on in shock and then turned and followed the Big Jock without a word. I realized as I looked at the mess that this was not for the faint of heart and got to work cleaning my son. I almost felt proud, if you can ever feel proud cleaning shit. Still in the dress I had worn for my son's baptism, I got down and began scrubbing. The tour and the drinks went on without me. Somehow, this had become the place I was more comfortable. This was real. Upstairs was the show. I didn't have to pretend I had it all together. I could be upset and still love God. I could cry. I could stink. My kids could too. I could be dirty. I was still loved.

There were some people who came into my life as a result of the letter, most importantly, Sarah. Sarah is about as good and genuine as they come. By that I mean she is real. She is true. She is love. God doesn't make many people with such an extraordinary capacity for love. She had tried for years to become pregnant and ended up losing several children to ectopic pregnancies. She told me I was stuck with her; that God had told her she was supposed to be my friend. She wanted to help. I couldn't refuse her help, nor could I begin to explain how difficult that would be. One weekend she decided to spend the weekend with us to help give me a break. Sarah is an interpreter for the deaf and wears hearing aids. After what was the most ridiculous and hectic morning, with crying from all five children and constant fussing from Benjamin, Sarah walked upstairs around 10 am and asked me in shock, "How long have you been awake?" I looked at her and said, "Since five. How could you not hear us?" We both laughed. So, there was a glorious benefit to being hard of hearing. She was not quite up to the insanity of child rearing yet. But she would get there, and quickly.

The pastor continued his series on faith. Trust Me to do something you don't see evidence is possible - seemed to whisper to me in every scripture. I prayed to God about what to do next. My prayers about autism were just to help sustain me. I had stopped praying for miracles. The Big Jock had decided to open additional branches of his mortgage company. I felt led to talk to him about taking a big step of faith to give a substantial amount of the money he was making to the church. I was shocked when he agreed. I think it was two weeks later that he came home very upset and concerned that Governor Roy Barnes had proposed a predatory lending law to restrict the rates and fees charged on mortgages. I remember thinking to myself, 'Isn't that regulated by the Department of Banking and Finance? How bad could it be?' The rates I saw advertised sounded amazing. What were the extra points and fees the governor was trying to stop? I asked questions and could tell from the response, something he was doing didn't sound right. I just didn't know what the lie was. The law passed. He and his employees left to open a branch in Colorado where there were fewer regulations. He began plans for a Florida branch. He was gone for a while. When he returned, he confessed to time with the boys that had gotten out of hand. He told me things he had done that were disturbing. Somehow this compelled him to share much more than I wanted to know. He confessed to me things from his college days that made me want to throw up. In addition to the sexual indecencies and nonconsensual sex there were other things. They would set girls up to steal from them while one of them was having his way with the unsuspecting victim. He confessed how he would drive his scooter around campus and when he saw books unattended, he would grab them and take them directly to the bookstore to sell for cash. His confession came with tears and prayers that gave an appearance of earnestness. He begged me to pray for him. So, I did. He talked about wanting to really live for Christ. I stared at this man. Could he change? It's hard to know if you should believe someone when they've just confessed to you. My prayer was for God to work a miracle in his heart. Scriptures of forgiving seven times seventy, turning the other cheek, washing the feet of the one who will betray you, loving your enemy - these were the words I knew well, tenets of Christianity. So, I prayed for God to give me more love. I was numb.

11

My God, Where Are You?

Deliver me, O Lord, from evil men; preserve me from violent men
who plan evil things in their heart, and stir up wars continually.
They make their tongue sharp as a serpent's, and under their lips is the venom of asps.
Guard me O Lord, from the hands of the wicked;
preserve me from violent men, who have planned to trip up my feet.
The arrogant have hidden a trap for me, and with cords they have spread a net;
beside the way they have set snares for me. I say to the Lord,
You are my God; give ear to the voice of my pleas for mercy, O Lord!
— Psalm 140:1-6

Despite his tears and new commitment, God didn't answer the Big Jock's prayer for money before the bills were late. The new laws in Georgia just didn't allow him to make the money he had before. The money worries consumed him. He had taken on so many cars and the ridiculously expensive home, and with the new regulations he couldn't make the same money. Not even close. His other branches were not doing as well as he hoped. He drank more and more and more. I learned to stay away. One day when he came home drunk, I told him he wasn't changing like he had promised, and he didn't do anything to help with the kids. Upset, I went to bathe Paul and Benjamin.

A while later, when I went to find Houston, I found him completely lethargic and unable to support his body. He was completely limp, and it looked like his eyes were beginning to roll back in his head. I screamed for the Big Jock to come help me. Terrified and crying, I told him I didn't know what was happening to him and to call 911. A look of horror overtook my husband. "He wouldn't shut up. So, I gave him his medicine," he said defensively. "What?" I shouted. "I already gave him his medicine today. How much did you give him?" It was two and half times the dosage. Houston was rushed to the hospital where the charcoal he was administered absorbed the toxicity in his sweet little body. All I wanted to do was hold my baby boy. I couldn't trust their father to do anything. I could hardly speak to him. Shortly after that I was making the kids peanut butter and jelly. He came up to me intoxicated and started saying all sorts of cruel things, trying to provoke me. He wanted a fight. I didn't say anything. He wanted a reason to explode, and my silence hadn't given him one. So, he headbutted the side of my face. The sudden sharp pain brought tears to my eyes. I didn't dare move. I kept staring at the slice of bread half spread with peanut butter. Bam! He headbutted me again. I did everything not to cry out and just turned and walked away.

One night I woke in a fright to the massive pressure of him on top of me entering me. Even in the dark I saw the evil on his face and tried to push his three hundred plus pounds off of me. I half cried, whispered and choked a "n..no". He rolled over and I did too. I cried silently until morning. Over the next few years, he did this repeatedly. I would wake to him on top of me or his fingers inside me.

He announced we would be moving. I asked about selling the house; he told me he had never bought it. It was just a lease purchase, and we didn't have money to keep paying it. I knew better than to remind him that I had told him it was too expensive or question him about why he had lied to me about buying it. There was a lot of shame in leaving a home we had been in only a year. A few women smugly told me it hadn't been wise to buy such an expensive home. It felt like some of them were secretly reveling in the satisfaction of seeing us fail. My cousin from my mom's side that had played with me as a little girl told me to never hold onto anything, to always have an open hand with whatever God put in it. Others said, "The Lord gives, and the Lord takes away, blessed be the name of the Lord." I shrugged my shoulders. People didn't realize I had not wanted all the show in the first place. I was guilty by marriage. I could have lived without the house and the shame. Houston had a way of not letting me hold onto much. We went to look for another home and I found one that was in our budget and perfect. It was just what I wanted, a beautiful Cape Cod style with three big bedrooms, a big yard, and a bonus space above the garage that we could eventually do something with. I tried to keep a positive attitude about the whole mess. I asked the Big Jock if he could help with the move this time since this was the ninth move and I had done all the packing and moving for every other move. Including the many moves from my childhood, my college years, and as a young family, I had moved 26 times in 29 years. The Big Jock agreed he would help on moving day. I started the process. It was exhausting with all the kids.

Morgan was getting quite the attitude during this time. She was incredibly smart and gifted, reading well above her age level and drawing beautiful pictures that others couldn't believe a young child could produce. But, if she knew what you wanted, she would do exactly the opposite. When a school wanted her to draw a family to assess her skills development, she, who could create remarkable pictures, drew stick figures with no detail. She might as well have given the teacher the finger. I knew exactly what she had done. When I asked her about it, she crossed her arms and pouted, no, huffed at me. She was routinely moody and disrespectful and didn't like to help. It was a constant drain.

On May 17, 2003 as I fed everyone at the bar top, Morgan backtalked me. I looked at the Big Jock who had been drinking heavily. In frustration I turned to him and said, "Aren't you going to say anything to her? Do you hear how she talks to me?" It was like I had called on Satan to appear, and he did. The hate in his eyes turned wild. "I would act like her too if I had a mother like you!" he seethed. His brow bent forward, and his massive shoulders swelled as he bent forward and came toward me swiftly. He cornered me and burrowed his head against my forehead with such force that the back of my head pushed against the back door and then his huge paw of a hand started strangling me as hard as one can with one hand. Hate poured out of his eyes, a lustful, powerful hate. He said so much that he had said so many times before. I got used to tuning most of the profanity out. The one that always upset me was, "No one wants you! Your mother and father didn't even want you!" When he finally let go, I opened the door and jumped in the car and drove off. For hours I drove around and finally tried to sleep in the Barnes and Noble parking lot. I prayed to my God. *What am I going to do? Help me, Lord. What do I do?* For hours I prayed in my minivan. Around 3 am on May 18, 2003 I went home. Trying not to make any sound, I got into bed. The hate was everywhere. Just like you can feel love, you can feel hate. As soon as I pulled the covers up, he boomed, "TURN THE ALARM ON!" I thought for a moment. I had to stand up to this. That had to be the only way for it to change. Very quietly I responded, "Please ask nicely." With a force I can't explain I was struck in the rib cage and was on the floor one second later. I heaved an enormous breath trying to decide what to do while my lung burned. I couldn't fight but I could not back down. I got back into bed. Five times he kicked me in full force to my ribs that three times landed me on the floor. I remember his disgust when he gave up his game of terror and violence. I know it seems ridiculous, but in that moment, I thought I had won some tiny victory. I had faced the monster and stood my ground.

On May 24, 2003, I got up early as usual to pack. At 9 am the Big Jock left. At 10 am, one of the volunteers in the special needs Sunday school class came to get Houston. At 10:30 Sarah came to get Benjamin. The Big Jock's sister and brother-in-law came to get Morgan, Reagan, and Paul at 11 am. "Where's the Big Jock?" they asked. I looked at them knowingly. "He said he went to pick up some things." His sister looked at me with her mouth open, jaw dropped. I looked back at her. My face said everything. She seemed uncomfortable. She asked about the mattress we were giving them. I told them where it was. They took the mattress and three of my kids.

At noon the Big Jock came home with a Chick-fil-A bag. He was shit faced. I glared at him. "What's your f..king problem?" he barbed. For the first time in my life, I stood up to him. This is what I did. I looked at him and said simply and resolutely, "You said you were going to help." What happened next happened so fast it's difficult to put it into words. The rage I knew so well glared back at me for less than a second before it took over. He came at me so fast I didn't even realize what was happening. In one second he had rounded the corner and had my neck in his hand. He was spewing things I couldn't catch and some I could such as - "OH YEAH!! YOU WANT MY F..KING HELP!! YOU F..KING SLUT PIECE OF S..T!!!" He held me up in the air and dropped me to the ground and picked me up by my hair and literally shook me by the roots of my hair like a rag doll, dropped me and then did it again. When you're in a violent moment you don't have thoughts. You just experience. I think that's something people don't realize. It's all just happening. You're not a person. You're a thing. It's happening so fast there is literally no time to process. He picked me off the floor and threw me into one of the green overstuffed chairs and in the same second pushed it to the granite overhang. With every ounce of force he could muster he burrowed his head into my forehead with his three hundred plus pounds of pressure while the chair pushed against the back of my head. The granite counter wrenched into the top of head in a trianglulated vice grip as he tried to crush my skull. I thought my head was going to explode. I couldn't even cry. I couldn't even think. I don't know what my limbs were doing. I felt like a rag doll, limp and unable to move. When he let go, he screamed, "I WANT A DIVOOOOORCE!!!!" I was in a crumpled heap in the chair. I tried to regain my senses. What had just happened? It was moments before I could speak. Finally, I said quietly, "Ok. But you're not getting the kids." He glared at me. "Oh yes I will!" He heaved and panted, and with a devilish smile thundered, "As soon as I chop you up into tiny pieces with a chainsaw, I will *definitely* get the kids." And as awful as it is to admit it, that is what I had to hear to try and get help.

I stood up and was dazed. I tried to think and really struggled. My head hurt so badly. I went to the bedroom closet to get clothes. I took some items and literally couldn't process what to do next. My mind went completely blank. I picked up a laundry basket. I tried to think what to put in it. *What do I need? Think.* I heard his footsteps. I turned around in absolute terror and he violently picked me up by my hair again and shook me around like a rag doll, a foot off the ground. With violent force he threw me to the ground. At this point I was bleeding. He screamed, "Oh, should I feel bad because I popped one of your zits?" Something in me said, LEAVE! JUST LEAVE! I ran to the garage, got in the minivan and left. I cried and cried. All I wanted was my kids. I drove to the McDonald's where I knew my sister-in-law had taken my kids. I walked in and saw the horror on their faces. I couldn't talk. Reagan, sweet Reagan came and kissed me and got on my lap while I cried. Paul, still sucking his thumb, nestled close to me. I couldn't stop crying. All his sister said to me was this, "Oh my God! Oh my God! Did he do this to you? Oh my God! D-! (her husband's name) Give her ten dollars!" I heard her and was utterly stunned. I looked up at her. She thrust a ten dollar bill at me and said frantically, "Don't call the police!!! Just don't call the police!! OK????" I swallowed back the vomit that her words involuntarily triggered. Ten dollars to keep justice at bay… It said everything. It said how much they thought of me. It said what they thought of right and wrong and those who are weak.[25] I had thought after thought after thought, so many I couldn't process any of them. I couldn't think of what to do next. Then I had an idea. A dear friend had moved just down the road and I went to her house. They had a few acres that was gated and quiet and was just what she was looking for at the time. I went to her house and she walked up slowly to open the fence. She came up to the car to say hey and saw me. "Oh my God! Did the Big Jock do this to you???" I couldn't stop crying. I felt bad for intruding on her, but I didn't know where to go or what to do. I was without a home. I needed a friend. I needed a lot more than a friend actually. I sat at her kitchen table and cried. Her husband came in and I heard him ask, "What's wrong?" His question made me even more embarrassed. He was such a good man. They were such a sweet, normal family. And here I was, such a freak, such a mess. My friend called shelters. They told her there was nothing available for someone with that many children. There was nothing available for autism. There were no answers. There was no room in any of the inns. "Katie, there is nothing. There is no place to go."

She decided to go back with me to the house to get some things since I had nothing. When we pulled up, he was on the riding lawn mower in the front yard riding in circles at full speed, over and over again. He wouldn't look at us. We walked in and I gasped. "Oh my GOD!" she gasped. A giant jar of Orville Redenbacher had been smashed and popcorn kernels were everywhere you could see. The furniture had been pushed against the front door and stacked on top of each other, teetering precariously. Other pieces were smashed. It looked like a madman had been let loose. My friend started grabbing anything she thought was expensive that he could break that could fit in the minivan. "Katie... This is bad! Really bad! Did he do this when you were here?" I shook my head. He had just tried to bash me. The insanity, chaos, and violence around me broke my heart all over again. I was frozen. She started to tell me what to get because I literally couldn't think of what to do next.

The volunteer from church who was watching Houston met me at church in the morning and exhaustedly told me how hard it had been to watch him for twenty hours. I nodded. She said she couldn't watch him any longer. It was too hard. I understood. My very religious friend saw me and my swollen eyes and demanded to know what was wrong. I told her. She gasped and said, "Has anyone prayed for the Big Jock?" I literally stopped breathing for a moment. Really? He's your big concern in this moment? Repeatedly through this process, I witnessed Christians very concerned about the state of my husband's soul who didn't give a rip about what he had done to me. It left me blindsided when I was already fighting to stay alive.

I went back to my friend's house with Houston after keeping him away and busy as long as I could. That night I slept in her son's bed with Houston, trapping him with my leg across his legs to keep him from getting up. He scripted Disney lines over and over for hours until he finally slept. I never took my leg off of him. I don't know if I ever slept. My good friend, wanting to help me, had called our circle of friends. There had been a meeting. What could they do to help? The intentions were good. But one of the reasons I had put so much effort into making a pretty front was that I feared their judgment and ostracism. As they gathered together to pray for me, the feeling I got was quite clear. There was no love. Some of the women who were in horrible marriages that had not become physically abusive suddenly became very austere regarding the sanctity of marriage and how wonderful everything was.

They never spoke to me again about the truth of what they were living through. Others who tried to live the perfect Christian life with the perfect everything shunned me. The invitations dried up completely after that. No one wanted the public scrutiny that accompanied the truth. Based on the silence, I was apparently the only one who had married an asshole.

---

[25] 'Cursed be anyone who perverts the justice due to the sojourner, the fatherless, and the widow.' And all the people shall say, 'Amen.' — Deuteronomy 27:19

12

Sleeping With the Enemy

He has put my brothers far from me,
and those who knew me are wholly estranged from me.
My relatives have failed me, my close friends have forgotten me...
All my intimate friends abhor me, and those whom I loved have turned against me.
My bones stick to my skin and to my flesh, and I have escaped by the skin of my teeth.
— Job 19:13-14, 19-20

The leadership at our church was notified so they could counsel and help save this marriage. I was terrified at what would happen. Would they believe me? Would he lie and sell them with his smooth talk? How would they help? What would the Big Jock do if I told the truth about how bad it truly was? A church leader who knew the Big Jock contacted him and told him not to go to the new home where the move had taken place. The keys to the new home were left and the furniture had been scattered in random rooms since the movers had no direction. That first day I set the television and VCR up for the kids and started moving furniture. The kids didn't ask where their dad was, and I didn't offer. That night I watched out the front window, lost in fear and thought. A pair of Porsche headlights turned into the neighborhood at full speed, and I looked in terror as they began speeding up the long driveway. I had left the garage door open, and I began to realize these might be the last moments of my life. His massive shoulders were bowed and ready to kill when he filled the doorway and walked in with the gait of a conqueror. He threw his keys on the counter and announced, "This is MY house! No one's going to tell me I can't come to my own house." Trembling I backed toward the couch and sat down. I sat on my hands so he couldn't see them shaking. He sat across from me and said, "So are we getting divorced?" I didn't respond. I didn't know what response he wanted to hear. I kept the truth buried deep - deep under duty, under motherhood, under the demands of money and Christianity, under friendships and dreams. Truth had no place when you're tasked with staying alive to do a job no one else would do. Still, as I always had, I measured every move. That's the only way to waltz with the wicked and live to tell the tale. He leaned forward to refresh his intimidating posture. "Do you think anyone would ever want you?" He chuckled with a wicked glee. "Five kids and one severely autistic. HA! No man would ever sign up for that. But I'll be just fine. I've got a lot to offer." And he leaned back as if that settled it, as if it became true because he said it. I sat silently. I couldn't take anything for granted. I never knew what could set him off. Then his voice dropped. He looked off to some far-off place only he could see. "I see demons." He waited for a reaction. I offered none. "They're real! I see them. I can see their eyes and they smile at me like they are coming for me." "You can pray for protection if you're scared," I said quietly. And silently, I did just that. God help me. God help me.

The next morning, I called the elder that had told him to stay away and told him what happened. They still didn't want me to call the police. There is no way to save the marriage once the police get involved was the consensus of the great ecclesiastical wisdom. The Big Jock was furious but agreed to stay with his sister for a few weeks. After a few weeks and some ridiculous counseling sessions, both where he demonstrated his rage and propensity to declare himself a changed man, he said he was sorry, so I needed to get to the business of going back to the way things were. I was reminded of my Christian duty to forgive and be a submissive wife and that love covers a multitude of sins. By July, he felt his penance had been paid. He showed up unannounced and rammed his body against the door. In the next second, there was a massive kick that shattered the door frame followed by a second kick where the door busted wide open. He told the church he wasn't leaving. It was his house.

From this point, I became a shell of a person. Pounds I didn't have to spare started falling off me to the point where I didn't look well. I remember him looking at me during all of this with one of his evil smiles and saying, "You've lost weight. HA!" The church just didn't get it. They told me I couldn't get divorced without their permission and I still hadn't provided any proof of adultery. If I divorced without their consent, that would be grounds for being out of covenant, for being barred from partaking in the Lord's table and any other dispensational grace the church had to offer. They spoke to me like a teenager who was grounded, not a faithful mother of five who was praying for her husband to stop being abusive. The Big Jock started telling the elders any time I spent any money. I would have conversations where I had to explain to a church elder that I bought towels, a forty-dollar vacuum, sunscreen, and a new bra because nothing would stay on me anymore, that the $22 I spent at L&L Management was Burger King for the kids on Saturday. They didn't question him about anything. I had no access to the money - to the accounts, to the mortgage, to any loan, just a debit card. He had told me that because I never owned anything, my credit would hurt our interest rate. When you're in a situation like this, you don't believe anything, but you also don't have any power to change the situation. Standing up for your rights becomes a gamble of life and limb. This is still not something that society recognizes. You are judged for staying, judged for leaving, judged for not defending yourself, judged for not being self-sufficient and independent, judged for having children. But no one helps. I call it the judgment of the safe. People have no idea how utterly destructive their judgment is until they have walked in those shoes. Many never will. Even more don't care.

There was one tiny event right after we had moved in that brought me some small comfort and trust in my heavenly Father. The former owners had left an older washer and dryer. I had a newer set and no room for two sets. I called an organization from church that provided home essentials for struggling families. I told her I had a washer/dryer set to give away. She was silent. "Wow," she finally said. I asked what she meant. "We have a single mom who has nothing, and we are moving her into a place. Another family was donating a washer/dryer set and they called me to cancel. This mom really needed this washer/dryer. She has nothing. I started to fret and then I remembered to pray. I said to Him, 'Well God, you know she needs a washer/dryer today. Since you took that set, I guess you'll be sending us another one so I'll just trust that You're going to provide another set real soon.'" She paused and continued, "That was this morning and then you called." Tears welled up in my eyes. If she only knew. But here in the middle of this awful mess, God was still answering prayers and letting me be a tiny piece of a blessing to some other hurting mom. It might seem like a very little thing, but the fact that He could be trusted to work events to provide a washer/dryer in one morning made me think, 'Maybe You really are listening.' And I started praying intently with a glimmer that something good could happen. I devoured God's word, everyday praying for miracles in my son and my spouse.

The next few years were a blur of trying to make everything look good to stop the judgment and the ostracism while internally I just kept praying and praying for miracles. Governor Sonny Perdue had overturned 130 years of Democratic party rule in Georgia in 2002 when he was elected, and the predatory lending law, one of the strictest in the nation was reversed. The money machine roared back to life. The Big Jock roared right back with it. He had a reputation to rebuild. There is really no explaining how much charisma and charm he has when he wants something. He was suits and smiles and big handshakes. I told him I was concerned this gravy train he was conducting wouldn't last. I noticed the prices of homes skyrocketing and everyone was refinancing to get the equity out of their homes. He laughed and said, "Isn't it great!" I told him people's incomes hadn't increased and the disparity would eventually catch up to the mortgage industry, especially when the teaser rates began to fluctuate. He laughed and looked at me like I was the stupidest person he had ever met. He explained like you explain to a child who's pestering you with questions you don't have time for. "There's a refi around every corner. My customer is the guy with a Marlboro stuck to his bottom lip. The country will never run out of that guy." Then he would laugh. His company grew and his ego grew too. He would try to charm every single waitress, even if I was sitting beside him. It was embarrassing. An old friend came to town and he took him to an expensive steakhouse where they partied on Louis XIII and drank until it was gone so he could give his friend the bottle. The trophies weren't just in bottles. Class A business space with all the corporate perks, business lunches and dinners, new servers, new furniture, new Porsches for his top men - he was going to rule the world. I was at home trying to raise babies and battle autism.

The world was not kind to autistic children in those days. In school and church, we were hidden far away from others so we wouldn't bother the "normal" kids. The reality was that I had to be hypervigilant, always aware of every circumstance and every possible thing that could go wrong. Sirens and alarms would make me panic and frantically look for Houston. Was there an unlocked door, any way to escape, access to water, an intercom system that could go off and leave him screaming and covering his ears, sounds that would upset him, were there babies with pacifiers he could grab, were there open food and drinks, videotapes, DVD's, something that could be a stick that he would obsess over? Houston would regularly take food off someone's plate as we walked by and angry parents would have to be pacified as I would repeat, "I'm so sorry, I'm so sorry," and then I would replace their food and keep a tighter grip on Houston while I carried Benjamin and herded the rest of them. "I'm so sorry. I'm so sorry." I said it at every furrowed brow, every ugly look, at every person slightly inconvenienced by son's noises, gestures, or behaviors. Years later, I had people tell me to stop saying sorry so much. I would gulp at the rebuke. My "I'm sorry" had become part of me, an unconscious defense mechanism, my way of protecting myself and my children from a world that didn't understand and didn't want to or have to. If you can, if you care to understand, if you have it in you to be empathetic, not sympathetic, try to imagine being aware of every sound, smell, and movement and having to react to protect and apologize for every single action that is not even your own. Try to imagine what that does to a human being. Try to imagine what your thoughts and feelings would be if it was you for an hour, for a day, for a week, for a month, for a year, for a decade, for two with no real relief more than a few hours. What would be left of you? It was not Post Traumatic Stress Disorder because at least then the trauma is over. There was nothing post about it. It is Perpetual or Permanent Traumatic Stress Disorder; the trauma knows no limits and just keeps going and going and going. The grieving never ends. Is it any wonder people give up?

Lovely mothers would bring all kinds of snacks to the pool for their kids with their many pool toys and Houston would not be able to resist. He was so quick, and he would dig into strangers' bags and take juice boxes from other kids. It didn't matter if he had just had one. He had to have them all. There was no such thing as full. He would take bites out of other kids' pool noodles while they were using them. It was exhausting. I tried to only go to the pool when other families weren't there so he would disturb less people. Other kids were as awful as their parents. The pointing, the rude questions, the revulsion if Houston would get near them while he made noises or flapped his hands. "Is *that* your brother? What's wrong with him? Why does he do *that*? Why does he keep saying that?" all with scrunched up, disgusted faces. My kids didn't have an answer. I was so glad my kids had each other to play with. Few wanted to play at our house. My kids didn't want to explain why their brother just appeared naked or why there was poop on the couch or why he would fast forward and rewind the same scene of a video or why he covered his ears, flapped his hands, bit himself or made those awful noises. At the pool, parents would notice his hands and try to hide their revulsion when they asked me, "What's that on his hands?" I would have to explain he had been biting on himself since he was two and was now grinding on the bones in his hands. When we got him gloves, he would chew through them. They would look at me speechless with mouths open or with eyes looking at the ground. Sometimes I might get the comment, "You're a strong woman." But more often I got the worst comment someone could possibly think to ask. It still makes me shake my head that people are so emotionally dense. They hadn't learned the lesson I had taught my kids, "If you can't say something nice, keep your mouth shut… Treat others like you want to be treated… How would you feel if someone did or said that to you?" They would look at me with a look of horror and disgust and ask, as if an answer to their cruel curiosity was required, "*What* are you going to do when he gets *older?*" I was always trying to be a lady. I couldn't punch them even though they deserved it. Another mom with an autistic son and a feisty spirit said to me, "You hold 'em. I'll hit 'em." I struggled for a long time with how to answer them in a way that didn't involve profanity. It actually took me years to find the answer. To other moms like me - use this statement, the world needs to hear this again and again. My answer to their crude curiosity was and still is this, "**My plan is for my son to spend his entire life with people who love him. In fact, that is the same plan I have for all my children.**" It was the first defense I ever felt really good about.

Then there was the running. Houston's age had accelerated his speed and his ability to problem solve through our efforts to keep him safe. His unquenchable obsessions ruled him. It was a while before I learned the technical term, elopement. You cannot imagine how fast my son can run. It is like something takes over and he cannot stop or pause the sprint button. He would sprint barefoot, across hot pavement, naked, it didn't matter. If he was running, you'd better catch him because he couldn't catch himself. I still remember Paul at four years old, chasing after him across the wide, sloping front yard, yelling in his sweet little voice, "Huuueeeyyy!!! Come baaaackkk!!!" We had so many locks and he would still find ways to escape. One day he went missing and I called the police before I took off running through the streets and backyards of our neighborhood. I remember realizing as I ran that my frantic fear had suddenly turned to anger. Unwittingly I was going through a horrific grieving process that had no end and so my mind, body and spirit had decided to adjust and move on to the next phase. Over the years I found myself responding with different emotions than would be expected for a particular incident and it broke my heart in a strange way, as if I had become an observer of eternal trauma on a human being. I remember thinking that I should probably take clinical notes. But I was not allowed the gift of grief. I had to keep going and relive it over and over and over again.

He was found running half dressed down the busy highway right outside our neighborhood with a stick in his hands, of course. I wept and felt grateful, relieved, numb, angry, hysterical, frantic, and ashamed. I began to almost feel separated from what was happening around me, as if I was watching a horror story that never ended.

One night or really morning at four a.m., we got a call from the next-door neighbor. They were furious when they had found Houston in their refrigerator. We couldn't figure out how we had gotten out since the alarm was still on. It was a mystery until one day, as I sat reading to my little ones on the couch, a little foot busted through the ceiling right above us along with drywall and insulation. That was his second attic escape. Once we began investigating, we found the intake vent in the room above the garage partly ripped off the wall and bent in half from the attic side into the room. He had crawled through the attic from the tiny crawl space in his closet, to the room above the garage that we rarely used, and out the backstairs that led outside.

Another time I was potty training Benjamin, sitting next to him in the bathroom giving encouragement to stay on the potty. For some reason, I had decided to get dressed up that day and was even wearing espadrilles instead of being barefoot like I usually was. There was a strong, terrifying, non neighborly knock at the backdoor. I was startled and saw a police officer standing at the back door. Immediately the familiar panic was triggered. My panic checklist went into high gear - 'I didn't hear the alarm. The crawlspace is drilled shut. He has to be upstairs. Have I heard movement? Isn't that one of his videos playing upstairs?' - all running through my head at high speed. Nervously, I opened the door and the officer asked me to step outside. I did. "Ma'am, are you missing a child?" he said in his most authoritative tone. I hesitated, unsure how to answer, "I don't think so. I'm not sure. I haven't heard any of the alarms go off," I nervously offered. Clearing his throat, "We found a boy that we think is your son." Terror raced inside. My breath stopped and instantly as I felt the chokehold on my heart. I knew the next words would be *and found him dead*. The officer continued as I braced for the worst news. "We found him NAKED-" And right as he said "NAKED," he turned and looked at the backdoor as Benjamin, who had decided he was done sitting on the potty, walked outside into the garage with no pants, pretty much naked. The cop looked at Benjamin, looked at me, looked toward the cop car, and then back at me. I put my hands over my mouth. "Oh my goodness, I'm potty training him." The cop tried to remain serious, but I could tell he was stifling laughter. They brought Houston out of the car and explained he had been found swimming naked in someone's pool. They warned about making sure the house was locked and I told them about the alarm system and some of the other incidents. I brought Houston inside and locked the door. I kneeled down and hugged him, thanking God. I looked at Benjamin dancing around with no pants and smiled. After all, "Life would be tragic if it weren't funny."[26] Once I got them both dressed, I started looking around for Houdini's escape route. I heard a breeze and followed it. There it was - an open window. I ran over and looked down at the drop. Unbelievable.

As I drilled all the windows shut, I started thinking about how smart my son had to be to figure out all these escape routes. I just knew there had to be something going on in that beautiful, cloaked mind of his. Something spectacular. I tried to teach him all that I could, but I had no idea what he was retaining. At school the teachers had told me they had to keep finding new hiding places for snacks or items he wanted. In later years, his high school teacher told me she had to keep using new passwords on the computer because he would somehow break everyone. Puzzled, she scrunched her forehead and said, "I even used my fiancé's birthday and I know he doesn't know that, but he still figured it out." We had similar issues at home. No matter how crafty I was, he was craftier. I remembered how he would spell the names of Disney movies with magnetic letters when he was two and a half. What did he know? What did he understand?

Two years later my non-speaking son would confound the administration at his school when he broke through their closed network to access a wild world wide web to find images of Mickey Mouse on Ebay. He had then sent the images to be printed in the school office. No one could determine how he had done it. When the principal took the pile of printouts to each classroom, the teachers all shrugged their shoulders until she got to Houston's classroom. Houston walked right up to her as if she was his personal courier and took the

[26] Stephen Hawking

pictures out of her hands. Her jaw dropped as she rushed to the computer he was on to find tab after tab of Disney imagery. They never could figure out how he did it. They awarded him the *Yes, I Can* award, which he promptly ripped off the stand so he could hold the cylinder in his hand. Then there was the time his teacher called me crying to tell he had just tied his shoes. I wept and praised God on my bathroom floor. I wept again and rejoiced when she called to tell me that out of nowhere Houston stood up in class during the announcements, put his hand over his heart and *spoke* the entire pledge of allegiance. It was almost as if, amidst the prison bars, he would escape for a moment to the outside world before the prison caught and swallowed him up again. Experts dismissed each moment with a liturgy of neurological skepticism, assuring me there was no hope. Like a hand squeezed at death or people seeing angels before they die, there was always a neurological reason to discourage anything they didn't understand, anything that allowed for hope. It was as if unbelief had become a belief all its own, and the ordained experts carried out the ceremonial discouragements and doctrines of the honored atheology.

In spite of their skepticism, Houston has made me appreciate the miracle of human life like nothing else in God's creation. It's all a wonder. In all the grasping, chasing, competition, ambition, and pleasure, people don't even realize the miracles of life all around us every single day. They don't know how many things have to work together to catch a ball, sing a song, write a sentence, make a friend, or to speak a single intentional thought. And yet every single one of those is an orchestration of a dozen or more coordinated body systems that work together to bring us an ordinary everyday miracle. Miracles, or an absence of them, that experts use to assess intelligence, assign limits and access to education, and determine the value of a life.

The ABLES test had concluded Houston had massive functional, intellectual, and language deficits. The school psychologist mirrored the diagnosis, prognosis and projection of the developmental pediatrician. What all the experts had concluded was there was no hope. That the sooner I gave up on hope and accepted the reality that my son was intellectually and developmentally disabled, the better life would be. The reports were so hopeless I could barely read through them. Every few years would be another round of pages and pages of rating skills questions scaled 1-5 that reaffirmed what the experts said, that hope was pointless. At age 18, when he had his adult testing completed, I wept at the results. Intellectual age 4-5 years of age. Translation - if you haven't already, GIVE UP.

Amidst all of this, I tried to create joy, happy memories, and beauty for my other kids. I had my girls in ballet and riding lessons across the street from our neighborhood. Morgan lived for three things: horses, drawing, and books. Reagan was ridiculously fun. I used to refer to her as Julie from the Love Boat. She directed all the fun. The boys followed every crazy idea she had. Her years of wearing princess dresses and tutus continued as if she really was blissfully unaware that anything was wrong. Benjamin was addicted to Buzz Lightyear and Paul was sweet and shy. They would play near me while I gardened and would run around our yard laughing. At night we cuddled on the couch and I read all my favorite novels from childhood to my girls, hoping the goodness of those stories would seep in. I was trying so hard, with everything in me, to love them all and raise them well.

The running continued. Houston's favorite therapist was getting married in Massachusetts, and we decided to have our second family vacation after the first tragic trip to Disney World before Benjamin was born. That trip was worthy of an installment in the National Lampoon's Vacation series, except no one died in the backseat. I was so excited for the trip to Massachusetts. We had bought matching khaki pants and button-down shirts for the boys, and the girls were precious. She had asked me to write and deliver a blessing. I was deeply honored and wrote the blessing as we made the long drive north. We stopped in Washington D.C. and for a day, everything was wonderful. Finally in Massachusetts, we caught up with our dear friend who hugged Houston tightly and asked if he remembered her. There was no response, no indication of recognition, and the hug was not returned. She didn't let that stop her. At the wedding the next day, a summer thunderstorm with torrential rains ensued. The ceremony started and for a brief moment I thought everything was going to be ok. When you have a child with severe autism, your assessment of what is deemed a successful event is a wee bit different than other parents' grading systems. Almost as soon as our friend walked down the aisle, Houston covered his ears and started crying which I knew would turn quickly to screaming or wailing. The Big Jock looked at me, pissed. Completely annoyed, he took Houston to the back of the church and before he could stop him, Houston urinated all over the church foyer. Cleanup was never the Big Jock's responsibility and he grew even more agitated. I sensed two ticking time bombs.

After the service, the Big Jock grabbed me to let me know I was to blame. There was no point in arguing. We went to the reception where I gave the blessing. For one brief moment I saw my friend's face full of gratitude and thought gratefully how I wouldn't have known her had it not been for autism. A half hour later I watched in horror as The Big Jock came back with XL cups filled to the brim with liquor and a splash of Coke. I quickly lost count of how many times he went to the bar and grew more annoyed that I was now babysitting five kids and a 315-pound former offensive lineman with alcoholism and a mean streak. Houston began to become unmanageable and started running around the reception in circles at breakneck speed. I could read the signs. I had already lost control. The next thing I knew, Houston had pooped all over himself and the Big Jock was in a drunken rage, barely able to stand. I gave our friend a hug and said goodbye, never knowing when or if I would ever see her again. I focused my attention on getting everyone in the car and back to the hotel. I cleaned up Houston and got everyone in bed. That night the Big Jock screamed obscenities for hours. Every attempt to ask to stop was met with a fresh wave. It wasn't until other guests started banging on the walls that he stopped. I felt numb.

When he woke the next day, he wanted to leave immediately for the condo we had rented on Martha's Vineyard. I tried to put the night behind us and just focus on the rare opportunity to do what other people do. The condo had no air conditioning because everyone leaves the windows open for the breeze. I hadn't even thought of that. It was narrow and two stories high. I went through the condo realizing how difficult it was going to be to keep a watchful eye on Houston. Benjamin was a toddler and Paul was three so there were a lot of little people to watch in addition to our escape artist. I couldn't get over how rough the ocean was this far north. The waves smashed onto the rocky beach and seemed to suck the whole shore underneath as they retreated into the wild roars above them. The second morning, my husband had started drinking again and his mood deteriorated quickly. I got the kids settled and asked him to watch Houston while I took a shower. He glared at me, "Hurry up."

I showered for maybe ten minutes. I got out of the shower and found my husband lying on the bed. Instinct had taught me well. "Where's Houston?" I asked. I tried not to sound panicked. "How the f..k should I know?" he retorted defensively. "You were supposed to be watching him," I said as I raced up the steep stairs. The girls were lazily watching television. "Have you seen Houston?" They shook their heads. After less than two minutes, I realized he wasn't inside the condo. "He's gone!" I cried. We both started racing around the outside of the condo and asking neighbors if they had seen him. Noone had seen anything. The police were called. I ran to the beach. In my mind, I knew we were close and his obsession with water could draw him to those raging waters. The day before at the beach, I couldn't let go of him because he would take off running on the beach. I knew one wave could swallow him whole and I would never see my sweet boy again. I ran and ran. My lungs burned. I sobbed as I ran. I prayed as I ran. *Please God. Please God. You know where he is. Please bring him back to me. Please God. Please.* I felt the ferocious waves crashing against every prayer my heart uttered.

This went on for hours. The police, other guests at the condos, strangers all of them, rode bikes, got in their cars, went out on foot, all looking for my son. Another guest had volunteered to watch my other kids. I was shaking. I couldn't stop. Hours passed. It would not be possible to explain the pain and prayers and the dark places my heart went during those hours. Death followed me like a black cloud, like vultures waiting for me to give up the fight.

A helicopter was ordered. A call came in. A little boy wearing only a t-shirt and nothing else with a handful of pretzels had been found at a cow exhibit. A policeman found me to give me the news. I bent over and sobbed uncontrollably. *Thank you, God. Thank you, God.* The police showed me the path he must have taken. As I looked at the enormous field he crossed, I saw what my son had seen. A big top circus tent far off on the horizon. He had gone to find Dumbo, the movie that he would watch obsessively and then scream and cover his ears. I was speechless. The next day, trying to salvage the vacation, we went to the beach and Houston took off running so fast it took the Big Jock a long time to catch up to him. I could see him fuming even in the distance as Houston pulled against him with every step. I saw my son screaming, pulling away, reaching for the great beyond. My husband didn't look at me, just ordered me to get in the car. The vacation was over. We packed the car and drove the 1,100 miles home. The only pictures we got were of us on the dock waiting for the ferry. The wind was rough, the skies were grey.

I was so grateful he was alive, but my every thought was *what if, what if.* Fear ruled. Over the next few years, there were countless more elopements. He seemed to know if I was in the backyard or in the shower or anywhere that I couldn't hear an alarm. He was found again walking down the highway our neighborhood was on. He was found in several neighbors' basements. When the firemen came, they said, "Oh yeah, we remember him. What was he last wearing?" I chuckled to myself, thinking, *who knows?* "Navy sweatpants fifteen minutes ago," I responded. Two days later, my neighbor returned the navy sweatpants from her basement. I realized how I responded to his elopements had changed. The constant trauma and fear made me skip to the next stage of grief at breakneck speed, almost as if a switch had been flipped. I began to get angry at God and teetered back and forth between accepting and finding joy in the pain, and demanding to know why He felt so much struggle was necessary. During the next escape I gulped down that initial shock, panic, and painful stranglehold on my heart and after a moment with that emotion, there was anger. I quickly realized anger was really a highly ineffective emotion. Almost as soon as I had let anger in, I found myself bargaining with God while I ran barefoot through backyards in a desperate search. "God, if you will just find him, You know where he is, You see all things, I will accept this. I will accept everything. I will stop asking for a miracle. I will stop asking to be loved." And that is how grief spun a perpetual prison whirling around my heart, spinning through every awful stage, day after unrelenting day. There was always a new devil of doubt, a new terror to spin me around again. Eventually, the constant trauma became despair. All I could do was love in pieces and keep going. The only thing that slowed Houston down was double deadbolts on every door, locked at all times, and screws on every window. I was actually jealous of parents who could let their kids just go outside and play or not have a deadbolt on the refrigerator and pantry. Their lives seemed so easy, so free. We were all imprisoned.

It took almost two years of doctor visits, evaluations, and paperwork before Houston was approved for the Deeming Waiver (Medicaid assistance). When he was finally approved, we found out that just like insurance, nothing related to his treatment was covered. After he had finally received the Deeming Waiver, he had it one year. His representative quit and his renewal paperwork was never sent. His award was cancelled. The thought of going through the process again made me give up on it altogether. Months of waiting for appointments with different specialists resulted in a string of psychotropic medications, each with a side effect worse than the original symptom it would attempt to target. He participated in a year long Risperdal study that did nothing except exacerbate other symptoms. The expert we took him to out of state had nothing for us. You could see he was used to dealing with less severe cases. When I called him one Saturday as Houston screamed and cried like he was being attacked, he acted annoyed. I apologized for calling him on the weekend but told him this was not normal, even for him. "Give him charcoal." That was all the medical community had to offer my son. Severe weight loss, loss of appetite, grey skin, dark circles under his eyes, chronic bed wetting after he had finally become potty trained, lethargy where he could not seem to move his body independently at all, increased stimming, increased hand biting, increased crying - I finally said no more. Drugs were not the answer. The doctors obviously had no clue, and I wasn't willing to let him be a guinea pig anymore.

After explaining the challenges to his teachers, they decided they would come to the house to help see what suggestions might help. The school had installed double sets of doors that required granted access. As they talked to me and I gave them the tour of our home, complete with the collapsed ceiling from the most recent Houston flood. They looked at me horrified. I shrugged my shoulders. Houston had destroyed more floors, ceilings, and walls than I would ever be able to remember. Destruction was just part of autism, along with no sleep, elopement, maddening repetitive behaviors and screaming, chaos, the judgment of everyone, ever present fear, and complete isolation. I called out to Morgan to stop the microwave, knowing from the sound and smell that Houston had put something in it. I raced upstairs to turn off another faucet I could hear running and answered their questions. I continued cooking dinner and answered Reagan's homework question while I talked to the teachers. Houston began wailing frightfully at a video and the boys were screaming for him to stop. I shouted at them to take the video out if he was upset and then went to calm him down. I returned to continue the conversation. I quickly excused myself as I smelled what I knew was another one of Houston's poops. Getting to him before he smeared it was always the goal. I finally asked if they had ideas to help. They just looked at me. "Katie, you're doing the work of a dozen people. I don't see how you do it. I don't think we have anything that's going to help." They were loving and so kind to me, but even the experts couldn't help.

13

Outcast

Even my close friend in whom I trusted, who ate my bread, has lifted his heel against me.
But you, O Lord, be gracious to me, and raise me up, that I may repay them!
By this I know that you delight in me: my enemy will not shout in triumph over me.
But you have upheld me because of my integrity, and set me in your presence forever.
Blessed be the Lord, the God of Israel, from everlasting to everlasting! Amen and Amen.
— Psalm 41:9-13

There were not a lot of people to turn to during all of this. I had begun to make friends with other women at church who had abusive husbands. We understood each other's chaos. We were all still married and the idea of divorce while raising our children seemed impossible and according to the church, unbiblical.

I should take a moment to explain another reality - women, Christian women. I guess that's what you call them. I thought I was one of them. I realized I didn't want to be. While there are many examples, I will share one to explain my point. I had already experienced isolation and exclusion, both from the revelation of my abusive marriage and the logistical reality of Houston's severe autism. The end result was the friendships I had fostered dissolved despite my ridiculous efforts to maintain them. One day I got a call asking me to go to the women's retreat for our church at Callaway Gardens from one of the women I knew. I was thrilled. I had not received an invitation to anything since the truth had come out. I signed up and paid for my share of the cabin. For weeks I held the joy of that invitation in my heart. During that time, I didn't receive a single call. As the weekend drew near, I wondered why I hadn't heard anything about the travel plans. Finally, I called the woman who had invited me. I asked what the travel plans were. There was a cold silence. "We don't have room for you. You need to drive yourself." I explained that if I left, I had to leave the minivan with the Big Jock and he wouldn't let me take his car. Then I asked how many people were in the car. There were three. "Why isn't there room for me?" I asked. "Well..." she said, with a piercing cruelty, "We need room for the cooler." "The cooler?" I asked. "Am I hearing you correctly? You invited me to fill your cabin to decrease the cost but it's more important for the cooler to get there instead of me?" Her response was to tell me to get a ride with someone else. So, stupidly I tried. I called a woman who had been my good friend before everything exploded and asked for a ride. "Ohhhh, no. I'm sorry. We don't have room for you. Sor-ry." The "sorry" was said in that sing-song way that lacked every possible ounce of sincerity. It was almost as if they had said, "Bless your heart. You thought we were going to include you?" And just like that, everything I thought was true was validated. I was out. They went to a women's retreat to learn about the love of God when they had missed every opportunity to actually *be* the love of God to someone who needed it so desperately. Obviously, I didn't go. I wept for a day. But the next day, I made an offering. I went to a nursery and bought two crape myrtles, flanking each side of the stairs to my front door.

> *Instead of the thorn bush the cypress will come up,*
> *And instead of the nettle the myrtle will come up,*
> *And it will be a memorial to the Lord,*
> *For an everlasting sign which will not be cut off.*[27]

Like I said, there were periods of my life of incredible faith. I decided I was going to put my trust in my God, in His promise that I would not be cut off. After that, I didn't call those friends too much. It was always me seeking them, not them seeking me. Which meant, we lost touch for the most part. It had a profound impact that I wanted to ignore, but the pain was still present despite how much I searched for silver linings. Resolutely, I told myself, God would be my everything. Within a short time, I would have to leave those myrtle trees, but to this day they still raise their branches by my old home. They know why they were rooted and whose tears watered them.

I was afloat, cast off and cut off. The future and the journey were a complete fog. It's not a little thing, a small insult, to be cut off from the chosen. It was as if God's people had cut the rope and pushed me into the sea with my children and a monster. There was no oar. Instead of "Ahoy" they said, "Pray" and turned and walked back to the feast. The storms roared. The boat leaked. The monster raged. The food ran out. The kids mutinied. Houston tried to go overboard. In the darkness, I kept searching for Jesus to call me to join Him as He walked on the waves. But all I could see was just blackness and an endless sea.

With few friends, I reached out to my dad. Over these years I grew closer to him and his soon-to-be wife. I depended on them for emotional support. It brought me joy to have my dad back. He told me my kids needed a father and thought everything would be fine. His new fiancé was sent directly from heaven. She told my dad he was wrong about a lot of things and began to educate him on the different idiosyncrasies of abusers and their tactics. I felt like I finally had the mother I always wanted. She gave me a book that changed my life, *Why Does He Do That? Inside The Minds Of Angry And Controlling Men* by Lundy Bancroft. I cannot recommend this book enough. It completely changed my perspective on one aspect of what I was living through. Now I just had to figure out how to stay true to my faith and my God while also doing what was necessary to save my life and my children. It might sound ridiculous, but that is the reality of where I was spiritually and where a great number of women still are. I began seeing things in God's word I had never seen before. I began writing furiously during this period and my thoughts were those of someone who wants to stop abuse and keep their family. I was still fully committed to staying married and trying to make it work, but I couldn't submit to an abuser anymore. Eventually my heart realized that keeping the family intact was a lost cause, but acceptance was still a few years away.

Somewhere in the middle of this journey, I was asked to put all my thoughts together by a counselor at my church. I told my dad, "I have to get this written and out of me while I still think this way. I'm changing the way I think and I'm never going back." For weeks I studied, thought, wrote, and prayed. In truth I was wrestling, wrestling with a thousand different thoughts.

One late summer afternoon, I sat on the front porch thinking through the philosophy of contentment and how to write about how this impacted someone like me in my circumstances. The sky was the deep blue of summer that seemed to have no end. Our home was set on a hill, and the porch was at the top of a long flight of steep stairs. From the porch I could see a huge expanse of sky. There was not a cloud to be seen except one. It was the strangest cloud I had seen. It was not the wispy cirrus that accompanied gorgeous skies or the low, flat gray stratus that would cover the sun. If it was anything, it was one layer of a lenticular cloud that had formed out of the clear blue, literally. Then I saw it. It was a castle. On the right of the cloud in grand detail with steeples and overlooks all in white was a castle overlooking the vastness of the cloud and the sky before it. Everything else about the cloud was flat, crisp, white as if it was an island in the sky. I looked away thinking that can't be. I read some more Jane Austen that I had brought with me. I looked up again to see if the cloud was still there, if the castle had vanished. But it was still there. I prayed and looked again. The cloud stayed motionless in front of me until the sun went down and I could see it no more. I had believed in smallness and acceptance my whole life. God, it seemed, wanted me to dream of castles and glory. His glory. His love. And this is what I wrote.

14

Justice Crying

Why, O Lord, do you stand far away? Why do you hide yourself in times of trouble?
In arrogance the wicked hotly pursue the poor;
let them be caught in the schemes that they have devised.
For the wicked boasts of the desires of his soul,
and the one greedy for gain curses and renounces the Lord.
In the pride of his face the wicked does not seek him; all his thoughts are, "There is no God."
His ways prosper at all times; your judgments are on high, out of his sight;
as for all his foes, he puffs at them.
He says in his heart, "I shall not be moved throughout all generations I shall not meet adversity."
His mouth is filled with cursing and deceit and oppression; under his tongue are mischief and iniquity.
He sits in ambush in the village, in hiding places he murders the innocent.
His eyes stealthily watch for the helpless; he lurks in ambush like a lion in his thicket;
he lurks that he may seize the poor; he seizes the poor when he draws him into his net.
The helpless are crushed, sink down, and fall by his might.
He says in his heart, "God has forgotten, he has hidden his face, he will never see it."
Arise, O Lord; O God, lift up your hand; forget not the afflicted.
Why does the wicked renounce God and say in his heart, "You will not call to account"?
But you do see, for you note mischief and vexation, that you may take it into your hands
to you the helpless commits himself, you have been the helper of the fatherless.
Break the arm of the wicked and evildoer; call his wickedness to account till you find none.
The Lord is king forever and ever; the nations perish from his land.
O Lord, you hear the desire of the afflicted; you will strengthen their heart;
you will incline your ear to do justice to the fatherless and the oppressed,
o that man who is of the earth may strike terror no more.

— Psalm 10

When I first began to write this paper, I was in spiritual and literal turmoil. My husband had become excessively violent, and I had been forced to seek help. Emotionally I was done, finished, spent, incapable of submitting to the insanity even one more day. The reason I was still there after all that had happened over so many years was because I thought I didn't have a choice. I didn't know there was a line. If I was going to honor and obey God, I thought I had to submit to anything that was thrown at me. If you knew all that is covered up and encouraged by the term submission, you would be amazed and probably devastated at the misuse of God's Word. This submission to sin stripped away my hope and left me lonely, broken, and bitter.

Anyway, I thought I was being obedient to the Word of God even though it seemed to make the situation worse. At church, a few remarks were made about my circumstances that seemed to be the precursor for yet another lesson on the role of a submissive wife. I spoke of my concerns to my counselor at church. She asked if I had ever written about my feelings regarding submission. I said, "Not exactly, here is what I have written." I then read to her the deepest burdens of my heart from my journal. She paused and then asked if I would write about submission. That is how I started this journey, and this paper is where God has led me. I didn't have a purpose when I began, other than to pour out all the ponderings and prayers I had made for years. Yet God began to expose His Word and His Will to me in an utterly new light. My focus began to change from seeking to be a Godly wife to seeking God's will. What thrilled me even more was to realize that right in the Word of God was the answer, not just to my pain but to so many others caught or trapped because they had been restricted to one part of God's Word. You see, God did not limit me to one truth the day I said my marriage vows. He wrote every word for me, and all I had to do was dig deep into His wonderful wisdom and find Him and all that He loves.

Right now, many women are taught that if they will just submit, serve, and love more this will make their husbands love them. I must emphasize that I absolutely agree that I am called to submit, serve, and love. Yet my submission is not capable of changing my husband's heart. That is a job the Holy Spirit has reserved for Himself. Also, I think we have it backwards. The Church did not submit to Christ, serve Christ, and love Christ to initiate Christ's love for her. Instead, He loved and died for her while she was dead in her sins. The Church, brought to life by this great love, then responded in love, service, and submission to Christ. Christ is the initiator, His bride, the responder. The same is true in marriage.

While I certainly speak forthrightly in this piece, it is by no means intended to offend, but rather to tell the truth and direct the hearts of His people to Him, His Word, and to all that He loves. You see, I also want to see God's covenant of marriage restored, and I want to see Christ's Bride, beautiful and righteous, standing bright like a city on a hill, beckoning to His World. Yet if there is to be cultural change regarding marriage and divorce, then it must begin His way, by defending what He loves and what He died for - me, the bride, the one made in His image. The way to do that is to seek truth, spoken in love, followed by justice, while always loving mercy, only then will righteousness follow.

***

For Our God Who Sees All, Even the Sparrows Who Fall

The kid's toy at Chick-fil-A this week was the Harriet Tubman cassette tape. I played it in the car for the kids, but it was I who was moved nearly to tears, but mostly to resolution. I could hear the crack of the whip and feel the hot tears and anger that fell with the injustice and cruelty she experienced. I understood her determination and conviction that "God gave me the right to be free or to die tryin'." I rejoiced at her escape and marveled at her courage to rescue her family and others. I could plainly see God's hand leading the modern Moses. When I listened to the remarkable details of how God provided and protected her missions, I was left with one undeniable fact, God wanted her to be free, and not just her, but her family and others, as well, just like He wanted His people free from Pharaoh's hand, just like He wants sex slaves free in Southeast Asia, just like He wants battered women released from their silent oppression.

I must confess I feel odd writing about submission. I know what it should look like. I have heard it from the pulpit, read about it in books, been wisely instructed on it, and seen it in other's homes. One dear friend commented she had no problem with the idea of submission because her husband did such a good job making her feel loved and honored. I was in awe of what she said. She obviously trusted him. It sounded so beautiful, yet I was hurt that my own marriage was so completely one sided. The love and honor I gave my husband were repaid with anger, cruelty, selfishness, and violence. Ideally, I thought, there should be a mutual love, respect, care, and dedication between two individuals joined into one covenant relationship, where each are equal in worth but different in duty and authority. The husband takes the role as the servant leader and the wife takes the role of helper, lover, and friend, willing to contribute support, or even follow as situations arise.

However, it does not matter what submission is *supposed* to look like or how a husband *should* treat his wife if that is not the reality. After hearing a few details of how my marriage worked my father exclaimed that was just not how a marriage was supposed to function; to which I replied that it didn't matter how things should be because that was just not the way things were; and I had no right, no power, and no authority to change anything. However pathetic or ridiculous that may sound, it was the down to earth truth. I am reminded of the reaction to Amy Carmichael's, Things as They Are, which was a frighteningly accurate account of the situation in India. The people of England scoffed, "Things can't really be that bad. Why would you write such things?" She responded, "Because it's true!"

For example, we in the United States proclaim that every human has "certain inalienable rights endowed to them by their Creator, and among these are life, liberty, and the pursuit of happiness." (Interestingly, Jefferson's original draft dubbed these rights as life, liberty, and property, which was omitted for a more elusive "pursuit of happiness.") We charge other nations with violations of these rights and yet their oppression goes on mercilessly. Why? It is such a simple concept. Unless someone in authority acknowledges and gives the people these rights, or someone with courage, strength, and conviction fights for these rights, they are just empty words that leave hearts and souls shriveled and without hope. The same is true in marriage. I have heard it said that marriage halves your rights and doubles your duties. But I know there are marriages where a wife's rights are stripped and her duties made into burdens, leaving her heart defrauded of any love or kindness, her body aching for tenderness or a gentle touch, and her spirit longing for peace and freedom from fear. I know because I have been this woman for eight years. For eight years I prayed for God to be enough, for grace to be sufficient, for me to be content with His love and Him alone. While I would love for you to think these prayers were motivated only out of a love for my Lord, in truth they were a cry for help, hope, and love in a desperately bad marriage where the abuse of my husband only grew stronger, bolder, and invaded new territory. Initially, there would be a few glimpses of hope after an incident, but even those vanished after a while, and he would act as if nothing had happened. Oh, and I had better act that way too. Unthinkable, you say; no, common. But what right does a wife have when her body and spirit are not her own, and she is not allowed the privilege of having feelings? She is to give everything and expect nothing while enduring cruelty and hate.

When I searched Scripture for direction all I found was duty, not rights - duty to forgive, submit, suffer, turn the other cheek, be kind, and love despite the circumstances, the number of offenses, or even the individual involved because this is what Christ did for us. How could I ignore the clear directives of Ephesians 5:1-2, 1Timothy 1:16, Philippians 2:1-16, 1Corinthians 7:1-16, Luke 6:27-31, Matthew 5:43-48, Romans 12:14, 1 Peter 2 & 3, and the 13th chapter of John? It seems clear that God Himself abdicated all His glory and rights thereof when He humbled Himself and came in the likeness of man, served, suffered, loved, and died. If Christ humbled Himself to death, what right or reason do I have to claim any rights when I am a recipient of His very grace by His very death?

I read and prayed all these familiar passages in God's word and begged for grace to live them. My own love was insufficient in the face of such day to day cruelty and selfishness. It was clearly obvious my only value to my husband was to keep house, raise his children, and be the recipient of any frustration he might be feeling. I guess the reason I found submitting so hard was because of what I had to submit to. I could give you some gut-wrenching examples, but I prefer not. Call it pride or maybe my last shred of dignity, but if you need to understand just how bad it can get, there are many stories out there. Anyway, it is not that I did not know how to submit. My childhood had trained me well. The best way to avoid the abuse was to keep a low profile, say nothing, zone out during a rage, and make sure everything was as perfect as possible. I am aware of how this all sounds, but my goal was never perfection; at best, it was peace at all costs. I sincerely wanted to be a faithful disciple and Godly wife and mother. Yet my efforts seemed so fruitless. I thought, maybe this was my chance to be broken bread and poured out wine, to spend and be spent. There is a passage by Oswald Chambers that seemed to settle the matter for me. "It is one thing to go on the lonely way with dignified heroism, but quite another thing if the line mapped out for you by God means being a doormat under other people's feet. Suppose God wants to teach you to say, "I know how to be abased"- are you ready to be offered up like that? Are you ready to be not so much as a drop in the bucket- to be so hopelessly insignificant that you are never thought of again in connection with the life you served? Are you willing to spend and be spent; not seeking to be ministered unto but to minister? Some saints cannot do menial work and remain saints because it is beneath their dignity." So, I submitted and served and gave and loved, all for Him. John Piper's quote, "God is most glorified when we are most satisfied in Him and Him alone," was another thought that kept me going. But I waned and grew tired of the nastiness.

By that time, I was frustrated with myself. Why can't I just be content with the cup God has given me? How dare I expect more than grace? Isn't that an insult to my Savior? I felt wronged and guilty simultaneously. I heard it perfectly verbalized in this statement: I don't deserve any better than what my husband is giving because I'm not perfect either, and I owe it to God to keep loving him into loving me. After all, love suffers long and love never fails. If I would just submit more or serve more, then he would be kind. Surely there must be something I can do to change the way he treats me. Why can't I just stop caring how I am treated? So I prayed again and again and begged God to change me and make me more loving, submissive, serving, and humble.

Now I know love is giving someone what they need and not what they want, and certainly love includes truth. But how can someone in the role of submitting, respecting, honoring, and serving expose a truth that would be considered disloyal, dishonoring, and disrespectful? The consequences of the truth are very high and very risky. *Justice is turned back, and righteousness stands afar off; for truth is fallen in the street, and equity cannot enter. So truth fails, and he who departs from evil makes himself a prey* — Isaiah 59:14-15. What seems so overwhelming about the whole situation is the hopelessness of it all. Once a woman realizes nothing she does will change the way she is treated, she begins to lose hope and die inside, especially when the only end to the cruelty seems to be her death or her husband's. She becomes bitter, cold, and resentful watching the years pass. She has no desire to touch or to be touched. The promises of God seem meant for someone else and she begins to doubt if God ever loved her and if *these are the plans He has for her, plans of peace and not evil, to give her a hope and a future- Jeremiah 29:11.* She can find no recourse. Her prayers seem to be unheard, and the church preaches submission and no divorce. She tries to get guidance from older and wiser women without violating the sacred code of silence, regarding marriage. Without hesitation, she is told that no matter what the issue, she is required by God to submit, with a smile on her face, serving hands, and open legs. No wonder she feels like a hated thing. She just wants to hurry up and die so she can be with the only One who truly loves her. I remember thinking the same thing Harriet Tubman's father said, "We'll be free together in heaven."

While God certainly promises freedom in heaven, He does not think highly of oppression on earth in any form. In fact, Scripture is filled with warnings and indictments against oppressors and charges for His people to root out injustice, end oppression, and to show mercy, such as Isaiah 58:6-10. Some use the Scripture in 1 Peter 3 to suggest that wives should submit silently to anything. However, the cross was not an act of submitting to wickedness and sin but submitting to the will of God. The cross was the ultimate act of truth and love, fulfilling justice, righteousness, and mercy. Christ did not cover up sin, submit to sin, or respect sin. He did not pretend that the sin wasn't there or make excuses for the sin. Instead, through the cross, He became the redeemer and deliverer of those living under the very sin He paid for with His life.

I realize, of course, that the church is trying to reclaim the role of a Godly wife in response to a century of feminism that they *believe* has wreaked havoc on our culture. Yet if you look to the roots of feminism, these women had something very different in mind than what has occurred. Besides the equality of all people, many suffragists had another goal - temperance, the absence of the angry drunk, or rather, peaceful, prosperous, loving homes where women would not be silenced or stifled in their pursuits of their God given gifts or abused and controlled by their spouses. They intended to clean up all the muck, some earning the term "Muckrakers," who fought to expose the corruption and injustices perpetrated by leaders, institutions, industries, jobs, and homes in that era. Susan B. Anthony, Elizabeth Cady Stanton, Mother Jones, Alice Paul, Ida Tarbell, and an incredible assembly of other women upheld a fierce movement, what we refer to as the Progressive Era, to change the culture and the way those who were not in a position of authority would be treated. They were not power-hungry feminists, but people who felt something must be done about the saloons and pubs where men would drink away the children's food and clothes and return home only to inflict their drunken anger on wives and children, and where women were sanctioned off from any participation in society outside of church, home, and tea. Why did the suffrage movement happen then and not at other periods of history? Personally, I believe it was in response to a situation made desperate by the Industrial Revolution, the influx of immigrants, and Westward Expansion. The injustices of the day ran unchecked, as did the abuse of those in power. But whatever the social or economic reasons for the problem, the cry was against the ugly reality in many families and communities, and the utter waste of human potential. They desired women and children to be free from the fear and oppression found in their homes and in society, and free to pursue their dreams. Neither men, nor state, nor church made much of an attempt to rescue women from their harsh, second-class reality, but instead lauded each other on proper roles, the authority of man, and the necessity of man to rule his roost and keep his woman in her place. Women sought to insert their voice - or vote - into the public arena, a voice of peace, reason, and equality, recognizing the value and dignity of both man and woman. If man would not save himself from his own debasement, then woman would save him whether he wanted to be saved or not. Although suffrage was won, not all the reforms of the day achieved their desired outcome, most notably temperance. While ultimately the American public decided they needed to drink, the Great Experiment (the 18th Amendment) did not end the oppression found in homes. It failed quite simply because liquor was not the root of all the evil they saw, sin was and still is. The problem the suffragists failed to deal with was sin - selfish, angry, violent, cruel, oppressive sin, from the one with all the authority. They had reasoned that by removing women from under the authority of men and drink from men, decency and dignity would prevail, and hopefully the ability of women to seek their fulfillment in avenues beyond the home. They recognized the difference of talents and desires beyond biology and pursued them. In this thought and endeavor, they were correct. For there is one thing that all people share despite their many personalities and gifts, their one singular purpose, their chief end, the glory of the Maker, Lord, and Savior.

G.K. Chesterton begins his book, <u>What's Wrong with the World</u>, with a theological discussion of the chicken and the egg. His conclusion is that the only purpose of the egg is to produce a chicken, whereas the chicken can lay eggs, amuse herself, inspire painters, squawk incessantly, or even praise God. So we are not only procreators, but creatures, bearing His image. We are not only products of the Fall, but knit, chosen, and redeemed by our Father as well. The life we live has purpose and dignity because God Himself died for us. *The life I now live in the body I live by faith in the Son of God, who loved me and gave Himself up for me-Galatians 2:20.* Yet many men treat their wives in such a way as to remove any hope of dignity or love. These women become diligent ants, scurrying to manage and repair all the angry footprints their husbands leave trying to squash them or keep them in their place. They cannot even begin to heal or deal with the damage to their spirit because they must prevent the next outburst, if possible or accept the mess as their fault, after all, "They are the one with the problem."

This environment leaves entire families scarred and shattered. The damage done to the children is extensive and is often passed down to the next generation for another lifetime of hopelessness and despair. So, wouldn't the dignity of Godly womanhood, the future of children and entire families, justice, liberty and the glory of our God be better served by destroying this tyranny, rather than destroying these women by ignoring their plight?

Now I have been taught ever since I was a little girl that grace is sufficient, that the only thing I need is Jesus. So I sat in my misery, trying to be content and grateful and silent, holding out for when I would meet my Savior and enter His everlasting grace. *I will wait upon the Lord- My flesh and my heart fail; but God is the strength of my heart and my portion forever* — Psalm 73:26. *The Lord is my portion, says my soul, therefore I hope in Him! The Lord is good to those who wait for Him to the soul who seeks Him. It is good that one should hope and wait quietly for the salvation of the Lord. It is good for a man to bear the yoke in His youth. Let him sit alone and keep silent, because God has laid it on him; let him give his cheek to the one who strikes him, and be full of reproach. For the Lord will not cast off forever. Though he causes grief, yet He will show compassion according to the multitude of His mercies. For He does not afflict willingly, nor grieve the children of men* — Lamentations 3:24-33.

I used to say to myself, "Well, if he does it again, then I'll do something." I'm embarrassed by how many times I said that statement. I remember the day I asked myself a different question, "Why won't I leave or at least say something?" Essentially, there were two reasons - pride and fear, but I also clung to the idea that I was being Godly; that a submissive wife keeps silent, just as Christ did, thereby glorifying the Father. I also hoped my silence and submission to all he did and said would somehow open his heart so that he would love me. It didn't. "They solace themselves that the enemy will be merciful. It is the madness of folly, to expect mercy from those who have refused to do justice," Thomas Paine.

What did work was truth, and the truth most certainly did set me free. How? By the power of our Lord, "For our Lord Christ has surnamed Himself Truth, not custom," Tertullian. Deitrich Bonhoeffer who was hung for resisting the Nazis said, "We cannot follow Christ unless we live in revealed Truth before God and man." By letting go of pride and fear and revealing the truth, I opened the doors to justice, and grace came rushing in to rescue me.

The power of truth astonished me. Not only did truth release me to deal with the sin and oppression in our family, it released me from resentment, and most importantly from having such a small view of God's amazing grace. The word sufficient in our culture has the connotation of "just enough." Yet that does not even begin to describe grace. For enough is as good as a feast- old proverb; and enough is an abundance to the wise-Euripides. I saw that His grace is not stingy, it is abundant. His grace is not meant for heaven only, but for this life we live through Him, as well. His grace is not meant for a stale and stagnant life, but for a life of feasting on the wonderful riches of His grace. But what does all this talk of God's grace mean to someone oppressed by sin? It means because His grace is so sufficient, so divine, so abundant, that I have a duty to fight and live for Him and His kingdom, to show others how much He loves truth, justice, mercy, and righteousness, by breaking the yoke of affliction and showing His compassion which fails not. I have the duty and privilege of telling how Christ died so we might know abundant life is found in Him and through the cross which stands for all that God loves, but I also have a duty to live it. "Always preach the gospel, and when necessary use words"- St. Francis of Assisi.

It's hard to know what to do when you are in the middle of oppression with an angry foot in your face. One thing is certain, though, God does not call us to do nothing. As Edmund Burke said, "All evil needs to triumph is for good men to do nothing." In 1776, a few brave patriots saw the oppression of the British Empire clearly and boldly confronted the evil they saw, declaring they would not submit to wickedness. They lost much because tyranny does not fall easily. As Thomas Paine wrote, "Tyranny, like hell, is not easily conquered; yet we have this consolation with us, that the harder the conflict, the more glorious the triumph... Throw not the burden of the day upon Providence, but show your faith by your works, that God may bless you." Martin Luther stood against the tyranny and deceit of the church and it cost him dearly. Martin Luther King Jr. dared to dream for an America free from hate and prejudice, it cost him his life. Harriet Tubman dared to flee oppression and risked her own life, time and time again to rescue others. These were people who acted on the truth of the gospel, that God came to free His people so they might know His wonderful works and the goodness of His love. Saint after saint has died defending and clinging to Truth. If they had been silent, done nothing, and submitted to the sin and to the lie, their lives would have been spared. But they chose to do and say something, the only something which could truly free them, Truth. They chose the hard road of truth with all its persecutions, so they would triumph in freedom and life.

In my own case, I had come to the sad conclusion that because of my circumstances I would never, could never tell the truth about what was going on behind closed doors. What I failed to see is that I was standing in the way of truth and peace and hope. My silence enabled my husband's sin to thrive. That was when God said, ENOUGH! He put my children in safe hands so I could not worry for them and stay for their sake. He left me with no home to retreat to and no money with which to hide away quietly in a motel while the storm passed. He forced me to swallow pride and fear and tell the truth to friends and turn to the church for help. He does not want the bride, the symbol of the church, to be oppressed one more day, nor does He want husbands, symbolic of Him, to have epitaphs that read, "Dead, but not forgiven," because of a life of cruelty. He wants His people free, free from fear, free from sin, free to speak truth, free to live, free to love, free to give, free to serve, free to feast on the wonderful riches of His boundless grace. Freedom is paramount to truth, for it is only in truth that freedom can be found. As the songwriter says, "All her sins were cast on Me, and she must and shall go free." So why are freedom and truth so important to God? Is it because freedom's price was so high, the life and death of His son, Truth, that He does not want to see it squandered or squashed? I think this must be why He rejoices to set the oppressed free, so they might taste a little of heaven's goodness on earth. As Harriet Tubman told her father who resisted being set free, "God has a different plan." He wanted them to see His goodness and His wonderful works. *I would have lost heart, unless I had believed that I would see the goodness of the Lord in the land of the living* — Psalm 27:13.

When I see all the problems and injustices in the world, it all seems so overwhelming. It's hard to know where to begin. Why should my suffering and oppression matter to anyone? Why should it matter to the church? Should I concern myself with justice or am I called to administer mercy by continuing to turn cheek after cheek, literally. Which brings God glory? Which is seeking after Christ? Eventually, it came down to Him; the most important use of my life was living the gospel of Jesus. But what did that mean specifically? Abide in Me. How do I abide in Jesus? By sitting at His feet, listening to His Word, with a heart willing to obey. Obey what? His revealed will in His infallible Word. What does His Word say? *Seek ye first the kingdom of God and His righteousness* — Matthew 6:33. How do I seek His kingdom and His righteousness? *Prepare ye the way of the Lord, prepare ye the way for the Kingdom- Mark 1:3. How do I prepare the way? But to do justice, and to love mercy, and to walk humbly with thy God* — Micah 6:8. What is His way, what is His righteousness, what is His justice, what does His Kingdom look like? James says real religion is helping orphans and widows and keeping oneself clean. Isaiah 58:6-10 — *Is this not the fast I have chosen, to loose the bonds of wickedness, to undo the heavy burdens, to let the oppressed go free, and that you break every yoke? Is it not to share your bread with the hungry, and that you bring to your house the poor who are cast out; when you see the naked, that you cover him, and not hide yourself from your own flesh? Then your light shall break forth like the morning, your healing shall spring forth speedily, and your righteousness shall go before you; the glory of the Lord shall be your rear guard. Then you shall call and the Lord will say, "Here I am". If you take away the yoke from your midst, the pointing of the finger, and speaking wickedness, if you extend your soul to the hungry and satisfy the afflicted soul, then your light shall dawn in the darkness, and your darkness will be as the noonday.* Apparently, God thinks standing up for what is right and not blindly submitting to sin is essential to kingdom building, to righteousness, to following Christ, and to freedom and Truth. *Let justice roll on like a river, and righteousness like a never failing stream* — Amos 5:24.

Where power and authority are abused and control is unrighteous, unjust, and unchecked, liberty, peace, and justice vanish, particularly when the oppressed are instructed to submit silently in the name of their Savior. *No one calls for justice, nor does any plead for truth. They trust in empty words and speak lies... Therefore justice is far from us, nor does righteousness overtake us* — Isaiah 59:4&9. The reason the oppression and abuse in the home is so destructive is twofold. One is because it entraps another generation to the heartache and patterns of oppression, whether victim or abuser. The second is because it is home, the place where you lay your head and eat your food, a place that should be a haven but is filled with hate and fear. For example, it is much easier to suffer under an oppressive regime if there are loving hearts and hands at home to ease the burden, to encourage, and to share compassion. But when home is horrible, it leaves women feeling helpless and hated and despair takes root. Abuse in the home also has a horrible social stigma to bear if one ever dares to tell. So pride aids in the silence.

Another important facet that creates an enormous burden on women is sex with your abuser. I remember calling out to God, "I know you want me to love my enemy, but why do I have to sleep with him?" Because of the intimacy of sex, it creates a much deeper wound. *For it is not an enemy who reproaches me; then I could bear it... but it was you, a man my equal, my companion, and my acquaintance, we took sweet counsel together, and walked to the house of God in the throng... He has put forth his hands against those who were at peace with him, he has broken his covenant* — Psalm 55:12-14, 20. I remember after a night of abuse, retreating to get breakfast with some friends. The conversation turned to marriage and one friend began saying how important sex was in reestablishing intimacy after a disagreement, and for the first time I didn't keep silent. Maybe it was because I was still so raw, but the words quickly spilled out of my mouth. I said, "Do you know what it is like to have sex with someone who is constantly cruel to you? It feels like they are peeing on you." That was pretty much the end of breakfast, no one said much, but then they prayed and prayed. A week later the dam broke, and yes, I will stake my life on the power of Truth.

In the church, women are taught submission and silence are what is required of a Christian wife, some from the pulpit, but mostly from other women. Home is hateful, and the church says stay at home. And I have to ask, why? Why is the rest of Scripture, the wisdom of God, not for me, as well? If I am going to seek Truth Himself and His kingdom and His righteousness and all that it stands for, then I will no longer be bound to one truth, but will bask in the full power of the Word of God which has no limits and no lack of wisdom, mercy, and love. Just as in the verses in Lamentations 3, which I quoted previously, the very next verse which God wrote for me as well states, *To crush under one's feet all the prisoners of the earth, to turn aside the justice due a man before the face of the Most High, or subvert a man in his cause- The Lord does not approve.*

Now I am no mathematician. I only have experience from which to speak. But if every 9 seconds in America a woman is abused, and the world considers this a serious social problem with far reaching effects, and the rate of divorce among evangelical Christians is higher than the rest of the nation, doesn't it stand to reason that maybe a substantial number of those cases of abuse are in the church, in the body of Christ? Maybe we don't hear about them because they are not here. Maybe we don't hear about them because they are dismissed as marital problems, or maybe women feel they are not free to speak the truth, and because of this blanket of submission the sin goes on and grows until she can't stand one more day wasted in this madness. I also must ask, isn't this what Satan would want, to encourage submission to sin and covering for sin, managing sin and excusing sin, so hate, violence, doubt, despair, and bitterness would thrive, thereby making the righteousness of the bride of Christ impossible? Aren't we to encourage each other to love and good deeds? How can this happen with such monumental sin controlling our homes. This is a crucial task for the church. Just as Old Testament high priests cleansed themselves outwardly and inwardly before entering the Holy of Holies, so we must take the power of the cross, Truth, and cleanse His bride. Why now? "If there must be trouble, let it be in my day that my child may have peace, and this single reflection well applied is sufficient to wake every man to duty," Thomas Paine.

There is a great song out right now that clearly states the mission of His church. "If we are the Body, why aren't His arms reaching, why aren't His hands healing, why aren't His words teaching? If we are the Body, why aren't His feet going, why is His love not showing? Yes, He is the way." Of course, there are risks, big, messy risks, and strong, smelly sin. However, we cannot fear bad reports if they are true, or turn from hurting people because they bleed. *He who justifies the wicked, and he who condemns the just, both of them are like an abomination to the Lord…It is not good to show partiality to the wicked, or overthrow the righteous in judgment* — Proverbs 17:15 & 18:5. We must do His work regardless of the cost. As Janani Luwum, shot for defying the cruelties in Uganda said, "Whenever I have the opportunity, I have told the president the things the church disapproves of. God is my witness." And as Mother Theresa said, "God does not ask us to be successful, just faithful." Or better yet, as G.K. Chesterton said so audaciously, "If a thing is worth being done, it is worth being done badly."

The Church must seek His righteousness which will not be found without Truth and cannot be attained apart from justice, for these are crucial to His Kingdom. "By perseverance and fortitude, we have the prospect of a glorious issue, by cowardice and submission (to sin) the sad choice of a variety of evils," Thomas Paine. I also must ask, what will the world think if the church stands up for righteousness and protects the oppressed of her own flock? *Bear one another's burdens* — Galatians 6:2. What will the world think if we not only preach the gospel of Christ, but live the gospel of Truth and love? What will the world think if we not only reveal our sin, but deal with and heal our sin with His redeeming, unfailing love? What if we, the bride of Christ, could be that place where people find out in very real life terms, *Come to Me all who are weary and burdened and I will give you rest* —Matthew 11:28, for we are His body. The church and the elders, responsible to God, must not rebuke women as they muster the courage to speak truth, but rather be a haven of safety and compassion for the ensuing whirlwind it will stir up.

Prepare the way; remove the stumbling block out of the way of My people — Isaiah 57:14b. If we are strong and courageous enough to take a stand on pornography, let us be strong enough to take on oppression in our midst and stop sin! As Christ said, "*Go and sin no more,*" for it is He who leads and guides us. The Church has even further instruction in Hebrews12:12-15, *Therefore strengthen the hands which hang down, and the feeble knees, and make straight paths for your feet, so that what is lame may not be dislocated but rather be healed. Pursue peace with all people and holiness, without which no one will see the Lord, looking carefully lest anyone fall short of the grace of God; lest any root of bitterness springing up cause trouble, and by this many become defiled.*

I have heard from every Christian with a soapbox that "the biggest threat to national security is the unraveling of the family." I agree but would take it even further; the unraveling of the family is a threat to Christ's bride, which He bought with His life. If this is true, wouldn't women, children, and families, the Body of Christ, justice, liberty, and mercy be better served, and ultimately saved, by destroying this tyranny rather than ignoring their plight. Because that is exactly what submission to sin does, sweeps the tyranny under the rug till she suffocates from the stench.

So, if the future of the Church, the family, and the child must be saved, so must the woman be saved from her present oppression. If the woman is to be saved from her present tyranny, then the tyranny must be revealed. If the tyranny must be revealed, it must be brought down. If the tyranny is to be brought down, then justice must prevail. If justice must prevail, then it must be the justice of the Lord. If the justice of the Lord is required, then it must be the Church that fights for it. If it must be the Church that fights for the justice of the Lord, then it must be through His power, His wisdom, His Spirit, and through Him, Truth. For it is He who died for her and it is His image she bears. "She is the human and sacred image; all around her the social fabric shall sway and split and fall; the pillars of society be shaken, and the roofs of ages come rushing down; and not one hair of her head shall be harmed," G.K. Chesterton.

I realize no one wants to open up and see how far the cancer has spread, but we are called to pursue His Kingdom and His righteousness. With the Holy Spirit to guide, we can walk this path. The result will be this, *Mercy and truth have met together; righteousness and peace have kissed. Truth shall spring up out of the earth, and righteousness will look down from heaven. Yes, the Lord will give what is good; and our land will yield its increase. Righteousness will go before Him, and shall make His footsteps our pathway* — Psalm 85:10-13. *For the day has come. The spirit of the Lord is upon Me, Because the Lord has anointed Me to preach good tidings to the poor; He has sent me to heal the broken hearted, to proclaim liberty to the captives, and the opening of the prison to those who are bound; to proclaim the acceptable year of the Lord, and the day of vengeance of our God; to comfort all who mourn in Zion, to give them beauty for ashes, the oil of joy for mourning, the garment of praise for the spirit of heaviness, that they may be called trees of righteousness, the planting of the Lord, that He may be glorified.* — Isaiah 61:1-3.

***

I wrote that paper eighteen years ago with all the hope in the world that change was possible. But nothing happened. It stayed the way it had always been. In the end I felt stupid and alone… Years later, my boyfriend read this paper and looked at me. "Wow…" He paused for a long time. "This isn't you anymore." He was right, I had changed. I no longer asked permission or sought the approval of others to make decisions for the wellbeing and safety of myself and my children, but it took me a while to get there. This paper was just the beginning. But there was something else that hadn't changed. God. God was still the same and He was still against injustice and abuse and for justice. He still chose justice and mercy as the preferred way to fast and worship Him. My paper was not a message the church was ready to hear. Some of the pastors who read my paper were deeply moved with compassion and saw how what they were teaching was being heard by women like myself. Other pastors told those of us who tried to explain what was going on inside families that these ideas threatened their theology. One told me I would never be satisfied. An elder who knew the details of the abuse I lived with, shrugged off the paper and said it was "mere hyperbole." I had feared not being believed, but to have my heart indifferently mocked and belittled was a bitter pill to swallow. I guess since it didn't happen to them, it wasn't that big of a deal.

A group of us tried to advocate for awareness on this topic and a shift in teaching at church. We knew churches should never have so much influence and control over the decisions people make for their own and their children's wellbeing, especially if they weren't helping those being victimized. Quickly we grasped the reality that churches were interested in saving the institution of marriage, not the people suffocating inside of one. The company line was to save all marriages at all costs. More times than I can remember, I made the point that God wanted us to save people. Marriage was made for people, not people for marriage; and if people were being crushed, they needed our help, not discipline and condemnation. There were moments when we thought change was happening and moments when it seemed all hope for changing their perspective was lost. I was determined to keep trying to help women like myself at least view their situation differently and yet still didn't have the courage to get out of my marriage. I am embarrassed by my continued efforts to try to make my husband love me. It went on long after our divorce. I kept trying to save a sinking ship while he kept trying to drown me in the deep end. The only hyperbole in my paper was how completely convinced I was that the truth would change him. The person it changed was me. When I reread my old letters, emails, and journal entries I hardly even recognize that young woman. She had a good heart, she was far too idealistic, and she sought to love - but she was trying to win over a wicked heart and that was never within her ability.

The entire ordeal changed me in so many ways. As I read God's word and saw this incredible God who loved justice and called His people to fight for it, I fell in love with God in a whole new way. My life might be hard, but I could follow God by fighting for the voiceless, for the oppressed. I began volunteering for justice organizations and advocating for our church to fight for the oppressed in multiple areas. I was shocked and saddened when I realized there was resistance to actually doing justice. *"Mercy triumphs over justice,"* I heard more than I care to recall. "Justice *is* mercy to those who are oppressed," I argued to those who wanted to pour mercy on oppressors.

The passion I had felt as a teenager watching the fight for freedom in Eastern Europe resounded again in my heart with several different faces. I used what little free time I had to focus on supporting the work of IJM (International Justice Mission) and on unwed pregnant women, trying to love them so they wouldn't feel so alone. God put two women in my life. One was an illegal immigrant from South Africa, bitter and unbelieving that God's grace was for her. The other was a young mother who was married with several children and had gotten pregnant from a one-night stand. I thought of my sibling that my mother aborted. I saw this very broken woman who had also been molested and couldn't settle her wandering heart. Her restless soul couldn't keep still. She resented the baby growing inside her and was angry at herself for causing it to happen. She resented her husband who wouldn't let her go. As I walked along with her on a road I knew was so difficult, I thought of how my mother had mocked marriage because hers hadn't lived up to the promises. "Peter Peter pumpkin eater had a wife and couldn't keep her. So he put her in a pumpkin shell and there he kept her very well." Those are *literally* the exact words my mother used to describe to me how she felt being married with a child to care for. I saw the same resentment in this young woman. I walked a fine line of just trying to be her friend and helping her find a place for the baby she did not want, but was, in great sacrifice, willing to carry for someone else to love.

15

Forgiveness With My Eyes Closed

Be kind to one another, tenderhearted,
forgiving one another, as God in Christ forgave you.
— Ephesians 4:32

Along with seeking justice, I knew God still required me to forgive. I contemplated how to seek justice, while still continuing to love and forgive. I thought back to my childhood. I knew my stepmother was not a safe person. As I prayed, I felt God's peace in forgiving her, and the right to still protect myself. I felt peace in praying for her to truly know God's salvation through Christ, but that was God's project, not mine. The damage she had done was extreme. What if she actually does become a true believer? The thought made me fearful. I remember having this epiphany in the middle of Target one day. I asked God, "Do we have no memory of the things people did to us on earth in heaven? Do we not care because Your glory is so abundant? Do the memories no longer cause pain or fear? Do we feel so safe in Your presence that even the memories do not cause us concern? In the light of Your glory, are we dwelling on our own sin, so we don't recognize the sin of others? Does our freedom from sin free of us from seeing the sin of others even while we fully acknowledge our own in the presence of a Holy God?" My heart and mind wrestled through different Scriptures. The Spirit spoke quietly to my heart when I was navigating through the toy aisles in Target. "They are wearing Jesus' righteousness. You see Him and His goodness. You can do that now too. See them that way." My wounded heart felt peace and joy at the thought. So that is what I prayed, to see people even more through His eyes.

It was in this frame of mind that I contacted my mother and grandmother and invited them to Thanksgiving. My mother brought her fourth husband who was a kind, simple man. I hardly recognized her. It had only been a few years and it was painful to see how she had deteriorated. The way she spoke and the things she spoke about were illogical, grandiose, and confusing. Sadly, I realized she knew very little about being a mom. My kids ran around each of them, trying to outdo their siblings in silliness, except for Morgan who tried to be a grownup. I so hoped their attention and childish joy would shatter the tense awkwardness. My mother's husband sat in a corner and videotaped her as the kids bounced around and performed. My stomach hurt intensely the entire time and I couldn't tell if it was my nerves or some kind of intuition. Two days later, she called me to thank me and graciously, I received her gratitude. I just wanted to show love; that was my only goal. Then out of left field she said, "Your husband is amazing. He's so strong and handsome. I'm so glad you found someone so powerful to marry." Politely, I thanked her. This was no time for the truth. Elevating her voice with even more dramatic inflection, "And you... YOU look exactly what I always imagined Mary, the mother of *Jeesuus* looked like! Beautiful!" finishing the statement with a dramatic gasp. In my head, I laughed out loud. Ridiculous. Absolutely ridiculous. Was this her way of ingratiating herself to me? I tried to do everything I could to respectfully express my discomfort. I kept a monotone. "Thank you, but I *really* don't think I look anything like what Mary looked like for a large number of reasons." She was on a roll. It was if she had slipped into some character from some play and I was the captive audience. Without letting me finish my sentence, "AND YOUR BREASTS! You have the most BEAUTIFUL breasts!!" Speechless, I literally couldn't even think of what to say. To think when I was serving them Thanksgiving and watching my kids play, my mother was analyzing my figure made me physically sick. In my head, I said one word. 'DONE.' That was the moment I knew for sure that it was ok to draw boundaries if someone wasn't safe, and to not be in relationship with people that should have held a place of respect in our lives. I never saw my mother again after that.

Three years later, she died. She had divorced her fourth husband who was still trying to love and care for her even though he had found evidence of someone else. When I went to her memorial, there was a video loop of her life. I was shocked and sad as I watched it. It was just one scene over and over. And the scene was a lie. The ONE afternoon that she had come to meet my children and watch them play repeated on a loop on the small chapel video screen to represent the story of her life. I could hardly watch or listen to the lies. It was all just a terrible loss of human life and potential. Her last husband sent me a thank you for coming, and I called him back to thank him for his kindness. He told me, "She really did love you." I responded, "From my vantage point, I think she tried to talk like she felt something that just wasn't there. I'm not upset. I don't think she could help it." He paused. "Yeah, I know what you mean. Based on what I found, I don't think she ever loved me either." I knew she was broken in a way that only God could fix. All the king's horses, all the king's men, all the Peters and their pumpkin shells, all the sonnets, plays, psychotropic drugs, alcohol, all the dreams of a better life - couldn't put her together again. I just hoped she was with the only One who could.

16

Courage

The LORD is my light and my salvation; Whom shall I fear?
The LORD is the strength of my life; Of whom shall I be afraid?
— Psalm 27:1

My friend Sarah was on her own journey of following God's heart by opening her home to foster children. There had been a set of four sisters, whom they had taken in, that the court had sent back to drug addicted parents. Despite being upset at the court's decision, Sarah and her huge, extended family bought new mattresses and clothes and filled their home with food and furniture. Then they prayed. The foster agency called them to let them know there were two brothers who would be sleeping on the floor of the agency if Sarah couldn't take them. Sarah's big heart could never say no. So two very traumatized young boys came to stay at Sarah's, and for the first time in their lives, they heard and felt that God loved them. But the trauma was severe, and Sarah learned that this kind of love was a long, long road. In the midst of this, the young woman I was walking with through her pregnancy told me she would feel better if she could pick the family to give her baby to. I told her about my friend Sarah who had always wanted a baby but had lost three, and how she was fostering now. She asked me to see if Sarah would be interested in her baby. I gave her Sarah's number and called Sarah to explain the situation. Ecstatic, Sarah couldn't even let me finish the question before praising God and shouting for joy. Apparently, the young woman had already called Sarah and asked her to take her baby. I was stunned at the speed at which this was happening. I tried to calm Sarah's exuberance since nothing, NOTHING was certain. Plans for them to meet were made. The story had the momentum of a freight train, and I was holding on to the back trying to keep up.

When I called Sarah to set up the details of the meeting, her mind had gone into full baby planning mode. She told me, "I always wanted to name a baby boy Joseph or Josiah because of the faith they had in our heavenly Father. They were both fully committed to God. What do you think of Joey?" Beautiful names, both of them, but I tried to caution her excitement. On the appointed day, I drove to pick up the young mother and we talked on the drive to Sarah's. The young mother told me, "I just wish this baby could have something that is from me, some little piece of me." "Like what?" I asked. "I was kind of thinking maybe, since it's a boy, it could have my middle name for a middle name. I have a boy name." "What is it?" I asked. "It's Jo," she said quietly. "Do you think Sarah would be willing to give him my name? Do you think she would name him Jo?" she asked pensively. I stared at the road ahead as tears welled up in my eyes. My heart cried praises to my God who had named this unborn baby when he had named this young woman over twenty years before. "Why don't you ask Sarah and see what she says?" was my quiet reply. Joseph was born. Sarah became a mom. The other mother from South Africa I was helping fell in love with her newborn and the grace she found in Jesus Christ. She and Sarah became friends in the process. There are precious pictures of those two babies from fifteen years ago, who are growing into incredible young men today, when once, long ago, all looked hopeless. It reminds me that God's view is much higher and much larger than ours. God was not even close to being done. The parents of the four girls that Sarah had previously fostered could not stop the substance abuse. On a court checkup, the girls were found with all the furniture and food gone while rats ran through the home. Parental rights were terminated, and the four girls went back to Sarah's. The parental rights of the two boys were terminated as well. Sarah went from 0-7 children in one year. The journey began. The freight train was at full speed.

At age sixteen, as I write this, Joey's whole heart is committed to his Lord and Savior just as Sarah always prayed. When I think of Joey, I think of so much. I think of believing in God's faithfulness when your heart has been broken by loss again and again. I think how God makes something so beautiful to bring Him glory out of what the world calls a mistake. I think how every single human life has eternal value no matter the circumstances in which a life is conceived, because every single life is made in His image whether we recognize it or not. I think He has so much fun letting us peek at how He weaves countless stories together when we are busy thinking He has forgotten us. And I think it all matters, the mistakes, the heartbreaks, betrayals, the broken parts and losses, the paths that go nowhere, the journeys, the joys - all of it, every mile and every tear matters.

***

While I still kept trying to be the good wife, good mother, and good Christian, The Big Jock's bizarre behavior and drinking had begun to get wildly out of control. At night on several occasions, he would look at me in wild terror and tell me he saw demons. I wondered if he had sleep apnea or if this was from the alcohol. I was always trying to find logical reasons for everything. At one of Houston's birthdays, I invited all my friends and their kids to celebrate at a warehouse with several bouncy houses. Even though he couldn't connect with people, I wanted his life and his birthdays celebrated. The place was filled with parents and kids. I asked the Big Jock to do one thing - watch Houston. Instead, he sat on the floor. At one point, as I organized cups and cake, I looked down to see a hand behind me. The Big Jock had one of the new Blackberries and was taking pictures up my skirt like a peeping Tom. He laughed when I saw him. My cheeks burned with embarrassment, but at that moment there was nothing I could do.

One night I went to a meeting for World Vision, and our team discussed how we could partner with airlines to combat human trafficking. (Last year I was in the airport and saw the exact signs we had discussed fifteen years ago. Who knows? Maybe all those prayers and seeds planted just needed a long time to sprout.) Anyway, I had been gone for three hours and that almost never happened. The Big Jock had been left in charge. When I got home, the house was trashed. There was an empty 1.5-liter bottle of Shiraz, over a half dozen empty beer cans and trash everywhere. I found him on the internet watching porn. Angry that I couldn't even trust him for three hours with the kids, I asked how he could have drunk that much in three hours. He immediately defended himself by attacking me and my parenting. For the most part, I ignored his ridiculous comments and furiously started cleaning up the mess of mac and cheese, fast food trash, and empty beer cans. He walked into the kitchen behind me while I washed and cleaned up the mess at the sink. Hearing him, I turned around and stood frozen. He slowly walked toward me with a knife aimed right at my face. He was bowed and hate boiled out of him. He held the knife a half inch from my left eye and just glared at me while the corners of his mouth turned up in an evil grin. I didn't dare move. He took the knife, still towering over me and not breaking eye contact, while he very slowly lowered the knife to the sink. His hand was still on the knife and the sinister smile spread across his face. I held my breath waiting for his next move. Still smiling, he walked out of the room.

I grabbed the phone and called a friend, telling her in a panic what had just happened. While the words were still tumbling out of my mouth, the phone was ripped out of the wall and he lifted me off the ground by the sides of my head and violently threw me around repeatedly. He finally left me alone, took the phone to the bedroom, and locked himself inside. I found another phone and called my friend. She told me the police were on their way. I gasped. I knew how he would react to the police. I knew he would consider it betrayal and would do everything to retaliate, even if I hadn't called them. Terrified, I waited on the phone and moments later they arrived. I also knew I couldn't go on like this. The police took my statement and saw the marks on my face. They sent me upstairs and asked if there were guns. I told them there were, but I wasn't sure if he had one on him. Benjamin was awake when I went upstairs. He climbed onto my lap and tried to tickle me. He slid down and did a silly dance before climbing back in my lap. I just wanted to hold onto him and never let go. He had no idea our life was falling apart downstairs.

The Big Jock was arrested and spent a few days in jail. I went to court to get a Temporary Protective Order. I remember standing there with my four-year-old in my arms who had a fever, while I held my five-year old's hand. The judge looked down at me from the bench with his glasses perched near the end of his nose. "Do you have a *JOB*?" he questioned. My mouth opened in shock. I tried to explain that I had five kids, that one was severely disabled, that my whole life was work, that… I felt stupid and small because I didn't earn a paycheck. I hired an attorney. When the Big Jock was released, there was enormous rage as I had suspected. "YOU THREW ME IN JAIL!!!... YOU HAVE NO F..KING CLUE WHAT YOU HAVE DONE!!... WHEN YOU WAKE UP SHIT IS GOING TO RAIN DOWN ON YOU!!!..." And more I can't recall. You grow numb to it after a while. I felt I couldn't enforce the TPO based on verbal threats alone. That could incite an even more dangerous reaction. My attorney urged a separation and not a divorce because he wanted to make sure I was certain. It was enough time for the Big Jock to do an enormous amount of manipulation.

My church decided I needed to go before a group of elders for filing for separation without their permission. I still didn't have proof of adultery and the rest wasn't grounds. During this time, the Big Jock lied to everyone he could about me. He became Disney Dad to the kids. He would refuse to make the payments required by the temporary support order and demanded to know what money was being spent on. He would barge into the house repeatedly and get on the computer, going through my email. When I would ask him to stop, he would scream, "You must have something to hide! You're seeing someone or you wouldn't have turned on me!!" Then he would try being super charming and kind. He would tell me how sorry he was and how he was changing and that he was so scared of losing me and the kids. One day, he cornered me in the bedroom when he felt I wasn't responding quickly enough to the waves of charm. He raped me. At the time, I was so abused I couldn't even call it that. Then he told my attorney we had slept together so the separation was void. I had to answer all these questions of my attorney that were so humiliating. He asked me if it was rape. I didn't know how to answer. Can it be rape if it's your husband? Even if you don't want it? Even if you hate it? Even if you're scared? Even if you hate yourself for not being able to stop it? I don't know how, but I pressed forward with the divorce. It took eleven months.

The church would initially not give me permission for a "Biblical" divorce. Abuse was still not grounds, only adultery. I made the best case I could which infuriated me that I had to share so many intimate details with only men as my jury in order to defend myself. But something good came out of that mess. I finally realized I may not get permission, and that was okay. I stopped letting other people speak for God when I knew He was telling me to RUN. Just like when the colonists first sought a righting of wrongs, their desire had been to set things right and make it a mutually beneficial relationship. But eventually, when that failed through repeated offenses, the colonists declared their independence. They were no longer asking permission, and neither was I. They took control of their future. And finally, I did too. I was terrified.

17

The World According to Autism

*"I will fight to take away your hope. I will plot to rob you and your children of their dreams.
I will make sure that every day you wake up you will cry,
wondering who will take care of my child after I die."*
— Autism Speaks "I am Autism" video

The Big Jock moved into an apartment and his younger brother moved to Atlanta to live with him. He continued the life of a Disney Dad, seeing the kids once every other weekend and other random times. There were so many women and he allowed these twenty-year-olds around my kids. I began to hear stories that made me sick. This is what I got for not wanting to be abused? On a trip with their dad to his sister's wedding the boys were thrilled to tell me they had been to Universal Studios. I knew this was not in the original plans, so I asked Morgan. She was afraid to tell me but finally shared that he had brought a bridesmaid into the hotel room and had attempted the unmentionable with the bridesmaid right next to our daughter while she was asleep. She had woken up and started crying. She was too young to know about such things and too innocent to know what to do. Universal was the "forget about it" gift to make it go away. My stomach dropped when she told me. He acted as if I was the one making a big deal out of nothing. I didn't know how to protect my kids when they were with him. Fear became part of me.

His tactics with me were quite different. He withheld money and still barged into the house as often as he wished. It was still his house, he told me. He was letting me live there. He regularly employed a fifteen-year-old babysitter who was the daughter of one of the Big Jock's employees. The mother of the babysitter was Italian with a mouth and a hair trigger temper. She made the Big Jock's younger brother her plaything for a summer of love. It was a circus. The babysitter was sweet and always seemed to be there when I dropped the kids off. One day when I arrived, the kids ran in ahead of me and the door was open. I walked in behind them. All the lights were off upstairs and downstairs. It was pitch black and silent. I called his name. Nothing. I stood there combing through the possibilities - he was late, he had forgotten, I had missed a message and he cancelled. And then two young teenagers trepidly walked down the stairs. I was stunned and confused. One was his babysitter, the other, a girl I had never seen with a similar young punk hairstyle. Neither could make eye contact with me. Shocked, I asked what they were doing there. "Oh, um we were just leaving. The Big Jock gave me a key. He lets me hang out here." *"Really? During school?..."* None of it sounded believable. They looked caught. "Ok. Do you know if he's on his way?" "No, we gotta go. Bye." They rushed out the door, never able to look at me in the eyes. The Big Jock showed up soon after and asked what we were doing inside. I told him the door had been unlocked and the kids had run inside. I told him the babysitter had been there with another girl and the place was pitch-black. He laughed his predatory laugh and said, "She's totally a lesbian."

My stomach hurt at his careless cruelty. 'Of course he thinks that,' I thought to myself. 'She's just a young girl trying to figure out who she is.'

During these years as I dealt with abuse, separation, divorce, and the aftermath that wouldn't end, life was very hard. The intimidation and abuse never stopped. And then there was Houston. I lived in a state of extreme hypervigilance for two decades and still do. There are so many things to be vigilant about, things you don't expect far beyond leaving a door unlocked. I had to get rid of the toaster for years because Houston set the kitchen cabinets on fire after putting a DVD of Cinderella in the toaster. He would put everything in his mouth - I'll leave it at that. You can use your imagination. He would chew dirty socks and other things that would leave us shocked. He chewed his clothes to bits. He would eat everything he could get his hands on - raw bacon, raw hot dogs, entire boxes of cereal. It was dizzying. Locks were on everything and somehow, he could sense when one was left unlocked. He unwrapped a 64-count box of tampons and pulled out all the tampons so he could fill his hands with the cardboard applicators - more sticks. Sarah offered to buy me an industrial size box from Costco and I just shook my head. "No. No. You don't understand. The more there are the more he will unwrap. I need the fewest amount possible to reduce the loss." No one could leave a gift out. He would open everything. After staying up until 4 am wrapping presents on Christmas Eve and going to bed exhausted, the kids came in crying a few hours later because Houston had opened everything. And he had. That Christmas and the next really took all the remaining joy out of the holiday. I couldn't find joy at all. I was too tired. Houston would barely sleep, and his siblings would get furious, screaming in the middle of the night for him to stop. He had minimal language by this time, but it was almost exclusively echolalia or scripting. Let me explain what that means. For hours at a time a loop takes over.

Coming to video January 2, 1998. Coming to video January 2, 1998. Coming to video January 2, 1998. Coming to video January 2, 1998. Coming to video January 2, 1998. Coming to video January 2, 1998. Coming to video January 2, 1998. Coming to video January 2, 1998. Coming to video January 2, 1998. Coming to video January 2, 1998.

Join us after the feature for our special presentation for a behind the scenes look at the making of... Join us after the feature for our special presentation for a behind the scenes look at the making of... Join us after the feature for our special presentation for a behind the scenes look at the making of... Join us after the feature for our special presentation for a behind the scenes look at the making of... Join us after the feature for our special presentation for a behind the scenes look at the making of... Join us after the feature for our special presentation for a behind the scenes look at the making of...

Stay tuned for our feature presentation. Stay tuned for our feature presentation. Stay tuned for our feature presentation. Stay tuned for our feature presentation. Stay tuned for our feature presentation. Stay tuned for our feature presentation. Stay tuned for our feature presentation. Stay tuned for our feature presentation.

Ichabod and Mr. Toad. Ichabod and Mr. Toad. Ichabod and Mr. Toad. Ichabod and Mr. Toad. Ichabod and Mr. Toad. Ichabod and Mr. Toad. Ichabod and Mr. Toad. Ichabod and Mr. Toad. Ichabod and Mr. Toad. Ichabod and Mr. Toad. Ichabod and Mr. Toad. Ichabod and Mr. Toad. Ichabod and Mr. Toad. Icabod and Mr. Toad.

Miss Bianca Rescuers Down Under. Miss Bianca Rescuers Down Under. Miss Bianca Rescuers Down Under. Miss Bianca Rescuers Down Under. Miss Bianca Rescuers Down Under. Miss Bianca Rescuers Down Under. Miss Bianca Rescuers Down Under. Miss Bianca Rescuers Down Under. Miss Bianca Rescuers Down Under.

Poor Unfortunate Souls. Poor Unfortunate Souls. Poor Unfortunate Souls. Poor Unfortunate Souls. Poor Unfortunate Souls. Poor Unfortunate Souls. Poor Unfortunate Souls. Poor Unfortunate Souls. Poor Unfortunate Souls. Poor Unfortunate Souls. Poor Unfortunate Souls. Poor Unfortunate Souls. Poor Unfortunate Souls. Poor Unfortunate Souls. Poor Unfortunate Souls. Poor Unfortunate Souls. Poor Unfortunate Souls. Poor Unfortunate Souls. Poor Unfortunate Souls. Poor Unfortunate Souls.

In between the loops bizarre noises would erupt out of him. The older he got the deeper the noises became. Some were cries. Others were guttural. There was a deep moaning wail that hurt my heart. It was the sound of a soul crying out, weary.

AAAYUU AAAYUU AAAYUU AAAYUU AAAYUU AAAYUU AAAYUU AAAYUU AAAYUU AAAYUU AAAYUU YOOP YOOP YOOP YOOP YOOP YOOP YOOP YOOP YOOP YOOP YOOP YOOP YOOP YOOP YOOP LILLU EP LILLU EP LILLU EP LILLU EP LILLU EP LILLU EP LILLU EP LILLU EP LILlU EP LILLU EP

Sometimes the sounds sounded like language, but not one I could understand. There were low mumblings that echoed everywhere while he stared at the ground, paced back and forth, and held his hand out towards the ground drawing an imaginary circle in perpetual motion that you couldn't stop. Like the earth spinning, round and round and round and round. I felt like a broken record. "Houston, stop. Houston, be still. Houston, shush baby, shush. Houston, don't bite. Houston, DON'T BITE YOURSELF. PLEASE! DON'T BITE! STOP BITING! Houston, calm down. It's ok. Calm down. Houston, stop jumping. Houston, stop flapping your hands. Houston, stop running. Houston, look at me. Houston, come back. Houston, no. Houston, don't touch. Houston. Houston. Houston." People would watch me as I tried to break the endless cycles he was caught in and would interject. "Houston, we have a problem," and laugh. His teachers said it A LOT, but with love and camaraderie. Others just laughed, relieved it wasn't them. The joke got old. I was well aware there was a problem. I never laughed. I was searching for the solution.

It's hard to hear God with this kind of a soundtrack. If I ever dared to hope, one of the loops or the wails or the low moaning snaps you back to reality real fast. You want to scream to cover the screams. Cry to cover the cries. Match the moans as your heart breaks. After I got my part time job at the mall while the kids were in school, I remember one day walking into the big open area by the elevator and I could hear my son's noises from what was easily 150 yards away and one story above me. He was on a field trip. I waited as the sounds got closer and closer so I could hug him. He wanted to come with me. I was on a lunch break. He started biting himself. I kissed him goodbye and went back to dressing mannequins, still hearing his voice echoing through the mall while I cried silently in the window of J.Crew.

The loops weren't limited to speech. He could write but would stim on written words too. He would write over and over and over and over and over.

Snow White and the Seven Dwarfs. Snow White and the Seven Dwarfs. Snow White and the Seven Dwarfs. Snow White and the Seven Dwarfs. Snow White and the Seven Dwarfs. Snow White and the Seven Dwarfs. Sno wWhite and the Seven Dwarfs.

Lion King. Lion King. Lion King. Lion King. Lion King. Lion King. Lion King. Lion King. Lion King. Lion King. Lion King. Lion King. Lion King. Lion King. Lion King. Lion King. Lion King. Lion King. Lion King. Lion King.

Mickey and the Beanstalk. Fun and Fancy Free. Mickey and the Beanstalk. Fun and Fancy Free. Mickey and the Beanstalk. Fun and Fancy Free. Mickey and the Beanstalk. Fun and Fancy Free. Mickey and the Beanstalk. Fun and Fancy Free.

Dumbo. Dumbo.

The Fib from Outerspace. The Fib from Outerspace. The Fib from Outerspace. The Fib from Outerspace. The Fib from Outerspace. The Fib from Outerspace. The Fib from Outerspace. The Fib from Outterspace.

He would write on every single piece of paper in the house. He wrote on birth certificates, his siblings' homework, his assessments, ANY AND EVERY piece of paper. I couldn't leave any pens, pencils, crayons or any writing instrument where he could find it because of his obsession to write on anything. He wrote on walls and furniture if he couldn't find paper. I had to learn to keep all important information in my head. This was before the days of reminders and calendars in your phone. The mental stress of trying to manage it all left me in a constant state of exhaustion and anxiety.

The video obsession became relentless, hypnotic, as he would fast forward to the same scene then rewind and watch it over and over again becoming more and more upset, obsessed. The worst was the firemen scene in Dumbo. Repeatedly I tried to remove the videos to reduce the obsession. Years later, when YouTube was released, controlling this obsession became impossible. YouTube was cocaine. The boys would try to block certain sites and links but like an addict, Houston always found a way. He would watch his videos in foreign languages if the link he wanted was blocked. He would take our phones, strangers' phones, break onto every possible computer. He would run behind counters in stores or offices trying to break into YouTube to stim. People would say, "It's fine. He can play on it," while I would shake my head vehemently. "NO!" They didn't understand they were giving him a drug more powerful than anything on the streets.

The other obsessions grew worse when he didn't have that one. He would bite himself so hard he would bleed. I would have a one to two second window where I could calm him enough to take his hand out on his own. Then a switch would flip and a force he had no control over would take over and wage war on himself. When I would try to take his hand out of his mouth, he would look at me maniacally, a mix of terror and hysteria and bite even harder shaking in ferocious strength. I would fight trying to wrench his hand out of his mouth once I could hear the grinding on his bones. At that point, there was no calming him. It was a rescue operation. If I got his hand out of his mouth, he would instinctively attack his other hand. I would be struggling to keep his hands away from his mouth as he made these bizarre yelping noises. It was something like "EEEEE YOPE YOPE EEEE OOEEE AAAAA EEEE." He would shake and tremble while he would lock eyes with you, his eyes so full of terror, or blinking oddly while he looked up and then down and up again while he made noises you knew he could not control. Sometimes his arms and legs would flail and kick in a vicious wild rage. Often, he would howl over and over. I would scream his name trying to reach him. Again and again. Then exhausted, he might cry, stim, or pant like he had sprinted a mile. I would weep. "GOD!!! WHERE ARE YOU??? WHY ARE YOU DOING THIS TO HIM??? HELP HIM GOD! HELP HIM! HAVE YOU NO MERCY? PLEEEEAAASSEEE!!! It is difficult to explain the emotional exhaustion that comes from physically fighting your child off of himself. Who do you get mad at? Who do you cry to? Who do you yell at? Who gets grounded? Where is the answer? And so it went, day after day and year after year.

Intentional language was limited to the names of a few foods and "puter" (computer) so he could look for Disney images in the days before YouTube. But even then, what seemed like intentional language could, in the blink of an eye, become another stim.

Burger fies. Burger fies. Burger fies. Burger fies. Burger fies. Burger fies. Burger fies. Burger fies. Burger fies. Burger fies. Burger fies. Burger fies. Burger fies. Burger fies. Burger fies. Burger fies. Burger Fies. Burger Fies.

The "r" sound is still hard for him today. If we didn't get him "Burger fies," he would start wailing and biting himself. More times than most, I would get him what he was repeating, having no idea I was feeding an obsessive body that ruled a captive and brilliant mind. If I told him to, "stop saying that," or "cut it out," he would repeat me in this high pitched squeaky, nasally voice. Having my desperate pleas for peace and sanity parroted back to me in a mocking voice felt like autism laughing at me. The mocking was in direct proportion to my agitation – or greater.

Stop saying that. Stop saying that. Stop saying that. Stop saying that. Stop saying that. Stop saying that. Stop saying that. Cut it out. Cut it out. Cut it out. Cut it out. Cut it out. Cut it out. Cut it out. Cut it out. Cut it out. Cut it out.

"Houston!" I would plead, "Please! Please STOP!" And his mocking voice would answer, "Stooooop. Stooooop. Stooooop. Stooooop." Then I would want to cry and often did.

His siblings would get so frustrated and scream at him in exasperation. In the middle of the night, one of his brothers scratched him in exhausted frustration. I lost count of how many nights during all those years and the ones to come that I would hear someone screaming, "STOOOPPP!!!" While I certainly tried to have limitless reserves of patience, sometimes the sheer unrelenting barrage of repetitive verbal stims and noises would overwhelm me and I would have my own meltdown. I knew he couldn't help it, but neither could I. There was no end. There was no help. There was no answer to my prayers.

I saw the easy lives of others and it stung. Deeply. I repented. Repeatedly. I saw kids Houston's age getting older and meeting milestone after milestone while we were left hopelessly behind on a merry go round named Torment. It's hard to explain what happened to my prayers for Houston. Slowly they stopped. Without intending to, I had given up. The weight of exhausted reality had won. I had finally accepted that healing would never happen. It was what it was. Those were the cards. Play them. To give up on your child takes a very long time. It is a failure unlike anything else. You can't even think about it in those terms. You frame it as survival. But you know. You know you gave up. Finally, after years of hoping and fighting, you accepted what the experts had told you all along. There was no hope. Accept it and get on with life. You listen more intently to the philosophies of suffering, sifting and weighing to see if there is a nugget of courage or perseverance you can use. You compare yourself to others who suffer, finding fault or strength. You don't know at whom to be angry. Yourself? God? The world for going on and not giving a shit? Your helpless child? The doctors and therapists for their indifference, ignorance, and mistakes? The pharmaceutical companies? The politics of a neurological condition no one understands? The schools? Who? Anger becomes pointless and exhausting, especially when you don't know where to point a finger. Acceptance numbs the pain. But as numbness goes, it doesn't let you feel anything. You watch life from a cage. Life doesn't want you to bother the important people out there in the world making a difference. Your child is a disruption and they let you know it's your job to make sure others aren't bothered. Today's efforts of tolerance and awareness are another world compared to what it was like in those early years.

I began to think of the world as us and them. I didn't like them. They didn't care about us. I'm being honest. At the same time, I LOVED people who lived this hard life. I loved all those broken bodies and the incredible broken parents who chased and fought, who carried and cried. They were my comrades. Without consult, I had been assigned to a clan - the broken people. I didn't know it then, but those were the people God had revealed Himself to in ways I could have never comprehended. In all the Bible studies, sermons, Christian books, and women's conferences I had attended for thirty years, God had been defined, explained, and the rules had been laid out. He was routine. God lives here in this place that we built, in this box. His purpose is this, what we say. He uses these people who know the right people and act the right way. His will is what people in charge want to happen. He wants us to spend His money on places, not people. He is worshipped this way, our way. He cares about what the people in charge say He cares about. For those of us on the sidelines of life, it didn't seem we had been invited to participate in God's kingdom. Children of a lesser god - that's what it felt like. Go to the basement, in the corner, where you won't disturb those who are here to worship.

18

On the Outside

And he will answer, 'I tell you the truth, when you refused to help the least
of these my brothers and sisters, you were refusing to help me.'
— Matthew 25:45

One year I got a very special and precious invitation from a mother who invited her twin daughters' good friends and their mothers over for a Valentine's Day tea party. I can't even begin to explain how precious it was. As the moms talked and the little girls played, we began exchanging stories. By that time I had gotten quite good at telling Houston's tragic stories and trying to find humor in them. Once I realized that two of the other moms had children with profound disabilities, I decided to tell some stories to try to lighten our loads. Of course, there were poop stories. Our hostess stood frozen staring at me. "Katie, did you write a letter to Pastor Q at Q church a few years ago?" I stared at her in shock. "Yes," was all I said. She put her head in her hands. "You don't understand. You don't understand. We had just gotten the diagnosis that the baby I was pregnant with had a chromosomal issue that was going to cause severe disabilities. I couldn't handle it. I was so angry and stunned and broken. I didn't know what we were going to do." She paused. "And then that letter. With all the awful poop." She paused again, holding back the tears. "That is how I've gotten through. Every time something happens that makes me want to cry, I keep going back to that poop letter. And here you are in my living room." I didn't know what to say. It was my turn to cry... My good God. Using the worst of me. For things I could not see. But He could. He knew.

After years of trying to be included, I saw that it just wasn't possible. There were a few amazing people who knew how to love at church, but not many. It was a place to learn theology and get connected but only if you had a respectable, controlled life, only if you had your shit together, and our shit was <u>literally</u> everywhere and on everything. I remember telling a friend how I felt. My life was too much of a wreck to make a difference. I just hoped that maybe people would think of Jesus if they knew me and know for certain that He loved them. But there didn't seem to be a place to do that. Going to church hurt so much. Even Chick-fil-A was a struggle. This was our reality. It wasn't just me. My friend, whose daughter is an absolute angel, was told by mall security that her older daughter couldn't play on the play equipment because it was designed for younger children. Infuriated, she told them, "My daughter IS three! She might be eighteen, but in her mind, this is where she wants to be, playing on a playground. Where is she supposed to go?" Her beautiful daughter, who might have weighed eighty pounds and was non-speaking, went around giving hugs to everyone who would receive one and sliding down slides while security stood near to protect all the important patrons from her. What you have to realize is someone went out of their way to leave their child and find mall security to report the eighty-pound, hug giving "threat." Maybe you think this was just one occurrence, but it's not. I have talked to too many other moms. I have heard too many stories. I have received too many looks. People are mean, meaner than you will ever know.

I would try to go to public places in the late afternoon so Houston could play in the play place without disrupting others. It was safe, completely surrounded by glass with a door that I could guard. One day at Chick-fil-A, I let Houston play by himself while I sat by the door inside the play place and flipped through a magazine. After a while a grandmother and a young girl, probably four or five years old, came in to play. Houston noticed her and her long bouncy curls. At one point he walked over to her and touched a curl before climbing up the slide. A few minutes later he slid down and walked over to the grandmother's purse she had left open on the bench. I could see his little wheels spinning looking for something to eat or spin and told him, "Don't touch. No Houston." He turned and there was the little girl again. He stared at her for a moment and then reached to touch her curls again. "No sweetie. Go play," I said quietly and looked back down at the magazine. A few moments later, the grandmother got up and left returning with the manager. The manager explained that we were not welcome because this place was for young children, because my son was touching a girl inappropriately and because I was reading a magazine and not supervising my son. I was shaking I was so angry. It took several attempts before I could remain calm enough to defend myself and Houston to the manager. The brazen choice of this woman to grossly exaggerate the truth for her own comfort and prejudice shocked and infuriated me. There were so many things to say I could hardly think where to start. When I told his teachers, they wanted to storm the restaurant. They lived it with me. They knew how people treated our kids. The end result is we don't feel welcome *anywhere - EVER*. Others get to experience the joys of life; our assignment is to not bother other people. The world is for them, not us. Eventually you adopt a bit of a cavalier attitude, but it's just a defense against the isolation and loneliness.

The judge's comments back when I got the Temporary Protective Order had a big influence on me. Being a mom of five young children and one with a severe disability, I needed a job to prove my worth, but all the other responsibilities remained. I got a job at J Crew. I remember being so excited when they gave me a raise to $11/hour because I had performed so well. It wasn't many hours, but I could drop Benjamin off at preschool, go for a run, go to work, pick him up and then be back home for the bus. One early morning while it was still dark outside, I saw a package at the front door. I thought I was seeing things. I opened the door and sure enough, there was a package addressed to me. Confused and curious, I opened the box to find a turquoise blue that I had only seen in ads. The word Tiffany stared back at me, and I blinked back tears. Was this a joke? Trembling, I opened the box to find a delicate silver chain with a silver heart. My friend who lived in Switzerland had decided I needed to know I was loved. I don't think people realize how much people need love and how much they need to know they aren't forgotten. It is one of the greatest gifts I have ever gotten simply because it told me I was loved. And I wasn't forgotten, I was treasured.

I wore that heart almost every day to remind myself I was I was worthy of something of value. I was of value. Someone else of value loved me.

As I dressed mannequins, I would let my mind wander. I tried thinking of ideas to solve problems, huge problems, world problems. It was a way to keep my mind occupied. I would come out of the store window with its blazing hot lights and tell my coworkers about the ideas. They would shake their heads in a bit of awe. "So that's what you think about in the window?" I decided to seek out some experts to see if my ideas had any merit.

Accomplished men were astonished. Others would defensively retort, "I would need to see the numbers before I could say it would work." I was advised to speak to several different lobby groups, and I did. I had ideas about economic policy, ways to reduce healthcare costs, ideas to help single mothers and abused women, and policies to promote an immigration policy that served everyone. I made several appointments, sent emails to the contacts I was given, and followed up with phone calls. The indifference was shocking. No one was looking for new ideas or solutions. It was all about money and power. I remember being stunned. All my idealism met reality. It's the kind of thing you hear is true, but the taste of truth was much more bitter than I had imagined. One of my coworkers at J Crew was studying for the LSAT. I began to think seriously of going to law school. Maybe that was the way to change the world. After she took the test, she gave me all her books. Right there in that bag was my future. At least that's what I told myself.

19

Lies and Loss

My heart is in anguish within me; the terrors of death have fallen upon me.
Fear and trembling come upon me, and horror overwhelms me.
And I say, "Oh, that I had wings like a dove!
I would fly away and be at rest; yes, I would wander far away;
I would lodge in the wilderness;
I would hurry to find a shelter from the raging wind and tempest."
— Psalm 55:4-8

The Big Jock had fallen in love with one of the blond twenty-year-olds. It was all so cliché. But being a cliché didn't stop it from hurting. I was embittered when I learned he had bought one of them a boob job and another one a pair of diamond earrings. I thought about the fake ring he had gotten me. It was salt in an open wound. I told myself not to care but I did, especially as he withheld child support, openly forced my kids to interact with his new barbie doll and became more and more manipulative with the kids. As Christmas approached, the kids wanted to see their dad. I didn't know what to tell them. He didn't answer any of my calls and they went straight to voicemail. Finally, I received a phone call that I almost didn't answer. The caller ID said Nassau, Bahamas. Bahamas??? It was him. I was shaking. "You went to the Bahamas?? You took your girlfriend to the Bahamas for Christmas and didn't get your kids anything? Or even tell them? They've been asking and asking, 'Where's Daddy?' Why would you do that?!" For a brief moment in time, the Big Jock felt guilty. He flew home that day and tried to make it up to everyone. My dad told me that he was definitely sorry and to listen to him, for the sake of the kids. I saw the pictures of the two of them in the ocean cuddling closely and felt the urge to vomit. He told me the trip had shown him he was being an idiot and that he missed his family. He finally realized he was the problem. He knew it would be hard but wanted to prove to me that he would do what it took to get his family back. I was numb. He said the same thing to my kids, and they jumped around hugging him.

I waited... I watched... I felt like the fool my circumstances forced me to be.

He took me to Miami. I realized it was more about him showing off to himself and even strangers how much money he had than it was about me. The truth was everywhere, even when he put on a big show, but especially when he put on a big show. It all made me feel dirty. *He* made me feel dirty.

His interest would wax and wane over the next few months. And then in April, his lease was up. At the same time, something akin to a coup happened in his office. He dramatically told me about a man he had hired who stole all his employees from him. They all stormed out of the office in a fateful coup de grace. I knew I wasn't getting the whole story. But at this point, I had stopped counting the lies. I came to the conclusion that if he was talking, it was a lie. Ironically, this all happened at the exact same time his lease was up, and suddenly he was crying to the kids and to me, telling us how much he missed us and wanted to be a family again. "Please, please tell your mom you want me to come home." The funny thing is, I didn't believe a word. I wasn't even terribly moved by the kids pleading with me. I was mostly moved by one thing. Fear. Money. The same stupid thing that had gotten me into this mess still held all the power. I knew the Big Jock. I knew there was a lie. I just didn't know what the lie was. I let him move back in until he could find a new place. He used the room above the garage as his new office. I began to search through papers when I could. I had to be VERY careful. Something wasn't right. The numbers didn't add up.

In July, he told me one of the truths. He hadn't been paying the mortgages or the car payments. The cars were being repossessed and the house would foreclose soon. There was no money. As a threat he added. "You need to go find a place now. If you don't let me live there, I'll make sure you never get a dime. I'll take care of myself before I *ever* take care of you." As you can see, it was true love. I saw my stupid little world crashing around me. All the drapes I had sewn and walls I had painted, the crape myrtles, crabapple trees, the English rose garden and massive three season perennial garden I had planted and worried about - it was all gone, just like that. There's a pool there now. I remembered the hand I was supposed to keep open so God could take out whatever He had put in it. It brought no comfort. Leaving the home I had poured so much love into, to make a special place for my kids, left a deep, deep hole. I was set adrift. Again.

I found an apartment in the same middle school district so Morgan wouldn't have to make new friends. Since middle school is already so difficult, that seemed like the best plan. And the Big Jock came too. For the second time in our marriage, we sold most of our furniture and belongings. In the process, some items were stolen that I was trying to keep. It was if the complete disaster of our lives was on display for everyone to see and loot. I had to shut something off inside me, unsure if I would ever be able to open it again. Another dream was dead. I thanked God and prayed, but my heart was numb. I counted my blessings, closed my eyes, and moved on.

Moving day to the new apartment was crazy, as moving days are with five kids. I had found an apartment in a gated community which I hoped would keep Houston safe if he escaped. I made sure our apartment was on the bottom floor so if he started jumping and making his noises, they would disturb less people. Toward the end of the day, I turned the water on for Houston to take a bath and play in the water. I thought that would keep him happy and busy for a few minutes. As I unpacked a box, I noticed I didn't hear splashing anymore. I dropped everything and ran to the bathroom. Empty. No Houston. I looked down the hall and the front door stood wide open. I yelled for everyone to start looking and ran out the door barefoot. My heart raced as I looked around me at the hundreds of doors and floors, twists, and turns, parking lots, gardens and the pool. Pool - even though it was gated I raced there first. The water sat still and clear and people sunbathed as my heart raced. I tried to calm down long enough to think where he would go. Then I heard sirens and I went into full panic mode. I raced toward them.

Across a divided highway I saw an ambulance pulling up to a police car and another car parked on the side of the road. With tears pouring and gasping for breath I ran up to them. "Is it my son?!! Is he ok?!!" And then the sobbing started. A police officer tried to calm me down and asked for a description. I gave them one and told them about the move and the bath and his diagnosis in between sobs. The Big Jock walked slowly over to the scene. The officer explained that Houston was fine. But, because a naked child had been running down the street, they had to call an ambulance to make sure he was okay. They put me and Houston in the back of the police car and drove us back to the apartment. It was a short ride but there was something symbolic and tragic about the whole scene. I stopped feeling anything. I was beyond numb. I went inside with Houston, got a picture for the cops, and gave them all my information in case he eloped again.

The Big Jock did one thing. He bought and installed a double deadbolt. I drilled into the refrigerator to install a keyed lock. The boys had introduced Houston to YouTube and unwittingly made his autism drastically worse. His obsessive-compulsive issues and loops became profound with unlimited access to every single Disney movie he could ever want. But there was nothing else for him to do. All therapies had to be stopped. There was no money for anything. The cars were gone. The Big Jock borrowed an old Cadillac from a friend of his. The back passenger side door wouldn't stay closed even if you locked it. I would have Morgan sit beside that door and hold it shut while we drove. People probably thought I was a grandma with how slow and cautious I drove. I have never been so grateful for seatbelts.

By this time the rest of the country was experiencing the Great Recession. Due to his line of work, it hit the Big Jock first. I remember hearing on the radio that couples who had divorced were having to still live together due to the crisis. I thought to myself sarcastically, 'You don't say...' The Big Jock vacillated between finding his own place and starting another company along with a number of other endeavors. He moved out and moved back in. He would not give me money for rent until we were served eviction notices. It became routine. This was how he handled finances. I would plead with the front office to give us more time. It was humiliating.

My dad offered to sell me his wife's minivan if I paid for the repairs to get it running. The Big Jock agreed as he found another place to live. I found the cheapest flight I could, flew to Minnesota, and drove back with the minivan. The exhaust pipe leaked into the interior of the car, so we had to drive with all the windows down at all times. There was also no muffler, but it was transportation and all the doors closed. While I had been in Minnesota, I read a book that belonged to my dad's wife that greatly impacted me, The Girls That Went Away. That whole two-day trip home, I thought about those heartbreaking stories and an idea was born. I didn't just have my own experiences to pull from, there were so many. I decided to use this time to study for the LSAT and eventually write a book - a testament, a voice for the unborn and a voice for terrified pregnant women, while I worked retail and raised my kids.

That minivan was the first thing I had owned since I was twenty and had bought my first car for $800. I was 35. It was the beginning of me getting my life back. I loved that it was mine, despite the issues the car had. I was cautiously relieved when the Big Jock found another place to live, and we moved his things. But it was short lived. I never got the real story about what happened. He just came back. His drinking was nonstop. I was living with a powder keg in close quarters with five kids and one who stimmed constantly. It kept getting worse. He would force himself on me. I would lay there hating him, hating life, afraid to move. He had gained more and more weight. I was suffocating slowly in every way a person can suffocate. The only thing that kept me going was my kids. One fall morning he went out to get coffee. He came back and did what he would do to me. I felt dead inside. He got up and took a shower. I went to his phone and saw he had been texting sweet love notes to the Barbie doll while he had gotten coffee and then had used me for his release. The violation I felt crushed my spirit. I started trying to help him find anything that would get him out, get him away from us. But there was nothing. No jobs, no opportunities, at least none that he would take seriously.

One night his friend came into town to visit, and they went out drinking. He came back, and I knew it was going to be bad. I locked myself in my room and prayed. He came in obliterated and raging. The locked door set him off even more, and he busted the door in. I laid in bed frozen and terrified. The next day I saw the damage. The doorframe was split and there was a huge hole about two feet wide that he hung his ties over to cover.

Morgan was in middle school and dealing with all the awkwardness and moodiness that comes with the age. She took most of it out on her little sister. Reagan would come crying to me, and I would try to teach her about turning the other cheek and killing with kindness while at the same time trying to teach Morgan that kindness was required and her cruelty to her sister would backfire. One of the moms from my old neighborhood was a designer and had seen my design, as well as the soft goods I had made by hand. She asked if I would sew all the soft goods for a home that would be featured in Coastal Living. The job was worth a thousand at least, but I did it for $250. It was hours and hours of meticulous work in a tiny apartment with all my kids underfoot. I used the money to buy the girls new bedspreads and give them an updated "cool" room. That helped for a moment, but the rift between them began to grow. Reagan had a very different way of dealing with her sister and fought back, which only made everything worse.

The Big Jock was still such a charmer to the public. I was quiet, watching the liar work, feeling more powerless and alone with every head he turned. One day we walked into Publix, and he stopped near the entry. With his winning grin and empty compliments, he charmed one of the middle-aged cashiers before pushing the cart toward the aisle. I followed behind, numb to everything. Suddenly the hood on my hoodie was jerked back and I almost lost my balance. The cashier whom he had flirted with looked at me sternly and dropped my hood. "You know he's one of the good ones, don't you?" It was an order - to be grateful for the good man who raped and abused but looked good in a suit and had a great smile and a firm handshake. I looked at her in shock. He really could fool anyone, which made all of it worse. He had a sadistic and vicious sense of humor, along with paranoia which grew worse with the alcohol. By this point, it showed up in horrifying ways. He was obsessed with sharks, snakes, aliens, and conspiracy theories. He would spend hours upon hours watching documentaries about these topics. Repeatedly I told him I didn't want the kids watching these things and to stop showing them scary movies. He would advance and tower over me with intimidating terror any time I told him not to expose the children to these things. I remember he took a picture of the skyline and brought it home in paranoid delight that he had proof of a UFO. "I have proof! I have proof!" he shouted. He showed me the picture he had printed that showed nothing but a highway, the tree line, a plane, and a cell tower. When I didn't react, it triggered his wild temper.

He was still obsessed with knives and guns. One day when Reagan asked about him sharpening a knife, he grabbed her hand and with brute force, held the knife over her hand like he was going to cut it off, then laughed when he let her go as if she couldn't take a joke. She was terrified. He would force the kids to watch movies with him that were very inappropriate for children. When I would object, it would ignite one of his rages. He delighted in terrifying them. The kids told me when he lived on his own, he had put pantyhose over his head and jumped out to scare the babysitter who was there all the time. With his macabre humor he would laugh at everything, no matter how sick, and accuse those who were offended of being no fun, banal, humorless, and prudish. You know, "You're no f..kin fun! B..ch! Can't take a joke. You wouldn't know funny if it hit you in the face. Why do you think no one wants to be friends with you?" that kind of stuff. *Memories...*

One night we went out to a cheap dinner to discuss his options. Cautiously, I urged him to consider moving back to Florida. He drank heavily but remarkably, there was no tension during the conversation. When we got back home the kids were glued to the television. No surprise. I went into the bedroom and found all the LSAT books I had been studying ripped to pieces. First, I gasped, then it turned immediately to weeping. My gut reaction to the destruction around me was that I was not ever allowed to have dreams. I was supposed to clean up shit, literally, and that's it. Upset, I went out to the living room to show my kids what Houston had done because they hadn't watched him. The Big Jock lost it. I don't know if Morgan gave him a look or if he didn't like the general attitude, but he absolutely went wild with rage. I was screaming for him to stop and raced to throw myself on top of Morgan. He suddenly stopped and panted with hate. He was bowed up and had the face of a devil. I just screamed at everyone to get in the car. We ran for the door and the car, and I drove, my head spinning. We drove to a parking lot and waited. None of us wanted to go back. I was so angry with myself for caring about some dumb books. I was so angry my kids had been scared and hurt. He had to go. I waited for hours and hoped he was asleep. Finally, we went back. He sat waiting in the dark with just one light on. He had burned something terribly and the place wreaked. He said one thing, and I knew it was a promise. With burning hate, he glared at me and finally threatened in his booming terrifying voice, "You better not have called the cops." I knew what he was saying - promising. Shortly after that he moved to Florida.

Free. Free at last. It didn't even seem real. I didn't know how to not be afraid.

20

The Weight of Everything

Is this not the fast which I choose, To loosen the bonds of wickedness,
To undo the bands of the yoke, And to let the oppressed go free, And break every yoke?
— Isaiah 58:6

Learn to do good; Seek justice, Reprove the ruthless,
Defend the orphan, Plead for the widow.
— Isaiah 1:17

Bear one another's burdens, and so fulfill the law of Christ.
— Galatians 6:2

A few weeks later when rent was due, I got an email telling me he had decided he was only going to pay $750 a month in child support for five kids. I emailed back saying that he couldn't make up his own rules and that I had never enforced what he was supposed to pay. He didn't care. He, not the courts, was in charge. He mocked my fear and questions. "What are you going to do about it?" I filed for child support enforcement. He was livid. "You threw me into two different court systems in two states! You're going to pay!" He paid $200 to keep himself out of contempt and then sued me for a downward modification to lower child support. He knew I had no money for an attorney. So I researched. I learned how to file a counter suit and filed for discovery as well. I also stood in line for food at our local community food bank. I had to be interviewed to be sure I fit the criteria and wasn't a fraud, milking the system. I was so angry. I didn't want their stupid charity. I needed it to survive. My God! They make being in need so shameful, such a judgment of your character and work ethic. I guess good people don't let this happen to themselves. I hated standing in line for hours in the cold before the center opened so I could have a better chance of getting decent food before they closed. I realized during this time that receiving is more difficult than anyone can prepare you for when you've been raised to work hard and be self-sufficient. Neediness has always been the great American sin. Your story has to be bad enough to deserve pity and provision, otherwise you deserve to suffer. But even if you "deserve" help, you better learn to pick yourself up quick.

When help is given, those who give act as if $300 paid to Georgia Power fixes every possible problem you could have forever. (Of course, the check has to be made out to Georgia Power, poor people can't be trusted with cash.) People who haven't lived it, don't understand the complexity of the problem. It's just easier for them to judge than try to understand what it feels like to live a life where you are always drowning. I have seen single mothers struggling. I have been one. I know the power of the whirlpool and the riptide. I have seen the generosity that comes wrapped in judgment and expectations. I have seen wealthy women enjoy the self-adulation that comes from giving to the poor without understanding sacrifice and definitely without understanding need. I have seen wealthy women become frustrated that a single woman who once received remains impoverished. Shouldn't she have pulled herself together by now? I have seen and I have known the pit that sucks you down and leaves you clinging just to hang on while the gracious judge from above. I have seen so much of the judgment of the safe - judgment from people who don't have a clue that hardship isn't just seasonal but can be a life sentence. Yet I have also known what it is to get a gift with no strings. Just love. One leaves you with awe and dignity. The other is a bitter pill.

Although I never got everything I requested in discovery, I did learn that he had deposited over $11,000 in his bank account the same month that he had sent me the letter saying he could only pay $750 to support five children. Eventually he decided he should play nice. He told me how sorry he was and how his attorney would represent us both. We talked on the phone, and he told me lie after lie. By this time, I was acutely aware that he lied like my stepmother, staring straight through me, with no fear and a weird lust in the power of deceiving someone. He came up with a horrible agreement. I'm still so embarrassed I agreed to this ridiculous order, but I felt I had no money and no choice. It was enough to keep me from being evicted. At the time I was actually proud of myself for filing the papers. The thing is - to fight a bully you need more than a pile of papers, you need to be wiser, have more resources, and be more intimidating than they are. I wasn't any of those things which is why I was such a target for someone who didn't obey the law. I thought if you stood for good and did good, the courts would be just. That was over ten years ago, and I'm still waiting for the courts. The courts are not unjust per se, they just are too overwhelmed to care about what is true or good. Time, not justice, is their currency.

One of the wealthy women who shopped religiously at J Crew went to my church and offered to introduce me to her husband who needed a writer. I was thrilled that I could work both jobs and still be available for my kids. I accepted a part time work-from-home job as a grant writer for a Christian development company. For anyone who doesn't know - that's the nice way of saying raising money for Jesus. So my days became working for J Crew in the mornings and writing grants in the afternoons. When the kids were in bed, I worked on finishing my book. Something incredible happened as I wrote that book. God took my hand and had His way. He said His piece. I took dictation. People who have never had the experience may not be able to grasp the power of it, the partnership, the dance of words that come from a place you never knew was inside you. It's magic. I remember some scholarly person telling me my words were too passionate and I thought to myself, 'Clearly you don't know God, do you?' I put my whole heart into that book. By that I mean, I listened and followed God and let Him use me, my story, my voice. But the love, even my love, that was all Him. My hope was that all I had been through and learned could be used for good. My hope was that it would save the lives of unborn children and their mothers. After an extraordinary effort it was finally in print, and I began to pray. For the cover I used a pen and ink drawing I had done when I was seventeen. When the Bough Breaks: Abortion and the Rest of Us. I included the economic policies I hoped would change life for those at the very bottom, struggling to survive. It was written to all of us, mothers, fathers, grandparents, preachers, doctors, the media… everyone. It was written from the voices of those who lose their lives and like in other cases of social injustice, it is the voices of victims that have the greatest power to right the injustice. So that is who I gave a voice to. *Open your mouth for the speechless, in the cause of all who are appointed to die.* [28]

I taught my children about the value of human life and our job to defend the oppressed, the fatherless, the poor and needy as if it was for Him. I told my kids to be smart, to make good choices, but that they never had to be afraid if something happened, that a baby is a blessing. Always. No matter what. I taught them that a person's value has nothing to do with how much money their parents have or the circumstances in which they were conceived. I took my kids to pro-life marches and helped with diaper drives and college presentations. I met with local pregnancy centers, volunteering in whatever capacity I could. Each Sunday I would write a prayer request for the unborn and for mothers for the church staff to pray over. I prayed for Christians to care about single moms and be a voice for the voiceless. I prayed for the church to love. I prayed for laws to change. I met with leaders, political and ecclesiastical. And silence answered its deafening, disinterested reply.

One day I received an email from my ex-stepmother. In the email she talked about the anniversary of the fall of the Berlin Wall and asked if I remembered how we had all gotten up together and watched it in our pajamas and how she had made popcorn. She talked about how cute and precious I was in my pajamas. I was livid. Even now, all these years later, she was still trying to rewrite the truth. I knew my brother had given her my email address with the very best of intentions, but I was NOT ok. I told him in great detail how my childhood actually was compared to his and how she had treated me. Angrily I asked him if she had even done the math before she had concocted her lie because I was sixteen and did not wear pajamas, nor was I woken up to eat popcorn while rubbing my sleepy eyes. I told him in detail of how I actually learned of the Berlin Wall falling and how I actually felt. I was so sick of liars and abusers. I was so hurt and tired of others not seeing the truth or ignoring it because it caused problems no one wanted to deal with. I wasn't doing the "Christian" thing anymore where you just keep letting liars lie and saying I forgive you. Oh, and would you please come back and poison me once more? No! I would forgive, but I would protect myself. I gave myself permission to use the wisdom of God and my own good sense to discern the actions of liars and wolves in sheep's clothing and guard myself against them.

The fallout was that my brother was angry at me. To him everything was about forgiveness, but he had never been preyed upon. He didn't understand my need to protect myself and had not experienced how vastly different we were treated or how strongly I felt. I sent the email to my dad too. My dad knew everything I said was true. We had grown close, and the reality of my childhood was hard for him to bear. He preferred to focus on the present. He sent it to my aunt, who I think was stunned. I do remember that after that she treated me like an adult she respected. Her respect stunned me. I hadn't realized it was something I wanted until I received it. Before then I think they still thought of me as a child and hadn't realized I had always been intelligent and cognizant of my stepmother's ability to manipulate along with everyone else's ability to be manipulated. Being a child meant you had to be silent and do what you were told. Suddenly I was an adult with the truth.

I was sick of manipulators. I seemed to have an inordinate number of them in my life. Even after moving out, the Big Jock could control and manipulate. One night around almost 11 pm, after he had moved to Florida, the front door opened. I was working at the computer and froze in fright as he walked into the apartment with his evil smile. What do you think I was thinking? Can you imagine? I couldn't even speak as he told me he was staying the night. I didn't know if he had a gun. I didn't know why he was there or what he was going to do. The entire night I just laid there in absolute fear, praying. He had called Morgan and told her to unlock the door for him. She had been too scared to tell me. The manipulation never stopped. It was everywhere and in everything - money, isolation, degradation, terror, but most horribly with my children. He had so many tools and so many ways to manipulate. After he moved out, he branched out and used gifts and spent money on the kids, and then lied to them about me. When they started using his words, words I knew by heart, to defy and defame me, I was truly scared. Over two decades I had experienced so many fronts, so many battles, so many years of defeat. It was all I could do to survive and still stand for something.

An old friend from my first class of my first semester of college called me when he was coming into town. He knew all my kids. He knew the Big Jock. He knew about Houston. He was a good Christian man. He wanted to know what had happened with my marriage. So I told him. At first, I was hesitant. I knew most Christians thought you should stay married no matter what. When I would mention anything about the reality of my marriage, I would get comments like, "Well, you chose to marry him - There are two sides to every story - No one likes a victim." After all, it's a lot easier to blame the victim than stand by her side. These comments kept me quiet, helping to hide the truth that made other people uncomfortable. What did it matter what I felt? As long as they didn't have to feel for me. But for some reason this time, I spoke up. I didn't give all the gory details, but I also didn't cover up for the Big Jock. There were facts and I didn't hide them. He asked a question that made me realize he was thinking along the lines of the typical Christian perspective - that you should never feel bad when bad things happen to you because other people have it worse. Self-pity was as sinful as self-defense. I knew he didn't understand. Empathy is an art safe people have no yearning to learn.

Gently, I called him out on it. I said, "You know, the only reason people say that is so they can absolve themselves of feeling or showing any compassion. It's just another way to make it the victim's fault for feeling pain. If I broke my leg, would I be wrong to feel pain? What if someone else broke two legs? Does that mean that my leg suddenly shouldn't hurt? I'm not asking for empathy or even sympathy, but don't tell me this shouldn't hurt because someone else hurts worse. And as for other people having it worse - yes. I am certain others have it worse. I just don't know them." He looked at me without replying, as if he was digesting what I had said. His last words to me were, "It could be worse." My irritation rose instantly, but then he added, "You could be him." He hugged me and said goodbye. Suddenly I realized how right he was. I could be a horrific, selfish, abusing, irresponsible, unfaithful, corrupt, nefarious, terrorizer. But by God's grace, His Spirit lived in me. That would never be my fate.

The girls refer to our time in that apartment as the worst years. They were awful. The A/C would break constantly and flood, so mildew began to grow. Maintenance would just run fans on the soiled mess, and the front office refused to replace it. Rats would appear constantly and got brave enough to crawl right up to Benjamin on the floor while he was watching TV. Morgan somehow got coerced by a predator on the internet. Fortunately, I found her hiding with the computer and unearthed all sorts of nonsense. She began to discover boys, and Reagan thought she should be able to do anything her sister was doing. My efforts to discipline and control the rebellion were a failed disaster, and only fueled her pubescent resentment. Houston would frequently break into the food. One morning I didn't know if I should laugh or cry. When I woke up, I found him sleeping peacefully on the couch. But clearly, he had thrown a party. There were empty Hard Mike's Lemonade bottles all around, an empty box of cereal, and an empty package of raw hot dogs. But he was sleeping. 'So that's the trick,' I thought to myself. Daily disasters and tears kept unfolding like a recurring nightmare.

The boys, however, were in the prime of their childhood. I had been blessed to find the boys a mentor who loved fishing and hunting. He was one of the strong, silent types who taught them how to be men who loved God and how to hate my Georgia Bulldogs. I decided not to fight that battle. For ten years he loved on my boys and taught them right, wrong, and the love of God. He is so much to them. As they grew up in the apartments they played constantly, running, and hiding in the gardens with other boys in the neighborhood. One family in particular became our second family. We were all in this fight for survival together and our kids adored each other. They were from Bulgaria, and I doubt if any people anywhere could actually be kinder and more authentic than them. I tried unsuccessfully to teach the boys how to play baseball and got them signed up on teams. They struggled to learn, and I was frustrated that, despite their dad being an incredible football and baseball player, he had never even tossed a ball with them. Houston would jump in the pool constantly, even in winter. As usual, I had to be tethered to him to keep him safe. Reagan was bullied at school, and it triggered something in that sweet, sweet girl. The next two years she struggled silently, and I had no idea. I had gone to the parents of the girl who scrawled hateful things about Reagan on our old minivan and they couldn't have cared less. I always felt she was angry at me that I wouldn't fight back and play dirty the way she saw everyone else getting their way. I would tell my kids in so many ways what I read in God's word, *"Do not answer a fool according to his folly, lest you be like him."*[29] She began to view the law of kindness as the foolishness of the weak. The powerful answered blow for blow.

On Reagan's twelfth birthday I was called to the school for an emergency meeting. I was notified of disciplinary action that would be taken because of a hate journal she was keeping. They called them diaries when I was growing up. I was also informed she had been cutting herself. When the counselor told me, I swear I heard glass shattering inside my head. How had I not known? How had I not seen? I have no memory of what I said or if I said anything at all. She didn't have an answer for why. If this was a cry for attention, why did she not want to spend time with me when I tried? Did one of the endless episodes of teenage angst on television spark this idea? We had recently watched such an episode and it seemed like another world. Were other kids doing this? Was she trying to get attention from someone else? Was there something else? My efforts got nowhere. I felt lost.

It's so difficult to explain those years. So many tiny things were happening that I couldn't see and couldn't control. It was like being caught up in a tempest on the sea. You are just trying to survive. You have no idea where you will land, but when you do, people look at you like it's your fault that you're naked, covered in fish guts, and don't have a penny or a passport.

My part time job expanded to full time, and I was working between fifty and sixty hours but for $3000 a month. I got paid a check once a month and was told by the owner that he was being generous, that it was really more than $3000 since it was all 1099. I wrote and wrote and wrote. I researched thousands of foundations and grant opportunities and created spreadsheets for every client. It was an exhaustive amount of research and writing that included well over 500 grant submissions and more development letters than I can even begin to count. When another grant writer was hired years later, he told the owner, "Do you even realize what she has done for you?! No one does this kind of research! No one!" But it didn't matter. I was working for a user. He played multiple games with paychecks and clients and the lies began to accumulate.

The clients were, for the most part, incredible men and women of faith, trying to acquire resources to do God's will. They were good people trying to do good things. The good that had drawn me to the job was that I could use my gifts to advance God's Kingdom. There was something honorable and sacrificial in this ideal. But the owner of the firm was not even up to Pharisee standards. At least they knew some Scripture. This man just knew people with money. He bragged about his secret sauce that was really just a hefty rolodex. *You are like whitewashed tombs, which look beautiful on the outside but on the inside are full of the bones of the dead and everything unclean. In the same way, on the outside you appear to people as righteous but on the inside you are full of hypocrisy and wickedness.*[30] I realized philanthropy was more like politics than church. It didn't matter that these religious nonprofits knew God, they needed to know people with money. That is the ugly truth. It is proximity and power, elbow rubbing and massaged egos that move the mechanisms of mission work, not what the mission is.

---

[29] Proverbs 26:4
[30] Matthew 23:27-28

21

What Happened to Men?

Fear not, for you will not be ashamed; be not confounded, for you will not be disgraced;
for you will forget the shame of your youth,
and the reproach of your widowhood you will remember no more.
For your Maker is your husband, the Lord of hosts is his name;
and the Holy One of Israel is your Redeemer, the God of the whole earth he is called.
For the Lord has called you like a wife deserted and grieved in spirit,
like a wife of youth when she is cast off, says your God.
For a brief moment I deserted you, but with great compassion I will gather you.
In overflowing anger for a moment I hid my face from you,
but with everlasting love I will have compassion on you, says the Lord, your Redeemer.
— Isaiah 54:4-8

I was CLUELESS about dating after divorce. In time I would learn just how ugly the game was. Although the vast majority of men were just as heartless as boys had been in college, I would find they were soulless too. I wanted to find a man who loved God like I did and didn't see that as a limitation to life. Jesus was a hard sell to a population who wanted to do whatever they wished to whomever they wished. Men "just wanted to have fun." I heard this over and over, literally. Fun had a very specific meaning - sex with a lot of different people with no commitment and an "anything goes" attitude. It appeared that men had reverted back to pubescence but with a penchant for porn. They called it freedom. If you didn't want to be treated like a toy, like a plaything, there was no availability. The message to women was very clear. Be like us. Give us what we want, or we won't give you the time of day. But I didn't want to be like a man. I didn't want to use people for pleasure and feel no remorse. I didn't want to be shallow. I didn't want to value net worth over character or ease and pleasure over love. Most of the time, women sadly lowered their standards to the point that they would allow almost anything just to not be alone. Men knew this. Responsibility, decency, kindness, and chivalry were no longer required and not even expected. They thought they had recaptured immortality but had actually lost any sense of morality. They all wanted to be ramblin' men. As one said to me after some appalling behavior, "I'm just being me." And "me" only had to think about "me".

Freedom meant there was no one and nothing else to consider. Men sought freedom, power, and glory and were glorified for it. Women sought love and were told they were stupid for it. How that must break LOVE's heart. Clearly someone else has men's ear. Any ideas who that might be? Apparently, the values we were all taught in kindergarten were just for those with two XX chromosomes. Somehow, someone had excused an entire gender from practicing decency, virtue, or even compassion. As if society was taking orders, it has condoned a world where boys never have to grow up and live for anyone but themselves, and each woman is expected to only live for the benefit of everyone except herself while also doing everything men are expected to do and be deprived of the only thing they truly want. So they despair. I will never understand why society keeps telling women to choose better instead of demanding men be better. After all, it's difficult to choose something that is almost extinct. I wish that was hyperbole.

Over the next fourteen years I would vacillate between clinging to hope that one day there would be someone perfect, just for me, no settling required, someone who returned the love I gave, or the overwhelming loneliness and fear that I would always be alone, that my son's autism would turn away anyone halfway decent. As the years passed, it became harder and harder to hope. I felt the years drain my youth. Reality left little room for dreaming of better days when every day there were fewer of them. The diminishing ratios of probability mocked me. Too many times I would come home after another discouraging date and the memory of the Big Jock telling me no one would ever want me would replay over and over in my mind.

There are far too many horror stories to tell, but this is a good one with a happy ending. A burly, drunk man started hitting on me while I sat at the bar after another forgettable first date. This drunk was the kind of guy you would politely acknowledge and try to ignore. He slurred a bit as he tried to flirt and asked how my date had gone. By this point I had developed some strategies and a sense of humor about how to handle situations like this. I decided Jesus was just the thing to turn him away. I started a conversation about God, and, to my great annoyance, he engaged in the banter. I honestly don't remember what I said. At some point he lamented over a big gulp of whiskey that he was too far away from God to come back. I asked him, "What did the father do when he saw his prodigal son coming home from a long way off?" The drunk man stared into his whiskey and responded to his reflection in the murky spirit he held in his hand. "He ran to him and embraced him." I said nothing since he had said it all. Then something eerie or supernatural happened. The piano man, who had been casually singing songs, called out like a dastardly devil, battling for a soul. "Sinners have more fun than saints!" boomed through the microphone and the speakers. Everyone was startled at the outburst. But the drunk man looked up in shock. He looked at me and then at the piano man. "Did that just happen?" he asked me in astonishment. He looked back at his drink and pushed it away. The angel had won. In that one moment sobriety and forgiveness took hold. Peace washed over his face and his eyes softened. "Thank you. I needed to hear that." I just shook my head in wonder. Good grief. 'Jesus? You're here too, aren't You? You really do love us sinners.'

But for the most part, fun won in the dating world. Freedom to treat people anyway they wanted was what men wanted most. Most of the men I met would ask me this series of questions. I literally can't even begin to put a number on how many people, men, women, and total strangers who never pause to think before they speak. Manners truly are a dying art.

Them: Do you have any kids?
Me: Yes.
Them: So, how many kids do you have?
Me: Five.
Them: Are they ALL from the same father??
Me: (Silently, inside my heart… ????? And then out loud but meekly) Yes.
Them: That's a lot of kids. You don't look like you've had five kids. Why did you have so many?

Me: It's a long story. There was a lot going on. (Their questioning made me feel wrong and shameful just for the number of children I had.)

Them: Do you not believe in birth control? Are you Catholic?

Me: I actually like children, especially mine.

In time I named it the 'Are you a slut or just stupid?' questionnaire. It took me years to be able to answer their impolite curiosity. I realized they were asking for information that would give them permission to judge me. If I answered one way, then I deserved what I was dealing with. If I answered another, I got pity which I also didn't want. 'What is wrong with people?' is the question I wanted to ask.' Many times I would fantasize of having the gumption to sarcastically reply, 'All five are from seven different men,' and leave them to ponder the mathematical ratio between my sarcasm and their rudeness. One friend told me I should have answered every single time, "NONE OF YOUR F..KING BUSINESS!" Right. True. But I didn't have any desire to be as crude as the captious who thought it was their right to judge. That was their heart. I had enough to carry and didn't see the advantages of having a combative, defensive spirit when I was such a mess. I couldn't help that I lived in a glass house, but I was wise enough to not throw anything. Anything at all. I had always hoped that by treating people the way I wanted to be treated, it would eventually cause reciprocation. From my perspective, it was a failed theory, but one I was still determined to follow. Of course, only God knows the mathematical probability of reciprocity. Houston would tell me later, "Jesus told me proving theories is proving what life is. I'm used to forging theories. The formula that I have proven is that the power to give is greater than the power to take." And without knowing that truth, just because Jesus said to, I gave all that was in me and kept hoping to see God's goodness in the land of the living.

The only other statement I hated as much as the one above is when people would say flippantly, "You're strong. You'll be fine." I wanted to scream, "NO I WON'T! I'M NOT OKAY! I NEED HELP! I'M DYING! I DON'T KNOW HOW MUCH LONGER I CAN SURVIVE!" It was their way of not giving a shit and thanking God it wasn't happening to them. It's kind of like someone in a lifeboat looking at someone who is still breathing, floating along in the water after the Titanic sunk and saying, "You're strong. You'll be fine." Translation - you're still alive so nothing, not even empathy is required of me. Cheers! Happy sailing!

I wish I had a way to do a brief but important public service announcement to help out all the people who still haven't learned how to consider others. Here it is.

Let me teach all the self-absorbed (sorry), empathy challenged people out there who say things like this. We're going to walk through this step by step like a lesson from Schoolhouse Rock. (I'm taking applications for theme songs by the way.) You should have learned it in kindergarten, but here goes…

Imagine the weight was on you. Can you feel it? How long can you carry it? How many nights or years can you go? How long can you carry Mount Everest while you're surrounded by people carrying a pencil who tell you, "You'll be fine." How many times will you watch people pass by on the other side of the road, so they don't have to be bothered and still retain your hope? What do you want someone to say to you? Is it "You're strong. You'll be fine."? I'm guessing not. The better statement is -- wait for it --"You're strong to have gone on this long. I don't know if I could have done what you have done. How are you right now, really?" Then stop talking and actually LISTEN to what they say. That means you don't let your mind wander, but you actually retain what they say and allow yourself to feel it. They will probably make a joke or a vague statement that isn't remotely close to how they actually feel because society has taught them people don't want to hear their sad stories. Possibly, they may wipe a tear away quickly because you sound like you might care and the flood waters of emotions are always right under the surface. If they do any of these things, say to them, "Is there more you don't feel like you can share but you need to?" No matter if they take you up on your offer to listen or not, the next step is to stay connected to them. Call them. Visit them. Bring them a bottle of wine or maybe tequila if necessary. Send them something to make them laugh. Include them. Don't stop. Stay connected to them. Don't make that their responsibility. The burden on them doesn't vanish because you were friendly once. Treat them like you would want to be treated if you were in their shoes. This is not rocket science and it is not difficult. It is simply LOVE. It takes time. It takes thought. It takes effort. It is what God requires of us. He never said accomplish, earn, prove you're the best. He said love and believe.

If I speak in the tongues of men or of angels,
but have not love, I am a noisy gong or a clanging cymbal.
And if I have prophetic powers,
and understand all mysteries and all knowledge,
and if I have faith, so as to remove mountains,
but have not love, I am nothing.
If I give away all I have,
and if I deliver up my body to be burned,
but have not love, I gain nothing…
So now faith, hope, and love abide, these three;
but the greatest of these is love.[31]

"Teacher, which is the great commandment in the Law?"
And He said to him,
"You shall love the Lord your God with all your heart
and with all your soul and with all your mind.
This is the great and first commandment.
And a second is like it:
You shall love your neighbor as yourself."[32]

---

[31] 1 Corinthians 13:1-3,13
[32] Matthew 22:36-39

22

Down in the Valley

This is the valley that I'm walking through
And it feels like forever since I've been close to You
My friends up above me don't understand why I struggle like I do
The shadow's my only, only companion and at night he leaves too
Down in the valley, dying of thirst
Now down in the valley, it seems that I'm at my worst
My consolation is that You baptize this earth
I'm down in the valley, valleys fill first...
It's like that long Saturday between Your death and the rising day
When no one wrote a word, And wondered is this the end?
But You were down there in the well, saving those that fell
Bringing them to the mountain again [33]

To avoid going into another extraordinary set of circumstances, I want to sum up a side story. My good friend who was also separated from an abusive alcoholic decided to send her very gifted and athletic son to school where he had the best opportunity to play and get a scholarship. This school became an incredible blessing for her son, and I was there with her for every pondering and prayer. She became invested in this school and seemed to know everyone. At some point she decided to play matchmaker and introduced me to someone in the school system that she thought I would love.

During those years I had begun running as a way to clear my head and cry in peace. When I couldn't run outside, I would run up and down the stairs outside the apartment for way too long. I lost toenails, and my hips and knees began to grind. Early mornings, late nights, it was a way to escape, to get my lungs to burn so badly I wouldn't care about the other things breaking inside me. We all have our drugs. That was mine. Anyway, because I was fit, she thought I would be a fit for this man. I was his type. He was separated and going through a divorce.

When I got dressed for my blind date, I told my friend I was very apprehensive to meet someone going through a divorce. She ASSURED me. "Oh my gosh! It's SO over! You have nothing to worry about. They can't stand each other." So, I met this man. He was wonderful in ways that most people aren't. We sat at a bar, and I sipped nervously on a beer. Eventually he got around to asking the question. "So, how many kids do you have?" I swallowed and paused before answering, readying myself for his wincing. He leaned toward me before I could answer and whispered, "I already know." I turned toward him surprised, and he was already smiling. "Tell me about them," he said sweetly. I melted. I told him about each precious little human being that held my heart. Then finally I told him about Houston. He told me about working in the special needs

---

[33] *Valleys Fill First;* By Edmund Cash and Aaron Tate. Copyright Cumbee Road Music and Wondrously Made Songs

department and about different kids he loved. My eyes must have been saucers. I thought, 'God, are there really men who aren't intimidated by severe disabilities?' We began to see each other. I remember the first time he got in my car, and I cringed in embarrassment having to explain that the windows had to stay down because of the exhaust that would pour into the car. I couldn't even look at him in the eyes. Parked beside the fuel pump, sitting in the stinking car, he picked up my chin and held it. He told me to look at him. It took me a moment. When I picked my eyes up off the floorboard, he looked in my eyes and told me he didn't give a shit what kind of a car I drove and that all he cared about was what kind of person I was and how I treated people. I didn't know that God still made men who saw people's hearts. As I look back, I think that was the moment I fell. I thought he was the answer to my prayers.

Six months later he met my boss at the company Christmas party. He was agitated and I didn't understand. When we left, he angrily asked in the parking lot, "How can you be you and work for that creep?" I was speechless. One of his gifts was he didn't see or look for good in people that wasn't there. He saw black. He saw white. He saw truth, or he saw a liar. Sometimes he kept his mouth shut about liars he worked with, but he always knew what they were. He told me he knew because he had demons too. I knew he did, but I overlooked them. I was forever handing out grace because God told me to or because that was how to survive. Did I even know the difference?

The rent at my apartment continued to rise to the point that I could no longer pay. The minivan couldn't pass the emissions test without an $850 repair. One of the families who were so kind to us paid for the repair so I could drive. That is how we lived for years, one emergency to the next, never able to take a breath or get ahead, filled with shame because we were always in need. I found a townhome in the same school district at a reasonable rent with a wonderful landlord. Shortly after I moved in, I got a call from the woman who directed the special needs class at church. She told me someone had given me a minivan and wouldn't tell me who. I kept guessing and she kept giggling. Nope. It might as well have been Jesus Himself. I never found out and I have never stopped being in awe and full of overflowing love and gratitude for whoever God used to bless me. I needed every blessing I could get. You see, that's real love, real generosity. It gives without rules, without measures, without expectation of praise for the giver or improvement from the receiver. It operates under the foolish idea that everything on the earth is the Lord's, and the gift is really from Him.

Reagan's problems began to snowball. She failed seventh grade and started cyberbullying a girl that was being mean to her. She was not going to let people be mean and get away with it. She would be mean right back. She didn't like my way of handling life and we butted heads. It all happened fast and furiously. I found out she was telling friends at school she had leukemia to get attention. She was furious when I tried to talk to her about it. A wall had risen, and she wouldn't let me near. I had no idea what to do so I talked to counselors and friends. The bottom line, when it was said and done, was that I decided to have her do online school and make up the work for both seventh and eighth grade in one year so she could stay on track. That was a mistake. One of my most horrible, awful mistakes. I had no idea what course of events that decision would set into play. All I can do is continue to wait for God to make all things new, to turn mourning into dancing and make beauty from ashes. He is the good gift giver, so I wait for Him.

That year, my sweet little girl got heavily involved in dangerous relationships that I knew nothing about. She spent the night at a friend's house and became involved with a 19-year-old, the friend of her friend's older brother. She was 13. I had no idea. I tried to let her see her friends as much as possible since she wasn't at school and little did I know, I was helping orchestrate the affair. The brooding hatred and cutting began to get worse. She watched disturbing videos online when she was supposed to be doing online school. The daily management of her schoolwork became an exhausting battle. Five hundred miles away, her father goaded her rebellion. I can still hear his laugh, his sick pleasure from her every defiant act. Any other father would have stepped in to enforce boundaries and protect his daughter from the wayward precipice of pubescence.

In another twist of fate, Reagan could not reenter school because of a technicality with the online schools. Being an administrator, my boyfriend helped get her enrolled in one of his schools forty-five minutes away. Reagan was so angry at me for putting her in another school. I did all I possibly could to make that year a blessing for her. I drove the forty-five-minute drive twice a day and worked off my laptop in a McDonald's playground writing grants. No matter what I tried, I couldn't reach Reagan. She loathed me. One night the police called to let me know they had found her behind an abandoned strip mall down the street with the now twenty-year-old. I learned how not far at all the law actually goes. Another day we called the police because Morgan's good friend across the street had seen Reagan get into a strange car. We were able to track her down and the police had another conversation with the twenty-year-old. And so, the year went on, one awful day after another. Eventually, Reagan started to love her new school, and I started to breathe easier. Maybe everything would be ok.

The Big Jock had not come close to keeping the ridiculously lenient agreement we had entered into three years previous. Every month I begged him to pay, and he offered excuses or insults. He had met someone new, gotten married, and had a baby in Florida. The kids were not invited to the wedding, which I thought was strange. I assumed it must have been a small, private affair. As for the kids, I wasn't sure if that was a good or bad thing. He told me he had a new family and that was his responsibility. After I filed taxes and received my refund, I used it to hire an attorney. I had him served w8.5

hen he dropped the kids off after spring break. He stormed into my townhome ready to kill me. Raging profanity and threats… I stood frozen, still afraid to move. The man who served him had been hired to protect me as well, but he literally ran to his car as the Big Jock's temper exploded in front of him. I didn't know what was going to happen. He decided the way to pay me back was to threaten my new relationship, my boyfriend's job, and his daughter's wellbeing. The end result was I had to withdraw Reagan from her new school right when she began to connect and thrive. So, she hated me again.

As for the man whom I loved, the drama of the entire fiasco ended our relationship for good. I will spare myself and the reader the anguished details of my heart breaking every day, but it was bad. I would have to remind myself to take a breath. Each one pierced. Short, shallow breaths were best. Deep breaths ignited those stupid salty tears that wouldn't stop. My friend who gave me the necklace told me, "Okay, this is bad. It's okay if you have a pity party but make it a short one. And keep that beautiful chin up." I nodded. She couldn't see I had started crying again.

The grant writing job went on for four years as all of this was going on. Two of my coworkers that I adored began to get frustrated with the enormous workload and the deceit of the owner. His lies were growing. We were Christians so we didn't talk about it. There were just looks. We knew it. We felt it. There was a unified discord of disgust. Lines of integrity vibrated within each of us. Conflicts with the owner were impossible to avoid. When they quit, I cried. I knew the end was near. They both had husbands to support them. I had no one, nothing, and was in the middle of a war. I knew he would direct all his energy on me. What would I do then? How would I take care of my kids? How would I take care of Houston?

He hired a replacement for one of my friends. A few weeks later he asked me to meet him at Starbucks. I got there early and was working on a new grant. When he arrived, I saw he had brought the new employee. In brief, he told me I had to submit to him. I told him I needed to be treated like a professional and paid for the work I did. He threw a piece of paper in my face and lunged forward trying to rip the computer out of my hands, seething, "IT'S MINE!!!" I sobbed and begged him to no avail to let me get my things off the computer. Everything, my whole life was on that computer. Every picture since pictures had become digital, every file and document I had created for court, every song I had downloaded, every beautiful thing I had written for God and His kingdom. It still sickens me when I think of all that was lost on that computer that I will never see again. With one final violent yank, he ripped it from my grip. He told me I would get my things back after I signed the non-compete he had thrown in my face. The new employee said in a completely calm voice, "Oh Katie. This is just business. Just sign the paper." She looked at me and then, as an afterthought, smiled awkwardly. I glared at her like you look at someone with no soul. "You call yourself a Christian? This is not what Christians do." With empty hands I walked to my car and sobbed hysterically. My former co-workers were in shock and could do nothing. "Trust God to right this wrong." That's what they told me. One even asked me, "Why don't you just sign the paper and get your things back?"

The next day my used refrigerator I had bought when we moved in died. I had no job, no computer, no refrigerator, no money. We used a cooler and bought ice and basic necessities. A neighbor that Reagan babysat for asked friends from their church to use their tithes to buy us a small basic refrigerator from Lowe's. I thanked God and thanked them and cried. I was so tired of crying. So tired of being in need. So tired of assholes. So tired of teenage rebellion. So tired of autism. So tired of being abandoned and alone. So tired of being poor and needy. So weary of praying for help and miracles and for God to stop the people who won by doing wicked and wrong. The good gifts that came in the midst of all of this were flickers of light that darkness engulfed at the first spark. Light and hope had no place here. My prayers seemed like screaming in space, snuffed out before there was ever a sound. Darkness pressed down.

Rescue me
I am drowning in doubt, I cannot see you
This water's deep
I've been treading too long, And now I'm sinking
Will you let me see if you are there? Will you let me see if you are there?
Comfort me
This fear is dragging me down
Deep in the darkness, Frigid sea
My whole heart has gone cold, I know I'm dying
Will you let me see if you are there? Will you let me see if you are there? [34]

And the silence, especially the vastness of it, swallowed me whole…

It was as if I was covered. I couldn't see Him. He couldn't hear me. I couldn't read God's Word because it was promises meant for everyone else. I couldn't read God's Word because it made me cry. I couldn't sing praises. I couldn't worship. God's goodness was for others. I was loving someone who had left me. I had loved. I still loved. My love felt unrequited. The silence of heaven broke my heart. I just wanted to be loved. Why Lord? Why do you hate me so? You treat Your enemies better than Your children. You let those who hate You destroy those who love You. Being in the company of Psalmists was no comfort at all. I needed Him to show up, not in the next life, but now, in the land of the living. In the silence there was only one thing I could do. I could not deny Him. I knew He was God. I kept going, with the weight of the world on my heart.

---

[34] *Rescue Me*; The Brilliance © Used with Permission

I've tried to stand my ground
I've tried to understand
But I can't seem to find
My faith again
Like water on the sand
Or grasping at the wind
I keep on falling short.
So please be my strength
Please be my strength
I don't have any more
I don't have any more
I'm looking for a place
Where I can plant my faith
One thing I know for sure
I cannot create it
And I cannot sustain it
It's your love
That's keeping me
Please be my strength
Please be my strength
I don't have any more
I don't have any more [35]

In the emptiness and pain of my ever-present grief, life never slowed down, my children never stopped living their own stories. That year and the year before I had reluctantly paid for Morgan to get classical singing lessons, afraid it was a fad I couldn't afford. At first the lessons were every other week, then every week, then a whole hour instead of just half a lesson. I thought it was one of those things she would eventually lose interest in, like horses, but it wasn't. She committed to singing, painting, and becoming fluent in French. Over those years, as my oldest went through the process of discovering her many, many gifts, she wrestled with her own insecurities. The wealth around us had made her feel secluded and the isolation necessary because of autism exasperated it. Some of the kids she knew had laughed at the tiny, outdated homes on our street when they dropped her off at home. There were other moments too that made our financial struggle something shameful she internalized. In an effort to feel like everyone else, she shoplifted trinkets to give as gifts and other items to feel like she had what others had. The backlash from it was devastating. I couldn't understand how she could let herself be tempted to steal, even if I understood how she wanted so much to fit in. It broke my heart. In the midst of it all her heart was broken by frenemies and then by boys. Like most mothers, I wondered if I was doing enough, or the right things, or maybe I was doing it all wrong. My dad would remind me they needed a father figure and that was the problem. I saw their father figure AS the problem.

To make Morgan's heart break even more, her father would give elaborate and extortionate gifts to Reagan - expensive guitars, soundboards, phones, tablets. My dad's wife once asked me when I told her about the gifts that he only got Reagan, "I don't want to upset you, but do you think the Big Jock ever molested Reagan?" I was shocked at the question. She explained that gift giving was one of the signs, especially when it coincided with other very risky behaviors with men so much older than herself. I shook

[35] *Please Be My Strength;* By Michael Gungor. Copyright Capitol Cmg Genesis o/b/o Worshiptogether.Com Songs

my head, more at the horror of the idea than with any certainty in my answer. She was wise. I knew that about her, and her question scared me. She went over a few things that were red flags - the gifts, the early promiscuity, the defiance, the ridiculous lies. By this time the Big Jock only saw them three times a year. I had thought the gift giving was to ingratiate Reagan to him and spur her rebellion to me. Anything else made me... the unknown of what if... I guess I can only describe my reaction to such a thought as what it must feel like to have your soul sucked out of you.

Morgan had started driving the old minivan to work at a local pizzeria to earn money. She was trying so hard to be grown up. When the minivan needed repairs, she called the Big Jock and asked if he would help her. She knew I didn't have the money. He told her "You're not getting another dime from me. My priorities are different now." Morgan sobbed and sobbed. How could he do that? How could he say that? I didn't understand. I don't know how I did it, but I got the car repaired. Then while delivering a pizza, she rear-ended another car and just like that, it was totaled. The hits kept coming.

23

Leaving and the Lost Art of Love

Beloved, let us love one another, for love is from God,
and whoever loves has been born of God and knows God.
Anyone who does not love does not know God, because God is love.
In this the love of God was made manifest among us,
that God sent his only Son into the world, so that we might live through him.
In this is love, not that we have loved God but that he loved us
and sent his Son to be the propitiation for our sins.
Beloved, if God so loved us, we also ought to love one another.
No one has ever seen God; if we love one another,
God abides in us and his love is perfected in us.
— 1 John: 7-12

Houston began going through puberty. For any teenage boy, this is a challenge. For a teenage boy trapped in a body he can't control, with no voice and no outlet, the onslaught of hormones ignites a chaotic typhoon of physical and emotional outbursts which he had no way of controlling. The self-injurious hand biting grew worse and there were new behaviors that required constant intervention to prevent them from becoming a new loop. Even though he would get naked when he shouldn't, he couldn't undress when he should. I would repeat simple instructions over and over and he would just stare at me as if he was in a trance, sticking his belly out, chin jutting out, and his hands resting on top of his belly. Even something as simple as getting in the car was a nonstop litany of repeating every single instruction. "Houston, get in the car." He would stare at me, paralyzed. "Houston, open the door. Houston, open the door. OPEN the door. Get in the car. Get in the car. Get in the car. Close the door. Close the door. Close the door."

The fatigue of repeating myself with no results, no improvement wore me down. I felt myself getting weaker, wearier, if that was even possible. I wanted him to learn daily skills. It was in every IEP (Individualized Education Program that is written and modified each year). But most of the time he was unresponsive to my instruction. The water in the shower made him go into a trance. He would spin his circles over and over like I wasn't even there. I felt like I was talking to myself. He had such low tonicity in his upper body and especially in his hands, I wasn't sure if he was even capable of pressing hard enough to clean himself. So even though I was supposed to be teaching him to take care of his body, I did it for him. What that means is that I have brushed his teeth, bathed his body, washed his hair, and cleaned every loose bowel which never has stopped being loose for long over 20 years. For those doing the math, that's well over 9000 times for each task from a very conservative estimate, which is a minimum of 36,500 acts of intensive physical caretaking. You can increase that number by a minimum of twenty percent, which is 43,800 acts, because of Houston's bowel movements, feces smearing, bed wetting, puberty, and chewing of clothes. There were also fingernails and toenails. Then he grew facial hair and eventually developed into a 250-pound man that needed everything done for him, every day. There were three to five loads of laundry to do daily and meals needing to be served/cooked/provided while I worked two to three jobs, raised, and loved my other children who resented helping with housework and meals like most kids do, and I had no money for anything. Remember — the judge didn't think I had a job…

There were some bright spots too. I would cling to those. Everyday Houston's teachers would send home a sheet with notes about how the day went. One particular day he walked in, went straight to the trash can, opened his bag, took out the papers, and quickly pushed them to the bottom of the trash can. His siblings had tried this trick with bad grades, and I recognized it immediately. I pulled the papers from the bottom of the trash and laughed out loud. It was a long paragraph about how out of control he had been that day. I called his teacher and told her he had promptly disposed of the evidence. It was funny but clearly there was more awareness of what he couldn't control than I realized. Another day he had written in the smallest and neatest handwriting on the wall near the computer, "Paul Potts." Paul Potts was a simple, humble British mobile phone salesman who had shocked the world by singing "Nessun Dorma" in a way you could feel in your soul. I had no explanation. This one stumped me. Had Houston seen Paul Potts and been inspired?

On one of the few trips to see the Big Jock I got a phone call from him telling me he was bringing them home early. Houston kept saying, "Mama Mama Home Home Home" so much that the Big Jock couldn't take it and brought all the kids home. I was stunned. He didn't speak except for verbal stims and echolalia. Although I hadn't heard it, I was in awe. Did he miss me? When they got home, he ran right past me up to his room to get on the computer. 'Well, he said my name even though I didn't get to hear it,' I thought. 'That's something.' Another day we were in the car and suddenly he picked up my hand and held his hand up to my lips for me to kiss him. I kissed his sweet scar covered hand and felt this surge of incredible love. For a moment, autism had lost its grip. Houston looked at me for the briefest of moments. My love. My son.

Benjamin and Paul had started wrestling. Finally, we had found a sport they could excel in. At night we would go to practice and Reagan or Morgan would watch Houston. I loved watching them wrestle. Their coach asked if I would become a trainer at his gym when he heard about my job loss. Unsure of what else to do and never wanting to write another grant again, I agreed. I started seeing clients at 5:30 a.m. every weekday, and Saturdays were wrestling tournaments. On Sundays I would sit in the bookstore at church. All the loss had begun to take a deep toll on my heart. The more I struggled, the more I felt the distance grow between me and God. It felt like He had turned His back and forsaken me as I was clinging to His hem begging Him not to abandon me.

I fought for every penny to feed my kids. I signed up for programs to help me with gifts at Christmas even though I had lost all interest in the holiday. I just did it for them. Slowly, it happened again. My heart almost seemed to pump purely to get me to the next breath. I knew God was real, but did He love me? I began to doubt His love. I saw Him bless those who destroyed me. I saw Him answer prayers all around me, but never mine. I saw others thrive while I withered. I saw others supported and loved and encouraged while I was very, very much alone. God might be good, but He wasn't good to me. I had proof. My heart broke. No, it crumbled. It was dust. All I could do was keep going. But I was so very tired. Actually, tired doesn't even touch it. Wearied is worn down but can keep going. Exhausted needs to catch its breath. Fatigued is the beginning of explaining it, the numbness, the loss of hope, the wondering where God is and why He doesn't answer, the heartbreak and loneliness of realizing the cavalry will never come. Seeing the long, joyless struggle laid out before me, life became something I just didn't want to do anymore. How much longer, God? Even You rested. Does it really need to be this hard, this heartbreaking, this lonely for so so long?

Around this time, I was asked to participate in a show that highlighted families dealing with long-term challenges. The idea was to create relationships with people in the surrounding communities who could help. When I shared the short version of my story in front of a room of strangers, they were all crying. I remember thinking to myself, "Why are you crying? That's not the half of it." They were trying to think of some way to help me, and the producer got frustrated. "Katie, most of the families are struggling because there is something they aren't doing right. But you're doing all the right things. It's just not enough. This is too much. Too much for anyone." She threw her hands up. One afternoon, a producer volunteered to watch Houston while I took Morgan to a Bible study at church. I got a call on the way back from a police officer telling me to come home immediately. This is what had happened. While I was dropping Morgan off at church Houston had gotten into the ranch dressing and spread it all over the kitchen, like ranch finger paint. The producer was so excited and ran to get her camera to film the mess. She left the door unlocked, and while she was filming the kitchen counter he ran. He broke into someone's home and found their Disney stuffed animals. The residents were furious and called the police. The police had tried to take them from him, and he had violently started biting himself. The police officer took me into my boys' room where stuffed animals covered Houston's bunk. "Ma'am, I need you to identify the animals that aren't his." I looked at the officer whose hands were on his hips next to his gun with his bullet proof vest massively bulking out, and I almost busted out in laughter PLUS tears. "So, I'm doing a stuffed animal line up?" I asked. "Yes ma'am." He was serious.

Identification was easy. All the ones that looked unused were definitely not Houston's. The producer apologized profusely. "Katie, it was like one second and he was gone. How do you do this? How have you kept doing this for this long?" Wasn't the answer obvious? I didn't have a choice. There is no choice when you love. Later, since the production team hadn't been able to help me like they wanted, she said to me, "Why don't you just do something you'll enjoy for a job? Start a company or just do something you like." I stared at her like she had just suggested I sprout wings and fly instead of drive a car to get from here to there. "How?... How would I make enough to pay for them and take care of Houston?" I shook my head in disbelief at the very idea. "I don't know. I just know you are going through so much and you need to figure out how to be happy." Right, happiness... That old thing. Her suggestion was like a cruel hot poker to my heart. Happiness - What a joke.

The biblical lessons I had been taught stressed that seeking happiness was seeking an illusion. Seeking God was the only right thing to chase. All else was foolish grasping for the wind. I had been chasing God, chasing to the point that I, breathless and frightened, stopped to see if I was the only one in this game. The joy that was promised from serving Him, seeking Him, resting in Him... it wasn't there. Was He? Have You left me, God? Silently I listened. My prayers were quiet just waiting to hear Him. I kept waiting. Laughter mocked me. Loneliness shrouded my heart. Silence. I was not to have joy. For whatever His purpose, I was to have affliction, delivered daily. Everyone had a quote to justify the suffering and why, as a sinner, I deserved nothing else or whatever else they could come up with because they actually didn't have an answer at all. It never occurred to any of them to just keep their mouth shut and give me a hug and let me cry while they poured me a drink. When I would hear the religious platitudes, I began to have a horrible visceral reaction. I was like Houston with my fingers pierced to my eardrums to shut out all the crazy religious jargon from people who didn't understand suffering that doesn't stop. Their religion and their desire to make sure I practiced it appropriately to their standards repelled me.

---

[36] John 13:35
[37] 1 Corinthians 8:1

PLEASE! PLEASE PEOPLE! I AM BEGGING YOU! You do so much damage and wonder self-righteously why those people don't come to church anymore. He said the world would know we are Christians by our love, not by our knowledge. *By this the world will you know you are My disciples, if you love one another.*[36] *We know that we all possess knowledge. But knowledge puffs up while love builds up.*[37] Don't tell hurting people they shouldn't want happiness, when your easy life is quite delightful and absent of suffering. Don't tell them that suffering is how God brings us closer to Himself when they feel His absence and His unanswered prayers. Don't tell people with tragic, long enduring suffering that everyone suffers and minimize their pain. Don't tell barren or abandoned women that Jesus is enough when you and your intact family of six just vacationed at your lake house for the summer. Don't tell people who are afraid they are going to be evicted or don't know how to feed their children that God helps those who help themselves when you have been a stay-at-home wife and mother for thirty years. Don't tell those who are abused to turn the other cheek when you've always been safe and don't know what it's like to live afraid every day. Don't tell someone who has never been loved that God's will is perfect and to be content with or without. Don't tell someone whose child is severely disabled ANYTHING AT ALL. NOTHING. No, not that one thing. No, not that either. NOTHING. If you haven't lived it, keep your mouth shut. And please don't compare your small inconvenient obstacles with people who live daily just trying to survive. These are not opportunities to quote scripture or your favorite theologian. These are not people for you to pity. These are human beings that God loves. And that's exactly what He expects you to do to them. Love them. These are opportunities to wash someone's feet. To give. To listen. To be there. To make a casserole. To love. But please keep your mouth shut unless you can make us laugh or help carry the load.

And in the absence of love, I felt the absence of God. So, I left church. I just couldn't keep chasing someone who didn't care to help when He could have. I put my Bible in a drawer with all the flowers from the gardens I had lost still pressed between its pages. It held pages and pages of verses I had researched and prayers I had prayed. Everything lost. Everything unanswered. I couldn't pray anymore. It hurt too much. I couldn't sing. My heart was too heavy to lift my voice. I couldn't even listen to a song of praise without feeling the weight of His abandonment. I decided I would seek things that made me happy, if I could ever figure out what they were.

> And in the streets the children screamed
> The lovers cried, and the poets dreamed
> But not a word was spoken - The church bells all were broken
> And the three men I admire most
> The Father, Son and the Holy Ghost
> They caught the last train for the coast
> The day the music died...[38]

24

Despised

You have removed my acquaintances far from me;
You have made me an object of loathing to them;
I am shut up and cannot go out.
— Psalm 88:8

For wicked and deceitful mouths are opened against me, speaking against me with lying tongues. They encircle
me with words of hate, and attack me without cause.
In return for my love they accuse me, but I give myself to prayer.
So they reward me evil for good, and hatred for my love.
— Psalm 109:2-5

Morgan had gotten a job at another pizzeria and asked me to work there. I felt like a failure. I was 38, working three jobs to survive, serving pizza with teenagers to put food on the table for five kids. My ex was vacationing in Hawaii. It was humbling in a crumbling kind of way to see people I knew from my former life and take their pizza orders. I resented their questions but tried to smile anyway. Over time I learned to accept it - the downgrade. I learned I could love people here too. So I became a mom of sorts to some pothead teenagers and old grumpy regulars who came in for Trivia Night. I would bring my boys when they needed to go to practice and one of the delivery boys would deliver my boys to practice. I would run to pick them up on a break, and they would sit at the bar drinking free coke and eating discounted pizza slices. The funny thing is they thought I had the greatest job in the world. We would go there in our free time because we could eat at a discount. It became a home, and the pothead teenagers became family. I actually liked them a lot more than all the nice people at church.

Before Reagan started back at our local school, I had a young college age friend that I was training take her shopping to help her pick out new clothes so she would feel beautiful and cool. I did all I could to help her find ways to reconnect and build healthy friendships. I have no idea how or why, but she became almost immediately attached to someone with chips on both shoulders and a moody, brooding, threatening countenance. He would give her black roses and morose music was the soundtrack to her life. I don't think I ever saw him smile. When I would try to correct bad attitudes by taking her phone, she would find every way around it. It was exhausting trying to enforce any discipline at all. When I took the boys to practice, I discovered she was sneaking her boyfriend over when she was supposed to be watching Houston. I went to talk to the parents to let them know what was going on and to get their help. They told me I had done the right thing. Their son came in while I was talking to them and charged toward me with rage on his face. The dad shouted for him to leave. The mother told me they had been struggling with their son and that he had anger problems. But then she told me that Reagan had told their son that she didn't have to worry about getting pregnant because I had forced her to have a hysterectomy. "What?? She said I did WHAT?? That doesn't even make sense. Who would do that? Who would say that? Why wouldn't you ask to verify such a ridiculous story?" The mother apologized for not talking to me and asking me. She said she knew her son wouldn't stop seeing my daughter and they couldn't control him. I knew I had no control either. Reagan was determined to say and do whatever she wanted. I was horrified, incredulous, angry, scared, and embarrassed by my daughter's lies. God, what else has she said? What else has she done? The parents thanked me for coming to see them and agreed to help their son take Reagan on real dates and not hide in his room with her. I took Reagan to the doctor the next day. The doctor, the nurse, and then I had long talks with her about using the pill and being responsible. She was determined to do adult things with the militancy of a delinquent teen.

Half a year later, despite trying to encourage a healthy dating environment between them, my heart sank as I read hateful texts about me from her boyfriend on my daughter's phone. Once again, I contacted his parents to ask for their help and to talk to them openly and respectfully. I explained that this type of malice toward me was hurting my relationship with my daughter and that I was trying to be supportive of their relationship, but this hatefulness could not continue. We met outside a Starbucks near my home and had a cooperative and helpful conversation. They apologized and the mother told me that she was a person of faith and that his behavior was not acceptable. She would do everything she could.

Houston turned 16. My heart was heavy. Time was passing and I saw all the moments lost. I decided to take him to Sky Zone, a trampoline park, to celebrate his birthday. There were no visits to the DMV, no harrowing moments teaching him to drive, no friends to invite over, no party to plan, no sneaking a kiss from a girl. I couldn't bear giving the same stupid gifts he got every year - jelly beans, Disney stuffed animals, and VHS cassette tapes that he couldn't even watch but would spread out all over his bed. His bedroom was a memorial to the entire cast of characters that Disney had ever created. It was tolerable when he was still a child, but those days were past. What do you do with a grown up that hasn't grown up?

At Sky Zone I sent Reagan out on the trampolines to jump with him because his jumps were so enormous, and he had no ability to control the power of his legs. He made a big loop and jumped in one place for a while. A cute girl came near him and said hi to him flirtatiously. Houston had always been a beautiful boy. Puberty hadn't changed that. As soon as she talked to him his hands flapped wildly and a huge cacophony of noises erupted out of him. The girl turned in horror and jumped away. Reagan kept jumping around with him. They made another loop. I stood by the side watching every single jump, never taking my eye off of him. He jumped in front of me, his strong legs propelling him high into the air. Another woman standing next to me said to the attendant, "Excuse Me! Excuse ME, SIR!" The teenage attendant turned to her. "THAT BOY! THAT ONE. Right there. You need to get him out of here. He's jumping too high. He has no business jumping like that when there are other people around." She pointed at Houston the whole time she spoke. I stepped toward her. "You mean this boy? This one right here?" She looked at me. "Yes!" thinking I was going to agree with her. My face turned like fire. "That's MY son." There was nothing diplomatic in my tone. I had had it with a world that wouldn't let my son be a part of it. "He's severely autistic. Today is his sixteenth birthday. We aren't doing what other sixteen-year-olds get to do. He's not taking his driver's test. He's not having a party or trying to kiss a girl he has a crush on. We don't get to DO anything. So even this, just jumping on a trampoline on his sixteenth birthday, you want to take that away from him too? What does he get to do? What is he allowed to experience in life? WHAT?! This is his birthday. We paid like every other customer. He's not hurting anyone. His sister is jumping beside him to keep him safe. What else do we need to do to make YOU happy?" The attendant grinned. I'm sure he had seen plenty of moms like this one. The woman's face was absolutely blank before she finally mumbled an apology and then uncomfortably added, "He looks like he's enjoying himself." 'No thanks to you,' I thought to myself. My stomach was sour the rest of the day. I really wondered if there were any good people in the world. I wondered if this was it. Were we to be lepers all our lives? Isolation does something strange to hearts.

One strange question I would get all those years about Houston was this, "So is he a savant? Is he like Rain Man?" Certainly with all this hard stuff there had to be a cool factor. Other parents with a severely autistic child understand exactly what I'm talking about. I would get so annoyed by this question. "No, he has the fecal smearing kind of autism. The getting naked all the time autism. The running away autism. The eating everything in sight autism. The repeating Disney phrases until we all want to scream autism. The making awful noises in the middle of the night autism. No, he is not a savant." Angrily I recognized how much the world idolized intelligence. Every time someone asked me this question it was a slap in my face and the mama bear inside me would growl. The world believed you were somehow more valuable if you could do something cool that others couldn't. I looked at all the smart, intelligent assholes around me and thought, intelligence is the last thing the world needs more of. What it really needs is kindness, empathy. If love had ever had its day, it was long past, a dying relic of a virtue replaced by performance and possessions. I developed a habit of responding to the question by asking people why they valued intelligence instead of kindness. Why was that the attribute to acknowledge and honor? My son was the most gentle human being and the only person he ever hurt was himself. Why wasn't his sweet spirit something to be honored and adored? Why didn't they consider my child to be just as valuable as theirs unless he could do something cool? It made me feel even more excluded. I disliked this world more and more. The more I saw higher minds honored for things that I felt were far apart from the teachings of Scripture, the more I saw people only care about what they possessed, what they accomplished, and what they knew all to impress others, the more I didn't want to belong. The world felt like the sorority of my college years. It looked great in the beginning. Inclusion and acceptance seemed like the belonging I had always longed for. But the longer I was there, the more I saw the ugly hearts behind the pretty faces, the empty, vapidness behind their wealth, the arrogance behind their knowledge, and the phony behind everything.

I was numb from all of my life, from all the different fronts I had to fight. I did what I needed to meet everyone's expectations. The gym owner's wife was a cruel, cold woman. She decided I needed to do more for less pay. I didn't say a word. I just cleaned bathrooms and mopped wrestling mats and listened to rich, whiny people cry because they didn't get enough sunshine in the winter months or beat their own chest because everyone was a failure who hadn't accomplished what they had. I kept my secrets to myself and smiled - politely. When the owner saw me change into the pizzeria t-shirt, shorts, and apron before I left for the day, he laughed his big, loud laugh. "You're waiting tables?!?" He laughed like it was the funniest thing he had ever seen, doubled over, and kept laughing. His laughter cut my heart deeply. I guess a grown woman serving pizza really was ridiculous. I already felt ashamed. That didn't help. I left quickly so he didn't see the tears he had triggered. That might have made him laugh harder if that was possible.

Somewhere around this time, I was notified that one of the non-speaking autistics from church who had already aged out of school had died suddenly at his day program. I was heartbroken. I went to the funeral. The father told how the violence and his son's out of control body had affected him and his family. He told of all autism had taken. He spoke of how taking care of his son had nearly destroyed him and how their family had to have round the clock help. He wept openly and couldn't continue speaking. One of the pastors stood and finished reading this father's letter. It wasn't a eulogy. It was the truth. I remember listening to this strong man weep and thinking to myself, 'That family had two parents, one stay at home mom, two neurotypical children, and one severely affected child with autism and they couldn't handle it. They needed 24/7 support. How much greater is the burden and load I'm carrying, God? It's just me. I'm doing the work of ten people while being attacked by my ex. Please God. I'm so tired. Please. Please help me.'

25

The Mustard Seed

He said to them, "Because of your little faith.
For truly, I say to you, if you have faith like a grain of mustard seed,
you will say to this mountain, 'Move from here to there,' and it will move,
and nothing will be impossible for you."
— Matthew 17:20

nother year passed quickly while I struggled to make sure we all survived. At the gym the owner insisted I get certified to teach yoga as well as Pilates, TRX and other certifications. I had no problem taking yoga but was apprehensive that in learning to teach yoga I might be introduced to some aspect of the practice I didn't agree with theologically. I had been taught to be heedful of practices that were spiritual and from other cultures. Even though I felt abandoned, I was still trying to honor God. I could tell most of the people in my class didn't come from a similar background. But they were good people and I loved them.

One day we were taught about beliefs and told to set an intention for our life. Inwardly, I rolled my eyes. I knew about belief. It didn't work. Very quickly I told myself, 'Be brief. Say as little about your life as possible. Keep your cards close to your chest.' I was the last person in the room to share my statement. I gave my vague and indifferent intention, and sarcastically added as an afterthought, "OH, and I would like for bad shit to stop happening." Sometimes the bitterness of my broken heart would expose me. The teacher stopped. "Why would you say that?" Oh crap. Undaunted and still refusing to share how badly my heart was broken I responded. "I know about belief. Beliefs are built on experiences. We believe what we have experienced. And that's what I've experienced, why would I believe anything else?" The teacher replied thoughtfully, "But good has just as much of a chance of happening as bad." I was unconvinced. She continued to challenge my doubt. Eventually she encouraged me to at least be open to good happening in my life. As I began to try to utter the words, "I expect," they got stuck in my throat. I swallowed the words. I couldn't say it. There was too much certainty, too much assurance. I quickly substituted hope. "I hope good things will happen." My voice trailed off toward the end. It was a whisper of hope, and even as whispers go it was weak. I didn't feel like I even had a right to hope for good in my life. The great discourager had trained me well and twisted God's Word to do it.

I looked at these men and women and noticed how many of them were so free. I envied their weightless cares and the way they could tease others and speak their mind so boldly. Not one of them knew or cared to know the fine art of or the dance steps to the eggshell waltz. I envied how easily they laughed and didn't bother with what other people thought. I know they admired me for other reasons, for wisdom, grace, and deep compassion for those who hurt. That didn't come from a spirit unhindered by wounds, but I wanted to heal so I could be at least a little bit like them, and I found I was willing to learn something that might help hope become real to me. The instructor gave me articles to read and exercises to open my heart to process some of the pain I held so tightly. The most important shift I would make in my life was about to happen and I had no idea. It seems small, infinitesimal actually, but the application and impact of this one truth changed everything. Look around you, the article instructed. What is real? You might point to a table, a chair, a bed, a book, a dress, a car, a lamp. But let me ask, what was this thing you think is real before it was a table, a chair, a bed, a book, a dress, a car, a lamp? I'll tell you. It was a thought. People think thoughts are not real things, but in reality, thoughts are what make all the things we think real and come into being. Everything you surround yourself with was first a thought before it was ever a thing.

I sat there stunned grappling at the enormity of this truth. Thoughts were things. Thoughts were energy. Thoughts were the power behind everything. For the first time in my life, I began to see the metaphysical impact on the material, not just at the beginning of time, but perpetually. This is how He created His world and how it continues. *By faith we understand that the universe was created by the word of God, so that what is seen was not made out of things that are visible.*[39] I began to examine my thoughts and what I was empowering with them. Sorrow, fear, despair, doubt, hopelessness. I called my very anxious friend and told her what I had learned. She exclaimed, "But KATIE! Look at what you live with! How are you supposed to not think those thoughts? That's all you're surrounded by!" I thought about it and responded, "I think it's a retraining process, like a muscle you've never used. It will be hard at first, but it will get stronger." "What do you do when you're having a negative or anxious thought? That's literally all I have." she asked. "I think you replace the fear with what you want, with something good, something positive. But I'm just figuring this all out." Slowly I was allowing myself to desire something more than I had been given. I began to question and challenge the doctrines of constant suffering that were so firmly rooted in my heart.

Did you come that we might just survive?
Did you come so we could just get by?
Did you walk among us
So we might merely limp along beside?
I was bound, I have been set free
But I have settled for apathy
Did you come to make me new
And know I'd crawl right back into the skin you found me in?
It's where I am, not where I've been
You make me want to live
You make me want to live
You came to shake us
And to wake us up to something more
Than we'd always settled for
And you make me want to live [40]

[39] Hebrews 11:3
[40] *Live;* By Nichole Nordeman and Jay Joyce. Copyright Capitol Cmg Gensis o/b/o Birdwing Music. Capitol Cmg Genesis o/b/o Birdboy Songs, Sony/ATV Songs LLC o/b/o Joyjayce Music Pub, and Sony/ATV Songs LLC

The next series of events all happened in very close succession as if God wanted to hammer home His point and make sure I listened to Him, not the darkness. I was surrounded by the darkness. It was all I saw and all I heard. But He found a way.

As I learned how the anatomy of my body intertwined with my spirit, I decided to do an energy cleansing to balance all that was disjointed and broken inside me. All of this was so weird to me, but it made sense that my spirit had its own anatomy. The session was about an hour. I just remember never being so relaxed and snoring so deeply and then there was this flood of energy from head to foot that shocked me as if my spirit had been in the off position and suddenly someone had turned it on, and the rusty pipes burst forth with pent up energy. I felt lighter. Then suddenly things started happening. At the time I didn't realize it, but now it is deeply evident that hope began to move in my life.

My friend who had heard the poop letter when she was pregnant twelve years earlier had sent out a letter saying that she and her husband were going to an autism treatment program in New England. They were going to believe that love could work a miracle, one tiny step at a time. They had decided to hope. I was curious and called her to learn more. She sent me a DVD to watch. A young man was being interviewed. He was delightful, smiling and answering questions. Clips of him as a child, trapped by autism and stimming, played while he talked about his life now. He had fully recovered. My jaw just hung open, very much like Michael Banks in Mary Poppins, "Close your mouth, Michael. We are not a codfish." I played the video of the formerly autistic young man several times, still stunned as if it was a dream. I got in the shower. I got down on the wet tile with water streaming over my naked body and wept violently, letting the sobs take over before I shouted at God. "DON'T!! DON'T GOD!! Don't you dare let me hope! I can't God! I can't! I've accepted it. OK? Don't. Don't do it. I can't take it. I can't take it. Please. WHY?? Why would you want me to hope after I've already been grieving for fifteen years? WHHYYYY??? That doesn't make sense. I can't. I can't. No. I can't hope. Don't let me. NOOOOO!!!" I cried and cried. It was the first prayer I had prayed in a long time. The truth was I was terrified to hope. I knew the risks. "Hope is a dangerous thing. Hope can drive a man insane." [41]

As I pondered this opportunity and considered if I should go to the treatment program, I shared the stories from the videos with one of the men I trained at the gym. He decided I was going and that was that. Whatever I couldn't cover, he would. His generosity overwhelmed and scared me. I was afraid to accept the offer. I was afraid to believe, afraid it wouldn't work, and afraid I would be wasting this man's money. I knew businessmen, especially ruthless ones who loved their money, expected results. But I was willing to accept the offer with grace and timidity. Isn't this part of believing in the good I want? Isn't receiving good, part of expecting good?

It was the Wednesday before Thanksgiving. Houston was 17. I came home from waiting tables. I had gone straight to the restaurant after a long day of training that began at 5 am. I laid down on the couch and covered up with the blanket. Paul sat in the chair next to me with his leg hanging over the arm of the chair. I was so utterly exhausted my body just buzzed, too tired to sleep. My mind was both foggy and furiously spinning. I wanted to sleep so badly. Houston came downstairs. He only came downstairs for food or to run back and forth and jump and make his booming noises. Very quietly, very calmly he walked by me and sat down at my feet. He sat completely still. He didn't rock back and forth. He didn't flap his hands. He didn't script from Disney movies. He didn't loop. He didn't make any noises. He just sat beside me - still - calm. I knew it was strange, but I was so tired I couldn't even acknowledge it. Then, in the silence, I felt his hand reach up to the blanket and tug very intentionally, like you would to get someone's attention. Then he spoke. "Mama." Astonished, I opened my eyes and looked at him. He stared straight back into my eyes. "I love you." The vastness of those words never spoken by those lips gripped my heart. I

---

[41] Shawshank Redemption

was speechless. It was the first time, the first time he had made eye contact on his own, the first time I had heard his real voice. The first time he called me by name on his own. The first time he told me he loved me. His voice was clear, the voice of a kind young man. There was none of the high-pitched squealing, the nasal sound, or the low guttural booming. It was the most beautiful sound I had ever heard - I love you. I couldn't speak. Paul just stared and then said, "Did that just happen?" I jumped up. I kissed him. I started crying. I started laughing. I kissed him again. "Houston! Houston! I love you too! I love you too." I jumped up and down and cried and laughed and ran shouting for the girls to tell them. It was one moment. One beautiful moment. My son, who was basically mute, had called my name and told me he loved me. And in that moment, I remembered what I had learned about thoughts and belief. Nervously, with faltering faith, the kind that is like shifting sands, I made a choice. I decided I would believe in a miracle. *I remain confident of this: I will see the goodness of the Lord in the land of the living.*[42] That means when I'm alive, not when I'm dead.

Soon after this, I pondered the idea, the possibility that if my thoughts had power, more people believing with me would have even more power. Some faithful might say, "Of course. Communal Prayer." But I had been to enough prayer meetings to know Christians didn't really have faith God would answer their prayers. They rationalized unanswered prayers. They asked. Sometimes they begged. They didn't believe. I thought of my Savior's words...

And Jesus answered them, "Truly, I say to you, if you have faith and do not doubt, you will not only do what has been done to the fig tree, but even if you say to this mountain, 'Be taken up and thrown into the sea,' it will happen." [43]

And Jesus said to him, "'If you can'! All things are possible for one who believes." [44]

He said to them, "Because of your little faith. For truly, I say to you, if you have faith like a grain of mustard seed, you will say to this mountain, 'Move from here to there,' and it will move, and nothing will be impossible for you." [45]

But let him ask in faith, with no doubting, for the one who doubts is like a wave of the sea that is driven and tossed by the wind. [46]

As Jesus went, the people pressed around him. And there was a woman who had had a discharge of blood for twelve years, and though she had spent all her living on physicians, she could not be healed by anyone. She came up behind him and touched the fringe of his garment, and immediately her discharge of blood ceased. And Jesus said, "Who was it that touched me?" When all denied it, Peter said, "Master, the crowds surround you and are pressing in on you!" But Jesus said, "Someone touched me, for I perceive that power has gone out from me." And when the woman saw that she was not hidden, she came trembling, and falling down before him declared in the presence of all the people why she had touched him, and how she had been immediately healed. And he said to her, "Daughter, your faith has made you well; go in peace." [47]

Although I didn't understand how belief had power, clearly God said it did, power to move mountains and make miracles. So I decided to put my faith out there and wave it like a flag, like a kid with a flag on a stick. See God? Do you see me? I'm trying. I'm trying to believe. Slowly, I began to dismantle the doubts that were woven into the fabric of my thoughts. I printed a collage of pictures that I had taken with the help of a friend and sent a letter to everyone I knew who might believe with me. The pictures included words I would tell myself over and

[42] Psalm 27:13
[43] Matthew 21:21
[44] Mark 9:23
[45] Matthew 17:20
[46] James 1:6
[47] Luke 8:42-48

over again to sustain my tiny seed of faith. *We live by faith not by sight.*[48] *The world is so full of possibilities that dogmatism is simply indecent.*[49] *Now to Him who is able to do immeasurably more than all we ask or imagine.*[50] This picture in particular I loved because it was the back of someone's t-shirt in the Social Security office.

I had been forced to sit in the Social Security office for Houston for hours, fighting for his benefits. As I sat in my chair wondering why life was so hard, this man sat directly in front of me. God found a way to bring me His promises when I wouldn't open His word. He put His word on a pillow. He put it on a poster. He put it on a t-shirt. He posted promises. He posted His love. And finally -

IT ALWAYS PROTECTS
ALWAYS TRUSTS
ALWAYS HOPES
ALWAYS PERSEVERES
LOVE NEVER FAILS. [51]

This is the letter I sent out in bright yellow envelopes in December 2013.

***

Dear Friends,

I have a favor to ask. A big one. But first I want to share some of my story. Fourteen years ago, my three-year-old son, Houston, was diagnosed with severe autism. It felt like a death sentence not just for my son, but for myself and my other children. At the time I begged, prayed, pleaded, and hoped to the point of utter exhaustion. Every night I researched treatments and spent countless hours trying any strategy that fed any glimmer of my rapidly dwindling hope. Those years are a painful blur. The experts are not kind to mothers when they don't know what to do. They label your child, offer no help, and dismiss you, all the while strongly scolding the folly of your hope. The further autism engulfed my little boy, the more pathetic and pointless my hope seemed. I finally believed the experts were right. I stopped praying for God to heal my son and tried to just accept it. I can't begin to explain how difficult acceptance is; it feels like quitting even if you've tried everything. Quitting on your child isn't an easy thing to do. Eventually, hope left, and I grieved a grief that cannot be adequately explained. It wasn't just the loss of my son, or even our future, it was the loss of faith – the ability to believe and hope for something your entire being longs for but can't see. I became realistic, sad, fearful, pushing back the avalanche of bitterness with a painful smile on my face.

Strange as it sounds, I think our culture condones those wise enough to live faithless. Realism, proof, statistics, logic – things I have great respect for – are the sacraments of a world that sees belief as a pastime for the simple minded. Hardened hearts are revered, and hopeful hearts mocked. Facing facts is the heartless advice thrown about by those individuals who don't ever really have to face them. The mere fact that those facts leave you breathless with despair and fear, feeling abandoned is either irrelevant, because it's not happening to them, or evidence of your weakness. After all it's your problem, not theirs. This is the mental dichotomy mothers of special needs children live with, trying to figure out a way to survive and face a future that terrifies them when they are already exhausted and grieving from the past. Yet it has not been the cold, indifferent, realistic view of life telling us our place is in the shadows where we won't bother normal people that has helped me or my son. In fact, the only thing that has brought any reprieve has been when people listen and love us, just as we are – very broken and messy, but as valuable as the most talented and accomplished of sons.

Although I have spent years taking care of my beautiful boy, chasing after him, dressing him, bathing him, feeding him, protecting him from strangers, defending his odd behaviors, answering the casually cruel questions, smiling at the impolite stares, and managing his education and

---

[48] 2 Corinthians 5:7
[49] Albert Einstein
[50] Ephesians 3:20
[51] 1 Corinthians 13:7-8

treatments, the grief has never left. Yet something else hasn't left either - the desire to truly know my son. In fact, as I now watch boys his age maturing, excelling, dreaming, becoming men, this yearning cries much louder within me. I desperately want my son, as much of him I can possibly reach, and hopefully all of him.

Recently, my wonderful friend, L-, who has lived with these same struggles, wrote a blog about her newfound hope for her daughter and their family. My heart soared as I read her words, "There's a school of thought that says if something seems too good to be true, it probably is. I was a student there for ages—that was me raising my hand at the desk in the front row. But now there's this: if it seems too good to be true, it's because of boundless love. It blows by everything in its path, with blinders blocking doubts and fears. There's a lot of potential energy here. So I find myself walking, no running, through a minefield of miracles. And realizing love's Author is really, really, big. Scary big... Skepticism, my bedfellow, has flown."

The short story of where her new hope is from, how, and does she have any real reason to hope, is the reason for my letter. There is a place in New England that has had success helping autistic children live improved and even normal lives. Their approach is very unique and is the opposite of traditional behavior modification approaches to autism. Instead of trying to pull autistic children into our world, we enter theirs. They believe social creatures can learn anything, so the goal is to help them learn to interact not through behaviorism but out of pure desire to be with and know the people reaching out to them. When I saw a video of one of these children who had recovered, I couldn't stop weeping. The very idea of being able to know who my son is was so beautiful and big there was only thing I could possibly do – hope. Immediately I felt lighter, happier. The truth is in our culture we have been conditioned NOT to hope, NOT to believe, NOT to expect or even consider the possibility of miracles. But a miracle is exactly what I want - I want to know my son, and that would be the miracle of a lifetime. So, in February I'm going to New England to learn how to begin this new treatment for Houston, and how to love him and connect with him like never before.

Naturally, I have met with some hesitance, pros and cons have been weighed, well-meaning caution has been offered. I have been warned not to get my hopes too high. Even my daughter discouraged the idea of getting everyone's hopes up only to be disappointed. Many have encouraged me that even a little progress is better than where he is now. That's true. However, even though I will be overjoyed with each tiny step he might take, and I love him exactly as he is, I want all of the autism gone. If he had cancer, I would want all of his cancer gone. It's like L- so aptly titled her blog, "Hope Untamed." I think as we gird ourselves against disappointment, we put limits on our possibilities, limits on hope, limits on what we ask from God. What a tiny view of Him and His love.

As for the bad things life has to offer and the disappointments, I have had more than my fill. I am well-seasoned, and I'm not afraid of being disappointed. So, this is where my mind and my heart are. I am tired of believing Murphy's Law is greater than God's power and love. I can't keep believing in a world where nothing good happens, where only little prayers for little things are answered. I will do anything to really know my son, anything. You would too. And I do NOT believe this is impossible for God. In fact, I believe He wants to answer the prayers I stopped praying so long ago. Back then there was a story in the Bible that said everything I felt for years regarding Houston. The Gospel of Mark tells of a desperate father who approaches Christ to heal his son. *And He asked his father, "How long has this been happening to him?" And he said, "From childhood. It has often thrown him both into the fire and into the water to destroy him. But if You can do anything, take pity on us and help us!" And Jesus said to him, "'If You can?' All things are possible to him who believes." Immediately the boy's father cried out and said, "I do believe; help my unbelief."* I have been that father, believing in God's power, but somehow unable to believe it could ever touch me, heal him – as if miracles were for other people. And that is my big favor. I am asking all of you to help my unbelief. I want you to believe that God will heal Houston. I want you to believe in a miracle.

For those of you who think I may be a little desperate or crazy, you should know the things that have already happened as we have started this process. A very kind and big hearted friend offered to help me with funding for my training at the center which was more than I ever would have asked anyone. Then last week, right before Thanksgiving, I laid down on the couch, exhausted, just trying to rest. Houston came and sat on the couch at my feet. That in itself is unusual. He has a difficult time being still and being quiet and usually likes to be alone. After a while he gently put his hand on my leg and pulled at the blanket. With incredible intention and clarity, he said, "Mama." I was startled. I opened my eyes and there he was sitting calmly and looking deeply into my eyes. And then he said it. "I love you." I couldn't believe it. He has never said I love you without being prompted or repeating me. There it was, so simple and yet so miraculous. Paul was dumbfounded. With Xbox remote in hand, Paul asked, "Did that just happen?" When you go 17 years never hearing that, you can't even imagine how incredible it is. In fact, it makes me believe even more is possible for him. So, I am daring to believe and asking you to believe as well. When we begin his program some of you may want to meet Houston and volunteer to help. Others of you might want to help me by believing. I need all of it, the help, the love, and especially the faith.

In Faith,
Katie

***

A few people called me or messaged me their support. I never knew how many people believed with me. I didn't know if it was one prayer once, prayers for a month, or one sweet thought on my behalf before it slipped away to never be thought again. I didn't know if some of those who received that letter were sad for me, shaking heads of pity, or rational, logical minds who knew better than to believe in the impossible. But I didn't care. I didn't care if I got some support or no support. I believed. My miracle was going to happen. My son would be healed. But there was a minefield I had to walk through.

An important part of this faith journey I had decided to embark on was considering the will of God and the role it played. You see, before I decided to rebel and believe, the way I had been taught was if you pray for something and it doesn't happen, then God's answer was "No" or "Wait" or "I have something better." And God always knew best. *For as the heavens are higher than the earth, so are My ways higher than your ways and My thoughts than your thoughts.* [52] I was taught to tiptoe to the throne of Almighty God and ask, Please sir, if it is Your will, please. But Your will, not mine, be done. And then accept whatever He gave with worship, love, and gratitude, trusting His sovereignty and His will - be it rubbish or rubies - for it is all for our good. For God chastens those He loves. I was taught it was sinful to look at what He gave others and to question it. So I did a lot of repenting and worked constantly on self-denial. It was an orphan mentality which is exactly how I felt. By this time I had concluded God gave good things to His real children and the leftovers were for the rest of us. "Prosperity gospel" and "name it and claim it" were grouped in the "garbage theology" that were mocked in my church as teachings for the weak and uneducated, along with "sharing and caring".

For too many, their theology was their pride, which was the worst kind. Their knowledge of doctrine became a way to pass judgment and preach, instead of love the broken. If you wanted anything and it became a yearning, your teachers, preachers, parents, and friends would question if you had made that thing an idol and ask if you loved it more than God. They would remind you that embracing suffering was a sign of

[52] Isaiah 55:9

maturity and holiness. Of course your prayers would be answered, but there's a good chance God's will would be to grant your rescue, justice, provision, mercy, and healing after you were dead. I heard that one a lot. I guess if you no longer had a body or any physical need to be provided for, that counted as answered prayer. To them death was God's answer to almost everything they didn't have a suitable answer for. I knew the passages of Abraham and Isaac. I knew the Hall of Faith in Hebrews. I knew so many things. It all added up to me feeling like I couldn't want anything that had already been taken or denied. *The Lord gives, and the Lord takes away. Blessed be the name of the Lord.* [53]

I had been taught a very strict doctrine of sovereignty and predestination since I was a child. I knew there was suffering because of sin. I knew God used what He hated to accomplish what He loved. I knew the Scriptures. I knew the logic. I knew the theology of unanswered prayers. I make these statements so that any of you who like to discuss theology as a pastime to show others your intellectual prowess instead of actually living the enormous implications of this paradox when life has been wicked and cruel, will actually give me the benefit of the doubt that I know what you're going to say. Please, please try to not intellectualize this. Please don't quote scripture. I am talking about my heart and its deepest longings. I am talking about watching my son be tormented in front of my eyes for decades and being unable to stop it. I am talking about crying out to God. I am talking about the silence and what I scream into it.

All my life I've tried to make everybody happy
While I just hurt and hide
Waiting for someone to tell me it's my turn to decide [54]

There were mountains of unanswered prayers, and I felt the withering weight of disappointment at myself for not accepting it with joy and becoming weary. *Consider it all joy, my brothers and sisters, when you encounter various trials, knowing that the testing of your faith produces endurance. And let endurance have its perfect result, so that you may be perfect and complete, lacking in nothing.* [55] *And let us not grow weary of doing good, for in due season we will reap, if we do not give up.* [56]

My religious instruction was rooted in accepting all things, not changing them, submitting and suffering, not challenging, and definitely never believing in something that seemed impossible, that's what foolish, simple minded people did. The decades of never-ending adversity had turned me into an expert at finding the silver lining and at self-emptying. Yet even after lining my whole world, it all felt like whitewashing a tomb and my heart would not stop wanting. Try as I might, I couldn't find my heart's off button. All I could do was keep telling my heart to shut up and force feed it what it didn't want. Smiling made my stomach hurt. It felt like a lie. More often than I can explain people would serve me another plateful of platitudes, a 'blessing in disguise' mini sermon while they thanked the good Lord my life had not happened to them. I viewed their words like a used tissue. No thank you. *Hope deferred makes the heart sick, but a longing fulfilled is a tree of life.* [57] God, will my prayers ever be answered? Even just one? How is it that none of my prayers are within Your will? What's the point of praying if You just do what You want anyway?

This was my cross I was told. The answer is right in front of you. If this is what is happening to you, then accept it and lay it at the cross. *Whoever finds their life will lose it, and whoever loses their life for my sake will find it.* [58]

---

[53] Job 1:21
[54] *King of Anything;* Words & Music by Sara Bareilles.© 2010 Sony Music Publishing LLC and Tiny Bear Music. All Rights Administered by Sony Music Publishing LLC International Copyright Secured. All Rights Reserved. *Reprinted by Permission of Hal Leonard LLC*
[55] James 1:2-4
[56] Galatians 6:9
[57] Proverbs 13:12
[58] Matthew 10:39

Then Jesus told his disciples, "If anyone would come after me, let him deny himself and take up his cross and follow me. For whoever would save his life will lose it, but whoever loses his life for my sake will find it. For what will it profit a man if he gains the whole world and forfeits his soul?[59] Or what shall a man give in return for his soul? Yet when I looked around me, I saw the same people telling me to accept my fate doing what they wanted, making things happen and having a glorious time in the process. If they got their way, God willed it. If not, it was still part of His plan, just a detour for some unknown but perfect purpose, and they went on chasing whatever they wished. Certainly, they genuinely had far fewer obstacles preventing them from doing so, but the point remains true. Very few in charge or in church were truly living this theology of passivism. More and more I saw people who prayed Your will, not mine but lived, "History will be kind to me for I intend to write it." [60] Few would ever admit they did exactly what they wanted. Then to justify their choices and God's approval, they would act as if a minor hiccup in their pretty and carefree lives was evidence of them bearing the deepest, heaviest cross, giving them the authority to teach others how to bear burdens. They would eagerly quote Scripture to sanctify their struggle as an act of God calling them worthy enough to suffer.

Church made the spectacle worse. There was always an aside in the sermons about how humble, trusting, and godly the well-connected were. I found I had no stomach for the show. Christendom calls this bitterness. I call it true. I felt like I was playing a game and was the only one following the rules. I was stuck eternally in Molasses Swamp while those who did what they wanted had stacked the deck and made it all the way to the Candy Castle every summer with pictures on Facebook to prove it, along with a tidy story of adversity to mark God's approval of their journey. Clearly, I was playing the game of life wrong.

The religious teaching about crosses focused centrally on changing your heart, so your heart lined up with God's desire for you. God's desire was whatever was happening, no matter how evil and awful. It was never about *breaking chains of wickedness, undoing heavy burdens, setting the oppressed free and breaking every yoke.* It was never about *feeding the hungry, bringing the homeless into your home, clothing the naked and not turning away from your own flesh and blood.*[61] That part of God's will was figurative or evangelistic, a tool for bringing people into the fold, definitely not for the people who were suffering and already in it. They used predestination and the sovereignty of God as a justification that excused them from demonstrating mercy or justice to those suffering right in their midst. They actively, brazenly cared more about non-believers than believers. Believers were supposed to carry their own weight and then some. Lip service was offered in exchange for doing His expressed will, despite the fact the God said, *For it is not the hearers of the law who are righteous before God, but the doers of the law who will be justified.*[62]

The church also never wanted to encourage the belief it was God's desire for someone to be healed. They mostly believed it was God's desire to teach us through suffering. But I had to wonder, why didn't Jesus, the very nature and being of God incarnate, even one time tell someone it wasn't His will to heal them or they needed to suffer more to learn some lessons before He would be willing to heal them? If he never taught that, why do we? Why instead did he, after teaching, healing, and demonstrating the compassion of God, say The Spirit of the Lord is upon me, because he has anointed me to proclaim good news to the poor. He has sent me to proclaim liberty to the captives and recovering of sight to the blind, to set at liberty those who are oppressed, to proclaim the year of the Lord's favor... And he began to say to them, *"Today this Scripture has been fulfilled in your hearing."* [63] Why didn't He just tell all the blind, mute, lame, sick, and demon possessed to just hold on, they would be free one day in heaven? Why instead did he literally create food to feed thousands out of his compassion and concern that they

---

[59] Matthew 16:24-26
[60] Winston Churchill
[61] Isaiah 58:6-11
[62] Romans 2:13
[63] Luke 4:18-19, 21

might grow hungry and faint?[64] If he was that concerned about people fainting from hunger, how much more concerned would he be about the torment my son was in? When John inquired who Jesus was, why did Jesus identify Himself as the Christ by His actions? *And he answered them, "Go and tell John what you have seen and heard: the blind receive their sight, the lame walk, lepers are cleansed, and the deaf hear, the dead are raised up, the poor have good news preached to them. And blessed is the one who is not offended by me."*[65] And most importantly, if the church was supposed to be the Body of Christ, why had the church largely reserved His mercy to the cross? Why did they believe the power of faith to do the work of Christ stopped there? And how did the outpouring of the Holy Spirit on the Body of Christ make us impotent to do the work of Christ? Something was missing.

When it came to prayer, the church too often believed faith was just making a request, not the assurance of it being answered, at least in this lifetime. That's when they would warn about "garbage theology" and the dangers of believing God would do the abundant or miraculous thing requested in faith. I never understood how believing God to do as He promised was garbage. I do believe there was genuine concern that prayers may not be answered, and they feared being wrong or looking foolish more than anything. I guess they didn't want to sound like TV evangelists or phony spiritual healers. It was beneath their dignity. They didn't want to provoke the critics because the goal was always to bring more to Christ. I always thought they feared the world and its mockers more than they trusted in the power of God to do the impossible. They preferred the encouragement realists and pessimists offered, with a side of both piety and pity.

They taught that while God may randomly grant a miracle, the days of God's people healing and being healed through spiritual gifts and the radical power of the Holy Spirit were over. They taught cessationism versus continuationism. "Fundamental Christianity has suffered great damage through the efforts of some theologians to excuse their own spiritual impotence through relegating everything supernatural into an imaginary transition period of dispensational truth, which cannot be scripturally proven. It can only be substantiated through their own interpretation of isolated passages and is perpetrated through blind traditionalism not unlike that which Christ faced."[66] To them the proof, that it was God's will to NOT answer even some of the most desperate pleadings and prayers of mercy, was the fact that they saw no change, no proof of answered prayer or even the possibility of answered prayer. It was never a lack of faith, after all they had asked, right? The petition had been submitted before God with the appropriate "If it be Your will." Isn't that faith? But was it? Wasn't faith trusting in who God is and what He wants? Is His will and His nature really so mysterious, so hard to determine? Pain, wickedness, and brokenness were everywhere. What was so hard to believe about that? Or was the problem really us and what we couldn't believe about Him and His faithfulness? *Nevertheless, when the Son of Man comes, will he find faith on earth?* [67] *O you of little faith.*[68] Was it possible that what was missing was our faith in His power and faithfulness to actually answer us?

The way His will had been taught to me was as if who He is, was very different than what He allowed to happen. This was the mystery that we just had to trust, which created a very shaky ground to stand on. It's not that big of a deal if your life is relatively safe and free of problems. But for someone who faced monsters of all kinds every day, it was so uncertain. I never knew what to pray or what to do. Was His will what was happening or who He was? Was I to give thanks for the evil done to me and those I loved? Was I to fight? Was I to submit and suffer? Was I to keep being broken? Was I to just accept and wait for something good to come out of something evil? Was I to wander aimlessly until something started to point to something that made sense in God's Word? Was I to demand logical proof before I prayed, before I believed anything at all? The proof was the hardest part to overcome. Basically, Christendom had become just like the world. We had to have some kind of

---

[64] Matthew 15:32
[65] Luke 7:22-23
[66] R.V. Bosworth, Preface to 1973 Edition of <u>Christ the Healer</u>
[67] Luke 18:8
[68] Matthew 6:30, 8:26, 14:31, 16:8, 17:20; Luke 9:41, 12:28; Mark 4:40

proof before we truly believed God's promise to answer our prayers and do the impossible. The way prayers were prayed were weak, you never knew what would stick, what His will really was.

It was a part of the same spirit that demanded proof to trust, the spirit that said, *Physician, heal thyself,* [69] or *You who would destroy the temple and rebuild it in three days, save yourself! If you are the Son of God, come down from the cross.* [70] This kind of faith puts limits on the will of God to do what we cannot fathom, or what is not answered quickly.

But beyond not understanding faith, that faith was assurance that God would do as He promised to us, even to me, even if no evidence could be seen, the point they missed was who God is. And despite all their focus on God's will, the church missed what His will is too. He has seven redemptive names that reveal who He is and what His will is, as well as what our redemption through Christ and through the Atonement includes. This is who God says He is: JEHOVAH-SHAMMAH "The Lord is present", JEHOVAH-SHALOM "The Lord is our peace", JEHOVAH-RA-AH "The Lord is my Shepherd", JEHOVAH-JIREH "The Lord will provide", JEHOVAH-TSIDKENU "The Lord is our righteousness", JEHOVAH-NISSI "The Lord our Banner" (victor), and JEHOVAH-RAPHA, "I am the Lord that heals you." Not I was or I sometimes, but I AM. He is the Lord who is present with me, who by taking on my chastisement is my peace, who is my Shepherd, who provides for me so I lack no good thing,[71] who is my righteousness, my Banner and victor, and my Lord who heals me, and my son. But just like salvation, all that God wanted to give me came through faith. Through belief I would receive the good gifts He wanted to give.

As if scales had suddenly fallen from my eyes, I sadly acknowledged that the church didn't teach how to have faith or hope beyond salvation at all, unless of course, it was the teaching on tithing and testing God to open up His abundant storehouses. Then they would teach profoundly about the power of faith. But in response to pain, loss, suffering, or injustice, the church taught acceptance. It taught how to experience suffering as holiness. It taught how we deserve nothing good. It taught against complaining and grumbling. It taught to grin and bear it. It taught God doesn't want us to be happy, just holy. It taught how to trust there was a greater purpose beyond our ability or wisdom to see, which meant that no matter how horrific, this was ultimately good for you. It taught God uses what He hates to accomplish what He loves. It taught sovereignty and submission. And it taught how to just hold on until you die. There was always admonishment against bitterness of course, because God's will was perfect. Having feelings or thoughts that were anything other than embracing your cross was a sin, proof of you distrusting God.

The ease and safety of the lives of those teaching these doctrines made their messages even less palatable. Convenient for them, I thought. Teaching acceptance of suffering meant they didn't have to help alleviate it or even have compassion for those who were crumbling under the pressure. If I heard one more person say, "Add your sufferings to the sufferings of Christ," or "These are opportunities for you to become more like Him," or "He is the potter, you are the clay, a vessel to be broken," or "God never gives us more than we can handle," or piously preach about the wilderness I was going to scream. If I heard one more person talk about humility or the still small voice, when I had been listening to a busy signal for over forty years, I just might hang up permanently. Again, I was told by another Christian that God only cared about saving men's souls and shouldn't be bothered with other prayers. I couldn't even respond because I could actually feel my heart

---

[69] Luke 4:23
[70] Matthew 27:40
[71] But those who seek the Lord lack no good thing. — Psalm 34:10b;
No good thing does he withhold from those who walk uprightly. — Psalm 84:11b
If you then, who are evil, know how to give good gifts to your children, how much more will your Father who is in heaven give good things to those who ask him! — Matthew 7:11
Who satisfies your years with good things, so that your youth is renewed like the eagle — Psalm 103:5

breaking inside me. Their teaching pushed me further and further away. I knew what my desire was - for my son to be healed. I didn't want to hear anything else. The truth was I did want to be more like Him, and Jesus got things done. He helped hurting people and He let nothing stand in the way of love, not sickness, not disabilities, not distance, not Pharisees, not demons, not even death. Christendom taught the way to trust God was by accepting the present. I chose to trust God by rejecting the present and believing in the impossible, by believing who He says He is forever, and what He promises He will do for all time. I didn't care if impossible took a while. I decided to embrace a different theology, even if others thought it was garbage, simply because my heart refused to accept anything but the theology of answered prayers, the intent of God that may lead me through a desert, but also rescues me out of it, and the presence of my heavenly Father who loves me and works miracles. I realized the only way to block the message of how to accept instead of how to believe was to not go to church, read a spiritual book, or talk to religious people. And that's what I did. Literally.

There was still one thing I had to deal with - the issue of God's will. God's will versus man's desire… I spent years pondering it. Desire is a funny thing. An invisible compass for your heart to follow. Who knew for sure if and when it was really your own desire or the Holy Spirit? As one sarcastic, wise old man said, "I find it interesting how so many young people feel God is calling them to the mission field in paradise and asking me to fund it. Why isn't God calling them to some place like Kazakhstan and asking them to pay for it themselves? I'd be more inclined to believe that God was speaking if there wasn't so much self-gratification in the assignment." Where did free will stop and God's will begin? Was He always just picking up after our messes and fashioning fine things? He sounded like a mom. Except He didn't get tired.

Since desire could so often lead us astray, where did it come from and when was it right to heed its call? Certainly some of the great sins in the Bible led to Christ and then to the cross. How much do we really choose for ourselves and how much is His sovereignty which uses our mistakes for His purposes? Where is the line between a grace that knows no bounds and hearts that are never satisfied? Years later, one of my sons would try to justify himself after betraying our family by saying, "Even what I did was meant to happen. Nothing is an accident. It's all for good. And you're supposed to forgive." Trying to point out that he was cherry picking Scriptures for his own purposes did not seem to dissuade his self-serving theology. It seemed that the lines shifted as often as the tides, as often as a fickle heart flickers. The truth was, despite Paul's admonition, *What shall we say then? Shall we continue in sin that grace may abound? Certainly not! How shall we who died to sin live any longer in it?*[72] there was a whole lot of "It's better to ask forgiveness than permission," amongst those who said they followed His call. Man did what was best for man and placed it as an offering for God to make good.

So I made the decision I would pursue what I wanted, whether it was His will or not. And I wanted a miracle. I was just going to take God at His word, *all things are possible for one who believes,*[73] and shut my ears to everything that conflicted with this no matter where it came from. By this time, something deep within me knew that there was something powerful and real in belief. It truly did make things become real. The belief was critical, but so was the action. Faith without works was dead. I had known that since I was a child. Works had always been taught as *'If you believe in Jesus, you had better be good and do good,'* for *If a brother or sister is naked and destitute of daily food, and one of you says to them, "Depart in peace, be warmed and filled," but you do not give them the things which are needed for the body, what does it profit? Thus also faith by itself, if it does not have works, is dead… For as the body without the spirit is dead, so faith without works is dead also.*[74] But now I realized that the combined power of faith and works was not limited to the spirituality of good deeds. The lightbulb itself was a thought, a belief that became real through hard work and effort. Buildings were just ideas that someone drew and later built. The beautiful

---

[72] Romans 6:1-2
[73] Mark 9:23
[74] James 2:15-17, 26

drapes, bed coverings, and pillows I had made were first an image in my mind that I crafted into being. Everything I saw around me was an idea, a belief made real by works. Why not believe in something, believe in a miracle I couldn't yet see? Maybe then the works, the way to make it real, would find me.

Whether there was willful disregard for God's will in my determination to believe, I'm not sure, but I did genuinely grapple with the fact that I wasn't asking permission. One comfort I had was the woman who had bled for twelve years. She didn't ask permission. She didn't ask if Jesus was willing. She didn't even ask if it would work. She just knew if she touched the very edge of His garment, she would surely be healed. She trusted that power was in Him. And Jesus, feeling the power leave Him, demanded to know who had touched Him. Clearly, even without His consent, it was His will and nature to heal. Meekly, she approached. He did not rebuke. He honored her great belief, telling her it was her faith that healed her. He restored her, erased her shame, and called her daughter.[75] The Syrophoenician woman challenged Jesus and refused to relent in her request for her daughter's healing, despite Jesus' intention to honor the covenant with Abraham and focus first on the children of Israel. *Then Jesus answered her, "O woman, great is your faith! Be it done for you as you desire." And her daughter was healed instantly.*[76] To the leper who implored, *"If You will, You can make me clean."* Jesus corrected him so there was no confusion about His will and said, *"I will, be clean."*[77] In fact, seventy percent of the recounted stories of Jesus healing people in the New Testament, Jesus, our Savior, attributed their healing to their own faith. Jesus never objected and told them that they might have faith but healing them was against His will for them. And the patriarch Jacob as well, he wrestled with God and refused to let go until God blessed him. For his will he was named Israel, for he strived with man and God and prevailed.[78] That was faith. That was works. That was belief in the giver of all good things and belief in their own desire as well. Their will mattered to God. So I decided, the hell with it. I'm going to desire and believe, and I don't mind wrestling or crawling in the dirt. I'm used to being on my knees.

After I made the decision to believe, an unusual and remarkable set of incidents occurred. Reagan had a friend come over to prepare for a History project. I took Paul and Benjamin to practice. It was a decidedly eventful night. When I returned home there were cop cars up and down my street. Immediately, I panicked. Houston was my only thought. The police finally allowed me to pull into my driveway. I raced inside to find my kids. Reagan reassured me Houston was fine. "He's upstairs, Mom. But MOM! The lady across the street who has all those massage parties, She was shot by the police! She shot at them. We heard gunshots and ran outside! They carried her out naked!" The teenagers were taken up in the excitement and I was horrified by it all. The friend's mother arrived to pick up her child amidst all the police activity. I explained what had happened and that it was mostly nice, poor people who lived here, and that the neighborhood was not a ghetto like the wealthier people referred to it. Maybe it was my vulnerability, maybe it was meeting Houston, but something I said affected her and she opened up to me. She told me she was poor too, single and struggling mightily, especially with her thoughts. Fear and despair consumed her. She saw her future as a slow, downward spiral. I shared with her some of my journey and explained to her what I had learned about thoughts, that everything material was first a thought and that our thoughts had power - good or bad. We could choose what we thought, what we believed about our future. Then I told her about the words that I never thought I would ever hear from my son. Tears rolled down her cheeks. "I think... I think you might be right." Then she asked if I had ever studied numerology. I said no. She told me that she was just learning but had discovered that certain numbers had significance and that specifically the numbers 11 and 1 had greater importance and power than any other numbers. She told me she had started seeing these numbers paired

[75] Matthew 9:20-22; Mark 5:25-34; Luke 8:43-48
[76] Matthew 15:28
[77] Luke 5:12-13
[78] Genesis 32:22-32

together everywhere and gave me five different examples. I listened and thought to myself, 'That's nice for her to be encouraged, but I don't know if I buy into numbers.' Still, I listened and kept my skepticism to myself. She gave me a hug and I went to bed, exhausted from another long day.

The next morning at 4:30 a.m. I sat on the couch to meditate per my yoga instruction. My phone chirped. 'Who could possibly be texting me at this hour?' I thought. It was a text from a friend I had not spoken to in over a year. That in itself was shocking. She knew nothing that had happened. I hadn't sent her the yellow letter, and she had moved to Tennessee. She said she felt the Lord told her to send me this verse. I opened the link. Hebrews 11:1. The numbers seemed to hover above the screen staring back at me. I gulped.[79] 'I don't believe in numbers though,' I told myself. 'I'm Presbyterian.' With the possible few exceptions found in the Bible, we don't acknowledge what we can't explain. The friend who sent me the verse was always talking about signs, to which I always responded by offering logical explanations and frankly, doubting everything she saw as evidence. Uncomfortable, I hesitated before I opened the link. Then I read...

Now faith is the confidence in what we hope for,
the assurance about what we do not see. [80]

The weight of it left my speechless. For me it was everything. A little love note from the God of the universe saying, "I saw that. I heard you too. So you don't think numbers matter? Everything matters. It's all in My hands. All of it. Numbers, broken hearts, autism... Go ahead. Be assured. Believe."

And I did. I believed in the face of more than I can explain. I believed in my miracle even when I struggled to believe in my miracle maker.

In February 2014 I went to the autism treatment program. The first day of the program they called my name out in front of the group. For a moment I was nervous. I didn't want any attention. 'Why were they calling me?' I thought. "How old is your son?" the speaker asked. "Seventeen," I answered apprehensively. There were a few gasps as people turned to look at me. I looked at the floor. I knew why. We had all been told there was a window that closed after which there was no hope of reaching your child, recovery, or rehabilitation. At Houston's age, all was assumed lost. My presence must have seemed foolish even among other desperate parents. "That's old. Why are you here?" she asked with a bit of a knowing smile on her face. Carefully I weighed my answer so I wouldn't look the fool I felt to be. Then something in me, my little seed of faith demanded to be in charge - aw fuck it. I spoke loud enough so they could all hear. "Because there is always reason to hope. Because I decided to believe." The speaker smiled. "Do you hear that everyone? There is always hope. Don't ever stop believing." Then the hope building began. I spent a week listening to techniques and watching films and began to adore all these other broken parents and their children I had never met.

At the end of the week, I met with one of the in-home therapists to come up with a plan. She cautioned me to be patient and to commit to the process. Then she said, "And I want you to remove all screens from your house. That's imperative." The issue and impact that videos had on them had already been discussed and I had literally wanted to just disregard it and pretend I hadn't heard their caution. Concerned, I responded, "But that's all he does. That's all he wants to do. He goes absolutely crazy without it." I felt the enormous pressure and impossibility of the task. "You have to. He's addicted, I'm sure."

So I went home and told the kids the plan. They groaned. Literally. They told me it would not work. They told me they were tired of watching me get my hopes up and trying to get theirs up too. I asked what

---

[79] Skeptics might refer to this as the Baader Meinhof phenomenon, the frequency illusion — except I didn't notice the numbers, they were sent to me at what can only be described as incredibly coincidental timing. And then there was the message within the verse itself. To me, it was God.

[80] Hebrews 11:1

would they want me to do if they were the one who was autistic instead of their brother. Would you want me to just give up and accept it or keep trying? They HATED when I taught empathy. They will tell you I said two things to them ad nauseum: "What would you want someone to do for you?" AND "The answer to 'Am I my brother's keeper?' is YES. You ARE." Who knows how many eyes were rolled over the years.~ I told them I would need their help, and they did help - for a little over two weeks. Houston's stims, hand biting and trying to break onto the computers, tablets, and phones was relentless. He made high pitched squealing noises, jumped, and howled while biting himself. It was all day, all night. It didn't slow down. Everything got worse. Eventually, they just let him have the computer. I was still fighting. I did what we had been taught and whatever stim he engaged in, I followed his lead. The techniques I had learned had us mimic their activity, so whatever he engaged in I did the same. When I did, he became furious with me. "No! No! No!" He would bite his hand in absolute rage, and I would cry. I would calm him down and wait for a new opportunity to follow his lead. Every single time it ignited a vicious cycle of self-injury. 'Why isn't this working?' I wondered. 'What am I doing wrong?' Eventually I gave in on the videos and let him watch them ad nauseum again. But I still thought she was right. This was definitely addiction. I just didn't have a clue how to treat it without him harming himself. The wonderful thing that happened was I wasn't defeated. I just knew what I was doing wasn't it. But I was going to find it, whatever it was.

26

Blinded by Faith, Labeled a Fool

There are times when faith and common sense do not align,
when hard core evidence of You is hard to find,
and I am silenced in the face of argumentative debate,
And it's a long hill, it's a lonely climb.
Cause they want proof, they want proof of all these mysteries I claim.
Cause only fools would want to chant a dead man's name.
I admit that in my darkest hours I've asked what if,
What if we created some kind of man made faith like this,
Out of good intention or emotional invention,
and after life is through there will be no You.
Cause they want proof of all these miracles I claim,
Cause only fools believe that men can walk on waves... [81]

O ver the next five years people would constantly make references to Houston, about the next stage in his life and all he still couldn't do. I found myself answering their questions very cautiously. My answers acknowledged the limits we all saw. But something had happened to my heart. I wasn't going to let the way things were get in the way of the way I wanted things to be anymore. The world calls this delusional. I would often add a precursor to my response. "I have decided to believe in a miracle. So until then we will do everything we can with what is available." People would nod their head with pity at the foolish hope of a mother with nothing, absolutely no reason to hope. I would see the look in their eyes and the way they would turn away from my very direct gaze. What did I care what they thought though? They hadn't waited seventeen years to hear their child say, "I love you." His words had become my bedrock.

"There are places in this world that aren't made out of stone.
That there's something inside…
that they can't get to, that they can't touch.
That's yours." [82]

Houston was getting older. There had been a succession of annual IEP meetings since he was four years old. The improvements were miniscule despite the constant ABA (Applied Behavioral Analysis) repetitions. ABA had been a failure and I had bought the lie for too long. Like most of the other parents, we considered it largely a waste of precious time and money. The only real success was when many of his incredible teachers pushed past the monotony with their creativity and their hunches and raised the bar, while trying to incorporate it into a format that gathered data and proved 80% competency. The minute

[81] *Fool For You*; By Nichole Nordeman. Copyright Capitol Cmg Genesis o/b/o Ariose Music Group Inc.
[82] Shawshank Redemption

goals seemed insignificant in the scheme of all the mountains still left to climb. But his teachers loved him, and I was grateful for love.

Based on how disruptive his noises and stims were and the psychological evaluations that identified his functional age as that of a 4–5-year-old with a comparative IQ, I never used any of my parental rights to fight for the least restrictive environment, for more extensive evaluations, for alternative communication methods, for inclusion, for anything. My son's access to education had been within my grasp to influence and control. But because I believed what the experts told me; I didn't fight for anything. Just like with God, my broken heart just submitted to my reality, and I accepted what I had been given. And that will always be my biggest and worst mistake.

At the time it didn't seem like I wasn't fighting for him. In fact, exclusion came in the form of a gift, an offering of extra help that I desperately needed. As the years passed and the gap between my son and other children his age widened like the Mississippi River, and the tests told me to not hope, the translation was simple - don't fight for anything you're not offered - ever. There was an unwritten policy. If your child needed massive amounts of help, they weren't competent and did not have a right to the education everyone else received. So my son received what they thought he was capable of. I did nothing. That's not true. I smiled politely. I agreed. It's my signature on every one of those IEPs. I didn't rock the boat. There are no words for this failure. If you are in my boat, DON'T REPEAT MY MISTAKE. FIGHT FOR EVERYTHING. YOUR CHILD IS IN THERE NO MATTER WHAT THE DATA SAYS!!! IF YOU HAVE TO, BE THE PARENT THEY HATE. BE THE PARENT YOUR CHILD NEEDS.

Now things were different. I refused to accept that this was all I could hope for. I was determined to believe in a miracle. God says *without faith it is impossible to please Him, for he who comes to God must believe that He is, and that He is a rewarder of those who diligently seek Him.*[83] Belief is difficult under the best circumstances. Believing in something that seems impossible, even foolish, that there is no evidence for, that others see as a waste of time and energy, well that is a whole different level. For a moment I want you to consider what it takes to believe in a miracle that flies in the face of facts, data, and an even harsher daily reality...

That believes the experts are wrong when they tell you to accept the status quo —
That believes when there is foul feces to be cleaned every day for decades —
That believes when you see your child smelling feces and covered in it —
That believes when you are running frantically for hours and can't find your child… again and again —
That believes when there has been no sleep for days… for years —
That believes when the flood waters won't stop, and the sky won't stop falling —
That believes in the face of noises that are incomprehensible to explain —
That believes when the stims won't stop —
That believes when there is nakedness in public —
That believes when the police show up again and again —
That believes when strangers judge you —
That believes when strangers pity you —
That believes when your child injures themselves every day with ferocity —
That believes when food is eaten raw —
That believes when pantries are emptied right after you fill them —
That believes when there is no food, no job, no car, no money —
That believes when full shampoo bottles are emptied into drains and syrup and salad dressings become finger paint for the walls, carpet, and furniture —

---

[83] Hebrews 11:6

That believes when food you have prepared is dumped in the trash —
That believes when you have to beg —
That believes when things you cared about are destroyed —
That believes when your other children resent how hard their life is and blame you —
That believes when you have heard the same three Disney scripts nonstop for days that have turned into years —
That believes when there is no money for more years than you can recall —
That believes when there is hateful, cruel abuse that never ceases —
That believes when there is no help —
That believes when there is no justice —
That believes when you've been betrayed —
That believes when friends are cruel and abandon you —
That believes when people who love God turn away —
That believes when you're gossiped about —
That believes when your strength is gone —
That believes even after you have a meltdown —
That believes when there is no rest —
That believes in spite of ever-present fear —
That believes when no one has the stomach to be your friend —
That believes when you haven't been held or kissed in years —
That believes when no one wants to hear what your life is really like —
That believes when you never get to dream —
That believes when your child's screams and terrors don't stop, and neither do yours —
That believes when everyone tells you to give up on your child —
That believes when the church tells you it's God will for you to suffer, and turns away —
That believes when the only sound you can make sounds like a wail that would embarrass a whale —

Could you believe in a miracle? Few could. It was a fool's dream. I decided — why not? I would be a fool. What did I have to lose? I clung to my belief in my miracle in spite of it all.

If you're reading this and your life is in a similar hopeless state, I want to tell you something important. If you need a miracle, then go ahead and believe in the goodness of God and His willingness and power to give you one. You don't need anyone's permission or approval to believe. You do not need an expert to give you permission to believe in God's faithfulness to do what the experts tell you He can't. You don't need favorable statistical data. He longs to show you how good He truly is. Close your eyes to the madness and pain around you and just believe in the goodness and faithfulness of God. He longs to show you how good He truly is. *Taste and see that the Lord is good.*[84]

---

[84] Psalm 34:8

27

Angels and Bureaucrats, Caesar and God

And he told them a parable to the effect that they ought always to pray and not lose heart.
He said, "In a certain city there was a judge who neither feared God nor respected man.
And there was a widow in that city who kept coming to him and saying, 'Give me justice against my adversary.'
For a while he refused, but afterward he said to himself,
'Though I neither fear God nor respect man, yet because this widow keeps bothering me,
I will give her justice, so that she will not beat me down by her continual coming.'"
And the Lord said, "Hear what the unrighteous judge says.
And will not God give justice to his elect, who cry to him day and night?
Will he delay long over them? I tell you, he will give justice to them speedily.
Nevertheless, when the Son of Man comes, will he find faith on earth?
— Luke 18:1-8

Social Security was the next battle. I had already been down this road. What a mess. First was the Katie Beckett Waiver battle that took a year and a half and was lost because a worker quit and didn't send the notification and renewal paperwork. One friend had told me condescendingly that there were resources I wasn't accessing and to apply for assistance. This was hard for me. I had been raised to be self-sufficient. I had heard the constant commentary about all the single mothers who live off the government. People hated the moochers, and I didn't want any other reason to be an object of disgust. I had guilt and shame just from going to a food bank. My pride kept me from applying for anything that was beyond the standard services. Finally, I applied for SSI, and Houston was approved because of my low income. I breathed a momentary sigh of relief. Then the development company that I had worked for over four years fired me. There are really no words for his actions. He loved pride, money and himself more than Christ. The owner then fought my unemployment and said I wasn't an employee. He sent his lady henchman and a cheap attorney to argue his case. He wouldn't show his face. I can only speculate he wanted to avoid lying under oath. I knew he didn't have a problem lying to people's faces. Their defense for me not being an employee was that I had published a book during the first few months of my employment when I was working part time, saying that proved my independent contractor status. The Department of Labor granted me unemployment retroactively.

Feeling a tiny victory, I spent an afternoon waiting in the Social Security office to update my income. When I was finally seen and explained what was going on, the Social Security worker looked only at the computer with a cold unmoving gaze, never at me. She wouldn't make eye contact. It was beyond strange. In a monotone voice she said since I was receiving unemployment, I had to pay back all the SSI I had received on his behalf since that changed my income. I asked how that was possible since unemployment benefits were a fraction of my income. "It's figured differently than regular income." No matter what question I asked, the woman refused to make eye contact or help me understand. Houston began biting his hands furiously. I left in tears. Then immediately following this event, Congress' new 2013 budget deal ended all unemployment. The stupid help I didn't want and had fought so hard for was gone. I was overwhelmed with fear. What a stupid waste of time, and now I owed the government money??!! The help that I hadn't been taking advantage of was a mirage. A lie with a mountain of paperwork and a guarantee of debt.

A few years before when Houston had turned fifteen, I had filed for the NOW/COMP waiver. I was warned the waiting list was long. That year, as I began the process of filing for adult Social Security, I took Houston to one of the board meetings for the Department of Behavioral Health and Developmental Disabilities on the southeast side of Atlanta. One of the social workers from school joined me. I saw several other parents whose children had aged out of school begging for assistance and explaining that one parent could no longer work and had to stay home with their child to provide 24/7 care. There was no help, almost no respite. I recognized one of the dads from the Special Olympics track team and Miracle League softball that I took Houston to every week. Finally, it was my turn. As I stood to speak Houston lit out like a cannon, wailing his low guttural noises, and flapping his hands wildly. He ran and took out everything in his path. Only the window of a huge conference room stopped his sprint. He jumped and made loud, disruptive noises while I ran after him and tried to calm him down. The social worker helped me stop him from biting himself and took him in the hall. I stood before all the people in charge and pled my son's case again. I got business cards of people with titles and exchanged emails. The officials were horrified by the truth of severe autism. I guess it looks different on paper. BUT… Despite their momentary compassion, there were policies. Because he was still in school, there would be no help.

Now that he was almost eighteen, I had to file for Social Security Disability for Houston. It was about an eight-month process in total. More psychologists, more experts, more testing. In one office Houston erupted into one of his jumping fits complete with sound effects, and the entire office shook like an earthquake. The psychologist immediately prescribed some kind of ADHD medicine for him with almost no explanation for what it would do. I told her we had never had success with meds, and she told me he was going through puberty and his body chemistry was different. As she handed me the prescription she said, "You really need something for yourself." No thanks. I'm already numb, I thought to myself. These drugs, like all the others, didn't help my son a bit. I was frustrated that these doctors prescribed psychotropic drugs randomly, without any blood tests to see if there are vitamin deficiencies, hormonal imbalances, metabolic factors or even to do a blood count or a brain scan. No one bothered to find out if he had too much serotonin before prescribing an SSRI. Not one doctor tried to be a detective. Not one doctor thought critically. Not one doctor cared. They were the bartenders of the pharmaceutical profession. What cocktail do you want? I was so tired of trying to understand the medical and neurological component when I wasn't a doctor, and the doctors didn't bother to practice medicine. I was tired of doing more study than those with degrees. In ten minutes after getting weighed, having his blood pressure taken and seeing him jump and flap his hands they wanted to prescribe a mind-altering chemical cocktail. And apparently, because I was exhausted and overwhelmed, I needed one too. Maybe I just needed help and hope. Maybe I just needed love. I had no faith in doctors.

That fall, after multiple delays and court extensions, my attorney finally negotiated an agreement with my ex less than 24 hours before our court date. He had to start paying the back child support immediately along with the continued child support. The relief was like a rushing river that I didn't know what to do with.

Despite the fact there was now a current as opposed to a dried-up bed, it never felt safe. I was still afraid he would do something. Stop paying. Lie. Attack me in some way I hadn't yet considered. It was like getting money from the mafia. There was just no way to feel safe. Was I supposed to be grateful?

One day I was called to Houston's high school to bring shoes. I always left at 5 am for my first job. Apparently, when the boys had helped their brother get ready that morning, they had put a shoe three sizes too small on him. They had to put him on the bus because I left for work so early and their sisters were already at school. I brought two pairs of shoes to school in case it happened again. It was embarrassing. I just wanted to be home, taking care of everything that needed to be taken care of. Houston had a new teacher that year. She had all the exuberance and love of a first-year teacher and Houston adored her. She practically bounced with joy. When I walked into the special needs hallway carrying shoes, she greeted me with that infectious joyful energy. "I'm so glad you're here! I wanted to show you something. She pointed inside a dark classroom with an overhead projector and a teacher at the front of the class. I peered into the darkness and saw Houston staring at the screen listening to the teacher. I was puzzled. "We've been teaching him age-appropriate curriculum for history and he's amazing. He gets every single question right. 100% on everything!" I stared at her like she had just told me my son could fly - 100%! "How is that possible?" I asked. "You've seen his evaluations." She just shrugged and smiled her gigantic smile. I got the feeling she didn't care one bit about his evaluations. She just was so excited to teach someone so eager to learn. "Keep teaching him, ok? I don't know what he's learning and retaining, but will you keep teaching him?" I didn't even know what to do with this information. All those old thoughts I had before started stirring. Again, I asked myself, is Houston smart?

The transition officer sent me the paperwork to fill out for guardianship for Houston. Reluctantly I started the paperwork. I had spoken to several parents about the process and had attended forums and discussion groups. I got several pages into the process. Then I read that I would have to take away his right to vote. I was sick, completely sick. What right did I have to take my son's rights away? This didn't even begin to make sense. The strangest thing happened. I couldn't do it. I couldn't even begin to do it. I knew what was logical, but it was not possible. My heart wouldn't let my hand do a damn thing. I couldn't write even one more word. I just got up and stuffed those papers somewhere I couldn't see them or find them ever again. All I could tell myself is, 'No. You can't. You're getting a miracle.'

Another time his teacher excitedly sent me a picture of him at the Hoops for Hearts event. He was arm in arm and surrounded by cheerleaders. I laughed out loud. I don't think anyone in heaven or on earth has ever smiled that big. It was a smile from deep within. He was gorgeous. Breathtaking. Happy. And obviously preferred the company of cute cheerleaders. Everyone who saw that photo was filled with joy. It was impossible not to be.

Later that month I picked him up from school for another psychological evaluation. One of the other non-speaking autistic students, with little body control, was being escorted inside while Houston was being escorted out. I chatted with the teacher with the car door open. When this young man saw me, he turned and tried to violently break away from the teacher. He pointed, no lunged toward me and did everything in his power to reach in my direction. He kept reaching and pulling away and was trying so hard to articulate a message as drool fell from his bottom lip. There was powerful determination in his movements as he struggled to convey something. He wouldn't stop reaching and pointing. The teachers were in shock. They had never seen him do that. I was in shock too. We all just sat or stood with our mouths open. I looked at Houston and wanted so much to ask him and hear his thoughts. But instead, I said nothing more than, "Hey sweetie. Put your seatbelt on."... My mind wondered and wandered about all the words they wanted to speak. "McDonald's. McDonald's," Houston said repeatedly. I snapped back to reality and smiled. "Ok, McDonald's it is. AFTER the appointment." I drove off and let my thoughts drift back to Houston's classmate. It was so powerful I knew it meant something. I had no idea that one day I would realize I had witnessed something miraculous, something of heaven and not of earth.

28

Unfolding

The eyes of the Lord are in every place, keeping watch on the evil and the good.
— Proverbs 15:3

For he looks to the ends of the earth and sees everything under the heavens.
— Job 28:24

O Lord, you have searched me and known me!
You know when I sit down and when I rise up; you discern my thoughts from afar.
You search out my path and my lying down and are acquainted with all my ways.
Even before a word is on my tongue, behold, O Lord, you know it altogether.
You hem me in, behind and before, and lay your hand upon me.
Such knowledge is too wonderful for me; it is high, I cannot attain it.
— Psalm 139:1-6

The owner of the gym had become more and more difficult to work with, more demanding, more irritable. I had seen him treat another trainer this way before and had a gut feeling he was looking for a way to get rid of me to cut costs. His wife, who never worked, was constantly badgering him, clients, and employees. Clients would have enough and leave after dealing with her, and she would tell her husband it was my fault, that they were leaving because of me. These people had become my friends and the accusation was not even remotely true. Still, it's never fun to be lied about. One morning, my 5 am client cancelled and when I reset my alarm, it didn't go off. I woke up late for the next client and ran to work as fast as I could. It was the first time in a year and a half I had ever been late. The owner wouldn't even speak to me. At the next opportunity, in a horrific rage, he began screaming that I was the reason all the clients were leaving. I left in tears. I came back and turned in my key. I was out another job. My boys were out a coach and a whole crew of friends. As my clients began asking where I was, the owner just kept saying, "It was time. It was time." "Sounds like you need to apologize," they told him. It was well over a year before he was able to gather up the humility to text me and say, "I miss you." "I'm sorry" was just too hard to say. His wife had taken all their money, ran up the credit cards and moved to California. Perspective is a powerful thing.

A friend got me an entry level job in commercial insurance. I kept my two other jobs because the pay was still awful. I saved all I could from the money I was now getting from the Big Jock. It was a while before I trusted the payments enough to quit one of the jobs. Benjamin later told me he had seen his father's bank account open on the computer during one of their visits around this time. There was over two million dollars in one account. When the Big Jock saw Benjamin looking at the available balance, he put his finger over his lips in the universal sign of secret keeping, smiling devilishly behind his fat finger.

Reagan's teenage angst was reaching catastrophic levels. You could tell she hated me with everything in her. Nothing I did worked, not talking, logic, warnings, diversions, extra-curricular activities, restrictions, youth group or yelling. When I cautiously pointed out how her boyfriend was controlling her, she would attack me saying I hated all her boyfriends. No matter what kind or corrective thing I did, she hated me. There was no win. I was pretty numb to her hate at that point and felt like she had been stolen from me. Watching my daughter get further and further from the person I knew her to be and being powerless to stop it was its own special kind of grief. The lying was nonstop. She lied when the truth would have been just fine. Her boyfriend would stare at me with raging eyes trying to burrow his hate into me. Everything I had read about teenage rebellion wasn't just true, it was worse. The Big Jock continued his long-distance manipulation. I really couldn't compete. I noticed she was developing a figure and thought how the hormones had to be playing a part in all her moodiness. She seemed to have a more extreme case. All she wanted to do was be with her boyfriend. She had lost interest in everything. Her cutting had gotten worse. For a time, I thought it was a phase she had outgrown, and then it was suddenly back again. I can't even remember all the tearful conversations and pleadings I had with her trying to help.

Morgan graduated that same year while all this was going on. She went to college to study vocal performance. All those singing lessons had stuck. My little girl wanted to be an opera singer and she had a *beautiful* voice. I know I'm her mom, but I'm NOT the only one who thinks that. I remembered my dad telling me that my mother had an incredible voice and how all of her family was musically gifted. At one point the Big Jock had given Morgan one of his many cars to drive. She found it came with some serious strings. If Morgan didn't make sure his new daughter received gifts and birthday wishes from her siblings, she was repeatedly threatened with having the car taken from her. The list of unspoken obligations that contained very loud and verbal threats kept growing. One day she called me crying, telling me she was sick of being manipulated. She just wanted to give it back, so she owed him nothing. I understood. She asked me to buy her a car. So, I financed an older Nissan, not nearly as cool as the fun cars her dad had, but totally hers without strings. She was happy. She worked hard. She was gifted. She was kind. She had the kind of empathy that went deep and did something instead of just saying something. She was following her dreams. If I couldn't follow mine, at least I could watch with wonder as this little girl I raised bloomed. And so I kept existing. I kept doing the next necessary thing while life spun madly all around me. 'God? Do You *see*? Do You see it *all*? Does it matter?'

29

Evil

Woe to those who call evil good and good evil,
who put darkness for light and light for darkness,
who put bitter for sweet and sweet for bitter!
— Isaiah 5:20

There are six things that the Lord hates, seven that are an abomination to him:
haughty eyes, a lying tongue, and hands that shed innocent blood, a heart that devises wicked plans, feet that make
haste to run to evil, a false witness who breathes out lies,
and one who sows discord among brothers.
— Proverbs 6:16-19

After years at a centralized high school the X County Board of Education decided to send all special needs students to their home schools instead of grouping them at a few central schools and having well-resourced programs. I didn't want Houston to leave the program. He had a new teacher who was incredible and loved him dearly. Everyone loved him there. The students had grown up with him since elementary school and the program was so well established that the neurotypical peers who mentored in the program treated the special needs students like family.

That summer Paul and Benjamin were playing football and while they practiced at the high school fields, Houston would sit and watch his videos on my phone while I ran stadiums. (By that time I had given up the attempt to eliminate screens.) When I was done with stadiums I would run with Houston on the track. Houston would take off flying far ahead of me, flapping his hands, running like the wind, and making very loud deep EEEEEEEEEEEE noises as he ran. It was impossible to keep up with him. One late summer night Benjamin came up to me during the middle of practice. He was visibly upset. "Mom, I just heard some kids mocking Houston's noises. I tried to figure out who it was, but everyone has helmets on, and I can't tell." He wanted to hide in shame and punch the mocker in the face at the same time. Like my son, there was nothing I could do to fight back. A familiar burn stoked my heart. I had really had it with people. Why didn't adults stop cruelty when they saw it in children? Why did parents not teach their children better? Why didn't they insist their children treat others like they would want to be treated? I was so sick of people who saw life as something to dominate and win at others expense.

Shortly after that was a meeting at the school for all the concerned parents of special needs students. I told the principal what I had just witnessed. I told them they had just taken my son from a school where he was loved and put him in one where he would be mocked and now my other children were in the position where they would have to be witnesses to their brother being mocked or be his defenders. I said they get enough of that on a daily basis. Other parents voiced similar concerns. It didn't matter. It was done. The decision was final. Someone with a degree and ambition, who wanted to shake things up to make a name for herself, had decided what was best for all of us. I had little faith in the students. One of the coaches knew of my concern. He told me, "I know you're concerned, but our students need this. They need to know the world isn't just about them. They need to learn how to love others who are different." I agreed, but I didn't want my son to be the sacrificial lamb for their learning curve.

In October I was recruited to another insurance company doing the same assistant work but getting paid a bit more. I jumped at the chance. I was told there was room for advancement and that thrilled me beyond what I can explain. It was a specialized field which made the opportunities for learning an industry more compelling. I had a wonderful mentor and supervisor. She was a single mom too and understood some of the struggles I faced. She also knew what hard work was and recognized it in me. I was respected, valued, and given an opportunity to learn and grow.

In February, at the age of seventeen, Reagan ran away from home. That's the short way of describing the drama. She would sneak off campus with her boyfriend into the woods. She was failing her classes. I was getting calls and emails from her teachers. My favorite was the one entitled - DEFINITELY NOT GRADUATING! The police told me they don't hunt down seventeen-year-olds. She kept breaking into our home when I was at work. She shattered windows. She vandalized cars. She spewed hate. A year earlier, after Morgan had left for college, I had put $6500 down on a new car for Reagan and her father had supposedly financed the rest. We had agreed she would help with her brothers as my workload steadily increased. After several acts of hateful defiance and drinking, I told her she was grounded from the car. She told me it was her car, her dad gave it to her, and I couldn't do anything. Anytime I tried to enforce any discipline the Big Jock would encourage her defiance. It was exhausting. I knew the only thing I could do was wait for the right moment. One morning when she wasn't watching I took the keys, and with only a few moments, ran down to the car. As soon as the beep of the alarm sounded, she came flying down after me. I already had the car in reverse and gunned it. She ran holding onto the door handle as long as she could. I took the car far away where she couldn't find it. She called the police and told them I stole her car and a dozen more ridiculous things. Then she was gone. She would call and text hideously cruel things trying to threaten me into giving her the car back. The Big Jock tried to file charges of car theft against me. My little girl who had loved me with her whole heart would say the exact same things her father would say to hurt me and laugh the same cruel laugh. My heart was broken.

When I searched her room, I found drug paraphernalia and a Ouija board. I was angry. I was scared. I found a ticket with a court date for several infractions. I had no idea where she was or what she was doing. Every time my phone rang, a surge of panic ran through me. I was in a constant state of intense anxiety, worried that each call could be the police notifying me that my daughter was dead. I hoped she would show up for her court date, so I went at the time listed on the ticket.

I sat in the courtroom and listened to the proceedings, watching the door, hoping for a sign of my daughter. A girl Reagan's age came in with her grandfather. Her head hung down sorrowfully. Her grandfather was a humble man with hands that showed a life of hard manual labor. His modest and simple clothing was clean and tucked into his work pants and belted. He trembled while he sat with his granddaughter. The girl's name was called, and she walked slowly to stand before the judge. The judge read the charges against her which were repeated probation violations related to drugs - opiates and heroin. The judge struggled as he told her gently, "It's because I don't want you to die that I am sending you to jail. This stuff will kill you. Do you know how many times I have had kids just like you stand before me for the exact same charges, and then I find out a few months later they've overdosed and died? I hate this part of my job. I know you're loved. Look at your grandfather." Tears were rolling down the girl's cheeks and her shoulders were trembling. "I only wish I could give you a longer sentence so you could completely get this trash out of your system. You don't have to have the same ending. DON'T have the same ending." He called the grandfather up to the bench. "Here is the name of a drug that could save her life if she overdoses. I want you to go to her primary care doctor and get them to write a prescription. Have them educate you. Don't put this off. Do it now. You might have to save her life and every minute counts." The grandfather's voice trembled as he said, "Yes sir. Thank you."

He embraced his granddaughter and they both broke down as the bailiff escorted her out of the courtroom and out of sight. The judge took his glasses off to wipe tears from his eyes. All of those people who had come to court to argue about running stop signs and speeding violations wept. Everyone was in tears. I was shaking, trembling at what might happen to my little girl. She never showed and an arrest warrant was issued. There was no escaping reality.

I kept texting and trying to reach her. After rounds and rounds of pleading with her and the gracious efforts of her teachers, she graduated. When I tried to hug her at her graduation, she pulled away from me like she didn't want me to touch her. It broke my heart. I could tell she was high. She swayed and her pupils were enormous. I smiled while I cried inside. She also broke up with the boyfriend who had controlled her every move for almost three years. He reached out to me for my help. I told him I couldn't reach her, and she wasn't listening to me. I stood in the back of the stadium as my daughter graduated and wondered how it could have gotten so bad. How can you give so much and love so deeply and be rejected? The next day she gave me a card saying to leave her alone, she didn't need me anymore. As she left, she pulled up her shirt to show me a huge tattoo of a tree wrapped around her rib cage. It was her flag of independence, and I was not welcome in her life. She flicked me off and left. That following morning at 6 am the phone rang. It was the county jail. She had been arrested. Two felony counts - felony theft and possession of cocaine. I felt like someone had knocked the air out of me.

The Big Jock actually called me and acted concerned. He said he was wrong for trying to help her rebel. Then he asked a favor. Could I please give him a few months of reprieve from child support and the arrearage payments? He told me a blurry story of confusing details that had resulted with him having to declare bankruptcy to protect himself from his investors. Realizing you never knew what the truth was with the Big Jock, I tried to get answers to some of the obvious questions. He rattled off two case numbers, so I was left with a piece of a puzzle but no idea as to what the truth was. I was mostly just concerned about Reagan and agreed to let him pause his payments for a few months. I went to the jail to wait. It's difficult to watch your child stand before a judge and post bond on her behalf. But that was my little girl. I might be shell shocked and numb, but it hadn't been the coroner's office calling me so there was still hope. She came home. Her crowd was a dangerous bunch. They did drugs, broke laws and didn't wear shoes. When I mentioned my concern, she would scream obscenities and slam doors. I caught one of her friends in my bedroom writing down all my information off my passport that had been hidden in a drawer. One day I found her curled up on her bed sobbing these gut-wrenching sobs that didn't have an end. Softly I pleaded with her to tell me what was wrong so I could help. She just shook her head.

After a few months the Big Jock asked to have Reagan's car returned to him. I agreed after he sent me a letter in writing promising to repay the down payment I had provided. I was in the process of trying to buy a home. I was so excited about buying a tiny ranch and fixing it up. I had plans drawn up, contractors retained. It was the third step in me getting my life back. Car, job, home. It had taken me ten years to get that far. Morgan drove Reagan's car down to Florida with the boys for their summer week with their dad. Then the Big Jock called me. He had started cleaning out the car and found two pill bottles prescribed to Reagan from 2014. They were drugs used in abortions. I was shaking. I drove to pick her up from work. HOW??? HOW??? How could she not tell me? How could she not let me help? All the events of the past few years raced through my mind like a merry go round gone wildly wrong. I had put her on the pill. I had nagged her about being consistent. I had told her she never had to be afraid. I had told her babies were blessings. I had told her over and over how much she was loved. I tried to think back to see if I had missed something, anything at all. She had hated me the whole time. She had shut me out. Had she heard *nothing*?

I told her I knew. She was silent. When we got home, she couldn't look at me. She sat on my bed and answered questions in a monotone voice while I tried to piece all the details together. Her boyfriend and his parents had forced her to have an abortion. The boyfriend had threatened to kill her or give her a Mexican abortion. The mom, the "woman of faith," had snuck my daughter out of school and driven her around downtown Atlanta to find a place that performed late term abortions. It had a big heart on the website when I looked it up. The father had sat my daughter down in his home and interrogated her about what her mother believed. Reagan told him, "My mom wrote a pro-life book. She took us to pro-life marches. She helps women who are pregnant." Never once did he ask her what she believed. My little girl was scared, scared of her boyfriend's father, scared of her boyfriend, scared of losing him too.

The father began giving orders. He told her he wasn't going to let his son's life get ruined. He ordered his wife to find an abortion clinic. He ordered his son to not let my daughter out of his sight. He ordered my daughter not to tell me. He ordered her to lie to me and ask permission to go to the Aquarium so she could be gone a long time without me questioning her. He orchestrated every tiny detail. In a monotone, all the details that she had hidden in her heart began spilling out of her. Her boyfriend would scream at her, "My dad had to spend all that money because of you!" He told her, "If you have that baby my family will sue you for custody. No one will ever approve of you as a mother." One horrifying abuse of power and manipulative act after another. I stopped her. I wanted to throw up. "Reagan! Fathers have NO rights. NO RIGHTS in the state of Georgia if they are not married to the mother. Did you know that? That was *YOUR* baby. No one else's! It was a lie! He couldn't have done anything at all. It was also coercion. I would have taken care of you and that baby. You *know* that! You know it. I told you over and over." I was shaking uncontrollably. I called the mom. I left a voicemail. "Reagan just told me that you took MY daughter to get an abortion when she was sixteen?? She didn't even have her driver's license. I need you to call me back immediately." Reagan continued in a numb monotone voice with the horrifying details. She had been 21 1/2 weeks into her pregnancy. She was so far along that a two-day procedure was required. I wish as you read this you could feel what I feel. It's not a word. It's a sound, a loud moan from underneath my belly button, deep within me that won't stop, that raises to a screech that has no end. It's the sound of a soul, my granddaughter's soul.

For the parental notification that was required by law, her boyfriend had instructed Reagan to use her father's name and provided an address for her to send it to - his friend Max. That's what she was told. She had been instructed by the father to list their address as her address. Her boyfriend had threatened her repeatedly and glared at her during the ultrasound, blocking her from viewing and glaring at her after he saw her face wash over with wonder at the sign of her child inside her.

After a while the father, not the mother, returned my call. I guess it was too much for her, considering she was a woman of faith and all. Isn't it interesting what she was faithful to? He screamed at me. "Why would she tell you now??!! Why would she tell you now?!" I explained that she hadn't; that the pill bottles had been found in the car. "Why would she keep those for all this time??" he screamed. "Clearly, she was upset and traumatized, and she had no other way to stay connected to her child. How dare you? How dare you take MY child without my knowledge or permission?" How dare you? Who does that??" He kept screaming, "I'm not going to have some stupid girl ruin my son's life. Ruin OUR lives. This is all HER fault!! It's all YOUR fault for raising a daughter like that!!" "This is MY fault?? You've got to be kidding me. I went to you repeatedly letting you know the relationship was not healthy. I asked for your help to enforce guidelines that were age appropriate, that were healthy. And instead, you helped your son threaten her, you coerced her, and you forced my daughter to have an abortion!! You sat there and lied to me and told me you would help them have an appropriate relationship. You told me that you would teach him how to be respectful and take her on dates and instead you went behind my back and destroyed my daughter and her child?? Your wife says she is this woman of faith, and she took my daughter out of school and drove her around downtown Atlanta to help her find an abortion clinic that specializes in late term abortions?? Who does that? Who takes someone else's child? She's MY child. Not yours. How do you follow God and help kill someone else's child? How can she even say that?" His screaming erupted again, "WHAT ARE YOU GOING TO DO??!! WHAT ARE YOU GOING TO DO??!!" His screams pierced my ear. "I DON'T KNOW!" I screamed back and hung up, shaking. Reagan just stared at me with her mouth open. "You defended me," she whispered. "YOU'RE MY DAUGHTER. Of course, I defended you. I LOVE YOU. Don't you know that? This is not your fault. Reagan, this is NOT your fault. I don't care what they told you. They lied to you." I sobbed.

I called the police. I paced. I wanted to scream. They went into my bedroom where Reagan was sitting curled up on my bed. They had me leave. She gave them her statement. I gave them mine at the kitchen table. They called the Big Jock and he told them what he had found and sent pictures. They were visibly disturbed and promised me a case would be opened, but there was little else they could do. The captain warned me that due to how long it had been he doubted there would be justice.

The first thing I did was get her medical records. For Reagan to return to the place that had become a gravesite was the beginning of uncovering and healing her deep, deep wounds. As for me, I was shaking I was so angry. We handed over our driver's licenses. Reagan timidly asked for her medical records. I stood behind her and stared at the woman behind the counter. I tried to measure my breaths. I kept my arms crossed to keep from shaking. I'm sure I looked like a mama bear whose cub was taken from her. I never broke my gaze. The woman behind the counter couldn't have been older than 23. She finally looked up at me and said, "I didn't work here when your daughter came here." "You work here now, don't you?" I flashed back at her. She laughed nervously. "Well, yes." I said nothing else. We were told to wait. I walked over to the waiting room. It was wretched. Women hung their heads down. It was deafeningly silent. I heard whistling. Startled at the sound, I turned and was absolutely stunned to see a young woman in scrubs coming from the back of the facility whistling and prancing as she walked. As if there was something back there that brought joy. My jaw dropped. I sat down with my daughter. All the magazines were untouched. I guess it's no time or place for celebrity gossip. I felt my skin begin to prickle fiercely like a thousand needles stabbing me over and over. I couldn't swallow. My stomach ached painfully. My hands were trembling. With everything in me I wanted to go to those women and tell them there was hope, that I knew how to get help. I wanted to hug them. I wanted to tell them it would all be ok. But I also knew that day was about getting the truth and seeking justice for my daughter and grandchild. I was face to face with the ugly research I had done years ago. I knew what they did with body parts of aborted babies. I was shaking thinking of what had been done with and to my grandchild. I couldn't stop thinking. My mind spun with the horror of it all, with the truth of it all. I tried telling my mind to stop. Stop. Stop. Stop. It wouldn't. Truth played a broken record.

We were escorted to two different rooms. In one, I asked to see the literature that was required by law. I showed it to Reagan and asked her if she received the counseling and literature the law required. The director was quiet and avoided eye contact, staring at her computer screen. "Just this," she whispered, pointing to one pamphlet. Did anyone tell you about other options? She shook her head no. "They wouldn't let me hear anything else." "Who?" I asked. She named her boyfriend and his father. It took everything in me to remain seated and silent. The director glanced sideways at me and quickly looked back at the screen. Still not looking at me, she commented that they have no way of verifying if someone gives them accurate information to abide by the parental notification laws, and the law does not require them to verify information provided to them. Inwardly I seethed. I wanted her to stop talking, stop trying to justify killing my granddaughter for money, stop trying to justify breaking my daughter's heart! My heart!!! In the second room, I gave the abortion clinic fifty dollars for my daughter's medical records which were stored offsite. My heart literally burned in my chest when I had to give them money. Was it blood money? No. It was a ransom for the truth.

Later that day, I was notified that the owner of the house I had contracted pulled out of the contract and sold it to someone else for more money. The owners knew my story. They had met my son. I wrote a letter pleading with them to reconsider. Greed won. I was surrounded by people doing whatever was in their interest. No wonder the world laughs at people who believe that good will win. Winners win, they take, and losers lose. All that working for good is a fool's game. The world's wisdom is rooted deeply in the survival of the fittest. Work for your own good. Destroy any threat. Take everything. And here I was believing in the invisible, impossible - the fool's dream.

A few days later the truth came via certified mail. It was worse than I thought. I picked my daughter up and gave her the envelope. I looked at her in shock as she ripped it open and started tearing through it. When she found the ultrasound picture, she held it to her chest and wailed in the passenger seat. I couldn't see the road anymore. The picture that pissed me off was the one of her empty womb. All three of their driver's licenses were copied and in the file. Despite the fact that our address was on my daughter's learner's permit, the boyfriend's address was listed on my daughter's information. It was the sam.5

e address that was listed on their licenses. Any idiot could have recognized there was coercion. I looked up the address where the parental notification was sent. Imagine my shock to find the address was a fraternity house at Georgia Tech. A friend of my daughter's boyfriend who was a member of the fraternity had forged the Big Jock's name. The clinic hadn't even waited for the time mandated by law after sending the notification before beginning the two-day procedure. Reagan began to share about what happened after and how her boyfriend treated her. She told me about the drugs she did to forget and numb the pain. We began to grieve together.

The second thing I did was get her in to see a counselor who specialized in post abortive trauma. Reagan loved her. I thought here is someone she can tell everything to, someone who knows how to help her heal. I sat in the car and wept. For that summer I took her every week.

One night I went to see my friend who had known me since the summer we first moved to Atlanta. We were in the same Bible class together and she had fallen in love with Reagan's bobbly head and giant blue eyes and the way she never cried and tried to smile and wave at everyone. When she told her son that night that her friend Katie was coming over, he asked, "Who's Katie?" She looked at him and said, "She's known about you before you ever existed. How do you not know her?" She told me that story and I just nodded my head. The divorce and Houston's autism had completely isolated me from the friends I had once held so dear. Loneliness had been enforced by circumstances and social pressures out of my control. She said, "I saw a picture of you on Facebook with a bunch of girls and I thought, "Oh good, she's got friends." I shook my head. "No. There are two women in that group of divorced women I would share secrets with, and life doesn't really allow us to even do that. I have no one."

I sat on her back porch and poured out all my anger and grief. I told her with assurance. "I know God's real. He knows I love Him. But God does NOT love me. There's just no way." I shook my head as a wave of grief welled up in my throat. "To me it's logical. He has all the power in the world to answer my prayers and He chooses not to. I do everything I can to stand up for the weak, to speak truth, and He allows my daughter to be destroyed and my grandchild to be taken. If you say you love someone and that someone keeps begging you to help them and you ignore them, not once, but over and over again for years and give them no relief when it's within your power to do so, but instead you help those who hurt her, HOW am I supposed to interpret those actions as love?? I cannot tolerate listening to all the *'suffering, persevering, His ways are higher than our ways, and all things work for good things'* people spew who haven't really endured much at all. God is MEAN to me. He's mean. He doesn't keep His promises, at least not to me. When is it going to stop? When?!!" And then, in case my friend dared to say let's pray, I added. "I can't talk to Him. I just can't." I felt anguish in every part of my body and spirit. In my heart I wanted to know where He was, why He wouldn't answer me. And yet, despite my broken heart, despite my anger, I missed Him. I missed feeling His presence. I missed just talking to Him. My friend listened and cried with me. She was a good friend.

It was all I could think about. I would try to distract myself with insurance quotes at work, but the pain laughed at my efforts to ignore it. Waves of grief would come, and I would run to the bathroom to cry in a stall. The crying brought on migraines that wouldn't go away. For decades, in an effort to stay positive, I had become a master at finding the silver lining. I knew the art of dancing in the rain. But now the truth laughed mockingly at my silly silver linings game. Life was black, there was no silver, and the music had died. Good was gone. The great thief had taken everything. There was nothing to cling to, no shred of anything at all. I reached out to one of my favorite pastors who had moved away. His wife had dealt with horrific post-abortive trauma, and he had posted about her pain with grace and love. I had to talk to someone, and this is what I wrote.

M-

As you know, my life is very difficult with burdens and struggles that most people will never experience. There is no rest and even joy is difficult, but I have always tried to have faith, count my blessings, hope, love people, look for the silver lining, etc. However, without going into great detail about my spiritual journey I will say my faith is so very fragile.

And now this... My daughter Reagan is 18, the same age as MG, the same age as SK, the same age as MM, etc. All of these young girls were raised with the same values, the same teachings, the same expectations, and standards and yet, my daughter is a freaking train wreck. Reagan barely graduated, chose all the wrong friends, has been a vandal, a drug abuser, promiscuous, a thief, suicidal, cruel. As a child she was the most precious human being I have known. She lived to make others happy. She loved Jesus. She was loving, kind, playful, wonderful. I can hardly stand seeing everyone sending off their daughters to college and all the congratulatory messages of raising precious young women as I am bailing mine out of jail for two felonies. I have not been able to understand it. How could this happen? What have I done? How did all of those stories taught, Bible verses and love produce this? I am baffled, ashamed, hurt. I get all the free will theology, but honestly, most of us believe if you raise children well, you should get decent results.

Then on Sunday, an old prescription bottle was found that was the worst thing I could have imagined. My daughter had an abortion two years ago. Obviously, this explains the horrible downward spiral she has committed herself to in earnest, but when I began to find out the details, I just am so out of my mind upset I can't even explain it. She was VERY far along in her pregnancy. When she told her boyfriend, he threatened to kill her or give her a Mexican abortion if she was too far along to have it taken care of, and that she wasn't going to fuck up his life. His parents, his

CHRISTIAN parents (the dad always referred to what a great woman of faith his wife is) coerced my daughter into having an abortion, had the parental notification sent to a local fraternity house (addressed to her dad which they knew was not the custodial parent) where a friend of the boyfriend who was a member of the fraternity forged my ex-husband's name on the parental notification required by law in the state of Georgia. I can't even pick someone's child up from school without a note and these people had the audacity to take someone else's child without her parents' knowledge, drive her to an abortion clinic two days in a row, and pay $1600 to kill my grandchild and burden her with the kind of emotional trauma that she will live with the rest of her life????!!!!!! When I confronted them, they screamed they were protecting their son, that it was her choice, that they did nothing wrong and had no responsibility or blame in any of this. This was all Reagan's fault and my fault for raising a daughter like that! I had to leave my son's orientation today because I knew there was a chance I would run into that mother. I can't believe these people. I can't believe this kind of phony faith where you don't do the hard job of helping people do the right thing. I don't understand a faith that is ok paying money to kill your grandchild, so you don't have your child's life derailed. I don't understand the kind of faith where you put all the blame on a 16-year-old who thought she was in love and was scared when you are the freaking adult! I don't understand, after I have spent my entire adult life being an advocate for young pregnant women, how God would allow my own daughter to go through an abortion with me never even knowing, never being able to help, never being able to love her and give her hope, never being able to give her the courage and the resources to make the right choice. I can't believe I was a grandmother and now I'm not and some asshole has no problem destroying that life. I can't believe my little girl is destroyed.

I don't hate them, but I can't even explain the emotion I am feeling. How do you do that? HOW? She is a stay-at-home mom and makes jewelry in her spare time in their luxurious home. I have been killing myself as a single mother of five children, struggling to make ends meet, working 3 jobs, fighting for child support, raising a severely autistic child that I have to bath, shave, wipe, everything. As an aside - after almost a decade of renting I thought I was finally going to get a home, a $130K home that I could fix up. A week before closing the seller took another contract for more money because the FHA process took longer than the length of the contract. So, I lost the house and the money the day after I found out I lost a grandchild. I guess I just want to know, WTF??? I don't want to hear some Christian platitude or some lesson about faith, suffering, or endurance that is going to make me scream. I am frankly beginning to believe that even though God is good, He is not good to me. I don't want to believe this but the disparity between what I see around me and what I experience is really hard to get past. When is life going to get better? When am I going to see His goodness in my life? Why do I see other people who do selfish things to hurt and destroy others prosper in their easy lives while they worship and sing praises on Sunday while my family struggles so deeply for so long? I do not know how much more, how many more times my heart can be broken. The things in this email are just the most recent in an unrelenting life of bad things that won't stop happening. Even though I had gotten to a place of peace about my circumstances and had been able to tell myself very hopeful, positive things, I am now having a difficult time changing my thought patterns and I know I need to. When I try to say good things to myself it feels like I am lying to myself.

Please tell me something that will actually help. I know because of your loving support of your wife that you understand on some level what I am experiencing. Frankly, I can't stand listening to most pastors. Right now, I can listen to you and SB and that's it. I realize I just unleashed an avalanche on you, and I am really sorry. I really am. This is not a problem I can go tell all my girlfriends about. One of my friends literally, just two seconds ago sent me videos of her two-week-old grandson. I can't stop crying. If you have nothing that will help, I understand. Again, I'm sorry and thank you.

His response.

Katie,

Thank you for giving me the gift of your heart. I read your message twice and I'm just sitting here trying to absorb the trauma, pain, disappointment, injustice, powerlessness, and loneliness that must be your unwanted daily companions. There really aren't any words to say. Romans tells us that the Spirit intercedes for us with groans that words cannot express. What you've had to walk through is so painful that I don't even know if there is any sane response beyond looking heavenward and groaning. There are simply no words that are sufficient to do the pain justice. Let me tell you what I do know. You are a good woman. You are an exceptional mother. You have been shit on time and time again and you've had every opportunity to quit, and you haven't. I doubt many of your friends have a clue as to how hard even one day of your life is. I'm proud of you and I am frankly in awe of the fact that you show up and do the deal day in and day out. I'm so heartbroken over your daughter. It's not your fault and it's not the end of the story. There is hope for her, I'm earnestly praying that God will do for her what no human can. That he will heal the years the locust have eaten and restore her. I'm just praying that you'll have the grace to love her and hold her like Jesus would. I can't fathom the level of injustice, evil, and outright hypocrisy that went into that family making the decision to do the abortion like that. All I can say is that God will deal with them. In fact, I'm praying that God will deal with them sooner than later. There is no covering up anything before the eyes of 'Him to whom we must give account'. That is not your fault. I don't always understand why I do what I do, so I sure can't speculate on why God does what he does. I know you're not alone in asking these questions. So many of the writers of the Psalms looked around and saw how basically F@#$ed up the world was and cried out, "WHY GOD??!! WHY do the wicked prosper?? WHY do the righteous seem forsaken?? WHY do you seem so far away??" I read that their pain was discombobulating, and their deliverance seemed distant. I also read that somehow, in God's presence, some peace found them. That's what I'm praying for you. Peace. Hope. One more day of staying in the game. You are a good woman, Katie. I'm so grateful that you trusted me enough to share with me a little bit of your pain. Your honesty and desperation are sacred ground. I don't have any answers, I only have the hope that the God who said, "I live in a high and holy place, but also with he who is lowly and contrite… to revive the heart of the lowly and to restore the heart of the contrite" will show himself to be faithful and true. You are not alone.

Your friend,

M

I started visiting attorneys. I contacted the Assistant District Attorney, former judges, the very best medical malpractice attorneys in the state, attorneys who had won cases like this in the past. The horrifying consensus was due to the time that had passed, her age, the lack of evidence of physical trauma, and the limitations of the law there was no "cause of action" they could prove. I was stunned at the limitations of the law. I was urged to close the chapter, accept defeat, grieve, and get on with life.

I couldn't even try to talk to God anymore. I couldn't read a verse. If I heard a worship song, I changed the station as fast as I could. I would drop the boys off at church. I couldn't step inside. At night I would repeat to myself one thing and one thing only. I love Him, but He doesn't love me. His plan for me was to give me nothing and then crush me. For a time, this became my belief system. I saw everything through this lens. I was alone. I was angry, angry that God didn't answer my cries for help, angry that people didn't help, angry that the justice system didn't work, angry at the ease all around me, angry that people bailed on me, angry that people only cared about themselves, angry at my anger. I realized I didn't like anger at all. To me it seemed an exhausting and pointless emotion for someone who had no access to power of any kind. The reality was I was too utterly exhausted to be angry. So I gave it up and instead let my raw woundedness feel the space. This is what despair feeds on. It's hollow and empty with a bottomless pit for a foundation. I refused to put an expectation of joyfulness on myself until something changed. It was an emotional compromise I made and a loneliness and darkness I really don't wish on anyone. I believed in one good thing. It was the only thing I clung to - that one day I would get a miracle for my son. I refused to let that go.

Reagan's battles with darkness continued. She couldn't stop hating herself, and she adamantly refused to forgive herself. I sent her to Rachel's Vineyard. It's a time and place for grieving, forgiving, and being loved. On the last day I got a message from her asking me to bring her guitar right away and inviting me to stay for the service at the end. I grabbed it and practically ran with Houston to the car, speeding the whole way. She played a song in remembrance of her baby at the service and told her story in brief. She named her daughter Elyse. Sweet Elyse. And for a moment, she had let me back into her world, into her heart. The years would continue with her letting me in and pushing me out again, with dramatic, raging outbursts, with pain no one should ever bear.

In the middle of all this Morgan called me as I drove to work after lunch one day. "Hey sweetie. What's up?" "Well," she took a breath and continued, "I'm pregnant." It was my turn to take a breath. "Oh Morgan. Well, a baby is a blessing... always. Don't worry about anything. We will figure it out. Who have you told? What did Jason say?" (That was her boyfriend.) "Well, he's freaking out a little. His parents aren't handling it well, but he knows how I feel. My friends asked me if I was scared to tell you and I told them no. I already knew what you would say. And you know what?" She chuckled. "That's exactly what you said." "Morgan, there is no way in hell I'm going to let you go through what I went through. No matter what, I'll be there." After a few more months she posted an adorable announcement on Facebook that I shared. Two days later my kids asked what people said about the announcement since Morgan was the first child from the group of friends from church to announce a pregnancy and her young and unwed status was no secret. "Um, I think there were fifteen likes and a few comments." They were shocked at the low like count. I shrugged and commented that the number of likes wasn't important. But then I heard through the grapevine that the disapproving housewives of Christendom were weighing in on my daughter's pregnancy offline. I had HAD it. I posted an ultrasound picture of my grandchild with this message and pruned my friends list.

Hello everyone,

I don't usually share my thoughts on Facebook unless it is something that matters very much to me. Facebook is funny. Some people use it a lot and post almost anything. Other people just post the big moments. I don't post too often but I try to like and comment on all the people in my life to let them know I care, I notice, and I'm happy for them even if it's just little moments. Just recently I posted about Houston's birthday and was touched by all the people who commented. But last week I shared that I was going to be a grandmother, that my oldest daughter was pregnant and only a handful of people commented or liked (THANK YOU VERY VERY MUCH FOR EVERY ONE OF THOSE SWEET WORDS). I didn't notice at first until a young person (of course) noticed how few likes or comments I had gotten for such big news. I shrugged it off - after all what do I care about that stuff, people are busy, etc. - until I realized that people were sharing the news outside of Facebook without a word to me. I am left to conclude the commentary amounts to shock and judgment, not kindness or joy. So for the record... I am very happy my daughter is having a baby! A BABY IS ALWAYS A BLESSING! ALWAYS! Even if it's a surprise. There is not only one set of approved circumstances in which to have a child. This child was created by God, is loved by God, has a purpose, and will be celebrated and loved. My daughter will not be made to feel shame because people don't approve of her circumstances. She is going to be an incredible mother. She will continue to sing brilliantly. She will be loved and supported as every mother should. I wonder if all those people who self-righteously judge realize that young girls abort their babies in order to avoid the shame and judgment they feel so entitled to bestow. Judgment doesn't make our society more wholesome, it makes it more cruel. Love to you, little one. I can't wait to kiss and hold you.

I was outside of the flock for sure and had NO desire to find a way back in.

30

Chaos, Baby Kisses, and Brokenness

Cause I am a sinner
If it's not one thing it's another
Caught up in words, Tangled in lies
But You are a Savior
And You take brokenness aside
And make it beautiful... [85]

Not surprisingly, the Big Jock never paid child support again. I would send letters pleading and received threats and excuses in response. I filed again. He hired a nasty attorney who thought a good tactic was to attack me even though he was in contempt. I had to file several squash orders to stop his legal assaults. The Big Jock always repaid grace with gunfire. He viewed every act of self-defense or justice as an act of aggression and responded in kind. Because of this, I would do everything I could before pursuing legal action. My heart would clinch in fright at the very sight of him and my mouth would go dry. I would forget how to speak. He knew it. When we finally got to trial, my attorney wanted to negotiate. I threw my hands in the air. "That's his game! He always wants to negotiate. I don't care if I get less. I want enforcement. I want a judge." My attorney loved negotiating too and so I got strong armed into another negotiation where I got nothing, and he got an extension. His attorney commented he hadn't paid her most recent invoice either. I looked at her incredulously. Are you kidding me? If he had paid me, he wouldn't have needed to hire and pay you. How courts allow fathers to pay attorneys instead of mothers has always been a head scratcher for me. I could say my prayers were unanswered, but I had stopped praying. Months later when I asked my attorney to pursue the case, he resigned. He was certain I wouldn't be getting anything, which meant he wouldn't be either.

My home became grand central if it hadn't been already. Morgan and Jason moved in with us and the boys moved to the garage with Reagan. There were eight of us in a three-bedroom townhome with my daughter's two cats to round out the circus. I had never had much to offer my kids, but I decided the garage would be the man cave my boys had dreamed of. The front door was an open door for all their friends. It smelled like boy, a whole different kind of teen spirit. The walls were covered with flags and taxidermy. They loved it. Countless kids slept over on old couches and carpet scraps, played endless rounds of games, ate ramen, cereal, and Little Caesars. I had been blessed over the years to become a second mama to many. Morgan's best friend since sixth grade will always be one of my children. It was home to everyone I could make it home to. I might not have much, but you're welcome to it, was my mama mantra.

During her pregnancy Morgan's blood pressure skyrocketed and her amniotic fluid dropped dangerously low. After being hospitalized she was put on bedrest. As she tried to manage her schoolwork from

---

[85] *Brokenness Aside;* By David Leonard and Leslie Jordan. Copyright Capitol Cmg Amplifier o/b/o Integrity's Alleluia! Music and Capitol Cmg Paragon o/b/o Integrity's Praise! Music

bed, she began to experience the hurdles the world has against single motherhood. She was shocked by it. I knew it all too well. I was proud of her for standing up for herself and her journey.

A few weeks before my grandson was due, I got an email from the woman who ran the special needs class at my old church. It was brief and horrific. "I am so sad to let you know about this, but B-'s mom killed her and then shot herself. This happened in a local hotel. Her father is totally devastated and shocked. Please pray… I am sick about this news." I had to read it several times before it sunk in. I was so angry, devastated. *How?* How could she do that to B-? We had seen B- every Sunday for at least fifteen years in our special needs class. She was always smiling. Her father brought her faithfully every single Sunday. Like his daughter, he was always smiling and had a kind word to say. For those of us with special needs children there was an unspoken understanding and camaraderie. I went to the funeral, and I saw many familiar faces from so many years past. The chapel was filled with love - good people who loved God and loved people. But the waste and tragedy of the loss weighed heavily on me. How was it that two special needs young adults had already lost their lives? Where are You God? *This* is Your plan?

Into this chaos my grandson was born. I didn't go to the hospital that morning to see God, but as I watched that precious, tiny human being make his entrance and my daughter's face of utter shock as they placed him in her arms, I felt His realness. My grandson's overwhelmed young father stood with tears running down his face and I felt His nearness. It was like He was looking over my shoulder and I felt the warmth of His gaze, but I couldn't look back. I didn't want to have any hopes or expectations ever again, even though it's hard to stay true to that when you hold a newborn's hand. Optimism, love, the hope, and wonder of new life began its work on my wounded heart. It's amazing that much goodness and power can be found in just five pounds. Houston held his nephew with the most precious tenderness and fed him. Life was new again.

During these years my boys became young men. They both had their awkward stages and were figuring out who they were. Paul was, by everyone's standards, tediously lawful. His brother and sister would groan and complain at his insistence on following every possible rule and pointing out their grievances, with the exception of chores. Benjamin was big hearted. They both excelled in wrestling and were respected by their coaches and teachers. I wanted them to learn how to be disciplined and passionate, courageous in the face of adversity, and how to fight even if you knew you wouldn't win. These were the life lessons I knew they would need. But there were problems too. They played too many online games and were on their phones too much. I had long given up that battle. I learned they didn't hear their names until the fifth or sixth time I called them. They wanted to eat out for every single meal. With my sad spur-of-the moment cooking, I really couldn't blame them. This was all just part of life. They were typical good boys with the temperaments and appetites of teenagers. The only thing that concerned me was the narrative I knew the Big Jock was feeding them. I heard statements all the time such as, "What do you even do with the child support?" Since I hadn't received any in a long time the question unnerved me. When I would tell them no to a request, their retort was, "The child support is supposed to be spent on us." The indentation in my tongue grew deep. I practiced breathing and biting the tongue that did not want to hold. Every now and then I could see the discontent and rebellion the Big Jock foddered. He could feed them any lie he wanted and all I could respond with was, "He hasn't paid *ANYTHING* in a year and was already deeply in arrears. I'm the one who's supporting this family."

I still taught cross fit type classes at 5 am and yoga for a little bit of extra money. The men in the class would tease me about my car saying, "You work out like this, and you drive that???" I would just shrug my shoulders and say, "Clearly I'm not struggling with my image. You can't beat no car payment." Then that faithful, wonderful minivan that had been given to me started having severe car problems and after four months in a row of expensive car repairs, a wheel that was about to break off the axle, and an electrical issue that disengaged the steering mechanism, my mechanic told me, "Katie, that's it. I'm not going to fix it. Go get a new car," and then added, "And get a car you like. Don't settle." I was so scared to buy a car on my own. I was astonished to find out I had good credit. I got a Jeep Wrangler. I was 43 and it was my first new car. I drove with the top down and emotionally was somewhere between crying and laughing. I was proud of myself. It was me. I had done it. As excited as I was, the car payment made me anxious. The budget was so tight. Saying yes to anything induced a mathematical fit in my brain. It's hard to be anxious and joyful at the same time. The boys didn't understand money. They just knew they weren't embarrassed to be seen with me anymore.

My dad lived near Canada and would try to see us when he could. The summer before he had taken a fishing trip to Canada that he wanted to recreate for his grandsons. It sounded amazing. As the year progressed, my dad reconnected with his roommate from college. His plans changed. He decided to take my boys to visit his old roommate in Philadelphia. It was not quite the trip they had hoped for, but my dad got them excited. Then Paul failed Algebra and had to take online summer school, which is about as much fun as a summer long tooth extraction. That means I got to continue the nagging that didn't work during the school year. Oh, the joy...

I had already prepped my dad that he would have to take on the role of homework enforcer to make sure Paul stayed on task. After I came home from dropping them off at the airport, I looked in horror to see that Paul had left my computer. I called my dad and anxiously told him. He assured me that his friend would have a computer Paul could use. During the week my dad called every day to tell me that the boys were constantly on their phones and that Paul was holding everyone up with his online homework and kept having to be nagged to complete it. I explained to my dad repeatedly that is exactly how it is at home too. It's just part of raising teenage boys. I could hear his level of annoyance increasing with every call. Finally, I told him, "Dad, they're not like I was. They don't love to learn like I did. They're just normal, but they're good boys." I called the boys and they told me they would try harder. I asked about the trip, and they told me that when they went to Philadelphia, the friend was yelling all kinds of things at people while he was driving and drove on the sidewalk. Paul told me how he was showing them how to make their computers and gadgets run faster. They told me that Pop's friend was really volatile, but they were still having a good time. Clearly not the fishing trip I had hoped for. On the evening of July 4th, I got a call from my dad telling me there was an emergency and he had to talk to me immediately. My dad could overreact, so I tried to stay calm. I could tell from his voice he was extremely upset. The boys were supposed to come home the next morning. When I called him back, he launched into a furious tale of how Paul had tried to break into his friend's bank account. His friend grabbed the phone from my dad and started screaming at me, "I know he did it! I know he did it! He cleared the history to cover his tracks. And I don't have a dog that jumped up on the computer! I know it was him! My password doesn't work, and I've been locked out! My mother left me a whole bunch of money and I can't get into my bank account to see if it's all there. I'm going first thing in the morning, and I'll PROVE your son tried to break into my account! I know it was him, this isn't even the first thing they've stolen this week." I responded, "Wait a minute. Please let me speak to Paul."

Paul got on the phone and his voice was quivering. "Mom, Mom. Pop is MEAN!" Mom, he's mean. I'm going to call Dad."

"Paul, that's a bad idea. Let me take care of this. First of all, I just have to ask but I know you, ok? Did you try to break into the bank account?"

"NO!"

"Okay. I believe you. Can you tell me what he was saying about the history?"

"Mom, you know I always clear the history. It makes it run faster."

"Yes. I do know that. What's this they are saying about you stealing?"

"Mom. Oh my gosh. There were some pork rinds in the pantry. We didn't know we weren't supposed to eat them."

I had to hold the phone away from me for a moment. I couldn't believe my dad was defending this insanity and not standing up for his grandson, but he had never defended me either.. "Wow. Ok. Try to calm down. I believe you. Ok?"

"Ok," his voice still quivered.

"I love you, Paul."

"I love you, too."

My dad got back on the phone, and I told him, "Dad, Paul didn't try to break into the account. I'm sure there is an explanation."

"There sure is. HE DID IT! The bank will have proof in the morning."

"Dad, are you sure it wasn't your friend forgetting his password after Paul cleared the history? That can clear passwords too you know."

"No, he didn't forget his password!"

"Did you ask him?"

"YES, I did! I know who it was. It was Paul and it was his father who put him up to it!" I kept trying to be rational and talk to him.

"Dad, seriously. I know I have told you how manipulative he is, but I don't think he would have his kids steal money from a stranger's bank account when they are visiting their grandfather. The more important issue is your grandson. You obviously don't know him. He is a rule follower. It annoys his friends and siblings. He just wouldn't do anything like that."

"His father would! Paul would do it for him."

The phone call ended with tempers and tears on their end, and complete helplessness on mine. I just wanted my boys back. That night Houston and I sat on an empty sidewalk far from the fireworks and watched the celebration of freedom in silence with the mosquitos. Joyless.

I have never been so happy to see my boys. They were visibly shaken by the incident. My dad called me that morning saying that his friend had gone to the bank, and they told him it was from that computer that the passwords failed. "Dad, that doesn't prove Paul was the one who put in the wrong passwords." "YES, IT DOES!" My dad seethed. We didn't speak for months. He sent a letter saying Morgan's shoplifting proved Paul's guilt as well and that I hadn't done a good job raising them and that they needed a father figure. They needed more discipline. Morgan was crushed to hear that was how he really felt about her. I wrote him back and defended my children's honor and my mothering. I finally called him trying to talk through the issues and bring resolution. I sat in a Fuddruckers trying to talk to him and tell him how he had done this to me as a child and I was not going to discipline my son with no evidence against him. "I AM THE EVIDENCE! I SAID HE DID IT AND THAT'S ALL THE EVIDENCE YOU NEED!!!!" Tears streamed down my face as I told him, no. Emphatically no. Him saying it was so, was no evidence at all. The silent streak continued.

31

Silent Torments

For I consider that the sufferings of this present time are
not worth comparing with the glory that is to be revealed to us.
— Romans 8:18

I had finally been able to afford dental insurance and took everyone. It had been years. The dentist said he thought there was an issue with one of Houston's teeth, but it was difficult to get him to be still enough to take the x-ray. To perform any procedure, full anesthesia would be required which wouldn't be covered. He mentioned that he wasn't licensed to do anesthesia and there weren't that many dentists that were. I put it in the back of my head to find a dentist who specialized in disabilities and anesthesia. When I called the dental organization that served Medicaid patients, I was told if they find a tooth that needs a root canal, they will just extract it. I was appalled. Why was it ethical to extract a tooth instead of repair one because someone was disabled??? I was infuriated. Shall we dismember them too?

Soon after that school year started, his new teacher that I had never met contacted me saying he took her hand and led her to the clinic and kept saying, "Tooth, tooth - hurt, hurt." Houston almost never complained of pain, so I knew it was serious. That was one of the odd things about autism. Their pain tolerance and threshold were enormous, frighteningly so. I took him to five different specialists. One of the endodontists said urgently, "The nerve is exposed and infected. You HAVE to get him into surgery immediately. But no one was certified to do it. In total it was over ten days of excruciating pain before he had his root canal, which a saint of a doctor finally did even though he had already said he had no openings. I had called his assistant pleading and pleading for an emergency dental surgery in the hospital. The dentist who finally performed the procedure told me that disability and dentistry, the need of anesthesia, and a total lack of understanding about how to care for this population was the dirty secret of dentistry. No one wanted to serve them. But we found a doctor who did. He healed instead of cut off. He saw value where others saw nothing at all. He saw my son.

The torment inside Reagan continued. There were constant eruptions, and it was obvious she was abusing alcohol and drugs. She was arrested while driving on a suspended license, and I bailed her out of jail. She didn't even seem grateful. It was like it was expected of me and she could still treat me any way she liked. Then there was a breakup that broke her heart. There were more drugs. Finally, there was an episode at work that ended up with her being admitted to a treatment center for depression and suicide. I went to visit her, and she spewed more hate. When she got out, she moved in with a friend and we rarely saw her. I remember being really excited when she came to decorate the tree at Christmas. I missed my baby girl so much.

At the end of the year, I was recruited by another insurance company for an underwriting position. I was thrilled at the opportunity to advance my career and make more money. Anything that would provide any relief at all was my constant focus. I was flown to Boston and sat through multiple interviews. I wanted the job but was upfront about my biggest concern. My son would be aging out of school within a year, and I knew I would need flexibility. The job offered some, but not much. I weighed the money vs the flexibility, the opportunity vs the safety of working with people I knew. My bills won. I gave my notice. The VP at my company was surprised and countered with making a spot for me on a new team. I discussed it with the new supervisor and told him what would make me stay was the same financial package along with the flexibility I would need as my son aged out of school. He told me the whole team worked remotely and that wasn't a problem at all. So, I stayed and outperformed their projections by a long shot. I developed more extensive relationships with brokers as well as the support staff and basically, tried to exceed everyone's expectations for service and standards. I helped train other members on the team and just tried to be a blessing in every way I could. They were as happy as they could be with me. My reviews were glowing.

The drama of Houston's teeth was how he started his last official year of public school. I had started the process of touring potential day programs for Houston for when he aged out of school and had finished the application process for the Georgia Vocational Rehabilitation program. I met with the most respected psychologist for autism who had asked me some questions and gave me some information about a learning method I had never heard of. He told me that one of his patients is able to communicate this way. He gave me the patient's mother's name and number. Along with all my other meetings, I met with this mother at a Dunkin' Donuts who told me her son had broken out of his shell and pointed to letters to communicate. She showed me paragraphs he had spelled that she had written down. I listened. I thought... maybe. But the doubts. I doubt her son is that severe. I wonder if it would work for someone like Houston. I don't know how I could do that with him all day long every day. He won't sit still for one minute. In my ignorance, I didn't ask much at all because it seemed so far out of reach and inconceivable. After I talked to her, I thought, well, maybe I could try that one day. It might work. Maybe.

Paul had one of those bodies that can toss a wrestler before he knows he hit the ground, which also made him great at tumbling. When one of the wrestling coaches recruited some of the wrestlers as cheerleaders for the co-ed team, I scrimped to put the money together for that too. I went to watch the parent exhibition with Houston. Two of the cheerleaders came running over to me and threw their arms around Houston. "OH MY GOSH! Houston! What are you doing here?" I looked at them. "How do y'all know Houston?" "Oh, we are mentors. We see him every day." "What's he doing here?" "Paul is his brother," I answered. They both looked shocked. "Paul? Houston is Paul's brother?" A chill ran through me, and I had three thoughts simultaneously. Benjamin had always been a part of the mentoring program. He loved all the special needs kids. He saw himself as their friend and protector. Paul had always been embarrassed of his brother, but to not even acknowledge him?! I was pissed. When I talked to him about it later, he just shrugged it off. The second thought was, 'Who are these incredible young women who obviously adore my son?' During Christmas break they came and got him and took them to their house and made cookies with him and just spent time with him. At the end of the year, he was invited to their graduation party. He had been included, even if he did have to have me there to stop the impulses. The list of people who loved my son was longer than I realized. The third thought was of that picture and his giant smile from a few years earlier. Houston most definitely loved cheerleaders.

32

The Miracle Pergola

And he who was seated on the throne said, "Behold, I am making all things new."
Also he said, "Write this down, for these words are trustworthy and true."
— Revelation 21:5

I focused on the pressing business of the day. I met with state senators about my son's status on the waitlist. It had been almost seven years and still nothing, not a word. The programs were awful, not because people weren't trying, but because they treated these adults like preschoolers. There was bingo, coloring, and mind-numbing vocational exercises because they had no ability to speak or control their body. The question that had haunted me his entire life now demanded a very real answer. What exactly was I going to do now that he was older? I heard stories of parents sending their kids away, stories of sterilization "just in case" something happened. By March I had seen all the programs, all the facilities. The ugly reality was more hopeless than I could have imagined. The last facility was a large campus that housed living quarters and a vocational program. You could drop your kid off and forget you ever had one. I asked about the independent living quarters and the security. I was told if they had issues with elopement, there was another house on the campus where they would be housed. She took me there. It was essentially a nursing home with locks. Elderly disabled people stared at televisions and people laid motionless in beds. Who knows how long they had been there.~ The final building was a ward with much more nursing staff. My arms began to get prickly, and I walked away from the crowd trying to get out as fast as I could. I asked if anyone's families visited. Our guide said sweetly and truthfully. "We become their family."

As politely as I could, I excused myself and got in my car. The second the door shut the sobbing started. I called my old friend that had long ago sent me the Tiffany necklace. "I can't send him there! I just can't! I don't know what I'm going to do but there is no way in hell he's going to one of these places! I just can't do it. It's like death." I broke down into more sobs. I really wanted to scream F*******CCCCCKKKKK at the top of my lungs. Even though she didn't begin to understand, she listened. She knew she had told me years earlier that one day I would need to do what was best for me. The advice was common and seemed sensible. But clearly, anything not best for him was not best for me either.

My grandson grew and we all loved him so. It was chaos with so many people but most of the time we gave grace to each other and pushed through. There was a baby crying, Morgan singing opera, Houston's constant noises, Reagan having a fit or playing her music loud throughout the house, and Paul and Benjamin gaming. As Morgan prepared for and approached her senior recital and her son's first birthday, she decided she would do something quite wonderful. She was growing into a woman of extraordinary grace. Despite the harshness from her grandfather, she invited my dad and his wife down for both the recital and first birthday party which was spring break. I was nervous with everything still unresolved. Paul told me he intended to be around as little as possible. I tried to make the place as nice as I could for the visit. I bought outdoor furniture, a fire pit and ordered a pergola from Target. And that pergola changed my life.

Early one morning as I sat on the bike at the fitness center, I read an email from a pastor at my old church. He said God had put me on his heart and he wanted to know if he could pray for me. It had taken the church five years to realize that I was a lost sheep, and somebody should look for me. I thanked him and spilled out the litany of awfulness and unanswered prayers. I told him that God wouldn't listen to me, so I had stopped praying. He told me he would pray.

That afternoon the boys and their friends agreed to take on the daunting assembly of the pergola that had been sitting unopened. When I got home, they were all shirtless and skinny, some on a ladder and others yelling and lifting the final pieces in place. There were only eight or so extra pieces that somehow didn't make it into the assembly process, so I decided this was definitely a win. I knew when to say good job. They posed on the ladder with embarrassingly white chests, showing off their muscles and I smiled at their youth and joy. Paul ran over to me and asked if I would take everyone out to eat. "Pizza???" I asked. "NO. No way. This project deserves way more than pizza. It was SO hard," he answered emphatically. I chuckled. "Chili's?" He conferred with the boys, and they agreed. And off we went. I wanted to get there well before the dinner rush. I looked at the pergola as I closed the back door and smiled. Little did I know, they had just erected my miracle.

Timing is everything they say. If they hadn't finished at that time on that day, if they had been ok with pizza, if I had suggested another restaurant, if they had wanted to go later, none of what happened next would have happened. Who knows what would have happened or if some version of this story would even be told.~

I drove to Chili's and Benjamin said, "Mom, why did you go to this one? We go to the other one." He was right. We did. But I had auto piloted to this location with absolutely no thought as to why. I went to call Paul who, at that moment, pulled into the parking lot in his friend's car. "Benjamin, look. They're here. Isn't that funny? They went to the wrong one too." So with a crowd of eight we filled up a booth and began to enjoy their thank you meal, the fruits of their labor. It was early, only 4:30 in the afternoon so the place was mostly empty. This was always the best time to go anywhere - when everyone else wasn't there. For two decades we had learned how to navigate on the sidelines of life. We lived in isolation, always making sure we didn't bother the general public. Houston, as usual, was watching videos on my phone. It kept him from stealing food off people's plates and making the noises that make people stare contemptuously. As we ate, the boys laughed and teased each other, and the hostess seated a father and son two booths ahead of us. From the uncontrolled body movements, I could tell the son's autism was similar to Houston's. Benjamin noticed too. He elbowed me and whispered, "Are you going to say something?" I nodded, "Of course." I knew they had likely intentionally come at this time of day too, like the woman at the well who came in the heat of the day to avoid the judgment of others. It was a way of life. Go to the back. Don't bother the normal people.

After the boys finished eating, I stood up with Houston and walked over to their booth. I always tried to reach out to others on the sidelines of this life. It was so lonely. Any kind voice was always a blessing. I said, "Hi. We were sitting over there and noticed you guys. My son is autistic too. I know how isolating it is and I just wanted to say hi." The father looked up surprised and called my name. I looked again, surprised to see a father from the church and special needs Sunday school class I had left so many years earlier. My face showed my surprise. "This is J-," he said waving across the table toward his son. I looked at the young man who had to have been 6'3". "That's J-! Oh, my goodness. I would never have recognized him. Wow!" The father wasted zero time. Zero. With urgency and excitement in his voice he asked, "What are you going to do with Houston?" Here was someone I could tell the truth too. "I don't know! I don't know. He ages out in October.

OCTOBER! I've been visiting all these places and they are awful. AWFUL. I don't know what I'm going to do. Honestly, I'm freaking out." The father slid out of his seat and his son followed. In the middle of the aisle at Chili's this father said, "I don't want to tell you what to do, but I want to tell you what we have done with J-. It has changed our lives. So, you see, they are in there." He turned to Houston who was stimming over a video on my phone. "Houston. We know you're in there." I looked at him and at Houston in shock. NO ONE had ever spoken to him that way. I realized that was the first time anyone had ever spoken to Houston as if he understood everything going on around him. He was 21 years old, and it was the first time he was treated intelligently or included in a conversation. The father continued. "We taught J- how to spell out his thoughts on these boards and now he can communicate. And you wouldn't believe it. They understand everything. They just can't control what they say."

I remembered the mom from Dunkin Donuts. "Wait. I think I've heard about this." My mind began to spin. Was it really true? I knew J- was very much like Houston. Could it work? The father continued. "Once he learned to communicate J- explained that he understood what we told him to do but he couldn't make his body respond or it would respond not the way he wanted so it looked like he didn't understand. For example, he would say 'park, park, park,' all the time. So we thought he wanted to go to the park. When he was able to communicate, he told us, 'I know I keep saying park. I just can't stop saying it. I don't want to go to the park.' Do you know how stupid we felt? All these years and we just kept responding to what he would say, and it wasn't what he meant. Can you imagine how frustrating that was for him?" I looked over at J-. J-'s body is very jerky. His arms, head, and hands are in constant motion. When I looked at him, he had wrapped his arms around himself squeezing them close to keep them still. He was using an intense amount of energy to keep his head still and he was staring into my eyes with such intensity that I can only describe it as the way a soul communicates when no words are possible. It was his soul to mine. I stared back with my mouth unknowingly ajar in wonder. I knew. It was real. His father continued, "I would love to have you come over and see for yourself. I'm not as good as my wife is on the boards. She would love to talk to you." I jerked back to look at him, not wanting to break my gaze with J-. "YES. Please. Can I have your number?" He gave it to me. It was time to go, but I didn't want to leave. I practically skipped to the car. Unexpectedly, hope had come.

With that in my mind, I went back to getting ready for my dad's visit. I was anxious. It was uncomfortable and awkward even from the first moment they entered. I could tell my dad wanted to pretend there wasn't a problem. He had a pride that didn't allow for bending, and certainly couldn't admit he was wrong. When I served dinner, he said surprised, "When did you learn to cook?" I held my tongue. "Dad, I was making meals as a kid. I just don't like to cook for picky eaters when I have no money, especially when I'm exhausted. It's not a lack of skill, just a lack of desire." Paul came in, shook hands, and left the house less than thirty seconds later. The tension was dense with everything unsaid. A comment was made mocking my name I hated. I rolled my eyes. His beautiful wife mentioned that he had really done me a disservice naming me the name of his abusive wife. My dad dismissed it with a wave of his hand. "AHH! Keeps her humble." A sharp pain stung in my gut at his words. I turned away. He really had no idea. When he asked if he could help with anything, I mentioned that he could help Benjamin set up the firepit and that one of my lamps had stopped working. Projects were his way of saying he loved me. He loved the challenges and loved telling me what was wrong. It's part of his perfectionism and even though I knew that, it was not what I wanted to hear. There was always something else being said. There was always a look, a judgmental, dissatisfied look. The fire pit was too close to the awning by three inches. There was no way these lamps could be rewired, and so on. I preferred grace, ignorance, and broken things. Let other people be perfect. I was just trying to stay alive.

Paul stayed away. He didn't want to be home. Saturday morning I dropped him off at Chick-fil-A where he worked, and we talked. He was angry and I didn't blame him. So, I called my dad from the parking lot trying to be a peacemaker, seeking reconciliation. I said, "Dad, I don't know if you realized that Paul hasn't been around." "Yes, I did. What's wrong with him?" His voice was filled with disgust. Very, very calmly, like I was tiptoeing toward a giant, I said, "Well Dad. He's still upset you accused him of trying to break into your friend's computer. He hasn't gotten over it." "Well, he DID." Finality, disgust, and judgment hung in the air. "No Dad. He didn't. I'm not going to convict him with no evidence." It was like I had ignited the nuclear button. "I SAY HE DID IT AND THAT'S THE ONLY EVIDENCE YOU NEED!!!!" What followed next was a horrifying loss of control on my dad's part. I will spare the reader. I screamed back the horrifying truth that had been my childhood. He denied and I declared. I went home and went to my room sobbing for hours. I told everyone that was still in the house what had happened in between sobs. We all decided not to tell Morgan since she was downtown preparing for her recital that night. I got an apology text from my father that didn't come close to getting to the truth. I knew him and I knew pride was running the show, no matter what the text said.

We all went to watch Morgan perform her senior recital. It was exquisite. Her heart was full. She had no idea of the drama and discord. My heart was a wreck. I could barely smile when I should have been absolutely joyous. My dad showed up to the recital and afterward acted like nothing was wrong and offered a handshake. I was incredulous. A handshake? I shook his hand and gave his beautiful wife a hug.

The next day was my grandson's first birthday. It was at the other grandparent's home across town. I couldn't believe my dad showed up. He smiled and shook hands and acted like he was the guest of honor. I sat on the back porch with Paul. I couldn't bring myself to go inside to watch the show he was putting on. When it was time for my grandson to blow out his first candle my dad was in the front snapping pictures. I sat against the wall on the hearth next to my daughter's best friend's mom. Because we had known each other since our girls were in sixth grade, she wanted a life update. In what can only be called discouragement, I told her the current set of problems. The one she decided to encourage me with was finding an attorney to deal with the Big Jock. She had just the name for me and promised to send it to me. I saw my dad shaking hands with everyone except me and Paul and leaving. I followed him out to the car. He opened the car door for his wife and as it shut, he saw me. Hatefully he said, "What do you want? Do you have something to say?" The hostility pierced my heart. "Yes. I want to say goodbye to her." "She has nothing to say to you." I welled up. "And I have nothing to say to you." I turned and ran inside crying - again. Morgan was livid. No one was going to hurt her mom. "That's it, Mom. I'm done. I'm not going to pretend like everything is fine when it's not, and he's not going to apologize, that's obvious."

So, it was this hurting heart that went to J-'s house the next weekend to watch him spell. They opened their home to me and explained the progression of the boards. J-'s mother graciously and patiently explained J-'s story and confidently assured me Houston was capable. The problem had never been intelligence, she explained. It was motor planning, sequencing, and control. The father added in anecdotes. "It's like if you never shot a basketball and someone handed you a ball and told you to put it into that basket way up there. You would miss. But what if someone said, 'Hold the ball like this. Use this hand. Bend your knees. Use this much pressure. Look at this point. Push this way. Jump like this.' Over time you would learn the motor control and the movements to put the ball in the basket if you kept practicing. These guys have no control of their intentional movements and must learn all of them. And the impulsive movements they can't stop."

While J- spelled he would flick a rubber spider in his hand and adjust his hat. Despite all the movement, his engagement and conversation were remarkable. His words said one thing clearly. SEE ME. HEAR ME. I'M

NOT MY BODY. J-'s mom showed me transcripts of J- and his friend B- who explained what their life had been like trapped in their bodies and what the boards had done for them. It left me speechless. My head was spinning. How could I have been so wrong, so clueless for so long? I choked back tears as the full reality of all Houston had been deprived of for two decades began to sink deeply through my being. Like the worst reel of instant replay, I began thinking of how we spoke to him like he wasn't there, how we treated him like a child. The realization tumbled down upon me like a rockslide. J-'s mom explained how it had taken over a year to break into open communication and how J- had endured so much trauma being trapped with no voice that there were months of weeping and remorse at all they had done wrong. But finally, he had been able to express himself and the difference was life itself. The three of them told me a story of such an incredible and life altering shift that the only way I can explain it is Jesus rubbing mud on someone's eyes. He was blind. But then suddenly he could see. And why? *It was not that this man sinned, or his parents, but that the works of God might be displayed in him.* [86]

I asked question after question trying to get a handle on what I was watching. Below are some of the questions from this first meeting.

Katie: How do you know this will work on anyone? Maybe it's just you and you're special.

J-: Mom, tell her about E-.

J-'s mom: If the answer is a long one, sometimes J- will ask me to explain it if I know the answer just to save time. E- was a speech therapist for decades before she learned to use the boards to help non-speaking people communicate. She went back to as many of her old clients as she could to teach them and every one of them has been able to use this to communicate. Soma is the one who taught her.

Katie: When did you learn to read?

J-: I was about four when I taught myself how to read.

Katie: What about loops? The constant stimming on Disney videos.

J-: Mom, tell her about loops.

J-'s mom: It's basically hard wired in their brain, and they don't have the motor control to stop it. It's like the messages are being sent but not being received by the part of the brain and body they are directed to. What we are trying to do with the boards is create new neural pathways that eventually will reduce those loops.

Katie: Do you know how to do math more complex than you've been taught?

J-: Math is not my forte, but I have friends who have not been taught any math and are incredible at it.

Katie: What about friends? Have you been able to make new friends?

J-: (He jumped up in his seat and got excited.) That's been the best part.

J-'s dad: The difference between before the boards and after is we had no hope and no life and now - everything is possible.

Toward the end I said to J-, "I know you have something to tell me. I can tell. What is it you want to tell me?" He began spelling rapidly and furiously. I watched from the side and could see him poke every single letter independently. His mom had to keep stopping to write down everything. She didn't say a word as he spelled. As he spelled, I noticed he hit the letter z. I thought to myself. 'What word is he spelling with a z in it?'

Here is J-'s message. Hope hadn't just come to visit; she had come to make a stand.

It is life changing and that is an understatement. Houston needs a voice. We all do. Don't let time or money deter you. Don't let the fact that you tried a Zillion interventions over the years that haven't worked make you gun shy. This is the real deal and it works. It is not a cure. We don't need a cure. We need a chance to live a life as who we are. I'm certain Houston is as excited for you to meet him as

[86] John 9:3

you will be. We are great people. We just need the same opportunities to be known that everyone gets effortlessly. I'm so glad you came and have an open mind. By the way my mom is fabulous at this and she should work with Houston and you.

There was only one thing to do. "Do the best you can until you know better. Then when you know better, do better."[87] I went home and walked up the stairs where Houston was stimming on YouTube videos. "I'm getting you a voice," I told him confidently. It was a declaration. He looked at me with a funny look like I had surprised him, and then he turned back to the screen. I told his brothers and they barely listened to me. I called Morgan and she gave me the typical warning. Don't get your hopes up. My heart declared within me, 'NO! HOPE is exactly what needs to get up and show up. NOW. The time is now. I WILL HOPE.' I felt deep inside me that hope was fire. It was the energy that moved my belief to make it real, a belief that had been sputtering in neutral for five years, present but without a direction. I wasn't going to ask the shadows what to do anymore. My face was turned to the light.

I called his teacher and excitedly told her. She told me she had heard of it, and it had been discredited. I responded, "BUT I SAW HIM DO IT! I saw him spell every one of these letters. No one was guiding him. Would you be willing to meet him? You've got to see this for yourself." She was noncommittal and unbelieving. She told me they are focused on reducing prompts and developing independent skills. I knew the IEP by heart. That was not what independence looked like. Independence was being able to direct your own life and have a voice. Independence was not putting socks in boxes and pushing buttons on a calculator with less prompts. Independence or really, autonomy was the goal - the ability to make decisions that affected you and request the help you needed to accomplish the goals you had chosen for yourself.

I told Paul and Benjamin they were going to meet J-. This time I brought Houston. Houston had my phone and the boys sat on a couch. I asked so many questions. I wanted them to see J- and believe in their brother. I wanted them to be as mind blown as I was. I wanted them to be as excited as I was to teach Houston. This was it. Our chance. Our answer to more prayers and tears than can possibly be told. I asked J-. "When did you realize you would be able to use the boards to communicate?" J- spelled, "I knew from the very first moment. But I couldn't control my hands or my fingers for a really long time. It was so frustrating trying to tell my finger where to point and it wouldn't do what I was telling it." I asked more questions. J- spelled out elaborate and intelligent answers. I was angry at Paul. Because it was taking J- time to spell his answers to the questions, Paul closed his eyes and began to drift off. Here was this young man, a year older than him, and Paul couldn't stay awake to hear what he had to say. Irritated, I told Paul to ask J- a question. Paul pulled himself out of his nap, and with no expectations asked him if he liked Marvel movies. J- spelled out that he had seen some but usually they were too violent for him, and he had a sensitive spirit. He explained he had to be careful what he exposed himself to. Paul's eyes opened wide. He hadn't expected him to know about Marvel, to have an opinion, or to know about anything. He said, "Wow." Benjamin sat taking in the whole situation and with each answer growing in awareness that Houston had been aware the whole time. Houston had stopped watching the phone and had looked at J- and then to his brothers almost as if to watch their response. J- told them about his incredible mind. "An autistic mind is a gift. Not being able to control your body is the curse." I asked J- one last question. I had read about photographic memories and of course there was Rain Man. I had read about synesthesia and that some individuals with autism have this very remarkable blending of senses. I wondered if Houston had some of these abilities. "Do you have any other abilities?" J- "Yes."

---

[87] Maya Angelou

We thanked them and got in the car. I asked the boys, "Well, what do you think of J-? Pretty amazing, isn't he?" "Totally. Do you really think Houston is like J-?" "Yes, I do." "He totally thinks we're assholes then." I looked at them and nodded, "Totally." We all were. The only thing I could do is everything, everything to make up for almost twenty-two years of being dead wrong.

I told my good friend that I had started dating about what I had seen. He said, "What's stopping you? Do it now." "I am. Nothing is stopping me. I'm going to a workshop that's scheduled next week." Even so, I don't think he believed. It takes seeing. He had held my hand when he read Houston's psychological evaluation. He knew what it said. I went to a workshop and ordered letter boards. When I sat in that classroom and watched the lesson on the monitor, I was astonished. These were autistics with severe verbal loops and fidgety bodies. I watched in shock as they completed lessons on complicated topics. One family came in and sat down next to me. A beautiful girl with dreadlocks sat next to her father as the mother got her sister situated with the instructor in the other room. The young girl told me that was her twin sister on the screen. They were sixteen. The mother came to sit with them, and the lesson began. The girl's body bucked, and she made wails that sounded like a fire engine siren. She smacked at the instructor, who ducked expertly, and her twin sister videotaped the entire time. Her parents watched nervously. The lesson continued. Although it took a long time, she completed a lesson and answered correctly, spelling out several things including "photosynthesis," all while her body moved wildly. Her parents sat next to me crying. Her father kept repeating photosynthesis and shaking his head. Her mother couldn't wipe all the tears of joy away. They just kept coming. "Let's go get cake!" crying and laughing as she said it and her daughter started jumping. I walked directly over to one of the organizers and said, "I need to schedule an appointment as soon as possible." Before leaving I talked to another mom who basically told me the same thing J-'s family said. "It changed our lives," and much much more.

33

Breaking Bonds and Seeing the Light

He will not grow faint or be discouraged
till he has established justice in the earth; and the coastlands wait for his law...
To open blind eyes, To bring out prisoners from the dungeon,
from the prison those who sit in darkness.
— Isaiah 42:4,7

After a year and a half Morgan, her fiancé, and my grandson moved in with her fiancé's parents. They planned on getting married in November. I waited expectantly for Houston's appointment, and I prepared for court. My friend had sent the attorney's information to me. I was still scared. I told my friend I was dating my concern about filing again. He told me I couldn't live my life in fear. "What's he going to do?" he gestured flippantly. I responded with all the fear I felt and all the rationality I possessed, "I don't know, but I promise you, he will do something. He always fights back harder than whatever he thinks was done to him. I just know it will be bad."

I remembered the story of his father demanding he never lose a fight. It was the mantra, the banner of his life. I remembered the frighteningly accurate psychological assessment from 2005 that my divorce attorney had been astounded by and so thrilled to have as evidence. *"(The Big Jock)'s perspective exhibits a disdain for the welfare of others, very little empathy, is self-centered and displays a socially intimidating manner. He is resentful, rebellious, antagonistic, and refractory. He is insensitive to the needs and feelings of other people - seemingly interested in how they can be used. He is also prideful, self-reliant, unsentimental, and competitive. His perspective on human relations is to outwit others and exert power over them before they can dominate him. He has a kill or be killed mentality and believes only vigilance and vigorous counteraction can put a stop to the malice of others. He is inclined to brood and harbor grudges. He is easily provoked and distorts and magnifies the actions and remarks of others into purposeful slander. Much of his aggressive demeanor and posturing comes as a result of his desire for power and control."* I was right to be afraid. The new attorney I had been referred to was not going to settle, she was going to fight. I loved her. I warned her. Finally I had someone who would fight for me. Trepidly, I filed for contempt.

For Reagan's birthday she invited me to hear her sing at Eddie's Attic. I almost never heard from her, so I was surprised and excited she wanted to include me. Houston came with me. When it was finally her turn to sing, I listened in astonishment. There was my tiny little girl playing furiously on her guitar and belting out a voice that had such power and intensity that people were absolutely stunned. But there was more. She sang her original song and my jaw dropped as I listened to the lyrics. It wasn't about her old boyfriend. It was about her dad.

Yeah this might seem just a little familiar
Well my whole life has been a little familiar
I had this dream that you were a shark
You came in through the roof
You ate my momma up

Big bad shark you ate my heart
And I don't know what to do
I don't want to be like you
I can't get over you

I remember when the book ripped
We all lined up to get whipped
Then it all ended with one great big hit
Big old shark you ate my heart
I'm always falling through
I don't want to be like you

Big bad shark you ate my heart
Now I'm always falling through
I don't want to be like you
I don't want to be like you

I remember you sat on the couch
Sharpening your knife saying goodbye to your wife
And your life and your kids and your everything
Hell we could have been your everything
But you let us all
You let us all down

Big old shark you ate my heart
And I don't know what to do
I can't get over you!

Big old shark you ate my heart
Now I'm always falling through
I don't want to be like you.

The book ripping, his insane violent rage, his obsession with knives and sharks, the constant lies… It was all there in that song and in my daughters' powerful voice. Her rage was all over that stage. But even though she had partnered with him to hurt me at one point, I realized there was hope. She was terrified of him. She didn't want to be like him. When she was done, I hugged her tight. "It was about your dad. I didn't know." There was so much I wanted to say and ask. Finally, she had cracked a window to let me back in. I knew I had to tread softly, or she would slam it shut.

I drove an hour into Atlanta for Houston's appointment. The appointment was in a small school with an orange door beside a stone church. The building was old and awkward, just the kind I liked with high ceilings, narrow hallways, walls that had settled unevenly, and two-inch-wide wood planks that creaked when you walked. Buildings like this always speak to me, whispering, 'oh the stories we could tell'. We were directed to a closed door and kindly told to wait. Houston jumped and with his massive frame, the whole building shook. His calves are like large logs and his thighs like tree trunks. "Telephone. Telephone. Telephone," he repeated with the urgency I knew meant he was close to biting himself. "No Houston. We have an appointment. No telephone."

The door opened. The young woman I had met at the workshop stood smiling at us and invited us inside the room. She closed the door behind us. "Hi, it's so nice to meet you. Houston, my name is Jacqueline. We are here at The C----S which is a school for students who learn differently." While she was talking Houston, in a loud and demanding voice, repeated emphatically, "Telephone. Telephone. Telephone." "No, Houston. I already told you no. You need to be quiet. You can't hear her." She paused and looked at me. "Oh, he can hear me just fine. He can hear everything." I looked at her, still not believing, still not understanding. "Houston, will you have a seat next to me?" He walked over to a small table seated under a small window placed high on the wall. The light streamed in brightly and beautifully. Jacqueline sat next to him and placed a pencil in his hand. She held up a black stencil board with the letters J-R. And then my life changed.

"Houston, what's my name?" He immediately pointed to the J. She picked up another board and he began pointing to all the letters in her name, correctly. She asked, "Where are we?" He spelled, "The C----S." My hands had flown to cover my mouth at the letter J. By now I was trying to recover from the shock. "Wait. How does he know how to spell that?" She looked at me, patiently trying to explain what to her was painfully obvious. "He knows how to spell. These guys tend to be great spellers." "But how? How did he learn? No one taught him." "He's been learning his whole life. Language is everywhere," she answered matter of factly. It was like she was telling me the mysteries of the universe as if they were flashcards.

My mind was spinning but my heart was spinning faster. She continued with a lesson. The door burst open and a beautiful young blond about fifteen years old ran in the room with a teacher chasing after her. "I'm so sorry to interrupt. She always has to meet anyone new," the teacher apologized. She went straight up to Houston and said eagerly, "Hi. What's your name?" Houston stared at her with obvious awe. Slowly, with very deliberate control he answered, "Houston." She started to ask more questions and the teacher guided her out of the room. I realized that was the first time, other than the failed flirtation at the trampoline park on his sixteenth birthday, that a girl had ever greeted him as an equal. He was 21. They continued with the lesson. Jacqueline stopped and turned to me. "Oh my gosh. His motor control is amazing. He's going to be great at this." I instinctively thought about all the impulsiveness and said, "He is?" She nodded and then told me it was my turn. 'Already?' I thought. 'I don't know what I'm doing.'

Step by step she walked me through the steps to spelling on the boards and being a communication regulation partner. She stressed posture. She explained the lessons were a teach/ask format with known questions, followed by semi-open where there were several possible known answers, and then open questions, where the answer could be anything at all. She warned me that open questions took the longest to attain from a skill level and explained that when the speller had less motor control, you reduced the cognitive and emotional demand. She stressed this would take daily practice. She stressed this would take a long time. She stressed board placement. She stressed how to correctly use prompts and gestures. She stressed to not touch them. She stressed to not lead them or tell them the letter. She explained motor planning and I just sat there with my mouth open. How could I just now be hearing all this? Why was he almost 22 and someone was just now saying these things to me? She had me do a lesson. It was on Edward Shackleton, the British geographer and explorer to the Antarctic and his expeditions. It was a story of remarkable perseverance and survival, and my son, who had been fed a steady diet of first grade material for almost his entire education, spelled the answer to every known question. There was a light in his eyes I had never seen. No. There was a fire in his eyes I had never seen.

I went home calling every person I could think of to tell them. I don't know if anyone believed me or not. I don't think I even cared. I told strangers. I told friends. I told absolutely everyone. Like the blind man who could see - who cares if you believe me. I can SEE!

My chains are gone
I've been set free
My God, my Savior has ransomed me
And like a flood His mercy rains
Unending love, Amazing grace

The Lord has promised good to me
His word my hope secures
He will my shield and portion be
As long as life endures

My chains are gone
I've been set free
My God, my Savior has ransomed me
And like a flood His mercy rains
Unending love, Amazing grace

The earth shall soon dissolve like snow
The sun forbear to shine
But God, Who called me here below
Will be forever mine
Will be forever mine
You are forever mine [88]

---

[88] *Amazing Grace (My Chains are Gone)*; By Chris Tomlin, Louie Giglio, & John Newton. Copyright Worshiptogether.Com Songs, Vamos Publishing, and Six Steps Music

Life Begins

This is the sound of life beginning
This is the song of the redeemed
It was the rhythm of Your dancing
That woke me from my sleep
This is the sound of hope returning
All Your children coming home
I can hear the sound of heaven
Singing over us... [89]

On May 21, 2018, I started my very first letter board lesson with Houston at our kitchen table. And sure enough, he spelled perfectly. It was one letter at a time - one exhausting letter at a time. I wrote down every word like they were the most precious gems I had ever been given. When we finished the lesson, I just shook my head as I looked at the list of words he had spelled. I could see the effort and the exhaustion. Just sitting up straight fatigued him. He would lean over to the left, and I would pull him center over and over again. I was a bulldog. I wanted more. He was going to get to open communication. Nothing was going to stop me from knowing my son. When he would stim, I would stop him. When he would try to bite, I wouldn't let him. I kept pushing him to spell. There were breaks but they were short. To me it made sense. Like practicing piano, it was so hard in the beginning to look at a note and make your finger hit the right note. But with practice, over and over, those neural pathways started to form and suddenly fingers could dance on their own all over the piano

May 24, 2018 — Houston almost walked in the graduation ceremony. His mentor that he loved had come back from college just to walk with him. They had a game she would play with him. She treated him with warmth and goodness. She considered him a friend. To her, love was an act. She had taken him to prom and to homecoming. That year the special needs program had chosen him as their Homecoming King and I had watched my three handsome sons put on suits, most of which we pulled together from Goodwill.

It was a special night, even with the limitations. For a few hours, he was just a guy at a dance with a friend who cared for him. The school had already decided Houston's name would be called first out of over 800 students. Just moments before they were about to call names, the skies opened up to a torrential thunderstorm and thousands of people ran for the gymnasium. With no hope of rescuing the event they decided to hold a reading of the names the following morning.

May 25, 2018 — The next morning his teacher met me on the football field, and I stood to the side. His friend was not able to be there, so his teacher took her place. The stands were only half full. There was no band, no music. It was anti-climactic. While I waited, I got a call from the Department of Behavioral Health and Developmental Disabilities saying that they would begin his assessment for the NOW/COMP waiver after

[89] *This is the Sound*; By Steffany Gretzinger and Bobby Strand. Copyright Bethel Music Publishing

seven years. I told his teacher. "You're never going to believe who just called me." When I told her she just shook her head, "Just in time." Then about five minutes later his principal read his name and my incredible son crossed the stage, shook his hand, and accepted the red diploma cover. Although he was still eligible to attend school until the last day of his 21st year of life, public education was over.

That afternoon I took him out to celebrate in his cap and gown. People were kind and for once didn't ask rude questions. It was almost like the cap and gown was a superhero cape. That was all they could see. Later we went to get yogurt. As we ate outside a young woman walked up to me with an enormous smile and said, "I was at the graduation. He was the first one to graduate. It's Houston, right?" I thought I was going to cry in my yogurt. Someone cared about my son and had noticed his special day. Then I saw the rest of her family walking up behind her and immediately I knew why. Her brother was like Houston. When you live it, you can recognize it a mile away. She introduced herself and then her mom and brother. He was in the same program with Houston. His mother and I immediately started swapping information. She had five kids too. Her autistic son was the youngest. I told her I had just started this new method to teach Houston to communicate and explained it. She half-listened just as I had done regarding other therapies so many times before. She told me how she felt awful about going on a trip without her son but his stims were so difficult they just couldn't handle it. It was easier for him to stay behind. I saw the exhaustion on her face. All I could feel was compassion for her, for her son. It was obvious how much that whole family loved each other. Right then, I decided I was going to make sure her son had the same opportunity Houston was getting. All of Houston's classmates weighed heavily on my heart and mind. This had to work. It had to.

Summer 2018 was the summer of spelling. As much as I possibly could, as much as Houston could stand, that is all we did. Every day I would take him to a special needs summer camp, pick him up after work, go home and spell until I knew I couldn't push him any further. As always days started at 4:30 am, I taught at 5:15 am, had coffee with the older gentlemen at McDonald's, got ready for work, took Houston to camp, worked a full day, picked him up, spelled with him, made dinner (usually something frozen), or took the boys for Chick-fil-A (they both worked there by this time), gave Houston a shower, went to bed. Most people don't realize summers are much harder on families with a special needs child. I had long ago resented the question people would ask, "So what are your plans for the summer?" 'Survive,' was always my thought. One special needs mom would always say the sight of the yellow bus at the end of summer was the most beautiful in the world. She called spring break the little s before the big S, like s was a dirty word. What people must understand is - We need help. It's hard. Too hard. For too long. We never ever get to rest. We never get to dream. We never get relief. We never get to live.

I spelled and spelled and spelled with him. I wrote down almost every word. In the beginning when he pointed to letters the pencil would struggle to make it to a letter and would sometimes hit right beside a letter or above/below it. I would make him get it inside the letter. Over time his accuracy increased. Words became phrases. I asked questions not listed and found he knew more than just the known questions. My yellow legal pad was filling up fast. The best way to describe this time was ravenous hunger. I would not relent on his lessons and drilled like a drill sergeant or a coach running all the way down the sidelines.

The end of June approached and finally my day in court arrived. I got so nervous like I always did. The Big Jock came in with a rolling cart and a 6-inch binder and boxes. That's what the acting world calls props. He pulled out a color-coded chart that was about five feet wide and then began to speak in his calm, salesman voice saying that he only was supposed to pay this amount and had actually overpaid by $500,000. Sometimes the lies are so bad that it leaves your head rattling because no normal person would try to create such a complete farce that has no factual basis in reality. He pulled out an affidavit from 2011 as his proof. I quickly got my bearings. Ok, that's what he's doing.

"Your honor, there were two affidavits. He's just showing you one. The other was for $125,000 that he never paid, and the interest has been accruing on both since 2006. In addition he has never paid for any of the medical or extracurricular expenses that he was ordered to pay, and he is severely behind on child support." I explained.

The judge looked at him, "Is that true?"

"Well, I uh… This chart shows-"

"Do you have proof? Actual deposits into her bank account proving your numbers on this chart?" she demanded.

"Uh, yes, I'll look for them." He began fumbling in his folder and said he had given me a lump sum in 2014.

"That's not how it went, your honor. That is the amount we agreed to in the 2014 agreement and part of that went to my attorney fees. That amount was included right here in the statements. There are no sums he has paid that are not listed and we have provided every deposit statement. We have also shown the amount of money he has had in his bank accounts and his spending during this time."

"We have some of the bank records, but there are multiple records missing that he still hasn't provided," my attorney added.

"Why haven't you been paying child support?" asked the judge.

"Well your honor, I'm disabled. I had a goiter wrapped around my jugular and they cut my jugular when they removed it."

The judge scoffed and rebutted quickly, "If they cut your jugular, you'd be dead."

His attorney interjected trying to fix the lie, "Nicked! They nicked his jugular!"

"How do you pay your rent?" the judge asked.

"My baby's mother pays the mortgage."

My attorney leaned over to me and whispered, "Did he just say baby mama?"

I bit my lip to keep from laughing outloud and whispered back, "He told me he had gotten married."

"Why can't you work? Why can't you pay her something?" the judge asked.

His attorney said something about it being admirable that I had been taking care of my children and the judge said, "HER? Her children? They are their children. Why don't we take their autistic son and have your client take care of him for a while and see what it's really like, give her a break. What about that?"

Panic was all over my face. I just started shaking my head no. As if Solomon himself was wearing that judge's robe, the judge turned her wise face toward my direction and looked at me with eyes that said, 'Hush honey, I would never let that happen.' She had made her point. The Big Jock's attorney said nothing at all. I spoke up. "Your honor, I am working two jobs right now trying to make ends meet and have worked as many as three over these years. I have cared for and financially supported five kids on my own. I have supported my adult daughter and her child as well. Both of my sons work part time, go to school, and participate in sports. Why can't he work one job?"

The judge looked at him, "Are you a deadbeat?"

"No, your honor. Through no fault of my own I had a company that failed because of grand theft."

"How much money do you have?" He pulled out a negative balance from a credit union.

"Do you have a degree?" she asked.

"Yes."

"From where?" she asked.

"From the U of -."

The judge stifled a laugh at the mention of the elite private school. Her voice had authority and judgment. "And you can't get a *job*? You have no excuse. Why aren't you doing something? Even minimum wage would be something. I'll tell you what. I'll give you three months. You give her minimum wage for three months due on the first and a $5000 lump sum the day before your next compliance hearing, which at that point you had better have a real job. All monies owed are still accruing. This doesn't change what you owe."

My attorney and I walked out in a bit of a daze. She grabbed me and said, "You did that. That was you. You did great!" Her paralegal called as we walked to the parking garage. She had found some filings against the Big Jock from the State Attorney in Florida. I asked her to send me the findings.

I drove to Houston's camp and parked. I pulled out my phone and began to read. Mortgage fraud and fraud against the elderly were definitive and there were additional pending charges. Much of the law referenced in the documents was regarding the abuse of the elderly. I recalled the psychological report submitted to court during my divorce. *"(The Big Jock)'s scores indicate that he can be very impulsive and will likely strive for immediate gratification of his impulses. He does not plan his behavior very well, and he may act without considering the consequences of his actions. His behavior often involves poor judgment and considerable risk taking. Often there does not appear to be any guilt associated with the aggressive behavior. Sometimes (The Big Jock) may feign guilt and remorse when his behaviors get him into trouble, but such responses typically are short-lived, disappearing when the immediate crisis passes."* He had agreed to pay $253,700 in reparation and fines to stay out of jail. Then I saw the date of the plea deal. It was ten days after he had told me he was having trouble with his company and had asked for a break from his child support payments. I sat there in the parking lot thinking so many things with a knot in my stomach. My stupid grace giving had believed another lie. What else did I not know? What else had he hidden?

When I got home, I was shocked to see Reagan there with her best friend. We hadn't seen her in months. The first thought I had when I saw her was the question from years ago. "Do you think the Big Jock ever molested Reagan?" Something said to me, 'Talk to her. NOW.' "Reagan, can I please talk to you in my room, alone?" She wouldn't make eye contact, but she nodded her head. In my room I closed the door and told her I had just been to court. "After court I was sent some documents about charges against him in Florida."

She practically shouted and for the first time she looked right at me, "What was it??!! What was he charged with??"

I was taken aback. "It was financial fraud. That's not what I wanted to talk about."

"What was it?? What did he DO??" she yelled.

Her insistence caught me off guard. "The part that got me was the fraud against the elderly. It just reminded me that he will do anything. He doesn't care who he hurts. Reagan, did your dad ever do anything to you that you were afraid to tell me?" She looked like a deer in the headlights. She looked at the ground.

"There was this one time in the shower." She paused, "The big shower, the one with the stone and the big window."

I tried to keep my voice calm. I was trembling. "Yes. I remember. You were very young, Reagan. Very. What did he DO?"

"I don't know. I don't know. I thought I must have had a fever because I was sleeping, and he got me out of bed."

"Reagan, *try* to remember. What happened?"

"I don't know. He hit my head. He hit my head!!! That's all I remember!"

I tried to stay calm, but I was not. I stopped and started my sentence several times. "Reagan, your father NEVER took care of any of you when you were sick. NEVER. And you didn't get sick very often. Can you please try to remember? Anything at all. Any detail."

She nodded and pleaded, "Can I *leave*?" I nodded and hugged her. She could barely hug me back. My head and stomach were spinning but my heart felt like it was on fire.

The next week I got a call from my boyfriend. The Big Jock had sent a letter full of lies to make sure I had no one to turn to, no one at all. I told him, "I'm so sorry. I'm so sorry. I told you. I told you he would find a way to hurt me." His mind was made. No one was cut out for this kind of drama and unwarranted hostility from someone they didn't know just for knowing me. He broke up with me. I found it ironic that it was always the people who flippantly told me to stand up for myself that were the first people to run when I did. Telling others to be brave and standing by them when they do are two totally different things. It was no small heartbreak. But like everything else, it went into that ocean deep heart of mine.

35

I'M IN HERE

*"Hope is a good thing, maybe the best of things,
and no good thing ever dies."* [90]

Houston had finished all the lessons, so I called J-'s mom for some guidance on getting more lessons and moving to one board. We scheduled a time later in the week to come over. One night I decided to try an open question. I had an idea. I took my legal pad and wrote down a whole bunch of sports. I read them all off to him. "Okay Houston. Which is your favorite sport? Now point to the board which has the first letter of your favorite sport." He pointed to the board with S-Z. He spelled out S W. There was only one word on the list beginning with those two letters, so I picked up the first board and he hit I. Then I picked up the middle board and he spelled M M. He finished spelling SWIMMING. My son likes to swim. All the floods and water rescues came rushing to my mind. Wow. Houston had always liked to swim. So I did a lesson on Michael Phelps. It seemed he knew things I hadn't taught him. I was puzzled. I would look up what he spelled and found it was accurate. He knew more than I did.

We went to J-'s house. His mom sweetly and patiently did a fantastic lesson on the history of the t-shirt on three boards. At the end of the lesson there was one question left. She held up the board with 26 letters which we had not tried yet. "If you could put any slogan on a t-shirt, what would it say?" She called out the letters as he pointed to them.

I M I N H E R E

She set the board down with an impressed smile on her face. "'I'm in here.' Houston, that's a great slogan." "I'm in here?" I repeated in shock. I think it was only a few seconds, but I thought for sure it was a full minute before I almost gasped those words as my heart stood in front of a truth so good, an answered prayer so deep that I could not fully take it in. "He spelled, *'I'm in here'*??" The weight of a soul, of my son's soul, hit me like a gale wind and left me stunned, speechless. My heart and my mind didn't seem to grasp it all. It was too wonderful. Oh my gosh. Houston, --- you're in there? OF COURSE! OF COURSE!... YOU'RE IN THERE! My mind was spinning. He's in there. He's in there. I called Morgan. I told the boys. I cried. I cried a kind of soul purging that would be difficult to put into words. It's the kind of cry that people turn their heads not to watch. The kind of cry that speaks of just how monstrous the burdens have been. I texted every single person I knew. I told his teachers. I was legitimately freaking out, but with hope. The door was open, and my son was standing there waiting to be known. Finally, he had a voice.

[90] *Shawshank Redemption*

"The human voice is the organ of the soul." [91]

And that is why every person has a right to voice their soul and have it heard, and why no institution, expert, or other person has a right to limit, dismiss, or invalidate the voice of another. PERIOD. It is also why you should n.ever stop hoping, no matter how foolish or long or impossible it seems. For God is good. He hears our cries and answers them.

Bless the LORD, *O my soul, and all that is within me, bless his holy name!*
Bless the LORD, *O my soul, and forget not all his benefits,*
who forgives all your iniquity,
who heals all your diseases,
who redeems your life from the pit,
who crowns you with steadfast love and mercy,
who satisfies you with good so that your youth is renewed like the eagle's. [92]

---

[91] Henry Wadsworth Longfellow
[92] Psalm 103:1-5

36

Beautiful Heart, Beautiful Mind

Let everything that has breath praise the Lord.
Praise the Lord.
— Psalm 150:6

July 3, 2018

I started expanding to history to make lessons. Since it was around the fourth of July, I did a lesson on the Declaration of Independence. Then for whatever reason I asked, "What is the famous line from the Declaration?" He spelled it out. "We hold these truths to be self-evident, that all men are created equal, that they are endowed by their Creator with certain unalienable Rights, that among these are Life, Liberty and the pursuit of Happiness." I sat there in shock. "How do you know this? How? Keep going." And he did - from the beginning. I would check his work against Jefferson's long sentences. I found one error in the use of an article but that was it. He spelled the following with Morgan watching.

"When in the Course of human events, it becomes necessary for one people to dissolve the political bands which have connected them with another, and to assume among the powers of the earth, the separate and equal station to which the Laws of Nature and of Nature's God entitle them, a decent respect to the opinions of mankind requires that they should declare the causes which impel them to the separation."

Over the next several days he continued.

"We hold these truths to be self-evident, that all men are created equal, that they are endowed by their Creator with certain unalienable Rights, that among these are Life, Liberty and the pursuit of Happiness.–That to secure these rights, Governments are instituted among Men, deriving their just powers from the consent of the governed, –That whenever any Form of Government becomes destructive of these ends, it is the Right of the People to alter or to abolish it, and to institute new Government, laying its foundation on such principles and organizing its powers in such form, as to them shall seem most likely to affect their Safety and Happiness. Prudence, indeed, will dictate that Governments long established should not be changed for light and transient causes; and accordingly all experience hath shewn, that mankind are more disposed to suffer, while evils are sufferable, than to right themselves by abolishing the forms to which they are accustomed. But when a long train of abuses and usurpations, pursuing invariably the same Object evinces a design to reduce them under absolute Despotism, it is their right, it is their duty, to throw off such Government, and to provide new Guards for their future security." [93]

[93] Declaration of Independence

Sometimes I would let him take a break. Barely. I was desperate to know all he knew. I was desperate to know him. Like a mother who hasn't gotten to talk to their child in two decades I wouldn't let up. The inquisition began.

July 4, 2018

I asked him, "Define inalienable."

He spelled, "Cannot be taken away."

"Why can't they be taken away?"

"They were given to us by God."

"Name two people responsible for the Declaration that died on the same day. What day did they die?"

"July 4th, 1826."

"Name them."

Jason, my future son-in-law was listening and interjected. "There's no way he knows that." Houston, as if to defy us all, continued spelling unaffected by the disbelief.

"John Adams. Thomas Jefferson."

"Who was the oldest person who signed the Declaration of Independence?"

"Benjamin Franklin."

"How old was he?"

"70."

July 5, 2018

"What did the colonies not want to be ruled by?"

"King."

"Who did the colonists try to make king?"

"George Washington."

"What did he do after he refused?"

"Farm."

"Where?"

"Mount Vernon."

"Where is Mount Vernon?"

"Virginia."

"What was the name of the King of England at the time?"

"King George."

"What were the colonies upset about?"

"Taxes."

"Name one of the taxes that made them angry."

"Stamp Act."

"Who did Jefferson father illegitimate children with?"

"Sally Hemmings."

Morgan covered her mouth in shock as she watched her brother come alive.

"How many children?"

"Six."

July 7, 2018

"Who inspired Thomas Jefferson as he wrote the Declaration of Independence?"

"John Locke."

"What was his philosophy of government?"

"Contract between the people and government."

"What do the people give the government?"

"Permission to govern."

"Who inspired John Locke?"

"Voltaire."

"What was Voltaire's philosophy?"

"Freedom of religion, speech, separation of church and state."

"Why did our founding fathers believe in separation of church and state?"

"The church abused its power and authority."

"Give me an example."

"Spanish Inquisition."

"Who else was influenced by Locke?"

"Alexander Hamilton."

"What was one thing he thought the new nation should have?"

"Centralized bank."

"What kind of government did Hamilton want?"

"Federal."

"What kind of government did Jefferson want?"

"State."

"Who were they both trying to influence?"

"George Washington."

"Who did Washington ultimately agree with?"

"Hamilton."

"Who killed Hamilton?"

"Aaron Burr."

"How did he kill him?"

"In a duel."

"What was Aaron Burr?"

"Vice President."

"Do you know other important documents?"

"Yes."

"Which ones?"

"Gettysburg Address."

I asked him to spell the Gettysburg Address. He spelled,

"Four score and seven years ago our fathers brought forth on this continent, a new nation, conceived in Liberty, and dedicated to the proposition that all men are created equal."

I videotaped. It took 11 minutes. I asked who wrote it and why they were fighting. He spelled, "Abraham Lincoln and slavery."

"Is slavery consistent with equality?"

"No."

"What attribute did Lincoln demonstrate?"

"Courage."

"Who assassinated him?"
"John Wilkes Booth."
"How do you know all of this?"
"Internet."
"What can I do to help you?"
"More letterboard lessons."
"Is it working?"
"Yes."
"How does it make you feel?"
"Glad. Happy."

I noticed that *Forrest Gump* was coming on television. I knew he had seen it. "What are some famous lines from *Forrest Gump*?"

"Life is like a box of chocolates. You never know what you're going to get. Stupid is as stupid does."

"What does that one mean?"
"You're as smart as your choices."
"How smart are you?"
"Brilliant."

July 8, 2018

"Why are we doing the letter boards?"
"So I can communicate and tell people what I think and feel."
"Tell me one thing you think and feel."
"I think I am too nice for my own good."
"I agree. What is one thing you would want to change?"
"I want people to treat me with respect."
"What do you want people to stop doing?"
"Stop treating me like I'm stupid."

At this point all I could do was tell him with my whole heart how sorry I was. How wrong I was. How I was the stupid one for not knowing. I asked him if he could... if he would forgive me. He spelled yes and hugged me. It was the beginning of absolution. I was determined to get back everything that had been taken. My son would get his life back.

Morgan, who had disinvited her father from her wedding, asked me if I would ask Houston to walk her down the aisle in November.

"Houston, who walks a bride down the aisle?"
"The father."
"Who do you think should walk Morgan down the aisle?"
"Paul."
"Morgan wants you to do it. Would you?"

Houston immediately put his fingers in his ears and put his head down. He stayed there for quite some time. I cannot begin to explain how much emotion, recognition, inclusion, love, and answered prayer were conspiring in that one moment and consuming my son's whole heart. For once the silence was full. It was love.

He lifted his head and picked up the pencil. He spelled. "I would like to walk Morgan down the aisle."

July 9, 2018

We sat outside at a table at Chick-fil-A, and he spelled the rest of the Gettysburg Address and I captured it on my phone. "Do you have a photographic memory?" "Yes." I just shook my head both in wonder and in sadness at all the years lost, at all he had been deprived of. Here was my son who had done the job of teaching and the job of learning all by himself.

"What other things do you want to learn?"

"American stories."

"What is a big story in today's headlines?"

"The boys rescued from a cave in Thailand."

"How many?"

"Twelve and one coach."

"Did you read or hear the story?"

"It was on the internet."

"What website?"

"Fox News."

I had used every single lesson I had originally purchased in the span of six weeks. Jacqueline had said I could make lessons from anything - History.com, Biography.com, National Geographic, The Wall Street Journal, old textbooks. So I began looking up This Day in History for lessons.

"Today in history the British broke the German code. What was it called?"

"Enigma."

"What year?"

"1941."

"Who invented it?"

"Hugo Koch."

"What do they call people who break codes?"

"Cryptologists."

"What message did the British break?"

"It was about German ground and air invasions."

"Tell me one thing you think and feel."

"I know my family loves me far more than this medium will allow me to say."

Morgan called and on speaker we discussed an earlier conversation with a mom who has a newly diagnosed two-year-old with autism. Morgan asked Houston what she should do. Houston eagerly took the pencil and spelled, "She needs to go to the hospital right now so he isn't autistic." My heart broke thinking about my frightened young son twenty years earlier realizing he was trapped. I asked if he remembered everything I tried to do to help him. He spelled, "I know you tried hard for a long time and it didn't work." I asked if he knew why. "No," he spelled.

July 10, 2018

"What is something from today's headlines?"

"Trump nominated Brett Kavanaugh to the Supreme Court."

"What do you think of the nomination?"

"I support the nomination because the court needs more conservative judges."

I laughed. "Morgan is going to be ticked off to hear you say that."

"Name one thing you think or feel."

"I want to know how to spell my feelings so I can have friends."

July 11, 2018

"Tell me one thing you think or feel."

"I make nothing. I have nothing. I am nothing. Happiness is not possible."

"That's not true!! That's not true at all!!! You are brilliant and kind and good! You are loved! Everyone is going to find out how brilliant and wonderful you are! You have so much to offer!

"I want you to stop pushing work on me."

"What work specifically?"

"Letter boards."

"Why do you want me to stop pushing you?"

"Because it is hard."

"What do you want that will make you happy? I know there is something. What is it?"

"To have a family of my own."

"What do you need to have a family?"

"A wife who is understanding of autism."

I read him a story of a young teen who also used the boards to communicate. She was brilliant and unreliably speaking, just like Houston. She discussed the pain of being isolated from friends, trapped in a body she could not control, having so many thoughts but unable to share them and being treated like she was intellectually disabled. I asked him if he wanted to meet her.

"Yes."

"Do you think that is a girl who is understanding of autism?"

"Yes."

"Is there another girl you know that you want to talk to so she can become your friend?"

"Yes."

"What's her name?"

"A-"

"Is she one of the cheerleaders who brought you over to bake cookies attmas?"

"Yes. You would love her. All she does is think of how to love others and love God. She thinks I'm handsome."

"Because you are. I already loved her the minute she came to spend time with you. Houston, happiness is possible. We just have to start seeking the things you want in your life. Let's make a list. Ok, we already have a family of my own, a wife who is understanding of autism…" I paused as I wrote down Houston's Happiness List. "What else do you want to make you happy?"

"I want an education in psychology."

"Why psychology?"

"I want to help others hear God in their hearts."

"Do you hear God in your heart?"

"Yes."

"What does He say?"

"He says that I have a purpose and that nothing can stop it so keep hoping."

"That is very different than what you said earlier. Do you have both thoughts?"

"Yes. I have both of these thoughts. One happens at a time."

"Does God love you?"

"Yes."

"How do you know?"

"I remember what He said in His word."

"When did you read all of this? Everyone wants to know because we only see you on YouTube."

"At night."

"Do you just remember what the Bible says? Is that the only way you know He loves you?"

"I am sure because ... I hear Him in my heart and because you taught me too."

As I watched him begin to spell his response there was a shift in where his hand went and what he spelled as if he was going to say something and suddenly changed his mind. Instinctively I knew he was holding something back, but I couldn't think of what it could possibly be. I guess when you hold your cards for two decades, you don't share them all at once.

"Back to your happiness list. What else do you want on your list?"

"Friends, so I can stop being made fun of."

"Who makes fun of you?"

"Paul and Benjamin."

I was livid. I knew he was right. Siblings can be mean, but they are equal, they can at least try to defend themselves. His brothers didn't view him that way at all. I asked, "Does anyone else make fun of you?"

"Other guys at school."

"Where do other guys make fun of you at school?"

"In the cafeteria."

"Do you want Principal Caresalot to do an assembly about it?"

"Yes."

"What do you want him to say?"

"That it is not right to make fun of people who are different."

"Do you realize you just spelled your feelings?"

"Yes."

"How does it make you feel? Does it make you happy?"

"Yes. Too much to explain on the board."

"Anything else?"

"I want you to get more money so everything will be fine."

"Me too. Me too..."

While all of this was going on, I was crying constantly. Every moment on the boards was momentous. I didn't experience the miracle all at once, but like light breaking into darkness and growing brighter with every brick that's torn down. The breaks in our lessons were now more for me than for him. I laughed to myself thinking, do the spelling coaches cry? Houston kept holding tissue up to my face and saying, "Hug, Hug." As I read his list back to him, he nodded his head in peaceful, quiet reflection. It was as if he needed me to encourage him. I understood. We all need that. He had been hoping on his own his whole life. Finally, his dreams had been spoken. The words of his heart had gone live.

Every day I knew my son a little more. It was as if each day I was being hand delivered a missing piece of this incredible human being who had been by my side all along.

July 12, 2018

"Goals are how to talk to girls."

"Do you know how to flirt?"

"No, I do not know how to flirt."

"Do you want me to invite the girls who came to hang out with you at Christmas?"

"Yes."

"Maybe we can work on questions you can ask them. Tell me something else about yourself."

"I am loving. I am brilliant. I have insight into deity. Everything is about Him. I owe everything to Him. One thing I have is family who loves me. In tomorrow a new love will begin."

"When you say, 'In tomorrow' what do you mean?"

"In heaven."

"Do you want to describe your insight or yourself?"

"My insight."

He paused for a long time. I asked, "Are you afraid to tell me?"

"Yes."

"Why?"

"Because what I see in God is amazing. Back one day I needed a change of scenery at school. Same day as any. So I was walking and I saw..."

He refused to continue with what he had seen.

"Ok, tell me something else."

"I have seen the naming of God's children for God's deity. In the Great Naming I had no family there."

"What do you mean? Are you saying we aren't there?"

"No. You are there. I had no family of my own."

"How do you know? Have you met your wife or your children?"

"No."

My thoughts raced thinking of how to encourage him while at the same time grappling with the gravity of what he had seen.

"Houston, remember what Jesus said? He said ANYTHING IS POSSIBLE. Did you hear that? Anything is possible if you believe. You have to believe. You have to believe you will have a family of your own. You have to. In fact, we are going to start right now."

So we prayed to our Father in heaven. We approached the throne. All those years I had prayed timidly with fear inlaid with doubt, and suddenly it was gone. My son was going to get the family he longed for. No - was no longer an acceptable answer.

That night I watched *Rain Man* with Houston. He sat still the entire time which was remarkable. After the movie we had this short conversation.

"What did you think of *Rain Man*?"

"It has so many similarities to my life. To know that others have experienced what I have experienced is so moving. Can I watch it again? I napped so I did not see all of the movie."

When we watched it the second time, he said this:

"At first I thought the people who took care of him were bad. Now I realize they were good people who took care of him. I feel there are good people who work to make a difference, who happen to have a gift."

"Why do you think his brother didn't fight to take him out of the home once he realized he loved his brother?"

"Because he knew he would be with people who care. But they thought he wasn't capable of making a choice because he repeated both choices. That was not his real voice. I want each person to have a voice so they can choose."

37

Thoughts and Wonders

I am the LORD, the God of all mankind.
Is anything too hard for me?
— Jeremiah 32:7

July 13, 2018

I did a lesson on some of the events following the end of World War I. On a whim I decided to keep going and see what else he might know. Because I was a history major, I knew enough of the history of the period to just start asking questions.

"Who was president during WW I?"

"Woodrow Wilson."

"What campaign was he re-elected on?"

"He kept us out of the war."

"What prompted the US to enter the war?"

"The sinking of the Lusitania and the Zimmerman Telegram."

"What was his contribution to the Treaty of Versailles?"

"His Fourteen Points."

"Did the US ratify the treaty?

"No."

"What senator blocked the ratification?"

"Henry Cabot Lodge."

Wow… That was enough for the day. I bragged to the boys about all Houston had spelled. Paul was obtuse. When I went upstairs, I found him on Houston's computer.

"What are you doing?" I asked. "I'm trying to find the searches where he learned all this," he answered. "Paul, he has been listening and learning his whole life. They did some history lessons at school too. He might have learned it there." Paul kept searching. "Paul, get off his computer." "I'm trying to find something to prove he learned all this stuff." "Paul, get off his computer now." He didn't budge. "Paul, why won't you believe in your brother? This is incredible." "There's no way he's this smart," he said defiantly. "That's it. Get out! Get out now. If you can't be supportive, you can at least get out of the way."

Houston sat on the bed very still. I sat down beside him. "Houston, can you tell me how you know so much? Do you have really great hearing or something? I know you have a good memory."

Very slowly he started spelling, almost as if he was contemplating his response.

"I am special."

"I know you're special, sweetie."

"I have many abilities. I can hear thoughts."

I made him spell it again. I rested my arm. It was incomprehensible. "Houston, are you sure? Are you telling the truth?"

He glanced at me and then started spelling, "You don't get the kinds of abilities I have if you lie."

"Ok. What am I thinking now?" I was still very irritated at Paul and was thinking, 'Paul is mean.' But I sat there in silence holding up the board.

Houston spelled, "Paul is mean."

I gasped. 'What about now?' I thought. In my mind I asked him the following question. 'What did your dad just do that upset me?'

"He sent that letter and your friend broke up with you."

Without speaking I asked Houston, 'What do you think I should do?'

"Say you're sorry," he spelled.

"I did. I don't think it's that simple, Houston."

"Say it again."

"How do you hear thoughts? What does it sound like?"

"It sounds like a voice in my head."

"Do you hear different voices?"

"Yes. I have been hearing my whole life. I hear everything. I hear Wi-Fi signals. I can hear thoughts the same as I hear voices. In the mind of an autistic we hear others' thoughts, how it sounds is just like a voice."

"What does Wi-Fi sound like?"

"Buzzing."

I called Morgan. I yelled for Paul and his friend to come to Houston's room.

"Morgan! You're not going to believe this. Houston can hear thoughts!"

Irritated she said, "No he can't, Mom. No. There's no way. I don't believe it."

"Yes! He can. He just did it. I'm not kidding. This is unreal!"

Paul walked in. I turned to him. "Paul, Houston can hear thoughts!"

"Bullshit. Prove it."

"Ok. Think something."

I turned to Houston. "What's Paul thinking?"

Houston spelled, "Dead men don't talk."

I turned to Paul furious. "Is *that* what you're thinking??" Paul shook his head and said, "Mom, he's not saying what I'm thinking. He's saying he won't tell secrets."

I turned to Houston. "Is that what you're saying?"

Houston spelled, "Yes."

"Ok. Fine. We need someone with a clean conscience." I sent a short glare at Paul. Paul's friend had just come back from a church youth camp and walked into the room in the middle of this revelation. "Mason, I want you to think something and keep thinking it and I want to see if Houston can hear your thoughts."

"Ok. Cool," he answered.

"Ready?"

"Yep."

Houston spelled out, "God is in my heart."

"Mason, is that what you were thinking??"

Mason's mouth hung open as he slowly began nodding his head. "Yeah, pretty much exactly."

"Morgan! Are you hearing this? Send me a text I want to see if he can tell me what you text."

She said in the background, "Jason, I need something to text."

I received a text and read it without letting Houston see anything on my phone.

Houston spelled, "Lord of the Rings," which is what Morgan had texted me.

"Morgan. Houston just spelled Lord of the Rings in front of all of us."

There was silence. And finally, "Holy shit."

"EXACTLY!"

July 14, 2018

Still reeling from the wonders I had witnessed; I didn't know where to start. There was so much I was afraid to ask. If he had been hearing everything all these years, then he had heard *everything.* He knew the things I had prayed and the excruciating pain. He knew how I longed to be free from it all. He had heard all my grief, my anger, my guilt. He had heard my resentment. I was overwhelmed with shame. Here I had been gifted the most incredible human being to raise and love and I had harbored so much resentment. I couldn't even begin to figure out a way to undo the damage of twenty years of what my struggle must have done to my son's heart. I hesitated and finally confessed. "Houston, there is just so much to say I'm sorry for. I don't even know where to begin. Honestly, I will understand if you don't forgive me. I didn't know. I just didn't know. I'm so so sorry. I always loved you. ALWAYS. I love you so much. I just hated what autism did to you and to me — well, to everything. I don't know how to take it all back. I'm so sorry. My God, what you must have heard... It's not you. OK? It's me. My weakness. My fear. Can you forgive me?" … And then I paused for a long time, afraid to ask. "Houston… What do you think of me?"

My incredible son, rooted so deeply in His heavenly father spelled, "I want to call in God's favor for every single moment that has been taken from us. He loves us and He keeps His Word. He will always be there no matter what. Do not always believe you are alone. Others are forever fighting for you and every time run to help you."

"It doesn't feel like it." My doubt had become my armor against hope and its long list of disappointments.

"I like that you are beautiful and loving and kind."

All I could do was cry and cry and cry. The fact that my son could hear my love in spite of all the rest humbled me more than I can explain. The weeping that went on that month had to have woken heaven, for it was not the same as the tears of past days. It was the wailing of truth uttered at last. It was the flow of justice that would roll like a mighty river. It was LOVE. He had come.

> And the Mississippi's mighty
> But it starts in Minnesota
> At a place that you could walk across
> With five steps down [94]

And that's pretty much how it all started. Just one voice finally being heard. That first night in bed, as I processed the miracle I had just witnessed, I suddenly and abruptly realized - Oh my word. They were right! Thoughts are things! They are as real as anything else, as real as a sound wave or a radio wave or a Wi-Fi signal and as real as the smell of a rose. Houston's brain just happened to be able to receive, but the thoughts were always out there traveling, moving matter in one way or another. There was no filter, no division between his conscious and subconscious. I realized how it was too much. Too much for anyone. Too much physically, emotionally, intellectually. For twenty years he had been standing under a Niagara Falls of input from the world and deprived of a way to process, share, explain, and ask for help. And yet, he was still kind. Who but God or someone who has seen God could operate aware of everything, even the worst things, and not retreat?

In wonder I sat there — complete awe mixed with a thousand realizations all at same time. I started thinking about all the books I had read about thought and belief that I had taken at face value. Before that moment I just thought it was something mystical that somehow affected the material. Then it hit me. Prayer! That must be why God said prayer with faith worked, why He repeatedly said it was your faith that healed you. Because thought was a real thing, an energy or force of some kind, and belief in His promises was the driving force behind it.

The implications were enormous. If thoughts were energy, then they were subject to the laws of energy, the first being that the energy of the universe is constant, as stated by the first law of thermodynamics, and could not be created or lost, just transferred. There were two types of energy, potential and kinetic. Hope and worry both had to be potential energy. But faith and doubt had to be kinetic energy since they were both active energy in motion. Internal energy (U) is the total potential thermodynamic energy combining both potential and kinetic energy within a system. Change in internal energy is defined as the sum or change of work and heat: $\Delta U = q$ *(heat = flow of energy due to a temperature difference)* + w *(work = force (mass x acceleration) across a distance)*. Since heat could be both exothermic or endothermic, I realized that heat could be negative or positive, much like our emotions. And there was no limit to temperature or emotion. Even absolute hot, the theoretical opposite of absolute zero, is not a limit. It is simply a point at which particles become so large that gravitational forces act differently on them. Theoretically, work was infinite as well. Although acceleration was limited by the speed of light, mass and energy were ultimately the same thing, so if mass was unlimited, so was the energy it created. Infinite mass equaled infinite energy and ultimately affected gravity, the electromagnetic pull or attraction between objects. And distance could never be limited, just as there is no limit between east and west. Since anything finite multiplied by something infinite is indeterminate or not defined, there was essentially no defined limit to work. More work, infinite work, or force across a distance in either direction, positive or negative could always happen, the gravity or attraction responded in correspondence to the change in energy.

But what did all this thinking about thought even matter? I realized for too long, because of pain that I cannot adequately describe, I had believed in God and not believed God. Yet the truth of His power was all around me. He had shown his limitless nature throughout creation. I thought about how in one acorn there are infinite potential oak trees. Ultimately, there are infinite potential human beings, which means there are no limits to the amount of love and faith we as a human race are capable of exercising. If the undefined limits of human love and faith had a force, a gravity, then it was transcendent, pulling us to LOVE itself. While fear and doubt weighted us to limits and laws, faith and love released us to do the impossible because with God all things *are* possible. They are possible because of His Word, His unchangeable nature, and His promises. Which made me think that if q (heat/emotion) is infinite and w (belief with works) is not limited or defined, then the change in internal energy (all combined potential and kinetic energy) is without limits: $q\infty + w\infty = \Delta U\infty$ ... *Or ΔU*(no defined limit). In other words, anything is possible (change in internal energy) if you believe (heat/emotion) and act (work) on that belief. But too often the potential energy was acted on by exothermic worry. People did not work believing God would keep His Word, and instead the work they did enforced doubt, fear, and unbelief, which yielded exactly what you would expect – Despair.

So I guess it is true that the energy of the universe is constant, but the constant was and is without limits. As my mind turned with the complexities and applications of what I had just witnessed there was one thing I could not deny. The unseen. It was real. And God, LOVE itself. He was real. He had no limits.

But the battle was real too.

July 15, 2018

Houston explained he couldn't get his mind to control his body. I thought, ok, maybe it would help if his spine was aligned and adjusted. Couldn't hurt. So I took Houston to my chiropractor. The whole time he was being adjusted he was giggling. Then he stood up and was extremely excited, jumping up and down so the entire office shook. My chiropractor just looked in awe and said, "Wow." I talked to the chiropractor as we were leaving, and he told me to take the magazines I had been reading while we were waiting because he was going to throw them away. As soon as I picked them up Houston snatched them out of my hands and said, "NO!" I was puzzled by that behavior. I picked up the magazines again and Houston snatched them again and set them back on the table. I took them to the car and put them in between the seats. Houston reached in and gave them back to the doctor who had walked outside after us. Strange. When we got home, I questioned him.

"What did you think of Dr. R, the chiropractor that you met today? Did you like him?"

"Yes. He is friendly and he made me feel better by adjusting me and he's a good person."

"I agree, but how do you know he's a good person?"

"He was kind to me rather than being judgmental. I could hear his thoughts."

"What did it feel like when he adjusted you?"

"I felt my body connecting with my mind."

"Did it help you control your body more?"

"Yes."

"Does it make the letter boards easier?"

"Yes."

"Why did you take the magazines away from me and say no?"

"You like pretty things too much."

"But pretty things make me happy! What's wrong with liking pretty things?"

"You forget about God."

"You're wrong. I do not forget about God. Beauty is something God made, and He gave me a desire for it. When I create, when I see beauty, I feel more connected to Him. This is a gift He gave me. I can't help it. It's just how I'm built."

He wasn't wrong that I was not thinking much about God, but it had nothing to do with beauty. It was my broken heart that had blinded me. Nevertheless, Houston's rebuke upset me. I wanted to defend myself, but nothing came to mind. What could I possibly say? He was right. I wasn't thinking about God. I wouldn't even talk to Him. I felt so far away from Him I didn't know how to find a way back.

38

Hidden Truths

For nothing is hidden that will not be made manifest,
nor is anything secret that will not be known and come to light.
— Luke 8:17

The eyes of the Lord are everywhere
keeping watch on the wicked and the good.
— Proverbs 15:3

And no creature is hidden from his sight,
but all are naked and exposed to the eyes of him to whom we must give account.
— Hebrews 4:13

For my eyes are on all their ways.
They are not hidden from me, nor is their iniquity concealed from my eyes.
—Jeremiah 16:17

For he looks to the ends of the earth and sees everything under the heavens.
—Job 28:24

July 16, 2018

Driving down Hwy 9 Houston called out repeatedly, "Family Store! Family Store!" That's what he called the Salvation Army because he couldn't articulate those words. I avoided it as much as possible because he would become absolutely obsessed over Disney VHS tapes. When the girls had first moved out, I had bought Houston a queen size bed and put the boys in the girls' room. By this point he was at least 240 lbs. and towered over me and had still been sleeping on a twin-size mattress. Morgan had painted him a picture of Dumbo and I had found a vintage Pinocchio picture to hang on the wall. It looked like a young child's room, but I knew he was thrilled to have his own room and his own space. He would line the bottom of his bed with at least fifty Disney VHS cassette covers. It looked like Disney had exploded on his bed. If I moved them, he would have a meltdown and bite himself, so I just let it be.

That day it took Houston an hour to pick two VHS tapes. He wanted seven. It took everything to manage his impulses in the store. I hated it. I wanted to leave all the Disney videos behind. Oddly, one of the videos he insisted on getting that day was the movie the Big Jock had been in when he was just a baby. He had always liked that movie and I always thought it was because his dad was in it. When we got home, this was our conversation.

"Why did you choose that movie?"

"Because my goals are to make something of myself."

"How does that movie inspire you to reach your goals?"

"He is a nobody who becomes someone important."

"Are you important?"

"Yes. I am important because I have special abilities. I want to be a hero. He was a hero."

"Do you remember meeting the star of the movie?"

"I remember he walked the football field with me."

"Houston, you were really young to remember that. How do you know that? Do you know how old you were then?"

"One."

"What was your first memory?"

"I was getting a laugh from Flubber."

I paused in shock because I knew EXACTLY what he was talking about. I also knew the moments he recalled occurred when he was only 13 - 14 months old.

"What did watching Flubber make you feel?"

"It made me feel merry."

That was true. I remembered it vividly. It was pure joy untempered. Still in a bit of shock I changed the subject.

"Tell me something else you liked about that movie you picked today."

"Another thing I like is how people told him he could not be a football player. But he became one."

"Did you know that your dad was in that film?"

"Yes."

"I thought that's why you wanted that movie." I thought to myself how his dad hadn't wanted to see the kids in over a year. So I asked, "Do you want to see him?"

"No. He's the worst person in the world and I never want to see him again."

I was stunned. Benjamin came downstairs. "Those are some pretty strong words. Why would you say that?"

As Houston spelled Benjamin came and sat down at the table.

"He molested Reagan. I heard his thoughts."

Houston turned to me. At first, I just sat there with horror on my face. I was scared to ask. I didn't want to know the truth. In my shock I couldn't ask.

Houston spelled, "I'm filled with RAGE!" Forcefully poking the board he turned to me and started shaking uncontrollably. I was so afraid to know. Benjamin sat in silence with his mouth ajar.

Houston continued, "He thought no one would ever know but I heard every single thought he had. He ran a shower and took her in it and forced himself into her."

At this point I began sobbing so violently that I couldn't swallow or breathe. The wails came from some place so deep that I didn't know such a place existed. My son, for the first time in his life, threw his arms around me and embraced me in a fierce hug, like a protector, like a hero.

At this point I did the excruciatingly difficult work of asking questions and getting details. It was the night I had run away in fear. It was the same shower Reagan had described which corroborated the timing perfectly. I asked what Reagan had thought. And he responded, "She thought he loved her and would do anything for her but she was fearful he would do it again. He thought she would never tell and God would not do anything."

Another incident Houston had witnessed involved the babysitter from the Big Jock's apartment, whose mother had worked for the Big Jock. I thought back to how she was there all the time and day I had walked in on her and her friend. I thought about the Big Jock's comment and his cruel laugh. It was unbearable to have my son spell out secrets he had been carrying his entire childhood along with everything else he had to carry. I wept for so much. I wept for my daughter, my precious baby girl. I wept that the Big Jock had hurt another young person. And I wept for my hero son. Not only had he been trapped, he had been trapped bearing the burden of knowing evil's most intimate thoughts.

Finally Benjamin spoke. "Mom. I need to tell you something."

I could hardly believe this was happening. He continued. "Last night I had this really scary dream of this big white snake. It was really unsettling. This morning I called dad and I told him about the dream. He told me that a dream about a snake means that a great truth about someone is going to be revealed."

"Are you serious?" I asked incredulously. He affirmed. Little did the Big Jock know the great truth would be about himself.

At that moment it was around 11 p.m. and the front door opened and slammed shut. Reagan walked in and was surprised to see us all sitting there. We were just as shocked to see her. I hadn't seen or spoken to her since June 28, 2018, when she told me about the shower with her dad. I didn't have any idea why she was even home.

I said as calmly as I could, "Reagan, Houston has abilities we were not aware of. His whole life he has been hearing our thoughts. Can you think of anything you have thought about that you want to share? Something that happened?"

Her face froze. It took a while for her to sit. Her head hung down. My heart was burning with injustice, fury, brokenness, and more emotions than I could identify at what had been done to my daughter, but I wanted to confirm facts. "Reagan, Houston says your dad…" I realized I couldn't say it. "I wrote down what Houston said. Here it is." I slid it across the table. She could barely look up at me. She took the pad of paper and read. When she was done, she kept her head down. "Reagan, is that true? Is that what your father did?"

She looked like one of my tiny China dolls from my childhood, so tiny, so precious, so fragile. All her hostility over all the years had momentarily vanished. She nodded. Her tiny, perfect chin trembled, and her giant blue eyes filled with tears even though they were unable to look at anyone.

I jumped up from the table. "That's it! We are pressing charges. He's going to jail!"

Reagan started begging me and pleading. "NO! NO! MOM! He'll kill you! He'll kill me! He'll kill Houston! He's a monster! NO! I won't! I won't testify!"

"Reagan, you have to! You can't be afraid. I have spent my whole adult life being afraid of him. That's how he wins. That's how he controls."

"I don't care if he wins! I just want him to leave us alone. I want you to stop trying to get child support. Just let it go! Just let him win. PLEASE!" Her pleas and screams took over everything. It's too painful to describe… I didn't know what to say or do.

"I want you to really think about this. He belongs in jail. You have to testify. I am NOT okay just letting him get away with this."

"No. It will be just like it was with the abortion. I'll go meet with all the lawyers and no one will be able to do anything. I'll think that people will finally be held accountable and then nothing will happen. I'm NOT going through that again!" At this point she became hysterical. I had to stop talking about it just to calm her down.

Despite my arguments and urgings Reagan refused. Houston wanted to spell and interjected, "If she won't, I will."

"Houston, that's not how the law works. There must be testimony and corroborating evidence. It's been so long there really isn't much else to go on."

Houston spelled to Reagan, "I'm sorry I couldn't protect you." She cried quietly and kissed her sweet big brother who loved her so much.

That night as I wept in bed, all the years with Reagan suddenly made sense. I looked for counselors who specialized in sexual trauma and called the hotline. I read what the signs were, and it was like reading a list of every single struggle I had with Reagan. How could I have been so dense? How could I have not known, not seen?

July 17, 2018

The next day I called and spoke with counselors on a hotline. They explained so much about what she was experiencing. I told them how hateful and hostile she was to me, and they confirmed that was a textbook coping mechanism, as was the cutting, the lying, trying to create other situations in order to process the pain, the promiscuity, the irresponsible use of birth control, the abusive boyfriends, the lack of self-care, the drugs, the abortion. Suddenly I knew why. My heart was shattered. Even though I was experiencing this miracle with Houston, my heart mourned for my little girl. Repeatedly I urged Reagan to talk to them. She refused. She wanted that lid sealed shut. The more I tried to get her to get help the angrier at me she became. Her self-destruction geared up again. The cutting became horrific. The sight of her arms ignited knife-like pains in my heart and my gut. I would look away to try to stop the tears, but it never worked. Why couldn't she just see what I saw? Why couldn't she see how beautiful and precious and talented and loved she was? Why couldn't she receive my love? Why couldn't she see the healing and love she needed and deserved? Why couldn't she see?

Thoughts of how evil the Big Jock was haunted me. I was baffled, sickened, angry. Hurt me? Destroy me? Fine. But my little girl???!!!! *God? Where were you? Why didn't you protect her? Why didn't you show me?* My sweet, joyful little girl. I felt like someone had taken my heart right out of my chest. I would try to stop the thoughts but couldn't. One day I suddenly realized why he had preyed on her. He knew it would destroy me. My children were my life. I was in shock realizing how insidious and how well his plan had worked. For years she had been stolen from me and I couldn't figure out why. The violation went to the core of who I was and what I loved. He knew it. My heart cried out for justice. For months I would just start crying at what seemed to be nothing. I never knew what would trigger it. People would call and I would have to fight to break the thought patterns to have a normal conversation without that storyline playing in the background. Not thinking about it felt like a dishonor to her pain and to the truth that Houston had been carrying for so long. I struggled to move past something when there was no justice. Reagan seemed to be stone. How could anyone do that to anyone? How could anyone do that to their child? How could evil be so *evil*?

I told the kids that the Big Jock was to be completely cut out of our lives. It would be cruel for them to maintain any contact with him after what he had done to Reagan. Paul refused. He said he didn't believe it. "I'm eighteen. I can make my own decisions," he answered defiantly. Houston spelled out to him repeatedly what he knew. He still refused to believe. After that Paul became a different person. He was present, but he wasn't part of us.

39

Faith with Sight

And in the last days it shall be,
God declares that I will pour out my Spirit on all flesh,
and your sons and your daughters shall prophesy,
and your young men shall see visions,
and your old men shall dream dreams.
— Acts 2:17

July 18, 2018

When I picked Houston up from camp, they told me they had been to an aquatic center and Houston had loved the dolphins. At home I asked Houston where they had gone that day.

"To see the dolphins."

"They said you loved the dolphins and were smiling and laughing."

"Don't give money before the show because no people would want to be the animals. Tears. They get treated bad. Every dolphin lives in a cage with no family. They were thinking love is not possible. Their calls to God are a melody for rescue."

"You can hear what the dolphins are thinking and feeling??? Are you serious?? Why did they think you were happy about the dolphins?"

"I was happy because Jesus told me that there was a star pointing to my healing."

Wonder became a daily occurrence as my mind tried to imagine what all my son had seen. He wasn't speaking in parables or dreams. His words were the statements of someone who has seen. This was all more than I can explain, realizing there was a world around me that I was unaware of that my son was completely attuned to.

When he began to fight me to stop working. I refused. I tried reasoning with him like I did my other kids.

"What's a coach?" I asked.

"Someone who is responsible for pushing you to become the best. They are helping you reach your goals."

"Do you see that I'm trying to help you reach your goals?"

"You don't reach your goals." I was shocked when he spelled that. My goals?? He was my goal. He was my whole life. That and surviving and maybe one day - happiness. I gulped at being reminded of dreams I had learned to bury, dreams that I was now being held responsible for not pusuing from the very person who made the pursuit of my dreams not possible. I was upset by his rebuke when I had given him my whole life, and no one had stepped in to let me pursue my goals - whatever they were. My heart ached. Was I to fight everyone and everything?

"Houston, what are you doing right now to me?"

"Fighting you very hard."

"I get that me pushing you is hard on you, but there is no way I'm going to stop or even slow down. Why do you think that is?"

"Because you love me more than anything in the world."

"So what should you do?"

"I should work very hard."

When the girls from school came to visit him, he was beyond excited. I had to bite my lip because he ran up to A and threw his arms around her. She had no idea. He had planned a whole list of questions to ask them, and I could see his anxiousness was making it harder for him to spell. From the list he made he managed to ask them where they were going to school, if they knew anyone, and if they were going to football games. Then he told them that talking to his mom all the time was lame and he wanted friends. The girls took him to Chick-fil-A and took selfies with him. He smiled like he was sitting next to his dream girl, like a boy whose dreams were beginning to come true.

When he got back home, I asked how it went. He told me, "It made me very happy to see them. They are impressed. It is wonderful to have friends. Chick-fil-A was too loud." I asked if he liked the headphones, I had gotten him a few days earlier at Wal-Mart in the gun section.

"Yes, it stops everything from illuminating."

"What do you mean when you say illuminate?"

"It means everything is at full exposure and it's terrible and it hurts."

"What hurts the most?"

"My hearing."

"If your hearing is the most sensitive, why do you listen to your videos and music so loud?"

"Not all sounds are the same, some are terrible. In my mind sounds are frightening noises, but my music is comforting."

Benjamin interjected, "Do you realize you react badly to Dumbo?"

"Yes, I know it has a bad effect on me."

"Why do you keep trying to watch it if you know you have a bad reaction?"

"Making my mind stop is too hard. Can we stop? I'm tired."

July 2018

It was Morgan's birthday. He had spelled a message for her birthday card.

Dear Morgan,

I keep a love for you in my heart that will never be comprehended. You are the most giving, loving person. You are so talented. Definitely keep pursuing your dreams. You will reach them. It is my dream for you to accomplish everything you have fought for. Far away someone feels the same as me. His name is Messiah. Happy birthday.

Love,

Houston

After Morgan read his letter out loud, I asked him how it made him feel to hear his own words and see Morgan's reaction.

"So proud of myself."

"You should be. It was beautiful. You may have a talent for writing. Did you know I'm a writer?"

"Yes. I know. You are the best writer I know of in America for sure."

"Wow. That's a bit of a stretch. I don't know that Twain, Hemingway, Steinbeck, or O'Connor would agree. But you definitely know how to give a compliment." I giggled to myself. I started to ask how he knew I was a good writer and then sat stunned realizing in that moment he had heard all my thoughts for all those years as I played with the beauty of words and tried to make words work my hope for the world. I was overwhelmed.

As the day continued and conversations flowed, Houston began to feel the power of his voice. Emotions and thoughts my son had held in his heart began flooding out of him. I can only imagine the psychological and emotional impact on a brilliant human being trapped in solitary confinement while the world offers him cartoons and cookies, and he listens to the true thoughts and feelings of everyone around him. That day an avalanche unleashed. He directed his justifiable fury at me. He rebuked me for my lack of faith, for my not talking to God, for bad choices in men, for not being brave. Morgan was angry at his anger and told him he was acting like a teenager and didn't understand all the pressures that had been put on me. But I understood - those thoughts, those emotions - they had to come out. It was a pot that had to boil over to calm down. In his anger he said one thing that cut me deeply, to my core, "All your thoughts are rotten."

I was devastated. I couldn't find words to express my brokenness. I didn't even want to know which thoughts he was referring to since apparently it was all of them. Once I realized he had heard everything over all those years, I had feared exactly this. I prayed, not asking for anything, just saying how sorry I was. I wept. I knew I was only human, with pain and burdens people couldn't even identify with, but to me that was just an excuse. I longed for the innocence and faith I had as a child. I stayed broken for a long time even as he poured love and absolution on me.

July 20, 2018

I approached the boards in trepidation. I was scared to know what he would say. But whatever it was, he had a right to say it. I owed him a voice. Even if it caused me pain, I would bear it. I would own it. I would listen and I would do everything I could to right two decades of wrongs.

Houston surprised me.

"I make many errors in judgment. I never meant to hurt you again. I will be considerate to you. I'm so sorry, really sorry."

"Houston, you have a right to be angry and a right to express it. You mentioned errors in judgment. Do you know what judgment is?"

"It means you know the right thing to do in any situation."

"Do you know why Morgan was angry?"

"She loves you and she did not like it when I was mean to you. After you talked to me and explained your hurt, I felt bad about everything I said. I feel forever terrible about it. You treated me with kindness and respect. I treated you disrespectfully. I sounded mean."

"Houston, I can only imagine the burden you have carried. You've never gotten the chance to talk through situations or have your perspective heard. This is all new for both of us. This isn't normal. Most people don't have the level of awareness you do. I thought all I thought was between me and God. I can only ask that you be patient with me as I help you get your voice. I promise I will do everything to make your dreams come true. I'm so sorry for everything. Houston, I'm scared to ask. But what do you think of me?"

"I think you are strong and you love God."

I began crying again. "I have loved Him my whole life, but I have felt abandoned by Him for a long time." Houston wrapped his arms around me and hugged me.

THE BOOK OF HEAVEN

I was in a perpetual state of wonder and weeping. Emotions and thoughts I had been unable to process because the burdens were too great to bear began to move within me. I wish I could say I just suddenly had hope and everything was great, but that's not what happened in my heart. Great wounds take time to heal. Maybe my faith would always have a limp.

July 21, 2018

When Houston woke up, he seemed sad. I asked him what was wrong. "I bring lots of different hurdles both physical and emotional. Brothers can't get free from dad. Besides fear lives the darkest and I'm scared he will find out." I asked if he was worried Paul would tell. He spelled, "He controls you both by fear and love in different ways. Go get Paul. Paul told." I was overwhelmed by all that my son had carried alone. I went downstairs and told the boys again not to talk to their dad, not to tell what Houston could do. Paul told me again he would do whatever he wanted. He would make his own decisions. I felt powerless to protect Reagan, Houston, and myself from a monster I knew all too well. And my son was indifferent, flippant, defiant despite all I had done, all he had seen. I knew for certain he was under the Big Jock's spell. How many of my children would I lose to him? How many would he destroy?

"I have nightmares about dad. I dreamed he knows I can hear thoughts. He was choking me telling me to say I couldn't. I'm scared he will know and hurt me." We prayed. I realized that all those years Houston had never been able to share when something distressed or disturbed him. He had never been able to share a good dream or a bad one. He had never been able to tell me something funny that happened or any of his fears or dreams.

I decided to focus on Scripture and see what he might know.

He spelled out Psalm 23 from memory. Then more love. He sensed my brokenness and without being asked any question he spelled, "I am not at war against you to be loved. People make decisions for love. I understand that. You are the greatest mom in the world. Nothing you would do could ever make me stop loving you."

I wept again.

July 22, 2018

He spelled 1 Corinthians 13 and the Preamble to the Constitution. I asked him what his definition of love was. He spelled, "I think love is kind, not selfish or mean."

"What is an example of love?"

"Christ died on the cross to pay for our sins."

As we drove around town Houston suddenly started pointing and shouted, "Johns Creek! Johns Creek! Johns Creek!" which is a neighboring suburb. The only thing in Johns Creek that I could think of where he might want to visit was our old church. I was stunned because he had never said those words before. I drove to the church and parked. Summer camp was in progress. There had been several additions to the church and while it was recognizable, at the same time it wasn't. We walked inside and as he turned to go to the bookstore where he had so often run, he stopped and looked at me. It was gone. There was a market with a café that served sandwiches, yogurt, and snacks. Metal tables and chairs filled the space and pleather modern style couches were scattered around the old church foyer. I looked to my right at the enormous staircase where I had found Houston standing at the top twenty years earlier. In my mind I saw him still so little and looked at him fully grown standing by my side. How far we had come…

The bookstore was now in its original windowless location tucked in a corner. I brought Houston over to say hi to the bookstore manager who had known me since my kids were babies. She didn't even know what to say as I told her about Houston's new voice. She had helped chase him down many times. She had heard the poop letter. She had seen my faith crack and dwindle. There were really no words.

When we got home, I asked Houston why he wanted to go back. He spelled that he wanted to see what it was like now. I asked him what he thought. He spelled, "It's cold." I agreed. It didn't feel like the church I had known. It was more like a convention center. But the chapel was still there I reminded him.

July 23, 2018

I read Houston blogs of other non-speaking or unreliably speaking autistics who spelled to communicate. The last blog was from someone I had already told him about.

He responded, "She is remarkable inside. I get excited when I hear about others communicating with letter boards. It inspires me to work hard so I can say anything I want."

"Houston, the message I hear over and over from these spellers is that they do not have control over their bodies and most of what people call their behaviors are not within their control. What do you think about that?"

"I agree completely. No matter what I do, read what I spell instead of my body."

"What about what they say about stims and stopping them?"

"You need to tell me to stop when I keep repeating storylines and biting myself."

"What else can I do to help you?"

"Have me appear and read a book to me. Break my habits by changing my surroundings."

"Houston, the biggest issue is the videos, especially the fast forwarding and rewinding. It has total control over you."

"Yes. I want you to stop me fast forwarding and rewinding."

"What else?"

"A must is for you to read to me. We need to work more on reading psychology."

"I also think we need to work on creative writing and defining words. I have no idea what you don't know and I'm really not sure how to go about this. Do you want to try?"

"Yes. Other autistics have a blog. I should too. Autistics can seem reticent, but they are really knowledgeable and lacking in communications skills."

"I cannot wait to hear everything you want to say. Let's try defining a word by giving an example and using it appropriately in a sentence. How about authenticity?"

"You display authenticity under lots of difficult circumstances."

"Ok, but that sentence doesn't really demonstrate the meaning of the word. Try again."

"Abraham Lincoln demonstrated authenticity every time he made all men free."

"Yes, he did! Yes, he did!"

July 25, 2018

After camp we met with the evaluators for the NOW/COMP waiver. There were three experts assessing his self-care and independence skills as well as a host of other assessments. They wanted to know about the giant calluses on his hands from twenty years of biting himself. I explained our daily life in detail. I called his teacher on speaker, and she gave her assessments to the evaluators as well. After that we just had to wait to hear their decision. I knew his ability to control his body and care for himself was almost nonexistent, but I still hated hearing everything he couldn't do. I was trying to believe and the ALWAYS, OFTEN, OCCASIONALLY, RARELY, NEVER questions were a necessary bureaucratic annoyance just to get help when it was painfully obvious to everyone how much we needed it.

When the assessment was over, I gathered up Houston's things and walked outside with the representative from the Department of Behavioral Health and Developmental Disabilities. As soon as I opened the heavy door, Houston dashed out at a full sprint with me yelling for him to stop. I was kicking my shoes off to start running and then he stopped and started jumping repeatedly. He jumped like Tigger and made his loud noises. The representative looked at me. "That's what you mean about elopement?" "That's part of it," I answered. "But he'll elope quietly too, and you'll never even know he's gone. I haven't been able to let my guard down in almost twenty-two years. It hasn't gotten easier. He's gotten faster and I've gotten older."

She didn't say anything. She just nodded. What could she say?

July 26, 2018

Every day was more and more. It was exhausting and exhilarating. We started taking a free online Psychology course on Udacity. Regarding the course content he spelled, "Emotional, behavioral, social. About social, I have awareness because I have observed it. I have two curiosities." I asked what they were.

"Why do people keep knowing the wrong thing and doing it anyway? Why do people alter who they are?"

"Houston, those are great questions with no small answers. The shortest answer is they want something more than they want to do right and they feel they will get something they want if they change who they are. Almost everyone is guilty of both of those at some point in their lives."

"I want to take AP Psychology. My must have is an education."

So I continued calling and emailing the principal at his high school every

day insisting on a meeting.

July 27, 2018

I picked him up from his last day of camp.

"How was camp?"

"It almost rained and I got a tan."

I chuckled because it was completely accurate. It had been one of those blistering hot Georgia days when the heat and humidity interacted and in the late afternoon, massive black thunderclouds moved in overhead. More and more I realized he was experiencing everything we experienced in addition to an even greater awareness of all that is true, both seen and unseen. His perspective, his faith, his kindness, his determination, and wisdom - they amazed me. Everything about him was beautiful.

"Camp is over. What are your feelings?"

"Glad. Now I can focus on psychology."

"Did you not like camp?"

"It's boring. They treat us like we don't understand anything."

"How do you feel about school starting?"

"I am determined to advocate for my fellow students who have autism."

July 28, 2018

"Have you planned what you are going to say to Principal Caresalot?"

"Yes."

"Let's hear it."

"About how I'm brilliant and I deserve an education equal to my cognitive abilities. I want to say, 'What do you want to ask me to assess my intelligence?' Whatever I know I have taught myself. You owe me an education. It is my right. I need to know you are going to help me and my fellow students with autism. The mocking of autistic behaviors by students in the cafeteria, I would like to speak at an assembly so they realize that just because we can't control our bodies is no reason to treat us like we are stupid or to be cruel. I want to be in AP Psychology. Poor fellowship with most of the student population. Why have we been isolated? Try to imagine what it is like for others to treat you like you are stupid just because you can't control your body. I yearn to control my body. So little acute understanding exists about autistics."

Then he told me again of his loneliness and pain because he was isolated from the world. I began making efforts to find and contact other autistics who spelled to communicate. He told me repeatedly he wanted to talk to other people. "Talking to you always is lame." I guess I wasn't that interesting. Clearly our perspectives were different. I thought talking to him was the greatest conversation I had ever had. I knew it was normal for a twenty-one-year-old to not want to spend all his time with his mother, but it was like I had finally been given my son and I couldn't get enough. One morning when I went to get him out of bed he spelled, "How long until I can live on my own?" I could have told him to be realistic and keep his expectations in line with his abilities, but his desire was very clear. A life of his own. So I responded, "I'm thinking six years, if you work really hard. He got up with the determination of someone who refuses to be defeated. I became focused on getting Houston a life.

July 29, 2018

"Make a sentence using copious."

"For federal measures you need a copious number of people to complete a task."

I cracked up. Yep. That's the definition of bureaucracy too. We continued his online Psychology course.

That night his brothers were teasing him. He wanted to fight back. He spelled and I texted. There was some teasing and profanity before Houston spelled, "Please keep your lust stories down tonight." He looked at me sheepishly like he had just tattled. But he was serious. "Oh my word…" Was all I could say. What he must have possibly had to listen to with this many teenagers for so many years. I felt awful for him. He just wanted peace - To hear his own thoughts, I'm sure, and not be interrupted - but still! I needed a drink after that one. Teenage boys…

July 31, 2018

We finally got our meeting with Principal Caresalot. My stomach was in knots. Houston was doing everything to try to stay calm. I heard him making a buzzing sound quietly. This was it. If there was a chance for anyone to go to bat for Houston within the public school system, it was this man. Principal Caresalot was approachable and kind. The students knew he cared, and they loved him. But most importantly, he was able to think and discern independently, advocate for students, and do what many never would. My sons wrestled him frequently at wrestling practice and respected him deeply.

As we sat at a conference table in his office, Principal Caresalot casually asked why we wanted to meet with him. I explained that we had found a way to teach Houston to communicate his true thoughts and that he was much smarter than his evaluations had indicated. I picked up the 26-letter board stencil and Houston began pointing with a pencil and telling Principal Caresalot how smart he was. He told him he had a photographic memory and many other things. The principal was in shock, like he had just seen monkeys fly. He turned to me in utter astonishment, "Ok, now I see why you wanted to meet with me. I needed to see it." After a moment of stunned silence, he began asking Houston questions. Other than Houston telling him he wanted to take AP Psychology and me insisting he get a new IEP; the meeting went in a completely different direction than Houston had planned. Principal Caresalot asked if I had told his teacher. I explained that I had been sending texts with the details of what he spelled every few days. He told me she was at the school, so I texted her and told her we were in the principal's office.

She came and sat down at the end of the table. She didn't say much but her eyes were wide with amazement. I did my best to answer their questions but there were many things that were still a mystery. All I knew for certain was that I was finally getting to know my son and he was more of a gift than I could have ever imagined.

When we got home Houston told me his teacher was thinking, "Maybe he really is smart." I told him, "Houston, it's up to you to prove it."

August 1, 2018

I read him several definitions and asked him to make sentences.

"Make a sentence with tenacious."

"Up deep in the Everest a fearless and tenacious team continues to climb."

"Officious."

"Families often gather and poke fun at the one officious member."

"Diffident."

"The child was diffident in his having to come out to play."

"Spurious."

"People who are spurious force others to give everything they want."

"Houston, that often happens when people are spurious but I'm curious why you say that."

"I've spent my entire life observing people. I know how people think who lie. My dad always lied. He would be nice to you and would laugh to himself, 'Now she will trust me.'"

My stomach seized. I realized my son had always known the truth, even when I had fallen for the lie. I was overwhelmed with the weight he had carried, unable to warn us, unable to share the truth, unable to be the eldest son.

August 3, 2018

J-'s mom had told me about a wonderful organization that was the idea of a non-speaking autistic like our boys. I went for a visit and was immediately hooked. There were spelling coaches and fitness coaches. They were using innovative therapies to help improve timing, motor planning, fitness levels, and communication. Recognizing the overwhelming effects of anxiety, they even had personal yoga training sessions aimed at balance, stress reduction, and body awareness. I was shocked. Where had all this awareness been all these years? Immediately I knew. Inside of those who were trapped. They were the ones who understood what they needed and what helped. They needed to be heard. Over the next two years, the center became a second home, and the therapists became family.

"What did you think of interactive metronome?

"Yes, the interactive metronome can help illuminate how I have a difficult time finding some letters on the letterboard."

"How? Why do you think that is?"

"Having a brain like mine makes letters difficult to find, but reading is easy for me. I am not limited by large numbers of letters or words. Reading on a screen is too hard sometimes. It blinds me. It's too hard to explain. Someday I will."

"What's your favorite way to learn?"

"Books, but it can be hard for my eyes."

"Do you have a hard time seeing? You pass all the eye chart tests."

"It's too hard. My blindness and my alternating eyes."

I had no idea what he was talking about.

August 5, 2018

Excitedly Houston spelled, "I age out in two months and I am so excited about my future. For my entire life I have made a daily prayer that somehow a way could be found so I could communicate. You and J- saved my life and I am so grateful. I have inside of me one thing made to accomplish, for I am made with a purpose. You will get your chance to witness it. Many miraculous things are going to happen. Keep filling yourself with knowledge of God's love."

"I'm trying, Houston. It's still hard."

"I had an idea. Maybe I could go to a college program."

"That's a really big goal, Houston. I'm not sure. I need to see what your diploma said. I don't know what's required and what is allowed. I promise I'll look into it."

"Impulsivity is a big problem for me."

"I know sweetie. I know."

I reached out to his teacher to see if he had a certificate of completion or a high school diploma. She got back to me and sent me a picture of his IEP with the designation of a high school diploma. I reminded her we wanted a new IEP right away as soon as school started.

When I told Sarah what Houston had spelled, she ordered him a t-shirt with "Created for a Purpose - Ephesians 2:10" printed on it. We went for a run. Houston flapped his hands while we waited for a light to turn. People stared at us from the safety of their car. I knew they were reading his shirt. From the way the woman looked down abruptly when she saw that I saw her staring at him, I knew she probably felt sorry for him or sorry for me. If they only knew…

August 6, 2018

"How was school?"

"I had breakfast in the cafeteria with my friends (listed his friends)."

We continued the online course and I suggested we investigate the courses available on I-University. The Psychology course was from Princeton. Houston was excited.

August 7, 2018

"My speech is a low mannerism for what I am thinking. Learning to live on my own is my biggest goal. Saying anything is far too difficult for me."

"That means you have to learn how to take care of your body and how to control your body. That's going to be hard. It's going to take a long time." Houston's growing to do list was all on me. It was overwhelming.

It was this day that Houston began to open up more about his faith and His relationship with God. I was unprepared. Nothing could have prepared me for what I would begin to hear. He told me he wanted to talk to a pastor. I asked if he wanted to talk to the senior pastor of our old church. He spelled, "No. I don't want to talk to him. I want to meet with Bill." Bill was the pastor who had prayed for me hours within hours of us meeting J- at Chili's. I was stunned. I didn't realize Houston even knew he existed. I emailed Bill that Houston wanted to meet with him, and we arranged a meeting. I asked Houston if he wanted to go to church. He spelled that it was too loud. Then he spelled something extraordinary.

"You can feel God's presence more in the silence than in the singing."[95] There are angels around wherever God's word is being taught. People think that God is far away but he is so close to us right now. Love is how He makes Himself known. Understand that He is more real than fear or guilt or hate or loss or distance or your awareness of Him. He knows that we want to be loved more than anything. So many of His efforts to show us love involve the same thing: knowledge of His love through family, knowledge of His love through others, and through the presence of His spirit. The love living in you is His. You will soon have faith. No prayer is unanswered in His world. I know this to be true. Dad will pay for what he did. You won't learn the reason right now. Love not hate is in this home. You must believe. Would you like knowledge of other things?"

"Yes. I want to know why." It was a demand, one that I had never gotten answered the many times I had cried to God. That day my mind was somewhere else. My heart was filled with loneliness and heartache. Even though a miracle was unfolding in front of me, I was still hurting. The Big Jock had refused to make the minimum wage child support payments and there was nothing that could be done until the compliance hearing. I hated living with this stress and how much thoughts of money controlled my emotions. Reagan's self-destruction and hatefulness broke my heart. She wouldn't let me get close. Her cutting had increased. Paul's growing rebellion, refusal to believe his sister or befriend Houston, and growing disrespect had become a daily grind. I knew he was still talking to his dad despite the fact that we were barely surviving because of him. I knew he was being manipulated and was incapable of stopping it. My broken heart wouldn't stop hurting from the breakup, and I was upset about not being able to talk to my dad and his beautiful wife that I loved so much. I worried about how I was going to continue to work and care for Houston and how on earth I would possibly get him a college education when I needed to work, and we still didn't have any funding to assist me. I was frustrated by how long it took for Houston to spell, how my arm would absolutely ache, and how my back had made it painful to hear my son's thoughts. Even in the midst of a miracle, I was full of pain and doubt. It overwhelmed me.

"Aren't you mad at God?" I suddenly blurted out one night through tears. "Aren't you mad that He locked you inside your body and kept you trapped all these years? Aren't you mad at all He took from you? Aren't you mad at what all He allowed to happen to us? Aren't you??" I began sobbing.

He didn't respond right away. Finally he put his hand on mine, which was how he let me know he wanted to spell. "When you say these things you make me doubt God's love. Those are the rotten thoughts." I wept more. Then he spelled, "When you've seen what I've seen, there is no doubt."

His face was so certain, so undeniably assured, it took my breath away. He's seen. He has no doubt. The full impact of his words sunk into my heart. 'Doubt?' I was in shock. 'That's what's rotten?' The doubt was my defense. Doubt is what made the world respect that I hadn't gone mad. I needed it to protect myself against unanswered prayers and disappointment. I needed it to protect myself from other doubters who question everything. Doubt was all I had. Doubt was my truth, proof of my intelligence, proof I had retained my sanity and rationality. NO ONE could not doubt in all of this. For a moment I pondered... If I stopped doubting... No. I couldn't. I shook my head.

---

[95] For God alone, O my soul, wait in silence, for my hope is from him. — Psalm 62:5

It is good that one should wait quietly for the salvation of the Lord. — Lamentations 3:26

"Be still, and know that I am God. I will be exalted among the nations, I will be exalted in the earth!"— Psalm 46:10

The Lord will fight for you, and you have only to be silent.

Be silent in the LORD's presence and wait patiently for him. — Psalm 37:7; Habakkuk 2:20

The Lord will fight for you, and you have only to be silent. — Exodus 14:14

For thus said the Lord God, the Holy One of Israel, "In returning and rest you shall be saved; in quietness and in trust shall be your strength." — Isaiah 30:15

And rising very early in the morning, while it was still dark, he departed and went out to a desolate place, and there he prayed. — Mark 1:35

After everything, my faith was still so fragile. I had only been able to offer Him that one act of faith in the face of impossibility. One faith beyond salvation faith. Just one. I didn't know how I could offer more. And my daring act of faith was huge. Wasn't that enough???

"God, why won't you just let me be rational and assess risks and probabilities. Why?? Why won't you let me have doubts? It's foolish not to. People already think I'm a fool for believing in a miracle. They think I'm a fool to pray for and seek justice. They think believing in the face of all this logic and facts is foolish, childish. They think I need to just accept reality. Do you know what they say about me when I say something positive or chase after wrongs to be righted? I'm so tired of being a fool. Why do You want me to believe You in everything??" Then I remembered a verse. *If anyone causes one of these little ones--those who believe in me--to stumble, it would be better for them to have a large millstone hung around their neck and to be drowned in the depths of the sea.*[96]

I was struck with the weight of my doubt, not just on myself but on my son. I wept even more as I realized the gravity of all my reasoning against God and the good that was always out of my reach even while it was rained down on those around me. I didn't know Houston had heard me all those years. I didn't know he had heard all my awful doubt. I never meant for him to hear me, but he had. My doubt had made my son question his heavenly father even though he had seen heaven. It was the most horrible thing I had ever done, and I had done so much of it. My unbelief had made my son question God's love. Is there anything more rotten? For the first time in my life I saw doubt as the destructive evil that it truly is. Could I give it up? Could I trust Him in everything?

> *And everyday I am swayed by whatever is on my mind*
> *I hear it all depends on my faith*
> *So I'm feeling precarious*
> *The only problem I have with these mysteries*
> *Is they're so mysterious*
>
> *And like a consumer*
> *I've been thinking if I could just get a bit more*
> *More than my fifteen minutes of faith*
> *Then I'd be secure* [97]

My prayer was soft. "God? You know what I've been through. I'm sorry I've doubted You. I don't know that I trust You, but I want to. I'm so sorry. Mostly I'm sorry for what my rotten thoughts did to my son's heart. Thank you for keeping him so close. He's needed You so much. But God, so have I. Will You please, please come close? I haven't felt You in so long. I need You. Please be near."

> *Cast out my doubts, please prove me wrong*
> *'Cause these demons can be so headstrong*
> *Make my walls fall, please prove me wrong*
> *'Cause this resentment's been building*
> *And burn them up with your fire so strong*
> *If you can before I bail, please prove me wrong...* [98]

August 8, 2018

I picked Houston up from school. He seemed so sad. I thought he had been teased or his senses were "illuminated," as he had described.

"Houston, you seem down. Is anything upsetting you?"

"My only insight is I saw heaven."

---

[96] Matthew 18:6
[97] *Shifting Sands*; By Aaron Tate. Copyright Msi Music Administration o/b/o Cumbee Road Music
[98] *Prove Me Wrong*; By Aaron Tate. Copyright Msi Music admin. o/b/o Cumbee Road Music

"Was that not good?"

"Either I have many good visions or a scary one."

"Houston, what did you see?"

"Roads or paths came together so many people could go to hell."

Immediately I remembered the verses in Matthew. I grabbed my phone and did a quick search. I read him the following. *Enter through the narrow gate. For wide is the gate and broad is the road that leads to destruction, and many enter through it.*[99]

"Houston, is this what you saw?"

"Yes. It was maddening."

"That was Matthew 7:13. You *saw* Matthew 7:13??"

"Yes." He put his head down. Clearly, he was upset. I was stunned. What else had he seen?

"You're wonderful to try to stop it."

What was he talking about? "Houston, I've tried to tell people about Jesus, but I don't know that I've done that much to stop anything at all."

"You are the talk of heaven. You have a band of angels who are always with you. They have to work to earn the right to guard you."

"What on earth are you talking about? I haven't done anything to deserve angels."

"Many lives are saved because of you."

"Are you talking about something I've already done? Are you talking about the book I wrote? It didn't sell that many copies. I don't think anyone is saved because of me, Houston. Please don't say that. It makes me uncomfortable. I don't deserve angels, okay?"

"They love you so much."

I got up and walked away. I was upset. I wasn't going to listen to this. I was so far from God. There was no way there could be angels with me.

I ignored what Houston told me. After a few hours I asked Houston to prepare a list of things he wanted to say in his IEP. I researched the IDEA ACT and read it to Houston so he would know what the law said. By law the IDEA ACT states that you "have a right to access the general curriculum to meet the challenging expectations established for all children." It also requires that "to the maximum extent appropriate, children with disabilities including children in public or private institutions, are educated with children who are nondisabled; and special classes, separate schooling or other removals of children with disabilities from regular educational environment occurs only if the nature or severity of the disability is such that education in regular classes with the use of supplementary aids and services cannot be achieved satisfactorily."

This was his list of points he wanted to make in his IEP meeting.

- I have a right to an education equal to my cognitive abilities and I have a right to not be isolated as well
- I learn differently but that does not mean I should not be educated
- You need to stop treating me like I'm stupid and treat me with respect
- Why isn't seeing believing? Is it because you usually hear a voice instead of see a voice?
- Education and friendship
- Everything I have a right to and access to the resources I need to achieve my goals
- Only I know how much has happened to fall into this spot where I can now say anything I want so now is the time to listen to me

***

"The difference between high functioning and low functioning is that high functioning means your deficits are ignored, and low functioning means your assets are ignored." [100]

August 9, 2018

It was the day of the IEP. At 11:33 am I got a text from Houston's teacher.

"Hi just wanted to let you know- I invited someone from AT as well as someone from speech aside from Kelly. Just wanted to have all hands-on deck."

My thoughts were 'AT… Assisted Technology maybe? Ok cool. I can't wait for everyone to see Houston communicate!' I replied, "Perfect."

That afternoon I walked into the classroom. I was shocked at how many people were in the room. I had been in a minimum of twenty IEP meetings over the years and this was triple the number of people that were usually there. I was immediately anxious because I didn't know how Houston would react to so many people. His anxiety was severe, and I didn't know what to expect. This was also the first IEP he had ever attended. Finally he had the opportunity to advocate for himself, and it was him against 6 adults. I had always had the best relationship with the schools, and I couldn't understand why on earth they had felt the need to bring so many people to this IEP.

A person I had never met before introduced herself as the head of X County Speech Services and immediately gestured toward the boards and said they didn't approve of ANY methodology, especially that one. She was surly and sarcastic. It was clear she was there to certify dominance and deny services, protect the coffers of X County. Here I was after never requesting anything in 17 years and all I wanted for my son was to be included in a regular class for his last three months of public education. All I wanted, more importantly all *he* wanted, was to access the education he had a right to, the one he had been denied. I was furious but I knew this was no time for emotions. This was my son's time, his chance to have a voice. I responded, "How can you say that when you haven't even seen him communicate?" My heart was beating approximately 200 beats a minute. I could hear it in my temples, in my chest. I couldn't hear my own thoughts my heart beat so loudly. I turned to his teacher and said, "Do you have a copy of my rights?"

That was always the first thing that a teacher would hand me in an IEP meeting. I used to joke with the teachers that I had so many copies of these I could use them as wallpaper. I hadn't even thought to bring a copy or review them. I tried to remember what the IDEA Act had stated. My mind went blank. Internally I knew we were sitting in an ambush, and I wanted to quickly review what my parental rights were. I hoped Houston would remember what he wanted to say because I couldn't remember anything that I wanted to say. His teacher printed off a copy in a font that was so small that the entire document was on the top right corner of the page. There was literally no way to read it. I was terrified. I didn't know what was going to happen and my mind raced as I scolded myself for not thinking of bringing an attorney. But I wasn't an enemy. Houston wasn't an enemy. We weren't trying to take anything. This was a miracle. A freaking miracle. What the hell was wrong with them? Why weren't they happy for us?

While his teacher was printing off the list, the young man who had pointed and lunged toward me when I sat in the car years earlier burst in the room. He was intent on something but was quickly pulled out of the room by a teacher. I looked up and smiled at him. The woman who had just attacked us said, "Who was that?" She was told and was surprised by how much he had grown. For that one moment she was soft, then she turned back to the agenda at hand. Scrutinize. My hand was shaking as I held up the board. This was it. *Please God. Please help him. Please.* I kept praying. Slowly, Houston told them he wanted to take AP Psychology, one letter at a time. I could see their eyes get big as he spelled. They asked what he wanted to do after school. He spelled that he wanted to attend college. They asked where. He spelled, "Georgia. Go Dawgs." He answered many other questions. Finally he asked a question to the head of Speech. "Why don't you believe me?" She turned and looked at him. Abruptly, sharply, with no kindness she snapped back, "I DO."

[100] Laura Tisoncik

One teacher teased him about his Bocce Ball performance and Houston spelled, "I'm not that bad at Bocce, coach." The coach's face froze. His teacher asked what about the other daily living skills they were teaching him. She reminded him how he struggled to do the simplest tasks. He spelled he still needed help with these skills because he didn't want to live with his mom forever. He told them about knowing math. I was shocked by this. He had only been taught single digit addition and subtraction using a touch point system and how to use a calculator to add purchases and make change. I thought to myself, 'How does he know math?' They asked him what other class he wanted to take if he couldn't take Psychology. He spelled, "US History." They agreed they could offer him access to that class. They insisted he had to use an iPad. I said, "He has just learned how to use a 26-letter stencil. This is all new. I don't think he's ready for that. That's just a huge leap for him."

I wished in that moment I had ten experts with me who could explain motor planning, ocular reflexes, regulation, and anxiety and how to manage the cognitive demand in those circumstances. But I didn't know enough to explain how even pointing to one letter was excruciating for my son. I did, however, think as he spelled, 'Don't they see how he's struggling? Don't they see his exhaustion?' It was obvious. I kept having to give him breaks. His body was limp at times and holding the pencil looked like he was holding a forty-pound weight and trying to point at letters with it. When I put my hand on his back his shirt was soaked with perspiration. I was angry and scared. His teacher suddenly asked, "Houston, what about yesterday in the cafeteria? What did you think of those boys?"

Houston spelled, "Dear Corrie, they were just having fun."

"So you think I was being too strict?"

"Yes."

I was puzzled and asked her, "What happened yesterday?"

His teacher replied that some boys were laughing, and spraying water bottles and she had told them to back away and not bother the special needs group. She was trying to protect her students from the wild boys. The question had come out of nowhere and I realized she asked to test him. I understood but I was pissed. No one had tested her awareness or intelligence. Finally it was over, and we left exhausted. We had walked into an ambush and won. Sort of. I hadn't ever considered that people wouldn't be happy for us. I hadn't considered there would be animosity and distrust. We left with a sad victory.

August 10, 2018

Houston's teacher called to let me know he had been approved for an iPad with a typing program that we could take home to practice. I explained again that moving to a keyboard was a huge leap that he was not ready to make. I offered to come in and show them how to use the letter boards so they could try practicing with him. I reminded her that Houston would be meeting the vision therapist to help us get approved for an Audiobooks program. They had to do an assessment that might take a while so he would be late the following day.

August 11, 2018

I took Houston out for pizza, beer, and live music. I asked him what he wanted to do that night and he spelled, "The best gift is most often alcohol." I cracked up. It was the same place I bought him his first beer on his 21st birthday. Because it was outside and he could stand and move around, it was much easier for him to not be dysregulated. We were shocked when Houston's coach, his adaptive PE teacher that had been with him at least six years, came running up to us and threw her arms around Houston. She hadn't seen him in ages. She had been his coach for years and worked with him on so many different skills and sports. She was just a beautiful mess, loving everyone and everything in her path. When I showed her Houston could communicate, she started crying. Houston told her how much she had done for him and how he loved her. She took him up to the front and started dancing with him. He was in heaven. He had been able to show his old teacher he had always understood everything. And here he was drinking a beer and dancing with his old teacher. It was one of the happiest moments. A complete gift. A moment, a person to treasure.

40

Sharing the Good News

How beautiful upon the mountains are the feet of him who brings good news,
who publishes peace, who brings good news of happiness,
who publishes salvation, who says to Zion, "Your God reigns.
— Isaiah 52:7

August 13, 2018

Monday morning 6:54 am - Text from Houston's teacher.

Good morning!! The more I thought about it this weekend, the more I think that it would be more appropriate to drop Houston off today and him and I will continue with the iPad based on the discussion that we had at the meeting. I hope Houston's appointments go well today!

7:17 am - My response.

Good morning. I forgot that he has another appointment in the afternoon so he will not be in today. While I understand your reticence due to the harsh stance that the county representative took and I also agree that ultimately, we want Houston on a keyboard, I am concerned about jumping so far ahead so quickly. I am afraid he will experience a great deal of frustration. Just communicating with a new person is difficult without the added challenge of all the letters being in a different place. If you want to use the iPad, I think that is great, but please try to find an app that has the letters in the alphabetical order until the two of you get a rhythm of your own going. My other pointers would be what I mentioned on Friday. Start with asking him to spell words just so you can start identifying his spelling patterns. When he pauses and can't find a letter, keep verbally prompting him to look for it. If he tires or starts spelling something that doesn't make sense, put the iPad down for a second and tell him to close his eyes and try again. Once you get a sense of his patterns move on to other questions - not easy at first obviously, until the two of you have a real rhythm going.

As an aside, it is disheartening that the school cannot be more accommodating and patient with Houston as he learns how to control his hands and eyes to communicate. I don't feel as if he should be expected to so rapidly adapt to us and how we want him to communicate. I feel we need to let him build his motor skills before we raise the standards. It's like, ok you stood on one leg so now you can run a race and jump hurdles tomorrow. You have seen him express how difficult it is to communicate and I just ask that you would do everything possible to make it easier for him to do so no matter what the county policy is. Having a voice is a basic human right, we should not make it more difficult for him to have one and erect unnecessary barriers.

7:24 am - Her reply.

I totally understand your concern- I will research apps that are alphabetical order today and tomorrow we will start by solely focusing on getting comfortable with each other.

7:25 am - Mine.

Thank you, Corrie! :)

We drove to the vision therapist. First were a battery of vision tests he had never completed before. I was fascinated. I had never considered there could be so many missing pieces in sight. When we finally met with the doctor, I assumed it would be like any other eye appointment. The doctor was a specialist. She looked concerned as she examined his eyes and said little while she worked. Finally she stepped back. Noticing the board in my hand she said, "When you're doing the boards does he lean heavily to the left?"

My jaw dropped. "Yes! He does. All the time. How do you know that?"

"It's his right eye. It suppresses. He's trying to accommodate. Here let me show you what he's seeing. She pointed to a picture on the wall with a paragraph. The letters were piled on top of each other with multiples of each word. This is what he sees. Let me try something. When his eye suppresses it doesn't function at all. He is momentarily blind in that eye."

While she rummaged through her lenses, I stared at the paragraph with my mouth open. *This* is what he's been seeing all his life?? I was getting nauseous just looking at it. I immediately realized yet another error I was making. When he leaned to the left, I thought he was trying to pull away from me and assumed he didn't want to work on the boards. I wanted to kick myself. How many things did his body do or did he do to try to accommodate a body he couldn't control that I had called a behavior? How many times had I misinterpreted his intentions based on what I saw and what I thought? How many ways have I been wrong? … Let me count the ways. Enlightenment came with a heavy dose of guilt.

The doctor inserted some lenses and asked Houston, "How's that? How many do you see?"

He spelled, "Three. They are still moving."

"What's he talking about?" I asked.

"Oh, wow. Yes, he has that too. So he doesn't just see multiples of everything. The images also move. Both eyes suppress but he definitely has more issues on his right side."

"What? He sees triple of everything, and it moves??"

"Yes. Prism glasses will help, but he's going to need vision therapy. The eyes have a great deal to do with their balance, spatial awareness, and ability to control their body."

"Um, yeah he is! Good grief. Houston! I had no idea!"

Then it occurred to me how, since he was little, people had been telling him to look in their eyes. Oh my word. If I saw six eyes that moved, I wouldn't want to look at anyone either.

The doctor tried one set after another with Houston spelling each time, "Still moving." Finally, he spelled, "It stopped. It's still." We placed an order for glasses and signed up for vision therapy. As I walked out, I forgot I had come in there for her to fill out a form for audible books for those with vision impairments. My head was spinning. Houston wasn't the only one who was gaining his vision. So many things about Houston, little things, began to make sense. When I explained Houston's vision issues to Benjamin, he told me that one day he had been talking to Houston and seen one pupil completely disappear and the other one get enormous. It had freaked him out. For Houston, it was all he knew, a body totally out of his control with no way to explain how it impacted him.

The vision therapist was across the street from the elementary school Houston had attended. Immediately after we left, he started saying repeatedly, "Sweet Gum! Sweet Gum!" I hoped his old teachers would still be there. We drove across the street and parked. It felt like home. Houston practically bounced out of the car and ran up to the door. Thanks to Houston and a few others like him, the doors were locked at all times to prevent elopement. We rang the doorbell and waited. I heard someone yell inside, "It's Houston!" And suddenly the door was open and filled with familiar faces - faces that loved Houston, that loved me, that had walked this walk with me and helped me potty train my son and so much more. Houston could hardly contain his excitement. I told him he had to calm down and spell for them.

"More than you have ideas you made me so happy. You kept trying to teach me. Don't do ABA. How would you stand to do the same thing over and over? Love. That's what you do well. That's why I love this school. Pray that we let little ones get the same opportunity. Know that good has come from all you taught me. Our prayers are for the ones who believe we aren't smart. Matter of principle to change their minds. It's good to show you what I've become. It will take all we have to change their stance. We are talking to everyone. Hope does work. Just look at me."

When he spelled, he would stop to jump and down and flap his hands. He ran off to the back of the school and found the pretzels that they kept in the same place from ten years earlier. He was smiling, laughing, jumping, spelling, hugging. The teachers were talking, crying, praising God. It was the most beautiful chaos I have ever seen. They were talking about ABA. "Of course they hate it! We hate it!" They were asking for information and how did I learn about this. They were literally praying and thanking God right there in the hallway that the boy they took care of and loved had become a man, a man greater than they ever thought possible. They were also praising God because their efforts had not been in vain. God had seen. God had heard. God had taken their love and made it speak.

That night I got so many Facebook requests from all his former teachers. Everyone wanted Houston stories. They made me remember how wonderful people can be.

***

Houston had continued to insist he wanted to meet with a pastor from our old church, so I followed up again with Bill and arranged a meeting. Everyone knew Bill was kind and patient, a devout man of God who prayed and loved others. He had very little hubris. All Houston would tell me was he had a message. After the vision therapist and Sweet Gum we went across town to meet with Bill. I was surprised when Bill told Houston it was nice to meet him. My heart dropped. I realized he had never met Houston because Houston had always been in the corner of the basement where the special needs class was. I winced remembering how the special needs class kept losing its classroom because other classes were a priority. It had felt like the leadership was focused on creating an environment to attract the wealthy and well connected. It had felt like they forgot Jesus' heart for the least, for the ones that were a disruption. But I remembered Jesus had said, *"Let the little children come to me and do not hinder them, for to such belongs the kingdom of heaven."* [101] All the things Houston had missed, all the people he hadn't gotten an opportunity to meet - It was my fault, my ignorance. I hadn't fought for inclusion. It was their fault that for too many years they hadn't seen these children the way God saw them. We sat in a conference room and Houston focused intensely on spelling. He really was on a mission. I was nervous because I had no idea what he would spell.

"This is God's word. 'The good I want is words of truth. Not singing. Not buildings. Prayer has come to Me to love your weak. Over and over My money goes to so many buildings instead of good. Love your people. Bill is called to hear.'" Houston paused, exhausted from the effort it had taken to quiet his anxiety and spell the words from the Lord. It had taken so long just to spell those few sentences. After a moment he continued, "I have seen the throne of God with majesty. Beauty cannot describe it. There are seals placed on Him. Jesus has good pouring out of Him. Heralds to Him are everywhere. The praises to the King of Kings move through the air like waves that keep coming." He slumped over and started repeating, "Coke. Diet Coke. Diet Coke." I told Bill that was all he had energy for. By this point I knew when he couldn't keep going. I didn't know what to say. Clearly Houston wasn't trying to be diplomatic. It was direct. At that moment, I wasn't sure if Bill believed Houston had seen heaven. Bill politely commented that, "It must really be something." Then he mentioned they were doing a series on compassion. I couldn't really say anything at all. He asked to pray with us and asked what our needs were, so I told him. He prayed for us. Houston was exhausted so I didn't ask him anything more

[101] Matthew 19:14

that night. The next day he told me Bill didn't believe him, that he thought I was just a mom loving her son and wanting to believe her disabled son had seen heaven. I understood. But I hadn't told Bill all Houston had seen or was capable of. When Bill called to check on me, I asked if he believed Houston and he said he did. I thought he was just being kind.

August 14, 2018

Houston attended his first neurotypical general education class - U.S. History 7th period. He had an aid who said he did great and only got a little antsy the last five minutes. Everyone wanted to know what he thought. As soon as he got off the bus, I got out the boards, excited to hear his perspective.

"Houston, did you like the class?"

"Yes."

"What did you like best?"

"Just being there was the best part. I love you. You are letting me live my life. Goals can begin to really change my finer desires."

"What do you mean by finer desires?"

"I mean I now have a chance to have a top education."

"Did you learn anything you want to share?"

"I learned that many different interests were responsible for colonists settling in the new world."

I texted his teacher his responses commenting, "I'm so freaking excited!!!!!"

She replied, "Oh my word! Can you ask him what they did in class?"

Houston spelled, "We read about colonists and the teacher told us that the truth is that colonists did not go there for freedom. They went there for better land."

August 15, 2018

We had one last place the transition coordinator wanted me to visit for an adult program. I had already visited but she wanted me to bring Houston. I was resolute when I met with the director. Houston began spelling and taking control of the conversation, clearly expressing his intellect, and acknowledging the difficulties he had with loops and controlling his body as well as expressing the type of assistance he needed and his goals for his future. The director went to get some of his staff to see Houston spell. I told the teacher that Houston was very smart and to ask him a question. The teacher asked, "What's your favorite food?" I wanted to throw my hands up in the air. Are you kidding me? Why don't you ask his favorite color too? "I said he's smart. Ask his opinion about politics or history." The teacher seemed confused and unable to come up with a question. As I watched him struggle to ask Houston an age-appropriate question for an almost 22-year-old, I realized how paralyzed we all are by appearances. I also realized how many more times I would have a similar encounter before the world would treat my son as anyone would want to be treated. Sight created its own blinders. I couldn't send my son here either. I knew I would only let him be around people who saw past his body to the magnificent man inside.

While he was at school his teacher texted me that he was agitated and biting his hand a lot. She tried to spell with him and there were only a few random words and his frustration escalated. I replied, "I really think we need to just have some time spelling words without anything else (questions). It took six weeks for him to open up to me. His first session with another spelling coach was awful but the next one was wonderful.

At my urging Houston's middle school teacher came over to visit that night. She had been with him every day for four years. We had recently seen her at the YMCA for a Special Needs yoga class I was teaching. She brought an iPad to record him. She looked at the board and consoled me before we started, shaking her head, "Oh Katie, don't get your hopes up."

"What? No, it's not like that. I'm not hoping. We're already there. He's communicating."

She looked at me in shock and began recording. He started spelling out how much she meant to him. She started crying. She told me, "Katie, I came here to tell you that there was no way this was possible. But I was wrong." She told me she felt awful for being so wrong. She asked if it would work for her daughter. Houston told her it would. After she left, she told me she kept thinking about all those years she didn't fight for her daughter, didn't fight for Houston, didn't want to make a fuss, didn't want to be the problem parent or teacher that made the schools angry, that she enforced the minimal standards that excluded all her babies from what everyone else got. I listened and tried to console her, "I did the same thing. I didn't want another fight. I was wrong. I should have fought for my son." She asked if she could post about what she had seen. She posted, "A big thank you to Katie for sharing her Miracle! I know Houston as if he were my own, but I don't. He is a man with big ideas, and he told them to me. I am overcome with joy to hear his voice." Later she posted the Maya Angelou quote, *Do the best you can until you know better. Then when you know better, do better.*" Exactly.

August 16, 2018

His teacher texted me and let me know his history book was in his backpack and that he had a project due. It was for the Hall of Fame. The assignment was to choose an American who had an impact on American history and write about them. Paul told me he had written about Ray Kroc. I went to Houston's bag and lifted the very first book out of his backpack - ever. I held that history book and wanted to cry. My son was studying. My son was learning. My son was included. The homework my other kids made dreadful was suddenly the most exciting thing I had ever gotten to do. For a few days we poured over his history book as I told him about different people in U.S. History and why they were important. For a moment he wanted to write about Lincoln. I discouraged it because everyone had written about Lincoln. I told him to pick someone that no one had ever chosen. On the cover was the picture of the Migrant Mother. He asked about her story. So I read to him from several different sources and even played an interview with her that she had done in her old age. I showed him how the original printed story did not have all the details correct. I discussed how important fact checking was in journalism. He listened like only a dry sponge can. Finally I asked if he felt he was ready to write his entry for the Hall of Fame. It took over 30 minutes of spelling, one letter at a time. I set my phone up against the bowl on the kitchen table and recorded the entire thing. When I sent his teacher the article, I sent the videos as well so they could see for themselves that this was his work. I wanted to make sure I had proof of everything he did. On August 30, 2018, he stood up with his aid in front of his U.S. History class of neurotypical peers. It was the first time he had ever been treated as an equal and allowed to participate. He tried to read aloud but his voice was so soft it couldn't be heard. At that point his aid read his report.

Hi. I chose to do my report on Florence Owens Thompson, Migrant Mother. Florence raised herself in Oklahoma. A native Cherokee by birth, she married Owens when she was 17. She farmed with him. Now after the dust bowl ruined his farm they moved to California with their five children. When she was pregnant with her sixth child her husband died of tuberculosis. She worked in fields picking cotton sometimes 400 to 500 pounds a day. She did anything to feed her kids. She had another baby. The camps did not have enough work for all the migrant workers.

Dorothea Lange took pictures not only for herself but for the government. Lange was in her car and saw a sign for a pea pickers camp. She decided to go look. She in some way found Florence and her children who were living on rotting vegetables. She took pictures of Florence.

Florence is famous because she knows poverty and refused to give up. Her picture helped save so many people from starving. When it was published it captured the hearts of the country. Florence lived a life poor in earthly things. God gave her something even better. He made her so institutionalized as a figure of motherhood and perseverance, dedicated to her children. Her failures. She had nothing. Respect is not given to the poor.

She deserves to be on our wall of fame because she is a hero. She is selfless and only took the pictures so Lange could help to alter their world.

That afternoon his teacher texted me. "His aid said he did great! He presented first and got a big round of applause!! How did he say it went?"

I asked Houston. Apparently, the applause had gone to his head.

"It seemed so wonderful when they clapped for me. So I want to next time save some pens for autographs."

August 18, 2018

At the center that morning Houston had been asked to run a sprint and had slowly jogged. I demonstrated and he still couldn't do it. The coach demonstrated. We tried several things. None of them seemed to work to encourage his body to move at a fast pace. The whole drive home I thought of all the chasing over the years and how he could run faster than the wind, how his teachers couldn't catch him, how he would run straight out of high-top boots, how I nicknamed his flights Forrest Gump fast. When I had signed him up for Special Olympics, he would sprint at practice, and no one could catch him. But in a race, he would barely jog and that was with constant encouragement. I always thought his refusal to run was willful since I knew he had the ability. Today I knew he wanted to run and show off for his therapists. He adored them. I didn't understand.

"Houston, I know you're athletic. I know you're fast. You run like the wind. People can't even catch you. You know we are trying to help you. Why couldn't you run today?"

"I admit I have athletic ability but I do not know how to control it. I can't access it. It just comes on me."

"Do you know what we can do to help you access it?"

"I learned that I need help to tell my mind where my body needs to go. I could not make my body move fast. I tell my body but it doesn't do what I tell it."

"I don't know how to tell it either, Houston. It seems like it doesn't receive or process messages. I'm not even sure which. Maybe both. Do you want me to start training you every day at the gym?"

"Yes."

So we started working out every day. I was a trainer, but this was different. Something in me knew deep inside it wasn't Forrest Gump's spirit in him, it was something greater. It was Eric Liddell's. The greatness of God was in him, but something was holding him back. I was training a body that couldn't direct itself in the tiniest ways that could make an enormous impact. But then suddenly everything would mechanize together in some glorious labyrinth of motor coordination and my son would run like eagles fly, and just as suddenly the coordinated movements would disappear as randomly as they had appeared. I was left to plug all the holes, and it looked much like Swiss cheese. I realized his core was extremely weak, but the disconnection and lack of power in his joints was extreme, especially his hips, elbows, shoulders, and wrists. I had always thought he had low tonicity in his upper body but now, as I had him try to do simple movements, I began to see there were far more things not connecting than I realized. He didn't seem to be able to find anything behind him or in his peripheral. Crossing his midline was an act of extraordinary focus and strength. He struggled to move different parts of his body at the same time. Even something simple like holding a light kettlebell upside down and extending it overhead made his stomach stick out and his upper back round backwards while his opposite hand would instinctively go under his belly, and his chin would tuck into his neck with his forehead scrunched and his eyes darting in all directions. I tried to get him to jump laterally over a rope and he couldn't do it without looking. Something was going on with his feet. I had always known that, but now I began to see the gaps and how one part of his body not working affected the rest of his body. He seemed to be lost and couldn't find his body most of the time. I had to prompt him verbally and sometimes with my hands for every single rep. Often he would look at me waiting, frozen, even though we had just done the exercise ten times, as if he had suddenly gotten lost and the fear had taken over. I would prompt him, and he would move. It was exhausting and frustrating to repeat myself that many times when the instructions and the tasks seemed so simple. I knew he understood. I remembered how his teachers had put "Reduce prompts" as one of his IEP goals. But as I watched him, I realized he didn't have the ability to initiate his movements. Somehow my directions, my prompts, were what he needed to move. He couldn't direct or prompt himself. What was going on in his body? What was going on his brain?

August 20, 2018

After school I took Houston to Chick-fil-A. It was raining and humid. He left his board in the car and I ran back to get it. He said, "No. No." I said, "Tough. The board's coming with us."

We sat in a booth. There were two girls in front of us studying on their computer. Houston was listening. I looked at the screen and saw A.P. U.S. History on the top of the screen. I asked Houston, "Do you want to talk to them about History?" He spelled, "Yes." So I said, "Excuse me. My son is taking U.S. History too. He wanted to talk to you. Both girls turned around to look and listen to Houston.

He spelled, "What are your thoughts on European exploration?"

They answered about the abuses of European exploration and how the Chinese thought their culture was superior to European culture.

Houston replied, "I agree and would add Europeans were the only ones that considered themselves conquerors." I had to stop myself from going "WHAT?! HOW DO YOU KNOW THAT??" At that point Houston's body acted out and I quickly explained that he was autistic and couldn't control his body. One of the girls with a dark curly ponytail and a sweet face nodded her head and said, "I know. My brother is autistic."

I stared at her. "Really?? Is he speaking?"

She cocked her head to one side and said, "Not really. He repeats things." I knew what she meant. Echolalia and scripting. Just like Houston. And everyone thought those were his thoughts.

"Come here. You've got to see this."

She stood up and walked over to stand on Houston's left side. Houston looked at me and with incredible determination and control began spelling with more rhythm and speed than I had ever seen. It was if he had mustered up every available ounce of energy within him and was using it to point. He spelled, "Your brother needs to learn how to use the boards. He needs a voice. He's like me. He's in there. My whole life I wanted a voice and now I have one."

She started crying and Houston jumped up and hugged her. Tears streamed down her face. Houston took one of her tears and put it on his tongue. She cried and laughed at the same time as I urged Houston not to take her tears. It was almost as if he was trying to catch them all. He held onto her arms and hugged her again. I explained as succinctly as I could how Houston had been trapped his whole life and how he had progressed to open communication because of these boards. She nodded while I talked and then wept openly. Suddenly the dam broke, and she began sobbing. Her friend hugged her, but she couldn't stop crying. We exchanged numbers while tears poured down her face. I said, "You HAVE to get your mother to call me. You HAVE to. Ok?" She nodded and then put her head on her friend's shoulder and continued to weep. The tears wouldn't stop. As Houston and I left I thought about my other children and the burden and sorrow that autism had placed on them. Watching that sixteen-year-old weep for a brother she had never gotten to know, the great immeasurable loss that autism had caused in family after family weighed like a boulder on my heart. I opened the door to Chick-fil-A and stepped outside. Purple skies hung heavy all around me. Then I gasped. Directly over Chick-fil-A was the largest and clearest rainbow I have ever seen in my life. Houston and I both stood staring for a long time, not wanting to leave. I knew exactly what it meant. God was showing me He's a promise keeper. Finally I asked Houston if he was glad, we had taken the board inside. He spelled, "Yes. That was heaven working." Then that beautiful son of mine turned to me and smiled. He looked deeply into my eyes and we both praised God in our hearts.

August 21, 2018

"How was class today, Houston?"

"Not so good. Some ages of kids took my reading materials away."

"What materials?"

"Some maps and yearbooks."

"Why did they take them away?"

"So I placed them on a table, more than I should have."

I chuckled. I remembered when I was a little girl and would walk a mile to the library and be so excited at all the books that I would check out, far too many for me to ever read in a two-week period but would bring them home anyway with my arms aching the whole way. I wanted to know everything. Apparently, he had the same itch.

"What did he teach today?"

"This is a people's president. So have some respect for Trump."

"What did the students say?"

"That he is going to ruin the country."

"What do you think?"

"I think he is making a difference."

At 4:56 pm I got a text from Houston's teacher.

"Has Houston been to Stone Mountain Park recently? Or does he enjoy going there?"

"He hasn't been in a long time. He loves going most places."

"He picked up a magazine I brought in today and on his own was adamantly saying 'Stone Mountain Park' and pointing to the picture."

We discussed it a little more and she said she would send the picture the next day. In her busyness and mine, we both forgot about Stone Mountain Park.

I texted the girl from Chick-fil-A. Her mom wanted to meet me but was sick.

August 22, 2018

"What did you learn today?"

"My (U.S. History) teacher said nothing comes from prejudice but hate and you need to accept others' differences."

"He's right. Tell me something you think or feel."

"You like having no time to yourself.

You like reading books to me that bore you so I can enjoy them.

You make me study so I can get better at life.

You have no life so I can have one.

You fear nothing so I can have a future.

You give everything to make me better.

You are the most remarkable mom in the world.

You treat me like a man with a future.

You have no idea how much I love you."

… Words I never thought I would ever hear. Words I didn't know had been thought. So I wept. Again. For joy.

August 23, 2018

"What did you learn today?"

"Men only recommend men to fight in war. But one woman took interest in learning to fight to serve her country. She took up arms to fight."

We were eating cherries. "Do you know the saying about cherries?"

"Life is like a bowl of cherries."

"What period of time are you studying next?"

"Frontier Time."

"Do you remember visiting Daniel Boone's homestead?"

"Yes."

"What do you remember?"

"My memories fall into two categories. One is for learning and the other is for fun."

"So is Daniel Boone for learning or for fun?"

"For fun."

"What do you remember?"

"It was very green. They thought of everything. Nothing could penetrate the inside."

I was stunned he remembered that. He had been a very young child when we visited. The walls of the homestead were incredibly thick to protect from all sorts of attacks. The details of the homestead resembled a fort with the amenities of home within. I sat back and marveled. Houston had always wanted to learn, always *had* been learning. He had always been curious. He had always been a sponge.

August 24,2018

"Tell me something you think or feel."

"Sometimes I need to imagine what it's like to be normal for my future and my hope."

"Ok. Let's work on that. Tell me about your future."

"I have a family of my own. I have interesting people to be friends with. I have a great career being a psychologist who solves crimes. Someday I have a girlfriend who loves me. I have control of my body."

"What do you think of your new glasses?"

"I love my glasses. It's so different than anything I have ever known. I am so happy right now. This is the most wonderful thing that has ever happened to me."

"What do you think of the world now?"

"It is so beautiful. I finally have an appreciation for how beautiful His world is and how tiny I am in it. I can hardly keep my eyes open. I go from awe to longing more. My mind is so much more calm now. I go for long periods of time saying to myself how this is going to make my life better. It is so different now and it does make some things harder."

"I noticed a few things. You keep taking the glasses off. You also are spelling slower."

"That's because I'm entering my mind the strangest of ways. My mind is only processing one image. The way my mind works trying to see only one thing is weird."

"Houston, I have a thought. You would always look at the ground. Is it because you saw multiple images? Did that make you feel more stable?"

"My looking at the ground makes me feel where I am."

August 25, 2018

My friend had invited us to ride on her boat for a lake day. On the way, I stopped at McDonald's to have coffee and get Houston some breakfast. He saw two men reading the Bible and headed over to them. I knew what he was thinking. He wanted to hear God's Word. We sat at the table next to them. They were reading a book that discussed creation theories and reading related Scripture passages. As he listened to the old men discuss creation, he spelled to me, "Do all Christ followers not believe the Bible?"

"It's a debate. Some people believe each day in creation represents a period of time and others believe it is a twenty-four-hour day. What do you believe?"

"It is what the Bible says. I've seen it. It was days."

"Do you want to tell them?"

"Yes."

I thought to myself, 'Well, this should be interesting.'

"Pardon me," I said to the gentlemen. "My son was listening to your conversation and wanted to comment."

"The world was created in days," Houston spelled.

I added, "I'm sure you want to know how he came to this conclusion."

Their curiosity was piqued.

Houston spelled, "I've seen it. The truth is time is circular, not linear. It's all happening at the same time."

I just shook my head. *What? What* had he seen?

The men discussed this theory briefly and referred to the book they were reading. Then they asked Houston, "So are you a Christian?"

Houston spelled out the most beautiful declaration of faith I have ever heard. It was the first time he had been able to tell the world where his hope and identity were found.

"I am a servant and child of Elohim. Jesus is my Savior and Lord."

"Where do you go to church?" They asked. They asked in a way that you knew they would judge what kind of a Christian you were by whatever answer you gave. A lot of Christians did that.

Houston spelled, "That's a good question."

Houston had apparently decided to throw me under the bus. I knew there was no way people who were safe and accepted could ever understand why I found church such a painful place to be. I interjected an explanation, "We are in between churches right now. I raised him in church. He was always in the basement of the church where they had the special needs classroom. He never got to go to services. I asked him recently if he wanted to go. He spelled that it was too loud, and he could hear God more in the silence than the singing. He also told me angels are present when the Word of God is being read."

One of the men said, "I think I've heard that before about hearing God in the silence."

Houston spelled, "He made all in six days. Are you His disciples?"

The men were surprised, and one responded, "We are. Good to meet you."

I said, "It was good to meet you too. We need to get going now." I got up and gathered our trash. As we walked away Houston abruptly turned and walked back to the men wanting to say something else. Not following was not an option. Houston spelled, "A good rule is if you are not sure about something believe the Bible just how it's written."

The men nodded their heads and we left.

In the car I couldn't stop thinking about Houston, what he had said, and the conviction with which he had said it. Clearly, he had an awareness that created boldness. That night when we got home, I asked him about it. "Can you explain why you believe in the new earth theory?"

He spelled, "Change happens fast on earth because heaven forces it."

"What do you think about all the scientific research that ages the earth and fossils as millions or billions of years old?"

"Reading books that say geological findings prove the earth is old presupposes our earth is old."

"I think now scientists use radioactive decay and quantum mechanics to come up with a scale to age the earth."

"Radioactivity and thoughts are both good ways to prove matter. Matter exists because of radioactivity and thought. Radioactivity has the same structure that thought has. It can be heard like thoughts can. Our efforts to work something to master the flow of power in the universe still cannot define the unseen."

"Can you hear radioactivity?"

"Radioactivity sounds like the waves that move heat. Most science presupposes there is no God. Proving their thoughts that science is their god they ignore the laws of radioactive movements in the universe, lost radioactivity, lost matter. Since energy cannot be destroyed and matter is energy, where does the lost matter go? They believe all matter and energy can be stored and measured. I write for TRUTH, not for the powerful who want to prove God doesn't exist. Love is energy. When will they measure the power of love on matter. Worlds don't just form, they form from matter and energy we think is lost. He weaponizes prayer. Where is the world's measurement of that energy on matter? Jesus told me, 'Time is not the work of physics, it is the work of my LOVE.' Are the laws of the universe static or do they work on His WORD? They walk a line talking about proving the power of the universe knowing that what proves the power has no limit."

"That's amazing."

"Knowledge of science is not my strength. Know going forward I want to know about everything."

"I think you probably know more than I do. You should write a book."

"To know I am making a difference is all I ever wanted. Yes, I want to write a book."

"How do you want to tell your story?"

"Back to the beginning. People will want to know what I was thinking."

"I know I do."

"What one person knows has the ability to bring many to God and stop others from perishing."

41

Hero Friend

LORD, you alone are my inheritance, my cup of blessing.
You guard all that is mine.
The land you have given me is a pleasant land
What a wonderful inheritance!
I will bless the LORD who guides me; even at night my heart instructs me.
I know the LORD is always with me. I will not be shaken, for he is right beside me.
No wonder my heart is glad, and I rejoice. My body rests in safety.
For you will not leave my soul among the dead or allow your holy one to rot in the grave.
You will show me the way of life, granting me the joy of your presence
and the pleasures of living with you forever.
— Psalm 163:5-11

August 26, 2018

I had finally been able to talk to the mom of the teenager we had met at Chick-fil-A. She had a thick Russian accent and told me she was an acupuncturist. She told me she knew there was something going on internally in her son because he would hit himself on his acupressure points. I thought to myself, 'My word. What else is going on in their bodies?' She asked if she could bring her friend whose son was also unreliably speaking. They had known each other for years as they both struggled to raise their sons. We met at Wills Park and sat on some of the bleachers in front of a baseball field where my sons used to play. First, I explained how we had learned about the boards, my conversation with J-, Houston's first lesson with a spelling coach, and his first independent communication, "I'm in here."

Then it was Houston's turn. Houston spelled, "So many of us want you to know we are in our bodies. Start teaching them. They want to get a voice."

One of the moms responded, "But they aren't smart like you. I don't even think our boys know how to spell."

"They can. I promise."

The other mom painfully confessed, "My son starts hitting me constantly in the car when I'm driving." Tears rolled down her cheeks. "I don't know what to do."

Houston the hero spelled, "Let me meet them. I can tell you if they are smart."

They asked if I would drive to one of their homes which was about 45 minutes away. So we went.

When we got there both boys were in the living room. One of the fathers was there, as well as an ABA therapist with picture cards hanging around her neck. The father was anxious and excited to meet us. They brought two dining chairs for us to sit down in the living room. One of the boys, St-, laid on the couch, while the other boy, E-, sat in a chair stimming. They were 13 and 15 respectively. The ABA therapist would hold up a PECS board (Picture Exchange Communication System) that the boys seemed totally uninterested in.

Houston had always refused the PECS boards. Apparently, when you're brilliant you want to say more than twenty words, and you find pre-school pictures insulting. At least that's what Houston says.

Suddenly Houston saw a book on the shelf that he used to stim on that was filled with Disney images. "Storybook! Storybook! Storybook!" He tried to lunge for the bookshelf, and I had to hold him back and physically sit him in the chair. They said, "Oh! He can hold it. Here let me get it for him." "NO," I said firmly. "He doesn't want it. That's his stims talking. Not him. Houston, do you want the book?"

Houston spelled, "Do not give me the book," while at the same time he said, "Storybook! Storybook!" repeatedly.

One of the moms said, "But he's saying storybook."

I explained, "His body and his mind are separate. He doesn't have control over the things he says. He has told me to only listen to his mind, what he spells, NOT to what comes out of his mouth. Other spellers have said the same thing."

"I don't understand," one of the moms said.

The dad said, "Don't give it to him. He doesn't want it. I understand. It's like me. My mind doesn't want to smoke, but my body has to." He turned to me. "Please keep going. This is the first time I have ever had hope for my son." I told Houston I knew this was hard and there were so many temptations for his stims, but he had to hold it together. I explained the process of spelling to communicate, how they needed prompts because they didn't have the ability to motor plan and also what I had just learned about Houston's eyesight. I explained how they needed to develop neural pathways and that it took time. I told them most importantly, above anything else, "You MUST believe in your sons. You MUST believe they are intelligent and understand everything going on around them."

Houston spelled, "Talk to them like they understand. Tell them they will get a voice that will change their lives."

As the father watched Houston spell, I could see he was overcome with emotion. He put his head down to choke back tears. He got a pad of paper and a pen. He wanted to know who to call. I gave him every resource I had.

The ABA therapist asked, "What about ABA? Did you find it helped?"

Houston spelled, "Some in the beginning when I was learning math facts, like all students learn some things. Then it was terrible all the things they drilled that I already knew. My teachers thought that was the only way to teach me. They were wrong."

One of the moms asked Houston, "What do you think? Can St- do this?"

Houston spelled, "Watch. He's listening. Give him a chance to show you."

The mom said, "I don't know. I don't know if he's smart."

I interjected, "Do you realize your son is reading an encyclopedia right now as we are talking?"

"He's just looking," she answered.

"I'm willing to bet he's reading that thing," I answered. 'He probably knows it by heart,' I thought to myself.

The other mom asked, "What about E-?"

Houston spelled, "Good. He's smart."

I urged them again and again, hoping we had shown them enough to make them believe in their sons. When I got home, I asked Houston, "What was St- thinking while we were there? Were you talking to him?"

"That wonderful soul was praying. St- loves God. He made this remarkable interpretation regarding one thing. 'The church is finally here. Now God will save us.'" My heart felt the weight of those words.

"What about E-?"

"He was writing on his hand with his finger. He was saying to me, 'Tell them we are here. Do it.' Then he did not believe it would work."

"When you met J- and his dad at Chili's and they told you about the boards, what did you think?"

"When his dad said, 'Houston, we know you're in there.' I said to myself, 'Is he talking to me?' I didn't believe after knowing so many lies to help me."

"So when did you believe this would work so you could communicate?"

"It was really when I met Jacqueline. I met a good friend that day. She needed to know my abilities. Right when she asked her name and held up the board something inside of me said, 'This is it.'"

"What did you think?"

"Help is finally here. Rebecca understands how a line of communication gives hope. Knowing that made me realize finally I was meant to have a future. Before it was just God telling me."

"Who is Rebecca?"

"She is one nice lady I met when I was like nine."

"Where did you meet her?"

"At school, in class. Rebecca made me notice people. These people kindly made me forget how horrible I felt by being my friends."

"Were these kids? Kids at Sweet Gum?"

"Yes."

I remembered how Sweet Gum made a gallant effort to teach kindness and compassion as part of the curriculum. Kindness was required. They had neurotypical students the same ages go into classes with autistic students and do projects and play together. I remembered running into former Sweet Gum students time and time again who recognized Houston and would give him a hug and talk to him at all kinds of random places. These were kids who had grown up being taught to love others. The programs at Sweet Gum always included a big presentation by the autistic students and the entire student body would watch and cheer them on. It was like that school had raised an entire community of kids who knew how to love. And now I heard what that had meant to my son, to be treated like a friend at school.

"Why did you feel horrible?"

"I felt horrible because nothing stopped the autism. Family stuff too made me know mom was strong most of the time. She made me know knowledge about the Bible I wouldn't have known. She made happy times. All the work she did and prayed, though the prayers were never answered, that gave me sorrow."

August 30, 2018

I taught a special needs yoga class that I thought was a disaster with Houston running to the corner, flapping his hands, and making all of his loudest noises. I asked him, "Do you like our workouts?"

"Today was killer. It really was something more meaningful than I can explain. I mean that now I need time. You must change me now. You know my sounds only keep me from being part of class. I want to learn yoga with you. I want to lose weight. So right now keep making me move. I want to look good. Yes, it's making me stronger so let's keep working out."

It was the day his presentation was due in U.S. History.

"Tell me about the report."

"First I held her picture. Then the teacher played my recording (of Florence). Next (my aid) read my report to the class. She presented so well that the class clapped so hard and loud. I about died I was so moved. You so knew that reading that piece provoked really strong emotions in people. So I want to know more about many things. My life is just beginning. Lots of kids took time to love me, umpire to regular kids."

"What do you mean by umpire?"

"Smart kids to knowledgeable regular kids."

"What did they say to you?"

"What a great job. You made me cry. You really are smart. Too many to remember."

"What did your history teacher say?"

"He really looked at me differently. He did not believe I was smart or knowledgeable. Yes, he was floored."

"I think Corrie is starting to believe you."

"Yes. She is, and I am getting better on the boards so more autistics can learn to communicate."

August 31, 2018

Houston mentioned his prayer to me.

"The prayer is being forwarded to God on time. I mostly keep saying only for God to help my friends."

"Can we talk more about yesterday when I taught the special needs yoga class? What about the twins in the class?"

"They talked to me."

"What did they say to you?"

"They said, 'You're like us. You goes less nose, noon to stone, snow stone stoop, lost into my stone, pray here snore poor stone.'"

"What on earth does that mean?"

"It means they were stimming."

"So sometimes the stims are words in your head?"

"Yes. The words in my head won't stop repeating when I'm stimming."

"Did you talk to them?"

"I explained you had taught me to communicate. Childlike responses followed like, 'No way! Not cool! You killer!' I was only in the class one minute and no one wanted to be my friend. That's why I got upset and ran off to the corner jumping and flapping. My good tries to help were totally a joke to them."

"Do you want me to show their mom the boards and tell her how you spell to communicate?"

"Yes."

And we did. For weeks I brought the boards when I taught special needs yoga until I finally got the chance to let Houston communicate on the boards with her. The twins were completely still. Houston told me later, "They told me, 'Ok. We believe you. So sorry.'" I realized the mountain ahead of us. Not only did parents not have hope, the kids didn't either. Houston and I both had been in that place, and it was our mission to change their direction and show them it was ok to look toward the light.

42

Friends and Foes

For those who live according to the flesh set their minds on the things of the flesh,
but those who live according to the Spirit set their minds on the things of the Spirit.
For to set the mind on the flesh is death, but to set the mind on the Spirit is life and peace.
For the mind that is set on the flesh is hostile to God,
for it does not submit to God's law; indeed, it cannot.
Those who are in the flesh cannot please God.
— Romans 8:5-8

September 2018
My attorney called me to let me know the Big Jock's attorney had emailed her to let her know he was not going to pay again, even though it was just child support at a rate of minimum wage. My attorney was livid. I felt the panic start welling up inside me. I couldn't stop the thoughts. 'God? Would there ever be justice? Would I always have to limp, scrape, save, and get further in debt? Would You leave me on my own forever? Would I always just barely survive? Was I only made for pain?'

The Big Jock's mother called Morgan and told her she needed to forgive her father and invite him to her wedding. Morgan refused. She also told me she was not inviting my dad. Her day was going to be happy, and she wasn't going to have anything that created pain or tension for her or her family. I was sad even though in my heart I knew my dad didn't have it in him to fix this. He would not admit being wrong. Morgan wouldn't sacrifice peace to pacify pride. She had learned to be brave. Her grandmother called it unforgiveness. My dad had a two-page rebuke for it. Morgan called it protecting her sister and her family. I had always meant for and taught my children to think critically based on certain ethical principles, but as I saw her apply her conscience and her heart, I was astonished. She called it loyalty. She called it love. She was a woman with a mind of her own. I respected it.

Houston had destroyed his shoes by walking on the heels. He did it to every pair. He would pull the insoles out and chew them to bits. That was just one of things he would chew on. He would smell dirty socks and chew on them. It was exhausting trying to keep things out of his mouth and cleaning him. He couldn't wash or wipe himself at all. I would have to prompt him repeatedly to put on each piece of clothing. He would usually stand and make circles in the air with his fingers while I would repeat myself. It was exhausting. Although I had been working for years on teaching him to brush his teeth and shave his face, the reality was his hands didn't have the ability to use pressure and if it required fine motor skills then he would just stare at me. But now he was 250 pounds so even though I had done it every day of his life, it was becoming increasingly difficult. These things didn't stop when he could communicate. But now that I realized he wanted to be independent, I knew I would have to work intensely on these skills.

I asked Houston about the shoes and how he always walked on the heels. He spelled, "My feet are the most frustrating." I asked him to explain. "I need shoes that are heavy but loose." "What about compression socks?" I asked. "No. It's hard to explain. I feel like I'm falling out of the bottom of my feet all the time. But the rest of my feet don't want to be squeezed." I couldn't even comprehend what he was experiencing. I took him to DSW, and we went to the work boots. We tried on pair after pair of the heaviest boots I could find. Finally we had narrowed it down to two pairs. The Timberland pair was much heavier, but they were a very intense mustard yellow. The other pair was a soft brown but not as heavy. I asked him to pick. He spelled, "This pair will look good with outfits but the yellow ones feel better on my feet." "Well, fashion or function? Your choice," I said. "I want the heavy ones. They feel so good. I can feel my feet." I took the shoes and had a thought. "Let me check something. Come with me." After some digging, I found the ugly yellow heavy boots in black. He loved them. "Houston, I didn't realize you were aware of fashion. I think that's awesome." Houston spelled, "The way you dress me is the worst. My wardrobe is awful." For a moment I didn't know how to respond. "Houston, I'm so sorry. I had no idea you cared. You chew your clothes to bits, so I never wanted to get expensive clothes. I thought you liked the Disney shirts, and I thought the polos looked nice on you. How do you want to dress?" "I want to dress like an athlete. That's what I am." So we went shopping. The girls got excited at the thought of helping him get a new look. We would hold up shirts and he would tell us what he thought. It was such a small thing, but it was everything. Finally, he was in charge.

Houston decided he wanted to try a church service to see if he could handle the noise. We started by sitting outside in the foyer and just listening. He told me, "Angels ride the waves of praise to the music." After church we were at dinner talking and Morgan asked if he might want to study theology. "No," he spelled, "I want to study psychology. Otherwise all this studying how evil men think would be wasted."

Later I asked him about that. He answered, "When dad would be nice, you would think it was true. He always laughed to himself and said now she'll trust me. He would stop being nice when you forgave him and he would pride himself and say, 'It worked.' He would always think, 'God won't do anything.' He would piece together lies to tell you. Our thoughts worked to love. His thoughts worked to be so mean. He rallied to get all money for loose living and stop you from ever having any. He would lie about how much he had to worry you to make you do everything yourself. Counting was big to him, as to how many women he screwed. It healed his pain to hurt them. It was lots of the best fun to him. Attacking you gave him such awesome power. Bouts of guilt he would drink to pretend to forget. He made bold statements with lies with everything he said to you. Making threats was his control, and knowing your goodness, they worked. All you could do was pray and love. That was how your goodness worked. Praying for him to find God was the right prayer but he didn't want to be prayed for. Force is all he prayed, to hurt others. Each time you prayed it had no effect on him. Just fierce thoughts hid all his pain. All power hopes to get more. All pride hopes others get nothing." [102]

---

[102] Their feet run to evil, and they hasten to shed innocent blood; their thoughts are thoughts of iniquity, devastation and destruction are in their highways. - Isaiah 59:7

For out of the heart come evil thoughts, murders, adulteries, fornications, thefts, false witness, slanders. — Matthew 15:19

They have said, "The Lord does not see, nor does the God of Jacob pay heed." — Psalm 94:7

He says to himself, "God has forgotten; He has hidden His face; He will never see it" — Psalm 10:11

The LORD detests all the proud of heart. Be sure of this: They will not go unpunished. — Proverbs 16:5

The proud and arrogant person—"Mocker" is his name— behaves with insolent fury. — Proverbs 21:24

In his pride the wicked man does not seek him; in all his thoughts there is no room for God. — Psalm 10:4

It was frightening to hear the soundtrack of a monster's mind, especially since I knew how smooth he could be, how convincing. I was also in awe of the courage my son showed in the presence of constant evil. There was so much to ask and so much I didn't want to know. I asked him if he could tell the difference between thoughts alone and thoughts with actions. "Yes. Years of hearing thoughts has taught me the difference. Thoughts alone float away. Thoughts with actions show up on a person. They carry them. For example, when you steal it shows up on your stomach as something hideous. You cannot imagine how disgusting my dad is." When I shared that with Morgan, her head hung down. "He's right," she said. "When I shoplifted that's where I would feel it, in my stomach. But I would do it anyway." I realized these actions must attach to certain related areas of our spirit associated with unmet desires, fears, or dysfunctions. While I had not yet begun to understand the energy (Qi) within us that flows through us, I was beginning to get a real awareness that far more was going on inside and outside human beings than could be seen or dissected.

September 7, 2018

Houston decided he wanted to start writing emails to make friends. He first wrote to A- who was off at college. The first thing he spelled was, "I'm writing and I'm stuck." I laughed. "Writer's block. You're nervous. Totally normal. Make a list of things you want to talk about." And he did.

Next, he decided to send an email asking to get to know one of the spellers whose blogs I had been reading to him. He was absolutely thrilled when he got a response on September 8th.

Dear James,

I'm Houston. For lots of my life I got really knowledgeable about so many things like History. You explained autism so well. Years of my life have been spent like yours, my mind forever trapped in my body. May freedom actually live forever in us. I know you mostly learn to deeply learn movements. Sometimes I struggle too in many similar ways. You would make a good friend to me. You rain knowledge about autism and love. You roam these little paths of wisdom. I really want to be your friend.

Houston

September 9, 2018 — A response!

Hi Houston,

So good to hear from you. Joyful when I hear from my people. I would love to be pals! History is cool and my favourite things to learn about are things that explain to me how people think - religion, leaders who I aspire to be like, and anything where my peers are in my online class with me. I love rock climbing and working out with my personal trainer to help connect my brain and body.

So excited to learn more about you and Skype soon.

September 10, 2018

Hi James,

You live similar to me in your knowledge and interests. God is so important to me. I make Him be kind to me proudly. Most of my life He let me rest in His promises. Now I have the voice to share what I know. What I know is amazing. You probably have visions too, really strong ones I suspect. Very few people understand God in the way He truly is. So my next question for you is how does He appear? Understand He appears to me as Lord on the throne placed at the right hand of God. See how He pours out His love to us in so many ways. You have special insight like I do.

Being autistic really makes my purpose so clear. Right now having autism is so tough. Tiny steps take forever. Another step of my progress is learning to control my motor responses and my body. All my energy goes to stopping myself from stimming. Love helps most, providing some kindness to me from my mom. She forgets everything so I can make progress. Sometimes I'm mean to her.

Sailing has always been a dream of mine, a long shot knowing how difficult it is to control my body. Rock climbing is hard too. My mom trains me to really focus and use my muscles. So I mention that post workout, so know my pace is really slow. You plan to invite me to Skype, but I'm worried I will take too long for you. So if you do please be patient with me.

Your friend,

Houston

Surprised by this sudden revelation to his new friend I asked, "You want to sail? I had no idea." Then I remembered an organization years earlier that would take special needs children and their families out on the lake in sailboats. I had taken Houston and remembered how calm he had been on that boat. I asked him if he remembered and of course he did. That was when his dream was birthed. I was in awe. All those years he had been taking in everything, dying for a chance to live and be a part of the world around him.

September 11, 2018

In his next letter to Houston his new friend shared his own purpose and calling and ended with this wonderful advice. "Please do not talk poorly of yourself. Keep being positive and moving forward. Negative thoughts are energy suckers. You are a beautiful being."

September 12, 2018

My attorney called to let me know the Big Jock's attorney had notified her that he was not going to pay the lump sum. The compliance hearing was scheduled three days later, on September 15, 2018. She warned him he was already in contempt, and this was another violation.

Around this time I reached out to several of the parents with children who were non-speaking or unreliably speaking that I had gotten to know over the many years in our community. I encouraged them to try out the center and I sent them the information to the spelling coach who had trained us. In truth, I gave the coach's email out like candy at a parade. I wanted everyone to know. I wanted everyone to have a new life.

September 14, 2018

My attorney called again. Her voice was shaking she was so angry. On September 13th, two days before the compliance hearing he had filed for bankruptcy in federal court. I didn't understand. Bankruptcy wasn't supposed to affect child support. She had to explain the law. She had been calling friends who specialized in bankruptcy law in order to advise me. Bankruptcies put a stay on all litigation in progress. Because federal court supersedes a county superior court, the compliance hearing would not be heard, but we still had to go to court.

September 15, 2018

We met at the scheduled time for our hearing. This was supposed to be my day where all his chances had been used up and the law would finally be enforced. The Big Jock was not present. His attorney presented the bankruptcy documents to the judicial officer. My attorney argued that this was a fraudulent bankruptcy and was filed only to avoid the enforcement of the compliance hearing. The judicial officer shook her head. "There's nothing I can do. There's a stay in effect."

"Your honor, can I ask a question?" I asked, shaking in anger and disillusionment. She nodded her head. "So that's *it*? He doesn't have to pay child support?? How can he keep getting away with this?"

"I am going to advise you to ask your attorney. I can't answer those questions."

Neither could my attorney. Outside the courtroom in the hallway I cried, "He always gets away with it. Always." My attorney was furious. "You need to get a bankruptcy attorney in Florida right now since that's where he filed to protect your judgment." So instead of finally getting financial relief I went further into debt to hire another attorney.

September 24, 2018

There was another meeting regarding Houston's communication with a new specialist. She insisted Houston needed to use a qwerty keyboard to communicate. By this time I had done more research and had actually taken the time to read the Americans with Disabilities Act. I was astonished at the forethought and breadth of this document and the rights that were protected by it. Now that I realized Houston had a voice, I knew how critical it was to protect it. In Houston's circumstances, the following particular points of interest and law applied. The bottom line was the county had used statements by ASHA, which is an organization that licenses speech pathologists, to base their refusal of services and the communication supports he wanted and needed. ASHA had no authority to deny my son's rights guaranteed by federal and state laws and X county had no right to deny his voice and rights based on an outside organization with absolutely no legal authority. This is in **direct** violation of the Americans with Disabilities Act and The Individuals with Disabilities Education Act.

According to United for Communication Choice who researched the events involving ASHA, "A small committee within the American Speech-Language-Hearing Association (ASHA) proposed that the organization take steps to prevent some people with disabilities from accessing their preferred and only effective means of communication. On June 1, 2018, an ad hoc committee proposed that ASHA adopt statements condemning two AAC training methodologies that teach individuals with motor-based communication disabilities how to type independently.

On July 16, 2018, a coalition of 23 national nonprofit civil rights and disability advocacy organizations asked ASHA's Board of Directors to withdraw the flawed and dangerous proposals. Some disability organizations wrote their own letters as well, including the Autistic Self Advocacy Network and TASH. Hundreds of individuals, many with disabilities, wrote in protest too.[103] In 2019 a large number of articles referencing multiple authors who spelled to communicate were removed from Wikipedia after an unethical editing war occurred among editors.[104] I was stuck by the power of darkness to discredit and silence so many voices. So much for freedom of speech. Why did they want so much to destroy the voices of the weak and uphold the voices of those with power and position? What was so threatening about what they had to say?

***

The Americans with Disabilities Act (ADA)

Ensure effective communication supports and services: 28 C.F.R. § 35.160 http://bit.ly/2uSO6jA

- "Shall … ensure that communications with [individuals] with disabilities are as effective as communications with others. … [and] shall furnish appropriate auxiliary aids and services where necessary to afford … an equal opportunity to participate in, and enjoy the benefits of, a service, program, or activity of a public entity."
- "In determining what … auxiliary aids and services are necessary, a public entity shall give primary consideration to the requests of individuals with disabilities."

Honor the individual's choice: 28 C.F.R. Part 35, Appendix A: http://bit.ly/2eDURi0

---

[103] https://unitedforcommunicationchoice.org/quick-facts/
[104] https://neuroclastic.com/2019/07/10/fc-rpm-and-how-wikipedia-became-complicit-in-silencing-non-speaking-autistics/

●"The public entity must provide an opportunity for individuals with disabilities to request the auxiliary aids and services of their choice. … [and] shall honor the choice unless it can demonstrate that another effective means of communication exists or [is not] required under § 35.164."

Public entity's obligations: 28 C.F.R. § 35.164: http://bit.ly/2uldT2i

●Public entity must provide the requested services unless it can prove in writing that the services would "fundamental[ly] alter … the nature of a service, program, or activity or [cause] undue financial and administrative burdens. … after considering all resources available for use in the funding and operation of the service, program, or activity."

●Even then, the public entity still must "take any other action" to "ensure … to the maximum extent possible" the individual "receive[s] the benefits or services."

The Individuals with Disabilities Education Act (IDEA)

Statute – 20 U.S.C. §§ 1400 et seq.: https://bit.ly/2usa4rA

Implementing Regulations – 34 C.F.R. Part 300: https://bit.ly/2nud2bL

●20 U.S.C. § 1401(1): "The term "assistive technology device" means any item, piece of equipment, or product system, whether acquired commercially off the shelf, modified, or customized, that is used to increase, maintain, or improve functional capabilities of a child with a disability."

●20 U.S.C. § 1401(2): "The term "assistive technology service" means any service that directly assists a child with a disability in the selection, acquisition, or use of an assistive technology device. Such term includes— … (C) selecting, designing, fitting, customizing, adapting, applying, maintaining, repairing, or replacing assistive technology devices; … (E) training or technical assistance for such child, or, where appropriate, the family of such child; and (F) training or technical assistance for professionals (including individuals providing education and rehabilitation services), employers, or other individuals who provide services to, employ, or are otherwise substantially involved in the major life functions of such child."

●20 U.S.C. § 1401(26)(A): "The term "related services" means transportation, and such developmental, corrective, and other supportive services (including speech-language pathology and audiology services, interpreting services, …) as may be required to assist a child with a disability to benefit from special education"

●20 U.S.C. § 1401(33): "The term "supplementary aids and services" means aids, services, and other supports that are provided in regular education classes or other education-related settings to enable children with disabilities to be educated with nondisabled children to the maximum extent appropriate in accordance with section 1412(a)(5) of this title."

●34 C.F.R. § 300.105: "Assistive Technology. (a) Each public agency must ensure that assistive technology devices or assistive technology services, or both … are made available to a child with a disability if required as a part of the child's—(1) Special education …; (2) Related services …; or (3) Supplementary aids and services …."

●34 C.F.R. § 300.324(a)(2): "The IEP Team must … (iv) Consider the communication needs of the child, … ; and (v) Consider whether the child needs assistive technology devices and services."

●20 U.S.C. § 1412(a)(6)(B): "**Testing and evaluation materials and procedures** utilized for the purposes of evaluation and placement of children with disabilities ... shall be provided and **administered in the child's ... mode of communication**, unless it clearly is not feasible to do so, and no single procedure shall be the sole criterion for determining an appropriate educational program for a child."

●20 U.S.C. § 1414(b)(3): "Each local educational agency shall ensure that—(A) assessments and other evaluation materials used to assess a child under this section—... (ii) **are provided and administered in the ... form most likely to yield accurate information on what the child knows and can do academically, developmentally, and functionally,** unless it is not feasible to so provide or administer."

Case Law – *K.M. ex rel. Bright v. Tustin Unified Sch. Dist.*, 725 F.3d 1088 (9th Cir. 2013)
●U.S. Court of Appeals for the Ninth Circuit <u>decision</u>
●U.S. Department of Justice amicus <u>brief</u>

***

The bottom line was Houston could choose his communication device and his communication method. The institution was required to follow his choice instead of the institution demanding he follow theirs. The speech representative didn't argue about Houston's intelligence. She just interrupted repeatedly while Houston was spelling, saying that she couldn't follow along. She repeatedly interjected that she had no idea what he was spelling even though I called out each letter as he spelled. It was rude. It was intentional. I was more than annoyed. I understood it could be difficult when you were watching a stencil from the opposite side, but all she had to do was come sit beside him, watch, and patiently recognize the words that he formed letter by letter. Instead she insisted, while he was trying to spell and communicate to her, that he needed to be on the same qwerty board the rest of the world used. In my head I thought, 'It's two weeks! He can't become fluent on the iPad when the light from the screen blinds him and the letters are in different places so that means new neural pathways in TWO WEEKS!' Finally, just to stop the ridiculous conversation and go home I agreed to let Houston try the iPad with their software at home and at school.

October 2018

As Houston had requested, we took the computer out of his room. We locked every access to the internet. He didn't seem to stim on two Disney videos, Mulan, and Hercules, so I would play those for him and removed the remote so he couldn't fast forward and rewind. He said they were heroes and he wanted to watch those videos. I was still waiting for him to be approved for the audible book program and I knew taking the computer away was going to have a big impact. The school had insisted we work on an iPad, so I did every day. I knew it was hard for him. Secretly I hoped he would make incredible progress and the school would acknowledge these techniques as a viable way to teach other students to have a voice.

When I took the internet away it was like I took him off heroin cold turkey. I realized he was seriously addicted. If a phone, remote, or computer was left unattended for even one second, he would immediately find the videos that triggered the greatest hysteria. The hypervigilance that I had been living with for two decades increased thirty-fold when we removed the internet out of his life. He could get to YouTube from an Xbox in seconds. When I would try to remove the remote or other device, he would completely lose control, biting himself to the bone, making wailing sounds, and sweating profusely. It would take hours to calm him down after two minutes of Dumbo. Eventually I noticed he began acting the same way with Mulan so I would only let him watch Hercules. Then the out-of-control body would even be triggered with

Hercules. I tried another film that was computer animation that he had previously had no interest in. I could see the anxiety spreading across his face and quickly turned it off. When I asked him about it, he spelled, "You cannot let me watch any animation. It is a drug." The more we enforced no animation, the worse his reactions were to it. One day the reaction was so violent it took three of us to get him to stop biting himself and making all the noises. I sat on the stairs and wept. I was so tired. I was trying so hard. 'God, why is getting harder? *Why?*'

October 4-5, 2018

Houston became violently ill. He was so exhausted he didn't want to spell. He just kept saying, "I'm sorry. I'm sorry." By the time he started feeling well enough to spell we had to start writing his farewell speech for graduation.

October 10, 2018

This afternoon Houston and I met with his teacher, the speech therapist, and the transition officer. I asked about accommodations that could be transferred to college, but mostly it was a summary of education meeting before an individual aged out of public school. They assessed Houston's intellect as age 4-5 years old with severe intellectual disabilities. I was shaking. "This is completely inaccurate! He's brilliant. Four and five-year-olds don't spell the complexity of words and language that he uses. Why is this in here?!" He's never even received the education he had a right to."

Houston spelled, "Are you calling me stupid?"

His teacher responded, "He received a free and appropriate education equal to his ability."

"What?! Are you kidding me? Houston received nothing. He didn't get an education because he couldn't communicate and had no control over his body."

"It was a free and appropriate education," she said in what felt like a robotic voice.

"Oh my gosh. I'm so angry. I'm so angry." I was shaking, trying to control myself. "I can't even think right now. How can you say that? Stop saying that! After everything? After all these years? After what you've seen? Are you kidding me? That's straight from some form from the X County Board of Education. He did NOT get an appropriate education equal to his ability! You don't even realize what his abilities are. You're so busy trying to uphold the county policy to NOT teach, NOT include that you've forgotten who this is about. It's about them! It's not about your policies and your budgets. It's about their lives! They matter! Don't you see that? Shouldn't you be excited that someone you once thought had all these limitations is proving you wrong? Why aren't you excited? Why aren't you happy? Why are you trying to put this label on him?"

She looked at me like a deer in the headlights. And that's when I realized that "free and appropriate" was the exact same thing as "separate but equal". I saw the enormity of the injustice of unequal education, of presuming *incompetence*. I saw the albatross of hopelessness it put on those students. Actually, this was even worse, these students were separated and intentionally withheld from any legitimate and meaningful education at all with no means of protesting, simply because they couldn't control their bodies.

Later I called the transition officer. She had only been there a year and was as appalled as I was. She said, "You know she's just doing what she's been told. You have to know that."

I decided the only thing I could do was reach every single one of Houston's classmates that I could and prove they were intelligent and that the school was wrong.

October 11, 2018

It was Houston's last day in public school. The next day was his twenty-second birthday. I planned a party and invited old teachers and other parents of his classmates that I knew to come to the school. Houston had promised his friends he would help them get a voice. He hoped that these adults would see his progress, hear his words, and be inspired. His teacher called me that morning and said she didn't want that many people to come. I held my tongue. Both Paul and Benjamin were able to get out of class for his very last hour in the special needs hall and hear his speech. It had taken him four days to write his speech. His teacher put together a slideshow of pictures, just a glimpse of the people whose lives he had touched. Houston stood in front of his peers, and we used the computer voice to read his speech aloud. Paul recorded it. Houston was ready to be a hero.

"So many thoughts. For so long I would pretend I was normal, but nothing could help me. Knowing I was smart made it worse. Understanding everything made me very depressed. My world was so little, so mundane, so boring. I know it is difficult to acknowledge I am most articulate and brilliant. Good people have given so much to help me but it wasn't enough.

Now my mind for many years was going in coils, looking for order but not making sense. I am determined to make my life matter. Now my most important goal is to make others perceive intelligent people for absolutely whatever fraction my friends can manage to share the brilliance that is coming from their minds. My friends need a voice just like I do. My friends are smart and have dreams for their lives just like I do. Now is the time to help them. Maybe I am here so many others have an opportunity to be something remarkable. Now I might still make noises right now but I am thinking intelligent thoughts. My family, this love has saved me. Soon others will want you to work with them so they can have their dreams come true. You must believe they are competent. Please make this a priority. My friends will amaze you. They just need a chance to show you. My mom tried everything. Nothing worked until now.

In my heart I am so excited to be an adult. Having a hope keeps me focused on pursuing my dreams to be a forensic psychologist. I am just beginning. My life has so much potential. I am going to have a family of my own. Nothing is impossible. My hope dates mostly to my relationship with my Savior. Finding faith for my most awesome intelligent ideas has made working to communicate so much more inspiring. Now everyone can hear my thoughts. Hear this. My tidings to you are thank you for your everything. To my friends, continue to believe others will find a way to teach you to communicate as well. Never give up hope."

I tried talking to one of the parents about the boards without much success or interest. Everyone hugged Houston and congratulated him. His middle school teacher had come for his last moment and I couldn't have been happier to see her. His classmate that had pointed with such urgency and barged into the IEP meeting wanted a picture with Houston. I was touched. I realized all these young people with severe disabilities had been encouraging and loving each other all these years. They were each other's secret keepers. It was this incredible network of love and faith and untapped potential that the world was completely oblivious too. I didn't want to leave them. As one of Houston's non-speaking friends explained to us later, "We can communicate in ways that most people do not understand. We have a special connection that I think was a gift from God given all the crummy things that come with autism. I can't explain it, but we feed off each other good and bad. It's our secret club I guess."

Earlier when Houston had been sick, his middle school teacher had texted me. "Did you know that there is a new Director of Exceptional Education in X County?"

I didn't.

"Well, I think Houston needs to go meet him. He knows Houston. He used to teach at the middle school when Houston was there."

"Would he remember Houston?"

"Everyone remembers Houston."

"Ok. I'll do it right now."

And I did. It took several emails, but I scheduled a meeting with him, and Houston began writing what he wanted to say. I sent the video of Houston's final speech and the Director asked if he could share it with his department because it was so inspiring. I was eager for every other parent and child's life to change. I was eager for all these teachers to know their students and push them academically. I was eager to help Houston keep his promise to his friends.

43

Manhood

He has made everything beautiful in its time.
He has also set eternity in the human heart;
yet no one can fathom what God has done from beginning to end.
— Ecclesiastes 3:11

October 12, 2018

Houston turned twenty-two. Morgan and I were so excited. For the first time in his life there would be no Disney videos, no jellybeans. They were banned. He decided for his birthday he wanted an adult bedroom, and he wanted all the Disney videos and toys thrown out. "No blue. No Disney. I want sailboats in my room. My animals really must go. Farther away the better. A cool room. I don't want to be a grown man addicted to Disney." So we stuffed five trash bags full of Disney stuffed animals, old VHS cassette tapes, and Magna Doodles that went to Goodwill. Then we redecorated. It's still not everything I want it to be, but I took him through Target and let him pick out his bedding. I let him pick his artwork. I let him pick his desk. "Knowing my style lets me choose what I want. My goal is to make my own bed every day." I got him a weighted blanket and he spelled, "My favorite is being weighted down at night." I found a picture of Mother Teresa with her poem Anyway and he said he wanted it in his room. Then he spelled, "That is bright in my doubt." After we got everything set up, he spelled, "I feel like a man."

People are often unreasonable, illogical and self centered;
Forgive them anyway.
If you are kind, people may accuse you of selfish, ulterior motives;
Be kind anyway.
If you are successful, you will win some false friends and some true enemies;
Succeed anyway.
If you are honest and frank, people may cheat you;
Be honest and frank anyway.
What you spend years building, someone could destroy overnight;
Build anyway.
If you find serenity and happiness, they may be jealous;
Be happy anyway.
The good you do today, people will often forget tomorrow;
Do good anyway.
Give the world the best you have, and it may never be enough;
Give the world the best you've got anyway.
You see, in the final analysis, it is between you and your God;
It was never between you and them anyway.[105]

[105] *Anyway;* Mother Teresa

And that is who my son is to his very core. He goes forward despite what people say, despite how he is treated, despite the awful thoughts of others he can't escape, despite being excluded, despite the countless obstacles, despite a body that betrays him. He pushes forward, building, believing, and loving all for the glory and love of God.

After several emails and petitions, Principal Caresalot agreed to allow Houston to continue attending U.S. History two days a week with Benjamin. He allowed this to take place from the goodness of his heart. He allowed me to work at a conference table in the front office while Houston was in class. The school could provide no assistance and if there were any problems Houston would not be able to stay. Benjamin would be his aid. The teachers were supportive and encouraging. When Houston would start humming or flapping his hands in class Benjamin would get nervous and tell him to stop. The teachers would tell Benjamin that Houston was fine and wasn't bothering anyone. Benjamin was trying to learn and trying to be there for his brother. He made Houston take notes. He reviewed material with him. It was remarkable how much love he showed. The other students were kind and didn't judge him. The teachers were friendly, open, patient, encouraging - basically everything you could possibly hope for in a teacher. So even though it was only two days a week, Houston completed U.S. History, his first class ever.

Houston had started vision therapy. Once a week we would get new exercises and would spend an hour every night working on convergence, peripheral, saccades, pursuits, increasing the strength and stability of his eye muscles. It was excruciatingly difficult for him, but he worked so hard and began to show the tiniest proof of improvement. I worked with him at night in addition to the six hours a week of training he received at the center and the hour every day when I trained him after work at the gym. One day his vision therapist told me about a functional neurologist that had come into the office and explained how he did a lot of work that was related to vision and overall brain rehabilitation using the principles of neuroplasticity. I had been reading The Brain That Changes Itself and was completely intrigued by someone who had knowledge and experience in this field. It was absolutely fascinating what incredible adaptability the brain had. I got his information and set up an appointment.

He was INCREDIBLE. His daughter had an infantile stroke and he had been able to rehabilitate almost all her lost function with different exercises focused on creating new neural pathways. I literally sat there with my mouth open while he explained how motor and vision affected the brain and why the brain needed complex movement to regulate itself. Then he got out a motor and a tongue depressor. After placing the tongue depressor on Houston's tongue he turned on the motor and the tongue depressor vibrated. He had me move Houston's limbs in patterns and had Houston look at a screen trying to follow movements both vertical and horizontal, what they call saccades and pursuits. The saccades have a critical function in the brain in organizing motor planning and sequencing and apparently Houston's were a mess. He did a test on Houston to try to follow a sequence of movements with his eyes. The computer tracked his eye movements. It basically looked like the worst plate of messy spaghetti you've ever seen. One eye was going one direction and would change direction erratically, the other eye was darting all over the place. I asked if I could use an electric toothbrush to stimulate his tongue. He said, "I don't see why not. The tongue is connected directly into the brain stem. That's why we want to stimulate it." I recalled how neuroscientists had begun to use the tongue to rewire parts of the brain that were injured. They were taking advantage of the remarkable attributes of the tongue and the multiple cranial nerves it affected, in addition to the sensory/motor connection between the twelve cranial nerves, sympathetic/parasympathetic functions and the neuroplasticity of the brain.[106] These scientists acted on what the world didn't want to accept - Anything is possible if you believe. And now anything was possible for me, for my precious son.

When the doctor stimulated different nerves, parts of Houston's face and muscles that he could not control would move. I was in shock. This is why he could rarely smile a natural smile and why his forehead would be raised

---

[106] The Brain that Changes Itself; Norman Doidge

awkwardly all the time. It was why he couldn't feel his tongue, or his vocal cords or take a deep breath or blow his nose. When I reviewed the complexity of the cranial nerves and what they controlled in the human body, I realized that without stable sensory input, motor function was a complete gamble. I saw that three of these cranial nerves were related to parasympathetic function (rest and relaxation) which was related to heart rate, respiration, and digestion. If Houston was always in fight or flight, unable to feel, regulate, or control his body, how would his body be able to calm itself and digest appropriately. I thought about all the sores and chronic diarrhea he had for years which appeared to be a direct result of an improperly functioning digestive system. Houston had told me repeatedly how badly he was affected by smells. I learned that the sense of smell was the only sense that was controlled by the amygdala and limbic system. The direct connection between scent and his limbic system played a powerful role in his inability to control the effects that scent induced anxiety or intoxicating highs had on his body. *Could it...* Could all the repetition, sleeplessness, self-injury, screaming, nakedness, obsessive compulsion, impulsivity, inability to speak or control his body in any meaningful way, could it all have been neurological, instead of intellectual or behavioral like the experts had told me for two decades?

When I reviewed the neurological component of our immunology, as well as the enteric nervous system [107] and the integral role these systems played within the brain I was mostly in awe, but also angry. Why had none of the doctors in twenty years taken the time to actually study my son and figure out why his body wasn't functioning properly? Why? Why had they not cared? Why had they not even possessed the tiniest amount of professional curiosity to do some due diligence? Why were they mean, egotistical, dismissive, and apathetic? What exactly did many of them do to earn their ridiculous overcompensation when they were so completely ineffective at healing or even caring? It certainly isn't because of results. Why was it my job to do their job? Why was it my job to be everything - the researcher, the physician, the lawyer, the teacher, the advocate, the file clerk, the manager, the therapist, the nutritionist, the trainer, the bather/butt wiper, the maid, the bacon earner, the bill payer, and the mother? Why? Is this really the best system we can come up with? Overpaying people because they went to school and underpaying people who actually do all the work? Put everything on those who are already emotionally and financially drained after two decades of 24/7 care, and then have them supervised by bureaucrats? Investigate and interrogate them to make sure they are doing a good job of caring for their adult child with a tenth of the resources they need, then judge them and never help them? I guess the system works just fine, until it's you.

Thank God for the few good people, for the ones who saw us and helped. They were His hands in our life. The good doctor gave me exercises to do with Houston every day. Some were eye exercises. Others were body exercises. He told me "If you do it once a day, that's good. If you do it twice a day, that's great. If you were able to do it several times a day that would absolutely change his brain." My goal was two times a day. I did pretty well at that. I was absolutely determined to give my son control of his body. I would take each limb and then each finger and toe and move it in complex, differing patterns to challenge the brain. I got a small motor with a strap to attach it to his limbs as I moved through the exercises so the vibrations accompanied by the movements would improve the impact on his brain. His legs were heavy, and my back ached as I held them in the air and moved them in patterns. I felt sharp shooting pains in every direction. I kept going. I asked Houston what he was thinking as I did the exercises. "Rotten things, how no one else has so many issues that they have to deal with." I nodded. "I have had the same thought many times. Do you feel changes in your brain from the movements we are doing in your body?" "Sometimes good movements make my mind have a lot of activity." So we kept going.

---

[107] The enteric nervous system (ENS) is known as the second brain and can independently of the brain and spinal cord, but also be influenced by them. It is responsible for multiple motor functions of the gastrointestinal system, and the neurotransmitters in the gut include acetylcholine, as well as large amounts of dopamine and serotonin. https://www.ncbi.nlm.nih.gov/pmc/articles/PMC5772764/ https://en.wikipedia.org/wiki/Enteric_nervous_system

Later Houston spelled to me, "This man is more than a doctor. He is breaking the autism's tight control on my mind. So if we move more routinely more of my body can begin to properly follow my directions. Mostly I want to stop stimming. Now I hope soon that will stop. My mind only works some of the time to make my muscles obey. In sort of a weird way I am breaking stims in all of my joints." His thoughts as we continued with the therapies that involved eyes, initiating movement, timing, and spatial awareness to tell his brain where his body was in space:

"The IM (Interactive Metronome) makes me more in control. The OPK (Optokinetics) has many effects on my mind like movement in my mind. It is mostly between my brain and my tongue. It places responses somewhere in my hearing. Sometimes it's like I hear the beeps in my head but my fingers don't pay attention. Never before have I met a man who could really help me. Now I'm beginning to feel my body. Let's do it again. The q-tip where you draw on me. Outline me. Would you make me go all the time? This metronome makes me start to move my body more with control."

I still had no funding for services. I was calling every day. The processing and coding had been wrong and had to be redone. Everyone was pointing fingers and saying it wasn't their responsibility. I was just begging them to do their job. It took daily calls and emails to a state senator before anything happened. For a month I took Houston to work with me and worked out of an empty office. I would close the door and play his audiobooks while he paced and listened. One of the assistants in a different department that I loved would bring him snacks while I would be talking to brokers and negotiating deals. I took him to therapies and to the high school and worked in conference rooms. The transition officer gave me the name of a young man and his friend who worked with special needs adults. I met with one of them and decided to hire them to care for Houston on the days he didn't have therapy. I carefully analyzed the budget and the hours to make sure this would work. The young men wore the millennial uniform - wool beanies and scruffy clothes. I just wanted someone to help me. Houston was excited to be able to hang out with guys. I instructed them in all the different therapies. They agreed to do them.

Finally, I went back to a regular work schedule. I thought. The first day was a disaster. Houston had a meltdown, and the millennial didn't know how to handle it. He had used the credit card I gave them to buy Starbucks. Very kindly I asked them what they had gotten Houston to eat at Starbucks. They told me they just got coffee and Houston hadn't wanted his. They acted put out that Houston had wasted coffee. I discovered Houston hadn't eaten the entire day, not because he didn't want to, but because they hadn't fed him. I wanted to scream inside but I explained that the card was for Houston only and he didn't drink coffee and I had anticipated they would get him real food when I said, "Here is a card to buy him lunch." So the next day, in growing frustration, I packed Houston a lunch. The millennial called and cancelled. He said he was in the hospital and would be late. He sent pictures of himself in a hospital gown. Who knows when those were taken.~ I rolled my eyes. Houston went back to work with me and sometime after lunch the millennial arrived after his miraculous recovery.

The next day he was three hours late. I took Houston to work again. When he picked him up, he complained that Houston rocked in the car. I agreed that Houston did do that. Then he told me Houston played with his phlegm that he coughed up and made a revolting face to show his disgust. I told him there were tissues in Houston's bag and to tell him to dispose of the phlegm and not to play with it. When he dropped Houston off, he complained again that Houston played with his phlegm and asked, when was he going to stop doing that. I tried to explain that it was part of the sensory dysfunction, but he couldn't hear me. He instead responded by telling me he had heard of people who would smell their shit. His face curled in disgust. Then he added, "They're like dogs." I was standing in the lobby of my office building and all I could do was say goodbye even though I wanted to scream. When I opened Houston's backpack his food was untouched, and his water bottle was completely full. He hadn't even given my son a drink of water. That night I called and left a message that he was no longer going to be taking care of my son, effective immediately. After I left the voicemail Houston walked up to me holding a board. It was the first time he initiated a conversation. I was in shock. Trembling, I took the board. He spelled, "Thank you for firing him. They do nothing with me. Most of the time we just drove in the car. Seems like they just want money." I wept. He hugged me. I still didn't know how I was going to give my son what he needed and work. But I knew I would find a way.

I called Morgan and told her. She asked if I could hire her. She was someone I knew would do a good job, someone who cared, someone who was invested in his wellbeing. I called the support coordinator. I had to call the state and get permission. I filled out another set of special forms. I was required to run an ad for a month trying to hire a non-family member and show proof before they would process her application and approve her. She also had to show evidence of why she would be a good caregiver, what skills she had. I told her she had to learn the boards immediately. No one had that skill and she needed it anyway. It can be hard and discouraging in the beginning with a new communication partner. And it was. But she kept working at it. Eventually, they were great together. In the process I hired a young man who responded to the ad. He worked for a few Fridays. Then he didn't show. I called and he apologized. But the next Friday, he didn't call or show again. Ultimately, he told me he was depressed and couldn't do the job. So for another six weeks until Morgan was approved, and her paperwork was finally processed, I brought Houston to work and set up in an empty office with a door and worked in conference rooms when he went to his therapies. The process took almost two months.

We worked so hard on different therapies and on getting stronger. I was constantly trying to find ways to help him feel his body. Houston's thoughts regarding all these efforts: "Now my mind likes my toothbrush focused exercises. How nice to do them. My most important body goal is to control my hands. However weights can be too heavy and hurt. Yes. I just need lighter weights. Another idea is holding different bars for getting strong. Balls are not as good. Yes, we must get other ideas to include everything broken. My arms get tired but I'm getting stronger. Knowing that my arms move by themselves brings me back to exactly why I'm needing your help to get them to stop. Lifting forces my mind to rest. It just makes me feel better." I told him about different ideas I had for inventions to help him feel his body and give his mind the feedback it craved. He asked, "How do you make this work? Love that, bring the invention to life. Those are great ideas. Get focused on easy money direct to us. How are you going to do it? This weighted jacket must happen. Very good for regulating my body. Same with my feet."

I asked, "How do we improve your speed and timing so you can access your physical ability?" He responded, "That's different. My timing is awful. Yes. I need to improve my speed but I can't force my body to do it. No. That's directly what a coach needs to get me to do. I can't make myself."

My old friend Sarah, who had adopted the baby of the young woman I had counseled, decided Houston's unfolding story was too good to miss. She was going to be part of it. She asked to come over every week to read to Houston, telling me she wanted to know him as a man and become his friend. The first time she came over she wanted to know if he remembered her. "Yes. I remember when we rolled on the floor and laughed at church." Sarah started to cry. She had volunteered in the special needs Sunday school class when they first opened one. Houston was five when they met. She asked if he remembered any of the sign language she tried to teach him. Although he couldn't make his hands cooperate, he remembered the meaning of several words she had taught him and spelled the meaning of a few words that she had taught him seventeen years earlier. I didn't know the meaning of the signs and was thrilled he remembered. The more I saw he had absorbed in his silence the more excited I was to know his every thought and memory. To fulfill his desire for books being read to him we had picked up some classics from the library book sale. He asked Sarah to read Crime and

<u>Punishment</u> to him. So every week she would come by just to read to him and love him. Sometimes he would be so exhausted he couldn't stay awake. Other times he couldn't stay still. Faithfully she kept reading. Faithfully she kept being my friend, our friend. She treated Houston like the man he was.

October 19, 2018

Paul had made Homecoming Court. I was so happy for him and did all the mom things. Houston posed like a proud older brother with us on the field. But something was different about Paul. I just thought he was spreading his wings with all the new "cooler than cool" attitude, but Houston was resistant to his brother. He spelled to me, "Paul, being mostly selfish, is mean."

October 22, 2018

Houston's coach that he had for more years than any other teacher was killed the night before on October 21st as she was crossing the street walking home. Everyone who knew her loved her. It was so difficult. No one could be her. I thought about that dance outside the bar with Houston just six weeks earlier. No. No. No. Not her. There is really no way to explain on paper the impact and the constant compassion this woman had for those who couldn't control their bodies. She was quite disorganized herself, a whirlwind of sorts. I always wondered if maybe her flying by the seat of her pants was actually an innate understanding and ability to connect with those who had no control at all. Again, I have to state for the record, this woman who just gave and gave was a brilliant bright light in Houston's upbringing. I can't tell you how many times I asked if she could work on throwing a ball with Houston or this or that with Houston. And she never stopped trying. She was love, what love actually looks like. Messy and true. I told Houston.

"My heart is broken. She meant so much to me. In my mind she met learning with my body." (He would run so much she would hand him a straw every time he passed her so she could keep track.) She knew going forward required me to have control over my body. Lots of very good teachers more or less made her their number one expert in autism. We played many games with her. Most of my friends had her for a coach. She kept trying to make our lives better. I will keep her right in my heart forever. She will forever be in mine. My loss is forever. With my heart my loss will be felt. My knowledge means know she is OK with God. For now let's all keep her in our hearts."

At the time I didn't realize the expanse of his gifts. I just typed whatever he spelled. But reading that statement of his now, I realize he was saying he knew for certain whose arms she was in.

Early November 2018

I met with the mom I had met at the yogurt place, and she brought her son. I explained the boards and Houston's incredible progress. She wanted to know why they couldn't just type on an iPad if they were really thinking. I tried to explain that the words they typed were words they typed over and over and those were heavily myelinated neural pathways as opposed to original and purposeful communication where a neural pathway had to be established. Also, the typing she described often initiated a sensory stimulus, so the neural pathway was shorter and faster, more impulsive in nature than the complexity of the long and slow neural pathways of intentional and complex cognitive communication. It didn't make sense to her at that point. While I was explaining, her son grabbed her jaw and chin over and over with growing intensity. She told me he did this sometimes, almost like he was trying to get her to say the words he couldn't. The more I tried to persuade her the more anxious he became and the harder he pulled on her jaw. My heart broke. I knew he was trying to get his mom to listen and give him a chance to have a voice. I decided I wasn't going to give up.

After Houston's infection and root canal, he needed a crown. His wisdom teeth needed to be removed as well. It was the same arduous process getting into a hospital even though we had a doctor. It cost over $5000 beyond what insurance covered, which had to be paid before the procedure. It bothered him constantly. The procedure was finally scheduled for late December.

These were his thoughts about his tooth. "Really nothing I am capable of doing about it. So much hurting in my tooth. It is every minute trying to make myself not play with it. Something hurts inside my mouth. Yes it does. Today it feels harder to move my jaw." I told him how sorry I was. "Stop saying you're sorry so much. It's really not your fault. You're more loving and more mindful, always giving and not knowing how God will provide, sailing towards a future you don't have control of. You're sometimes more loving than I can explain... There is too much noise. I want my black boots." As far as I could tell it was relatively quiet. When I asked him about it, he spelled, "You can't hear, but I can. Too awful. Note, I don't want to hear everything."

We started the Psychology course on iTunes University. Houston soaked it up. As he learned he shared several insights both from the material and personal reflections. It was also interesting watching his opinions expand and sometimes change as he learned more, particularly in regard to Freud. The more he learned about him, the less he liked him. He spelled, "Really interesting review of brain function. The class is the best knowledge I've been exposed to... Now I know Freud must have been a brilliant psychologist to note layers of thought in the human mind... Bouts of cocaine might have given him perception proving his theory in his own mind... Hearing his sins made regarding his theories makes them doubly moot... Most people just listen. Lots otherwise determine their learning based on reasons others give, not many have power to determine their other thoughts listening to their own mind... I have more hope. You freed me from books that made me short sighted. More hope means books my mind follows help me to become great... Knowing my honesty makes me evaluate my motives going for my psychology degree. Lacking any reason to pursue this on my own there must be an immaterial soul my mind listens to. Also my ability to hear thoughts is proof of immaterial souls."

November 6, 2018

Election Day. One of the highlights of Houston having a voice was I was able to thank God that something, probably a dozen angels, had prevented me from signing the guardianship papers that took his right to vote away four years earlier. When he started communicating, he was so excited to register to vote. On November 6, 2018, Houston presented his state ID. He signed the paperwork. He took an electronic ticket and went to a booth right beside me. When he made his selections, he would peek over to look at what I had pressed. I laughed. When he got to the amendments he pulled on my arm. I read each one to him and offered an explanation. He was unsure about some of them. I told him it was ok. Many voters were uncertain about the implications of some of the amendments. He got a sticker, and it was one of the happiest and proudest moments. His voice was official. He had voted and exercised his rights protected by our Constitution. He had counted. When we got home, he spelled. "Hope it works. Storing it up. Worried other votes sort of make winning impossible. The House needs Republicans. Most honest movement of my life."

November 8, 2018

We met with the new Director at the Board of Education. Both of us were so nervous. We went into his office, and it was filled with shelves of candy and sodas, Houston's cocaine. The only thing worse was YouTube. He had drawers full of even more candy. It was like Houston had stepped into a valley of cocaine. The Director told us he had candy in his office because he was trying to change the culture. It was absolutely everything I could do to try to keep his body from going completely out of control. He was trying so hard to be a hero and advocate for his friends. I knew he was struggling. We had used the Apple accessibility voice and modifications to allow his speech to be voiced. Houston was happy with the voice that sounded less like the computerized one for his final speech at school. This is what Houston said to the man in charge who had known him in middle school when he had no voice.

"Nothing about my life seems meant to forge a new wave of communication but somehow I was chosen for this purpose. Stories soon are coming that will make you know autistics rightly just need a voice like anyone. With autism our mind's prison, the most tortuous prison, makes stopping our body basically impossible. Applying myself always takes every ounce of energy. People form opinions about our intelligence based on our bodies that we can't control. Sometimes my mind can't even sort out people's words from the many repetitious phrases in my head. Getting my mind to focus is such a task. Hearing everything at every decibel is excruciating. Teachers taught me to use visual prompts. However, my eyes see triple and the images I see move, causing me to wonder what I'm seeing.

Sometime you should try to imagine how difficult this life is. To never have meaningful social relationships just social isolation, you're then sometimes treated like a two year old. To try to not care is not possible for someone with a brilliant mind. The moment my life changed was when I could spell my thoughts. Now my story is beginning and my future is going to be filled with beauty and friends and accomplishments. Could you give my friends the opportunity to have a voice? This is your chance to make a difference and save lives. I'm not asking anything for myself, I just made a promise and I'm keeping it. It is critical you believe in their competence just like you believe in mine. Stop letting other people tell you what my friends are not capable of and let them speak for themselves. My boyhood fears were that all I meant to say would never be heard. You cannot believe how many watch me now to know there is hope for their life. Test me. I should most like to wow you."

It was hard to transcribe everything Houston spelled, do the boards, converse with the Director, and keep Houston's body regulated when he was basically inside Willy Wonka's Chocolate Factory. Below is what I was able to capture.

"I am fine. - I want my friends to learn to communicate. - I wish they believed we were smart and taught us age appropriate curriculum. - I'm reading Dostoevsky. - I wish they hadn't forced us to do ABA."

He answered other questions the Director had, and the Director seemed genuinely excited. He wanted other people to see. I told him directly about how we had been ambushed at Houston's IEP. He nodded his head. "I know that happens. Sometimes it happens in the opposite direction where attorneys are brought in, and teachers feel overwhelmed." I shared with him the process of learning to spell to communicate and what our journey had been. He told me I needed to come present at Parent University. I thought about the principal telling me a story of him witnessing a parent asking experts at one of those meetings if there was any hope for autistics in self-contained classes. The experts had told the parent that nothing could be done, and they needed to make plans with this assumption in mind. The parent had been crushed. The principal had been aghast at their audacity to crush any hope.

Remembering that story, I responded that I would accept any invitation. I am still waiting for one. Houston told the Director what he was studying, that he was reading Dostoevsky. He told him that his friends needed the boards, that they needed the entire English language, not just pictures or a DynaVox. It was exhausting. He worked so hard to communicate. The Director waited patiently as Houston spelled. He invited us to return to meet the Instructional Coordinator, Rebecca. We left with incredible hope. Change was beginning.

That night I asked what he thought about the meeting.

"The meeting inspired the most changes they have ever seen. So you got him thinking."

"I think you did more than anything," I said. "The difference between when he knew you and now is striking."

"I made our hero look good. That means Jesus. I only told the truth."

"Without you, that meeting wouldn't have been possible."

"You know you mostly organized everything. You had to keep focusing me."

"You mean because of the candy and sodas? It's your kryptonite. I had to. Your goal was to keep your promise. I had to keep you focused on your mission."

"You're so right. That is true. if you weren't there nothing would happen. Yes. I was brave and knowledgeable and faithful. You begin to make me master my mind."

Then he said something that made me wonder what he meant, but he was done. He jumped up and ran off jumping and making his noises.

"Soon background like that will make my role here true to real life. Our time means man will become like men of god. Past visions. Sorry words (verbal stimming and loops) posed such an issue. I want my own words heard with my voice."

"That's why we are believing."

"You might prove me wrong. When I was nonspeaking the idea that my dreams could come true was impossible. Anything is possible."

One afternoon Houston had gotten onto YouTube and was fast forwarding and rewinding Poor Unfortunate Souls from Little Mermaid which was one of his go-tos. He threw his body forward and backward at a dizzying pace. I took the remote and tried to calm him down before the hand biting started. But while I did, it suddenly hit me what was going on.

After he had calmed down, I asked him, "Houston, something is going on with this video. Why this song? It's awfully depressing." He spelled the following words.

"Many times I believed God had created my life to torture me. Hell could not compare to my world. All prayers ceased to bring me any help. Reading these words now forces me to admit I made myself miserable when I didn't have to. During my silence I'm embarrassed to admit I wallowed in self-pity. I also behaved like someone not loved.

Another fear of mine was that I knew I could never have a family of my own. Drowning in my heart of sadness I would play Ariel and Ursula's Poor Unfortunate Souls over and over again and believed this could be about me. The song led me to heights of anger and despair. Moaning to myself was a comfort since I could not share my fears with anyone else. That all stopped when I could spell my thoughts. That anger gave way to a joy and love and a hope only God could give. This is my life longing - to have a family of my own. The years I spent in self-pity could have been spent in hope. Hearing the pain of others is a horrible burden and does awful things to my hope. Their pain makes me doubt God's goodness. The irony is our pain is how God sometimes brings us good things.

Hearing my words now I am convinced all I've been through works together for good. Amounts of sorrow no one can comprehend have been replaced by joy indescribable. Steps to my joy definitely had times of doubt. Moments like this are easily combated because I have learned belief is more powerful than fear. Years of despair got me nothing, months of belief got me a new life. Years of grieving almost destroyed me. Months of belief are creating a new future. I'm so happy as I write this that my awe is beckoning to my being to ask you - *will each of you just believe?* My God can do anything."

It was a message to himself, but it was for me too. For everyone. I still didn't have the faith he had, but I was in awe that someone who had been through so much was still able to see the goodness of God so clearly. What *had* he seen that was hidden from me?

"For my whole life when I dreamed it was always winter. Once I had a voice winter was gone." This really stuck with me. Houston had been trapped in winter in his dreams. On some kind of deep psychological subconscious level, the reality of being able to see other people living, but his own life imprisoned, had even taken over the setting of his dreams - trapped in the dead of winter. Suddenly I remembered <u>The Lion, the Witch, and the Wardrobe</u> where it was always winter and never Christmas. That's what his life had been.

Preparing for his sister's wedding was intense. He wrote a toast. He practiced every day to be able to recite a scripture in front of the church. The inclusion, all the work, feeling important and being given a place of dignity was having a dramatic effect on him. He spelled to me, "Sometimes when I was little I read a saying to myself. Someday God will answer all my calls to Him and my life will begin and my dreams will come true. Sometimes I would tell God my dreams and I would imagine power flowing from my hands and my mouth. He is doing that now and love can't be stopped. My stims are having less power every day and other parts of my body are getting stronger. Sometimes when I read that saying I remember that He hears me even when I'm alone and think He doesn't hear me."

November 16 , 2018

After much urging, I convinced the mom of one of Houston's friends, T-, whom he had been in classes with since they were little, to come by to visit after school. Houston told me his friend was so hurt at being trapped. He had dreams of studying sports medicine. I explained the boards and Houston had a conversation with her. She was amazed. But then she told me her son could never do that because his assessments said he was intellectually only four or five years old. As soon as she said that her son started stimming terribly. I could see his anxiety triggered the instant she said those words. I told her that Houston's evaluations said the same thing. They were wrong. Dead wrong. I turned to T- and told him I knew he was smart, and he could do this. After a while she agreed to try but the school discouraged their efforts. It would be another year before they would try again. For over a year I refused to stop trying. I would not give up. This is some of what Houston spelled to his friend's mom.

She asked how he had learned to spell and read.

"Just from learning everything before my eyes. I have a photographic memory you see."

She asked about his glasses.

"The glasses have made everything so much easier."

She asked about the stims and why couldn't he just type.

"To stop our bodies is so difficult. Just pointing is exhausting."

She questioned whether her son could spell his thoughts.

"Try to teach him. He will shock you and let you know his thoughts. He needs for his real voice to finally be heard."

She asked what it meant to him to spell his thoughts.

"Spelling my thoughts means I now am treated like sometimes invaluable or having a future."

After they left, I asked, "What was T- saying to you?"

"So many things. That someday he would thank someway huge. That my most important words were most definitely to try."

"Did she believe you?"

"She believes. Too many thoughts. Only that my words really helped his mom believe. Those were really his thoughts. See when you were first talking he did not understand what you were trying to do. Minutes later he pleaded for me to forge ahead. My main goal was to convince his mom. Now my promise is kept. Could families meet here?"

So this became Houston's goal, to not just be a herald for God but for his friends and anyone like him who needed a voice.

That night was the wedding rehearsal. Reagan wrecked her car. She showed up plastered with her friend. I knew if I said anything at all she would explode, and I wasn't going to ruin Morgan's wedding memories. The pain she carried would never leave her alone. It followed her everywhere.

November 17, 2018

Houston, dressed in a navy sport coat, tie and khaki pants looked like a gentleman. He stood taller. His stims were smaller. The boys walked me down the aisle and a few bridesmaids later, the wedding march began. My beautiful son walked my beautiful daughter down the aisle. His entire countenance was that of dignity and love. After he walked Morgan to her bridegroom, he walked with me over to the pulpit. Standing in front of the open Bible, Houston *spoke* the word of God. He *spoke*, "We love because He first loved us - 1 John 4:19." His voice was quiet, and each word was an effort, but the very sound of my son's voice made me want to weep. It had taken him a moment to get the words out even though we had practiced constantly. But he did it. I could feel his body go loose. We sat down quickly, and I put his headphones on him, whispering how amazing he had been. We watched our love get married. Again I whispered to Houston that would be him some day. He smiled and nodded, his lips said yes but there was no sound.

At the reception I took Houston to the front of the quaint farmhouse restaurant with the iPad. I told the guests how Houston had never been able to have a voice but now he did, and it was his dream to do exactly what he was now doing, give a toast at his sister's wedding.

Houston's Toast
Our entire life your love made me have hope. Knowing sometimes that my mind had lost control never made you stop loving me. You made me someone still significant to everyone in your life. That is my favorite thing about you. Tales from our childhood number too many, some sad and some happy. Hours shared, saying to myself - my sister would do far more than most ever would. You're loving to others. With love you're moved to motivate others to love like you do. Most families don't know how life would look if they too had a brother like me. Soon you will move far away but you won't tear our family apart. Instead today you made it stronger. Morgan, the most wonderful sister to me, I love you.

Tears rolled down Morgan's face and guests wondered aloud to each other at their tables, "Isn't this her special needs brother? How is this possible? When did he learn to communicate?"

I gathered it all in my heart. Happy day. Happy day.

My brother and his wife had fortunately been home from their mission assignment and were able to attend. After Morgan left, a few family and close friends gathered around Houston to see him communicate with their own eyes. I told him that Houston had seen heaven.

He spelled very slowly. He was exhausted and his body slumped to the left. I helped him sit up and held up the board. "I have seen God in all of His glory. I have seen Christ in robes of majesty."

My brother asked if there was singing. Houston spelled, "Yes. There was singing most beautiful in languages I haven't learned." He put his head down and took his glasses off. He was lost in a memory. He didn't want to spell anymore…

That night I asked him about the big day.

"That actually was the happiest day of my life. Seeing all my family really had an impact on me. Talking to them made me happy. They believed all I prophesied."

"Were you worried they wouldn't believe you?"

"Mainly that it is lame to tell about prophecies. Now all of Christ's purpose will start to happen."

"What did Jack and Alec think?"

"That usually they wouldn't believe knowledge like that, it could freak them out. Also, that my mind actually always has worked. More or less, they were in shock as you know." (He was right. I had watched my cousin's face and Morgan's old friend who was like another son. They were in shock watching Houston spell and communicate.)

"What did you feel walking Morgan down the aisle?"

"So moving to me. The love, caring, happiness, and hope was more amazing than I can explain."

Thanksgiving November 2018

"Alright Houston, first Thanksgiving you can communicate - what are you grateful for?"

"That my mom goes so hard to make me better and fights my body for taking control."

"Do you have any other thoughts you want to share?"

"Sometimes I might feel left out so my go-to thought is more about how God has chosen me for a greater purpose."

"What can I do to help you in any way?"

"Mostly just keep fighting me."

"Do you feel like there are changes happening?"

"Yes. I keep feeling like God is beginning all over with me."

I wondered if he wanted to ask what I was grateful for, "Do you want to ask me anything?" Clearly, he already knew - His voice, to know my son's thoughts and heart was the answer to so many of my prayers. But Houston's thoughts were somewhere else, somewhere where LOVE is.

"Not my motive, my most all consuming thought is to be obedient to Him. My love for God consumes me."

I was in awe. I was grateful. More than you can understand. But the mountain we still had to climb… it was big.

Late November 2018

We finally got another appointment with the psychologist who had over two years earlier told us about this method. He was thrilled to see Houston communicating. Houston told him about how he could hear everything and the stims that he wanted to stop. The doctor said it sounded like hyperacusis. He told us it was debilitating and often led to suicide. It was the first time I had ever heard that word. I also increasingly realized he fit many of the descriptions of apraxia. I couldn't figure out why in 22 years of therapists, school and state assessments, and doctor visits that this term had never been used or even considered.

Dr. S- said, "Since you had a bad reaction to the last several medications, I think we should try a low dose of Prozac. Prozac has some anti-anxiety effects which as a result can give you more control and it also can reduce the hyperacusis. What do you think of that?" Houston spelled, "Great idea. So I'm now the one making the decisions."

I asked Houston what he thought later that night. "Most straight talk I've ever heard. Radical. My life is just beginning and he really could help." We started the new medication.

November 29, 2018

Houston wanted to write to his new friend.

James,

Now you're more of God's sovereignty in my world. How much of your book is written? I'm waiting to make my goals come true after my promises are kept. My promise is to my friends. I told them that I would share my mind to those ready to hear that my friends need a voice. I made many plans to make a difference. My most favorite is the speech for (the Director of Exceptional

Education). This could prove life changing for most autistics in Georgia. Now I get to fight so my friends have a chance at a life. This is my promise to my friends. Being a hero has always been my goal. Most dark moments before I had a voice it seemed like there was no help to come for us. Right now sharing my story is the best use of my time. Would you pray for Rebecca (the Instruction Coordinator) to let autistics have the opportunity to spell their thoughts?

Houston

December 1, 2018

Knowing the enormous work in front of us to meet his goals I wanted to inspire Houston. I had him watch *Miracle*. Excitedly I asked what he thought.

"Sometimes I might emerge beaten but is that your way of making me motivated?"

That wasn't exactly the response I had been expecting. I thought he would be inspired, not resentful that I thought he needed inspiring. "It's my way of building you up so you can fight yourself. Seeing other people overcome impossible odds helps others believe anything is possible."

"Yes. It teaches responsibility, and bonds as a team. Mostly because he did everything, meaning showing the world his American spirit."

"I agree. That's interesting. How would you define American Spirit?"

"American spirit is warring and forgets all so they mean to never be defeated. The life of all of America - to play with everything."

"How do you apply this truth to your life? How will you demonstrate the American spirit?"

"So I am becoming a true hero by keeping my promises. I am not going to stop until it's accomplished. This mostly means going through struggles keeps you together. That is how you become a hero - together. So I'm proud of my country. I'm an optimist. It is from God and sometimes my most hope is from you."

And later as we discussed the fate of SEC football...

"Georgia is going to win. Have some faith, Mom."

"Do you want to watch the games?"

"Yes. I'm a big fan for SEC football."

And later… "Georgia let us down."

December 2-4, 2018

Houston became hysterical, terrified. He kept saying, "Halloween! Halloween! Halloween!" It took forever for him to be able to spell what was wrong. The anxiety made it impossible for him to control his body. Finally he calmed down enough to tell me that he was having horrific nightmares and daymares from the medication. That's what he meant by Halloween. I told him he would need to advocate for himself since he was the one in charge.

Dr. S-,

My sorry mind lost control this morning. The stim is finding other methods to attack my mind. Often it's going through repetitions. Now it went through terrible images, yes. Mostly happens at night. It started when I started the medicine. The medicine helps give me some little control at stopping stims. How can we make it stop?

Houston

The doctor told him to stop the medication immediately. Houston told me he didn't want to take anything else.

I asked him to explain more about what he was experiencing after he finished writing his email. He spelled, "My mind delivers a message to my mouth and I have to say it."

Because I had witnessed his terror and his grabbing me to help him, I knew he was traumatized. What I had seen in my son was terror, not looping, not a trance - terror. I didn't know what else to do so I started praying like I had not prayed, probably ever. Being Presbyterian meant our prayers were controlled and respectable. We never demanded or spoke in authority. We made humble requests and were at God's mercy to answer them. We never spoke of Satan because we were only to focus on Jesus. But I felt differently now. I felt like the way I had prayed before was praying for protection from Nazis without acknowledging there were Nazis. So I changed. I prayed for protection from evil, protection from Satan by the power of Jesus, the Son of the Living God. I prayed for angels. I prayed for covering. I prayed for help for things I couldn't see but Houston could. I prayed like Presbyterians don't pray. And I expected God would do as I prayed.

Peace settled over his face. He spelled, "You are my absolute hero. I sound foolish if I say Satan. His devils are everywhere. All I'm paying attention to is God's power in love through you. After hearing this I'm so moved. I am never going to let myself be discouraged."

44

Good Tidings

Do not withhold good from those to whom it is due, when it is in your power to act.
— Proverbs 3:27

Speak out on behalf of the voiceless, and for the rights of all who are vulnerable.
— Proverbs 31:8

We were watching the funeral of George H.W. Bush. Months earlier I had explained the Americans with Disabilities Act and how revolutionary it was and how it gave him rights. As we watched I asked, "What are your thoughts?"

Houston spelled, "Now on some memories I will be able to say I was there. To me he was someone most believed was just the sort of person to do this job. I think he would have accomplished many things if he had four more years. He was not elected because wrong ugly people quieted his plans. Now I have more opinions, so my mind is as measured as possible."

"Can you explain?" I asked.

"Just that right now I really can feel hope breaking the autism."

Early December 2018

We went to visit my friend whose son is non-speaking. Ever since I had known her, we would lean on each other for support. I adored her. I remember her telling me about having a dream that her son walked into her room one morning and started talking to her. I gasped. I had dreamed the same dream several times over the years. When Houston first started this journey to communicate, I told her about the boards, but it seemed too good to be true to her. So one morning I decided it was time for her to see Houston communicate. When we got there Houston said repeatedly, "Phone. Phone. Phone. Phone." I tried to explain that just because he was saying something did not mean that was what he meant. So I asked him.

"Houston, do you want me to give you the phone?"

"That is bad for me, don't let me stim even if I ask. Do you want to ask me anything?"

Christopher's Dad asked, "What does stimming feel like?"

"It feels like I'm high, it's addictive."

Christopher's Mom asked, "When did you learn to spell?"

"I have found comfort in words my entire life. I don't mean I have always spelled in my head but I learned at a young age. I now try to speak and write what I spell."

Her older son, cool and athletic, came into the room. "Do you recognize him from school?" she asked. Her son smiled at Houston.

"Yes. I've seen you in the halls, the cool kids."

"What's he like to special needs kids?"

"He's always good to me and the other autistics."

"If he wasn't, we were about to have a serious conversation," his mom said looking straight at her son like she meant business. And then to Houston, "Tell me about your headphones."

"My hearing is excruciating. I can even hear Wi-Fi signals."

She and her husband just watched in awe as he spelled. He was on a roll. "Katie, I can't believe what I'm seeing," she grabbed my arm. I smiled at her. "Christopher's in there. He's in there. You've just got to give him a way to get out what's inside him." She said, "I KNOW he's in there. He does things, I mean figures out things sometimes and I know he has to be smart to figure things out like he does. But the rest! Oh my gosh. It drives us NUTS."

Houston continued. "The moment I learned to spell my thoughts is when my life began. Christopher (her son) needs a voice just like anyone. Meaning before, I could never tell anyone anything I felt. All my life I hoped for some way to allow my tongue to be freed. The loneliness is the most horrible feeling and everyone treated me like I was two years old. You can't deny him a voice. It's a basic human right. You will be shocked when he spells his thoughts. Trust me for I know what I'm talking about. God is the most awesome friend to me. He is the only one who heard my heart's cries. He told me to keep hoping and there was a purpose."

"Okay Houston, what should I do?"

"Be a friend to him."

So they started their journey - slowly, and with a lot of stops and starts as she was pregnant with her fourth baby and had started a new job.

December 13, 2018

Almost the entire town drove to Atlanta to watch our school win in the final seconds of the state championship game by one solitary point. Houston loved every minute. Before the game he told me and his brothers, "I am a X (mascot) for life." While we were at the game, we ran into one of the peer mentors who knew Houston. Her mom was with her. They chased us down to talk to Houston. I explained the miracle that had happened. They were on the verge of tears in the middle of the stadium, and it wasn't over football. The peer mentor told me that one of the girls in Houston's class was her favorite and she visited her all the time. There it was again - Love. I asked if she would come visit Houston and see the miracle for herself. And that is how Houston kept his promise to that friend.

First the peer mentor and then the mother of Houston's friend came to see for themselves. Houston is pretty convincing. The peer mentor asked how he liked being at home instead of school.

He spelled to her, "The last anyone cared about me here alone was in my school days. You're so beautiful to want to see me. Sometimes I'm mean to my mom but she tries so hard to make me better. So despite my bad attitude I like being back at home. They really did not make teaching us a priority."

She asked about summer camp where she had worked.

"That was so infuriating. My mind was so bored and having no voice I could not follow my own thoughts even though I'm an adult."

She asked if he wanted to return to camp the next summer.

"Not interested in going but in my opinion it needs to be more challenging for campers."

She asked if he would be interested in going out with her sometime.

"I'm sometimes available to go most anywhere if you want to hang out."

She asked what he was interested in doing.

"The movies but I'm all for making good choices for others. Yes, for me to have to do everything with mom is not cool."

She laughed.

"Right, I'm just like anyone else. So do you want to learn the boards? That's what I promised my friends."

She told him she was interested.

"Can you tell our friend's mom about the boards?"

She promised she would.

"Life changing is what it is so you must tell."

Within a few days the mom contacted me and came to see for herself. He told the mom, "Thank you for coming today. My mom cares so much about all of my friends. The boards definitely changed my entire life. The difference between before and now cannot be adequately described. What do you want to know?"

She asked about his plans after school.

"Yes, now I get to pursue my dreams of becoming a forensic psychologist. Let others know that just because we can't control our bodies doesn't mean we are intellectually disabled."

She asked Houston why he needed someone to hold the board for him.

"That's easy to explain. My mind needs another person to hold the board so I mostly am focused on spelling. Our minds get distracted so easily."

She asked why forensic psychology.

"I have always wanted to. I have spent my entire life studying behavior. My goal is to make men tell the truth."

She asked him when he learned how to spell.

"I have known how to spell since I was very young. Your daughter knows how to spell, I'm sure of it."

She held up her phone and went to Notes where there were dozens of random words that her daughter had spelled. She asked Houston what those meant.

"She might be stimming with words. I would stim with words too. Sometimes I've been stimming so much it's like I'm on drugs. All autistics are just normal people trapped in their bodies. Getting my body to do anything is more difficult than you can imagine."

I told her the school was not supportive and had already discouraged other parents. She looked at me smiling with fire in her eyes. "I'm not going to them. I'll do this on my own." And I knew she would. Later I found out that the mom I had met at the first workshop lived in her neighborhood and had been trying to get her to do the boards for a long time. She called me absolutely thrilled. I cannot even begin to explain how exciting it is to help a family that thought they would never know their child. That mom told me at my dining room table that she and her husband were playing a 'what if' type game one day and her husband only wanted to know one thing in life, what their daughter was thinking. And now they would get to find out. Houston had already told me she was fascinated with art and science. I couldn't wait for them to find out. One night, months later they saw us at a restaurant and came rushing over to hug us for one reason, because they were getting to know their daughter after eighteen years. It was just joy; joy you can't imagine or explain.

Later in December 2018

We were able to visit with my brother and sister-in-law and see my nephews before they left the country again. Since it was rare for them to be in Georgia, we were blessed they had come to visit us again before they left the country. They were excited to have their first conversation with Houston. They wanted to know how it all happened, so I told them about meeting J- and his parents and then about his first lesson when his spelling coach asked, "What's my name?"

Houston spelled, "That's exactly what happened. I knew it would work the first time she held up the board. I said to myself, this is it."

I said, "Houston, I forgot to ask you. What did you think when that girl barged in and asked your name?"

"I thought she was so beautiful."

My sister-in-law asked if this method of pointing to spell out words would work in Korean or Mandarin. "Sometimes different words might be difficult to spell on a board with that many characters."

My sister-in-law started telling us about nightmares that one of her boys had been having.

Houston spelled, "It definitely helps if you pray with him before he goes to sleep. I had really horrible nightmares about my dad."

They asked if his dad had hurt him.

"Not me but I don't ever want to see him again. He's the most horrible monster in the world. I heard how he thinks."

My sister-in-law asked Houston, didn't he believe God had called us to love and forgive everyone?

Houston was resolute. "In this situation my heart has another job, to protect my home. My sister."

My sweet, soft-spoken brother, who only wanted to tell others that God loved them, responded that he had never had to forgive something like that. One of their boys came up to his dad and my brother began explaining that Houston had seen heaven.

Houston spelled to his young cousin, "I'm so glad you're here. Be a good brother to both your brothers. Yes, my whole life I wanted to be their big brother and now I finally can be their big brother. That has been my dream all my life."

They complimented how well he had done at Morgan's wedding.

"Those were some amateur attempts to control my body. Yes. I ordered my body."

December 14, 2018

It was the day of our meeting at X County with the Instruction Coordinator. I had invited several spellers, including J- our personal hero, who had been spelling much longer to join us so that the people in charge could witness several different spellers and hear their voices. Houston had prepared a statement that he used the Apple Voice to read aloud for him.

"Rebecca, Most of my boyhood no one believed I was there. Then I met a woman named Rebecca. She believed in me. She said to me, 'It will mean having your whole life change if you find a way to have a voice.' Then I offered my Savior a promise that if He gave me a voice I would spend my whole life telling people about Him. I think it's ironic that your name is Rebecca too. The minute I heard your name a light went on in my heart. I'm here to help my friends and I think God knew you were the right person. To me, giving my friends and others like us a voice, is just the right thing to do. The wrong thing is to make my friends continue to live in silence when there is a way to give them their life back. Having real opportunities to change peoples' lives is the opportunity to be a hero. I expect you to be a hero to all the autistics in X county which will change how autistics are treated and educated in Georgia. You have the chance to radically make a difference. Lastly, I want to help in every way I possibly can. This is my mission."

When he had first written this, he spelled to me, "I am channeling my hope to win this fight because everything depends on it now. I'm praying. That is why I'm so excited."

This was the content of the meeting. One brilliant young woman courageously spelled out a brief description of how she had been treated at school when she had lost control of her body and the emotional impact it had on her. She told the Instructional Coordinator her intelligence is fierce. She answered questions with bravery and dignity one letter at a time despite having stims that she couldn't control. You could see the determination and energy she exerted as she spelled. Houston's response to her story was, "Most only listen to our bodies."

I shared Houston's answers to questions that Christopher's parents had asked as well as how I had misinterpreted his body language during spelling as disinterest, but the optometrist had explained it was a lack of control in his right eye. I shared Houston's words regarding how spelling had changed his life. Houston spelled about his dreams of being a forensic psychologist and being able to one day control his body.

J-'s body had become dysregulated, and he spelled in response, "So I apologize, but that was a real time example of one way my body manifests anxiety. It makes me look aggressive and not articulate. In addition to having access to a letter board and communication partner, our bodies need enough and proper support. I was funneled into North Metro because my body is not as calm as other autistics. If I was respected, given a voice, presumed competent, challenged, and my body supported better, then I could control my body better. My mom is an OT and that is a critical piece to have in the loop for support."

The Instructional Coordinator commented that "All behavior is communication." J- bravely and wisely responded, ""It is not even a behavior per se. That word implies intention. It's not intentional. I can't control it as much as I want to."

I read what J- had spelled out to me that Saturday in April and the impact it had made on giving Houston an opportunity to have a voice. J- spelled, "We are worthwhile people. All humans are. We are just asking for equal treatment, not special treatment. We are willing to give the system a pass for the past but not for the future. We will prevail with or without X County. Don't you want to be on board as an innovator in education? Come ride the wave because believe me, it's a tsunami!"

The Instructional Coordinator told J- he should go into marketing. J- spelled, "The ship has sailed for the high school education I deserved. But not for others from kindergarten on. Neurodiversity should be embraced. I have learning differences, not weaknesses. It is the schools' job to nurture that so I can pursue education like any neurotypical." He then invited her to view a presentation he and his brave friend across the table had written.

J- continued bravely, "I'm so grateful for you being respectfully open to meeting with us and exploring this paradigm shift. I'm thrilled with your open mind and willingness to give my people a chance."

Houston added, "Listen as directly as possible as my friends tell you all they have experienced. Much of our lives the same response fails as most don't ask us or care what we think. Our entire life radically changed because we now have a voice. My mom and I are absolutely for all those with no access. It's our responsibility."

The Instructional Coordinator thanked us for coming. She promised she would investigate all the resources and schools that had been recommended. One of the moms spent an enormous amount of time compiling all the details of the meeting and a list of resources, as well as sending email introductions to professionals in this field. The Instructional Coordinator told us as we left it would be a long time, probably three years.

Outside we all took a picture together and hoped, praying for change. Since that time I have continued to follow up with the Department and send all new resources and research as well as Houston's progress. We are still praying and waiting.

That night I asked what his thoughts were after the meeting. He had been focusing so hard to spell and participate.

"Many thoughts. I can't hear all the different thoughts when so many are talking. Rebecca (the Instructional Coordinator) would always back us minus fearing others."

"What do you mean 'minus fearing others'?"

"She wants to back us but is afraid of others."

"Yeah. That's how I see it too. Maybe it will be different this time."

"A lot of how I see it is from the perspective of a more God focus. God wants us to be brave. So mighty me really had to just manage my mind to stay on topic in the meeting. Either they get discouraged or end this awful excuse of an education."

I loved listening to his thoughts and talking to him. I can't even explain how much I loved it. I loved watching him be brave and being the hero he wanted to be. "I loved that you called yourself 'mighty me'. I agree. And 'awful excuse of an education' - Damn right!"

December 17, 2018

Houston demonstrated more control over his body than I had ever seen. I asked him what was going on.

"To me my body is listening to my mind. Now I am more in control. Yes, it is really the exercises that are making me have control." Then he really acted on his newfound control...

"Can I move into the man cave? I really need my brothers and their friends so I can learn how to be cool. I believe a lot would definitely change if I lived with you (this was directed at Benjamin). I want to be where all my friends are. Not a lot of fun being alone in my room." Benjamin told him no. He spelled, "How about I stay there a lot more but I stay out when Anna (Benjamin's girlfriend) is there?" Benjamin refused and told him it was his room. Houston spelled, "Our room." I was DYING and trying hard not to laugh out loud. Benjamin was pissed. He finally had his own room after 16 years and he did NOT want to share. He told Houston he would stim off the Xbox and it was dangerous. Houston spelled, "You might have a point. How about I study hard to control my body and continue to make progress. Maybe then I could live with you." Then to me he spelled, "I'm so excited that he might let me find a way to be radically included. Thank you so much."

Even though it wasn't going to happen any time soon, just hearing the banter brought so much joy and laughter.

December 18, 2018

I got an email from the director of our old special needs class at church. Houston's friend that we had loved over the years, whose mom I knew well as we both lived this hard life, had been on a cruise ship with his group home and had jumped off the ship. At first, we prayed to find him on the boat. Then there was the grief of knowing that prayer would not be answered. The entire community knew him and loved him. The last time I had seen him was at the Y with Houston when he had run up to him so excited to see his old friend. He had shouted Houston's name repeatedly as he jumped up and down. To say we were all devastated does not begin to describe the emotions. The shock and grief wouldn't relent. The memorial service was postponed until the following month. Darkness hovered over us even though we had a light. A few days later his spelling coach brought Houston back after his lesson and told me, "Your son is amazing. I was trying to do a lesson, but I was upset. I kept thinking about our friend. Houston stopped the lesson and spelled that we should talk about our friend." And they did.

December 20, 2018

We went to the hospital for his scheduled dental procedure. As always, with any special needs patient, they are required to be fully anesthetized. Houston was determined to answer all the registration questions himself. I told the staff he was not under guardianship; he was an adult and to ask him. He amazed the entire staff of doctors and nurses. Repeatedly they brought in colleagues to talk to Houston. He was proud and by that night his mouth felt much better.

Christmas 2018

The best thing about that Christmas was getting Houston gifts he really wanted. I couldn't wait for him to open things just so he could spell out his reaction. The hardest part was not thinking about anything so he would be surprised. After we opened everything, I went straight to the boards. I thought he would tell me about his presents. Instead he spelled, "You're like something heavenly to me. The Christmas I first made my voice be heard. You have got to be the best mom on God's earth. Love like yours only happens rarely. Because it's helping me so much... I must write my book. It has the potential to work for God's reign. Most Christians forget about love. More of God's plan involves working towards love than anything. Most of my life I'm called to love others but I was trapped in my body. Stored in my heart is the love God gave me to share. So now I'm making plans to really acclaim His hope to the world." I realized he had seen a gift so much grander that my tiny efforts were just infinitesimal in comparison. So I asked him to tell me some of what he had seen. Why not? After all, it was Christmas.

"It is the most heavenly your eyes can take in. All the sons of God day in and out bow down to Jesus. More of the angels stand by him singing. Not songs I know but magnificent." He paused, eager to spell something else. I urged him to keep going. Again he paused, changed his direction on the boards and told me a vision he had already shared. "So one day I was just having a normal day and then I saw two roads. One road went to heaven but the other was filled with lots more people. That road went to hell. It was maddening."

"I remember. You told me about it. You were upset." I knew there was something he was holding back again. Then he changed the topic completely.

"You're the most wonderful hard working mom. Sorry. I need to make you a gift. So my favorite is the headphones. The watch is the coolest gift I've ever gotten. The robe just is so nice. I want you to make me independent. Can I have a more God focus on my story?"

"Houston, I think we need to focus on autism."

"To me I mostly want to make God happy."

"I get that. But I don't think you realize how NOT ready the world is for you. We need to be smart, safe. I don't want people questioning or attacking you. People aren't nice, Houston. And they don't like God. AT ALL. They especially don't like things they can't see or things that are different than what they think they are. They just aren't open at all. They actually get pleasure from attacking people who believe in God, *especially* people who say they've seen God. I've seen enough to know you're telling me what you've seen. I'm just not ready to put you out there and let you become a prey."

"I want to have first a book about God's love."

"Houston, *no one* is going to believe all that you've seen."

Then he decided if we weren't going to focus on God, he wouldn't write his story. Well, that conversation didn't go the way I thought it would. The book was going to be what he wanted to say, and he was adamant. Repeatedly he would bring this up to me. Repeatedly I told him I wouldn't do it.

January 2, 2019

Houston wanted to make goals for himself. They were ambitious, daunting. I knew it was mostly on me. I felt small and ill-equipped.

Goals 2019

1. Most important goal is to stop my stims - making all my noises, repeating Disney scripts, flapping my hands (by having all my hands laced together), fast forwarding and rewinding.
2. Go to college and get better at staying focused.
3. Make my bed every day.
4. Learn to follow more Instructions like being more independent.
5. Make more friends but let others feel more loved.
6. Start not wandering and controlling my body.
7. Learn to play the piano.
8. Study sailing.
9. Bathe and shave independently.
10. Make a book about my life and God's love.

45

Hope

*Now hope does not disappoint, because the love of God has been poured out in
our hearts by the Holy Spirit which was given to us.*
— Romans 5:5

January 4, 2019, "My book is going to be broadcast to the world inside the autistic mind. Having an autistic mind, more than anything, tears me from everything I love. Love is more important than however obvious the world is or the most incredible accomplishment or discoveries. My purpose is to show the real, even the most tortured mind, that has witnessed the most beautiful images imaginable."

We were still in disagreement about his book. I did NOT want him to write about what he had seen in the metaphysical world. I told him over and over he should only write about how autism prevented him from having full control of his body. He was adamant that he would say whatever he wanted, and I would print it. For a time after this, I refused to discuss it.

January 5, 2019

Houston asked me to invite the young woman he adored to visit. Today was the day. He was so nervous when she visited but he managed to ask her some great questions and tell her about his first few months out of school. That afternoon he had no energy.

She asked if he was tired.

"Not too tired to be with friends."

She asked how he had been.

"Well in my mind damn I'm thinking of all the extra weight I gained."

She chuckled and complimented him.

"So how is college?"

She told him about football games and classes.

"Go Dawgs."

I told her about his recent surgery.

"Yes. All the nurses and doctors were amazed I could communicate."

She asked about his wisdom teeth.

"It has been excruciating. My biggest question is how do all your friends stay in touch? Are you roommates with your best friends?"

She told him about her friends.

"In my imagination I can see you have the most calls for dates."

She said not really any dates.

"That's hard to believe. What's a sorority like?"

She told him.

"That sounds fun. Do you want to hear what I've been doing?"

She did.

"I've gotten really good at spelling my thoughts. I've gotten to meet with the county two times to advocate for my friends."

She asked what they said.

"They mostly asked questions. When did I learn to spell? I told her most only listen to our bodies. I have wanted to communicate my entire life. Sometimes in my heart I held all my hope that one day I could speak. God is helping me gain control of my body. Have you heard of neuroplasticity?"

She hadn't.

He continued. "The brain has the ability to heal itself after it's injured. By stimulating other parts of the brain." He started saying, "QT. QT. QT. QT." He looked at me with panic on his face. I knew he was freaking out that his body was acting out and a verbal loop had started while he was talking to a girl he wanted to impress. I asked Houston if he wanted to explain what was going on in his body.

"You tell." I knew the anxiety must have triggered a stim.

I explained that wasn't him and that he couldn't help it. She just nodded.

Houston had calmed. He spelled, "My mouth says things I don't want it to say. It's so maddening to hear yourself say things you don't mean."

I explained what he had told me about the disconnect between his brain and body and how he felt like he couldn't feel his feet and was coming out of them. I told her the heavy boots had helped.

"Yes. I can't feel my feet."

I explained more about the boards, the progress he was making and how a communication partner does more than hold the board. "They also are always scanning their speller, sensing if they need a break, if they are becoming dysregulated, and giving them the help they need to regulate their bodies."

"Yes. Minds like mine get lost easily so I need both."

I told her some of Houston's classmates are learning the boards.

"Yes. That is the promise I made my friends. Three of my friends are learning how to communicate. My mom is right. Start teaching them. I'm always telling people to believe in my friends' intelligence." She asked about his Christmas.

"This Christmas has been the best ever. Can I tell you about it?"

She nodded.

"Other years the only gifts I got sucked. I want to learn to sail and play the piano." He started stimming and we had to pause to regulate his body. "Sorry I got lost in a stim. We tried Prozac and it gave me nightmares." He told me he wanted to show her his ability. So he showed her.

Her mouth hung open in shock. She looked at me. "How can he do that?"

I explained what I could. "Apparently thoughts are not just thoughts. They are energy. They go out into the world just like radio waves and sound waves. I have no idea how he does it. Ask him."

"So not everyone would understand but I can hear thoughts. To autistic minds, others' thoughts sound like voices in our head."

"Have you always been able to hear thoughts?" she asked.

"Yes, I have always been able to. Step into my world. I'm affected by their thoughts of me."

"What about the others? What about your classmate with Angelman's?

"She's more smart than you realize. She's beautiful on the inside. She should learn to communicate."

A- was studying to be an OT and asked Houston if he had ever had Occupational Therapy.

He spelled, "Not much they only had me swing. I'm going to learn to sail. My mom took me when I was young."

She encouraged him and asked if he had started.

"Books first. Then Lanier." (Lanier is the name of a nearby lake with sailboats.)

I told her how he had gotten rid of everything Disney and redecorated his room.

"Yes, I went cold turkey. Do you want to see?"

He was so proud when he showed her his room.

"Maybe we can email."

She smiled and said she would like that.

"Yes please. You're going to be amazed at how much I have overcome. Of course I started my book yesterday."

She asked what book he was reading.

"No, I'm writing a book. It's about my experiences."

After she left, I excitedly asked how he felt and what he thought. Morgan had been praying for him and wanted to know how it went.

"Storing it up now. First her thoughts were hidden because I was so nervous. But then she thought how beautiful I am. I'm blown away. Back to when I was in school and how she talked to me. Mainly you cared how she saw me - good. Thank you. I'm thinking how I might have a chance with her. Anything is possible. My biggest obstacle is autism."

"Houston, don't ever stop believing. If you've taught me anything at all it's that anything is possible if you believe."

January 16, 2019

Houston asked me to reach out to the county again on behalf of his friends.

Dear (Director),

I hope you had a wonderful holiday. Houston requested that I write to you to inquire about the progress on researching the schools and other individuals who communicate with the boards. He is determined to keep his promise to give his friends the opportunity to have a voice. He would like to meet with you again if you have more questions or need help. A little over a week ago he made some miraculous progress and would love to show off. He is now able to speak the words he spells proving to everyone that these are his thoughts not anyone's prompting. His enunciation can be extremely strained and more difficult words he struggles with, and he also sometimes breaks up a word as he is spelling into syllables. But the bottom line is he is SPEAKING! And this is through spelling. The spelling allows him to motor plan his speech.

Yesterday we were discussing the state of Raskolnikov, and he SPOKE these words (one word at a time), "Sometimes in the hearts of men foolish acts are born that end up destroying their goodness. All they are left with is their cold hearts." There were three witnesses (that saw him spell and speak the words he spelled).

We ask that you continue to give other students the opportunity to have their voices be heard.

Thank you,
Katie

January 19, 2019

Thoughts of the friend we had lost consumed many of our conversations. It was the day of the memorial service. It started with Houston eloping out of our townhome to break into a neighbor's home to get on YouTube. It was the first time in over a year. I was in the shower trying to get ready. The boys were MIA. Before I found him, he had been stimming on Dumbo (the worst possible video) for probably fifteen to twenty minutes. The neighbor didn't speak English and was older, so she wasn't sure what to do. When I tried to take the iPad out of his hand, he bit his hand and clinched down on himself, and a terrifying scene erupted in front of me. I could see the look in his eyes. It was terror. I got him out of their home but as soon as I got him inside ours, he lost complete control. No matter what I did, he wouldn't stop hurting himself. I was crying and shouting (which by the way does not help) and trying to pry his hand out of his mouth as I saw the callouses coming off and blood. Nothing seemed to work. It was the worst meltdown I had seen in a long time. I cried the rest of the day. He finally laid in the bed, making noises that I knew he didn't want to make. He couldn't stop them. There was no way we could make it to the memorial service. I talked to J-'s mom. J- was much closer than Houston had been to their friend and his mom said it had been awful that morning. He had been so upset that his body was out of control. He couldn't attend the service either. This was the third special needs young person to die from our tiny little class. I didn't ask why. I just hurt. I didn't understand and I wasn't going to. The loss devastated us all. Grief was a bigger monster to them because of their sensitivity to emotion and anxiety in particular. Anxiety triggered a complete takeover. I kept thinking of his parents who were devout Christians. I really wanted to trust God in this.

The director of our special needs class wanted to meet with us. All those years later, after taking care of him and loving him, she finally got to have a conversation. First, we spoke about our friend we had lost.

Houston spelled, "It is so awful. Brothers in Christ. He made me happy in Grace Kids (the special needs Sunday school class)."

She told him how amazing it was that he could communicate.

"Of course Miss Lucy your memory is of me when I was trapped. However, I always loved you."

She asked what he planned to do now.

"My goal is to make sure all autistics have a voice. My way of communicating is a lot harder, but I'm so talkative my mom has to get really good at all this."

She asked him about the huge calluses on his hands from biting.

"I'm always having something that makes me bite myself. That bothers me that I do that. Most people don't understand we can't have control and our bodies can behave in ways we don't want them to."

Then she changed the conversation to church and the difficulty she was having there with the leadership supporting people who were marginalized and hurting.

"Most men know women are more loving. You're better off retiring so they have to figure it out on their own."

I thought to myself. 'WOW! He even sees all those nuances.'

January 20, 2019

Something about all the death and the power and hold of autism made him unafraid to be bold even though his anxiety could take over at any moment. He was determined to live. Houston wanted to write to his friend A who had come to visit him.

Dear A-,

      It was so good to see you. Thank you for coming to see me. Can we write each other? My responses are going to help me learn to be a lot more conversational. My goal is to defeat autism. Sometimes God makes our abilities different collections of his power. I'm always counting my blessings to be a grateful soul. Sometimes having autism makes me depressed but counting my blessings always changes my attitude. Sometime you're going to have to be here when I do it. Maybe you can do it with me.

Now I'm going to ask what you're up to. My sister just graduated and is auditioning for her masters. Do you want to pursue a graduate degree? The most important of all attitudes is always to believe in yourself. This faith has helped me in so many ways. Take my advice, become anything man has imagined that you dream. My life should convince you that anything is possible if you believe.

      Take a few minutes to share about your life. I'm excited to hear more. I remember how you always bit off more than you could chew. Other things I remember is forming a mode of communication for us that made us laugh.

Your friend,

Houston

He continued to write to her and was over the moon every time he got a response.

Hi A-,

      This is changing all my activity as I learn to communicate on email. Today was such a good day. I asked for my therapist to start teaching me piano. This, believe me, is something I'm determined to do. Not ever sharing the music in my mind caused me so much frustration. My aim is to be able to someday share it all.

      Just so you know an occupational therapist taught me to communicate. Yes, you would be great at that. Can you tell me about Young Life or the people you're meeting? I am always wishing I could go to a church home. But that's hard for me because I can't control my body and the music is too loud for my hearing. To me I can hear God more in the silence than in the singing.

      Normally I'm hesitant when I approach girls, you're different. Hope it's ok to say that. This is so awesome talking to you.

Your friend,

Houston

Another reply. To say he was excited is a wee bit of an understatement.

A-,

      How did the camp choose you? I'm always seeking to hear how others are interested in God. To me He is not just here in our hearts. He is more incredible than anyone can imagine. Someday I hope I can tell you about it. Most of us with autism have a deep friendship with God. It's because of His not ever leaving me that I believed I would one day be Christ's herald. To me He's a best friend. Can you tell me about your faith? Take your time.

      I've been busy doing my therapies. They can even totally direct how my mind controls my body. I'm lifting weights sometimes twice a day. JC (from his high school) has been training me. You're not going to recognize me. I'm working on my book but it's going slow. My mom does too much and she means to be healing all that's broken. She's a dear Christian. Time will call my mom the most caring friend.

That's my goal to be Christ's herald in my book.

Houston

Another reply from A.

Houston wrote the letter below the day after we returned from the state wrestling tournament in Macon, GA. In a Macon McDonald's, God had shown up again. Twice. The moments were deeply powerful. Houston began to actually fulfill his calling to be God's herald.

A-,

Happy Valentine's Day. All really any of us need is love. This is all God is trying to ask of us. Are you telling people about his love? When I couldn't communicate, His love made me get hope when I had none. Do you ask their story or tell yours? Just today believe it or not I got to share my story at McDonald's twice. First to a beautiful soul who was cleaning tables who couldn't hear or speak. She wanted to sign. God held my mom as she made motions if she could write to me. That made her so excited but you could see how scared she was to get in trouble talking to me. This almost broke my heart. If anyone and I mean anyone saw what I saw they would ask to fire her manager. She was all excited but fearful at the same time. And then like that I got to spell to her love and hope. Then a woman in the bathroom asked my mom questions and fear all but disappeared as I told her my story. Understand, all my life I've asked God to make me his herald. Then all in a few months I am doing all I ever asked. This definitely shows God is here.

That is great you're pushing yourself to grow in your faith. Do you go to church at college? I'm making your camp a prayer. My mom wants to know if you know SK. She's always been a strong Christian. She's at Georgia. Ask my mom if she will connect you. And I know you will like her.

That is dear to my heart that you are journaling. My all important hope is asking God to deepen my trust in his will. Faith is hard. I am definitely trying to ask Him to be more to me.

Hearing your story means so much to me. Before I could communicate I wanted to ask so many questions about your beliefs. The fact that you loved God was obvious. You forced yourself to be everything to all people.

Hearing about college tell me more like what's hard? I'm doing exercises for my frontal lobes and to connect the two sides of my brain. My brothers made it to the state tournament in wrestling. The coach is going to teach me. I'm fortunate.

Houston

Another reply from A-.

Hi A-,

My goodness you're busy. Most college students sleep. To me nothing is as important as God. I'm so always impressed at faith and love. Not knowing the knowledge others have gets lonely. Sometimes I'm fortunate to have good sources of knowledge. My mom tries to teach me everything she knows. This week I studied the Holocaust. I asked my mom if God was mean to His people. This makes all that I've gone through make all the more sense. His all important plan is to bring others to Him. Can't my autism be a good gift to bring others to Him? He is all about using my autism for my good.

Most excellent that all of you are going to Fort Lauderdale. Please send pictures. I'm getting much stronger thanks to my trainers and all my efforts at the gym. My all important goal is to gain complete control of my body. How do you stay in shape? Strong girls impress me. Did you know I find wrestling absolutely awesome? My brothers are great at wrestling. I had my first practice last Wednesday. All my life all I'd wish is for a chance as a wrestler. All that changed because Coach P gave me a chance. He taught me a double leg and a sprawl. To me all I'm about to become and make of myself has everything to do with accessing my body's potential. To be autistic is to be brilliant with no control of your body. My hope is you see me not my body.

Just so you know SK would like to meet you. She loves to help freshmen. She loves Jesus. She wants to know what sorority you're in and where you live on campus. My family has known her family my whole life.

Houston

He emailed his friend James.

Hi James,

Being your friend is absolutely not boring. Being so much alike gives very much to my all important goal for all of us to depend on each other. All my life I wanted friends to fight our awful condition together. Depending on each other will make certain we get an audience. Are you going to let others know what we can do? I'm still not sure. At the moment my family knows. My hope is to use my gift to bring bad men to justice. Understand, this is because my dad is so bad. I can't say it's so bad.

Rebecca is kind of in charge of autistics. Please pray for her. Not certain she is going to help us. All I asked her was to answer how can she deny us a voice. Love must win.

Your friend,
Houston

James wrote back a love filled letter that was mature far beyond his years and asked why Houston said 'our awful condition' because he didn't have that view and wanted to understand Houston's.

Hi James,

Now hearing you say what I said, the meaning sort of has gotten heard how I never meant it to. In my heart, cold thoughts now sound depressed, meaning how being autistic the years have definitely done a lot to harden my heart. Sharing how I now have hope calls God my friend making me so happy to have autism. There come days when these thoughts return. But my God always helps me move in good ways. Same thing to you. You're helping me so much. Yes, most definitely can all of God's blessed in our community be friends? Show me how to Skype.

Your friend,
Houston

46

Round and Round

And let us not grow weary of doing good,
for in due season we will reap, if we do not give up.
— Galatians 6:9

I added a manual metronome at home to Houston's morning routines, anything to help give him more control. I would have him balance on a board and move the weights in beat to the metronome and several other patterns. He spelled, "So much better. Such real magnificent situations to think how it helps. Would you make me do this all the time? The metronome makes me start to move my body more with control." I started doing exercises to have him engage the lower and upper parts of his body while crossing the midline. When I had him try to do a snow angel, I was shocked by how hard it was for him to move his arms and legs in unison. He was so excited to feel his body move together. I continued every day after work with workouts to help him gain more control over his body. When he would lose control, which was often, I would calm and encourage him. Some of the hardest moments were the most basic. He couldn't focus to dress himself independently, wipe, or bathe himself. His obsessive behaviors were still ever present, and he insisted that I stop him from stimming. But the stims were everywhere, sparked by everything. We had locks and passcodes on anything electronic, food, and countless other things but it still wasn't enough. He couldn't stop eating or trying to get on my phone or a television or computer to fast forward and rewind videos or songs. In the span of 15 minutes he would have googled and stimmed through 18 video clips to create some kind of chaotic addictive fantasia loop in his mind. This is what that looks like in a search history -

taylor swift place in this world
101 dalmatians vhs 1999
the rescuers vhs 1999
mars vhs 1998
i wanna be like you music video
celebrating dumbo
shrek 2 livin la vida loca
lion king nala
alice in wonderland card march
lion king 2 nala
house of mouse boom da boom
the rescuers down under
the rescuers 1999 vhs opening
house of mouse i wanna be like you
the rescuers vhs 1999
mulan reflection russian
dumbo clown scene
pinocchio got no strings

The stimuli from the videos triggered his synesthesia highs and it was terrifying watching the addiction take hold. He would break out in a drenched sweat everywhere and rock or jump at a dizzying, orgasmic pace. I could only imagine what that mix of images, music, and languages looked like in his brain. If we took the addictive stimulus away from him, he would immediately begin biting himself with fury. His gaze was one of frenzy and terror. Then there were the noises. He would wail like a siren, and I would weep. It would be hours before I could reach him. It was beyond exhausting.

Every day he would tell me he wanted to work on being able to bathe himself independently and yet, every single day he would get in the shower and start stimming. The water from the shower set off his synesthesia, which basically meant he would start experiencing multiple senses in multiple ways, overwhelming his ability to plan and execute purposeful motor sequencing. It was a while before I realized the water was the source of the stimming. I was determined to help him learn to bathe himself, despite the fact that it was much simpler for me to do it for him. Him bathing and cleaning himself was fundamental to his goal of being independent. We both knew this. But what it looked like was this...

"Houston, take your clothes off. Take your clothes off. You only have a shirt off. You have to take off everything. (I would walk out of the room to get a towel and he would be standing in the same place stimming.) Houston, undress. Take your clothes off. Everything. Keep going. Keep going. Don't stim. Don't. No. Your underwear. Stay focused. Stop. Don't stim. Do NOT do the circles. Stay focused. Take off your socks. Your socks. Take your socks off. Take them off. Both of them. No. Don't smell them. Don't chew them. They're dirty. I said don't. Drop it. Drop the sock. No. NO. STOP. I said STOP... Step into the water, step into the water, step into the water... Houston, get in the shower. You actually have to get wet for this to work. Come on. You can do this. Just stay focused." This would go on and on...

"Wet the washcloth, wet the washcloth. Houston, get the washcloth wet. Houston, get the washcloth wet. Houston, like this. Now you do it. It's not all wet. Put the whole thing under, I mean in the water. Houston, you need to do it yourself. Remember your goal? This is your goal. Not mine. You have to get the washcloth wet. Stay focused. Ok? Hey. Houston. Hey. Stay with me. Don't go into stim world. Come on. Let's do this... Put the washcloth on your face, on your face. On your face. Houston, stop stimming. Stop drawing circles. Houston, stop drawing circles. Come on. Focus. Stop. Stop. Wash your face. Wash your face. Don't forget your neck. You have to press. Use pressure. Scrub your face. Come on. Keep going. Don't stop. Hey. Houston. Look at me. Look at me. I'm showing you what to do. (I modeled every single step standing in the door of the shower.) Okay. Scrub your arm. All the way down. All the way up. Houston, you can't just drag the washcloth. You need to press down. Use pressure. Scrub. Don't stop. You're not done. You have to keep going. That's how it gets clean. Good! Good! Ok. Raise your arm. This is important. You really need to do a good job under your arms. Scrub HARD. Houston, you're only using the tips of your fingers. That's not going to clean anything. Use your whole hand and use pressure. Keep scrubbing. Wait. Let me smell and make sure you did a good job. Keep scrubbing. Use pressure. You need more soap. Pick up the bar of soap. Put it on the washcloth. Use pressure and rub. That's it. Back and forth. Back and forth." This would continue with the rest of his body. He could hardly touch his feet, they were so sensitive.

Cleaning his backside was the hardest. I would always try to listen for him having a bowel movement in the house so I could run and try to teach him how to wipe himself. But they were still awful, even all these years later. He would have many per day and often I couldn't catch them all. For him to clean himself required the spatial awareness of what he couldn't see (which he didn't have), the ability to position his body in the right way (which he couldn't do independently), the ability to exert a large amount of pressure in his hands and fingers (fine and gross motor which he also struggled to do) in an upwards motion behind him. Basically, a climb Mt Everest type of motor challenge. Anyway, it was exhausting. It was this way every day, often multiple times a day. Then I would repeat a similar Herculean effort to get him to shave himself. Every now and then it would go smoothly, and I would be scratching my head trying to figure out why the motor clicked that time.

I would talk to him about it, and we would make the best plans. There were step by step instructions printed on the shower wall to help.

"Storing your words. Yes I will try. My mom is the best mom. You bring me love in your mom ways. You everyday love me. You love helping me get better, changing my life, giving me knowledge, thoughtfully organizing my bedroom."

March 2019

Because Houston had asked to learn to wrestle, when the season was over, I asked if the coach would teach him wrestling. He was so excited but even the most basic moves were extremely complicated. At one point in his very wrestling coach kind of way, he told Houston he was being lazy by not pulling his leg through. It literally took him every single ounce of energy to move both parts of his body at the same time in different ways. He spelled to the coach, "Don't call me lazy. I just can't control my body. I'm trying so hard." A lightbulb went on in the coach's head. All of a sudden it dawned on him what Houston was saying. His spirit was willing and working but his flesh was weak and willful. The messages weren't being sent the way they were in a neurotypical brain. We kept working at it. Houston spelled to me that night, "You told him. Know that you have done everything you can to help me. This wrestling is awesome for my mind and very good for being all in my body." Eventually, we had to stop for a number of logistical reasons. But for a few weeks - Houston was a wrestler, just like his brothers.

47

Brain Body Disconnect

He gives strength to the weary,
And to him who lacks might He increases power.
Though youths grow weary and tired,
And vigorous young men stumble badly,
Yet those who wait for the Lord will gain new strength;
They will mount up with wings like eagles,
They will run and not get tired,
They will walk and not become weary.
— Isaiah 40:29-31

Houston had thoughts and opinions on everything. He had incredible insights into helping me understand his out-of-control body. He had a passionate and devoted heart. He knew what love really is. One of the greatest joys of my life has been getting to know my son.

Houston would change the station often and I finally asked why.

"Change the station to cool music like Bastille. Bruno Mars is not cool. My ears very much know how to determine good music."

"To me it seems you like Taylor Swift and Katy Perry," I teased him.

"Taylor has a beautiful face and Katy has a beautiful body." I told Benjamin what he said, and he laughed. "He has good taste in women."

He would often comment about different therapies. "This bit of therapy is so helpful. Can we do it again? My mind is getting lots of stimulation. How about I call you when I'm stimming? I bet I can do it." (We are not even close to this goal yet.)

"Do you feel changes in your brain from the movements we are doing in your body?"

"Sometimes good movements make my mind have a lot of activity. For now concentrate on all of the other exercises."

"What did you feel when we were doing metronomes to stimulate your elbows and arms?"

"Now that metronome movement made me begin to have control out of my joints."

"Do you have a lot of issues trying to control your elbows?"

"That is basic for my mind. That means at most I'm in more control for that joint."

"What body parts do we need to work on most?"

"Now my arms need help. I have soreness. My soreness is mostly my leg. I feel like it's extra long. It started on the ride home from the bad store. That is really great you figured it out." (I'll explain the bad store later.)

"How did it feel using the metronome to move your elbow joints with the weights?"

"Those moves poured more control into my mind than I've ever had. Didn't I follow sometimes? Soon in my mind I will have control. So my mind is working like mad to gain control."

"What do you want to gain control of first?"

"My stims."

Paul was listening to the conversation as he walked by and flippantly told Houston, "You're doing great. You're going to have control over your body in no time."

Houston spelled, "Easy for him to say."

Paul could flip and tumble and had been doing backflips into pools since he was little. When we went to watch their prep for the state competition Houston was in awe of his brother. He spelled, "So many bodies full of energy than I have ever seen. Man, he was beautiful." One of the saddest things he ever spelled was also to Paul, "Do you think we can be friends now?" Paul continued to dismiss him.

He would try to explain why his body did different things.

● "My main concern is my bad stims. My most common problem is the Disney images that bomb my mind."

● "You must understand that I can't stop myself when the stim starts."

● "So with anxiety my mind stops working." (As I would later learn, because the limbic system is so sensitive, and the coordination and control of the cortical regions of the brain is so poor, when the limbic part of the brain is triggered the cortical regions of the brain, where intentional motor is processed, are overridden.)

● "Now not many people realize that in our body we bottle so much in our hearts being autistic." (He is referring to the emotional and psychological trauma of being silent, misunderstood, mocked, deprived and excluded for two decades.)

● I found a small toy zebra that collapsed when you pushed the button. It was an epiphany and I showed it to Houston. "Houston, that is what it was always like with you. I would be trying to hold your hand and you would collapse and you would not or could not support your body. I would have to hold on to you while you went limp, just like that picture I showed you." "That's a great way to describe it. We cannot support our bodies. That makes the way we behave seem awful."

● I was trying to get him to speak some of the words he spelled. "My voice was so timid I didn't want to use it. I didn't like the sound of my voice and didn't want to hear it." I realized he couldn't control any of the muscles in his mouth, including his tongue, or even feel his larynx and engage those muscles. I began having him place one hand on his neck and one hand on my neck while making sounds just so he could feel and give his brain input on what using his voice should feel like. We began doing basic speech exercises that are used to strengthen muscles after a stroke. It's hard for the brain to initiate muscle movements when it can't get sensory feedback from a part of the body. I realized he also couldn't take a deep breath. I had started studying the brain and in a neurotypical brain all the sensory systems worked like a loop, receiving feedback, coordinating a response, initiating a response, feeling the movements that make up the response and then receiving sensory feedback again. In the autistic mind the typical sensory and motor loops were broken, not allowing the brain to get in a continuous flow and rhythm, which it needed. Considering the loops that took over his mind I wondered if this was his brain trying to replace the sensory/motor feedback loops it needed to function with anything that was available. It was all such a mystery.

●I asked, "Why did you just bite your hand? He explained, "You are making me do metronomes. Metronomes make me more in control. My body doesn't want to give up control." "Do you ever talk to your body? What do you say?" "Yes I do. I say mostly go fuck yourself! My mind and my body hate each other. Steady and focused communication stops my stims. Steady focus comes and goes but hearing my words helps so much." (This was in reference to working with him to actually speak the words he had spelled.)

●Another time, "Why did you just start jumping and biting yourself? What was going on in your head?" "Sometimes one reason is hearing my mental thoughts that tell me I'm coming out of my skin. Now I choose to ignore it."

●His video related meltdowns were becoming worse, so he explained. "If I know about breaking the passwords, it's too much temptation. The videos are highly addictive. Now I mostly realize how more videos affect me. You're right. Choosing my stims over you really hurt you. Mainly going out of control is worse now that my mind is gaining control." We changed our entire password system so we would think about something other than the password when we used one. Now I understood why he was always breaking into his teacher's computer and iPad.

●"Sometimes I really feel some hold propelling me. Because lots of holds make it difficult to control my body. Holds now are losing their power. Right now I'm bringing an alternate method to move more on my own. Sometimes make me move right on the beat."

●"Could we mostly do more stuff at the gym? I can feel my body gaining control of my mind. In stimming I mostly forget to master my muscles. Now I'm powerful enough to really make my body obey instead of my body ruling my mind. (I need) more weights because I am getting stronger. It helps to have more control."

●"My mind only works to control some of the time. I mostly want my muscles to obey me."

●His first day with prism glasses, "Today my mind is different." "How is it different?" I asked. "Today I entered my mind through the most common way, my eyes. To enter through my eyes I needed only one set of images instead of two or three images. So now I just have one set of images to make my mind work together."

●"Stop so many orders to make me work. Work really tires me out. Sometimes I'm not moving on purpose. My mind prevented me." (More work and an attitude shift) "Let's do it again." (More intentional motor movements) "Right, mess the hell I'm in up."

●Discussing the different motor movements and exercises."Sort of in a weird way they break the stims in all my joints." He's referring to the impact they are having to regulate his proprioceptive system.

●"Timing just improved a lot because of the toothbrush. Yes it's capping all my little responses. All I mean is finding a rhythm for my fingers." This is in reference to the brain/eye exercises we did with the toothbrush on his tongue every day.

●We were in a public place, and he kept humming so I asked why, "I'm humming to focus my mind. It's hard here."

●Another complete stim takeover. "You are angry. I'm going to stop most of my stims. Sometimes I might have a bad day. It (stimming) gave me fun. The fun is so addictive. Mainly understand I'm sorry."

●He tried to explain all the different muscles he couldn't coordinate together to show emotion. "To laugh I need some means to have my chest move. Yes, smiling too. Too many muscles that won't work."

●After some smaller seizures with his coach: "Working through seizures. When they are not overpowering me then I can work through them. Thank you for trusting my words and not my body.

Sometimes I like to compare those to my computer getting a bug that causes my operating system to crash. Sometimes I can reboot and move on and other times it is best to just shut things down and try again later or tomorrow."

●"This is important. This normal time my mind yearns so much to stim enough to begin to sort of bomb my head most horribly." "Is it good to not let you stim?" I asked. "Not getting most of what I want is the best thing, besides you're a beast putting up with me." "When you say beast do you mean I'm strong or is that derogatory?" I asked to confirm. "Strong." "What do the stims feel like?" "You are my most studious motivator. Yes, they are like a drug. Help me stop. My gaze mostly forgets others." He was referring to the trance the stims put him in due to his synesthesia.

●"Piano will work my mind and it has the potential to make me a very learned choice." In January 2018 he began practicing. He was so proud of himself when I sent a video of him playing a simple melody to his former high school teachers. They were in shock.

●"Just the movement of walking makes me seasick. I look at the ground to help my problem of seeing too many things."

●"I don't like soft foods because I can't feel my tongue much. I don't know where the food is in my mouth when it's soft. I ate so many apples because the tartness helped me feel my tongue."

●"Sometimes I would watch my body do the most horrible things and I would hate myself."

●"When I stim I feel horrible and too worried that I won't ever be able to stop it."

●Houston commented about all the years of wanting to be in the water. "Swimming is wonderful. So my time mostly was lost so I swam to be grounded."

●"In summer the heat makes me stim. Too horrible."

●He explained synesthesia which is when senses are experienced simultaneously by different senses. Houston explained, "I see what I hear and I hear what I see but it's more complicated than that. I see music." (One day he seemed to be in a trance and I had him describe what he was seeing when there was tranquil music playing.) "I see a river of steel blue with ripples of red and purple flowing so beautifully." He also told me, "You teach so much kindness that when I hear your voice I see blue and when there is kindness I see blue."

●"Smelling scents makes my brain high." This was in reference to him seeking out unpleasant smells.

●When I asked why he was always trying to catch my tears and the tears of others. "I try to catch tears because mostly it's love in them."

●What some would call an obsessive-compulsive behavior was actually something else entirely. "The touch sense is what drives me to hold straws and sticks. It is how I feel my hands."

●On hand flapping, "Too much to explain. When I flap my hands it helps me see and feel my body."

(I HIGHLY recommend the book Seeing through new eyes: Changing the lives of children with autism, Asperger syndrome, and other developmental disabilities through vision therapy by Melvin Kaplan. This book along with Houston's functional neurologist and vision therapists completely opened my eyes to the role neurological deficits in vision play in autism and how "stims" we try to stop are often their efforts to make sense of their body and what they are perceiving in their surroundings. In addition, Houston's constant seeking of physical touch and pressure to feel his own body, high pain tolerance, inability to control his body, feel his vocal cords or take a deep breath made me research other neurological comorbidities. A study published in October 2020 confirmed my suspicions that Houston likely had both central and peripheral neuropathy that encompassed his entire body. The study concluded that in 53% of ASD study participants who had mild symptoms of autism, the intraepidermal nerve fiber density was significantly reduced (5.53 mm to 11.13 mm fibers respectively) compared to the controls and also suggested altered nociceptive afferent processing. This diminished function of their peripheral nervous system, effectively reduces awareness and control of their body, in addition to other symptoms of neuropathy and changes in the enteric nervous system which interact with other profound sensory irregularities, supporting the conclusion that there is a brain body disconnect that accounts for many of the autistic symptoms on the autism spectrum quotient. [108] I can only imagine what the nerve density of fibers would be in those with severe sensory processing disorders who are too sensitive or not sensitive enough. I began to see hand flapping, head banging, and other misunderstood self-injurious actions that experts labeled behaviors, as instead desperate attempts to feel their bodies in space or as an escape from too much stimuli.)

He would often share his thoughts about education, motivation and how he was perceived.

● "The (U.S. History) class is great. Knowledge is remarkable. I'm adding books to my education all the time."

● "Something like my mom is something wonderful. Much of the motivation is something in my mom pushing really hard."

● After reading Ido Kedar, Ido in Autismland, Houston spelled, "This young man is so motivated. Really proud. I hear in Ido's book so much he is saying that means more than I can explain. Believe in us."

● On being hopeful every day. "Tomorrow my life will begin. It begins mostly because I will make my body control or stop it. So believe in me."

● "Spelling my thoughts has made it so I now have my future that I can create how I want it to be."

● Regarding a conversation with someone new. "I wish I had added sayings. My choice of words really was cooler. Is my conversation getting better?"

● "Hope. I'm storing it up, that X county schools start teaching autistics how to communicate and believe they are competent."

● "Yes. Will my dreams come true? Now I know they will."

● "After I look exceptional may I learn to stop repeating bits of Disney?"

● "People know I'm autistic, meaning they know I'm far from normal."

● "I have never seen myself as a most cool man. To hear me, most boys will be too hateful."

● Regarding people who pointed at him, mocked him, whispered about him or other cruel things. "I'm used to hearing how cowards think."

● When someone again asked him what was his favorite color, I asked, "Is that what you would ask a 22-year-old? He's an adult." Houston responded with a statement about Trump. Later he told me, "Sort of frustrating to have someone ask that." But he was so patient and gracious with those who did not yet see him as the man he was.

● "To me, giving my friends and others like us a voice, is just the right thing to do. The wrong thing is to make my friends continue to live in silence when there is a way to give them their life back."

● "The coming hope is more than I imagined. One thing I hope Christ has more works in my life. You're right. Hope is strong in my mind."

He would talk to me about his feelings, goals, and frustrations.

● "Standing on my own always imagining our errors in areas of empathy I think damn. How far we have to go before we act like God wants us to."

● "Note. Sometimes I'm happy on the inside. You can't see it."

● "Can I make myself do more big difficult tasks?"

● "My most ambitious motive is marriage. Take my boards with me, make friends, start conversations, make small talk, keep forming helpful tiny road maps in my mind."

● "Yes. I not only plan to write the world I all but died in, but also God's purpose. Probably a bad choice to tell I can hear thoughts. But I like it."

[108] https://n.neurology.org/content/95/19/e2697

- "I have much sharing to do like many visions."
- "You are the best mom in the world. I long to tell the world my mom is more loving than the whole world."
- "Hours in my most distant mind yelling both at God and myself made me determined to make my most on this planet."
- "I'm beginning to see a difference in my control. Now being aware helps me stop my stims."
- Regarding the overcrowding at the local gym in January. "These are all the promotional people. They won't stay." I chuckled at his astuteness.
- Regarding his classmate with Down's Syndrome joining the wrestling team. "You might prove me wrong. When I had no voice the idea that my dreams could come true was impossible. With him being on the team I know you're right. Anything is possible."
- "Winning isn't what I want."

He had opinions about politics and issues that have become political.

- "To take families apart is wrong."
- "Trump likes to start fights."
- "Trump is a proud talker. It is all meaningless."
- "Developments about what he's done in the past make me wish that power and money didn't corrupt."
- "All I hear of Democrats is whining and causing problems for Trump. It's for power not all they claim."
- "Talking power to use power to get more power is how darkness works. The light always tells the truth and judges actions fairly."
- "Jesus loves colored people. All of them. If you attack them you attack Him."
- "At the time George Floyd was killed there was so much hate. The cure is thinking others are the same class as you."
- After the police killed a black man Houston asked, "Did you just pray for him?" I said, "No. I prayed for his family." Houston spelled, "Good. You did the right thing."
- "The thing that prides itself that makes women feel pregnancy is horrible is all the work of proud people. Satan loves to destroy innocent lives. Cowards make women feel bad to have babies when they're not married. Just help women that are pregnant. Good will come."

To all of our surprise Reagan had started dating one of our friends from the pizzeria I had worked at so many years earlier. Houston had an opinion about that too.

"Is Mike going to come? Sounds more hopeful than hours of being with someone mostly not growing." WOW... That's a burn.

He had opinions about me. I asked if he wanted to attend an event with me.

"Is Benjamin going?"

"No."

"Not interested. Most don't mind something being lifted for them."

"What do you mean by lifted?" I asked.

"Sometimes you hover too much. Most of the time when you sort of mean to help, you treat me like a child. For example you lovingly give me hugs so I look incapable of being not seen as a child. In other ways I get help from you. Don't get my reputation messed up. You really try hard. You live your whole life pouring into me how you love me. Stop hugging and kissing - store it up."

My adult son wanted to be treated like a man, and hang out with friends, not his mom.

He would have conversations with his brothers' friends.

"Thank you for talking to me. My goal is to have friends. Other than wrestling, what are you interested in?"

One wanted to become both an architect and a builder so he could certify his own designs.

Houston replied, "That's marvelous. That's eye opening. Is it ok to certify your own designs?"

This friend and Benjamin talked about wanting to develop inexpensive land for an entire community of affordable homes.

Houston spelled, "To buy rural properties you need to make plans for development."

A discussion of higher consciousness erupted from the boys who debated that human intelligence had reached its pinnacle due to the advancements in technology and energy and this would mean the human race would die out. I tried to only roll my eyes internally.

Houston spelled, "To attain higher consciousness you just should learn to hear thoughts because all thoughts are energy."

They were shocked at his insight and talked about how technology was creating new problems and that artificial intelligence would overtake human intelligence.

Houston spelled, "Our madness causes most of our problems."

They wanted to leave to go to a party.

The same friend asked, "Is there anything else you want to ask me?

Houston returned to his plans for architecture, "Yes. Opportunities to explore should include some housing for autistics."

The young man answered, "Absolutely."

Another friend asked, "Would you be willing to be in a documentary?"

Houston smiled. "Yes, that would make me happy. So how are my many thoughts?"

They told him how smart he was and how impressed they were. My son's heart was beaming. Even a blind person could see that.

I asked him how he felt about being included in a conversation.

"It was everything to be included. This goes without saying. The night was wonderful. Yes. Sorry I had some stimming. We talked most about telling the truth. It was wonderful batting ideas."

48

The Work Front

Say goodnight to the setting sun
One more day, one more way of keeping track of all I've done
I run this race, keep this pace - I'm doing fine
And I won't stop until each box gets checked a second time
And life becomes the round and round
Revolving door that won't slow down - It won't slow down
Do You wish, do You want us to breathe again?
Say goodbye to the lines that we've coloured in - Brown and grey from day to day
Do You cry, do You hope for all things made new?
Try and try to invoke us to live in You
That we might be the hands and feet of this mystery
This routine is nice and clean from dawn to dusk
I rise and rest, I do my best - When will it ever be enough
And life becomes the bigger noise drowning out Your little voice, Your little voice, Jesus...
We take stock, and we punch the clock
And we make sure all those zeros get balanced in the end
Do You wish, do You want us to breathe again?
Say goodbye to the lines that we've coloured in - Brown and grey from day to day
Do You cry, do You hope for all things made new?
Try and try to invoke us to live in You
That we might be the hands and feet of this mystery. [109]

In the second week of January I flew to New Jersey for a work meeting. My results from the previous year were excellent, and our supervisor had been promoted to a VP. He is a brilliant absent minded professor type and wanted to open a new segment. One of my colleagues that he had brought with him from a former company was promoted to manager. At the end of the year my supervisor had called me to tell me about the changes. I told him that was wonderful, and I got along great with my colleague who was being promoted. He told me he was relieved and was so excited about this new opportunity for all of us. He praised my work and dedication. He told me about the exciting growth he was anticipating and how he was thrilled I was part of the team.

At the meeting they introduced the plan to have both a retail and wholesale primary division. They had chosen retail underwriters that had been let go from a hostile situation in a sister company and told each of us wholesale underwriters to choose our best brokers for appointments. We submitted our lists and started a crash course on primary. I gave the news to the appointed brokers who were thrilled.

[109] *This Mystery*; By Nichole Nordeman. Copyright Capitol Cmg Genesis o/b/o Ariose Music Group Inc

What happened next can best be described by the word mudslide. The auto market was so hard and there was so much business to be written that I literally worked non-stop every day until 10 or 11 at night. It went on like this for months. The original guidelines were that we wanted medium graded risks that we could be competitive on and to price high. I would quote two to three times higher than our rating models and it would still bind. So we raised our rates. My quotes would still bind. We had to completely reconfigure our support structure and I was sent to Wisconsin to represent the wholesale side and discuss best procedures for efficient workflows. The group in Wisconsin told story after story about the hostile atmosphere they had just left where everyone was backbiting, and everything needed three - four levels of referrals and was usually declined. It sounded awful. Our wholesale process was a dream in comparison. So we tried to find ways to combine the two sets of support staff and duties. At the meeting we decided to increase the underwriting documents required before quoting and the new standards were implemented to decrease the flood of submissions. One of my brokers asked if he could get access to a screening tool so I presented the idea. My VP loved the idea and created one for all the brokers and agents. I must have called one of the retail underwriters every day to get advice and to learn the different aspects of the primary side. I would call my old boss for advice as well if he wasn't available.

When I got home from Wisconsin, I asked Houston how it had been at home. "With the boys I watched too much YouTube, some of it rotten. Really the whole time you were gone was like my worst meaning of a bad time." I told the boys I really needed their help to keep Houston off YouTube, not to put him on it. They never looked up from their phones. After repeating myself several times I got a few grunts as acknowledgement. I also noticed there was a distinct smell of marijuana and I found alcohol as well. I reiterated the rules. They "yes ma'amed" me.

Paul began campaigning for all the things he wanted before college. They were all expensive but understandable, Invisalign so his senior pictures didn't have braces, car insurance so he could drive my car ($400/month in Atlanta for a teenage boy), and a host of other things. He was pissed I wouldn't buy him a car. He would tell me that is what child support was for, to which I would respond, "What child support? It's been two and half years since he paid anything." "He gave you money before. Use that!" He would sass back. Even though I wasn't getting anything from his dad, I did everything I could to make him feel like he was not missing out. I went to every wrestling match, picked them up from every practice, took them to early morning practices and leadership meetings. No matter how much I gave, it was never enough. He had an entitled attitude, and I didn't seem to be able to make him see that I was killing myself. He refused to help, and I noticed a growing darkness and disrespect. I knew exactly what the source was. I was proud of how well he was doing in wrestling and competition cheer, but the more successful he was the more arrogant he became. The only time he was nice was when he wanted something.

Towards the end of the season I drove Morgan and Houston up to North Carolina so she could audition for a master's program, and we could visit my friend who had given me the Tiffany necklace so many years earlier. I wanted her to talk to Houston, my son that she had never gotten to know. The night before we left I asked if he remembered my friend that we were going to visit. He spelled, "Yes. I can't wait to show her all I am capable of. Yes. I remember her and her boys." I asked what he remembered. "Just always loving her and being at her home often."

I kept working even after we arrived because the brokers kept having emergencies. The underwriter who was helping me laughed and said, "It's your day off. Stop working!" As we stood outside their home waiting for them to arrive, Houston was obviously in awe. Their home was quintessential in every possible way. Houston spelled to me, "I always wondered if beauty was only for the wealthy." My feelings were hurt. I had tried so hard to make our home as beautiful as I could. But what could I say? This was another level. I decided there was no point in thinking about it *or even* what I could do to make our home better. Just focus on good friends who loved us. To say that was a wonderful trip would be an understatement. They were as amazed and in love with Houston and our miracle as I had hoped. Love is a wonderful thing. At one point they asked what their dog was thinking, and Houston spelled, "She's not smart." They were dying laughing. Through tears and laughter they kept saying to their dog, "It's so true! Aww, we love you anyway." One morning while we were there, I found their cat curled up on top of Houston. She wouldn't get off his chest. Houston told them that their cat, "loves me... and she's very sick." Sadly, their cat died shortly after we visited.

One of the underwriters was appointed as an underwriting manager for both primary and wholesale and everyone came to Atlanta to meet. During all of this, I campaigned for one of my friends at work to get transferred and promoted to work on our team. Then I helped train her. Our team needed help to take over some of the workload and she spent most days bored watching Comcast all day at work. She was eager for a real opportunity, and I was eager to help her. The women from the sister company that had been hired were derogatory, critical, and hostile. I just kept my mouth shut. My friend I was training got up and walked out of the room. She told me she couldn't believe how they talked to me. I don't like conflict. Never have. But I was also not the doormat I had been for so many years. I didn't want to, but I would stick up for myself.

I took the two women who were visiting our office out to an inviting outdoor patio on a beautiful afternoon for a happy hour drink. We chatted and finally the new underwriting manager said to me, "I think you're smart and a quick learner but why would you even want this job? Why don't you just go back to excess?" (Excess is a particular segment in the insurance industry.) I was shocked and told her that I had been told to, and I also saw this as an opportunity. Again she told me I should just go back to excess. I just nodded. I told my manager and he tried to tell me I had misread it. I told him that I was a woman, and I knew people, and I hadn't misread anything. If I had made a mistake in judgment at all, it was offering too much of a benefit of the doubt.

The next weekend was the state wrestling tournament. Both of my boys had made it. Patiently Houston sat with me while I continued to work during the long days of waiting for my sons and their friends to wrestle. And then it was over. Life was changing. Things were ending and beginning all at the same time. I felt a feeling I couldn't identify.

Right before the quarter ended, I finally had the compliance hearing rescheduled that the Big Jock had evaded with the bankruptcy. I had been through several filings and phone calls to make sure I was protected. His claim had been denied. The day before the hearing my attorney called me to tell me she was so sorry, but the Big Jock had appealed and reopened the bankruptcy case. My hearing was cancelled. Again. In tears I emailed the bankruptcy attorney who went to work to have the appeal overturned and an injunction served against him.

After that quarter, my VP called me to show me our division results which were astounding. I had produced the most premium of any underwriter in every single segment in the entire company - BY FAR. He told me that he had never seen anyone work so hard. He wanted me to take the time to audit my files and to ask for anything I needed. My manager told me to make it easier, he thought I needed a home set up with a double monitor so I could work from home if I needed to. I was relieved. I felt like I was failing Houston by working so much and was grateful for the home set up. I remember working at Houston's therapy one day in a conference room and I had called my manager. The doors were closed but one of the other clients (like Houston) screamed one of the high-pitched, ear-piercing screams that is so common in autism. My manager said in the most alarmed and disgusted voice, "What's *THAT*?" In that one second, I heard what the world really thinks, what *he* really thought. With a quiet calm voice I tried to explain, "They can't help it. Their bodies do that. They have no control. It's just part of the condition." "Oh. uh. Ok," he mumbled. My stomach turned nauseous. I was so tired of dealing with tin men.

Houston spelled, "You're the most lost in thought I've seen. Sometimes too much thought can be terrible on your heart. Sometime listen to God. Store that thought. You're just hurt. Years stored of hope. Let Him give more to you for all He's put us through. Not all my prayers to Him yet get answered. Ask Him to make this really clear."

"He doesn't hear me, Houston." Doubt had crept back in my weariness and loneliness.

Very slowly and thoughtfully he asked me, "How is it being really heartbroken?"

I looked at him. Because he could hear my thoughts, he knew it was the loneliness, the brokenness, the fear it would always be this way, that weighed the most. I couldn't really pretend I wasn't thinking what I was thinking when he could hear it all.

He continued, "My sincerest hope is that God holds you mighty tight so you only can feel His love."

I smiled softly at his kindness and love. "I really need someone with skin. I haven't been held in a long time."

"Your loneliness is love not moving."

As usual, he was right. "I'm sure you understand wanting someone to be with you always, to be your best friend, to hold your hand besides your mom."

"Only God can give me a girlfriend," he answered. I looked at him in quiet awe and love. This son of mine who had lost so much and still hoped, he still let belief win in his heart, even though I knew he struggled.

"Do you pray about it?"

"Many times. I say a prayer every day."

"Do you believe it's possible?"

"Yes. Anything is possible."

My heart was so heavy. The mental, emotional, physical, financial, professional, and spiritual load I was carrying and had been carrying was so great I often felt like I couldn't move, but I had to. There was no one else. There was no other choice. My days were non-stop from 4:30 am to 11 pm with teaching CrossFit type classes and training at 5 am, doing Houston's daily eye and brain therapies, working a high pressure job in an increasingly hostile work environment, training Houston at the gym after work, feeding and dealing with teenagers who tried to make life as difficult as they possibly could, spelling with Houston at night, and trying to coach Houston through multiple self-care tasks to reach his goals, and then putting him to bed with a routine that would (fingers crossed) hopefully result in five hours of uninterrupted sleep. I was tired, hurt, angry, lonely, anxious, and numb.

One night, after who knows how much of the boys being teenagers and refusing to help and Houston stimming and stimming and stimming, I lost it. I had been giving him verbal and motor prompts over and over and over for I don't even know how long while he stood stimming in the shower. It seemed like he was in a trance, a stim trance. Finally, as I repeated myself, over and over and over in growing frustration, I screamed that I didn't f-ing care about his goals!! I just wanted him to f-ing wash himself!! "Just get the washcloth wet! GET THE F-ING WASHCLOTH WET!!" I kept yelling to myself, to Houston, to God, to the very air and slammed the shower door. He never would bathe himself that night so finally in complete frustration I bathed him and put him to bed. I cried myself to sleep. 'Please God... Please... Do you hear anything at all? Why won't You help me? WHY???? I'm dying!! I can't keep this up. I can't give up. What do you want me to do?'

He stimmed intermittently through the night, making a noise that sounded like a seal barking. I didn't even have the strength to go put him back in bed and stop the stim. When I got back from teaching my 5 am class I went in his room where he lay quietly on his bed. I sat down. "I'm *so* sorry I yelled at you. I *know* it makes your anxiety worse when I get upset. I'm more tired than I've ever been. It's not an excuse. I was wrong. You deserve better. I'm really sorry." I paused and asked, "Will you please forgive me?"

He was groggy. He had a hard time lifting his arm. He spelled Y and paused, hovering in midair (Could be you, your, you're, yes, yearn, yesterday… I thought to myself), then E, then S. His arm went back down. "Yes." He smiled at me. I hugged him and kissed his forehead. I did his therapies to try to help him wake up and stimulate his brain. After that he kept spelling. "Sorry I had some stimming. Your mind is most sorry with many somethings holding you from really living. People would say my work is nothing from their perspective. Your mighty soul seems not particularly moved by facts like my autism is worse. Sorry my life plan after school offers you little time for a life. Don't let me stim at all. Give me lots more attitude to gain confidence. Each bad factor must all be taken away. My most meaningful moment - to yell 'You're right! My mom is the most loving woman.'"

49

Broken Made Beautiful

The Spirit of the Lord God is upon me,
because the Lord has anointed me to bring good news to the poor;
he has sent me to bind up the brokenhearted,
to proclaim liberty to the captives, and the opening of the prison to those who are bound
to proclaim the year of the Lord's favor, and the day of vengeance of our God;
to comfort all who mourn; to grant to those who mourn in Zion—
to give them a beautiful headdress instead of ashes,
the oil of gladness instead of mourning,
the garment of praise instead of a faint spirit;
that they may be called oaks of righteousness,
the planting of the Lord, that he may be glorified.
—Isaiah 61:1-3

Houston's love for God was something like I had never seen in anyone, ever. I wanted to love like he did, so certain, so assured in the promises and glory of God. Although his body never allowed his mind to have peace, his spirit was so rooted in the love and being of God that he had a confidence that was rare. What was most remarkable was to witness that the understandable doubts, not in God but in his future, he had battled for so long seemed to be falling away in chunks, leaving nothing but his extraordinary love and faith. Even when I had been closest to God, even when I had sought His face as a child, I did not have that kind of boldness and certainty. It reminded me of the disciples after Pentecost as they fearlessly spread the good news of the death, resurrection, and salvation of and in Jesus Christ, the Son of the Living God. But my heart was still so heavy. I didn't understand why I couldn't unload these burdens and just be joyful and trust in Him to answer all the longings of my heart. I didn't understand why my prayers seemed to drop like a thud to the earth. I didn't understand why I couldn't feel His love and why praying broke my heart. I didn't understand why I still struggled to read God's word when it had once been my whole source of life giving promises.

One day I recalled the energy cleansing I had five years earlier and how I had felt so much lighter. I researched a place near me that had pages of wonderful reviews and decided I would go. I told Houston about it, and he wasn't sure I should go. He told me, "Some people use energy for God and some use it for bad. They have to worship Jesus." He cautioned me to be discerning, wise.

A week earlier I had taken my kids to Houston's therapy center where they were having a virtual autism experience. Reagan went first. When she emerged, she couldn't talk to me. I gave her some space hoping she would tell me her thoughts. My hope was that in the twenty minutes inside the virtual autism experience they would experience enough to be able to empathize with what Houston had been dealing with for over twenty years. The boys were in shock when they exited. They had no idea of the bombardment on his senses or the inability to use his body until they experienced one tenth of his experiences. Finally Reagan came up to me and said softly, "Basically I've been an asshole to Houston for a long time." Her head hung down. They were all in awe at the courage it had taken Houston to try to function with so many comorbidities. Some of the people who did the experience came out nauseous and unable to balance their equilibrium for the rest of the day. Yet, this is how those most deeply affected by autism live every single day, while listening to others ignore, despise, pity, or mock them and even listening to others question why they need support from a communication partner and doubting if their words are their own. What kind of a faith loves in these conditions? What kind of a spirit believes? The kind that God shows Himself to.

The morning I met Suzanne for a consultation I felt such ease. The place was peaceful and there were pictures of angels and Jesus. Even though there were angels and demons in the Bible, protestants by and large ignored their existence. We were too intelligent, too knowledgeable, arrogant, or purists to incorporate the existence of anything other than the trinity into our theology. The exclusion of the spiritual realm was so heavy handed it felt wrong to talk about anything other than the trinity. I always felt the reason we did not ever talk much about angels or demons or the spiritual realm (even though these are mentioned repeatedly throughout the Bible and in Jesus' ministry) was because of the conflict between Catholics and Protestants, and also because psychology had become the modern-day doctor for our darkness. We didn't need to do any spiritual cleansing, we had drugs for that too. Who needs church if you have good health insurance? But in fairness to people searching for help, church had lost touch with individuals completely. They cared about the buildings, the leadership, and the institution, not the body of believers, and even less about one member who dared to be in pain. That *was* a pain.

As I walked through the center to meet with Suzanne, there was a room with stones displayed and a room for solace and meditation. What I had was a list of questions. 'Why were there stones here?' was first on my list, and 'What is the deal with angels?', but I forgot to ask once we started talking. Suzanne was wonderful and warm, professional, and intelligent. She began asking me questions to see where I stood in my understanding of energy. I said, "Before we get started my son wants to know if you believe that Jesus is the Son of God. Do you worship Jesus Christ?" She smiled. "Yes, I do. I have believed in Jesus and been saved since I was a child. I attend North Baptist. I have found that learning about energy in creation just expanded my faith and my love for Him." The more we talked the more I sensed she had a mature faith and a deep understanding of Scripture. She continued with her questions to see where I was in my awareness of energy and our human connection to it. I chuckled. "My son hears thoughts. I'm very aware that there is energy. You don't need to convince me. He has told me some really amazing things." I gave her examples. She was stunned, but excited to hear. I told her that my son had told me that he was concerned about me coming here because some people use energy for other purposes and sometimes those purposes aren't good, in fact, they can be bad. I felt an urgency to let her know where I stood, with Christ, with Christ alone. She looked at me in genuine respect and interest. "He's very astute," she said. "Energy is as much a part of God's creation as the physical world. And just like the rest of creation, people can use it for good or evil. All I am is a tuning fork, focusing the healing energy of God's love where He wants it to go. It has nothing to do with me. I am here to point to Him, but I always try to get a sense of where people are in their journey." I thought about the disciples and how their ministries to proclaim the Gospel focused on redeeming the spiritually dead and healing the physically sick or disabled through Christ's work on the cross. They always did both. Jesus taught them to do both. I thought about the spiritual gifts of the Holy Spirit and how healing was one of those gifts listed in the Bible that not only wasn't practiced or acknowledged, but that traditionalism in the church basically mocked as the hope of fools or practice of charlatans. I thought about the laying on of hands of the elders and the anointing of oil over the sick. I wondered if any elders today really believed it would work. The disciples did. They believed.

Suzanne asked why I had come, and I told her the burdens and weight on my heart that I just could not release. She explained that we have an etheric body as well as a physical body. She described how we have blood running through our bodies, just as we have energy running through us as well. The traumas we experience have an energetic impact on our spirit that often manifests physically, emotionally, and mentally. I blinked back tears knowing how much I must be carrying. She told me there would be homework and wanted to make sure I would commit to all the work of healing. I agreed. I was ready. The next week I got started.

When I arrived the next week the first thing she did was pray to our Savior, then she put her hands on my feet. I felt a rush of movement all the way through me starting at my feet, similar to but softer than what I had felt at Houston's baptism. Slowly she felt my etheric field and told me what she found. She seemed to understand parts of me that I didn't. It was as if she knew the anatomy of my spirit and where each painful memory had lodged itself. Lots of trauma at my root chakra and all kinds of imbalances everywhere, as well as a heart chakra that was reaching out, extended. Suddenly she asked if I had a traumatic experience with my mother. I choked as I tried to talk. I realized instantly that she was in tune not just to me but to my Heavenly Father who was telling her that. I told her the truth about my mother and my stepmother. She began working to balance energy from the traumas. She had already told me that healing happens in layers, just like the hurts that caused the wounds. I could feel things within me moving dramatically. When she would move her hands a sudden flood of tears poured out of my eyes even though I didn't feel the rush of emotion that would accompany that many tears. It seemed like she just pulled out whatever had been stopping them up. There was so much to unearth. It was like I was hidden under boulders in an avalanche. When she got to my crown chakra, our connection to Yahweh, to our Maker, the Living Word through whom I and all things were made, I started weeping. She hadn't said anything.

Finally she asked me to sit up and asked permission to place her hand on my head and pray for me. I agreed. When she did, I felt a force push through my entire body and out my spine that was as powerful as a firehose on full blast. Suddenly there were gobs of tears and gunk coming out of my nose as I started trembling uncontrollably with the force that propelled through me. When she took her hand off my head I turned and looked at her. "What was *that*?!" I asked in astonishment. She smiled, "That was the love of God." "Will you do it again?" I asked. And she did. It was even stronger the second time. I felt like my soul was being pressure washed with love. I didn't want it to stop and was slightly afraid I might lose control of all bodily functions since all my faucets seemed to be on full blast. When she stopped praying and removed her hand from my head, I was a tear-soaked mess and had to use all her tissue to clean myself up. But I was beaming. She looked at me astonished. "I wish you could see your face right now. You're glowing."

She gave me homework and told me to walk barefoot in the grass (grounding), sit against a tree, take Epsom salt baths (she explained how osmosis works with energy), drink lots of water, eat fruits and vegetables, meditate, and pray as often as I could. "Don't be surprised if more energy moves. We did a lot of work today." Then she added as an afterthought. "I think you should take Houston too, to walk in the grass. It would be good for him." I went home and walked straight up to Houston in the kitchen who had been melting bread and cheese one after another nonstop. He stopped and stared at me with a puzzled expression.

"What is it?" I asked him. "What do you see?"

"What did she do to you?" he spelled.

"Why do you say that?"

"My entire life you've been nothing but blue."

"I'm blue?"

"Yes. Your aura is blue. You are the bluest blue of the ocean and the bluest blue of the sky. Everything about you is blue. Your blue is so blue your blue has a blue halo."

For a moment I sat there in awe… again. There were just so many questions. "So can you see everyone's aura?"

"Yes, but you've always been the bluest blue."

"Well, what color am I now?"

"You're blue and purple!" He spelled purple with emphasis and added the explanation point.

"Huh…?" I didn't know what to make of that. I told him we were going to go to the park.

When we got there, I found a grassy area where we could walk. I took off my shoes and socks and then his. As soon as his foot touched the grass he started shouting, "NO! NO! Shoes! Shoes! Shoes!" Something was clearly going on. Then he started biting himself badly and making the seal barking noises when I got his hands out of his mouth. I grabbed both hands and started walking with him in the grass. I made sure we stepped in soft clover as much as possible. He kept making the sounds and violently trying to pull away to bite himself. People were staring at us. I just ignored them. We kept walking. After about fifteen minutes I felt the tension in his body ease. I let go of one of his hands. He kept walking. Finally we sat against a tree barefoot. I was still for the first time in a long time. I still had a love affair with trees. I remembered how I used to sit in trees for hours and read books, how The Giving Tree had spoken to me on such a spiritual level as a child, how trees somehow made me feel covered and safe. Now I was learning that they actually produce an electromagnetic field and vibrational frequency. Maybe that's why they felt so good to play near, I pondered.

After a while Houston spelled to me, "My most awesome mom. I finally feel poking in my feet. I've never felt my feet like this before." "What do you mean poking? Do you mean the grass is poking you?" "No, the poking is on the inside." I contemplated what might be happening inside him, inside me. Maybe the nerve endings were being stimulated and waking up, maybe the energy inside him was moving. But it was incredible that walking in the grass could be so powerful in a body that he couldn't control. I looked at the clover in the spring grass and asked Houston, "Do you know what four leaf clovers mean?" He spelled, "Some say good luck. My thought is they are part of God's majesty… (and later to his spelling coach) I wonder if some of that Irish drinking made three leaf clovers look like four leaf clovers more times than not." I smiled at his wisdom. As I sat against the tree, I felt something rise up through my chest and force itself out of my mouth. It was the same kind of uncontrollable force that you feel when bearing down in labor or a purging that will not be stopped. Houston and I both looked at each other.

That week it happened again when I took an Epsom salt bath, several times when I was driving, and I instinctively rolled down the windows. I started having diarrhea, strange tastes in my mouth, and a migraine like I had never had before. It happened again when I was meditating. It was a huge wave of force that seemed to have left me, and it left me wobbly, dizzy, stunned. At that exact moment as I sat there unsure of what had just happened, Houston came bursting into the room like he was there to rescue me. He looked first at me but then instantly he turned as if he was startled by something else in the room. He stared with his mouth open at exactly the spot where I felt the force that left my body was hovering. He kept staring at this space, that to me looked like nothing but air, mouth still open. Finally, he came over to me, "Oh my word. All the good love pushed out all the gross energy." If you had felt what I felt, you would understand that what he said was spot on. Whatever trauma or burden or bad energy I had been carrying was exactly that - gross energy.

During the week at one point Houston spelled out to me, "Keep healing. I can see you healing." I asked what he saw, and he spelled, "There is more purple." So I asked where he saw the purple, "On your hips." I was astounded. That was where she had focused so much work, on my root chakra which is at my hips. So I kept healing. Even after just one week I found when I prayed, I had peace.

The following week I went to see her again. I told her about Houston's first reaction to walking barefoot and then how it had changed. She didn't know for certain but definitely thought it could be energetic as well as nerve related. I told her about everything that had happened to me, and she nodded explaining, "It's the love of God. It vibrates at such a high energy that the negative energy literally can't stay in the same place because the frequency of your spirit has changed." She asked me to think of my thoughts and emotions in terms of energy levels. How much energy did I feel when I was happy or joyful? What about when I was grieved, depressed, wounded, or when I felt shame, envy, or sorrow? As I reflected, I realized she was right. One set of emotions not only changed how much energy I felt or exerted, but it also directly affected what kind of thoughts I had. It was all related. The more I focused on receiving and giving the love of God, the more I would experience a shift towards a lightness and brightness that rooted into my being. *Do not be conformed to this world, but be transformed by the renewal of your mind, that by testing you may discern what is the will of God, what is good and acceptable and perfect.*[110] I told her I needed more of His love. Lots more. I needed to know how to receive it in bucket loads like I was standing under a waterfall of His love. Other than Houston, there was no one in my life pouring love into me. I had been giving out so much for so long. My weary spirit needed the peace of His presence, the power of His love. I needed to want *not,* not because I no longer had desires, but because they had been fulfilled, because I walked with Him in green pastures and rested by quiet waters, because He had restored my soul, anointed my head with oil, guided me in paths of righteousness and delivered me from evil. I needed to feel the safety of His refuge under His wings. Too long had I been left wandering alone. There were more shifts in my heart that day and the energy moved again. When she got to my crown chakra, she didn't say anything, but I started crying again. Big, giant tears.

Because darkness and evil had been such a constant in my life, I had grown weary of trying to see good, and truthfully, weary of trying to see God in all the pain. Darkness had been telling me for years to be angry, anxious, bitter, hurt, doubtful, and lost. But mostly the darkness whispered constantly, "Give up. There is no hope. God doesn't love you. Look at what He's done to you and what He generously gives to others. He doesn't hear you. Give up. Walk away." It required a massive amount of discipline to not look at the obstacles anymore but instead allow His love to heal my broken heart and transform my thoughts.

My homework was to continue with my other practices and get a diffuser and some specific oils. She told me the oils were extremely important for changing the energy of a home. She was highly educated on the science behind the oils and energy, and I found it fascinating. She explained that plants, like other living things that God created, have defense mechanisms. What we think of as fragrance is actually a set of chemical components with a variety of attributes that affect the chemical and physical world. Some of these oils are extremely potent because of their chemical composition. She explained that the oils have a vibration that can be measured in Hz. Different oils have a different Hz and by placing those oils on specific energy points on our body we can assist the energy flow and balance of energy within our bodies. Before I left, she told me she had a gift for me. She pulled out a small fabric bag. Inside were three polished stones. She told me the names of each one - carnelian, spiderweb jasper, and hematite. She said she had cleared them in a special way and prayed a passage out of Acts over the stones. I just looked at her like she was handing me a joint at a party.

[110] Romans 12:2

Clearly, I was supposed to be grateful, but I didn't know how to use one. "What am I supposed to do with them?" I asked. "Anything you want," she answered. "You can read about their properties and then decide what you want to do with them. You can put them by your bed. You can keep them in your purse. Whatever feels right to you." My thoughts at that moment… 'This is weird.'

When I got home Houston came up to me with the board. "What did she do to you this time?" "Why? What color am I now?" I laughed at my own joke. But he wasn't joking.

"Now you're every color. You're like a rainbow."

A few hours later I took an Epsom salt bath. I took the stones out and set them beside me while I researched them on my phone. As I sat soaking and reading, my bedroom and then my bathroom door burst open. Houston started pointing and demanding loudly, "STONES! STONES! STONES!"

"Houston, go. I'm taking a bath."

"STONES! STONES!" He pointed and looked at me with urgency, with fire in his eyes. He was not going to leave. I picked them up and handed them to him. He ran out of the room.

I sat there in my tub, completely confused by what had just taken place. What on earth did he want the stones for?

I got out and dried off. I took my time getting ready trying to focus on praying and being mindful. Then I walked down the hall to Houston's room. He was lying on the edge of his bed and the three stones were lined up on the edge of the desk next to his bed, inches away from him.

"Houston, what's this about?" as I motioned to the stones. "Why did you want the stones so badly?"

He sat up and looked at me earnestly as if he knew this was his moment. He swung his legs over to make room for me to sit down.

"The stones are alive."

"What are you talking about? They're stones."

"When you're autistic you're a magnet for all energy - good and bad. These stones have good energy. I need it."

'Energy?' I thought to myself. 'From stones?' I thought more and then asked him, "Ok. But why do you need good energy? Is there bad energy here?"

He pointed with forcefulness. "YES. Dad's jerseys."

I stood up with my mind spinning wildly. I knew what had just come out of me was from being beaten down by darkness which literally op*pressed* itself into me. How much gross energy could the clothes that darkness wore carry? In great ignorance I had hung three of his jerseys in my boys' room thinking it made them proud of their dad's collegiate accomplishments. Instead, I had been decorating their room with darkness. I told Benjamin what had just happened. Something had changed in Benjamin through all of this, and as much as Paul was running from me, Benjamin was running to me and to his big brother whom he now considered his best friend. Benjamin took every picture of his father out of the house that he could find, and I gathered up all the jerseys. I took Houston with me to the post office so he could address the label himself. He nodded with conviction when he handed it to the post office worker.

Feeling quite good about the changes when we got home, I asked him, "So is the house full of good energy now?"

Without hesitating he spelled, "No."

I was crestfallen. "Why? What else is there?"

As I watched him spell my stomach clenched. "Your bed. It's sick."

My bed. My bed… The place I laid wallowing in the heaviness of grief for hours every night, the place where he had done unspeakable things to me. The place where he had laid for years. I was literally sleeping in and wrapping myself in the remnants of his darkness instead of the remnants of life and love. Right then I decided it was time for change. I was getting rid of it all, the whole room. I was starting over.

The next day was Sunday. I was sitting on my bed meditating and Houston was lying down beside me which didn't happen too often, probably because of the sick bed. While I was meditating my hands began to vibrate intensely and at the same time Houston jumped up and ran out of the room. I felt the same overwhelming flood and rush of goodness and power come over me like it was pouring straight into the top of my head. It lasted at least ten seconds. For ten seconds I was flooded with some unseen power that was so high and full of power that I couldn't move. When it subsided and my hands stopped vibrating, I wanted to cry with joy. That was the emotion. It was joy. I got off the bed and went downstairs. Houston was waiting for me with the board.

He spelled, "How did you do that?"

"What did I do?"

"The angels told me to leave now because God was coming to love you. Now you're the most beautiful I've ever seen you. You're gold."

"I'm gold?" Tears came to my eyes and rolled softly down my cheeks. I smiled. I laughed. I hugged my son. My God had come to pour His love into me. My God had come to pour Himself into me. My God had found me.

I got rid of everything. I didn't even care how much I got for the furniture. In the process of cleaning out one of the drawers I found a necklace that had larger irregular clear beads that had broken. I put the broken necklace and the beads in a Target bag and left it on the kitchen counter. My thought was I would give it to Morgan to see if she could help me fix it. Houston kept trying to take the bag. I kept taking it back and telling him to leave the bag where it was. Without realizing it, I had missed one of the beads when I put them in the Target bag. That afternoon when I went into his room, I found one of the clear beads next to my stones that he had claimed for himself. I said, "Houston, what are you doing with that bead? How do you even know if it's a stone? It could be glass or plastic." He sat straight up and reached for the board. "Not only is it a stone, it's the bossy stone." He pointed with force, emphatically. 'The bossy stone? What is that supposed to mean?' So I looked up clear stones and found the one that seemed to match the beads. Clear quartz - one of the more significant attributes of clear quartz is that it magnified the power and energy of the stones around it. 'Oh my word… the bossy stone.' What impressed me so much was that his description was not something you would find in any kind of reading material. It was the description of someone who was witnessing and experiencing the power of its properties. And he had been so sensitive to the energy that he had found the one stone all by itself. I took all the other beads from the Target bag and placed them around the other stones. He laid close to them as if he was soaking them up. Then I recalled when he had been little and was constantly filling his hands with stones. His little body had been trying to get what it needed even at that age.

I had purchased some palo santo which is a wood used for clearing and I burned it in every room of the house, especially mine and Houston's. The garage was difficult. Houston told me all the boys who came over brought bad energy. He told me, "Boys' thoughts are awful. They only think of how to do things to girls." For a half second, I chuckled. At least I had confirmation of what I had always suspected. I knew sadly that didn't change with age. I recalled Anne Frank's sad realization, "Boys will be boys…" I knew only God could change men's hearts, but it broke my heart that they saw no need to treat women with respect, no need to be good and honorable in all things… Where had all the good men gone? I focused on the environments I could change. I bought a mattress from Mattress King and had it delivered to my empty bedroom. I called Houston into my room and held up the board. I asked him, "How is my room now?"

It was empty. There was nothing except a queen size mattress on the floor. No dresser, no tables, no bedding. The only thing I had purchased besides the bed was an oil diffuser and some oils for us both that Suzanne had recommended. I had put the oil and water inside and turned it on. His eyes were smiling. He spelled, "It's beautiful. There is so much good energy." The oils were from a family company where everything was organic and ethically sourced. Some of the bottles had Scripture on the labels and they were all sourced organically. I felt like the word and power of God had been infused into the oil. That night we both slept the whole night. Quietly, peacefully, in His arms. It's hard not to think that energy had something to do with it after over twenty years of middle of the night stims and terrors.

When Houston had told me the stones were alive, I emailed Suzanne to tell her. She, very matter of factly, wrote back and told me that Houston was right. The stones are alive. They are as alive as the earth is. Stones are just pieces of earth, and like the earth, they have vibrational frequencies. It was like I had been walking around God's creation oblivious to most of it. I had limited myself to what I could see even though I knew and believed in the unseen. When I realized the unseen was actually interacting with the seen on a physical level that could be measured, I have to say I was in more awe than I have ever been at God's creation.

I told Sarah about the stones. She was in just as much shock as I was, but then she texted back. "He said the stones would cry out if we didn't praise Him." I looked up the verse to read it with totally new eyes and ears. *As he was drawing near—already on the way down the Mount of Olives—the whole multitude of his disciples began to rejoice and praise God with a loud voice for all the mighty works that they had seen, saying, "Blessed is the King who comes in the name of the Lord! Peace in heaven and glory in the highest!" And some of the Pharisees in the crowd said to him, "Teacher, rebuke your disciples." He answered, "I tell you, if these were silent, the very stones would cry out."* [111] Oh my word… I had always thought that passage was figurative, but it was literal. Then she sent me the passage of the description of the New Jerusalem. *The wall was built of jasper, while the city was pure gold, like clear glass. The foundations of the wall of the city were adorned with every kind of jewel. The first was jasper, the second sapphire, the third agate, the fourth emerald, the fifth onyx, the sixth carnelian, the seventh chrysolite, the eighth beryl, the ninth topaz, the tenth chrysoprase, the eleventh jacinth, the twelfth amethyst. And the twelve gates were twelve pearls, each of the gates made of a single pearl, and the street of the city was pure gold, like transparent glass.* [112] From that moment I began to see the stones ALL over Scripture. In fact there are 1704 references to precious gemstones in the Bible. I read about the first high priest, Aaron (the brother of Moses) and the breastplate of judgment he wore that had a stone for each Hebrew tribe and two additional stones for communicating with God in the Holy of Holies. [113] I discovered this breastplate of gemstones is where birthstones have their origin.

How had I missed this all these years? How had I not referenced the twelve stones of the breastplate with the twelve tribes of Israel and the twelve stones of the New Jerusalem with the twelve apostles? And without even meaning to, I started pouring over His word again. He was so gentle and artful getting me back into His word that I had to laugh. It was almost as if He had set out breadcrumbs for me to follow Him home. Even all these years later, His word could be fresh, wonderful, and new. And then I remembered what He said, *"Behold, I am making all things new."* Also he said, *"Write this down, for these words are trustworthy and true."* [114] And me too, and Houston, He was making us new too.

There was a gem and mineral wholesale exhibit and show that month at the Cobb County Civic Center. I took Houston. He was overwhelmed. He spelled to me that there was so much energy in that room. There

---

[111] Luke 19:37-40
[112] Revelation 21:18-21
[113] Exodus 28:15-30
[114] Revelation 21:5

were so many stones I knew nothing about, and it was hard to know where to begin. There were certain stones he gravitated to more and certain stones I wanted. The magnetic hematite in particular he insisted on getting. Then I found a table with black tourmaline. Both of us picked up a piece. For the first time, as I held it in my hand, I felt it. It was strong, there was a warmth coming off the stone. I looked at him astonished. He smiled and nodded. The woman behind the table looked at us and asked, "It's strong. I'm curious what you're going to do with that." Houston spelled that he needed the protection. She smiled, "That's the right stone, then." I marveled that there was a world of people who knew these things. We walked to another table, and I heard a squeal of excitement and delight as a young woman was dragging her boyfriend with her and looking straight at me with a giant smile on her face. She ran up to us. "You use the letter boards! Oh my goodness! I can't believe I'm seeing someone use the boards! I'm just learning how to be a communication partner. This is amazing!" I introduced her to Houston, and she couldn't contain her excitement. She asked if she could try to communicate with him. I was nervous Houston would not be able to spell for someone new in a giant room with people everywhere, thousands of random thoughts and high levels of electromagnetic energy. But in that moment, with someone who knew the correct principles and best practices he amazed me. She asked him what stone he had purchased and with perfect precision and timing he spelled, "black tourmaline." We were all ecstatic. Houston smiled proudly and gave me one of his very light touch hugs. We won a door prize and Houston was able to get even more stones. He wouldn't let them go. The whole way home he kept them on his lap and smiled, not a grin, but one of his gorgeous smiles that makes me smile because they are so contagious. At home he set them next to the other stones. He spelled to me, "Binary. The stones are binary. They protect and they give off good energy. How stones work is they pattern their force to what they were made to do with our prayers." I began anointing him with oil each night before bed and praying with deep conviction about his greatest longings. Houston had dreams and goals. He told me, "Your superpower is loving people. Mine is believing."

Around this same time we met up with a bunch of the teenagers from the old pizzeria who were now almost out of college. Houston was able to communicate with them for the first time. They huddled around him and asked him questions while he answered and explained what his life had been like and how much he had wanted to be their friend. In one night, he became the coolest guy they had ever known. They wanted his opinion about everything. And I mean everything. I mentioned that he could see auras and they all wanted to know what theirs was. He spelled to me, "Seeing auras is the least favorite of my abilities." They told him that it was so cool. He began to feel his uniqueness and was treasured for it. They didn't care that he flapped his hands or made strange noises or repeated things. They saw him behind the stims. It changed him on a deep level to be accepted by neurotypical peers that he had always wanted to be included by. He drank beer with them and in his heart, he thanked God for the incredible miracles he was living. The miracle of acceptance, the miracle of friends who treated him like he was smart, the miracle of beer with friends. Life would no longer be lived alone and in silence. That night he spelled to me that it was one of the best days of his life.

Houston was very particular about what I should do with the stones. After I cleared them, he told me I was supposed to talk to them. I felt very weird, but I did what he told me. Another time I researched each one and read out loud what each of the stones was supposed to do. Houston looked at me strangely. "What are you doing?" he spelled. "I'm telling them what they are supposed to do like you said," I answered. He got a big grin on his face. "Silly mom. The stones are wired. They know what they are supposed to do. You are just supposed to tell them what you want. The word of God and His praises power them." Apparently, it was the equivalent of me telling trees to grow leaves and birds to fly. I was clueless. The more I studied, the more I realized they were like computer chips that would run the program written. Then I remembered Houston had said stones are binary, just like the language of computers. That's when it dawned on me, Silicon Valley, they already know and use the electromagnetic qualities and frequencies of stones.

I decided to put the stones in the earth to charge by absorbing the electromagnetic energy in the ground, just like we were doing for our bodies. I was reading all I could about energy and the earth. The next day I went out to dig them up before I planted flowers. My sweet neighbor and her daughter were looking at the flowers, so I gave her some and helped her plant them. Finally, as it got darker, I said, "Look, I don't want you to think I'm weird, but I need to dig up my stones while we talk." Without missing a beat she said nonchalantly, "Oh, are you charging them?" I was shocked that she knew about stones. I told her about Houston, the boards, and the stones. She was fascinated. Then she asked if I had ever gone to a myofunctional therapist. "A *what*?" I asked. She told me there was an incredible one just a few miles from us. So I called and took Houston.

The myofunctional therapist was an older woman who was so dedicated to her patients and to battling apraxia and for the voiceless that she couldn't/wouldn't stop working. Apraxia - there was that word again. I still wondered why NONE of his teachers or speech therapists had ever mentioned these specialists or even these different neurological conditions. As a matter of fact, why hadn't the neurologist? The myofunctional therapist evaluated and tested Houston. She explained that over seven body and neurological systems had to work together cohesively in order to speak. Seven. Seven miracles the rest of the world took for granted every time they spoke. Seven miracles my son had prayed for relentlessly over twenty years. Almost immediately she told me he had a reverse swallow. Again, "A *what*?" She explained the developmental process and how the tongue and swallow were actually related to the control of the entire body. In infancy the tongue is down for easy swallowing of milk. As solid food is introduced the tongue rises and presses against the roof of the mouth which is where it sits most of the time in a constant isometric state, sending information to brain. She continued. The tongue was one of the few muscles that was connected to the right and left hemispheres of the brain contributing to the ability to incorporate movement on both sides of the body as well as coordination and strength. She demonstrated. She had me stand with my arm held out at my side and my mouth closed. She pushed down and told me to resist. I did. My arm stayed extended. Then she told me to open my mouth wide with my tongue down. She pressed on my arm, and I couldn't resist at all. My arm fell immediately. My mouth was still open in shock. The neurological and motor impact of the tongue was extraordinary.

As she continued to talk, I recalled the Scripture in James about taming the tongue and how horses were controlled by a bit and ships by a rudder. Certainly James had been referencing the power of the tongue to wage war and destroy others by words, but I marveled that it was true both physically and relationally. There was a literal component to those words that I had never known. *Likewise, the tongue is a small part of the body, but it makes great boasts. Consider what a great forest is set on fire by a small spark.*[115] 'God,' I whispered in my heart, 'You're amazing. I had no idea. Words… they are power. More than I ever knew. And oh how much your enemies do not want these who have been your witnesses to have any words at all.' My spirit stirred within me, and I seriously began to wonder, 'Is this spiritual? Is this why so many have tried to silence and discredit these incredible people? Because they've seen the unseen? Otherwise why would they care?'

After a few visits she recommended we no longer use the gun range headphones that Houston wore to limit all the painful sounds he hears and get fitted for musician earplugs. We contacted an audiologist and made an appointment. I explained to the audiologist that Houston had hyperacusis and he could hear Wi-Fi signals and other frequencies. Houston spelled to her how painful everything is to hear. "Note I don't WANT to hear everything." She didn't think he had hyperacusis. He flinched when she did one audiology test. However, when she put him in a soundproof booth and spoke to him with the decibels set to a higher

[115] James 3:5

range, he was perfectly fine. He didn't put his hands over his ears and flinch in pain. After the testing she gave her diagnosis. He might have sensitivity to frequencies that would indicate hyperacusis but much of the issue was a neurological condition called misophonia which triggers an emotional or physiological reaction to certain sounds. The reactions can be anger, anxiety, panic and can also trigger the fight/flight/freeze response. But in Houston's mind, the list of sounds that triggered him encompassed almost all of his environment.

In the human mind hearing and movement are intricately linked. The ear, through the cochlea and vestibule, actually transform stimuli from the environment, acoustic frequencies, into mechanical energy, which is transducted into hydraulic energy, and then electrical energy. The electrical energy in turn becomes motor processing and movement. This is why hearing music often makes you start swaying and dancing, or empowers you to greater physical exertion, because the frequencies literally become energy. The complexity of auditory processing of high and low frequencies between the vestibule and cochlea attributes to the production of an enormous amount of the energy our body uses for multiple motor and cognitive processing. High frequencies contribute to speech, language, retention, executive functioning, and processing speeds. Low frequencies contribute to attention, behavior, emotions, balance, and coordination. But what if an ear and brain are taking in too many frequencies? What happens to the conversion of all these frequencies to energy? What if that is only one of many senses that are also taking in too much? What if another sense isn't taking in enough? What then?

The enormous challenge of these combined comorbidities in the human mind cannot be overstated. When anxiety is triggered, the reptilian brain essentially takes over and cuts off access to the frontal lobe where intentional, purposeful motor is processed. We experience anxiety as immobility, stage fright, not knowing what to say or forgetting what to do. The reason is simple, to survive, the brain is focused only on motor functions that will protect as opposed to more complex, rational, and planned functions. In addition to this ever-present issue of painful anxiety triggered by almost every single sound was Houston's inability to feel where he was in space. This is what is referred to as vestibular function and is actually the most primal sense we have. Vestibular function, proprioceptive function, hearing, and vision are intricately linked. We sense where our bodies are before we process other sensory information. The nerve fibers in our skin, the equilibrium in our ears, and visual receptors send all of this information to our vestibular organ which tells the rest of our body where we are in space and then sends this information to the proprioceptive systems in our muscles and joints. This is the most fundamental sensory/motor loop. Think of a newborn baby when they are lifted, or a blanket is taken off of them, their limbs instinctively react as if they are in a free fall. Terror takes over their bodies. This is the vestibular system acclimating to an environment outside of the womb and why swaddling newborns calms them. As the brain develops and processes correct sensory information, newborns begin to respond to the same sensory input with appropriate proprioceptive movement. In individuals like my son, a neurological event occurs that creates a sensory processing disorder. From that point normal sensory information in their environment is processed as nociceptive or noxious stimuli. The result of this is primal - not feeling their position in space, which in turn triggers massive anxiety (think falling off a building kind of fright and panic), functional - no input or wrong input to the nerve fibers, muscles and joints (when you receive wrong or no information the body cannot initiate movement and you experience pain in very different ways), and then emotional (people treat you like you are incompetent or a behavior problem because of a body you cannot control and you have no method to effectively communicate your experience). The type of sensory information their brain processes is what would be considered nociceptive, where they have high tolerances to pain including temperature or other harmful sensory input, but extreme sensitivity to other types of sensory input, like how sound could be excruciating and how the water in a shower felt like thousands of hot needles poking my son's scalp. Houston's life was a constant barrage of unseen physical, neurological, and emotional agony. Yet all the experts would do was create a behavior plan and encourage drugs. You don't have a problem. You are a problem.

Without the neurotypical sensory/motor loop that uses appropriate input and output, the autistic brain finds other ways to loop. Often these loops become addictive and take over their impulse control. Because of their inability to control their body, which is a neurological sensory/motor dis-integration, they are denied basic human rights, treated like a toddler, isolated from society, and trapped in their own body with no voice, no way to even explain what the problem is. The only escape is their fantastic senses that lead them to Never-Never Land, creating a sensory high that they use to distract themselves from the pain of their lives.

Combined with Houston's visual impairments, his hearing was having an acute effect on the rest of his body. The overload and underload of sensory information his brain was trying to process and the lack of integration of sensory and motor processing resulted in his vestibular and proprioceptive systems not functioning even remotely how they are designed to function, which affected his ability to control the rest of his body. This was in addition to the constant state of anxiety and addiction he lived in. The audiologist told me that scientists were beginning to theorize that in autistics with a wide range of comorbidities and lack of control, that there was no divide between the subconscious and the conscious, that they were aware of everything. I just shook my head, feeling deep remorse for not knowing and being unaware of how to help him for so many years. I was overcome with compassion at the pain he had endured without being able to tell me all these years. It amazed me that despite all his pain he still loved so completely. His spirit was completely gentle, and his heart was kind even though he had been denied everything. He told me some of his friends struggled with anger, anger at God, anger at everyone. Then he added, "I knew the best thing was for me to be loving so I would be treated well." And he was. The only person he ever attacked was himself. Who was this giant of man? How could I have ever been so blessed as to be his mother? One step at a time we would find the answers we needed to give him the life he deserved.

The next time I met with Suzanne she was amazed by how much lighter and happier I looked. I knew I was changing. There was still so much to heal but my heart was ready. That day we dealt with the loss of my granddaughter, Elyse, and how I had lost my daughter too. At one point I felt like someone had reached into my heart and was pulling it out of my chest. I felt like there was a knotted mess that someone was tugging at violently and my body was trying to hold on to it. Tears began to tumble down the sides of my face. Then a wailing noise from somewhere deep within me poured out of me. I tried to choke it back, but it came out anyway. I was deeply embarrassed by its ferocity, by its honesty. I felt exposed and free at the same time. It didn't ask my permission to come out and I seemed incapable of stopping it. It was like my heart was finally unburdened to mourn, to speak, to feel the horrific injustices done to my child and grandchild, and even to me. My heart refused to be quiet. Finally Suzanne placed her hands near my crown chakra. Like someone had turned the spigot on, my eyes started flowing again. Suzanne thoughtfully remarked, "Do you realize every time we get near your crown chakra you cry?" She was right. I thought about it and then I told her, "I've just felt abandoned by Him for so long. I thought 'I loved Him, but He didn't love me.' I just love Him so much and it hurt to never have my prayers answered and to keep being attacked." I have no idea why but after I spoke those words, I didn't feel that way anymore. It was the strangest thing. It simply didn't make sense to keep thinking that way. I stopped. I started believing God loved me more than I could imagine.

50

Glory Beckons

The earth is the Lord's and the fullness thereof, the world and those who dwell therein,
for he has founded it upon the seas and established it upon the rivers.
Who shall ascend the hill of the Lord? And who shall stand in his holy place?
He who has clean hands and a pure heart,
who does not lift up his soul to what is false and does not swear deceitfully.
He will receive blessing from the Lord and righteousness from the God of his salvation.
— Psalm 24:1-5

With the growing joy inside me and the tiny sprouts of hope in my spirit, I told Suzanne I knew I needed more healing, but I had to get Houston in to see her. Houston had told me, "Yes I'm excited to meet her." So that was the next step. Houston was ready to meet the person who had helped unburden the depth of sorrow from his mom. When I brought him in for his first appointment just to meet her, I had to laugh. Houston's first question to her was as straightforward as you could get. "Do you love Jesus?" He was leaning forward in his chair, trying with all his might to hold direct eye contact with her. She smiled at him. "Yes. I do," she told him, with confidence and certainty in her voice. He leaned back in his chair. She had passed the test. He was ready.

As she asked questions Houston would spell out answers. Then out of nowhere he spelled, "Are we keeping you from something?" I looked at her confused. "Are we keeping you from something? That's what he just spelled." Her jaw dropped. "Oh. Oh my word. You said he could hear thoughts. But oh wow. I'm so sorry. I had someone call right before you got here about a scheduling issue, and I was trying to not think about it and be present. But my mind kept wandering to how I needed to call her and how was I going to fix it. I'm so sorry. Do you mind if I make a call?" I said, "Not at all." I looked at Houston and laughed. "You are something else. I guess she believes you now." When she got back, she told us that she had believed me but to actually experience it was something else entirely. She was deeply moved. I told her he could see her aura and she asked what it was. Houston spelled, "Each good healer is turquoise. You are not just turquoise. You are the most marvelous turquoise." She told us how interesting that was because she loved turquoise and held out her necklace. I told her that other people had said the same thing when Houston had told them their aura. We discussed the best way to do the sessions since Houston couldn't communicate without a partner. She gave us a set of questions to answer that would help her in the sessions. It turned out that these questions were the next step in my journey of discovering the mysteries my son was witness to.

Suzanne scanned his energetic field and gave me an extensive list of questions for Houston to answer covering many emotional topics. She asked about feelings of security or insecurity in his childhood. Houston spelled, "My first memory of feeling unsafe is when my dad forced me to stuff apples in my mouth. My too wired mind, not my body, makes me feel unsafe in many situations. Hearing people's thoughts that are not nice to me makes me anxious. In many places where it's too loud I'm anxious. Many times I get anxious, radically so, for unknown reasons. Our home still has some bad energy in it." "Where?" I asked. "The garage. Not all that is us. It's bad guys who come over. The worst is in the boys' thoughts. Most only think bad things, very bad things." There were questions asking him to describe what made him feel safe. "Still think of my mom when I want to feel safe. Steering so many people to good is the real miracle of her life. That is why she, not me, is the hero."

When he was asked about trauma, he was most focused on his sister. "Reagan. It started when she was little. You heard what happened." He told her about the things that made him feel ashamed. "I'm so many types of sorry for losing control of my body so many different times. Errors in every part of my life still every day stay with me and tell me I'm worthless. I'm so sorry to my heart broken mom for what she gave up. She, most definitely, took the worst of it." She asked him what he wanted to change and heal. He spelled, "The storing of my emotions needs to stop. One emotion I have often is total yearning for a family of my own. This yearning consumes me the most. Testing over and over again if I still have faith is my longest struggle. Telling you this makes me so happy. My other emotion is my low self-esteem. To others I am embarrassing. Not only does that hurt, it steals my confidence. I'm actually intelligent, different. Healing this raw pain is too much for me. Sometimes real mean thoughts towards others happen in my mind when I see others who have everything."

He also described his feelings about how much I was expecting of him and how difficult it was on him because he depended on me so much and couldn't get away from all my thoughts and feelings. "End our coping together. Every day I'm dealing with your emotions and mine. Not only that but in total honesty, it is hard to meet all your expectations, like so much therapy. Is that too much to ask? Time to tell you the big thing. Will you be mad if I move out some day? Don't hate that. Remember that all my time is with you. I'm so tired of having to go everywhere with you. OK you can stop crying now. I'm done." He looked so relieved when he shared all of these thoughts as he had truly unburdened his heart.

I was crying. "Houston, I want that for you. I know we spend too much time together. But you're out of school and there is no one else willing to do the job. Morgan does what she can. I know you want your brothers to help but they are really being resistant to learning the boards. I want you to live on your own too, but it's not going to happen if we don't work hard. The therapies are rewiring your brain and giving you back control. Even though it's really slow, we have to keep them up. I will try to go easier and not do so many." Very sweetly he reached over to kiss me. "What was that for?" "To make very sure you know I love you," he spelled.

Another time he asked me curiously, "Do God lovers all walk in faith?"

I responded, "I think they all do. But just like me they have good days and bad days. Sometimes the bad days last a long time. Some have more faith than others. It must've broken your heart when I spent all those years in doubt thinking God didn't love me."

"Watching you be so hurt almost utterly wounded my heart. God told me He takes His most wonderful, favored through the worst pain to lay a formula of strength they cannot have on their own. It had to happen to work the really wonderful plan that Jesus has worked."

There were also times when he was frustrated. At one point I asked him an important question. "If you could be a normal neurotypical young adult, but you weren't able to see all that you've seen in heaven and the metaphysical world, which would you choose, to be autistic or to be like everyone else?" He looked at me and then back at the board. "I would choose to be autistic. What I have seen about God and heaven is beyond compare." With wonder I let the weight of his words sink into my heart. "Then you're blessed," I said. "I am too. I get to be your mom. I get to watch this miracle right by your side." Everything I thought for over two decades had shifted. Autism was our blessing, not our curse. What I had called a monster had made my son a prophet. But I wasn't naive. The pain the blessing had caused was more than most will ever understand or experience. The fullness of Houston's life and story were just beginning. I knew how high that mountain was, and we were still looking up from a dark valley. All I could think was how wasteful and dark all my doubt had been. Houston had pointed to where my focus needed to be - up, heavenward, Him.

His time with Suzanne was deeply special on so many levels. He could feel the energy moving dramatically. I sat on the floor totally still and even I could feel the energy moving in the room and rush through me just being near it. On one occasion he sat up and wanted to spell with me immediately. We had tried to have his session with me waiting in another room, but he wanted me with him. Outside the window there were men cutting down a tree. Houston spelled how he kept hearing the tree crying. It was upsetting to him. With immense compassion and intuition she was able to work with his remarkable perception to balance his energy and release some of the trauma he had stored for decades. She showed me how to use oils to calm his anxiety, drumbeats to move his energy, and tapping to stimulate his parasympathetic nervous system.

When I got home, I asked Houston so many things. First, he spelled, "Stored in my memories so in the future I will never forget. She is marvelous." I also asked him to share more with me about what he sees and hears. I wanted to know about the trees. And I wanted to know about heaven. He spelled, "Trees pour their divine love to us." Thoughts of my favorite trees as a child and the story of <u>The Giving Tree</u> filled my mind... all those loving trees. "Trees pray Jesus comes back." I recalled the scriptures...

> *For you shall go out with joy, and be led out with peace; The mountains and the hills shall break forth into singing before you, and all the trees of the field shall clap their hands. ---* [116]

> *Let the heavens be glad, and let the earth rejoice: let the sea roar, and all that fills it: let the field exult, and everything in it! Then shall all the trees of the forest sing for joy before the LORD, for he comes, for he comes to judge the earth. He will judge the world in righteousness, and the peoples in his faithfulness.* [117]

> *For I consider that the sufferings of this present time are not worth comparing with the glory that is to be revealed to us. For the creation waits with eager longing for the revealing of the sons of God. For the creation was subjected to futility, not willingly, but because of him who subjected it, in hope that the creation itself will be set free from its bondage to corruption and obtain the freedom of the glory of the children of God. For we know that the whole creation has been groaning together in the pains of childbirth until now. And not only the creation, but we ourselves, who have the firstfruits of the Spirit, groan inwardly as we wait eagerly for adoption as sons, the redemption of our bodies. For in this hope we were saved. Now hope that is seen is not hope. For who hopes for what he sees? But if we hope for what we do not see, we w6ait for it with patience.* [118]

'Oh my word,' I thought, 'The trees... they long for Jesus too.'

[116] Isaiah 55:12
[117] Psalm 96:11-13
[118] Romans 8:18-25

I think that I shall never see
A poem lovely as a tree.
A tree whose hungry mouth is prest
Against the earth's sweet flowing breast;
A tree that looks at God all day,
And lifts her leafy arms to pray;
A tree that may in Summer wear
A nest of robins in her hair;
Upon whose bosom snow has lain;
Who intimately lives with rain.
Poems are made by fools like me,
But only God can make a tree.[119]

It was all beyond comprehension... I started researching. I discovered that biologists, naturalists, foresters, and ecologists had uncovered a great amount of evidence that trees not only talk but are part of a common network and community that share resources and protect each other. They found even plants responded to sound and processed sensory input. Suzanne Simard has written on this topic extensively in The Language of Trees and given TEDTalks, as well as other biologists, most notably David George Haskell in The Song of Trees. The more I learned about matter and energy confirmed that everything is energy vibrating at different frequencies across an electromagnetic spectrum, most of which is not perceived by our senses. But it's still there, moving, working, connecting all around us. Mass is just energy compacted in a way that our senses perceive it. "Mass and energy are both different manifestations of the same thing – a somewhat unfamiliar conception for the average mind."[120] Yet some of the slowest oscillating manifestations of energy, humans, insist that if they can't see it and measure it, it must not exist. "I can calculate the motion of heavenly bodies but not the madness of people."[121]

As I began to experience the movement of energy within me, witness it in Houston and others, and feel the healing power of God's creation, I was reminded of a quote from a victim and witness of the Rwandan genocide.

> "We had a lot of trouble with western mental health workers who came here immediately after the genocide, and we had to ask them to leave. They came and their practice did not involve being outside in the sun where you begin to feel better. There was no music or drumming to get your blood flowing again. There was no sense that everyone had taken the day off so that the entire community could come together to try to lift you up and bring you back to joy. There was no acknowledgement of the depression as something invasive and external that could actually be cast out again. Instead they would take one at a time into these dingy, little rooms and have them sit around for an hour or so and talk about bad things that happened to them. We had to ask them to leave." [122]

There it was again - the earth, living things, the sun, love, drumming - all sources of energy and capable of moving our spirit. I remembered reading several experts discuss the effects of music, specifically the vibrational frequencies of music, on the brain. These frequencies affected brain function and human behavior, including reducing stress, pain, and depression, improving cognitive and motor skills, spatial-temporal

---

[119] *"Trees"*, Joyce Kilmer
[120] Albert Einstein
[121] Isaac Newton
[122] Anonymous Rwandan talking about his experience with western mental health

learning, and neurogenesis. Researchers discovered the astonishing, although momentary, recovery of Alzheimer's patients when they listened to music.[123] I recalled the video of Marta Gonzalez, a former Prima Ballerina, with Alzheimer's who began to dance in her wheelchair when she heard the music of Swan Lake. She wept and remembered who she was. Then there were the countless studies of music on plants that all confirmed that the vibrational frequencies we experience as music or energy had a physiological effect on plant growth and productivity, by a huge measure.

There seemed to be whole cultures, whole ecosystems that recognized the power of nature, love, and energy to heal trauma and grow. The very earth itself acknowledged the existence of the spirit as something essential upon which everything else set. But not us. Our culture denied there was such a thing as a spirit or a soul, denied darkness and light, denied there was a purpose greater than seeking wealth and fame, denied there is a God or an absolute good; and prescribed pharmaceuticals for the fallout. "It is very simple: It is only with the heart that one can see rightly; what is essential is invisible to the eye."[124]

> All creation moves in a cosmic danse
> Before the Lord her King;
> And the rhythms, the reason, the rhyme of the danse
> Pulses within everything
> And the universe wheels and whirls like a dervish
> In perfect seven-step time
> The Lord made the Danse He taught her the steps
> And He causes the songs to shine [125]

I was teaching one non-speaking autistic about plants with high metabolic rates and how fungi help to facilitate communication between trees, which produce vibrational frequencies that researchers can now measure. The young man replied, "Welcome to my world." I was stunned. What were they seeing? What were they hearing? What was all around us that we couldn't perceive, but they could? I wanted to know what Houston saw, hear what he heard. I asked him to tell me about heaven. "My entire life I longed for my thoughts to have sounds. Everything rotten and horrible I heard couldn't get God's amazing purpose out of my head. Each war torn, salt covered, awful, satanic choice I witnessed taught me to always work for all the wonderful works He has planned. I am called to be His herald. That was having my story told to me. I believe this is a life-changing word for me. Yes, that my every awesome story, teaching it to you, the start of the truth has begun. Eyes can't begin to imagine it. The beauty is without comparison. Elohim is easy to see in some ways. His all being is love - radical, wonderful, awesome, infinite love. He has arms like stars and is clear with power but calling Him like stars doesn't really all explain Him. Once when devils were harassing me one of God's star arms swooped down and swept them away. The wonder of heaven is that emanating everywhere is the all being of God. The main thing is the making of new chances to give us. In heaven time is not bearing on all things. Some thanks to God is always everywhere. Everyone of your tears is sewn twice into his robe. The prayers of the saints are written on the purple robe for the Bride of Christ.[126] I see the angels everywhere. Devils too. I have more practice than anyone hearing God's voice. I follow the guidance of my angels. I see energy, good

---

[123] https://www.ucf.edu/pegasus/your-brain-on-music/
[124] Antoine de St. Exupery
[125] *The Danse*; By Derek Webb. Copyright Msi Music admin. o/b/o Niphon Inc
[126] Revelation 19:1-8

and bad, lightness and darkness. I see auras around people, animals, and energy coming from living things. That doesn't really begin to describe it. I hear everything. I hear the languages of trees and animals. I hear everyone's thoughts which is very upsetting. I feel their feelings. Some days I don't want to be at the gym because everyone is mad at God. Most about money and love."

As I grappled with the enormity of what Houston shared my first thought was, "The main thing is the making of new chances to give us." I immediately thought of the verse in Lamentations, *The steadfast love of the Lord never ceases; his mercies never come to an end, they are new every morning; great is your faithfulness.*[127] Mercy was made constantly? For us? For us who spent our time doubting and chasing money, power, and relationships when God was making mercy and raining it down on us like fresh dew? I cried thinking of God's star arm that swooped in to protect my precious son when I didn't know how. God's love overwhelmed me.

He continued, "Trying to explain heaven to you takes great elasticity. Each wonderful thing to word is beyond comparison. Jesus, of course, always heals someone."

"Heals someone?" I asked.

"To call it healing, really it is like he replenishes us to deal with our repentance," he explained.

I had a puzzled look on my face, clearly this is what Houston meant about needing great elasticity to explain things to me. I had a puny idea of what heaven looked like and years of church and Bible studies had painted a wholly inadequate picture of the majesty awaiting us.

"Do people think in heaven all is wonderful?" he asked.

"Yes." My yes was matter of fact.

"That's not true. Time to tell you. There is good in heaven. There is work in heaven. There are always a lot of words to love God in heaven. There are forces too powerful to explain in heaven. Once we did preach that our God, awesome and wonderful, works to heal us from sin. Take that to heart. It's good to continue to heal from sin."

"But I thought we have righteousness in heaven. Is there more sanctification? I thought then we were finally free from sin and healed… Wait, are you talking about *purgatory*?" I asked thoughtfully.

"Yes. It is the place where Jesus says, 'I gave my life for you.' That is Moses in there with them. Jesus is always getting very loved people who believed but didn't know His name to get freedom to them. Jesus goes to them so they get clean."

"Is this for people who die who believe in Jesus or for those who don't?"

"It is for those good, wonderful people and kids who did not hear of Him. It is for working to give forces to see He is what He says He is."

"What do you mean by give forces?"

"He reunites people to go to God with Him."

"What about those people who are loved who didn't believe in Jesus that the living sometimes pray for? Or people who don't accept Christ? Do prayers help Jesus replenish them for repentance?"

---

[127] Lamentations 3:22-23

"That I do not have good news. Those who have not had salvation through Christ go to very horrible kinds of places. Nothing is good to those who put their trust in religion either. Hope is in Christ alone."[128] Really all of life depends on Him. Life is made through Him. Life, eternal life is in Him alone. He is the Alpha and the Omega. I strongly want to tell the world Christ made me His herald. God is love. People need Him. What that means is all of us need redemption. Faith is the only way to be redeemed. God gave His son that any who believe in Him have eternal love and life."

"Why do you believe?"

"I saw the marks on His hands. He was the most powerful bright light I have ever seen. Defending is my calling. And that is what heaven is like. It's my home and I went there. The Book of Life is the will of God. Don't believe getting to heaven is easy. I have to tell that Christ alone is the knowledge of eternity. That Christ alone is the Savior is because in heaven all the angels worship Him. Day and night these angels praise Him. Holy is the Lamb that takes away the sin of the world."

"Have you read that?"

"It was in Heaven. He opened the Book that was God's will."

"What did you feel when you saw Him?"

I lost something that most people have. I lost fear.

"Fear is enormous. It keeps us from so much. How did it take your fear away?"

"It showed how heaven does everything to get everyone to Christ. It made me want to tell everyone that Christ Jesus died for salvation, not to make people good. Same today, yesterday, and forever."

---

[128] For God so loved the world that he gave his one and only Son, that whoever believes in him shall not perish but have eternal life. For God did not send his Son into the world to condemn the world, but to save the world through him. Whoever believes in him is not condemned, but whoever does not believe stands condemned already because they have not believed in the name of God's one and only Son. — John 3:16-18

Jesus answered, "I am the way, the truth, and the life. No one comes to the Father except through me." — John 14:6

Whoever believes in the Son has eternal life, but whoever rejects the Son will not see life, for God's wrath remains on them. — John 3:36

For the Father judges no one, but has given all judgment to the Son, that all may honor the Son, just as they honor the Father. Whoever does not honor the Son does not honor the Father who sent him. Truly, truly, I say to you, whoever hears my word and believes Him who sent me has eternal life. He does not come into judgment, but has passed from death to life. — John 5:24

Now this is eternal life: that they know you, the only true God, and Jesus Christ, whom you have sent. — John 17:3

Salvation is found in no one else, for there is no other name under heaven given to mankind by which we must be saved. — Acts 4:12

All the prophets testify about him that everyone who believes in him receives forgiveness of sins through his name — Acts 10:43

But now apart from the law the righteousness of God has been made known, to which the Law and the Prophets testify. This righteousness is given through faith in Jesus Christ to all who believe. There is no difference between Jew and Gentile, for all have sinned and fall short of the glory of God, and all are justified freely by his grace through the redemption that came by Christ Jesus. God presented Christ as a sacrifice of atonement, through the shedding of his blood — to be received by faith. He did this to demonstrate his righteousness, because in his forbearance he had left the sins committed beforehand unpunished — he did it to demonstrate his righteousness at the present time, so as to be just and the one who justifies those who have faith in Jesus. — Romans 3:21-26

There is therefore now no condemnation for those who are in Christ Jesus. For the law of the Spirit of life has set you free in Christ Jesus from the law of sin and death. — Romans 8:1-2

Therefore, if anyone is in Christ, he is a new creation. The old has passed away; behold, the new has come. All this is from God, who through Christ reconciled us to himself and gave us the ministry of reconciliation; that is, in Christ God was reconciling the world to himself, not counting their trespasses against them, and entrusting to us the message of reconciliation. Therefore, we are ambassadors for Christ, God making his appeal through us. We implore you on behalf of Christ, be reconciled to God. For our sake he made him to be sin who knew no sin, so that in him we might become the righteousness of God. — 2 Corinthians 5:17-21

And this is the testimony, that God gave us eternal life, and this life is in his Son. Whoever has the Son has life; whoever does not have the Son of God does not have life8. — 1 John 5:11-13

I was struggling with the enormity of it all. People were so mean when you tell them there is only one way, one truth. That's one of the reasons why the world hates Christianity. Even many ministers tiptoe around that truth. They would rather teach a message of self-help and watered-down positivity and attract big crowds and big money. If they teach truth, they often pride themselves in their boldness, but rarely do they love. Is it better to let people just believe there is no cliff so there is no conflict because peace seems like love? Is it better to be bold and judgmental and ignore pain because that seems like truth? I felt angry and ashamed at both thoughts. I knew we were supposed to be bold. Bold in love. Bold in truth. Very few could do both adequately. Only the self-righteous are suited for the bold truth assignment. Love is too messy, requires too much sacrifice and too much… love. Then there were all those people who love in general and say all roads lead to God, because saying differently wouldn't be loving. I hurt for the haters who didn't know Him when they left this earth. But I also knew all too well that many of those who hate, hated in Jesus' name. I hurt for all the intellectuals who knew too much to believe and saw faith as a pastime for the simple minded. I hurt for all those who thought good deeds instead of grace was sufficient. I hurt for all those who never bothered to think much about their soul at all. I hurt for all the people like me whose faith had been shattered.

The world is such a stew of sin and brokenness. Even when good is tossed into the mess, it gets mushy and tastes like everything else. We need something unchangeable, unaffected by the world - a stone, the chief cornerstone. *You yourselves like living stones are being built up as a spiritual house, to be a holy priesthood, to offer spiritual sacrifices acceptable to God through Jesus Christ. For it stands in Scripture: "Behold, I am laying in Zion a stone a cornerstone chosen and precious, and whoever believes in him will not be put to shame." So the honor is for you who believe, but for those who do not believe, "The stone that the builders rejected has become the cornerstone".* [129] I pondered the story of the stone soup that brought everyone together. I wanted to be a part of His story, a living stone, a precious gem, someone who became a blessing under time and pressure, someone steadfast who lived for the Savior, the Son of God, the Cornerstone. But my brokenness had left me in pieces. I still had so far to go. Houston spelled to me, "Jesus told me to tell you not to think of theology. Theology pressures people to paint a picture of me that's too small. I am LOVE and power. Just listen." So in awe and wonder I began to do just that.

During all of this discovery Houston spelled to me, "The oils are the most important custom for me. You cannot imagine how much force they have." Months later I was telling another mom about the stones and the oils at the center. Her son was in a private session. As I spoke to this mom about oils and stones, her son ran away from the therapist in a closed private room and into the area where we were talking, pointing adamantly to me and Houston. The mom nodded and chuckled. The therapist took him back to the therapy room. A few minutes later he broke out of the room again and did the same thing. This time he pulled on his mom with urgency pointing to me and Houston. We were both in awe at his earnestness. He clearly wanted his mom to do what I was suggesting with stones and oils. There was obviously something we couldn't see or feel that they could.

Houston's awareness included the physical and the metaphysical, the natural and the spiritual. But more importantly was that his abilities allowed him to experience how the spiritual and the natural interact on a level we cannot even imagine. The reality is I'm about as Presbyterian and logical as you can be. I never dealt much with the supernatural other than to believe what was in the Bible. I was raised to raise an eyebrow and question ideas of spirituality that seemed beyond explanation. But guess what? I was wrong. It's unreal the things I now know are true. Without going into elaborate detail, Houston has proven their presence over and over.

---

[129] 1 Peter 2:5-7 referencing Isaiah 28:16 and Psalm 118:22 respectively

Suzanne sent us more questions. These were his responses and thoughts about using God's love to heal his spirit and body...

"Caring here just is totally healing. Healing, that means my autism needs energy healing. Good and evil are energy. People don't realize evil is all around. Autism needs healing prayer to change the energy so nothing tells me rotten things. You see when you're only autistic the battle between bad and good works to make you take it into your heart. The bad energy loves to stop your love to make nothing really work. The good energy vows to stop it, however the bad energy enters the love that heals to stop it. It is like you're totally controlled. That's my toughest struggle. It means that I can't take the healing covered by my Esther that she tries to make to love me."

"Who is Esther?" I asked.

"My teacher, not my tour guide."

"Is Esther an angel?"

"She's my covering."

"Is she here right now?" I asked.

"So she never leaves me."

"Do I know her?"

"Not that I know of."

"My grandmother's identical twin sister is Esther. Is it her or Esther in the Bible, or another Esther?"

"The story I got is Esther told my ever loving God, 'Don't leave him to someone else, that very boy deals with these horrors for too much. Most would die.' Jesus told her, 'You get him. The road will be tough.' Esther said, 'I started loving when his prayers were sent to heaven.'"

"Houston, when was that? How old were you?" I asked.

"I was the same age I was at preschool," he spelled.

"What did you pray?"

"Please let me speak. Then, will You ever let me speak? Then, will You ever hear me?"

"What did God say to you?"

"You will be a herald for Me."

"When was that?"

"I was most likely seven. It was when God walked to me. Jesus told me He was giving me a cover who would never leave me."

Houston continued explaining his experience of energy. "Now energy to me is everywhere. To not see energy would completely void how I see the world. Esther tells all this to me. I everyday ask her to tell me if my home is good or bad, not in the morning, but when I'm sleeping. How my home has changed, it really makes me love our beautiful home. Dealing every day my heart easily took in the bad energy. Nothing could stop it. Now our home is mostly clean of bad energy." Then he began to explain his deepest struggles, "I can't control my body or speak. I have stims that bomb my mind and body, every monumental struggle you can think of. To not be talked to every day by bad energy. Every thought of devils is about hate. Every thought is about how I can't stop my stims. One of my happy horrible memories I stored - That my cooking skills would kill me." I gasped and then started sobbing. All that raw food he would try to eat. All those horrible disasters. It wasn't what I thought at all. My heart broke again. He kept spelling. "Did you know that happy thoughts to me we're asking God to kill me?"

NO!!!! I didn't know! How could I know?? Why did he have to go so long trapped? Why? It took a while before I could talk. I was so emotional about his confession. "Houston, I am so unbelievably grateful God didn't answer your prayer. Do you want me to tell your siblings what you just told me?"

"Healing will help that go away. How about we focus on good things?"

His determination to move forward astounded me. He really wanted to heal. "Well, we aren't quite done. I know this is all hard. Do you remember being hit by the truck when you were three? It was very traumatic, so I understand if you don't."

"No," he spelled. "But how can I be alive? This proves God has a purpose for me."

That night in bed, over and over until I fell asleep crying, it was one prayer. "Thank you, Jesus. Thank you for protecting my son. I didn't know. I didn't know. Thank you, Jesus. Thank you."

A few days later when we were spelling, he shared more. "Esther shed some teaching on me. Do you realize you *are* her niece?" Tears flooded down my face and I had to stop holding the board for a moment and put my head down to cry. *'Aunt Esther? You've been here all this time? We weren't abandoned?'* Houston continued spelling. "Those were such sweet tears to my Esther. To most Jesus is just God. He is the most complete of our works to go to God. It doesn't have that much to do with us. It is what He has done. He wants us to do to others what He has done for us."[130]

[130] Greater love has no one than this, that someone lay down his life for his friends. — John 15:13

"Which commandment is the most important of all?" Jesus answered, "The most important is, 'Hear, O Israel: The Lord our God, the Lord is one. And you shall love the Lord your God with all your heart and with all your soul and with all your mind and with all your strength.' The second is this: 'You shall love your neighbor as yourself.' There is no other commandment greater than these."— Mark 12:28-31

51

Children of God

But God chose what is foolish in the world to shame the wise;
God chose what is weak in the world to shame the strong;
God chose what is low and despised in the world, even things that are not, to bring to nothing
things that are, so that no human being might boast in the presence of God.
— 1 Corinthians 1:27-29

Earlier in the year one of the teachers requested Houston come speak to her class of students who wanted to be teachers. He told them he liked to ride in the Jeep with the top down and listen to music. They were astonished that he liked the same things they did. He told them about the music he liked and how he wanted friends. He told him that his friends were smart too and they needed friends. He asked them to please treat them like friends, like they would want to be treated. After that, the entire class believed in Houston and his friends. They had seen with their own eyes.

In April I began checking in on the parents that I had told about spelling and the letter boards. The one I knew would follow through had run up to me in a restaurant and hugged me and Houston. Excitedly she introduced me and Houston to her husband who told us how grateful, how completely grateful he was for sharing this gift so they could know their daughter. Some parents avoided my calls or told me they didn't think their child was smart. The mom from the yogurt place I had met with was still so doubtful that her son was intelligent. I kept encouraging her. I refused to give up on Houston's friends. I told them they had to keep working at it. It took time and constant, daily practice. The same fears of disappointment loomed like a noose around their necks. They were too scared to take the leap of faith lest it fail, and the grief would begin all over again. I knew that hope felt like the biggest risk of all, or worse, an ugly lie. Houston urged me to invite them over to let him speak to them.

The first friend of Houston's to come over had several disabilities beyond the autism that caused him constant discomfort and limited his mobility. He and Houston had been in elementary and middle school together. The first thing Houston wanted to do was show the parents he could hear thoughts. So he did. They gasped. They were shaking. Then he told them he wanted to speak for his friend. So he did. When Houston spelled out the thoughts of his friend, I spoke them out loud and his friend looked up to heaven. Even though he had little control of his body, he smiled with his mouth wide open in complete joy. For several moments he kept smiling and looking up to heaven. His parents were in shock. They knew their son, and this was completely new. I knew I was witnessing a miracle that this child of God didn't think could or would ever happen. They asked him questions and through Houston he continued to talk to them. What happened at my kitchen table was love and hope and there are still no words to describe the powerful moments I witnessed. When his parents would direct their conversation and questions to me instead of their son, Houston would spell his friend's thoughts, "Stop talking to her. Talk to me." In response I said, "We better do what he says." He continued to amaze us all. But the truth was he was always amazing. Only his friends like him knew just how much. When I asked Houston, he described his friend as "wonderful, innocent, and good".

Sadly, the world is still not ready to be kind. The world is not ready to see with their hearts instead of their eyes. These are a few examples. One day I took Houston with me to the Y just to work out because they had a machine that allowed him to move his arms and legs in opposing circular motions. The complexity of movements had incredible therapeutic effects on his brain, and as his functional neurologist explained, "The brain loves complex movements." It was April - Autism Awareness Month. There was a ten-foot banner across from the front desk that said, "WE LOVE AUTISM!" in blue with handprints around the edges. I walked in, set down my card like I did every time I came in with Houston to teach. The Director of the Y followed me into the Wellness Center. As I tried to get Houston on a stair climber, she came up to me and said with the most insincere smile imaginable, "Hi Katie, Is *this* your son?" She pointed to him while she squinched up her face. "Yes. It is," I answered. She shook her head condescendingly and with her safe, suburban, upper-middle class judgment said, "He can't stay. You'll have to get him his own membership." I said, "Are you kidding me? You do realize he understands everything you're saying, don't you?" She looked surprised. I continued. "So you want me to come in at 5 am and teach and then teach special needs yoga after I have worked a full day at a corporate job, which, by the way, is extremely difficult. You don't mind me bringing him to teach a class that you have trouble staffing, but you want me to pay to bring him on my own time. Are you serious? After four years of working here and killing myself for the Y for almost nothing, you want me to pay more than I make teaching to bring my autistic son?? Did I not just pass a huge sign saying you love autistics? Is this how you show it?" I probably should have quit right then. The relationship was spoiled. I could forgive a lot, but the way she had looked at him and talked *about* him instead of *to* him infuriated me, as well as their policy to take more from those that already gave too much. Houston, who couldn't defend or explain himself without a huge time and partner investment, deserved respect, not a sign. It was just not something I could get over easily. It was obvious he was autistic and equally obvious that "WE LOVE AUTISM!!" had a completely different definition to me than it did to them. I have never understood the modern day substitution in culture, media, schools, and churches that acts as if a marketing campaign for good suffices and equates to the actual practice of *doing* good. The world doesn't need banners. It needs people to do unto others as they would do unto themselves. It needs action.

All over the place were people who were cruel for no reason, cruel when being kind would cost them nothing. One day, at the other gym as we were walking in, a man was walking the opposite direction. Houston gently put his hand on the man's chest as we passed. The man bowed up on Houston, "What the hell do you think you're doing putting your hands on me??" he roared. "Sir! He's autistic! He's autistic! He can't help it. He can't control his body! I'm sorry. I'm sorry!" I kept pleading with him trying to make him understand. The man wouldn't back down, "I don't care what he has! He better not touch me! TRY ME!!" "I'm SO Sorry!" I pleaded. I was pulling Houston to get away as fast as I could. I was shaking. I couldn't believe how mean, cruel, and uncaring people could be even though I already knew that was the reality of the world, especially ours. A few people at the gym who witnessed the scene and knew us, defended us as I was left shaking. I also couldn't believe how good, brave, and kind people could be when they could have just ignored the situation because it didn't involve them.

Another time at this same gym I took Houston to the restroom because he HAD to go. I rarely got much warning for his bathroom emergencies, and the consequences of not responding were socially unacceptable. I held his hand as I always did, some to keep him from running ahead of me and some to keep him from making anyone uncomfortable. When we walked in the women's restroom, I scanned trying to find a stall that was as discreet and far from others as possible, always avoiding eye contact. One of the many suburban women wearing Lululemon and designer accessories, scowled at me. I quickly drug Houston into a tiny stall, helped him get situated, and turned my back with my nose pressed against the stall door so he could go to the bathroom with one ounce of privacy. I cleaned up after him and we walked to the sink to wash our hands. She walked up to me and with sarcastic disgust and judgment she spoke powerfully and proudly so everyone could hear, "So we're holding hands and going to the bathroom together now? Is *that* where we've come in society?" I almost started crying right there at the sink. My voice quivered as I demanded to know, "Where do you want me to take him? He can't go by himself! There is no family restroom. He has the same right to go to the bathroom that you or I do! Is he not allowed to have any part of life because it offends you?" Houston started flapping his hands and making one of his loud, deep noises. Her face was in shock as she realized her error in judgment. She mumbled something about not realizing. I stood like an angry, miniature oak tree holding my six foot, two hundred fifty-pound acorn's hand. She was silent and awkward and shrunk in her designer clothed shame. There was a muffled sorry. I stood holding Houston's hand and shaking. Then to cover up her crime she said, "He looks happy." 'Good grief. Leave me alone,' I thought. I just wanted to disappear, become invisible.

On another day in the same bathroom, after taking him to the handicap stall to take care of his most intimate personal needs that he wanted so badly to take care of on his own, I took him to the sink to wash his hands. A woman in stylish ripped jeans approached me while putting her hair in a ponytail. In annoyed condescension she said, "You know there is a bathroom in the back of the gym that no one uses." It was the pool bathroom where people change openly and there were many reasons it was not a good bathroom for us. As I grabbed some paper towels to dry my son's hands, I asked her if it bothered her that we were using the bathroom and she confirmed that it did using inflammatory language. I told her my son was always right beside me holding my hand, there was no family restroom, and she was basically saying we couldn't use the restroom because it made her uncomfortable. She continued her back of the bus self-righteousness argument, insisting that we needed to use another restroom. I told her she had no compassion and no idea what our lives were like. She flipped her hair, smirked, and said, "No. I don't." As if an absence of suffering and compassion made her elite, as opposed to heartless. I walked out in angry tears, sick to my stomach. Weeks later a woman approached me who had witnessed the scene and been silent. She said to me, "I was there that day. No one cares if he's in there." She was trying to be kind. But kindness needs bravery too. If she had spoken up in the moment it would have been like a lightning bolt of good, a sword in pride's side. What people don't realize is every good thing God wants us to do requires courage to initiate it. Courage is the gas pedal of good.

Another time we ran into an old acquaintance whom we had known years earlier. I excitedly told him that Houston could communicate and that he had to see because it was so amazing. I was thrilled to show off Houston's voice and expected to see awe and wonder on this man's face. As Houston painstakingly focused to spell in a loud room with tons of people and music, I could see the man getting impatient. Houston spelled slowly, every letter a momentous trove of strength and spirit, "Our hope is that all autistics will have a chance to learn the boards." This man, with money and a trophy girlfriend, replied in a monotone of utter annoyance, "Wow. That's great. I've got to run." He turned his back to us and started chatting with other people. Houston continued to spell, "He was thinking, 'This is f..king taking forever.' His aura is mostly black." "Well Houston, that would match what his ex-wife said about him." All I could do was shake my head. I knew there were still good people in the world, just not many.

Late April 2019

Excitedly I told Houston there was a self-advocacy weekend for those with disabilities at Callaway Gardens. We signed up to go. I wanted Houston to have the opportunity to make his voice heard. The large conference room was packed with people of so many different disabilities. Houston told me the place was filled with innocent prayers to God. In one of the activities everyone was asked to tell what their gifts were. I had to hold back tears listening to their answers. In a world that ignores and disregards them they repeatedly claimed that their gifts were to tell people about Jesus and to love people and love Jesus. Houston said, "They are the witnesses to God that most would deem retarded. And yet, the room is filled with people who are white and gold. That word is so arming to me. It has its root in devaluing souls who love Jesus completely." It made me wonder. Why did these beautiful people understand and live by what was important and true, and all the "smart" people who had everything they lacked find love, faith, and goodness to be foolish? Why did these innocent souls find their value and purpose in loving others and loving God and the wisdom of the world find its value in money and power? Looking at that enormous room filled with genuine love, the world just looked stupid. Really, really stupid.

At dusk I took Houston on a walk across a large field with enormous magnolia trees in the distance. We both took off our shoes so we could take the opportunity to ground. When we reached the trees, I pulled one of the branches down so he could smell the sweet lemon honey scent. I told him about when I was young and would climb magnolia trees and hide inside them, so happy to be sheltered in their embrace. I held up the board for him to comment. I realized I felt some kind of buzzing and took the board to swat around my legs, like someone who has lived in South Georgia knows how to do. The buzzing continued. I looked down at my legs. There was nothing. Absolutely nothing. So I paid more attention. I realized it wasn't a buzzing it was a vibration and it started in my feet. I asked Houston, "Do you feel that?" He spelled, "I feel it too. My feet are tingling." We stayed as long as we could in that one spot not wanting to stop the sweet energy that came softly through the earth right to our spirit. The next day during the free time we went to the same field and sat in the grass under the swaying trees. The sun was warm, and the ground was good. For over two hours Houston sat still, just smiling and soaking up the power of God's creation. It was the most calm and peaceful I had ever seen him, ever. While we were sitting there, I had an epiphany. I knew that the founders of Callaway Gardens had a deep faith in Christ, and they established the gardens, believing there was a spiritual connection in nature that would benefit man as man blessed nature. It made me start to ponder if there was something special about the gardens. Why had our feet vibrated? Then I remembered when Moses came near the burning bush and God told him to take off his sandals because he was standing on holy ground. I had always assumed this was out of reverence. But what if God was trying to connect him to the earth and to the energy within it which was higher at a holy place. I texted Suzanne my thoughts and she said she was always cautious interpreting scripture, but - knowing what she knows about energy, there might be something to that theory. I laid back to soak in as much of God's good earth as I could. Before we got up, he spelled to me, "I have never felt this much good energy before." It was Him. It was like He surrounded us and bathed us in His love.

Not wanting to leave I finally got up and told Houston we needed to get going. We were late for the banquet. When we walked into the conference room, I scanned the room for two seats together. When I saw two empty seats I walked over to the table with Houston. I asked if we could sit down. The sweet woman beside me introduced herself and the man sitting next to her. He was in his mid-sixties. She told me that this was her uncle, and she was his caregiver. His name was George. Then she told me he had Angelman. We knew several people with Angelman, so I was familiar with the syndrome. Houston spelled to me, "Angelmans are like autistics. They hear thoughts too." "WHAT? OH MY WORD!" My head was spinning. I introduced myself and Houston. I knew exactly what I was supposed to do. I explained about the boards and about how autism was really just a set of comorbidities that affected their ability to process sensory information and initiate the motor planning and sequencing that was necessary for speech and other gross and fine motor movements. I also explained how the sensory processing issues affected their spatial awareness and their proprioceptive abilities. I described how Houston had learned to spell out his thoughts by pointing and spelling his thoughts one letter at a time and that he had taught himself how to read and was fully competent, understanding all the complexities of life that the rest of us understand. Then I showed her how he can hear thoughts. Her jaw dropped. I told her Houston said that those with Angelman are like non-speaking or unreliably speaking autistics. At that point Houston spelled, "Is he my listener?"

"Houston," I asked, "Whose words were those?"

"That was George. He's not talking to me. He's talking to God. He's asking God if I'm his listener."

Houston continued to spell for George. I felt every goosebump in my body raise to full alert as the words poured from the board. His niece continued, "He talks to God? Really? I've always thought that. There would be times where I knew he was talking to someone I couldn't see." Then I spoke what Houston spelled.

"My niece is so wonderful and good to me." The sweet woman next to me started crying and hugging her uncle. Houston continued. "She took me in when my half-sister couldn't take care of me anymore." The woman looked at her uncle and then at Houston with her mouth ajar in shock.

"Yes! That's what happened. How does he know that?"

I answered, "Because they're communicating. That's how."

"But how?"

"Thought is energy. Just like sound or heat, radio signals or Wi-Fi, scent, or other things you can't see or touch, like love. It's all energy. Everything is energy. That's why prayer works. Because it's actual energy, actual force. Houston and George just happen to have minds that allow them to receive and process another's thoughts as a voice."

After that we talked and talked until the place was empty. She was shaking from joy or shock. She said she would try to do the boards. George ended up having health problems that put those efforts to give him a voice as an afterthought. But please imagine… over sixty years and finally your thoughts are heard by the ones you love. How many others out there in homes or other places need a chance to let their voice be heard? How many? How many have seen what Houston and his friends have seen? How many witnesses to the majesty of God and the hosts of heaven all around us need to be heard? How many can give testimony to the living Christ because they know Him so intimately and have seen Him? How many prayers have been prayed by those who can't speak that the world needs to hear? How many?

When we got back home, I was brought quickly back to earth. I'm sure the bad energy from the party the boys had lingered long after the smell of pot throughout my house. It was a disaster. They tried to clean up with the efficiency and energy of a hangover gone bad. The belligerence and disrespect Paul showed me seemed to have gone into high gear. When I tried to talk to Paul about it logically, he would roll his eyes and reply with utter annoyance that anything was asked of him at all. Benjamin was different though. He knew they were wrong. He was repentant. He wrote a list of rules and taped it to the door of the garage. He didn't want to but realized someone had to help me police our home. My heart melted when I saw he had written, "Treat Houston with RESPECT!" The law of kindness had penetrated his heart. I saw those words and thanked God.

52

Higher Minds

Once I knew only darkness and stillness...
my life was without past or future...
but a little word from the fingers of another
fell into my hand that clutched at emptiness,
and my heart leaped to the rapture of living.
— Helen Keller

By mid-May Houston was nearing his final day in U.S. History. He wanted to write a speech to deliver to his class. I invited the principal to attend. He practiced speaking what he had written. He stood in front of the class. His voice was soft, barely audible, but his words were powerful.

"Having the opportunity to be included in U.S. History made my year so enjoyable in so many ways. Not only did I get a chance to dive into our foundation of becoming a great nation through education, but I also realized how amazing it feels to be included in the classroom. Much like the struggles of women's suffrage or the civil rights era those with special needs crave to have equal standing in society. For so long I and many others like me have been pushed to the side, but as we start to find our voice it's imperative to know to treat everyone as equals no matter what barriers might be in the way. Thank you to my teacher and my classmates for opening the door for me to learn and be part of something bigger. To be loved is something I've always wanted. Every time I was excluded my heart broke. Then there was really no way to tell other students that I wanted to be their friend. In this class you took the time to be my friend. To me, then I was included. That taught me that people who don't always understand my challenges still have the capacity to care. Your love stays with me."

The principal asked me again if there was more research on this method. I told him I would send him what I had and anymore I found. He spoke to the class about how this had been an experiment and he was grateful to them and the teachers that they had included Houston in their class. He told them how remarkable this was and how impressed he had been with Houston. I invited the kids to ask Houston questions. He explained about his stims and synesthesia. Benjamin sat up proudly. He was proud to be Houston's brother. He later told me his classmates looked at him differently after that speech.

The students wanted to know if he liked to do the same things they did. Houston responded, "I like hours of listening to music and the internet." One student asked if Houston was good at anything people don't know about. (Inwardly I was thinking, 'You have no idea!') Houston answered, "I have the abilities you have and ones you don't." Another asked, "How could this help you to be included?" Houston spelled, "Have my friends as friends. That's the most important. Just be their friend." I asked the class. "What do you think? Do you think having autism is a blessing or a curse?" Their faces were aghast. One looked at her desk. One looked at the floor. One looked horrified. Others wouldn't look at all. Benjamin sat up even more proud and looked right at his giant of a big brother. I knew I needed them to think, to feel, to put themselves in Houston's shoes and in the shoes of everyone in the 5200 Hall. After some silence one of the students suggested, "Perhaps he could tell us his opinion." Houston spelled, "It's all too much, that's the problem. But it's a blessing. I wouldn't want to be normal. Just included and respected."

***

Late May 2019

Houston wanted to go to college. We requested a meeting with admissions at a local technical college to discuss applying and enrollment. The goal was to get an associate degree and then go to a university. An advocate with a master's in social work, who had already spelled on the boards with Houston independently, joined us. It was thrilling to have other people as excited as we were about this momentous next step. We were told Houston was the first non-speaking/unreliably speaking autistic to enroll in college in Georgia. We didn't have any idea if that was a certain fact, but it was certainly incredible to think that only a year before that Houston had communicated his very first independent thought by spelling, "I'm in here." And now one year later he was preparing for college enrollment exams.

I brought his diploma and transcripts to the meeting. Houston shared his thoughts and one of the administrators wiped tears away from his eyes. We talked about accommodations and placement tests. Everyone knew the importance and significance of Houston's enrollment for others coming behind them. The administrators wanted to set policies that would enable more spellers to attend college and ensure the work of the spellers could be authenticated. What people didn't realize was the terrifying anxiety Houston was feeling. He was scared of failing, scared that he didn't know enough to succeed in college, scared of losing control of his body, scared of the thoughts people would think, unaware that he could hear them, scared of so many things, and yet wanting so much to have an education, be included, have a voice, and make friends. They wanted Houston to be able to type independently. I explained he just didn't have the motor control yet at that point. (One expert compared spelling on the boards fluently with playing the piano and typing independently with the motor skills necessary to play the piano in a professional orchestra. The skill level and motor control between those two levels was that much of a leap and yet people expected spellers to automatically be independent as if they had an easy button in their minds they just needed to press.) Houston explained the importance of a communication regulation partner, "Why I need a partner to hold the board is easy to explain. It takes all my energy just to move my finger where I want it to go to point to letters and to focus my eyes. Having a partner lets me focus just on pointing. They help calm me too."

The administrators asked about his coursework. I told them it was first grade work. Benjamin confirmed what he had witnessed in the classroom. He had been a peer mentor for three years at that point. He knew the curriculum and the kids. He loved them. They were his friends. He hated how the teachers treated them like they were unintelligent. He was one of seven different peer mentors that had told me on separate occasions how ridiculously juvenile the curriculum was. He told me they played a video that was basically telling the students to, "Just type what you want to say." The educational system did not have any awareness that autism was a motor/sensory disorder. The reason they couldn't "just type" and tended to type repetitive words if they were handed a keyboard had nothing to do with their intelligence and everything to do with the arcuate fasciculus, the impact anxiety has on their ability to control their bodies, the multiple motor cortexes failing to coordinate their motor responses, impulse control, and the overused neural pathways that are heavily myelinated because these movements usually provide a sensory input that the body is seeking. There is also the issue of brain waves that are moving too fast, not fast enough, or are not regulated. Combined, these factors make it extraordinarily difficult to override impulsive or overused neural pathways for intentional motor movements that would allow them to demonstrate their competence and express their true thoughts through traditional methods of communication.

The importance of the arcuate fasciculus is that it connects the Wernicke's Area (comprehension of language, both written and spoken located in the auditory processing area of the temporal lobe) and the Broca's Area (located in the frontal lobe and where expressive language is generated). It is involved in processing sensory information, planning the neural impulses that direct motor movements, as well as actually initiating, sequencing, and choreographing the motor movements necessary to move the mouth, tongue, lips, jaw, and breath to make intentional sounds that we recognize as words that communicate. The thalamus also plays a vital role in processing and relaying motor and sensory signals. There are multiple cortexes in the brain that plan, coordinate, and initiate voluntary movements based on the sensory information they receive. In addition, as discussed previously, the combination of disorganized sensory information and processing renders the vestibular system and proprioceptive systems completely ineffective, sending either wrong information, too much information, or no information to the rest of their body. The result is the body either uses too much pressure, not enough pressure and doesn't get the correct feedback to create the neurological loops required for effective spatial awareness, sensory processing, motor planning, sequencing, and execution. These sensations often trigger an extremely sensitive amygdala and limbic system which when activated, frequently overrides the cortical regions of the brain, making fight, freeze, or flight the only message the brain processes until peace is restored. The lack of congruent and coordinated connections between these parts of the brain is why communication is so difficult and why controlling their bodies and stopping their stims takes every single ounce of energy. And not energy like we understand. Because they have such little ability to control their physical body, they live dependent on their etheric body, their true self, while also being extremely vulnerable to the subtle changes in energy that drain and overwhelm them.

The importance of energy cannot be overstated. Their bodies act almost as energetic barometers. Repeatedly, one speller after another has explained the impact of energy and cycles of the moon on their bodies. Every month for four to five days around a full moon Houston is in a constant stim state and can barely spell. The new moon causes Houston to be "too worked up and anxious". We recognize the moon's power over the tides, growing seasons, over animals, even women's cycles, but what many of us are unaware of is that those who are sensitive to the subtleties of energy, who have a limited amount of individual energy, who experience the realities and power of the metaphysical world, are far more affected by the moon and the metaphysical, something that is unseen to most of us.

One beautiful August day Houston spelled, "I cannot explain to you how much energy there is in the stars today." When I researched, I discovered there was a particular celestial event occurring that I had no awareness or knowledge of, but Houston could feel it. There is also the energy of Wi-Fi signals that bombard their bodies. So constant and ever present, Houston described the EMF's generated by Wi-Fi signals as "a buzzing in my ears and a weird sort of power in the air." Some days he would give me clues to what was trying to pull him back and engulf him again. "The radiation is weakening me." I watched in horror as my son could barely hold up his arm to spell. Then his eyes started blinking uncontrollably - - seizure.

Other parents told stories of increasing seizures as well the severity of them. When he was able, he told me to turn the Wi-Fi off in our home because it was pouring into him, and to make him walk in the grass every day no matter what his body did. I realized the invisible kryptonite in the air was sucking the life from my son so other people could watch movies at a higher speed. I couldn't control the heavens or even the outdoors, but I could control our home. Suddenly I was mad. Are my son and the others like him just collateral damage for the pharmaceutical industry and the telecommunications industry? I realize no one wants to corroborate research or testimonies that contradict profit and progress. But are corporate profits more important than the lives of our children? Do people not believe because it's not their child, not their life? Do people not want to know the effects of widespread use of multiple electromagnetic frequencies on people, plants, and animals because they enjoy the freedom these technologies provide? When did we all agree to this? I don't remember that consent form. Did I forget to vote? Where are the environmentalists? Where is Erin Brockovich??!!

While corporations that stand to profit from wireless technology mock any concern over the potential biological effects of increased RFR and non-ionizing electromagnetic radiation on human beings, animals, and plant life, those responsible for researching the effects of technology are singing a very different song. As of May 17, 2021, over 417 scientists and doctors who have conducted peer reviewed research on effects of EMF have signed the 5G Appeal and request for a moratorium on the roll-out of this technology. The article in Scientific American detailing the dangers was titled, *"We Have No Reason to Believe 5G is Safe"*. Doesn't that make you feel better? In addition, the research that was used to approve the current standards of exposure limits were based on research conducted in the 1980's that did not measure the biological impact of radiation, only the behavioral impact of increased radiation on rats. Since then over 500 peer reviewed studies have found harmful biological effects from RFR at frequencies that were low enough to not cause significant change in heat. These experts have written over 2000 articles and letters in professional journals explaining the dangers of RFR and wireless technology. There is proven research about the harmful effects of 2G and 3G, although not for 4G or 5G because governments have been uninterested in funding research and slowing progress. The shorter range of 5G technology requires far more towers. Now we are being bombarded by 4G and 5G radiation levels simultaneously. "Numerous recent scientific publications have shown that EMF affects living organisms at levels well below most international and national guidelines. Effects include increased cancer risk, cellular stress, increase in harmful free radicals, genetic damages, structural and functional changes of the reproductive system, learning and memory deficits, neurological disorders, and negative impacts on general well-being in humans. Damage goes well beyond the human race, as there is growing evidence of harmful effects to both plant and animal life."[131] But what also hasn't been considered is the effects of multiple levels of RFRs on those who have neurological conditions and seizure disorders. What about them? Where are they supposed to live? Why is their health not important? Why is their life not important? Why should they have to experience ongoing seizures and be forced to take psychotropic pharmaceuticals with horrifying side effects because you want your Tik Tok video to play without pausing? Why? When is society going to realize that sometimes innovation goes too far?

In addition to the onslaught of man-made electromagnetic frequencies bombarding them is the power and impact of the thoughts and emotions of others on bodies that are basically Verizon cell towers for all that energy. The reality is neurotypicals consciously perceive 4% of the energy in their environment. That's right. **You** perceive 4% of the energy in your environment. There's another 96% that you think isn't there because you are not consciously aware of it. But individuals like my son, well… I don't even know if he could put a percentage on how much his brain receives and processes. It is beyond comprehension. But people want to say it isn't there if I can't see or touch it. What that actually is, is a statement of ignorance about the nature of energy and our own limitations. Only the slowest, most dense forms of energy are mass,

[131] https://blogs.scientificamerican.com/observations/we-have-no-reason-to-believe-5g-is-safe/
http://www.5gappeal.eu/the-5g-appeal/

and the normal range of sound, vibration and light perception by neurotypicals represents a fraction of the wavelengths and frequencies perceived by other species.

One day as Houston struggled to spell on the board, I became more and more anxious, feeling like the heavy cloak of autism was pulling him under. He finally spelled, "You cannot understand how much energy I'm feeling coming from you." I had to let that reality sink in deep. He was not only feeling his own emotions, but mine as well, without the ability to regulate the effect they had on his amygdala and limbic system. The reality of emotion is, even we can sense the emotions of others and be affected by them, without one word ever being uttered. Emotion is simply exactly what it says it is E=Energy and Motion - Energy in Motion. So someone's annoyance, judgment, voyeurism, greed, jealousy, arrogance, pride, hate, lies, doubt, and anger have a profound effect on autistics as waves of the differing emotions and thoughts of multiple people bombard them. In the same way, peace, love, joy, faith, humility, kindness, empathy, serenity, hope, generosity, compassion, and truth have an incredible power and strength that resonates deeply within them. It is these incredible people who truly experience, in technicolor, the real spiritual battle raging wildly around us all. Autistics have all 1200 high-definition cable channels in full technicolor running and the rest of us are operating off three grainy, black, and white channels from a tubular television. Arrogantly, we think autistics are oblivious to reality. Yet the truth is it's us that is blinded by our ignorance and lack of foresight and compassion.

I remember one night with our friends from the pizzeria when one of the guys joined us who hadn't yet experienced Houston's abilities. They all wanted Houston to tell what his aura was. The young man sat with arms folded, apparently indifferent, stoic, stable, a rock - the coolest of the cool kids. I called Houston over and instead of spelling colors Houston spelled, "Tell him to calm down." I looked at the rock of a young man. Puzzled I said to him, "He said to tell you to calm down." We all looked at him, confused. He seemed so solid and sure. He fell forward and put his hands on his head exclaiming, "HOW DOES HE KNOW THAT??!! I'm freaking out inside." I just looked at Houston in awe. "You're an empath too?" "Yes, I feel everything."

Even the rain Houston experienced as energy. With each shower, whether it was thunderous flood waters, steady and heavy, or light and misting, Houston would always lose himself within himself. I asked him to explain what was happening. "The rain is water in my mind, tears of purple and gray from heaven that heal the earth with prayers inside them. The prayers are energy and they tell the earth what to do." I remember he told one of his therapists, "God is everywhere. Energy is everywhere. He is all around us." Truly everywhere.

***

After looking over Houston's accommodations our local community college invited Houston to apply for admission and he began preparing for the placement tests. I downloaded every practice test and the app. I talked to his spelling coaches at the center. They quizzed him over and over during sessions. Morgan helped. For hours every day over the next six weeks all we did was take practice tests. First, we focused on reading comprehension and grammar. I was shocked by how well he comprehended but I quickly noticed the skills he lacked. He did not understand the nuances of test taking and wasn't looking for funny wording that could easily lead you to make a wrong choice. The other factor was his anxiety and the time it took. He couldn't track because of his many visual issues, but at the same time having a photographic memory made him take in an overwhelming amount of information at once, making it difficult to focus on one sentence or to go back and refer to different points. It was almost all memory and he had to decipher it, which was exhausting and actually a disadvantage in this environment. I remembered how Ido Kedar explained how he didn't want to read visually, only audibly, because his mind was already too filled with the visual imprint of pages and pages of words that were exhausting to comb through. These brilliant individuals were actually taking in too much, not too little.

53

Gone

A wise son brings joy to his father,
but a foolish son brings grief to his mother.
— Proverbs 10:1

June 4, 2019

At the end of May, Paul graduated and turned nineteen the next day. I did everything I could to make it wonderful. All these young men I had known since they were in middle school stood in my stairwell with their caps and gowns and it was surreal. Paul had made the competition COED team in college and all he could think about was getting out. He became cocky and cruel. Every day Benjamin was complaining about something Paul had done. He would sleep until two in the afternoon, vape and get high. Everything was a mess and if I asked him to do anything he would snap. I really began to think the marijuana was much more of factor than I realized. No matter how many times I laid down the rules, he broke them. I didn't know what to do. The posturing had begun to look frighteningly familiar. I began to fear my son.

On this afternoon when I got home from work, Benjamin was complaining about his brother again. The garage was filled with teenagers. He had already refused to do what I asked him and to help with Houston. I asked to speak to him outside and told him the attitude needed to change, he needed to stop sleeping so late and help around the house. There was back talking and eye rolling. "Is this just because I wouldn't watch Houston?"

"No, it's not, but since you brought that up, you haven't shown any interest in getting to know Houston or learning how to use the boards."

He screamed, "BECAUSE I DON'T WANT TO!! I'm leaving and I just want to hang out with my friends."

Earlier Houston had asked him to learn the boards and said, "Then will you be my friend?"

It made me nauseous that one of my sons was treating his brother that way. As he stood glaring at me outside our front door, I tried to reason with him and said, "If he was deaf, it would be the same as you refusing to learn sign language. How would you feel if it was you? What would you want him to do? How can you refuse to learn? He's been trapped in his body over twenty years and he just wants to have his brothers as friends."

He screamed, "I'm so sick of you! All you ever do is nag me!

"If you did anything, and I do mean anything, then I wouldn't have to repeat myself. It only seems like nagging because you never help."

He walked off while I was talking and I said, "Wait, I'm not done talking," and put my hand on his chest as he walked by me.

He threw his hands up and with the scariest scowl that was a mirror image of his father shouted, "I'M LEAVING! I'M DONE WITH YOU!"

Just like that he was gone. He gathered what he and one of his friends could gather and left. I wouldn't see him for almost a year. Other friends who had basically become my other children were yelling at him and telling him he was wrong and to apologize. No one could believe it. Afterward they told me about how he had changed over the last year. They told me so many things to try to comfort me and shed light on his behavior. But I knew what the real issue was. It was the Big Jock. He had swept in, stolen, lied, and destroyed. It was what he always did. I was scared my son was gone for good. What his friends were able to see on social media was that Paul had gone to Florida with the Big Jock. That terrified me like I can't explain. Houston told me to pray. I didn't have the same reaction as I had in the past. I prayed every day. I prayed for love, light, and truth. I prayed for protection and for his eyes to be opened. I prayed for my heart - my son was unwittingly carrying it. Paul tried breaking into my accounts. The other kids insisted I get the locks changed. '*What* was happening? *Why* was this happening?' I prayed. Old prayers, new heartbreak.

> *My son, if sinners entice you, do not consent. If they say, "Come with us, let us lie in wait for blood; let us ambush the innocent without reason; like Sheol let us swallow them alive, and whole, like those who go down to the pit; we shall find all precious goods, we shall fill our houses with plunder; throw in your lot among us; we will all have one purse"— my son, do not walk in the way with them; hold back your foot from their paths, for their feet run to evil, and they make haste to shed blood. For in vain is a net spread in the sight of any bird, but these men lie in wait for their own blood; they set an ambush for their own lives. Such are the ways of everyone who is greedy for unjust gain; it takes away the life of its possessors.*[132]

June 12, 2019

The Big Jock's second bankruptcy filing was denied. The appeal was set for a court hearing and was denied as well. The judge issued an injunction against him to prevent a bankruptcy procedure from putting a stay on my contempt/compliance hearings or anything related to my case. I got another hearing. It was almost a year since the original compliance hearing.

The other judicial officer had retired and there was a new one. The Big Jock pulled out the ridiculously wide spreadsheet he had given to the first judicial officer a year previously and claimed again he had overpaid by over $500,000. My attorney, in rapid fire succession read the decision the court had reached the previous June, listed the arguments that had been disproven with our evidence, and then listed all the discovery that had still not been provided. My attorney was livid. I loved her. No one ever talks about how amazing it feels to finally have a real defender when you've been the target of relentless evil and vicious attacks. That's what a hero is. They show up when no one else will. They show up when the enemy is powerful. They show up and do the right thing that no one else wants to. They don't bargain, negotiate, and shake hands with evil. They don't stand down. They stand up. They understand evil. They know evil never rests and never grows tired of doing evil. They know evil thinks hurting others is sport. A hero fights to take them out of the game. Heroes are the only way the world will change.

The judicial officer was as calm as could be. The Big Jock told her that one of his children had actually chosen to live with him. It had been eight days since Paul left. I could actually feel my heart swell and grow hot at those words. The pictures on social media showed Paul bragging about a used Mercedes his dad had

---

[132] Proverbs 1:10-19

given him. I knew who was buying and who was being bought. Paul would find in a few months his father was a liar, what he gave he would always take back. After asking the Big Jock questions and listening to his ridiculous lies, the judicial officer ordered him to be incarcerated and placed a $20,000 purge for his release. She said to him, "Do you think we haven't seen this before? Do you think we don't know you've manipulated the legal system to avoid supporting your children? No. You're going to jail." I walked out of the room and cried. I hugged my attorney. I can't even explain the feeling from that moment. The goal of wicked people is always to wear you down and crush you, to make you so tired you give up on justice. For whatever reason, maybe stupidity, I didn't know how to quit. Often, like in the case of Reagan, I had no legal recourse. But I promise you, and every one of the people who have sought to destroy me or my children, I have learned the power of belief. Every day I approach the throne of God with confidence, seeking truth and justice, and I have His assurance that my prayers will be answered.

One of Paul's friends came over that night with a bottle of wine. He told me it was from his mom and to celebrate the beginning of justice. Morgan and Reagan cried. Reagan's tears were painful to hear. She couldn't talk. But there was a relief in them. Benjamin was in shock. I think everyone was shocked that finally there was some action by the court. Unfortunately, there were limits to what the court could do. I knew his parents had millions available, so I knew it was possible to pay the purge. After two weeks a hearing was held. There had still been no payment. He claimed he had no money, and no one would help him. The judicial officer lowered the purge to $10,000. Morgan and I both checked the system every day to see if he had been released. We were both afraid of him coming to kill me. Benjamin told me he would defend me. I told him he didn't understand how his father worked. He would never have the chance. I called the police and they explained they could patrol the area if he was released. I knew too much about how his mind worked to not be anxious. Houston had told me that around the same time Reagan had been molested, his father had drunkenly put a gun to Houston's head when he was making all his noises in the middle of the night and whispered he was going to kill him. Monsters are mean.

One day when I was asking, where had God been, and why had my prayers not been answered, Houston spelled, "Dear Mom, God protected you from being killed." I asked what was he talking about. Houston spelled, "Do you remember *Little d?*" I nodded. Benjamin said, "I remember him!" If my ex was the Big Jock, *Little d* was the Small Jock, his sidekick, his henchman. I just thought their partnership was limited to using women and financial scams. Houston continued, "Before he moved Dad tried to get *Little d* to kill you when he was gone." Benjamin and I both were speechless. Knowing all the details going on at that time, it was frighteningly conceivable. He was obsessed with *Forensic Files* and *Snapped* and seemed to take a sick delight in those shows. Houston continued, "God kept *Little d* from doing it. God protected you." I didn't know what to say. I was quiet with the weight of it. I thought mostly how awful it had been for Houston to carry this all by himself, unable to tell me or warn me. The plans of men... They think God does not see. *Only fools say in their hearts, "There is no God." They are corrupt, and their actions are evil; not one of them does good!* [133] How much had I not seen the hand of God or seen His wings surround me?

[133] Psalm 14:1

Every word of God proves true;
He is a shield to those who take refuge in Him.

Once God has spoken; twice I have heard this:
That power belongs to God,
And that to you O Lord, belongs steadfast love.
For you will render to a man according to his work.[134]

I lift up my eyes to the hills. From where does my help come?
My help comes from the Lord, who made heaven and earth.
He will not let your foot be moved; he who keeps you will not slumber.
Behold, he who keeps Israel will neither slumber nor sleep.
The Lord is your keeper; the Lord is your shade on your right hand.
The sun shall not strike you by day, nor the moon by night.
The Lord will keep you from all evil; he will keep your life.
The Lord will keep your going out and your coming in
From this time forth and forevermore.[135]

[134] Proverbs 30:5; Psalm 32:11-12
[135] Psalm 121

54

The Prey who Pray

Deliver me from my enemies, O my God;
protect me from those who rise up against me; deliver me from those who work evil,
and save me from bloodthirsty men.
For behold, they lie in wait for my life; fierce men stir up strife against me.
For no transgression or sin of mine,
O Lord, for no fault of mine, they run and make ready.
— Psalm 59:3

July 1, 2019

Without the Big Jock paying one cent the courts were forced to release him. It had something to do with the constitution of Georgia not being a debtor's state. Another court date was set for late October, so he had an opportunity to find work and pay child support. What a joke. I found the law to be wholly inadequate in my life. Real wrongs were met with nothing at all. People could abuse, threaten, refuse to pay, lie, steal someone else's child and there was little that could be done. That night I was scared. I knew he would retaliate and blame me for the time he had spent in jail. I just didn't know what he would do. I slept with my door locked. I prayed with Houston and called out to heaven for legions of angels to protect us. I put oil on my doorposts and continued to pray for heaven to come down and completely surround me. When I finally stopped bustling about, I got a board to spell with Houston. As he was spelling, I felt something brush against my leg. We were standing in an empty hall. I looked down. There was nothing there. I knew something had touched me. I asked Houston, "What was that?" He spelled, "There are so many angels I can't count them. I can't see my Esther for all the angels." Even though I was scared, I knew I was not alone.

The next week I went on a business trip. On the way there Morgan called. There was sheer panic in her voice. "MOM, someone from the Department of Adult Protective Services just showed up at the house." They said they got an anonymous report that Houston was being abused. I told them there was no way and that is why you left our dad. You have to call him!" I heard a whirling, swishing in my ears as my body went into some kind of hyper anxious state. I couldn't speak. I couldn't think. — I had known so many other moms, great moms, heroic moms, moms who still have scars from their children and from the system, who had told me their secrets when they had experienced this very specialized trauma. There are really not words for the emotional wounds it leaves. It's another one of the unspoken secrets of autism, the constant fear of your child's violent or reckless body resulting in someone, with no real idea of what your life is like, making a report to authorities, as if surviving this nightmare wasn't enough. These parents can't trust anyone, especially not teachers or strangers who make false assumptions and accusations. Or like in my case, a predatory and vengeful ex-husband can make a phone call full of lies, and you have no recourse. At any moment, some local authority can swoop in, without compassion or understanding, and wreak havoc on your life, your familiy, your child's life, and your good name. Isolation becomes self-preservation. They can't tell anyone how bad autism truly is. They live under the mandate to control their uncontrollable child, a shroud of shame, and in constant fear that their child's out of control body will result in the interference of a judgmental and compasionless bureacracy that has no earthly clue or concern what they have lived through and without. A brave face, a forced smile, and your story locked up inside your broken heart are your only armor. — I had to start taking short breaths just to keep breathing.

It took me a few minutes before my mind could calm down enough to think. The Big Jock. He had just been released. This was his payback. I called the department back and went through the interrogation after stepping away from a business meeting. I told them I knew who had called and why he had made a false report. I explained what was going on and that he hadn't even seen my son in two years. I gave the names of all of Houston's doctors and therapists. I was physically nauseous for weeks. The next time I took Houston to the center the owner told me they had called her to interview her about my treatment of Houston. I just hung my head and told the story. I was so incredibly exhausted from being his prey. I was so ashamed of having drama follow me when I really wanted a quiet little life. I was so worn down. It crushed me to have accusations against me that I knew weren't true, that *he* knew weren't true. It made me paranoid of what else he might do. I was just so tired and terrified. No one seemed to care that I was human, that I was a soul who wanted and needed things too. It seemed society's role was to judge me, not help me. No one ever prepares you for a life where you have to do the work of twenty people and be perfect at every hour of the day, with no resources and never make a mistake while strangers judge if you can take care of your grown child. But thank goodness, I prayed. I was going to trust God.

Late June - Early July 2019

Houston took three placement tests. I was his communication partner for the testing. There was a scribe who sat with us to facilitate and monitor the testing procedures. He was so nervous. I wasn't worried at all until we did the math portion. He had to show his work on a letter board that had numbers on the opposite side. He had to spell out each step and then solve the problem. We had been practicing and he had done well. But my anxiety about math was pretty much all I could focus on. I knew he could feel my anxiety. The day of that test started off well. Two thirds into the testing Houston started spelling strange things that made absolutely no sense. I asked the administrator to pause the test so I could find out what was wrong. He spelled, "My mind is being bombed with hot air balloons. I can't focus." It was the images he kept telling me about. I put my hand on his back and his shirt was dripping wet with sweat. I realized he was flushed and about to go into a full meltdown. I asked if we could take a break. When he stood up, he started jumping, rocking back and forth, making his noises, and then bit down on his lip. I grabbed his hand as he reached up to bite himself. We walked outside in the sun while I told him to focus on breathing. I prayed aloud. I had him do his cross-march exercises to help regulate and focus his mind. I recited Scriptures and sang some hymns. I got him some water and asked how he was doing. He was ready to finish. When all the results were in, he scored out of a possible 120: Reading Comprehension 112; Sentence Skills 105; Math 113. Houston was going to college. After he heard his test results he spelled, "Teaching me is the beginning of my destiny. Don't ever count me out. Always believe everything is possible."

Houston kept adding to his list of new activities to help him get back the experiences he had missed. Riding a bike was high on his list. But it was so complex, both the motor initiating and sequencing, using enough force to turn the pedals, and steering the bike when you have limited depth perception and eye suppression. Being two hundred and fifty pounds he needed a sturdy bike, but he also needed it to sit upright since he didn't have any core strength. In addition, it had to have a frame that could hold adult training wheels. It took a lot of searching but we finally found an old Huffy with high handle bars. Houston couldn't stop jumping for joy. After work and after the gym I would take him on the flattest road I could find to teach him. He couldn't hold himself up and leaned heavily to the right. I ran along beside him pushing his midsection to hold him and the bike up and encouraging him to pedal every single turn, while the mosquitoes bit me, and the humidity made it difficult to take deep breaths. Finally, one of the training wheels snapped off in pieces. All 250+ pounds of Houston and the bike crashed into me. Maybe I shouldn't have but I started sobbing right there in the middle of the street. I started cursing. I picked up the pieces and kept sobbing as I steered the bike, held the pieces, and guided Houston back home. It would be another $400 to purchase and install a huge heavy balancing frame that could support his weight. I just wanted help. I was so tired of doing everything by myself. It was all too much.

July 14, 2019

My friend L- and her husband brought their beautiful daughter over. Houston was tired but determined. He showed them his ability and their jaws were on the floor. They had known him most of his life. Then I asked their daughter if she wanted to tell Houston anything that I would speak aloud to her parents whatever Houston spelled that was from her. The words Houston spelled were drastically different than the words Houston used so there was absolutely no doubt it was her. She didn't waste words and her parents knew what she said was true. Then there was her body language, which I knew astonished her parents. These precious moments changed their lives. To every single parent Houston spelled to, trying to convince them to give their child a voice, he had one piece of advice. "Core beliefs are the most important. You must believe. It was my mom believing in me that made me know she would not stop until I had a voice." At one point their daughter didn't want to leave. This precious child of God knelt in a corner in my living room and wouldn't budge. I asked Houston what was going on. He spelled, "She's talking to her angels." Her parents were… well, they saw. They knew it was true. Her sweet father right before he left the frantic scene, looked at me directly and said one thing. Just two words, but it was so sincere, so earnest, so full of hope as if Houston and I had lit a fire. With an emotional impact that I am inadequately describing the father said, "Thank You!" He said it with his entire being. There was nothing casual about it. On the way home my friend from so many years ago, who had first connected with my life through a letter about poop seventeen years earlier, texted me. She told me, "I am processing, more like spinning. There is no question we saw something extraordinary this afternoon." She asked many questions. She wanted more research. But she was willing to believe in her daughter's competence. Then she shared, "My favorite part might've been when he looked at me with a gleam in his eyes. That. Speaks. Volumes." I knew exactly what she meant. It was like when J- had looked at me. His eyes had spoken directly to my heart. There was no questioning their message. It was simple, "Believe me. We are in here."

July 27, 2019

Houston's friend Devon from therapy and his parents came over to visit. Devon spelled to Houston, "What do you want to talk about?"

Houston responded teasingly, "You're trying to make me choose."

Devon's mom told Houston to throw it back to him. Everyone chuckled. Houston accepted the challenge. "Let's talk about spiritual things."

Devon tugged at his shirt excitedly "I would love to talk about spiritual things. It's all I think about, and my friends only want to talk about it a little bit. Do you see the darkness or just the light?"

Houston sat up tall and spelled, "I see everything. Neurotypicals believe. I've seen."

I nervously decided to tell what I had learned and experienced about energy. They stared at me with straight faces and didn't budge. I thought they would make some dismissive, skeptical statement like, "Well, that's interesting but…" Instead the parents looked at each other and then at me, "After what we've seen we believe you." I didn't ask what they had seen. Devon's mom said that Devon said their house is evil. Houston spelled, "It is. Your house is the most evil with bad idols." Devon spelled thanking Houston for confirming what he had told his parents. I took them upstairs to show them Houston's stones. Devon sat on Houston's bed, and I put the hematite in Devon's hands. The instant I put the stones in his hands ALL of Devon's impulsive movements stopped immediately. His hands and arms were still. His neck was still. His parents looked at him in shock. His dad tenderly sat down next to him and told him how amazing it was to see him so still and at peace. The biggest, most beautiful smile spread across his face. I couldn't take my eyes off him. The change had been instantaneous. His mom wanted to know where to get stones. Immediately I gave her the information to get in touch with Suzanne. We were all in complete awe. They began their own journey of hope and healing. Out of respect, that is their incredible story to share.

There was another frightening moment that happened with the unseen that left me unsettled. There are more details to this story that are private, and we are respecting our friends and their story. This is what we can share. While visiting a friend, Houston had told me to take him outside at the same time I felt that strange tingling on my arm. He told me he had seen devils and they had stared and harassed him. More remarkable things happened that confirmed this family's experiences. It was beyond explanation. As soon as we left that friend's house I drove as fast as I could with Houston to the church Morgan loved that was close to our home. Their services reminded me of the services from my childhood where people knew each other's names. They were kind, there was order, people were good. I drove there praying the whole way. I parked in the back of the church parking lot where there was a small rock garden with Scriptures on some of the stones along the path. I read them aloud as Houston and I walked slowly towards the large stone in the center. We sat down on the large rock and took off our shoes. We began praying and called for His protection. It was a quiet, hot Georgia summer day. We sat in the stillness. Then I realized my feet were vibrating again. I asked Houston if he felt it. "Yes," he spelled. I stared in wonder at our feet and then in wonder at the sky. We both felt Him.

August 6, 2019

After over two years and more phone calls and emails than are remotely reasonable, someone from Georgia Vocational Rehabilitation came to our home to do an Assistive Technology assessment for Houston. The meeting was supposed to be an hour. There were so many facets to consider due to his unique sensory needs, the meeting ended up taking two and half hours which flew by. I realized as soon as she left, I had missed a weekly conference call. I called and explained. I wasn't terribly concerned as I had never missed a meeting in the four years I had worked there. Other people missed meetings all the time. I could never have imagined at the time how costly that mistake would be.

August 10, 2019

Earlier in the spring Sarah wanted to take us to a special worship service where people were experiencing extraordinary healings. She brought one of her deaf friends and Joey along with us to the first service. Even though the place was absolutely packed and extremely loud, Houston spelled that he wanted to sit in the front. He was captivated when he watched the worship. Afterward there were people at the front praying for anyone who wanted prayer and anointing them with oil. People pressed on all sides, and I knew I needed to get him out of the crowded church. We went to wait in an empty hall. Sarah came to check on us and asked Houston if he wanted to be prayed over. He spelled, "Yes. The angels said the man in front is supposed to pray over me." That was who everyone was trying to get to. I told Houston that it might not happen. How little did I know. Sarah left to try to reach him. She came back about two minutes later. I was sure she was going to say there was no way. She smiled her huge, kind, happy smile and said, "He'll be right here." "Really??" I asked. "Yep. I walked in and he was standing alone, and I told him there was someone out in the hall that needed prayer. He dipped his hands in oil and started walking this way."

Right then he walked up behind her. I gestured to Houston and told the pastor his name. Houston sat up, ready to receive. The pastor anointed my son's head with oil and prayed deeply over him. When he was done Houston wanted to talk to him. The pastor had never seen a letter board. Houston asked him if he had loved God his whole life. The pastor nodded and said he had loved Him since he was a young boy. It was almost as if Houston was testing his sincerity and the depth of the pastor's faith. Houston told me he wanted to show him his ability so the pastor would believe that he's seen heaven. And Houston did. The pastor was speechless. Then Houston told him he sees angels and has visions of heaven. The pastor's eyes were wide with the reality of what he had just witnessed with his very own eyes and heard from Houston's board. Like Helen Keller signed into a hand the vision, beauty and intelligence of her spirit, Houston similarly pointed with his finger the things his tongue was unable to speak. The spirit of God was upon my son. Everyone felt it. Everyone there saw it as he spelled out a small speck of wonder he had seen. The pastor was quiet for some time. Finally he spoke, "We have seen healing from autism. It's not all at once. But it has happened. Almost like they walk it off." He turned to Houston and told him that he had to come back. As he walked off Houston told me he was praising God for what he had seen, and that God's praise was constantly on his lips. Houston spelled, "He was thinking, 'I never thought I would ever see something so wonderful. Telepathy. Divine telepathy. Praise God! You are so good!'"

At lunch that afternoon Houston wanted to talk to Sarah's friend who was deaf. He spelled, "What's it like not being able to hear?" Sarah interpreted the conversation in sign language. Houston was fascinated with Kenny. He had what Houston wanted, stillness, peace, silence. The conversation went from Houston's index finger, to my voice, to Sarah's hands, to Kenny's hands, to Sarah's lips, and then back to Houston's index finger. He told Houston that it was great. Peaceful. Houston spelled, "It sounds amazing." He desperately wanted rest from all he couldn't stop hearing. Houston told him his aura and he looked up the meaning of the colors. "This is me! This is me exactly," he signed to Sarah. He texted his wife and she was stunned at how accurate it was. Houston adored him.

The next service Sarah took us to was the North Georgia Revival. Again, it was loud with the cheers and shouts of praise. I was worried Houston would start stimming. I tried to get him to spell, and he kept pushing the board away. I noticed he was staring directly at the water in the baptismal pool. His comment when he was watching the baptisms was that "Emanating from the water is the best energy." Of course that might not seem like much but when I was watching him, he couldn't take his eyes off the water and didn't want to spell - he was mesmerized by the energy of the water. Finally he spelled. "It's wonderful. Heavenly. Angels are telling angels to answer prayers."

I looked around the crowded jubilant room. "How many are there?" I asked.

"To tell how many angels - it's as many as can fill the room. So many they stand waiting to get in." The lights were turned off. Houston continued to spell with barely any light, "Darkness can't extinguish the shine from the angels." I felt like I was on the edge of heaven.

He was allowed the opportunity to be baptized for healing. I took the letter board into the warm water with us. He spelled his name to the pastor and then spelled, "I'm here to be totally healed. I am autistic. I want to be in control of my body." The pastor read off the letters as he pointed to them and then spoke each word and sentence as he finished. After he spelled "body" he put his hand down. The look of accomplishment and love that spread across his beautiful face could only be matched by the joy of the pastor's face as he prayed for and baptized my son. Spontaneous worship broke out. I wept. But how could I not. Strangers were weeping and they didn't even know the young man they were watching was already a miracle.

Sarah decided we needed to take a break from Dostoevsky and read another book, Josiah's Fire, the story of a young autistic boy who had also seen heaven and had prophetic abilities. It took us several weeks to read the book between all the other things we were trying to accomplish. There is really no way to describe all the remarkable pieces of his story and all he described about heaven and the angels here on earth. So - read the book. Heaven is not like anything you imagined. Also read Jesus, Josiah, and Me so you can get a glimpse of how remarkable these young people are and how great a God we serve. The first independent words Josiah spelled were not "IM IN HERE" like Houston. Instead they were, "God is a good gift giver." Can you say that? Can you be trapped in a body out of your control, with no voice, with so many challenges, and yet still bear witness to the goodness of God before you have even hit double digits? Would those be your first words? Well, they were his. He continues to share the wonders of heaven and of God to anyone who has ears to hear. He has said things like "Trials are for truth not for suffering." How, may I ask, does a child who isn't a decade old have this kind of wisdom unless it was given to him or shown to him? So when I finished reading the book to Houston, I asked him, "What do you think?" Houston paused. Finally he spelled. "What he said is true." Apparently, while we've been limiting and isolating children significantly affected by autism, by keeping them in secluded classrooms and giving them no access to the education they have a right to, God has been taking a few of them on tours of heaven and sharing with them the greatest secrets of the universe. As usual, we got it wrong. But in His goodness, He got it right. He saw their hearts and showed them His. Then I remembered, *I will pour out my Spirit on all people. Your sons and daughters will prophesy, your old men will dream dreams, your young men will see visions.*[136] And they had.

Autism is Limited by Who I Am in God

By Josiah Cullen, written at age 13

Autism says, "I am a giant"

God says I am wonderful in power

Autism says I am failures

God says I am hurrying to save

Autism says bang the air with losses

God says truly I am director of a band of angels

Autism says value this foster care of you

God says you are attuned to light up my family

Autism says find a ruined fan to watch the blades turn

God says I am the wind

Autism says do a furious fit to sit in ropes of pain

God says I break every iron chain

Autism says fuss until the morning rises

God says give me your night so I can share mysteries

Autism says bait a hook held in a passive hand

God says throw the net on the other side of your boat

Autism says value this dinner of sameness

God says I prepare for you a feast

Autism says give a huge sound to no effect

God says I put words in your mouth since I thought of you

Autism says build a nice little tower of blocks

God says I am your strong tower and your safety

Autism says find a minute to be ticked off by a timer

God says I will show you the expanse of time and space

Autism says right and left and right and left

God says you stay on paths I lead you, and run

Autism says aim low and get some nice stickers

God says aim high and final truth is totaled for you

Autism says vines are terrifying in a jungle of so much stuff

God says I am the vine of connection and you are tied to me

Autism says ban the future of the human faithful tongue

God says I am the Word on this life

Autism says raise the gate of joy to give no satisfaction

God says joy is the fundamental of strength

Autism says fear the unknown and rely on patterns

God says trade up for promotion all of your days

Autism says futility is a durable day if you are good

God says you are fully alive when you are serving

Autism says double down on your boldness to nitpick

God says voice the attitude of mountains moving in faith
Autism says drive a durable wedge between you and others
God says love as I love and be a light in the world
Autism says build a fight to face more going and hoeing
God says I am a burden lifter and go with you
Autism says fun is given only to be taken somewhere else
God says beautiful gifts are from the gift giver himself
Autism says drive and drive to find a direct gate of alone
God says face a good day in major friendship
Autism says do a sad game of humor to be seen
God says you have never seen the love I hold in endless supply
Autism knows functional stories of things that don't matter
God tells the wisdom of the ages to judge the foolishness
God says be still and know I am God

Autism has never been the answer I need to my life in this world. God faithfully might ban this way of thinking to give me assurances. He is my tunnel vision. I need his direct light to say my life is full and I am open to a very mighty life in gifts he gives and taught to dare to be huge in him instead of small in autism. Finally, my gifts are built in listing what they are and are not. I am totally lighter now. This is my fundamental justice to say stars in the sky open to the faith of a nimble joy to dare me to praise the maker of my life. I am daily handed my rights. I am choosing him.

Autism is limited by who I am in God.

55

Siege

For we do not wrestle against flesh and blood, but against the rulers,
against the authorities, against the cosmic powers over this present darkness
against the spiritual forces of evil in the heavenly places.
Therefore take up the whole armor of God,
that you may be able to withstand in the evil day,
and having done all, to stand firm.
— Ephesians 6:11-13

August 12, 2019

Houston started college. He was taking two classes and Morgan was his communication partner. The first class was English 1101. He told me that he did alright, and the students were shy. The teacher asked them to do an exercise where they couldn't speak, to which he commented, "How ironic." Regarding his second class he spelled, "It was awesome. Everyone was so nice to me. That teacher told me she would help in any way. I was all nervous but I didn't need to be. Nothing to ask them yet. But that will be changing once I start learning. Once my talking starts I will be unstoppable. Remember I have no limits. Anything is possible."

Houston had taken some of his stones to class with him to help keep himself calm and protect him from the negative energy of the others. Oliver, Morgan's son, my precious grandson, loved playing with Houston's stones and lost all but two of his magnetic hematite. Houston needed more. I didn't ask him what I should do, I just drove us to a local shop that sold stones so Houston could choose new ones. It was weird. I walked the aisles with Houston asking if he saw any he wanted. Strangely, he didn't seem interested in anything. I asked the manager if they had any magnetic hematite. The manager was surprised when he realized they had none. I stood in the middle of the shop and held up the board. Houston spelled, "My angels are holding out their wings blocking me. Esther said not to touch anything. There are idols in this place. There is evil here. Take me home now." A chill ran through me even though it was almost 100 degrees outside, and the shop didn't have great A/C. I looked behind me. I hadn't noticed there was a second half to the store. There were literally idols everywhere. I grabbed Houston's hand and ran. The whole way home I prayed and told Houston how sorry I was. I started crying. I thanked our angels. I thanked my Savior. There was just so much I didn't understand. Houston explained to me that the stones radiate what they absorb, good or bad. I remembered stories other families had shared about stones in bad environments that corroborated Houston's actions. Frightening stories. It was overwhelming to realize there were all these forces that my son was witnessing and being affected by daily. It was also overwhelming to realize how fully determined and prepared His angels were to protect us.

It was around this time that my good friend invited us over to her home. She had a pool and loved having friends visit. It helped her not to think about the hurt and dysfunction in her home. Her heart just wanted to love. It was always hard to take Houston places, but he was excited to go swimming. We talked and talked, and Houston calmly shared his thoughts and wisdom with her. While we there she wanted Houston and I to see a machine she had bought. We went upstairs through her large, beautiful home and into a bedroom. Next to the bed was a small machine with dials and she showed us how you could change the dials for different frequencies for things you wanted. Houston walked in the room and left immediately. I kept glancing at the door, feeling the strong urgency to follow Houston. As she talked my entire body tingled overwhelmingly with that uneasy prickly feeling. I couldn't let her finish. I interrupted and told her, "I don't have a good feeling about this. You don't need this in your home. You need to pray. You don't need a machine." I hurried to Houston. He stood frozen in the hall, staring at what seemed like an empty hallway. He spelled, "There is something here. Take me outside." I grabbed him and sprinted down the stairs and out the back of the house.

By the time we got outside Houston had become unglued. He was jumping, running, and his body thrashed back and forth wildly. His face was in absolute terror and the sounds were beyond terrifying because they were sounds of horrific fright. My friend ran out after us and started crying when she saw Houston's reaction. She kept telling me she was sorry. The difference was that stark. I grabbed onto Houston with both hands while his body bucked violently, and I pulled him to my car. I told my friend I was leaving NOW. Even in the car Houston was breathing and panting like he was still being chased. I recited Scripture and prayed while I was speeding home as fast as I could with the top down. Once we were home, I did everything Suzanne had taught me to do while praying Scripture. I called out for the angels of heaven to surround us and protect us. I remembered something about salt. I put salt all around the perimeter of our home and in his room. By this time Houston was lying calmly in his bed. He spelled to me, "Esther left me. She's never left me before. They were trying to get to me and she and my angels fought the devils." "Is she ok?" I asked. I was horrified and humbled. Actually, I was ashamed. "She has wounds. She is healing. We are never allowed to go back there." I nodded my head. I called my friend and told her we could never come back. She had seen. She understood. She had thrown the machine out, opened the windows, saged, and prayed for hours, reading Scripture out loud until she fell asleep. From that day she began covering her home in Scripture. It started with one verse and then she realized she needed God's word to surround her. She literally taped Scriptures to every wall of every room she used. Her husband would take them down and throw them in the trash and she would write them down and tape them up again.

Sometime later Houston told me about devils. "The devils know to trigger my stims."

"How do you know it's them?" I asked.

"They gather to opine that God prides Himself in making poor people miserable. The things they say gets my anxiety going which triggers my stims."

I asked, "Do you hear them only or see them too?"

"I hear them mostly. Sometimes they make themselves appear weird. They try to tell you it's your idea."

"Can you tell when they've put the thought in your mind and when it's yours?"

"The difference is what I think will always make me pray to Jesus. What they propose is to forget God."

"I know you saw them at Devon's. Did you ever see them on your dad?"

"Yes. He had so many terrible ones making him proud and most vicious."

"Did you see them anywhere else?"

"The worst were the ones at your friend's. Getting a portal was stupid."

"I know. She knows."

Mid-August 2019

While I was working upstairs, someone rang the doorbell. Morgan was with Houston at school. It was someone from the Department of Adult Protective Services. They wanted to interview Houston. I told them they already had, and I had already been investigated. My stomach turned. The young woman, half my age with dreadlocks and a clipboard, told me there were new allegations. The sick nauseous feeling welled inside me. Truth didn't keep me from being attacked repeatedly even if the accuser was over 500 miles away. I told her when Houston would be home. She could ask him herself. She came later in the day. He sat down and put his hand on the table. She leaned over and picked up his hand and looked at his nails. I knew right then. It was the Big Jock. He had an obsession about having absolutely no white showing on my children's nails. He used to scream at me with terrifying ferocity if my children had any white on their nails at all. Morgan would bite hers to the core, till she bled. The woman from Adult Protective Services asked about the calluses on his hands. He spelled that he bit himself and had for many years. She told Houston he didn't have to live with me. My heart dropped to a place so deep inside me that I wondered if it would ever come back. I blinked back tears. Houston spelled that he did want to live on his own when he could take care of himself but right now, he wanted to live with me. He told her I was the most loving mom in the world. She told me I was accused of kicking Houston out of the house and locking him out and hurting him. I told her that she could wait until Benjamin, my youngest son, was home and interview him and that the reality is we have to lock the house to keep Houston inside because of the danger of elopement. She looked around our home, at Houston's room, at mine. She saw the intimate details of our lives. I told her I knew who it was that accused us and why he was making these allegations. I showed her the court orders, the incarceration, the bank statements that showed how he moved and hid large sums of money, and examples of how he threatened me. I showed her how my son had left and tried to break into my phone and Gmail accounts.

While I was showing her all this documentation Houston came up behind me and put his hand on my shoulder. Then he reached down and took my hand and just held it. It was normal behavior for him but then I realized she was looking at the tenderness between us. It wasn't even a thought for either of us but she was wise and she knew. She was kind and good and smart and true. I knew it in my heart, despite what lies I knew she had heard, she was… well, if that woman was put in charge of all the people with special needs then the world would be in a much better place.

I asked how many times someone could submit false accusations to harass someone in their system. She told me that it was not uncommon for people to use their services to harass others. She told me there were limits and after a certain number of investigations, they could prosecute for false reporting. She gave me her card and left. Houston gave her one of his sweet, soft hugs and smiled at her. When I asked him about it, he told me to trust God. With a heart of fear and hurt, I did. *I call on the Lord in my distress, and he answers me. Save me, LORD, from lying lips and from deceitful tongues.[137] Deliver me from my enemies, O God; be my fortress against those who are attacking me. Deliver me from evildoers and save me from those who are after my blood. See how they lie in wait for me! Fierce men conspire against me for no offense or sin of mine, LORD. I have done no wrong, yet they are ready to attack me. Arise to help me; look on my plight!.. See what they spew from their mouths- the words from their lips are sharp as swords, and they think, 'Who can hear us?"... But I will sing of your strength, in the morning I will sing of your love; for you are my fortress, my refuge in times of trouble. You are strength, I sing praise to you; you, God, are my fortress, my God on whom I rely.[138]*

[137] Psalm 120:1
[138] Psalm 59:1-4 , 7, 16-17

August 16-18, 2019

The friend who had sent me the Hebrews 11:1 verse years earlier wanted a group of us to meet together at the Billy Graham lodge in Asheville, North Carolina for a weekend of teaching by my favorite pastor. He was the one who had endorsed my book ten years earlier. I stood in line to talk to him. When I reminded him who I was his face lit up in surprise and my heart filled with goodness. I had to fight back the tears. The fact that he had that reaction meant so much to me. Over the weekend he taught on revival. Just for the record, this is not something Presbyterians preach on - EVER. And yet, here was this old Calvinist explaining why there was a revival coming and what the markers of a revival were. As he said, "Aslan is on the move." He taught about how Christians mess it up and how to treat people who don't have clothes or politics like yours. He taught how to love like Jesus would. He taught love and truth like he always did. Listening to him teach about how love meets truth made me feel like I was listening to the teaching of Jesus. And that's how it should always be. On the last day I was able to get a moment with him and remind him of my story and my son.

Very briefly I told him that my son that had smeared feces and run around naked was now able to communicate in detail about heaven and that there was a real miracle going on in the autism community. While he gave his last talk, I wrote him a summary of the story you've already read. I walked down and handed him my pile of scribbled notes, a handwritten glimpse of a miracle. As I was writing my friend kept elbowing me asking, "What are you writing???" I just shrugged, "The truth."

August 19, 2019

My favorite pastor emailed me in response to the letter I had handwritten. The message was compassionate and clear. *Write the book.* I didn't respond because I didn't want to write a book. I didn't want Houston to write one either. I wanted to stay safe. If there was one thing I knew about people, it's that they were really mean. I could count on it.

August 20, 2019

It was 8 am. I was already ready for work and just waiting for Morgan to get there so I could drive to work. Even though it was August I was having a good hair day which was shocking to me. I thought to myself, 'This never happens at this time of year.' I finished up Houston's therapies. I heard Morgan coming in yelling, "Sorry I'm late. You can go now!" I grabbed a board and asked Houston if he had anything to say before I left for work. He spelled, "All the angels do is talk about you." I thought, 'I don't have time for one of these conversations.' I said, "Ok. I love you." I hugged him and kissed him and ran out the door. I yelled to Morgan that I loved her. I jumped in the car and headed to work. The tension was so toxic at work, I didn't want to be late. Fortunately my commute was short, so I wasn't too worried. I got in the left-hand lane. Because I lived close to the FedEx distribution center, I knew there were a lot of trucks that backed up to make the first left hand turn. Even though there was an officer there to stop traffic for the trucks turning left out of FedEx, the left-hand lane was the faster lane. The cop wasn't stopping traffic, so I cruised along. And then there was a split-second flash of black in my left peripheral and an explosion in the same second. It was like my mind registered this:

Bl - (not black just bl).

Massive head on explosion (the force of Mike Tyson punching my face, stomach, and arms at full velocity and force simultaneously).

Impact creates a violent force to the right.

Enormous PUSH backwards pushing me into the seat and also to the left which physically doesn't make sense.

Explosive impact of another car hitting me from behind and the side as if the car was at an angle.

Impact sends car airborne.

Car flips. Intense PUSH and PULL as if my body went the opposite direction of the car.

Car flips again. Same forces all so fast I couldn't determine what was what. But for certain I felt myself being held down, especially my head. My head was undoubtedly pushed back.

Car stops violently...

The explosions wrung in my ears. Smoke and a weird smell I have never smelled before were everywhere. I heard hissing. The windshield was shattered, and my Jeep bent in half. Air bags hung lifeless in the air. Glass was everywhere.

I was shaking. I put my right hand down to try to push myself up, but it didn't register correctly in my mind because it felt like gravel under my hand. It was. It didn't make sense. I couldn't get a sense of where I was. Someone was yelling at me not to move. I realized my head was on the rollbar. The car was crushed lying on its side. Someone grabbed my yoga mat off the road that had been in the back of my car and put it under my head. They asked me if I was ok. I didn't know. My ears were ringing so loud I couldn't focus. I tried to think. 'Am I ok? Check body parts." My face and my arms felt like they were on fire. I tasted glass. My foot -- my foot was stuck under the pedal. My sandal was in a contorted position strapping my foot under the pedal and the straps on top of the pedal. Someone was yelling at me to give them a number to call. I couldn't think. 'Is my foot broken? What do they want? What's Morgan's number? My arms... My arms... Houston. Houston.' I don't know where her number came from, but I heard myself giving it to the man who was crouched down talking to me by my car. He called Morgan. He kept telling me she wasn't answering. I think I whimpered. I told him to call again. I saw someone standing with blood in between his eyes running down his face looking at me in fear. He was terrified. I didn't realize at the time that was who hit me head on.

There was more shouting and sirens. I looked at the street. All the contents of my purse were scattered across the pavement. I was cold and hot and scared and crying. First responders had arrived and were telling me I had to get out on my own. I could tell there was an urgency to this particular point. The man calling my daughter was still calling. No answer. 'How is there no answer? I just left the house. I know she's there.' They were trying to talk to me. I don't have any idea who it was or why it made sense, but someone stressed to me that it was extremely important that if I could I needed to get out of the vehicle on my own. They wanted me to tell them what was keeping me in the vehicle. In shock I was still trying to process. "My foot's stuck." They talked me through pulling my foot out. It was like I couldn't see how to move if that makes sense. (I realized later that the stress prevented me from organizing the motor planning and sequencing movements like Houston experiences 24/7) I couldn't support my weight at all. Everything seemed disconnected. Finally I told them if they pulled me out far enough, I could crawl. I got my leg out and my phone slid out from some hidden place while the rest of my belongings were all over the road. I remember thinking, 'My phone survived??' My car is demolished but my phone is fine.

When I was pulled out my legs went limp while men grabbed my arms. My feet were twisted underneath me. It took everything to pick each foot up and take a step. My arms felt like they were on fire. I saw a woman lying on the ground face down on the grass. My stomach was sick instantly. 'Please God. Please don't let someone be dead. Please don't let someone be that hurt.' I couldn't tell what they were doing to her because they were moving me so fast. I saw the man with the blood on his face again. I stopped and told someone to 'get the letter board.' It was lying in the middle of the road. I couldn't lose the letter board. Seriously, it is the alphabet, and I could have made another one. But in that moment of delusion and barrage on my senses, I didn't care about my purse or my yoga mat, the intense burning on my arms, the blood on my clothes, or my face or arms. I wanted my son's voice. That was all I wanted. As they put me in an ambulance the man trying to call Morgan ran to the EMT's and handed me the phone. I told her I was in a horrible accident. I didn't know what was happening and to ask the EMT's. All I knew was I was going to the hospital, and I didn't need an oil change anymore. I called a friend at work and told her. I didn't want to be late or be in trouble. There was no way I would make the conference call. The EMT was so calm, I felt foolish for crying. I decided I needed to pull myself together. I spent the ride praying and crying quietly.

I was taken to the hospital and treated for related injuries. The impact had both bruised and burned the Jeep logo from the steering wheel into my forearm. I looked rough but I was ok. The police officer came in and asked if I knew what happened. I told him I saw a fraction of a second of black before everything exploded. I knew I had been hit a second time and there were several flips. He crossed his arms across his chest and with a serious look told me, "I don't know what to tell you. People don't survive that. I never get to talk to someone after an accident like that. I really don't know how you're alive. Clearly you're not ready to go." He explained that someone had been stopped to make a left turn into FedEx and the car that had hit me came up behind that stopped car too fast and swerved into oncoming traffic (me) to avoid rear ending someone. The force was so powerful it pushed me into the lane beside me which was when the second collision happened. Then my car started trying out for the Olympics Gymnastics team. He told me the driver just had a gash on his face even though his car was totaled. I asked about the woman I had seen on the ground. He told me she was older but there were no life-threatening injuries. "I really can't explain it," he said, shaking his head.

After some time I finally got to see Morgan and Houston. She was sweet and loving, concerned. Houston was… well he was chill as could be. Then she told me. "Mom. I have to tell you something. First of all Oliver had my phone which is why I wasn't answering. (Explains a lot) Anyway, it was so weird as this man was telling me my mom had been in an accident, I heard the sirens through the phone AND driving by. It was surreal." I agreed that would be weird. "MOM! That's not weird. WAIT TILL YOU HEAR! I got to the hospital as quick as I could. It took the EMTs a while to get you here. I was getting more and more anxious while we waited. No one had any information. I got the board out so Houston could tell me what he was feeling or thinking. He spelled, 'Calm Down. She's fine.' MOM! HE KNEW!! I looked at him and I said to him, 'YOU KNEW!' He spelled, 'Don't be mad. It had to happen.' Do you hear that??? He knew!!" I was stunned. What could I say?

When I finally got to talk to Houston, he told me, "It had to happen. I'm sorry I didn't tell you. They wouldn't let me." I thought back through the morning. "This morning you said all the angels do is talk about me. What were they saying?" He told me, "Don't be mad I didn't tell you. The angels told me I couldn't tell. It had to happen for God's wonderful plan to work. The angels were giving out jobs to protect you." I remembered how after the first impact I felt an enormous force pushing me into the seat right before the second car hit me and my Jeep started flipping. It was flipping like a tin can, but I didn't move like the car did. Then Houston told me that the angels loved me and that I had a band of angels. I didn't understand it all. Why would there be a band of angels when for so long it had felt like God had forsaken me? I asked Houston and he said, "God covered Himself to not let your prayers come to Him. I wondered if He had stopped loving you too." "But why? I needed Him," I asked. "Trust Him. All of your prayers will be answered." I went to bed that night in wonder, praising God and thanking Him. What else did I not know or see or understand? Here I was, in my bed, safe and sound. Hurt and sore, but ok. I knew there was no way I should be alive. Today I had seen the hand of God. I knew that too.

When I emailed the pictures to my pastor friend, he commented that maybe God was keeping me around to *write that book*. So of course I didn't. In my defense, God seemed to have told other people to tell me to write the book as it came up in conversations almost daily. Inwardly I would roll my eyes. I told God I was willing to write a book, but I needed to be free of all other obligations. There was just no way I could keep up the pace with my massive workload, Houston's therapy schedule and then add to that, writing a book of such tremendous vulnerability and wonder. I reminded God there was also the issue of money. It seemed settled - at least to me. Now was obviously not the time. It was impossible. I don't say that anymore.

I took the rest of the week off work just to rest and handle the logistics of the accident and replacing my car. The guy who hit me had minimum limits and had totaled two cars besides his own. It was wonderful I had not been seriously injured. When I had some time, I asked Houston what I had been wondering. "Houston, how much do you see what hasn't happened yet?" He spelled, "Time is all happening at the same time. The angels open windows to let me see some things. Other times they tell me." "Ok, I have another question. Why do you tell others the names of their angels, but you won't tell me the names of mine?" I asked. "They will not let me," he answered, and then he added, "They love you." I had learned I was supposed to trust that was a very big deal, a very big love.

I'm not certain where this next idea came from, but I decided I needed to be bolder in my faith, bolder about my prayers. I bought a pink linen box and lined every available space of the interior with the promises of God. I poured Scriptures into my heart like I hadn't in years. As I searched through my old Bible, I saw verse after verse after verse underlined and notes I had made in the margins. I recalled the anguish I had felt and the prayers I had prayed. Something stirred inside me. Some of the flowers from my old garden were still pressed within the pages. Every verse I read felt like reminiscing with a dear friend. There was something deep and transcendental in the pages, as if God was sharing His heart with me as more than a child, more than a friend. Most importantly I treasured the countless words of God's love for me, that *The LORD your God is in your midst, a mighty one who will save; he will rejoice over you with gladness; he will quiet you by his love; he will exult over you with loud singing.*[139] The breath of God stirred my spirit. But it was the love of God, something human words have not yet been quite able to pen, that grasped tightly of my heart. Suddenly, LOVE just seemed to appear when it had been absent for longer than I could remember. I wish I had better words for it. It was peace, belonging, intimacy, and a net - a really big net. For only the love of God would be able to hold me tight. The tempests that had roared for so long wanted to rip me away or rip me to pieces. Blindly, I walked toward what I hoped, what I believed. Satan cackled. Jesus dug deep.

---

[139] *Zephaniah 3:17*

56

The Earth is the LORD's

For by him all things were created, in heaven and on earth, visible and invisible, whether thrones or dominions or
rulers or authorities—all things were created through him and for him.
And he is before all things, and in him all things hold together.
— Colossians 1:16-17

Something in me wanted to understand more deeply the power and importance of energy in a way that resonated beyond the physical to the innermost layers of the spirit. Houston told one of his therapists who came to help us with his vestibular program, "God is here. He is everywhere. Energy is everywhere. It's in everything." He said it with the certainty of someone who sees it every day. Energy, I discovered, really was everywhere. I went to discuss learning about energy in people and environments from the woman who trained Suzanne. I got up early to teach yoga and then went to meet her. When I got home Houston was waiting at the top of the stairs with a letterboard and a giant smile. 'This should be interesting,' I said to myself. He spelled, "Did you meet the wonderful Grace?" He was giggling. "Good grief. Obviously, you know I did. Do you think I should do this? Do you think I should study energy?" He smiled and looked at me, and while still smiling spelled, "It is what is supposed to happen."

So in October I would begin a brand-new adventure that years before would have been inconceivable. With a cross on her neck and the love of Christ in her heart, Grace taught us how to become aware and in tune with the information our spirit was sensing around us, to quiet the analytical and listen to the spiritual, and mostly to trust what our spirit sensed. This was difficult for a Presbyterian. Presbyterians had rightfully been dubbed the Frozen Chosen of Christendom. Knowledge was their pride and focus. Sensing was not a skill I had *ever* been encouraged to develop. So with trepidation, I began to learn the art of listening, sensing, and trusting, instead of scrutiny, dissection, and proof.

While I had always known I was a soul who had a body and not a body that had a soul, I began to realize the enormity of this truth. The auras that Houston saw were not an outline of our bodies, but our etheric body that emanated within our physical body and outward as well. The sensations I got about people and places, many times before a word had ever been spoken, were actually the transmission of energy, positive or negative, to my spirit which had a far greater ability to perceive than the limitations of my physical senses. Throughout this process I learned to trust my gut, my intuition, the Holy Spirit's leading, and move beyond the limits of rationalization to the courage and confidence that accompanies being led into the unknown by the unseen Almighty Maker of Heaven and earth, and maker of me too.

There was so much to learn. Energy, I learned, was simply the movement of information, codes, and frequencies, which create oscillations that are vibrations and patterns that relay information. Because of Houston's sensitivity to stones I started there. I read about how quartz was used in watches, computers, and other technology applications because it is piezoelectric and can transform energy from one form to another, converting electrical signals into mechanical force and mechanical force into electrical signals. I read how Goodyear even had plans to use piezoelectric materials to generate electricity from moving tires and how scientists were using these energetic properties in surgeries and other applications. Stones had other properties too, they were dielectric, meaning they could be an electrical insulator that can be polarized when there is an applied electric field. Other qualities included piezo luminescence and piezo magnetism. It was an entire field of science. Each stone was a combination of different essential elements with unique properties and frequencies that interacted with each other. I remembered when Benjamin found a giant piece of white quartz in the woods and brought it home. Houston was mesmerized, "I can't explain how much energy it has. It is pushing the power of other energies." His words didn't make sense and I made him spell it three times. No sense at all, that is until I read about the unique *conducting* qualities of quartz crystals. I thought of a conductor, both in heat and in music and realized how accurate his description was "pushing the power of other energies." Once again, I was confronted by evidence that he saw and felt the pulsating vibrations and subtle energies because of his sensitivity to energy. His description was of someone experiencing the energy, not of knowledge from books. He was witnessing the conduction taking place, the "pushing the power of other energies." I needed to know more. I read how crystals were being used in LED, LCD, computers and microprocessors, optics and laser optics, infertility treatments, surgeries, micro electrical mechanical systems, motors, sensors, actuators, solar energy, and many other emerging technologies.[140] The more I read, the more I came to see stones as the first computers in the most raw and natural state. Energy was everywhere and in everything. It operated according to its unique characteristics in that particular piece of God's creation.

I researched the technology behind the MRI (magnetic resonance imaging) that uses the magnetic and vibrational oscillations of a person to take pictures inside their body. I read about how humans both receive and transmit energy and are in a constant state interacting with the energy in their environment, most of which is unseen and also why we, with our electromagnetic makeup, are affected by electrical power lines, fault lines, EMFs, etc. I read about the anxiolytic, anti-inflammatory, anticonvulsant chemical makeup in some essential oils such as asarone, carvone, citral, eugenol, and linalool (to name a few) that appear to modulate the GABAergic system of neurotransmission and alter ionic currents through ion channels,[141] and realized that these chemical reactions were why Houston kept insisting that "the oils are the most important custom for me."

I read about the Chinese discovering the Qi, the electromagnetic forces that flowed within each human being, just like it flowed through the rest of creation. Houston had told me about the direct current, as opposed to alternating current, that flows inside us and how his was very weak and unstable, almost like a battery going dead that was about to lose its charge. He kept insisting, "I need more direct current." I read about the Schumann Resonance and the vibration of the earth at 7.83 Hz and our homo sapien vibration of 7.7 and how the earth's frequency affects brain development in children, as well as why we feel so much better when we are out in nature and our body becomes more in line with the earth's vibrations. The entire electromagnetic spectrum is a combination of the electric currents and magnetic fields ranging in vibrational output. Human beings are only able to perceive a small amount of this information through our senses because we have limitations to our receivers. From sound waves to gamma waves, everything is vibrating, moving, transmitting information. Visible light (what we see) is only a fraction of the entire spectrum with colors simply being light waves vibrating at different frequencies. For example we recognize that dogs and other animals sense and hear frequencies we don't. They have even discovered that plants emit sound, and some have a metabolic rate so high they produce heat. We have limits. But the energy is still there even if we don't perceive it. Just like with God.

[140] https://en.wikipedia.org/wiki/Piezoelectricity
[141] https://www.hindawi.com/journals/ecam/2019/6216745/#abstract

The electromagnetic frequencies of the human brain can be measured at different frequencies Alpha, Beta, Delta, Theta, and Gamma, helping us operate our bodies through these five states of consciousness. The connection between the earth and mammals is extraordinary. When I saw how similar the frequency of mammals is to the earth, I pondered if maybe it is because God made man out of the same substance as earth and breathed the breath of life into us. I thought about the elements of the earth and the composition of the human body. I already knew we were 96% water so that would certainly account for elements of hydrogen and oxygen, but what else? "Almost 99% of the mass of the human body is made up of six elements: oxygen, carbon, hydrogen, nitrogen, calcium, and phosphorus. Only about 0.85% is composed of another five elements: potassium, sulfur, sodium, chlorine, and magnesium. All 11 are necessary for life. The remaining elements are trace elements, of which more than a dozen are thought on the basis of good evidence to be necessary for life.[1] All of the mass of the trace elements put together (less than 10 grams for a human body) do not add up to the body mass of magnesium, the least common of the 11 non-trace elements."[142]

I compared these elements to the elements of the earth's composition. The main components of soil are nitrogen, phosphorus, potassium in addition to sulfur, calcium, and magnesium, in addition to trace elements. Soil receives hydrogen, oxygen, and carbon from water and the air. Each element carries a different frequency interacting with other atoms of other frequencies. The emission spectrum of a chemical element or chemical compound is the spectrum of frequencies of electromagnetic radiation emitted due to an atom or molecule making a transition from a high energy state to a lower energy state. The photon energy of the emitted photon is equal to the energy difference between the two states. There are many possible electron transitions for each atom, and each transition has a specific energy difference. This collection of different transitions, leading to different radiated wavelengths, make up an emission spectrum. Each element's emission spectrum is unique. [143]

Then there was water. I read about the studies on the molecular structure of water conducted by Masaru Emoto who claimed that human consciousness, emotions, prayer, and music actually changed the molecular structure of water molecules. His thesis related his findings to the fact that human beings are composed of 96% water, so the impact of our emotions on our molecular cell structure would be significant if his thesis is true.[144] Life was literally moving all around us between all living things, all the time. What was so fascinating was not just the presence of all these elements but the vibrational frequencies transmitting information, and the impact of that transmission from the unseen to the seen.

Then there was the earth itself. "In 1953, Professor W.O. Schumann of the University of Munich was teaching his students about the physics of electricity when they discovered that the earth's cavity produces very specific pulsations; the vibrational pulse of planet earth.

In 1954, measurements taken by Schumann and Dr. Herbert König, who later became Schumann's successor, confirmed an earth frequency of 7.83 Hz. In the years to follow, investigators worldwide began to research what had been dubbed "Schumann Resonances". König compared human EEG recordings with natural electromagnetic fields of the environment. Eureka! They discovered that indeed there was a correlation between Schumann Resonance and brain rhythms. This relationship between earth frequency and brain waves was then studied by researchers around the world.

142 https://en.wikipedia.org/wiki/Composition_of_the_human_body#:~:text=Almost%2099%25%20of%20the%20mass ,sodium%2C%20chlorine%2C%20and%20magnesium.
143 https://en.wikipedia.org/wiki/Emission_spectrum
144 The Hidden Messages in Water; Masaru Emoto

Dr König carried out further measurements of Schumann Resonance and eventually arrived at a frequency of exactly 7.83 Hz, which is even more interesting, as this frequency is one which applies to mammals. For instance, septal driving of the hippocampal rhythm in rats has been found to have a minimum threshold at 7.7 Hz (Gray, 1982)."[145]

And then there's the heart. I defer to the experts...

The heart itself gives off 2.5 watts of power which is much greater than any other organ of the body, including the brain. All the other organs come in tune with the heart. The heart, as it processes emotion and fluctuates in vibrational frequency, becomes the bridge between the spiritual and the physical.

***

"The heart is the most powerful source of electromagnetic energy in the human body, producing the largest rhythmic electromagnetic field of any of the body's organs. The heart's electrical field is about 60 times greater in amplitude than the electrical activity generated by the brain. This field, measured in the form of an electrocardiogram (ECG), can be detected anywhere on the surface of the body. Furthermore, the magnetic field produced by the heart is more than 100 times greater in strength than the field generated by the brain and can be detected up to 3 feet away from the body, in all directions, using SQUID-based magnetometers.

Prompted by our findings that the timing between pulses of the heart's magnetic field is modulated by different emotional states, we have performed several studies that show the magnetic signals generated by the heart have the capacity to affect individuals around us.

Every cell in our bodies is bathed in an external and internal environment of fluctuating invisible magnetic forces. It has become increasingly apparent that fluctuations in magnetic fields can affect virtually every circuit in biological systems to a greater or lesser degree, depending on the particular biological system and the properties of the magnetic fluctuations.

One of the primary ways that signals and messages are encoded and transmitted in physiological systems is in the language of patterns. In the nervous system it is well established that information is encoded in the time intervals between action potentials, or patterns of electrical activity. This also applies to humoral communications in which biologically relevant information also is encoded in the time interval between hormonal pulses. As the heart secretes a number of different hormones with each contraction, there is a hormonal pulse pattern that correlates with heart rhythms.

In addition to the encoding of information in the space between nerve impulses and in the intervals between hormonal pulses, it is likely that information also is encoded in the interbeat intervals of the pressure and electromagnetic waves produced by the heart.

This supports Pribram's proposal discussed earlier that low-frequency oscillations generated by the heart and body in the form of afferent neural, hormonal and electrical patterns are the carriers of emotional information and the higher frequency oscillations found in the EEG reflect the conscious perception and labeling of feelings and emotions. We have proposed that these same rhythmic patterns also can transmit emotional information via the electromagnetic field into the environment, which can be detected by others and processed in the same manner as internally generated signals."[146]

***

---

[145] Excerpt from Article: http://www.schumannresonator.com/
[146] McCraty, Rollin, Science of the Heart, Exploring the Role of the Heart in Human Performance Volume 2, HeartMath® Institute, 2015, page number, www.heartmath.org

There are studies which go even further to demonstrate how human touch and human connections affect blood pressure, transmission of information, and brain waves. Thought, emotion, and the body itself are all pulsing and transmitting information constantly with others and our environments, which are transmitting their own information. The universe as well vibrates wildly in a push and pull of force and power, magnetic and electrical fields. Quantum physicists continue to delve into the mystery of the unseen.

One morning I woke up thinking about the law of thermodynamics and death. Where does the energy in our bodies go after we die? It doesn't just disappear; it has to be transferred somewhere since energy can't be lost. The physical matter of our bodies no longer has an electrical charge after we die. Where has the energy, where has the spirit gone? For me this was logical, scientific reasoning to prove life after physical death, and as well that the gravity of our souls either transcended our spirits to LOVE, or in rejecting Him, weighted us to all we wanted instead of Him.

The more I studied energy the more I saw the connections between our bodies and our spirits, our connection to and the impact of the energy that surrounds us in nature, as well the impact of different traumas and choices on both. Two invisible diametric opposites. One our Creator through creation, providing for us, inspiring us, healing us, and loving us in every way possible. Evidence of His love, goodness, and faithfulness were everywhere, in all things, even the smallest details. In my studies I had been reading everything I could about *faith and how faith comes from hearing, and hearing through the Word of Christ.*[147] In at least twenty different places in Scripture, God referenced the ears and hearing to understanding truth and receiving faith, such as Jesus' frequent words, *"He who has ears to hear, let him hear."* Why would He keep saying that faith comes from hearing? Then I recalled how our ears turn acoustic frequencies into energy. His Word, the Word who created us and all things, who crafted the ear, His living, breathing Word actually turned into energy after entering our ear, but energy of some supernatural kind when our spirit and heart received it, when we let it root and received the exponential grace that came *from* the living Word. I was in awe. Just as our eyes turned toward light, our ears and hearts turned toward truth.

Then there was the opposite, the trauma, the fear, the darkness and hardness that wouldn't leave. Why were these reminders of our brokenness so difficult to shake even after Christ paid for every debt? We were supposed to live like we were free. We were supposed to be mighty in power and authority, joint heirs with Christ, princes and princesses of Almighty God. Why didn't we live like that? Was it because the trauma, fear, shame, and darkness, our old bedfellows were literally on our body, slowing us down, stagnating the spirit and energy that flowed within us? The unseen materially affected the seen, both those saved and unsaved. The truth was, most of us didn't act like we had been forgiven. We didn't act like we were loved. We didn't act like living without fear was even possible. In fact, that was a foolish thought. Trauma after trauma befell and we just kept running for shelter. For me I knew the reason was because I hadn't heard, and thus didn't truly believe, it was God's will to bless me, heal me, sing over me, rescue me, answer my prayers. There was only the constant concert of how unworthy I was, not that God yearned to give me good things. There were people like me who had been freed and still lived like orphans. There were safe people with easy lives who lived looking down on others. And there were also people who still lived according to the dark. We didn't know how to shed the darkness and the pain. Craig Miller's work in <u>Breaking Emotional Barriers to Healing: Understanding the Mind-Body Connection to Your Illness</u> made sense after what I had learned.

---

[147] Romans 10:17

Then there was sin. I thought back to Caroline Myss' statement that, "Liars don't heal... Dishonest people, people who lie, people who have moral crisis and do not get it, people who blame others for things they do and they know it, people who make choices and they know another person is going to pay for the consequences of that choice and they are conscious of it, they know for a fact that they are saying something that is not true and they know another person is going to be hurt by that, people who deliberately say things to hurt somebody - believe you me - your body knows you did that. Your mind knows you did that. Your heart and soul knows you did that." But I realized Jesus had taught the exact same thing, He just worded it differently. *You hypocrites! Isaiah was right when he prophesied about you: "These people honor me with their lips, but their hearts are far from me. They worship me in vain; their teachings are merely human rules." Jesus called the crowd to him and said, "Listen and understand. What goes into someone's mouth does not defile them, but what comes out of their mouth, that is what defiles them"... Don't you see that whatever enters the mouth goes into the stomach and then out of the body? But the things that come out of a person's mouth come from the heart, and these defile them. For out of the heart come evil thoughts—murder, adultery, sexual immorality, theft, false testimony, slander. These are what defile a person; but eating with unwashed hands does not defile them.[148] - Do not be afraid of those who kill the body but cannot kill the soul. Rather, be afraid of the One who can destroy both soul and body in hell. [149]- What good will it be for someone to gain the whole world, yet forfeit their soul? Or what can anyone give in exchange for their soul?[150]*

As I uncovered piece after piece of His hand in all creation, I was filled with awe at our Creator and how He had created His world to connect to us and help us heal and feel His presence. I marveled at how He knit us, spirit and soul together, material and immaterial, finite and infinite dwelling the same space. I was astonished at His presence, power, and hand that touched everything, even the - no - *especially* the invisible things, bringing truth from darkness and hope from despair. And I was overwhelmed by His relentless pursuit of us... of me... of my shattered, doubt filled heart and His capacity to bring good out of anything. Slowly, bit by bit, I felt like the scales had fallen off and finally, my broken heart could see. I saw LOVE.

[148] Matthew 15:7-10, 17-20
[149] Matthew 10:28
[150] Matthew 16:26

57

Genius, Like God, Is All Around Us

*"You can't come up with a formula to
change the way you experience the world."*
— Alicia Nash

After my car accident, I had taken the rest of the week off to recuperate, three workdays. It was the first PTO I had taken that year except for the two half days I took off for court and the day we traveled to North Carolina to visit my old friend. One of those nights I watched a movie with Houston. When it was finished, another movie started. I looked through my phone and glanced up as numbers scrolled quickly and flashed across the screen. "Oh look, it's π (*Pi*)," I said nonchalantly. I looked over at Houston and he was sitting forward with his eyes glued to the screen watching the numbers intently. It looked like he was calculating or confirming something the way his eyes moved. He was absolutely mesmerized by the screen in a way I had never seen. I grabbed the board that was on the sofa table behind the couch and scooted close to him. I asked him, "What's going on?" He spelled out, "That's what goes on in my mind. I see numbers everywhere and in everything." I was stunned and asked more questions about his aptitude for mathematics. "Math is like words to me. Teaching math to me as words just was understood right away." I said, "But you've only been taught single digit addition and subtraction and how to use a calculator." I just stared at him. I couldn't get over it. What was going on in that brilliant mind of his? As soon as I could I talked to a mom whose daughter was similar to Houston with an incredible aptitude for math. She nodded and explained that I should read <u>Born on a Blue Day</u>, which is about an autistic with incredible mathematical awareness. He just sees it, like Houston explained. She recommended I meet with a math teacher who had worked on the boards. This brilliant woman had a doctorate in math and would be able to help us decipher the extent of Houston's abilities.

It took several months for that meeting to actually take place for various reasons. But the results were more miraculous than I could have imagined. We met her in the old school where Houston spelled for the first time. As we passed the door I smiled. It was the door of hope. At a conference table this incredible teacher asked me to explain what I knew Houston knew. I told her about the touch point system in the schools where they teach addition and subtraction by counting the number of points on each number. She asked what else. Other than a calculator to add prices, that was it. I told her about the π (*Pi*) movie and Houston's reaction. She said, "I think I have an idea." She wrote the quadratic equation on a small white board and said to him, "I'm just trying to get an idea of where you are. I'm sure you can do more but let's just start here." And while my jaw dropped Houston solved it quickly and spelled out the answer on the number side of the board. The instructor grabbed a board with statistics symbols and quickly showed him the symbols on the board. He solved a high-level statistics problem. She told me that an acceptable answer would have been 1 or 2 but that he had done the exact number which was .96. At this point it was like she and Houston both were speaking

Mandarin to me, and I sat there unable to even comment. Then she put a calculus problem on the white board. 'Calculus?' I thought. 'Oh, I'm definitely going to record this. No one will believe me.' And I did.

The question was $\int_1^e 1/x \, dx$...

She had Houston spell out what he was going to do before he solved the problem, which he did. Then he solved the problem. $= \ln e - \ln 1$. She said, "*Well*, actually to be accurate what do you need to add?" He spelled out, "Absolute value."

I - Was - In - Shock. She told me he needed to be in a high-level math class, not remedial anything. Later Houston spelled to me, "It was the most wonderful moment. I was proud." And this is the kid whose school and psychological evaluations determined he was intellectually disabled at a four- or five-year-old level and only deserved a "free and appropriate" education that was limited to counting and grocery shopping.

This incredible teacher asked him months later to comment about the experience. Houston spelled, "Most of my life numbers would talk to me. The numbers are interposed in the world sort of like forces going on behind the scenes. I see them leap to move with all the movement that uses power. Really, the entire world is numbers orchestrating power. Good power finds numbers and equations that prove themselves true. Numbers tell so many stories. Creating work to sort out all the numbers is putting equations together so we understand the power used to move matter. When I met with my new teacher, losing the battle of creating these equations by myself was lifted. Getting to sort out the numbers on a board was wonderful. I used that to prove to myself that the numbers I see are true. Not only was that work with her the long awaited proof of my purpose, it showed others how brilliant I am. Start to work with numbers to show the world how smart we are."

I sent the video to several of his high school teachers. There were really no words. Everyone was amazed. But not one of them said they had been wrong. Which makes me ask… Why is that so hard? *I was wrong.* I was wrong about what I thought was true for almost twenty years even though I was committed to believing in a miracle that actually did come true. What was/is everyone so afraid of? Why are some afraid of giving people a chance to have a voice who have never had one? Are the experts and educators afraid of what they will say?

Clearly, there is no way that the testing measurements currently used can be trusted to accurately test the intelligence of someone who cannot control their body or the extraordinary amount of sensory information that is being processed in their mind. The experts mistakenly believe impulsivity and stims are a choice these individuals willfully make and both the proof and limit of their intelligence. When you think about it, every single current evaluation method of intelligence requires the ability to control your body - speech, writing, sign language. None of the testing allows for accommodations for those who lack purposeful motor control and have sensory impairments. Without that control and reliable sensory input, people just assume the individual doesn't understand because their body gives wrong answers or no answers.

I remember one of the never-ending evaluations for Houston when he was 18 was a picture with a bunch of leashes and dogs. The psychologist kept asking Houston repeatedly how many more leashes were there than dogs. At the time, I didn't know he saw three sets of images that overlapped and moved. He looked at me with sadness and looked again at the picture, unable to tell me what he was seeing, unable to explain to me that he understood complicated mathematical concepts and that dog counting was beneath him. The psychologist scribbled in his notes and made his determination. I sat in heartbroken silence, hating my life, and wondering how strangers had so much control over me and my son. I sat ignorant of the beloved genius beside me and of his equal heartbreak. Houston failed their test. But really, I failed. The doctor failed. The system failed for one simple reason - we failed to see past the end of our noses. We had to see to believe. Proof was more important than equality or dignity.

The fact that these intelligence tests were first developed by eugenists as a means of identifying and sterilizing the "imbeciles, the feeble minded, and other undesirables" and to justify genocide and racism, seems to have been completely lost on society. The inadequacy of these tests to measure creativity, emotional intelligence, work ethic, as well as hope, motivation, and countless other essential human attributes, seems to be irrelevant in our Darwinian quest to stand on someone else's shoulders and play king of the mountain. Yet we still look to these tests that inspired genocide to try to prove superiority and inferiority and dole out access and resources accordingly. Where is the virtue in that? Where in this human rating system is the equality and inalienable rights that we say we believe in? Where?

I remember in the movie *Caddyshack,* the pretentious Judge Smails tries to provoke the naturally gifted and unaffected Ty Webb to reveal his golf score. When Ty doesn't take the bait, the perplexed judge asks, "Well, how do you measure yourself with other golfers?" The six-foot four-inch golfer looked down at the tiny man who wallowed in power, position, and prestige and replied, "By height." It's absurd really. All of it. All our efforts to say some are more valuable than others because of something we arbitrarily judge externally is ridiculous, hurtful, and wrong. Why can't we just treat others (all others) like we would want to be treated? Why can't we just love?

The moral, ethical and legal choice would be to presume competence for everyone. Period. The worst that could happen is that you teach students who are non-speaking or unreliably speaking something that they won't need and don't understand. Of course neurotypical students are taught information they don't need, won't use, and often don't understand because we presume they are capable of learning something they haven't yet been taught and give them access to education which gives them opportunities to make choices. But if you can't control your body you have to prove your intelligence and earn the right to the education everyone else gets freely. This is a remarkably unjust policy in a country that presumes innocence to those indicted for breaking laws and equality as a fundamental attribute of humanity. When *incompetence* is presumed, we deny these citizens of their lives, their liberty, and their pursuit of happiness.

The least dangerous assumption holds that "in the absence of conclusive data educational decisions should be based on assumptions which, if incorrect, will have the least dangerous effect on the student."[151] Douglas Bilken stated that, "Presuming competence was nothing less than a Hippocratic oath for educators." Educators will argue that those with disabilities need life skills and vocational skills. I agree they need life skills but would call it purposeful movement that encourages independence and/or autonomy. They do not need vocational skills for monotonous jobs though if that is not what they want to do with their life. That's a choice, and it's theirs, not ours.

For a moment put yourself in their shoes. Really try to imagine it. That's how empathy happens, when we feel what others feel. Slowly let this reality penetrate your heart …

Because YOU can't control YOUR body YOU receive no education past the most basic elementary material. YOU are denied any opportunity to be included socially, athletically, intellectually, romantically, communally, or even in a worship service. Imagine YOU are secluded in a classroom and treated like YOU are three and taught the same material for fifteen years. Imagine YOU are prompted to obey like a dog with visual prompts and applauded with "Good job!" and skittles. Imagine all YOU are given to enrich YOUR life is children's books and animation. Imagine someone else makes every single decision of YOUR life. What YOU will eat. What YOU won't eat. Where YOU will go. What YOU will wear. What YOU will learn. What YOU will do with YOUR time. Where YOU will live. Who YOU will spend YOUR time with. What music, shows, and books YOU will listen to. What YOU will do with the rest of YOUR life. And because YOU can't communicate what YOU really think, YOU have no say. How would YOU feel?

---

[151] Anne Donnellan, Education Researcher 1984

Now… What do *YOU* think we should offer and provide *THEM*? … At the same time, the best thing that can happen when you presume competence is that you teach hungry, brilliant minds and give them opportunity and hope. The alternative is what my son and his friends experienced, being brilliant and deprived of everything because they were trapped inside themselves. Often people mention Stephen Hawking when they talk about non-speakers. I think this comparison is inappropriate for this population. No one ever treated Stephen Hawking as if he was unintelligent and deprived him of opportunity because of ALS. The real comparison is Helen Keller. Before she was given access to language she was treated as if she was not intelligent. The moment she had a way, a method to communicate, her brilliant mind exploded with the output that had been trapped inside her. "A person who is severely impaired never knows his hidden sources of strength until he is treated like a normal human being and encouraged to shape his own life… Education should train the child to use his brain, to make for himself a place in the world and maintain his rights even when it seems that society would shove him into the scrap-heap… The chief handicap of the blind is not blindness, but the attitude of seeing people towards them… Science may have found a cure for most evils; but it has found no remedy for the worst of them all – the apathy of human beings."[152] It is time we offer this same opportunity to those who have dysregulated bodies, who can't speak or can't speak reliably, and give them access to an entire language instead of twenty pictures, as well as the opportunity to decide their own destiny. Instead of being their governors, we could be their friends.

"To one hampered and circumscribed as I am it was a wonderful experience to have a friend like Mr. Clemens.
I recall many talks with him about human affairs. He never made me feel that my opinions were worthless. . . .
He knew that we do not think with eyes and ears and that our capacity for thought is not measured by five senses.
He kept me always in mind while he talked, and he treated me like a competent human being.
That is why I loved him." [153]

---

[152] Helen Keller
[153] Helen Keller commenting on her friendship with Mark Twain

58

Serendipity

Even though I walk through the valley of the shadow of death,
I will fear no evil for you are with me;
your rod and your staff, they comfort me.
— Psalm 23:4

Early September 2019

Houston and I went to watch *Peanut Butter Falcon,* which is about a man with Down's Syndrome escaping a nursing home to chase his dream of becoming a professional wrestler. After the movie I asked him what he thought of the movie and held up the board. I thought he would comment about what his dreams were or about how he identified with the main character. Instead he spelled, "I want to talk to the people sitting next to us." Feeling self-conscious and embarrassed (but knowing NOT to ignore his requests) I got their attention and said that my son wanted to talk to them. The gentleman turned around, looked at me and called me by name. I was shocked. He recognized me from my old neighborhood, the one we left in such shame and sorrow. I fumbled my words, still stunned, explaining that the boy who ran around the neighborhood naked was the man standing in front of them and that he wanted to talk to them, and I didn't know why. Then we began to converse.

Houston told them a bit about his life, and they told us a bit about theirs. Both stories are hard. They lost a beautiful, vibrant young daughter, Carly, from pancreatic cancer in her early thirties. The pain she endured had crushed her entire family. They felt the full measure of anguish of watching their beloved suffer and die before their eyes when they couldn't do anything to stop it. The grief covered them like a heavy veil, blurring and darkening all of life as they traversed how to go on, how to smile when everything made them ache. Their tremendous and courageous faith in spite of their loss, their determination to keep praying for everyone they loved and telling the world of the goodness of God is evidence of how powerful and good the love of God can be even in our darkness.

Houston's story was quite different. His grief, trauma, and imprisonment had come first, and his freedom and joy had finally arrived twenty years later. Houston told them about his life and then about his Esther. Kari gasped when he spelled Esther, as this name has very personal meaning to her. Houston told us all later that Kari's angel's name was Esther too. There was just so much in that moment. It's difficult to explain but clearly, we began to see glimpses of stories being intertwined in supernatural ways, not because of some great event, but because all of our spirits just belonged together. Kari and Mark shared more of their daughter Carly's life and death. It was and is a great and heavy loss. With loss you keep still, you keep quiet… You love. It is Houston's hope that people realize that despite the unbearable pain and loss in life - God is good and loves us more than we can understand. It was overwhelmingly obvious we needed to stay in touch and exchanged numbers. They gave me a copy of a poem Carly had written in her youth, long before her fateful prognosis.

***

Epitaph of a Songstress

"My life has been a rich and royal hue…"
I kept my eyes and ears open and learned what the world had to teach me -
painted in shining gold and silver thread entwined on the tapestry of life,
that magnificent tapestry of past, present, and future, truth, beauty, freedom, and love, with its brilliant colors
and shimmering fabrics, and its serene countrysides and vibrant cities, vast swelling oceans and towering,
snow-peaked mountains,
love and hate, war and peace, and death.
But there were times when I did not see what life was throwing in my face,
when I sat pensive and sorrowful, worrying over what I had lost -
"I had some dreams, they were clouds in my coffee…"
Life slipped past me like water through open fingers,
and I awoke one morning on my deathbed.
So I say to you, the future,
keep your eyes and ears open and learn what the world has to teach you:
study the great tapestry of life - love it, hate it, but do not ignore it.
Life and love are too easily lost to sit and worry over clouds in your coffee.

***

When I read Carly's poem to Houston, he had many thoughts. He told me Jesus and his angels had told him to talk to the people sitting next to him in the movie theater. That much seemed pretty obvious. The request had come out of nowhere. It was the equivalent of a server asking a guest if they would like dessert and the guest responding they would like to meet the man who grew the potatoes they served. Clearly there was some story being woven and Houston was obedient to whatever role he was called to. More and more I felt I had become a chauffeur to an eccentric who gave me addresses only on a need-to-know basis. He was directing. I was trying to keep up. All Houston had seen had made him offer every part of his heart to seeking the Kingdom of God. He didn't question God like I did. He obeyed. He trusted. Houston, more than any person I knew, lived the great commandment, to *love the Lord your God with all your heart and with all your soul and with all your mind and with all your strength.*[154] Clearly God had something to say *about* Carly and *to* Kari and Mark - so I wanted to listen.

As always, his words to Kari and Mark were profound and full of faith. "Each tear is counted twice. In some wonderful real way doors to her are open. Esther says I'm someone to prepare healing for the families left behind. It's wonderful wishing you and too many other lives real calmness as darkness tries to take our hope. Count your time without Carly time to get His wonderful, great hope to be with her again. Teach yourselves to be more in God's beautiful love. To count your love to Christ every day is the way to be with wonderful Carly. Do your sight a lesson and hear instead of see. Taste instead of touch. Yes, you'll see her that way for certain. Each soul that loves Christ does carry our wants to Christ. Do your best to always bring your Esther in the times of the worst hurt. Esther has cast so much pain away. Esther said to erase those worries and to hope in your eternal savior. Over time you don't always love like you should. Esther says to be good and love all the more. Each soul seeks Him always despite their awful unbelief."

---

[154] Mark 12:30

September 2019

College was wonderful and a struggle as well. Classmates would greet him at school and at Chick-fil-A and ask him questions. He loved that he was leading a way for others behind him. But there were also hurdles we had not anticipated. Houston had never had to write a three-point essay. His style was formal, and his word choice was unique. He and Morgan would argue about his paragraphs. Morgan would tell him he needed particular points and to edit other unnecessary details. Finally having a chance to tell the world his thoughts, he didn't see why he should write the way the professor wanted him to. It was his voice. Morgan would say, "MOM! Can you please explain to him why he has to do what the teacher is requiring??" I chuckled at the question, the situation, the sibling argument, Houston's stand of independence, his lack of awareness of educational expectations in regard to grades, and the fact that his compliance had limits. I explained it another way. "Houston, you can write whatever you want. But if you want a grade that will help you become a forensic psychologist, you have to write what they want you to." He was *VERY* annoyed, but he did it. The more I pondered it, the more I wondered why education is the way it is. Why does it test in a way to trick? Why does it say you must write our way? Why does it demand proof of skills before it allows access to knowledge? Why not just say here it is - Take! Eat! See that it is good! I love that heaven is like that. Everyone loves an open bar. Everyone loves a feast. The invitation is to everyone. The offer of His table is there. *Come, everyone who thirsts, come to the waters; and he who has no money, come, buy and eat! Come, buy wine and milk without money and without price. Why do you spend your money for that which is not bread, and your labor for that which does not satisfy? Listen diligently to me, and eat what is good, and delight yourselves in rich food. Incline your ear, and come to me; hear, that your soul may live.* [155]

School was often painful. Sometimes Morgan would text me that class wasn't going well. In one of his classes they were working on essay writing and would discuss different articles that were topic ideas. There were days when he would try to hum to tune out all the thoughts of others to focus. Some days a verbal stim would get triggered and it was not possible for him to stop it. His humming and stimming made some students think cruel things toward him because of the sounds he couldn't stop. This escalated his anxiety. On the days he had energy and peace, he would do beautifully, and other days he would become completely overwhelmed.

"Read my essay. No later. Don't talk to me more... Not having a good day, look... (Trying to write his essay) 'The cultural impact of coke on young adults,' "I need to go home. My brain is, everything is, everything on me is hurting."

Another example, "'Terrorism in terror... The use of terror as an attack and retaliation'... I'm really not not ok... I am stimming... Go home. Pleading you."

As Houston explained to his U.S. History class, sometimes it was just too much. He would come home on days like this and throw himself in bed. He wouldn't be able to move, his system was so overloaded.

Another event around this time was that we had the opportunity to meet with others who were beginning to advocate for communication rights. Non speakers and unreliable speakers were asked what they wanted to change. Below is Houston's list.

- Start asking us to participate in school and letting us learn
- Every day ask us to understand material
- Teach us what everyone else gets to learn
- Each student sees that we are counted as stupid. Coping with false ideas about us every day is as challenging as the inability to control our body
- Teach others to communicate with us
- Don't talk about us around us
- Have the rationalization that autistics are retarded taken away

[155] Isaiah 55:1-3

September 12, 2019

At the center and at the gym Houston was working extremely hard to overcome many of his initiation and motor challenges. He was so ridiculously proud of himself when he was able to execute a 30" box jump. He was making progress.

I was struggling mightily. Work continued to be a pressure cooker. Almost every quote I submitted for approval was denied. My brokers were increasingly frustrated. There were several incidents when a retail underwriter in our department wrote a large and profitable account that we had declined because it didn't fit our guidelines. This is what you call a double standard, also - unethical. The brokers complained that my manager would act like he was their best friend and then stab them in the back. They complained there were double standards. I didn't know what to do. No matter how hard I worked or how pacifying I tried to be, it was a slaughterhouse of egos. One morning as I went to work out, I prayed in utter frustration to God. I told Him how tired I was. I just couldn't keep going. I needed help. The job I had I worked so hard for and been so good at had turned sour. That afternoon when I got home from work, having completely forgotten about my prayer, Houston spelled to me, "God heard your prayer for rest. It will be answered." I asked how - *how* did he know I prayed that. He explained he didn't have to be with me to hear my thoughts and that thoughts were not limited by distance or space. It was all energy, and he was connected to me. I just stared at him in wonder. If someone had ever told me this would be my life, I would have *never* believed it. But that's God. He's doing something else entirely. My job is to approach His throne and believe.

59

Shooting Angels

"You have enemies? Good.
That means you've stood up for something, sometime in your life."
— Winston Churchill

These six things the Lord hates, yes, seven are an abomination to Him:
A proud look, a lying tongue, hands that shed innocent blood,
a heart that devises wicked plans, feet that are swift in running to evil,
a false witness who speaks lies, and one who sows discord among brethren.
— Proverbs 6:16-19

Late September 2019

I got a call from Morgan one afternoon right before lunch. She was freaking out. Her voice was shaking out of control. She had gotten a call from the Adult Protective Services agency. She told me there was a video of me yelling and cussing at Houston. Her voice was trembling with emotion, "It was Paul! It was Paul, Mom! You can tell it's him filming. He gave it to Dad and Dad added all these awful lies on the bottom like a subtext. *MOM!!!!!* It's awful! These lies are AWFUL, MOM!! They were asking all these questions and threatening to take Houston. Dad sent it to them, and he posted it on YouTube!!! I'm so upset. I can't take Houston to class. He's stimming. He said to take him home now!! He heard everything!! He's freaking out too. I told them over and over, that's not my mom!! I told her. I told her what you're like, Mom. I told her you do everything and that it was my dad and my asshole brother. I told her about everything. I told her everything he's done to us! MOM? Are you there? Are you listening? They want the number of everyone who knows Houston."

.... There was a loud ringing in my ears and a hollow place from my heart all the way to my feet. My throat clenched. I could hardly speak. I felt as if I had been dropped into a cavernous pit. Nothing came out when I opened my mouth. I was stunned by how low and quiet my voice was, as if the power, the very breath had been knocked out of me. I felt the same suffocating clench in my chest when my stepsister dropped me to the ground on the seesaw. I couldn't speak, breathe, think... I tried - I tried to ask a few questions. I couldn't think of what she was describing. The ringing in my ears pierced my heart. Morgan said she could tell the video was old because all the old furniture was there and because of what I was wearing. Very quietly I got off the phone. I sat motionless for a long time, stunned. Then I remembered the night I had been so angry and had started yelling in exhausted frustration that I didn't care anymore and I just wanted him to bathe himself. Was that... Was my worst moment on the internet? Shortly after that Reagan called me yelling that they had called her too. She had told them the same thing Morgan had said. She told them they couldn't understand how completely frustrating Houston could be, that he understood and had told our mom to make him bathe himself but then wouldn't respond. She told me she would never speak to Paul again. She was shouting into the phone, escalating in furious indignation. Then she yelled, "THAT'S IT!! I've had it with Dad attacking you! I'm going to file charges!" I was still in shock. I told her we needed to really think about this and how dangerous this would be. I realized there was a storm of evil approaching like I had never seen - and I *had* seen, so I was scared. We had switched places.

When I got home from work, Houston was waiting for me. He stood in the hall and spelled out, "Are you ok?" Here it was, one of those rare moments of him initiating conversation and I couldn't say anything at all. I shook my head no and let the tears I had been holding in all day run down my face. But I still couldn't make noise. It was like someone had pushed the off button on my voice. Houston continued, "Do you know what I'm going to do? I'm going to testify." My son was trying to be a man when his brother had betrayed us all. I told him he couldn't. He was too vulnerable. He had to stay safe. I wasn't sure if it was shame, fear, or betrayal that made my entire being shake uncontrollably. All I knew was I hated my life.

I called my closest friends and shared the link. My kids showed their friends and I got call after call from them telling me they know what kind of mom I really am and how hard it has been raising Houston. Sarah said the video wasn't as bad as I thought. So many people were trying to love on me, but all I felt was shame. The problem with shame is it feels like truth, like a branding that can never be washed away or redeemed. The frustration that triggered my outburst was not something you can explain to people who haven't lived with severe autism for two plus decades. You can't explain how beaten down and defeated you really are. You can't explain how the very fact that you have any hope at all is actually a miracle. You just can't explain. I wanted to hide. I wanted to go away and never come back. I hated my life. I hated that I had been beaten down and abused and had so much taken from me when all I had tried to do was love other people. I hated that evil kept winning. I hated that my destruction was sport to evil, to revel in his power. I hated that even though I had worked so hard to believe and do the impossible, evil still struck blow after blow. I felt like I could hear evil laughing as it pushed the knife deeper.

> *How long, O Lord? Will You forget me forever?*
> *How long will You hide Your face from me?*
> *How long shall I take counsel in my soul,*
> *Having sorrow in my heart daily?*
> *Consider and hear me, O Lord my God;*
> *Enlighten my eyes,*
> *Lest I sleep the sleep of death;*
> *Lest my enemy say,*
> *"I have prevailed against him",*
> *Lest those who trouble me rejoice when I am moved.*[156]

I asked for some moms who love and care for incredible, gifted people like Houston to give me their thoughts on what our lives are like, the impact of severe autism, and the juxtaposition of living every minute with the brilliant human being you love and the disorder that rules the chaos. Before you read take a moment (compared to decades) and consider this ...

"Here are my shoes. Take a long walk. Talk to me when you get back."[157]

Mom 1) Autism is nothing but a thief. It steals not only my daughter's ability to function appropriately and the ability to speak, but it also steals joy and normalcy from the moments in life that so many take for granted--birthdays, holidays, family outings, church, even just a trip to the

[156] Psalm 13:1-4
[157] Anonymous

grocery store--severe, nonverbal autism makes everything exponentially more difficult than it should be. At any moment, in any situation, all hell could break loose and we all know it. It steals family, sleep, and health and hope... It holds all of our lives hostage... 'The thief comes only to steal and kill and destroy...' John 10:10. It steals joy, destroys lives and families, and there have been many times I thought about ending my life or both of our lives... I would never do it, but Satan has whispered it to me many times.

Mom 2) I used to believe in God but I don't anymore. I don't blame my loss of faith directly on autism but it is hard to believe in a God when my son and my family have suffered so much. It is just easier to believe that there is no one in charge up there and that our suffering is just something that has randomly happened, through bad genes, environmental triggers or just the luck of the draw. Autism has robbed my family of many things that others take for granted. My son will never drive a car, get married or have children. My dreams of having a fulfilling and satisfying career will never happen. Instead, my career has been dictated, by necessity, to be a full time caregiver to my son. My husband will never get the carefree vacations he has always dreamed of for the two of us in our retirement because quality respite care is difficult to come by and many caregivers would not be able to handle my son's outbursts and aggression. My older son will always remember the times I could not be there for him because I was driving his brother to endless therapies or dealing with one crisis or another that are part of life with autism.

Autism hasn't all been bad but it has mostly been bad. I remember the first time my son was able to tell me that he loved me. He was 14 years old. I remember the triumph of when he learned to ride a bike at 12 years old. I remember being so proud of him when he was finally able to print his name. He was in middle school at the time. And I remember when I finally felt like I could say that he was "potty trained". He was also in middle school at the time. He is 23 now and still requires occasional assistance in this area.

But I also remember the time he defecated in the middle of a baseball field in the middle of a baseball game when a caregiver was supposed to be watching him. He was five. Or the time he ran across the road at the beach and almost got hit by a car after escaping my grasp at the age of six. I have permanent scars on both of my knees to remember that incident by. Or the time at a hotel pool when he walked by a toddler who was standing near the edge of the pool and impulsively shoved her in. Of course she couldn't swim and both her parents and I jumped in to save her. Luckily, we were able to get to her quickly. After profuse apologies and trying to explain his disability, we left in a hurry. He was eight years old at the time. I try to forget the time we were riding a ferris wheel at an amusement park and I realized that he really needed to go to the bathroom. After frantically trying to get him to sit down in the seat and pee in a water bottle and failing to do both of these things, others on the ride finally realized that something was wrong and stopped the ride immediately to let us off. After cleaning up the pee out of the seat and apologizing again, I carried him away as fast as I could, thankful that I would never have to see these people again. With autism, parents learn to do a lot of apologizing. I've also learned not to make eye contact with people. It makes dealing with the crisis at hand easier.

Gradually my son's behavior changed from being reckless and impulsive to being aggressive, destructive and impulsive. He has broken windows, kicked in a glass door in school, kicked in a particularly hated teachers car door after running off of the playground (yes, he knew what car was hers and targeted her car. That cost us $1500 to have fixed). He has broken his fathers finger, blackened my eye, hit us countless times, screamed at us countless times and bitten and hit himself countless times. All out of frustration of being unable to communicate with the outside world. Throughout his childhood, he has developed many destructive coping mechanisms and I developed PTSD.

Then life changed for him and our family when he learned for the first time to communicate his thoughts and feelings via a letter board, painstakingly pointing out letter by letter to form words and give me my first glimpse of the person who was trapped inside his body. He was 22 years old. And he was only able to accomplish this due to the perseverance of the author of this book, who realized the potential our children had and would not give up until I started the process of helping my son find his voice. She never stopped telling me what an incredible, and an incredibly intelligent person my son was and that he was just waiting for me to help him come out of his wordless prison.

You see, it took me this long to get to this point because, throughout his whole life, I listened to the autism "experts". I was told by a developmental pediatrician that he was "intellectually challenged" and I believed him. I was told by his teachers that he could not understand abstract concepts and I believed them. I was told that he was not able to do age appropriate school work and I believed these "experts". These well-meaning people had autism all wrong and still do. I was told that he didn't pick up on the stares and smirks that ignorant people would give him when he acted "autistic" in public. Well, he did and he does, and it cuts him to the bone. Almost everyone I came in contact with had it wrong about autism, including me. I fault myself for believing them and not having enough belief in my son.

Now we now see light at the end of the tunnel and hope for his future. Learning to communicate his thoughts and feelings on the letter board has been life changing for him. We have hope that his aggression will lessen as he learns to communicate with us rather than lash out . He can now further his education and we can try to make up for the many years he wasted in special education classes. Since he has learned to communicate, I am realizing just how intelligent he is and how wrong I was about so many things concerning his autism. As his mother, I should have understood him better and I didn't. It is a bitter pill to swallow.

As I write this, I am sitting in a hospice room watching my mother die. My son has insisted on being with me every step of the way. When I asked him how he was dealing with this whole process, he told me that being in a room with so much raw emotion and grief was extremely painful for him but that he knew that he had to be there with me and for me. Bravery comes in many forms and I am grateful that I finally recognize it in my son.

Mom 3) This journey with autism leaves me so often with this: our lives are filled with dichotomies. For a woman who has lived a life where my yes is yes and my no is no, it rocks your world. My son woke up this morning and was dying to share with me a note on the letterboard. To write the note he wants to share, I have to give him constant commands to attend and to finish what he started as his body wants to buck away. What he finally writes is like the wisdom of sages or prophets, deep waters, and yet immediately afterwards he decides he must throw open the fridge door and dig into the grape jelly, straight up. Then his dad declares that he is going to use his lunch break to take my son out for fast food and to a nature trail that he loves. It takes both of us about 45 minutes to get our little philosopher to simply wear pants. Then he insists to Dad on the letterboard that he wants to go to Chick-fil-A and tells him exactly what he wants. Only to drive a double distance to fulfill that request for him to refuse to eat one bite. Showing his maybe/maybe not attitude about the nature trail, they finally push through and after a few minutes my son is actually enjoying it, feeling oneness with nature, and they are doing well. And as I am writing this, my husband tells me that our son just tried to take his pants off.... Yes, this is autism. When the fleeting thing I call "flow" is found, it is euphoria, but wow the frustration to just be in alignment with what one thinks and what one does is unlike anything I have ever witnessed. I love to see my son when he feels free. I love to see our family when we get those moments that feel "right," though so fleeting.

Mom 4) Autism. The ride. I think of autism in many ways but the two I think best explain to others what autism is like is - it's like being on a daily, hourly, monthly, yearly rollercoaster that's constantly resetting and going on different tracks; and the second comparison I use is it's like living a double life.

The first analogy is pretty easy to explain, yet hard to understand if you're not a rider. Life before autism for me was easy, like a toddler ride at a theme park. I got on. I hear the twinkly music playing, my kids are smiling, squealing with joy, then we got off. One child might get upset because they dropped their ice cream, but these small issues were manageable and easily fixed. Whew, life was easy although I didn't think that at the time.

With autism I'm on the ride that just doesn't stop. I have to get on another ride and another and another. Some of these rides are briefly beautiful and joyful and I totally appreciate those times. I really try to… But then I get on a ride that throws me from side to side, up and down, you get splashed with an unknown substance, there's a physical assault and the ride just keeps going. Those brief seconds, hours, days of joy are what keep me holding on because I know somehow it will come around during dark tunnels of the ride. It's always in the back of my mind. I"m still on this ride. I can't get off, my child can't get off and the operator of the ride doesn't know how to stop it - meaning cure it. So I hope, pray, try every doctor, supplement, voodoo, and especially prayer I can use to help me and my son hopefully get off the ride.

Living two different lives is the other way I feel about the ride. I have two neurotypical children and you have to interact with their peers, other parents, teachers, etc. It feels like being another person. I almost feel like I'm cheating on my child if I enjoy stepping into that other world. Most of the time I find it shallow because things that others find important just don't matter to me. I am dealing with something that is so fundamental and basic. I can't fathom having to really truly care about something that in my world is small and meaningless. I have to feign interest in things I don't care about. Some things help take my mind off something I deal with every hour of every day and again I feel guilty even trying to have alternate interests because I think I should only foucs on helping my child. It's a really weird struggle. I'm not the person I was when I entered the ride turnstall. She has left the park never to return. I'm a better human by my standards, but I just don't know how much I have to give to others. Autism takes that from me.

Mom 5) When Katie asked me to write about autism before spelling, I said, "Sure, consider it done!" What I didn't count on though, was having past traumas and painful memories come flooding back every time I sat down to write. Even after all these years, thinking about the past before spelling is emotionally draining.

I have twin boys, one neurotypical and one atypical, meaning non-speaking autistic. I remember getting the official AUTISM diagnosis, after watching my son slowly regress over a year. I knew there was a real issue, I just didn't realize how significant of a role autism would play in our lives. Like most parents, I was in the "I've got to fix this" mode, yet no matter what I tried or what new therapy I put my son through, nothing helped. We worked with talented therapists and well renowned doctors for years but could not get what we desperately wanted, COMMUNICATION.

As a speech language pathologist (SLP) I was shattered that I couldn't help him more. I was angry at the world; I was also angry at God. I felt betrayed, like my prayers had been ignored. I did not know that things were about to change.

I found out about spelling from a fellow speech therapist while doing continuing education. I did not know her prior to this conference. She told me she had just been to another continuing education conference in Texas where this mother (Soma Mukhopadhyay) had come up with a method for teaching her son to communicate using a letterboard and maybe it might help my son too. I then received a text during that same conference from another SLP (and friend) who had seen a Speech therapist (Elizabeth Vosseller) doing this exact type of work in Atlanta and that she would be coming back to do another workshop next month. So long story short, let's just say the advice given to me by these two SLPs would end up having a profound effect on our lives, most importantly, my sons. And I am eternatlly grateful to both Soma and Elizabeth for their dedication giving autistics a voice.

So, what does life look like now after spelling? Life looks hopeful, exciting, and full of possibilities. My son is fifteen now and is working towards earning a high school diploma. He has friends, a girlfriend (also a non-speaking autistic who spells) and a huge support system of professionals and spellers from all over the world.

I am overjoyed for my son and his friends, but I cannot say I am at peace. It is impossible to feel at peace when spelling is not accessible to MOST non-speaking, unreliable speaking or minimally speaking autistics. I cannot be content knowing that autistics are enduring, in silence, archaic and trauma inducing therapies. These outdated practices must be stopped. For me, the day when autism is recognized as a SENSORIMOTOR difference and when ALL autistics are presumed competent and given access to spelling as a means of communication, is the day I will be at peace.
- *Libby Ingram*

Mom 6) It brings us to utter despair and hopelessness, then to the feet of Jesus where every hard thing will be used in one way or another. It's a life of living in quarantine but then connected to the most amazing people; we need each other!

Mom 7) In the movie Hacksaw Ridge, there's a pivotal scene where the soldiers are making their way through territory where the enemy is dug in trenches; trip wire & mines embedded into the terrain & snipers are hiding to stop their advancement & progress. But, with his bible as a weapon, he safely navigates through each obstacle, while saving lives (most of whom didn't believe or had given up). So, is the life of raising a child with autism. Everyday as a parent, you suit up in your Christian armor, armed with the Word of God. Only difference is you're navigating with your child tucked securely in your arms. Each step you make, you're consciously aware there is hidden danger, traps, and snipers along the way. Many of whom are in the form of the medical institution, or the educational field. But, with the protection of almighty God, you safely move forward knowing one day, the battle will come to an end & you; your child, spouse will rest in the arms of our almighty Father. On that great day, The Father will wipe every tear from your eye & say, 'Well done my good & faithful servant, well done.'

Mom 8) I remember sitting in my living room one day…I was day 3 of 21 in a complete fast for healing for my Ady. I was exhausted. Hungry. Irritated. Debating on breaking my fast. Besides, how many times had I prayed for a miracle or a sign that she was in there? But this time I somehow knew God's justice would prevail. As I was sitting on my couch folding a load of laundry, I saw handfuls of ashes from my fireplace being thrown across my living room. A cloud of black dust would settle on every piece of furniture and my wood floors. I quickly sent her to the bathroom to wash her hands while I attempted to clean up the mess she had made. After about 5 minutes had passed, I noticed the water was still running in the bathroom. When I walked in, the entire bathroom was flooded with water mixed with an entire bottle of soap mixed in creating an amazing bubble bath two feet tall in my bathroom. "Ady go to your room!" I moved quickly to grab a dozen towels to dry up the water. The second the towels hit the floor, I felt my heart begin to race so fast and I knew I had again arrived to the hypervigilant world of autism mom! Then, the sound of shattering glass- I ran with speed towards the sound of the glass, as I saw her standing over the glass just staring at it with such a look of satisfaction. I took her by the hand, and led her to her room and went and took a seat on my couch and there I shut down, but not before we finished the episode with my beautiful child climbing on the couch next to me and defecating on my sofa. "God I can't do this anymore. If this is the life you've called me to live, I just can't…"

As I was sobbing on my couch, I felt as if I had hit some sort of breaking point. I texted my pastor which I had never done and simply told him "I am not ok. Ady is not ok. We really need prayer." What I didn't tell him was that I felt five seconds away from checking myself into a psych ward. The words he texted me back would resonate in my heart forever. "We will be fighting with you and for you in these 21 days and beyond. We have already seen warfare increase as we move into this spiritual advancement of God's kingdom. We have decided that we will not be moved by what our eyes see, but only what the cross declares and provides… Psalm 103:1-5.[158] We are declaring those benefits over Ady, and praying for joy and peace to be poured out over you and in you, your husband and kids. I want you to stand up and begin to praise God. There is a powerful exchange when we put on the garment of praise for a spirit of heaviness. These are the hardest times to praise, but there is a beautiful exchange that goes on when we put on the garment of praise for the spirit of heaviness. *'We have not been given a spirit of fear, but of power, love, and a sound mind.'* [159] Love you guys!"

So right then and there, I stood in my glassy, soot filled living room and lifted my hands and praised Him. Tears streaming down my cheeks. I knew in that moment, somehow things would be different very soon… Fast forward two years. God brought RPM (Rapid Prompting Method) into our lives, and with it came communication. For us, this was a miracle in itself as we didn't think that she was in there. As she began to open up about her world, we were astonished! We would come to learn that this beautiful little girl didn't see anything the way we saw it. Instead, she saw bursts of fired lights all around. She could see energy in motion, whether that be people, objects, music, emotions- angels! We went through a season of rejoicing. But soon that rejoicing turned to an extreme guilt that we spent so many years not knowing… Speaking in front of her as if she couldn't hear us. Leaving her out of family board games and conversations. A million instances, similar to the ones I described earlier, began to make sense. I can't imagine being in a body that was here, but not seen nor understood - I might be pooping on the couch next to my mom too if it got her attention. What we do know in all of this is that God is so incredibly faithful. Oh and that fast? I am confident we broke some chains during that one.

— Chrissy, mom of Ady (11) and non-speaking.

Well? How do our shoes feel? What if you could never take them off?

---

[158] Bless the Lord, O my soul, and all that is within me, bless his holy name! Bless the Lord, O my soul, and forget not all his benefits, who forgives all your iniquity, who heals all your diseases, who redeems your life from the pit, who crowns you with steadfast love and mercy, who satisfies you with good so that your youth is renewed like the eagle's.
[159] For God gave us a spirit not of fear but of power and love and self-control. - 2 Timothy 1:7

I know it doesn't seem like much but with a broken, shattered heart I put those prayers, prayers for my lost son to come home, prayers for justice, prayers for all the love that had been lost, prayers for my son to be healed, I put them in my box and prayed. I spoke those prayers like they were already true. I chose to believe, to trust with a broken heart.

> *But I have trusted in Your mercy,*
> *My heart shall rejoice in Your salvation*
> *I will sing to the Lord,*
> *Because He had dealt bountifully with me.*[160]

We discussed the matter of Reagan filing charges at length. I told her she needed corroborating evidence. Her word was NOT enough considering how much time had passed. Morgan found their old babysitter that Houston had mentioned. She called her and asked if she remembered anything, anything at all. The details she shared were about lots of women and inappropriate behavior but nothing that substantiated the details Houston and Reagan shared. I said, "Well, that's it. There's nothing else we can do."

Houston went and laid down on his bed. Later I went to check on him. He was despondent. His eyes were open and his stare was empty. Sadness, grief permeated the room. I went up to him and asked him what was wrong. "Do you believe me?" he spelled. "Yes, Houston. I believe you. But we have to have evidence," I said, trying to encourage and explain things to him. "I'm telling the truth. I want to testify," he kept insisting. I realized he was demanding the opportunity to be the hero, the big brother, the good man that he knew he was inside. He was trying to be brave. I was trying to keep us safe.

I told Morgan to ask him what had happened in detail. I wanted to see if he told the same story. He spelled to her the exact same story he had told me twenty months earlier, word for word. Morgan had never gotten all of the details and was extremely upset when Houston shared them. "Stop! Stop! I won't hear anymore!... I just can't." She had the same kind of gut wrenching, revolting, soul cringing reaction. For the first time in my life I understood why Houston put his fingers in his ears with such force. The sound of evil makes your body stop working. I asked her, "Do you believe him?" With tears and anger, she nodded and said, "YES!"

Reagan called the babysitter and asked her to meet at a coffee shop. She asked me and Houston to come with her. We made small talk. I let her and Reagan catch up. She was turning twenty-nine shortly. I took Houston aside and asked him if he was sure. "YES." I asked again if he wanted to go through with this. "YES," he spelled. So we sat outside in a park that was part of the coffee shop grounds. We explained everything that was happening. She told us the Big Jock had reached out to her recently and asked her to partner with him in a business. She invited her mother, the Big Jock's former employee, to join her but then changed her mind after seeing the charges against him in Florida. Inwardly, I thought it was very strange that the Big Jock would reach out to a former babysitter from fourteen years earlier. What kind of a connection did he have with a girl he knew as a teenager that would make that appropriate? I told her we needed corroboration of Houston's memories and any other details she might remember. Reagan told what she remembered. Houston spelled out his memories and then turned and looked at her. Her first response was amazement that Houston could communicate. He showed how he could hear thoughts, then she started crying. Her tears surprised both me and Reagan. We looked at each other with the same thought. Usually the response was joy or astonishment. Then Houston told her his memories. She shook her head and told Houston that had never happened. It was quiet. Houston studied her. He told me, "She has no memory of what happened," as fifty different thoughts bombarded my brain. I said nothing to him in response. I apologized repeatedly for asking if she had any memories that would corroborate what Houston and Reagan remembered. I told her we just needed any information that might help us. Over and over again I asked -- if she had any memory of anything to please let us know. We thanked her profusely for meeting with us. We all hugged when we left. She promised to do anything she could to help us. The conversation was gentle. We did all we could to talk about something difficult with a spirit of meekness and love.

My feelings were mixed. I knew Houston was telling the truth about his memories and he was upset she did not remember. The whole situation made me hurt. I prayed for us. I prayed for her. I prayed for truth. I wondered if there were roofies involved. There was no way to know. The former babysitter called me that afternoon and told me her mother wanted to talk to me and was making wild threats. She asked if I would please explain the situation to her mom and get her mom to understand we were just asking if she remembered anything that would confirm what Houston remembered. She warned me her mother was like a Pitbull and was seeing red. I remembered that from fourteen years earlier. She had the kind of temper best suited for street fights and paybacks and prided herself on playing dirty. She had an executioner's mentality. It didn't matter that her daughter was twenty-nine.

I wanted to do all I could to let her know we were trying to get information to hold the Big Jock accountable and that was our only concern. Nothing else. No one else. For one hour and forty-nine minutes this woman used every conceivable word to threaten, defame, spew venom, and twist. My hope had been to explain the situation as requested. She saw my questions as a threat that must be repaid with destruction and venomous hate. Morgan listened with me to her ranting on speaker for over thirty minutes. She wrote notes to me telling me to just keep saying you're sorry you asked. After Morgan left in anxious tears, I realized I needed to record the vile and insane things this woman was spewing. I was able to record fifty-four minutes. It is too graphic to put in print. There was nothing I could have said to make her understand our purpose was to ask for help or to convince her Houston had been competent and aware of everything his entire life. For most of the time I said nothing at all. She kept trying to throw something at me hoping I would react as violently as her with equal vulgarity. I wouldn't. She swore to destroy me because I had dared to ask if something painful was true. That night she sent messages on Facebook to the Big Jock, to his family, and to us that distorted, twisted, and mocked. Her threats were not veiled. We had asked for help finding the truth. We were repaid with vileness and hate. Vengeance is not something innocent people do. Innocent people want the truth. They want justice. There was a sickening, helplessness that took over our family. She sent more threats the next day. I knew better than to respond. Rational people don't understand this type of Jerry Springer behavior. They don't understand that hate sees every act of self-protection or justice as a threat, and views finding the truth or self-defense as an act of aggression. Basically, nothing stops them until their bloodthirsty lust for destruction is satisfied.

October 7, 2019

The former babysitter's mother called, and I didn't answer. She had texted me earlier that her only mission in life was to expose and punish me for the lies and atrocities I committed and that I was a manipulative, crazy bitch. She had ended her cruel text with a sarcastic and devious "have a GREAT DAY". On this day after she called, she sent a Facebook friend request (I deleted and blocked but it was too late. I hadn't thought of turning on any privacy settings.). Then she texted, "I got you… hook, line, and sinker on video. Good luck psycho bitch." --- I could hear her evil laugh. I was shaking. *Who does that?* I knew which video. YouTube had removed it but obviously the Big Jock had posted it again. I went to work the next day just trying to keep busy and not think about what might happen. I kept whispering prayers to my God.

At work my old manager that had become my friend told me she needed to speak with me immediately. She explained that the aforementioned mother had sent her an ugly email and a link to the video. I couldn't breathe. I texted Morgan to look on YouTube. Sure enough, there was an updated version. The narrative at the bottom of the video was profane, slanderous, libelous, and maliciously false. But to make it worse it listed my phone number, email, address, work email, work phone number, the company I worked for and every piece of personal information available and invited viewers to harass me. I was shaking when I went to the police with my friend to submit a report. They told me I had to file a TPO. While I was there, my current manager called me in a threatening voice telling me I had missed another meeting. My voice quivered as I tried to explain. My friend and former manager from work who was with me at the police station did what little she could to support me, but at least she stood by my side. I could hardly talk. I was shaking uncontrollably. I tried to explain. I tried to stop crying. I wanted to run away forever. I found where to submit internet crimes and sent it all to the district attorney as well. I started another privacy complaint with YouTube. The Big Jock didn't care about posting a video of his son naked and stimming on the internet. His only goal was to hurt me and destroy everything he could. That woman didn't care about distributing a video of my autistic son naked without his consent. She just wanted to destroy and hurt me because I wanted to find the truth, whatever it was…. God? You're still there, *right?* You still see everything, *right?*

> Listen to my prayer, O God, do not ignore my plea; hear me and answer me.
> My thoughts trouble me and I am distraught
> Because of what my enemy is saying, because of the threats of the wicked;
> For they bring down suffering on me and assail me in their anger.
> My heart is in anguish within me; the terrors of death have fallen on me.
> Fear and trembling have beset me; horror has overwhelmed me.
> I said, "Oh, that I had the wings of a dove!
> I would fly away and be at rest.
> I would flee far away and stay in the desert;
> I would hurry to my place of shelter, far from the tempest and storm." [161]

Throughout the day I got phone calls and texts from friends telling me they had received a horrific message and a link to the video. She had sent it to most of my connections on Facebook in Messenger. One of the other special needs moms that I loved dearly texted me freaking out, so I called her. "Katie!! That's all of US! We all have moments like that!! It's not possible to be perfect all the time. Autism is AWFUL! It never stops! People don't get it! Unless you've lived it you have no idea!! I'm testifying!! I'm testifying for you. Who the hell is this? Who would do this to *you*?" So I had to explain. Again and again. At least one stranger took the opportunity to text me and harass me.

The next day I went to court to file the TPO. It was an all-day affair. Way too many people were there dealing with violence and threats. Reagan and Houston went with me. Morgan did her best to try to determine the right address to have the woman served. Houston was remarkably calm. He spelled to me, "So many people here are thinking to make plans if they die. It's so sad. They are scared." Here we were to protect ourselves and Houston wanted to pray for others. So we did. While I was downtown at the county courthouse the Vice President of Human Resources at the company I worked for, called me and asked me what this video was about. The woman had sent the video my ex-husband had made to my corporate headquarters. Even if I tried, I don't know that I can adequately describe the emotion that came over me at that time. I tried choking back sobs so I could try to sound professional. At one point I couldn't take a breath. In short gasps I explained

[161] Psalm 55:1-8

what was going on. Morgan called and explained as well. It was such a horrific assault I just wanted to never return, but I needed that job to provide. No, I needed that job to survive. They put me on leave and used the opportunity to revoke the appointment of my largest brokers who had been the most outspoken regarding the double standards. They shut down my computer access, "So I could focus on healing." They insisted I take advantage of a counselor for the emotional distress of the situation. I knew there was nothing a counselor could do but I went anyway. For days I couldn't eat or sleep or think. All I could do was pray and cry. 'Do you *see*, God? *El Roi*? [162] I'm trying, Lord. I'm putting my trust in You. The wicked run unchecked, but I will praise your name. I believe You will use this for good... for me.'

> *Be not silent, O God of my praise! For wicked and deceitful mouths are opened against me, speaking against me with lying tongues. They encircle me with words of hate, and attack me without cause. In return for my love they accuse me, but I give myself to prayer. So they reward me evil for good, and hatred for my love.* [163]

My friends were in shock. No one really knew how to help. One of my more realistic friends said, "Start looking for a new job. They are going to find a way to get rid of you. You'll see." She had replied back to the woman's horrific messages and defended me and found out for herself how cruel this woman could be. Knowing someone had defended me made me weep for a different reason. That friend knew what love and truth looked like. But mostly I was in a fog, a deep pit of darkness, floundering for light.

There were three total attempts at serving this woman. All failed. I had to move on and trust God. Reagan, in a moment of unquestionably poor judgment, called her to ask her to stop harassing me. "Oh no Reagan. No. No, you didn't..." I gasped, horrified when she told me. Reagan was hyperventilating on the phone, she was crying so hard. "Mom! She told me I *wanted* my dad to rape me and that I was begging for men to f..k me!!" I could feel her body shaking through the phone. Her fragile heart couldn't take it. Of course, that's the kind of pain this woman was after. I knew how those minds worked. They love the fight, and lust for blood. You never, ever engage with a person like that in any way. They know how to use words as weapons. More than swords their words are like acid, like venom.

Reagan went to the police to file a report regarding what her father did to her, and I was called in to give a statement. Houston and I both gave one. The police wanted to know how Houston knew certain things and Houston had to show them how he knew. The investigator was in shock and uncertain how to proceed. They worked with an advocacy program but ultimately, because we couldn't find a communication partner to work with him in a legal capacity, nothing ever happened. We tried for months to find someone who was independent, and willing to help us. The law had so many limits. I did realize though, that this was another area of civil rights that was under the scope of people with disabilities, their right to give their testimony with independent and trained practitioners and not have it discounted because they couldn't speak or write independently and had other sensory/motor issues.

That weekend there was a storm. It seemed the rain wouldn't stop. It got louder and louder and finally on some subconscious level I realized it wasn't rain. I woke up and I just knew. I ran out into the hall and was standing in water. The sink in the boys' bathroom was pouring water and the water had reached everywhere. Houston had left the water running in the middle of the night. He hadn't caused a flood in years. The boys' bedrooms were soaked but I hadn't even begun to see the worst of it. Water poured down the stairs like a riverbed and in horror I saw the carpet, the hardwoods, everything sitting in ankle deep water. It was too much to even take in as I looked around. There were cords plugged in all around the water. I turned off everything and called Benjamin. He wasn't in his room. It was three in the morning and he wasn't home. He

---

[162] Hebrew: רֹאִי אֵל -The God who sees me
[163] Psalm 109:1-5

answered his phone and told me he had just left for a walk a few minutes earlier. "Well, that's a lie," I said. "Get home now. You'll see how I know you snuck out a long time ago." It was worse than when he had snuck out to drive to downtown Atlanta and I had been called out of bed to talk to another dad in the middle of the night in my robe. He and his friend walked in and were in shock. The ceiling bubbled ready to explode at the seams and the wood was lifting and warping before my eyes. The cleanup and the drying out process took days. The carpet mildewed quickly and had to be thrown out. Friends brought industrial fans to help. I was so tired. I wept. I didn't have any answers other than to trust God. I had no more strength. Sarah sent me Scriptures and worship songs. I hid in His praise. There was no other place to go.

One interesting thing happened when I was washing load after load of towels from the cleanup. I was folding towels while Houston stood behind me and I came across one that was from the awful trip to Miami with the Big Jock fifteen or sixteen years earlier. I stared at it in disgust. Something in me said, "Throw it out now!" Without questioning or second guessing the thought, I grabbed the towel and ran to the dumpster outside. I threw it in with a strange satisfaction. When I came back inside Houston was jumping up and down with excitement, smiling from ear to ear.

"What are you so excited about?" I asked.

"You heard me," he spelled, giggling.

"That was *you*? *You* told me to throw it out?" I asked.

"Yes. It has the most hideous energy. But you can hear me."

"I don't know if I heard you. I just felt that it had to go immediately."

"That was from me."

Again I just shook my head in utter amazement. "What did the hideous energy look like?"

"It looks like piss."

"Yeah, I don't need that in our home."

I started searching for a cross I had found but had never worn because I never got around to getting a chain. Under the bathroom cabinet I pulled out a small bag and emptied it out on the counter. I gasped as the cross fell out along with my wedding ring. I didn't even realize I still had it. I called Houston over. If an old towel was piss yellow and Houston had said, "Your bed. It's sick," I couldn't imagine how sick my old wedding ring was. Something that was supposed to symbolize love and faithfulness had become a symbol of his hate, lies, and the abuse that had stolen peace and innocence from us all. I called Houston over and said only one thing. "What do you see?" He spelled, "Don't touch it. It is horrible. You cannot imagine how disgusting the energy is." It went directly to the dumpster and everything in my home was scrubbed. I played hymns of praise and read Scriptures aloud in my home. Someone asked why I didn't sell it. It wasn't the kind of energy I wanted anyone to have - ever. I didn't want the money from it either. It just needed to go. There is no salvaging darkness. Only God can do that. I'm not Him.

60

Carly's Gift

He will wipe away every tear from their eyes, and death shall be no more,
neither shall there be mourning, nor crying, nor pain anymore,
for the former things have passed away.
— Revelation 21:4

October 13, 2019

Mark and Kari invited us over. I was still reeling from all that had happened. Morgan brought her family and Benjamin came along. They were all doing everything they could to love on me. None of us had any clue God had decided to join us for lunch. When we entered their beautiful home Kari showed Houston a picture of Carly at her wedding and later at her reception. He was looking at the picture and told me her aura was white and mauve. I told them from what I remembered that white was purity, innocence or connection with God and mauve was related to faith and quiet modesty. Then he spelled something I was unprepared for… "Carly is here." "She's here? Are you sure?" I asked, completely shocked. "Yes." Kari was crying. None of us really knew what to do. We sat at the table and they started asking questions. Houston delivered messages from Carly that had been given to the angels for Houston to spell. The messages were for her husband and her family. Morgan and Kari took notes. Houston acted as messenger to a family in great loss with great love that had no place to go.

Carly's message to Kari & Mark: "Pray for David. He needs to have faith. When the knowledge of His plan is worked, you are going to be more in love than ever."

Jack, Carly's brother, had been deeply sorrowful at her death and the horrific pain she went through. He had held her hand when she died. Kari told us the painful details of those last moments, a husband in anguish pleading with them to pray for his beloved when he didn't/couldn't believe, brothers heartbroken at the sight of their sister in bitter agony, and parents completely grief stricken and clinging to Christ when a world without their daughter was not a world they wanted to know.

We talked about not understanding God's plan and the pain we had all experienced. I shared the story of Houston telling me my thoughts were rotten and how grieved I was by that statement. Houston reiterated what he had shared with me privately.

Houston spelled to me: "Calling your thoughts rotten was my way of saying your doubt is rotten. Doubt is how Satan prevents us from receiving God's love. Don't worry. Happy days are coming."

Kari asked Houston: "Is Carly with the baby that we lost?"

Houston: "All families find each other in heaven. Carly is with her sibling. Teaching about God's love is my purpose. Even this is all for your good. Esther told me to tell you to read Scripture. We can learn to trust Him. Esther tells me,

"I can tell her your God has words of love to give you. Be very good. Be with Him every day." Esther says to prepare to find works of His love to you. He is showing it to your family."

Kari asked Houston about what he has seen.

Houston: "Yes, I see everything. Neurotypicals believe, I've seen. When you see what I've seen, you'd believe. I understand this is hard to believe. It's a real thing."

I told them about energy and Houston's reaction to the stones I had been given. I even told them about "the bossy stone". Kari disappeared for a moment and returned with several small stones. She said Carly had given her these stones. Kari told me she had been concerned they were "new age" when Carly gave them to her. I explained that they were earth, pieces of earth, and that they had unique properties. I shared with them some of the Scriptures. I knew one of her stones was rose quartz, and one was dalmatian jasper. I wasn't sure about the others. Jasper is one of the stones listed in Revelation in the foundation of the New Jerusalem. She was touched that one of these last gifts from her daughter actually had far more significance than she realized. Kari asked us to return to speak to some other moms who had lost children and promised to read Josiah's Fire.

When we left my head was spinning. I was in awe at why or how God was using us. But there was no denying He was there with us all. Later Kari emailed me with questions for Houston about the incredible afternoon. "Houston, did you know Carly would be there?" He spelled, "No. Her beauty was all I was aware of. There were angels with her. The words were spoken to angels, good angels. They told me what she said. I stated exactly what I heard." "Did she say anything else?" "She said thank you for telling them about the stones and our families are destined to be friends."

That next week I decided to use some of my time off to clean out some closets. As I searched through boxes, I gasped at what I found. It was the China dolls my Aunt Esther had given me when I was four years old that I had cherished all through my childhood. I had taken them away from Morgan when she was a child because she had broken their porcelain hands and feet. They had been in a box for sixteen years. Houston was at class with Morgan. I took my dolls and placed them on his dresser in a corner. Then I left. A few hours later when I got home Houston was asleep in his room. I woke him up excitedly and took him downstairs. "Did you notice anything different in your room?" I asked. He rubbed his eyes sleepily and yawned. "Do you mean the dolls Esther gave you? She was filled with tears and wonder when she saw them." I just sat there with my mouth open. Too stunned to ask anything else. It really was Esther. I had never mentioned or even really thought about the dolls since Morgan had broken them in elementary school. I wasn't alone. God really was here with me. Jesus really did love me. There must truly be angels all around.

I asked, "Did Esther tell you she was a missionary?" Houston spelled, "When I asked her what she did, she told me what she did before didn't matter. It does not compare to what she does now."

October 21, 2019

Two days before the compliance hearing my attorney notified me that the Big Jock had gotten a new attorney who requested the hearing be cancelled and informed my attorney the Big Jock had entered a plea deal with the US District Courts. His mother had hired one of the most expensive defense attorneys to handle the federal charges against him and hired a new attorney in Georgia to help him escape child support but had refused to help him pay any of the money he owed for child support. He had told the court on multiple occasions no one in his family had money or would give him money. In the federal plea deal the Big Jock had admitted to multiple counts of wire fraud, tax evasion, and perjury to avoid a trial and a lengthier sentence. In the months that followed, the court sentenced him to three years in federal prison. He had known he was indicted and facing prison when he lied at the child support hearing, when he still refused to pay, when he created the horrible videos and posted them online, and when he conspired with the babysitter's mother. Hate doesn't know how to stop.

October 23, 2019

The Big Jock did not appear for the hearing and a bench warrant for the immediate arrest and incarceration was issued. His attorney for the child support case filed for a new trial. It was utterly exhausting. He was sent to federal prison before an arrest was made.

Reagan wept. It was the second moment of justice we had known. Even if it wasn't for what her father had done to her, it was still something, some hope that God would right it all.

Nov 9, 2019

Houston and I went to Kari's house to meet two of her friends battling the grief and loss of their children. By this time Kari had read Josiah's Fire and was encouraging others who had lost someone to read it as well. Kari took notes.

Houston asked Elizabeth & Krista: "Do you muster the courage to go to God to find the answers to your fear?"

Elizabeth: "No. I am just living. Living and working."

Houston: "Dealing the words to our wounds all works to make God our source of love to our torn hearts."

Kari asks Houston: "When and how did you come to faith?"

Houston: "Each time that I would cry out to Him, Jesus heard me. Days were all too awful."

Krista asks Houston: "Do you feel better now that you can communicate?"

Houston: "Each awesome day, He is making me to be His herald."

Kari led a reading of Invocation to the Holy Guardian Angel prayers.

Kari asks Houston: "Did you like those angel prayers?"

Houston: "Each was too wonderful. The best teaching. Divinely tell your faithful angels the things of your core beliefs."

I commented: "Core beliefs are very important to Houston. He tells everyone, 'Core beliefs are everything.' Houston, Why are core beliefs so important with angels?"

Houston: "When you start to deliver your torn heart to Him, God will make His most wonderful angels work to hold you in their arms. The doubt prevents our angels from helping us."

I asked Houston: "What do you say to me when bad things happen?"

Houston: "Everything is to your good. You just need to trust Him."

Kari asks Houston: How did you learn of the name of the angel, Esther?

I told the story of Esther, Houston's cover, not an angel. Esther was my great aunt, my Grandmother Ruth's twin sister, and had died long ago. Because of Houston's isolation, he dealt with much darkness. So, Esther has never left Houston's side except for one time when the darkness threatening him was so bad, Esther left just long enough to help protect him.

Houston's message to Elizabeth: "Esther said that your angel tells her to tell you more than you think. Each tear that you have cried, they have been twice sewn to His robe. Over these years, not one tear has escaped the love of God."

I told the women how Houston and I had prayed before coming to dinner to prepare for meeting Krista and Elizabeth, knowing of their losses and shared our conversation.

Houston: "Do you think I am going to be able to pour out God's love to them?"

I asked Houston: "Do they have reason to hope?"

Houston: "Time to tell you, when the tomb was empty, that is when our hope, too magnificent to explain, began."

Kari asks Houston: "Did you have the experiences of school in heaven like Josiah described in Josiah's Fire?"

Houston: "Each time Jesus took me to heaven, something I would learn. Jesus told me my story would steady many wounded hearts. He took me to the start of teaching to make me see that the world took shape from His words. Everything happens at the same time, leading to eternity. When you are not sure, you should believe exactly what the Bible says."

Krista asks Houston: "Is Logan okay?"

Houston: "Don't worry. Your son is there with me." That's Jesus speaking.

Elizabeth asks Houston: "Is Jose okay?"

Houston: "I went to God and my God moved one tear to work this wonderful truth. My son, don't worry. The one we want to hear about. He is in the arms of my Son. The taste of truth is too sweet."

I told the story of how I thought for a long time that God's promises were for other people and how I thought that God was mean.

Houston: "Do you believe He is doing this out of love?"

My response to him was simple.

Me: "What else could it be? That's what He is."

A few days later Kari excitedly told me about the joy that Houston's words and Josiah's Fire had brought to the friends she had shared the story with. She asked us to meet her son, Jack, and his girlfriend. We all played frisbee golf on a gorgeous autumn day. Houston tried so hard to throw the frisbee. Jack was most definitely wondering why his parents wanted him to meet this random mom and autistic son. It wasn't hard to feel his reservation. We sat at a park bench and Houston told them a little bit about heaven and the hope we have in Christ. What he shared shocked them. Houston's words brought wonder, tears, and most importantly, hope. Kari wanted us to meet her extended family. The Saturday after Thanksgiving we went to their home to meet their family. I shared Houston's story and how we had reconnected with Mark and Kari. Houston told them the names of their angels and shared so much with this family that the doubt and pain so well rooted seemed to disappear off their faces right in front of us. The day was astounding and precious as I saw what hope, the hope Houston was pointing them to, could do. Houston spelled to me, "They are such good kind people. They will see God's goodness."

Dear Katie & Houston,

Each time we are together, I am humbled & awed by how much we are already seeing God's goodness! That vision I had years ago is unfolding. At that time, there was deep conflict in my family, some had not spoken in years. I was on the verge of a nervous breakdown over it. Mark gifted me time to go to my yoga class on our anniversary and so I was using the meditation time to pray for Mark.

This was my vision — After I felt the warmth of God's presence and love in response to my prayers, I became an observer of my body from the side (in the position I actually was in with my hands open at my sides), seeing myself still and floating in darkness. I could see only one wing on me from that viewpoint. I let my defenses go. Then my body began to spin centrifugally super fast and flashes flew out of me. They looked like sparkling shards of broken glass. I realized that the shards were all the things I had never forgiven. They had been killing me on the inside.

Then Mark was there. Though I still observed from the side, seeing that he too had a wing, I could also feel that we were barely touching each other at the tips of our noses, fingers and toes. We began to fly. I felt air rush past us as we flew, barely touching, at supersonic speed through darkness. It was amazing!

Then I was suddenly back in my body and floating, but upright. I was holding hands in a circle. Mark was across from me and we were smiling at each other. The circle included two at our left and right. It was our children and just as I realized the fourth one, holding my left hand, was the baby that we had lost and I started to turn my head to finally see her or him, I saw as I moved my eyes from Mark that behind him was an ocean of people. It took my breath away to see the incredible multitude of the Communion of Saints. My vision ended then with the sound of the bell. The line the instructor read was, "We are all angels with one wing. We need to cling to each other to fly."

I contacted all my family right away and said we have to resolve all the conflict. We all drove to meet at a centrally located home in NC and had a family intervention weekend. We painfully hashed it all out. After we all forgave each other, love finally grew in our family. The rocky road did not smooth out overnight. But our family is unrecognizable now from what it was then and I and others have been released from intense suffering.

The vision and after-effects assured me that all our family would eventually be in heaven, but I knew God's plan included hard work on my part. I stopped going to yoga because that vision gave me so much work, I did not want to make myself available to more assignments from God, haha!

My prayers prioritized Carly, because I knew she would be the first to die, plus Mark, as he is the best part of me. It seems like faith slipped for those who I prayed for less than those two during those years. Since Carly's home-going, I have focused my prayers on our sons, David and all their future wives. What a gift to see this new focus of my prayers being answered through you two! Your family will receive even greater crowns of glory because of what you are doing for us and for the growing circle of others in all our lives. Truly, you both are the Lord's heralds! Thank you to all your family.

With much love and gratitude,
Kari

Feb 16, 2020

We had dinner with Kari and Mark and the conversation and questions continued.

Benjamin talked about the new Tesla and the much anticipated Tesla truck with automation and accessibility features of new vehicles. Houston wanted to be included in this cool conversation.

Houston: "I want a Tesla too. I think that will be great."

For a moment Houston was just a guy talking and dreaming about cars, and with all the progress in automation and accessibility in cars, driving was not the obstacle it had once been. Then Kari wanted to ask about heaven.

Kari: "Are you getting direction from heaven about what to say?"

Houston: "It is Jesus telling me what to say."

Kari: "What are these messages that Jesus wants relayed?"

Houston: "Pray. Most of what He told me I have not told. Good question."

Kari: "Is the BOOK of Life that you refer to in the page you wrote referring to the Bible?"

Houston: The words of the BOOK of Life take up heaven."

I showed a painting of an open book with streams of words and light swirling up out of it that represents the BOOK of Life to help us picture what Houston means. I noted that in Revelation, Jesus is the only one worthy to open the seals of the BOOK.

Kari: "Where did you learn calculus?"

Houston: "I see the numbers going to work. I don't get to learn it."

Kari: "So you are figuring it out yourself?"

Houston: "Yes. Math - it only plays the most important role in getting our lost world to recognize that He is God. Most of what is physics is all the power of our God fighting Satan. It is throughout the universe."

Kari: "So that means Satan operates elsewhere?"

Houston: "Satan is throughout the universe too. Satan is not everywhere like God, but he can go many places. That's what I mean."

Kari: "In the vision that I had of seeing Mark and I flying in darkness, my view was from the side, so only one wing was visible on each of us. I do not remember seeing wings later in the vision, when I was in a circle with our family in heaven. I had previously always pictured angels with wings and saints without wings. Does Esther have wings and if so, are they similar to angel's wings?"

Houston: "My Esther does not have wings. She wears a white dress. They are the post-loves that love when they have died. They find their purpose in powerful love they give to work to help us. Post-loves. That means they use their after-life to love us. Some have love-jobs and some have other jobs. Wings are from our works. The work we do on earth has value in doing God's will. Really, too much is placed on our life now. Heaven is the most incredible place and Jesus tells us He makes heaven our home."

I added that in a sense, Esther is working here, near to Houston, rather than in heaven, so it may be different for saints working in heaven.

Kari: "Isn't earth important in that here we say either yes or no to God, determining if we are saved or not?"

Houston: "That is true."

Kari asks for her brother, Sean: "What are the wings of angels like?"

Houston: "There are angels too wonderful to explain that hover over the world and angels that look like us. The angels ride the words of praise."

Kari asks for her brother, Sean: "Did God create life on other planets besides earth?" and "Are the stars and other planets for our benefit or for others?"

Houston: "Most definitely, the power of God just doesn't stop with earth. I have not seen it. My opinion is that knowing how powerful God is that He would create other worlds too. Most definitely, God is everywhere."

June 2020

Kari had questions about COVID-19.

Houston: "Over the world, Satan tries to destroy. Just work to tell the truth of God and Jesus. The virus scares. I mean that the world needs to hear the truth of God."

Kari asked Houston to share about Jesus and Mary.

Houston: "Our thinking does not have a lot of the saints. The truth, even the saints mean something in heaven. It is good sharing the work of the saints."

Kari: "And Mary is the queen of the saints!"

Houston: "Yes."

Kari (excitedly with exuberant joy): "Yes, she was the first disciple and taught us how to follow and love Him." Kari asked Houston to share about his interactions with Jesus.

Houston: "The way He talks to me is with preaching the Word to me all the time. Our sharing the story that Jesus wants to share gives Mary the love she deserves. Jesus welled up with hurting when He was dying at the sight of Mary. Be praying that we put all the saints, every one of them in our mouth."

I described how Houston talks about the importance of what comes out of our mouths and then referred to Matthew 15 - What is in your heart is what makes you clean or dirty.

Houston: "Jesus is creating an army."

61

Fruit

And other seeds fell into good soil and produced grain,
growing up and increasing and yielding thirtyfold and sixtyfold and a hundredfold."
And he said, "He who has ears to hear, let him hear."
— Mark 4:8-10

L ate one night I got a call and a man with a Russian accent was on the other end. He asked if I remembered him. It was the dad who had choked back tears as Houston had spelled. It was the dad of the young girl who had wept in Chick-fil-A. It was the dad of E- who still had no voice. I gasped when I realized who had called. Of course I remembered him. He continued, "I had lost all hope for my son until I met you and your son. Please tell me again. Please tell me everything. This ABA is just babysitting. It does nothing." So I did. It was such a gift from God during that awful time to know that our efforts to give others a voice were still stirring, to know that God was still working. I continued to answer his questions. He had a fire in his voice. I knew he wouldn't give up.

Sometime later I got a call from St-'s mom. She told me that E-'s father had insisted she take her son to a coaching session. It was with great resistance that she finally relented and went. She continued with a trembling voice, "Then I saw the light in my son's eyes. I saw a light I had never seen before as he spelled right in front of me." Silently, tears rolled down my face as she shared the first moment of joy and hope she had known. "Katie! I've been wrong! I've been wrong all this time. I treated him like he could know and understand nothing. How much life I have kept him from..." I could hear her choking back the same tears that had choked me. I told her I understood the regret, but regret had no place now. Hope was in charge. Doubt was the enemy.

November 3, 2019

I kept calling T-'s mom. It had almost been a year. Houston determined it was time to show T-'s dad as well. We invited them both and after much encouragement they agreed to come. Once again, they were amazed at Houston but couldn't believe their son was competent and capable. T-'s dad left and we continued to talk. I pleaded with T-'s mom to try again. We stood in the foyer. Houston faced the stairs with his back to us, flapping his hands. T- faced the bathroom with his back to us, verbally stimming. Finally, almost with exasperation, T-'s mom said, "OK! Fine! I'll give it another try." As soon as she said that Houston and T- turned around to each other and embraced. It was extraordinary. T-'s mother turned to me with her jaw dragging the ground, "ARE THEY *FRIENDS*????" I smiled. "Yes. They have been very good friends since they were little. That's how I know T- wants to study Sports Medicine." "WHAT??" Her voice was quivering as she fought back tears. She texted me later about the impact seeing Houston and T-'s connection had on her and what she now believed was possible. She couldn't stop thinking about it. She had seen a glimpse of her son's heart and just like that, it one instant, hope had sparked, life had begun. Nothing would stop her. Like Houston said over and over again, "Core beliefs are everything."

I ran into one of the other moms who had been struggling to get going on the boards with a lot of stops and starts. She told me she thought the lessons were too difficult for her son and she had decided to just have him spell easy words. I was in no mood for doubt, for dumbing down and limiting these brilliant young people. While climbing at a fast and furious pace on the stair climber in the middle of the big corporate gym, I declared, "That's it! You have to see this." I turned mine and Houston's machines off and jumped down. I ran to get Houston's board. Right there in that moment surrounded by weights and treadmills Houston showed her his abilities. She started crying. I told her that her son was just as capable as Houston. I looked at him and he was smiling sheepishly. His parents embraced him and after that his spelling took off. When they asked Houston what their son wanted to read Houston told them their son wanted to study the Bible. When I was able to, I did a simple known question from Genesis on the boards with him and he spelled quickly and perfectly. His family was amazed and when I went to give him a hug goodbye, he kissed me. I understood. His family finally believed in him. I had gotten to bring hope, hope to them, hope to him. I cried happy tears when I got in the car. Houston squeezed my hand and smiled at me. At home he spelled to me once again, "Core beliefs are everything. They had to believe." A few months later his mom called me excitedly to tell me that he kept spelling he had friends. After several times of asking him who his friends were, he spelled. "C - H - R - I - S - T".

The two mothers I had met, because of the young girl at Chick-fil-A, wanted to meet with me. They had so many questions.

"Can I keep letting him watch Blue's Clues?"

"No. Fill his life with age-appropriate material."

"Is this a stim?"

"Yes. The stim is seeking sensory input so seek ways to give him sensory input that does not become a loop. Look for ways to replace stims with purposeful motor actions."

"How long will it take before he can communicate?"

It depends on many factors but the more you practice and the more you believe the faster he will get there. Remember, it's like practicing piano. How soon you will be able to play is often directly related to how much and how often you practice, as well as his motor control. You are creating neural pathways. Remember how hard it is to get your fingers to play a note at first, but after time the neural pathway is there, and you can increase the complexity of the music your fingers play."

"What about self-care?"

"That's all motor and sensory. It should be practiced daily."

"Don't I need to teach him all the things he has missed?"

"Yes and no. They have been learning the whole time and sucking in everything around them. They are like sponges. But yes, there will be holes in their education. The best approach is to teach age appropriate and interesting material and in time you will see where there might be gaps."

I told them they had to believe in the competency of their children. The idea of hoping in their children after giving up all hope was so painful, and they gave me all the reasons why this was still such a struggle. They asked question after question about Houston. I read to them what he had written. They wanted to know how he knew so much. I kept explaining that they hear everything. One of the women was a trained acupuncturist who understood the energy that flowed through the body as well as energy's connection to the physical body. Suddenly she looked at me and I saw her face change as the lightbulb, the brilliant lightbulb of awareness and hope went off in her mind. "They can hear thoughts, can't they?" I didn't answer, I just looked at her. "They've heard everything?" The weight of it sunk into her heart. She was quiet and then she said slowly, "I came here tonight for hope... for inspiration to keep going... I got it." The last thing I told them was, "Your belief in them, your determination... That is what will make all the difference."

One evening I asked Houston if he wanted to watch Harry Potter. He spelled, "Yes. The books are better." I started to ask him when he had read Harry Potter and then stopped myself. Morgan! He had heard Morgan, my voracious reader, read the entire series along with who knows what else. I called her and told her what he said. "MOM! He's right first of all. The books are better. But - he heard me! He heard me reading! WOW!" Exactly. With awe I pondered how he had been listening to me read God's word for so many years, listening to me as I wrote, listening and learning, soaking up all that we soaked in. How awful that for years I had stopped reading God's word and he had not been blessed with the comfort of hearing the words of truth in his own home.

62

The Joy of the Lord

Count it all joy, my brothers, when you meet trials of various kinds,
for you know that the testing of your faith produces steadfastness.
And let steadfastness have its full effect,
that you may be perfect and complete, lacking in nothing.
— James 1:2-4

November 18, 2019

My manager had called the week before and acted like everything was fine and they were excited for me to get back to work. He kept asking if Paul had called and admitted what he had done. No, was my honest and heartbroken answer. When I went in that day, I was cheerful, a little nervous, but upbeat, expecting good. Writing about this makes me physically nauseous. A person at work that I had befriended told me I was basically stupid for listening to Houston instead of protecting myself. Safety and security were the only things that some people valued. Explaining why I believed my son and why I needed to seek justice for my daughter exhausted me, but I was mostly viewed as stupid. I had become a plague. Three individuals from upper management had flown across the country to visit our office. I had no clue what was about to happen. I was taken to a conference room where I was told that I couldn't be trusted to work from home. Their big piece of evidence was that I had repeatedly been MIA for conference calls. (I counted in my head, the technology assessment, the car accident, the morning at the police station - three, three events completely out of my control.)

I listened in shock and deep hurt as they lied and twisted the truth. I defended myself against their lies. I told them I worked more than anyone and my results proved it. I asked how I could have written over $9M in new business if I wasn't working and that the other underwriters had written a third of that. I told them that the whole reason I accepted this job and not the other one was because of the flexibility to work from home that I needed to care for Houston. Tears I couldn't stop streamed down my face. My heart battled for truth as my brain battled to be professional, to survive. In my mind I thought about the people I worked with. I knew other coworkers who napped and watched TV at home during the workday. I knew the manager sitting in front of me, lying to me about me, would go for bike rides and mow the grass during his workday. I knew they were setting up an impossible situation for me where they could fire me for working from home, which I knew was inevitable.

Suddenly I had no authority and almost no brokers. When my manager saw my tears, he excitedly leaned forward and said, "If you want to quit now, we can offer you a severance package." His eagerness made me sick to my stomach. I needed time to think. I knew I had no choice. My ears were ringing. I tried to explain about Houston's care and that I needed to work from home. I explained how that was the only reason I had decided to stay and not accept the other job offer almost two years earlier. He heard nothing I said. With all the composure and courage I could muster, I went to our business dinner that night. No one could look me in the eyes. So the push out began. The next morning I went to my desk and wrote a detailed response defending myself against the allegations. I asked the manager to read it. I asked the Vice President to read it. My manager just rolled his eyes. "I just need a response. Are you going to stay?... If you are, then you have to sign this. You're agreeing that you have to work in the office and be granted permission anytime you need to work from home." I couldn't stop crying as I signed the lie they forced me to agree to so I could keep feeding my kids and paying bills. The most senior executive walked over to me and smiled before shaking my hand and telling me goodbye. I felt the way someone feels when the person who cuts off your hand wants to shake it first. I doubted I would ever see him again.

When the IT Department couldn't get my system to open up after shutting it down, I was written up for not working and told to use one of my PT days since I hadn't worked, even though I had spent the whole day on the phone with IT. For three months Morgan exercised every amount of energy to make sure she was with Houston all day during every workday so I could be at the office. No one in my department was there. They were at home. No one wanted to talk to me. With almost no brokers, there was almost no work. Every day, sitting at that desk, I just prayed. I asked colleagues in the industry to help me find another position. I talked to headhunters. I waited. I knew it was coming.

One day Morgan's eye got infected, and she had to go to the doctor. I told her if I worked from home, I would lose my job. The idea of asking permission was humiliating and terrifying after the way I had been treated when I my computer wouldn't work. I just couldn't bring myself to do it. Morgan couldn't open her eye, she had to go. So I worked from home. At four p.m. on the dot on January 21, 2020, I got a call from my manager who had been an underwriter just like me only a few months earlier. Also on the phone was the Vice President of Human Resources, and the Vice President who had hired me and promised me flexible working conditions as well as praised me repeatedly for my performance and hard work. The former underwriter and months old manager told me I was terminated, effective immediately for not getting permission to work from home that day. The Vice President of Human Resources listed my severance packaged and said they wouldn't fight the unemployment. The speed of it proved it had obviously been prepared, written, and choreographed to perfect corporate symphony. The sweet man who had hired me said absolutely nothing at all. He didn't have the stomach to be cruel to someone whose work ethic he had praised, to a single mother of five with a disabled adult child who was the sole provider for her family. He knew it was all wrong. But bravery and compassion are not corporate values. And cowardice is easier than courage. It is easier to stay quiet and live with indigestion. At least for a time. So he did. And the world spins madly on.

Sarah had just arrived to read to Houston when the call came. I put it on speaker so I wouldn't have to tell her what was happening, and she could hear for herself. The first words out of her mouth, "The Lord God is your provider, not them." I nodded and wept. I praised my God for a future that terrified me. Into the dark unknown I walked. Houston sat down on the bed and wiped my tears. He handed me the board and spelled, "The good has begun."

The joy of the Lord is my strength... But when you seek Him and walk away from security, you are climbing mountains. When you're that high the air is thin. God gives just enough for only one breath at a time.

My flesh and my heart may fail,
but God is the strength of my heart and my portion forever.
— Psalm 73:26

Many are saying of me, God will not deliver him.
But you, O Lord, are a shield around me, my glory, the one who lifts my head high.
I call out to the Lord and He answers me from High mountain.
I lie down, sleep, and wake again because He sustains me.
I will not fear though tens of thousands assail me on every side.
— Psalm 3:2-6

63

Empty Hands

What then shall we say to these things? If God is for us, who can be against us?
He who did not spare his own Son but gave him up for us all,
how will he not also with him graciously give us all things?
Who shall bring any charge against God's elect?
It is God who justifies. Who is to condemn?
Christ Jesus is the one who died—more than that, who was raised—
who is at the right hand of God, who indeed is interceding for us.
Who shall separate us from the love of Christ?
Shall tribulation, or distress, or persecution, or famine, or nakedness, or danger, or sword?
As it is written, "For your sake we are being killed all the day long;
we are regarded as sheep to be slaughtered."
No, in all these things we are more than conquerors through him who loved us.
For I am sure that neither death nor life, nor angels nor rulers,
nor things present nor things to come, nor powers, nor height nor depth,
nor anything else in all creation,
will be able to separate us from the love of God in Christ Jesus our Lord.
— Romans 8:31-39

I spent the first weeks of unemployment scrambling to network, make connections on LinkedIn, update my resume, and file for unemployment. I knew what I was supposed to do - WRITE THE BOOK - but I was terrified. 'Lord, isn't there another way? No one is going to believe the truth. I don't want people to be mad at me for telling it. I don't want to be exposed. I don't want to relive it. I don't want to be attacked again. Can't I just hide?' Houston was adamant. Morgan was insistent. Sarah was expectant. The gentlemen at McDonald's repeated every day, "Write the book." A chorus of others who knew me joined the mantra. Finally, I relented. After much encouragement by those close to me I started the book. A friend told me, "Before I knew you and Houston, I referred to God as the universe or the source. Because of you, because of your story and your faith, because of Houston, I now call him Jesus. The world needs to hear this story." So I began to write my story, God's story in my life. It is my offering to Him, so that through our testimony you might believe. Please be gentle. It's my heart. My life. And it's true, all of it.

I hung my head, for the last time
In surrender and despair
Before I'm dead, I'll take the last climb
Up the mountain, face my fears
The time has come, to make a choice
Use my voice for the love of every man

My mind's made up, never again
Never again, will I turn round
Though they may surround me like lions
And crush me on all sides
I may fall, but I will rise
Not by my might or my power or by the strength of swords
Only through your love my Lord
All that's lost will be restored [164]

Houston spelled to me, "The Lord makes fertile our thanksgiving to Him. He really thanks you're making His book. Your thoughts - those He loves. Your story that you hate - He loves your story. He says, "Walk to My soul. That is where the talk to hear Me is. I'm somewhere that hearts hope in." As I struggled through painful parts of my story he spelled, "The love that you give heals. Work the truth to tell what the story is. The times when our faith is tested the most are the times when it feels like our Father has looked away. The walk to more trust comes with more good. Believe it works for good. The patient all see that what they pray is answered. Hope imparts power to build astounding faith to keep the work of good working. His love roots in the words we pray. Nothing is good to those who put their trust in religion. Hope is in Christ alone." So I wrote and prayed, prayed and cried, praised and rejoiced.

I raise a hallelujah, in the presence of my enemies
I raise a hallelujah, louder than the unbelief
I raise a hallelujah, my weapon is a melody
I raise a hallelujah, heaven comes to fight for me

I'm gonna sing, in the middle of the storm
Louder and louder, you're gonna hear my praises roar
Up from the ashes, hope will arise
Death is defeated, the King is alive! [165]

One day Houston was in the car with Morgan and started shouting in earnest, "Cross! Cross! Cross!" She called me on speaker so I could hear. I told her to bring him home so I could figure out what cross he was talking about. He told me to take him to the cross. I drove to several churches but didn't see an outdoor cross that made sense for him to be so eager to see. We prayed again at the stone garden. That wasn't it. Finally, I drove to our old church, and we sat by the pond. After a while I looked behind me at the church and there on the back of the building was an enormous cross that I had forgotten existed because it faced the direction I never drove. Directly above it was the tower and the room where Houston had been found after searching for hours when he was little. I was in awe. What had he seen? Who had he been reaching for? I remembered another young autistic with no words who had been found on the edge of the roof of his two-story home as if he had been trying to fly with angels. *Because you have made the Lord your dwelling place— the Most High, who is my refuge no evil shall be allowed to befall you, no plague come near your tent. For he will command his angels concerning you to guard you in all your ways. On their hands they will bear you up, lest you strike your foot against a stone.* [166] Despite everything He was with us. I knew that now. He could be trusted. I knew that too. I took Houston's hand and walked into the quiet, dark chapel with only the light from the stained glass to fill the space. We knelt down and worshipped. In the silence I felt His presence. I heard His love. After so many years, I had come home.

---

[164] *Rise*; by Joshua Wallace. Copyright Tunecore Digital Music
[165] *Raise A Hallelujah*; By Jonathan Helser, Melissa Helser, Molly Skaggs, & Jake Steves. Copyright Bethel Music Publishing
[166] Psalm 91:10-12

Through this time I have learned even more, as if each day the veil is pulled back a little bit more. God and heaven, our home, is far more wondrous than we can imagine, and His hand is working in ways we cannot fathom. One of the first things I did when I started writing was to call my old church and ask for a recording of the sermon when the poop letter was read almost eighteen years earlier. I knew it needed to be part of this book. It took me a little bit of time to give the resource director a time frame to research. I narrowed it down to August 2002 and the first sermon of a new series. She finally found the sermon and sent me a recording.

The sermon began "What would you do if you could give God anything? Anything at all." The pastor then proceeded to teach that the greatest gift to God is a gift of faith, that *without faith it is impossible to please God.*[167] He asked if we could conceive of having the faith of Noah to build an ark when it had never rained, or the faith of the widow who gave her last meal for her and her son to the prophet Elijah. He explained that, "It's that kind of major league demonstration of faith I would like to offer God and I know you do too if you're His child." Then he said, "In light of the teaching of Hebrews 11:1 it makes a whole lot of sense that faith would be the kind of gift we would like to give God." I stopped the recording immediately. — Hebrews 11:1?? 11:1? I played it again. Hebrews 11:1 - There it was. I was in shock. It had always been there. He had always been there. Faith had always been the currency of heaven. Faith was always what He had wanted me to offer Him, trusting Him to do what couldn't be seen or explained. This was twelve years before God gave me that tiny miracle the night before Thanksgiving when Houston said I love you for the first time. It was twelve years before God had a friend text me at 5 am the morning after I heard about 11 and 1 and had ever given numbers a thought at all. It was eighteen years earlier when my pastor had written this sermon days or weeks before I had even written the poop letter. I hadn't even heard the verse that Sunday in 2002 when I was struggling to believe at all. But it was always there. Promising. Moving. Loving. Bringing about the confidence and assurance for the very miracle I longed to become true. Hungrily I read Hebrews 11.

As I wrote the truth of my life, I was afraid and ashamed. Houston spelled to me one morning, "Courage protects the truth by telling it. Fear trusts in the same thing that has power. This power is proud to worry those who trust fear." So there was really nothing to do but press forward in spite of every emotion within me.

One night Houston asked to go to a bar to watch football, have a beer and eat steak. Bartenders would always be shocked by his orders. When he ordered Hennessey, the bartender asked, "How does he know what Hennessey is?" Despite how many times I explained that not speaking does not equate to not comprehending, it still baffled people that inside a silent or stimming mouth was a vibrant and brilliant mind. Of course I had been guilty of the same misconception. The world has still not been able to stop judging books by their covers. We live in a world that is blinded by sight. That evening there were twelve screens blaring and appropriate fanfare for a SEC game. Houston's stims started and despite all my tricks to calm him, nothing worked. The whole night, the whole meal, was a disaster. I was so frustrated. It seemed the prison doors were trying to shut us in again. When we got home, I asked him what had happened. He was upset he had lost control of his body. His face was heartbroken as he spelled, "I'm normal inside." Those words broke my heart. I knew he was. Actually, he was so much greater than normal. I couldn't imagine his pain and fear as he longed to just be a twenty-three-year-old man on a Saturday night. How terrifying it must be to feel himself losing control and be unable to stop it, unable to tell me what was causing it, unable

[167] Hebrews 11:6

to show people who he really was, unable to just watch football and drink a beer. When he was able, we discussed it more.

"What was going on? What triggered the loops?" I asked.

"Nonsense words. The stims wouldn't stop. It's loops, looping that keeps good thoughts from forming."

"How are you?"

"Mostly I'm fine. But my thoughts, long over thought, are hoping to get out of my mouth. Care. That is what love does. That is what works. Thank you. In His love you are caring. Could you help me get more friends? I don't want to have to go everywhere with you. Men don't go watch football with their moms."

"I know. But we need more people, no, we need more *men* who will learn to use the boards, especially since there are more males who can't speak reliably. Honestly, men need to learn to love and think of others. They need to stop chasing money, pleasure, power, and glory. But we also have to change the way people see those who can't control their bodies. They need to be included in life."

"Hopefully men will want to be part of doing something revolutionary. I am happy to share my life."

"Of course you are Houston. Of course you are."

"Friends are everything."

"You're right. They are."

We walked at the park almost every day. I would have Houston wear his Delta glasses while we walked which use sunlight to regulate brain waves. One day we passed by the batting cages and I could see kids pointing at Houston and elbowing each other. When we turned the corner, I saw one kid grab his friend to make him look at Houston. I stopped and faced him. "Did you want to ask a question?" "Umm... Uh... those are cool glasses." I took them off Houston. They were falling apart and made out of paper and had tape all over them to hold them together. I had taped tongue depressors to the glasses to replace the paper arms that had fallen off. "Really? You think these are cool? They are taped together and just barely staying in one piece. These are Delta glasses that use light to regulate brain waves." "Oh uh, does he need special glasses?" "Yes. He does. These are to help his brain and his body work together. The next time you have a question, please ask instead of pointing behind someone's back. It's not kind." We continued to walk. Houston refused to put the glasses back on. He told me, "People think awful things about me. I'm used to how cowards think." My heart broke for my son and his friends. The world was still so stupid, so full of people who can't see past the end of their nose and never imagine there is something different on the inside than what they see on the outside.

After begging to go out for dinner one evening, Houston sat staring into the parking lot like he was watching something intently while his favorite chips and salsa sat untouched. This was completely uncharacteristic of him. I asked him what was going on and I could barely get him to look at the letter board. Finally he told me that he was watching an angel fight a devil. "The angel is destroying the devil. Do pray now. Your prayers give the angels power." So I prayed.

Later Houston told me, "When you pray, the words of God that have more power are 'The WORD, LORD, Master, Prince of Peace." I asked, "What about Jesus? Isn't Jesus a powerful name?" "Yes. It's not as strong as Prince of Peace. All the words of God provide Nowhere shame that he won't hear. The use of 'The WORD' slows the work of Satan. Other names are Immanuel, Adonai, Good Shepherd, Savior of the World, Chosen One, Alpha and Omega, The Beginning and The End, King of Kings, Lord of Lords, Crown of Thorns to Deliver Us, Son of God, God in the Flesh, Four Horsemen of the Apocalypse, Lamb of God, Lion of Judah, Son of David, Root of Jesse, Jesus the Name Above

All Names." Watching the names of the Son of the Living God pour out onto the letter board in front of me with my autistics son's finger was mind blowing. What had he *seen*? What had he *heard*? It changed the way I prayed. My prayers became more powerful, more commanding, more full of praise. My tears turned to purpose. My fear turned to faith. My mourning began to learn a new song. Without intending to, I became glad, the kind of glad that comes from some place that can't be seen. It was just there... In the midst of it all God placed two scriptures on my heart. My heart praised my God, my Savior. I believed His promises were to me.

Strengthen the feeble hands, steady the knees that give way;
say to those with fearful hearts, "Be strong, do not fear;
your God will come, he will come with vengeance;
with divine retribution he will come to save you."
Then will the eyes of the blind be opened and the ears of the deaf unstopped.
Then will the lame leap like a deer, and the mute tongue shout for joy.
Water will gush forth in the wilderness and streams in the desert.
The burning sand will become a pool, the thirsty ground bubbling springs.
In the haunts where jackals once lay, grass and reeds and papyrus will grow.
And a highway will be there, it will be called the Way of Holiness;
it will be for those who walk on that Way.
The unclean will not journey on it; wicked fools will not go about on it.
No lion will be there, nor any ravenous beast; they will not be found there.
But only the redeemed will walk there, and those the Lord has rescued will return.
They will enter Zion with singing; everlasting joy will crown their heads.
Gladness and joy will overtake them, and sorrow and sighing will flee away.[168]

Bring out the people who are blind, yet have eyes,
who are deaf, yet have ears!
All the nations gather together,
and the peoples assemble.
Who among them can declare this,
and show us the former things?
Let them bring their witnesses to prove them right,
and let them hear and say, It is true.
"You are my witnesses," declares the Lord,
"and my servant whom I have chosen,
that you may know and believe me and understand that I am he.
Before me no god was formed,
nor shall there be any after me.
I, I am the Lord,
and besides me there is no savior.

---

[168] Isaiah 35:3-10

I declared and saved and proclaimed,
when there was no strange god among you;
"You are my witnesses, declares the Lord,
"that I am God."
Thus says the Lord,
who makes a way in the sea,
a path in the mighty waters,
"Remember not the former things,
nor consider the things of old.
Behold, I am doing a new thing;
now it springs forth, do you not perceive it?
I will make a way in the wilderness
and rivers in the desert. [169]

[169] Isaiah 43:8-12, 16-19

64

The Sound of Faithful

"No halfheartedness and no worldly fear
must turn us aside from following the light unflinchingly."
— J.R.R. Tolkien

When I was writing about my grandmother and her faith, Houston spelled, "Esther said Ruth thought the cancer was God's punishment for not becoming a missionary." When he spelled that, I suddenly recalled a long forgotten memory of my dad telling me about being seventeen and his mom's death. He told me the lump had been the size of a grapefruit by the time she had gone to a doctor. They told her there was nothing they could do and she had interpreted the fateful prognosis as God's judgment for not going to the mission field. He had told me a pastor had tried to comfort her with wise counsel in her distress. I had completely forgotten that story until Houston shared it with me. How would Houston know this unless Esther had told him? I quickly went back to that part of the story in the beginning of the book and added those details. Still in awe at these wonders, I asked if Esther remembered when I went to see her before she died in the hospital. Houston spelled, "Esther told me she saw what your stepmother did to you. She saw how she treated you." "But does she remember seeing me?" I asked. "I only came in the room briefly. I was upset and frightened." Houston continued, "She told your dad to divorce her." I was stunned. I knew that statement could only have come from someone who had been there. Despite how many times Houston shared things, I was still in awe each time. It was like finding old love letters that I had never gotten to open.

I went to meet another mom with a non-speaking daughter a few hours away. When I stopped for gas, I saw I had gotten a text from J-'s mom asking for Houston to respond to what J- was struggling with. I took out the board. Without pausing and without me asking anything he started spelling, "Tell J-'s mom to tell him, 'Always believe that all is for our good.'" Soon after Houston replied to his friend's message of faith, J had spelled to his mom to ask Houston to elaborate, "Our focus is to be faithful to God's calling. He wants us to pray to give up fear. We need to walk the talk. Love your keeping the faith. Love your keeping steady."[170] Houston continued, "He wants us to trust Him. God is performing a miracle. Wait on the Lord. Watch what He does." The faith of these young men and their unwavering trust in God's ability to work His good humbled me. My doubt, however logical and justifiable, seemed foolish compared to their faith.

One day the subject of Reagan's baby, my granddaughter lost to abortion, came up with Houston. I realized he must have known the whole time and felt powerless listening to the events unfold and not being able to tell me. I asked him and he spelled, "It was the worst moment of my life. I thought God was as mean as a demon to allow that to happen when you had worked so hard to save babies. That pushed me into despair even though the angels told me to pray to fight." I told Houston I had asked God why He would do that when for so long I had fought for the voiceless. It had made me feel an even deeper abandonment from God. He shared, "I waited making my body and soul depend fully on love. 'Would your Holy Father have physically done that?' I asked myself. 'Power is changing,' the angels told me. 'That wonderful baby is with Rahab.' Everyone prefers to believe God works the worst for good. Jesus is fighting always to protect us from evil. Trust how love hasn't forced itself. That is God in the flesh. That is Jesus." As we talked about it, I realized I trusted God to bring justice and to answer my prayers. I just believed Him. I felt His presence and that made everything, even the worst of things, ok. The peace and the trust that had appeared in my heart shocked me. 'Where did that come from?' I wondered silently. Houston started spelling even though I hadn't asked him a question. "He wore something to hide from you so your prayers couldn't get to Him. He wanted your heart so worn out with worry to change to one of soft trust. Then when your heart had most of your worry gone, He worked a miracle. Now your prayers are getting answered."

My dear friend texted me as I shared these stories. She said, "The evidence of His love is all around us... but in the darkness it's hard to find our way out. It dawned on me that it doesn't mean He wasn't there across the entirety of our experiences... it just means we couldn't get to Him. Katie... I'm watching a miracle unfold in your life and when I sit down to pray for you and visit the body of doing life with you for twenty years... it leaves me undone. Because as someone who loves you, so much of what you've walked through makes me want to turn away from the pain and emotional torture that are chapters in your story. I don't pretend to understand or like the road you have traveled even though I know He was and is a loving God... and the Holy Spirit protected you from things we can't know... (that doesn't even sound right to me but I know it's true)."

For a moment I was astonished. I had always known she loved me. But there were many things I had kept to myself because I realized the brutality and despair of it was repulsive to people with safe lives. But her words in parentheses struck me. I had never told her about Houston's revelation that the Big Jock had asked the Small Jock to get rid of me. Those words had been given to her by the Holy Spirit and it humbled me when

---

[170] For the eyes of the Lord run to and fro throughout the whole earth, to show Himself strong on behalf of those whose heart is loyal to Him. — 2 Chronicles 16:9

He who is faithful in what is least is faithful also in much; and he who is unjust in what is least is unjust also in much. — Luke 16:10

Have I not commanded you? Be strong and courageous. Do not be frightened, and do not be dismayed, for the Lord your God is with you wherever you go.— Joshua 1:9

Do not be anxious about anything, but in everything by prayer and supplication with thanksgiving let your requests be made known to God. — Philippians 4:6

Therefore I tell you, do not be anxious about your life, what you will eat or what you will drink, nor about your body, what you will put on. Is not life more than food, and the body more than clothing? — Matthew 6:25

Let not steadfast love and faithfulness forsake you; bind them around your neck; write them on the tablet of your heart. So you will find favor and good success in the sight of God and man. Trust in the Lord with all your heart, and do not lean on your own understanding. In all your ways acknowledge him, and he will make straight your paths. Be not wise in your own eyes; fear the Lord, and turn away from evil. — Proverbs 3:3-7

And those who know Your name put their trust in you, for you, O LORD, have not forsaken those who seek you. — Psalm 9:10

Be faithful until death and I will give you the crown of life. — Revelation 2:10

Our soul waits for the LORD, he is our help and shield. — Psalm 33:20

Delight yourself in the LORD and He will give you the desires of your heart. Commit your way to the LORD, trust in Him, and He will act. — Psalm 37:4-5

You keep him in perfect peace whose mind is stayed on you, because he trusts in you. — Isaiah 26:3

When I am afraid I put my trust in You. — Psalm 56:3

Blessed is the man whose trust is in the LORD, whose trust is the LORD. — Jeremiah 17:7

Behold, God is my salvation; I will trust, and will not be afraid; for the Lord God is my strength and my song, and He has become my salvation. — Isaiah 12:2

He is not afraid of bad news; his heart is firm, trusting in the Lord. —Psalm 112:7

I read them. I replied back, "I want to turn away from it too. I'm supposed to start writing my part of our story. I feel ugly as I remember it. I don't know the reason for so much darkness or pain. It has kept me isolated from God and from even the company of others. I know people turn away from me because the whole mess of it makes them uncomfortable. I can conjecture that the enemies of God see Houston as a threat and destroying me is a way to prevent his story and all he has seen from being heard. But whatever the reason, it hurts more than I can adequately explain. I long and hope for the beauty He's revealing. It IS coming."

65

Glory

I saw the Lord, high and exalted, seated on a throne;
and the train of his robe filled the temple.
Above him were seraphim, each with six wings:
With two wings they covered their faces, with two they covered their feet,
and with two they were flying. And they were calling to one another:
"Holy, holy, holy is the Lord Almighty; the whole earth is full of his glory."
At the sound of their voices the doorposts and thresholds shook
and the temple was filled with smoke.
"Woe to me!" I cried. "I am ruined!
For I am a man of unclean lips, and I live among a people of unclean lips,
and my eyes have seen the King, the Lord Almighty."
Then one of the seraphim flew to me with a live coal in his hand,
which he had taken with tongs from the altar. With it he touched my mouth and said,
"See, this has touched your lips; your guilt is taken away and your sin atoned for."
Then I heard the voice of the Lord saying, "Whom shall I send? And who will go for us?"
And I said, "Here am I. Send me!"
— Isaiah 6:1-8

I had always noticed the strange reaction dogs had to Houston. I was no longer surprised by it. Once we went to a friend's house and her chocolate lab would not stop jumping on top of him and licking his face. The entire evening he would not leave Houston alone. Houston would smile and giggle at the attention. He spelled, "He knows I am someone close to God."

At the gym there was an assistant dog in training that would often be there when we would arrive. The dog would lay still while people would pet him, unphased by anything. But when I would walk in the gym with Houston the dog would immediately get to its feet and start wagging its tail. The dog would look at its trainer and edge as close as he could to Houston. I remembered the dogs that would come to the school when Houston was younger and how the teachers told me how incredible it was watching the dogs with Houston, as if there was something going on between them. As I watched the dog's obvious attraction to Houston, I recalled the dog that had practically jumped on top of Houston when he was little. The dog was so enormous, and Houston was so small I had been terrified. Now I began to wonder if something else was going on that I didn't see.

When COVID-19 began and the gym closed, Houston and I went to the park as often as we could. It was difficult without a routine, without much of anything that kept him focused and regulated. I told him his outbursts were putting us all on edge. Sarcastically he spelled out to me, "You're preaching to the choir." I laughed. No kidding. As we walked in the different parks around the area, the dogs we walked past would pull and lurch to get near him. Owners would pull back on their dogs and apologize. Over and over they would tell us that their dog doesn't act like this. In time I would just say, "It's ok. Dogs love him." Houston would always smile, knowingly.

One day we sat in the grass soaking up spring. A woman was throwing a ball with her dog. When the dog saw Houston, it ran over to him and barked nonstop. The owner apologized and picked up her dog walking further away. She tossed the ball. The dog ran, picked the ball up in his mouth, turned in the opposite direction and raced to Houston, giving the ball to him. She apologized and tried again. Repeatedly he ran to Houston, dropped the ball, and barked incessantly and earnestly. She poured water for him and he wouldn't drink it. All he wanted was Houston. Finally she picked him up to leave and he struggled to free himself, looking at Houston and continuing to bark. When they left, I asked, "Houston, *what* was that about?" He spelled, "He kept saying to me, 'I am not worthy. I am not worthy to see glory.'" I began to really wonder what on earth the dogs could see. What did Houston see? I asked another mom with a child similar to Houston if her daughter had ever said anything about dogs. She told me that dogs reacted strangely around her daughter and that her daughter said dogs are much smarter and aware than we realize.

On another walk we passed a small dog we had seen frequently that would always chase after us, while the owner would pull him back. This particular morning the owner stood by a tree talking on her phone. The dog took off after us. This time I stopped, turned around, and knelt down. Houston stopped behind me. The dog barked furiously and intermittently growled. The oddest part was his tail. It wagged like an independence day flag. The owner came up to us and asked, "Ok. What is going on? Why does my dog chase after you when he sees you? He does it every time. And now! Look! He's barking, growling, and wagging his tail wildly. Those things don't go together. What is it?" I looked at Houston and then at the tiny dog. Houston was perfectly still. I said, "I think your dog can see my son's angels." And that's how the conversation began. I told her our story. Her mouth fell open in astonishment. "This is a movie!" I shrugged my shoulders. Then she looked down and exclaimed, "Look!" I looked down and her dog was standing right in front of Houston but had tucked his tail between his legs and his head was bowed to the ground. Houston stood perfectly still. The dog was shaking uncontrollably. She picked him up, holding him in her arms, and he continued to shake. Houston gently pet him but he couldn't stop shaking and when he looked at Houston, he immediately buried his head back down. After saying goodbye we continued our walk. When I could I asked Houston to tell me what had just happened. He spelled, "It was my angels. They are ten feet tall. Their wings are enormous." When you're ten inches tall and covered with fur, ten feet covered with wings must be quite something. But it was more than that. I had witnessed someone seeing glory, someone who couldn't lie or exaggerate or dismiss or pretend he hadn't seen. Awe had overtaken him. There seemed to be two reactions, boundless love and joy... and fear and trembling.

> *Wherefore God also hath highly exalted him, and given him a name which is above every name: That at the name of Jesus every knee should bow, of things in heaven, and things in earth, and things under the earth; And that every tongue should confess that Jesus Christ is Lord, to the glory of God the Father.*[172]

> *For it is written, As I live, saith the Lord, every knee shall bow to me, and every tongue shall confess to God.*[173]

[172] Philippians 2:9-11
[173] Romans 14:11

I have sworn by myself, the word is gone out of my mouth in righteousness, and shall not return, That unto me every knee shall bow, every tongue shall swear.[174]

And I heard every creature in heaven and on earth and under the earth and in the sea, and all that is in them, saying, "To him who sits on the throne and to the Lamb be blessing and honor and glory and might forever and ever!"[175]

As I pondered over the wonder of it all I suddenly remembered S- from years ago as I waited outside the school to pick Houston up in my minivan. I remembered his pointing and reaching toward the top of my car as he wrestled and pulled away from the teachers. Excitedly, I asked Houston about it. Houston spelled, "S-'s title is a Reacher. What S- was doing that day was reaching out to God to pray to pour out the Spirit of God."

"What's a Reacher?" I asked.

"A good person who prays all the time."

"Why did he point toward me that day?"

"Your angels welled their wings to wave at him."

"So it was just because they welled up their wings?" I asked.

"Your angels are like wonderful triumphant angels. That is promised to those who pray all the time, who are pray martyrs, that they will see wings of glory to God. The love we prayed was for works of wonderful miracles."

I was embarrassed by my lack of understanding the majesty and glory of God. I thought about all the miracles I was witnessing and about behavior I had once thought didn't have an explanation. "Houston, what about that day S- broke into your IEP meeting? What did he say to you then?"

"He told me to pray for my angels to help and to pray for us to all have a voice. He told all of our friends to start praying."

"Did they?"

"We all prayed."

I was stunned. His friends had prayed for a miracle, for them to be given a voice while those with power and position fought to keep them silent. God had sided with them, with the weak, with the ones who trusted in Him. What fools we all were, blind fools. Those the world cast off were the ones Jesus had chosen. *A man once gave a great banquet and invited many. And at the time for the banquet he sent his servant to say to those who had been invited, 'Come, for everything is now ready.' But they all alike began to make excuses. The first said to him, 'I have bought a field, and I must go out and see it. Please have me excused.' And another said, 'I have bought five yoke of oxen, and I go to examine them. Please have me excused.' And another said, 'I have married a wife, and therefore I cannot come.' So the servant came and reported these things to his master. Then the master of the house became angry and said to his servant, 'Go out quickly to the streets and lanes of the city, and bring in the poor and crippled and blind and lame.'*[176]

There was an entire world, a feast of God's love, power and presence that surrounded us, that we were oblivious to, and those the world disregarded were the real heroes and power brokers of all that was unseen. They accepted His invitation to believe the impossible. By the way, you can too. The invitation is for everyone. I thought about it more and more, as if I was getting clues and piecing the miraculous truth together. From the words of J- to me, Houston now had a voice. From Houston's voice I knew at least twelve other young people who were non-speaking or unreliably speaking were beginning to break the chains of silence. They had seen. They had prayed. They had believed God was good and would answer their prayers. I wept. My God was good. He had heard our cries. This was just the beginning. And that's when it hit me. We had been taught to

---

[174] Isaiah 45:23

[175] Revelation 5:13

[176] Luke 14:16-21

only hope in a measure equivalent to what was probable. It made me truly feel the depth of logic and statistics and its effects on us. It was one of Satan's most effective tools to limit, disempower, demoralize, constrain, and effectively remove our confidence in the promises of God. We actually only allowed ourselves to believe in direct proportion to what the statisticians said was possible. With our love for control and predictability, we had made the past the limits of our future. We had allowed statisticians to become the predictors of our future and turn our eyes from the promises of our omnipotent Creator and Savior. But God never taught probabilities, only possibilities. He proved impossible over and over again with His actions when He walked among us. He was never limited by the past – past numbers, past infirmities, or past events. And with Him ALL things were possible. But how? How do we attain tically impossible, the unattainable? His word was clear. Through believing the unbelievable.

As I poured over and pondered all these miracles of the unseen, I remembered Houston's teacher texting me and asking about Stone Mountain and Houston's insistence. I had forgotten to ask him. So I did. He spelled, "We are asked to pray on a mountain. Stone Mountain has more energy than you can hope for. The force was incredible on Stone Mountain. It holds the prayers that are prayed there. I prayed to pour the Spirit of God on me." And God did. We decided to return to Stone Mountain and brought some friends. I put my hands on both young men and prayed. I called out to heaven for their healing. Houston jumped up and tried to run off the front of the mountain. I ran to chase him to keep him from falling off the edge and had to pull him back. His friend lay prostrate on the mountain top and wept. It felt as if I was watching something surreal take place right in front of my eyes. Urgently, I asked Houston what was going on and he told me, "Our prayers took flight. The mountain took our prayers and told God our prayers moved it." To His name be glory.

Have I come too casually?
Because it seems to me there's something I've neglected
How does one approach a deity with informality and still protect the sacred?
Cause you came and chose to wear the skin of all of us
And it's easy to forget you left a throne
And the line gets blurry all the time between daily and divine
And it's hard to know the difference

Oh let me not forget to tremble
Oh let me not forget to tremble face down on the ground

Do I dare to take the liberty to stare at you?
Oh let me not forget to tremble
What a shame to think that I'd appear even slightly cavalier in the matter of salvation
Do I claim this gift you freely gave as if it were mine to take with such little hesitation?
Cause you came and stood among the very least of us
And it's easy to forget you left a throne.

Oh let me not forget to tremble
Oh let me not forget to tremble face down on the ground
Do I dare to take the liberty to stare at you?
Oh let me not forget to tremble
The cradle and the grave could not contain your divinity
Neither can I oversimplify this love[177]

66

Washed in the Water

Now why do you delay? Get up and be baptized,
and wash away your sins, calling on His name.
— Acts 22:16

Sarah wanted some of her friends to meet Houston. One was and is grieving deeply over the sudden loss of her husband. The other I had met years ago. She is a skeptic. She is one of God's chosen, a child of Abraham who sat on the fence when it came to Christ. I began sharing how Houston said that our actions stay on us energetically. I added, "No wonder it takes the blood of Jesus, the Christ, to cleanse us from our sins." I held up the board for Houston to participate in the conversation and he spelled, "They stay on us until we are baptized. The baptism washes us clean." Sarah and her friend made sounds of shock. My jaw dropped. Oh my word. For baptism was the act of obedience and faith that kept Sarah's friend on the fence. But I was in shock as well. I remembered how Houston had stared with intensity at the baptismal waters and told me about the wonderful energy coming off the waters that he couldn't take his eyes off of. I remembered the flood of power that had washed over me at Houston's baptism.

Suddenly even the sacraments made sense. These were not just symbolic gestures or rituals of a religion. They were acts of obedience that were an actual transfer of the love, holiness, and grace of God. Love, despite being unseen, is a real thing, an energy like thought that moves without the limitations of time, space, and matter. No wonder Jesus said, *"Very truly I tell you, no one can enter the kingdom of God unless they are born of water and the Spirit. Flesh gives birth to flesh, but the Spirit gives birth to spirit."*[178] How powerful the spirit, the cleansing, and the grace must be when the spiritual transfers through the physical, when the love given to us is from LOVE Himself. And the Eucharist... the incarnation of LOVE being offered to us and for us, to be in us... do we even grasp the presence of God in this exquisite offering of His love? I remembered how I had many times not wanted to take the Lord's Supper because of the pain in my heart and the abandonment I felt from God. Each time I did, my eyes would become a water faucet and my heart would rear its raw wound. Something truly incredible, celestial, majestic happened, something exalted that wasn't of me at all. The vulnerability of having to trust God and receive His power and love in spite of the pain, that was much of my resistance.

I realized how stupid I had been, how I had kept myself from the hope God was trying to pour into me, how I kept myself from His healing love. And yet God had kept being good, kept healing, kept offering Himself.

Then God began to pour His wonder on our small Mexican alfresco dinner through his servant, Houston. To the new widow who was grieving Houston offered comfort that the prayers she couldn't even utter were still heard and answered. She knew what he meant. The pain was so great she hadn't been able to pray, just scream, and weep. Houston's angels had told him. Her tears came with gasps for air. At one point Sarah's other friend tried to test Houston's abilities by trying to trick him, but he shot back the truth so fast it astounded us all. That night he

[178] John 3:5

told me, "That was all for her." Later he told me to pray for her. "Jesus gave me a list of Jewsish people to bring His love to. She's the first... All God's chosen people, the Jewish, have a cloud of angels with them."

As I reflected on it all, I thought about the last meeting we had with Bill. He was diligent about checking on us and praying for us. Before the last meeting I had asked Houston if he was going to show him his abilities. Certainly then he wouldn't doubt Houston's messages were from God. Houston was stoic. "We'll see," he spelled. This time we sat at the same conference table and Bill asked how things were going. I told him all the struggles and adversity I was facing with my job, my son, and my ex. Bill then read a passage out of Hebrews. The whole time Houston had been remarkably quiet and still. When Bill finished reading Houston spelled, "Is that Hebrews 11:3?" Bill said it wasn't and then read Hebrews 11:3. *By faith we understand that the universe was created by the word of God, so that what is seen was not made out of things that are visible.*

In shock I realized what God, with Houston's obedience, had just orchestrated to prove. The unseen.... The seen is made from that which is unseen. I jerked my head back at Houston and asked excitedly, "Can we show him now?" Houston spelled, "YES." So we did. As Houston spelled Bill's words written down secretly, Bill's jaw dropped. "How?" he asked. I looked at him and smiled. "Thought is a thing. It's a form of energy. It's unseen but it's still energy. This is why there is power in prayer, why prayer works." He had to sit he was so stunned. "Can I tell people?" he asked. "Not unless there is a real reason," I answered. Later Houston told me, "The angels told me you did wonderful." "Houston, God and His angels need to protect us. People are going to attack us." He just looked at me and smiled his sweet smile. Peace, he had the peace that surpasses understanding. But he had seen. It made all the difference.

67

Receiving

I'm standing at your door - My heart is calling yours
Come fall into my arms
You're weary from it all - Been running for too long
I'm here to bring you home
I'm reaching out I'll chase you down
I dare you to believe how much I love you now
Don't be afraid - I am your strength
We'll be walking on the water dancing on the waves
Look up and lift your eyes - The future's open wide
I have great plans for you, oh, yes, I do
Your past is dead and gone
Your healing has begun - I'm making all things new [179]

April 3, 2020

As the shut-in continued, I consumed myself with writing this book. There were more tears than you can imagine as I relived it all. But I was praying and trusting and walking in faith like I hadn't in a long, long time. I had begun to feel His presence and His love ever so slightly, like a seed taking root. Slowly, softly my heart began to feel lighter. I remember being utterly shocked one day when I sang a song of praise. 'Where did that come from? What was happening to me?' I wondered. On a beautiful April afternoon as we were walking in the park, Houston kept trying to turn around and stand in front of me, bending over to look at my heart. I would pull him back beside me, but he kept doing it insistently, almost urgently. Finally I was annoyed and self-conscious. I stopped on the trail and demanded, "What? What is it? What are you doing Houston?" He didn't hesitate to tell me, almost as if he had been begging me to ask him. "There is something like a seedling growing out of your heart." "What?? A seedling?" I chuckled and kept walking - but slowly, thoughtfully, wondering what Houston was seeing and what on earth was God doing to my heart. Later Houston spelled to me, "The power has turned." "What do you mean?" I asked. "The words you started praying to believe. Walls that pushed our prayers' power have fallen down. Prayers to God without love really are wasted. Love is what powers the prayers. Teaching to pray with love is working to actively put faith in God. Do pray with faith in using that to turn your prayer to love." Love… My prayers for most of my life had been born from fear. But then God's love and peace had overtaken my fear and replaced it with faith. *There is no fear in love, but perfect love casts out fear. For fear has to do with punishment, and whoever fears has not been perfected in love.* [180]

---

[179] *Dancing on the Waves*; By Scott Cash, Frances Cash, Kyle Briskin, and Andrew Bergthold. Copyright Angie Feel Good Songs, Capitol Cmg Genesis, and Bay 19.
[180] 1 John 4:18

A month later I asked Houston if I still had a seedling growing out of my heart. He spelled, "No. It's a whole tree now." I gasped excitedly. "What is it?" "The tree is continuing to grow where your belief is." Belief... All I could think was, "Wow... Faith... like a mustard seed." So I kept on believing. Doubt was no longer welcome. The old stories of radical, powerful faith in the Bible became alive again in my heart. David only needed God and a stone to slay a giant. Elijah could call on God to defy the laws of physics. Men could walk with angels in a fire and not be consumed. The mouths of lions could be shut. A jar of oil would not run dry. Ravens would feed a prophet. A virgin would give birth to a Messiah. One boy's lunch could feed thousands. Jesus could pay a temple tax from the mouth a fish, quiet storms with His word, make blind people see, lame people walk, cleanse lepers, give the mute a voice, and make the dead live again. He could and would forgive all our sins if we believed in Him. And Peter... Peter could walk on water if he believed and kept his eyes on Jesus instead of the waves. Which meant I could too. *I could dance on the waves...* The wonder and power of all that was possible made my heart leap. That's when I realized all the half-truths, self-reliance, limits, laws, and logic of the world that I had trusted in had been discarded. My faith had been reborn. I had become a child again who trusted her father. I was His. He was mine. He had borne everything, my sin, my sickness, my wounds, my separation, and my son's. And as the very best of fathers, He delighted in giving us the very best, rejoicing over us, and showering us with His lovingkindness. By His wounds and His blood we were free. By accepting His resurrection and love, He freely gave us all that was His, which is everything. He was all I would ever need. Not because I lived a life where I accepted depravation, not because there were no battles to fight or struggles to face, but because through faith in His goodness and faithfulness every longing and need was fulfilled. The simplicity of trusting in the only one who is everything filled my heart. With Him anything was possible.[181] I had... no... I was Zoë.

May 18, 2020

The phone rang and I saw Paul's name on the caller ID. The previous attempts to connect with him had ended horribly. Horrifically is the better word. There had been almost nine months of him completely ignoring all of us. None of his siblings wanted to speak to him or allow him back home. Because of the pandemic I knew he had nowhere to go, but the truth was he scared me. He was volatile, unpredictable, and dangerous. When Houston and I had visited him at school, hoping for the best, hoping for love, his demeanor was frighteningly familiar to the Big Jock's.

When we had tried to reconnect with him earlier in the year, he had shown us his dorm room and I gasped when I saw the quilt I had made twenty-four years earlier on his bed. Even though I had made the quilt with love, my stomach turned at the sight of it. I was physically repulsed. Instantly I thought about my bed that Houston said was sick and realized Paul was wrapping himself in the same sickening energy that surrounded his father, without a relationship with God to protect him. Needless to say, during that visit he had lashed out with the same hateful language and posturing that had made the Big Jock so intimidating. The evidence of drugs and alcohol that gripped my son and strangled him were everywhere.

---

[181] To those who struggle with belief in the miraculous power of God to heal and to answer our prayers, I strongly urge you to read Christ the Healer by F.F. Bosworth. Although I came to my faith in God's power to do the miraculous in an unorthodox and defiant manner, the theology of God's willingness and ability to heal is rooted in the Atonement of Christ and character of God. This classic should be read and practiced by every believer. It is my prayer that both the spiritual and physical power of the Atonement would be experienced by every believer.

As the nighttime bleeds into the day
Tomorrow spills across the sky
And the sun's a harsh reminder why
We are feeling barely human...
We got drunk on this unholy wine
To deliver us from our old minds
The promise of a better time
'Til we're feeling barely human
We don't know what's good for us
'Cause if we did, we might not do it
Who knows where our limits lie?
We won't discover 'til we push it
'Cause the devil's got my arms
And it pulls me back into the night
Well, I should just walk away, away
Oh, it grips me [182]

When we returned home, I asked Houston about the quilt and if it had the energy of his dad on it. Houston spelled, "Now I understand more of how evil infects. It makes you get used to how that energy feels so you don't realize the difference and you forget what love feels like. He's been sleeping and wrapping himself in darkness." Despite his continued wild, cruel, and erratic behavior, I ordered him new bedding and told him to throw everything else in the trash. Then I prayed and prayed.

When the phone call came two months later, he begged for the chance to be part of our family again and to come home. At first pride had been his method of self-preservation. He refused to think about or acknowledge the destruction he had caused. But now shame had taken over and he couldn't face the ruins of his wrecking ball in our lives. I knew both of these were the enemy trying to keep him from being forgiven and loved. My other kids told me not to listen and not to let him come back, all except for Houston. We made the long drive across the state and loaded up the car. Paul was nervous but there was a softness and humility that had been absent for two years. There was still so much to unravel, but my prayer was being answered. I was very quiet, prayerful, watchful. As I turned onto the highway I was met again with God's faithfulness and presence, for there before us was a rainbow that stretched across the entire Georgia skyline and followed us for miles and miles until the past really seemed to be past us. There was no doubt, that rainbow was for me. And very slowly, very timidly my son came home. The unraveling of manipulation and the darkness that had choked him would take time to heal, but my son who was lost had been found.

And the son said to him, 'Father, I have sinned against heaven and before you. I am no longer worthy to be called your son.' But the father said to his servants, 'Bring quickly the best robe, and put it on him, and put a ring on his hand, and shoes on his feet. And bring the fattened calf and kill it, and let us eat and celebrate. For this my son was dead, and is alive again; he was lost, and is found.' [183]

***

---

[183] Luke 15:21-24

The effects of all the years of trauma, attacks, loss, and struggle to survive had left me shattered in more ways than I can explain. I was working so hard to heal. I had so many regrets and guilt for the person I thought I should have been, for the things I should have done with my life. I still felt like a failure. I had accepted God's forgiveness but had never been able to really forgive myself for not living up perfectly to the ideals I believed in. Many of my generation were raised with perfection, not as an ideal, but as a requirement. The taunts of the enemy were ever present. They had been the soundtrack of my life while I had tried to sing a song of praise to my Savior. It was exhausting repenting for sins I had already repented for, battling with a torrent of lies, while trying to remind myself of God's love and forgiveness. Without ever experiencing and receiving love in the natural, I was left trying to make all the pieces fit by sheer faith with a chorus of taunting reminders playing in the background. Trembling before the holiness of God doesn't produce feelings of worthiness, it produces repentance and worship. And God deserved both - my pure worship, my whole heart, my whole life. But I still longed for the tender, gentleness of God, the comfort and acceptance of a child before their father.

One day Houston told me, "Jesus told me that you --- because --- did that to you." It was a secret I had shoved deep. It was true. Houston continued. "Jesus knows how hard you tried to obey Him. He knows what they did to you. He loves you. Everything is forgiven from the cradle to the grave." This message of love from my Savior that understood all that had happened, that had seen the hidden things, that did not condemn me, that loved me in my weakness even though my name had been destroyed, it made me weep. Shortly after that I came across a quote that spoke to my heart. "Forgive yourself for not knowing better at the time. Forgive yourself for giving away your power. Forgive yourself for past behaviors. Forgive yourself for the survival patterns and traits you picked up while enduring trauma. Forgive yourself for being who you needed to be."[184] I asked my Jesus for permission to forgive myself and did just that. I let it go. The strangest thing happened. Within an hour a certain prayer that I had struggled to truly believe as I prayed came out of my heart with conviction and certainty. I stunned myself. 'Wait a minute,' I thought… 'I really believe that. I know that is a certainty, not just a hope.' When did that shift happen? Tears filled my eyes as I realized I had stumbled upon a mystery, that somehow God's love, His forgiveness that explodes in every direction when we forgive in return, and the power to actually believe without doubt were intertwined in some kind of powerful way that I would not have been able to recognize if I had not experienced the fundamental shift. *Then Jesus said to the disciples, "Have faith in God. I tell you the truth, you can say to this mountain, 'May you be lifted up and thrown into the sea,' and it will happen. But you must really believe it will happen and have no doubt in your heart. I tell you, you can pray for anything, and if you believe that you've received it, it will be yours. But when you are praying, first forgive anyone you are holding a grudge against, so that your Father in heaven will forgive your sins, too."* [185]

Love, faith, hope, truth, forgiveness, these were not just Biblical doctrines. They were actually a powerful exchange of God's power and energy in us, for us, through us. I was no longer allowed to be a slave to fear or hurt or shame. I was astonished. What invisible, imperishable powers were in these incredible forces that were tossed around like halfhearted slogans in a world where wolves roamed wild, devouring the children of God with lies, fear, hate, envy, guilt, pride, and doubt? All these theological concepts were actually the mysterious unseen forces of the universe. I went to Houston's room to help him get ready in a state of wonder. He spelled, "Satan has been making you hate yourself a long time so you wouldn't receive God's love. Each thing told you, you can't be loved. It is how hate works. Jesus said it is what has been keeping all of your prayers held up. They need the heart to be open to His love." The gravity of his words weighted deeply, like an anchor in my heart. My good God. *For the mountains may depart and the hills be removed, but my steadfast love shall not depart from you, and my covenant of peace shall not be removed," says the Lord, who has compassion on you.* [186] - So friend… forgive… forgive others, forgive yourself, open yourself up to receive His abundant, infinite love.

[184] Audrey Kitching
[185] Mark 11:22-25 (NLT)
[186] Isaiah 54:10

Joyful joyful, We adore thee
God of glory, Lord of Love
Hearts unfold like flowers before thee
Opening to the sun above
Melt the clouds of sin and sadness
Drive the dark of doubt away
Fill us with the light of day...[187]

Joy had come. That is exactly what my Lord and Savior had done, melted the clouds of sadness and driven the dark of doubt away. And I found that it was true. *Do not grieve, for the joy of the Lord is your strength.*[188] It most certainly was.

May 21, 2020

It had been two years since Houston's first letter board lesson. Within a few weeks of that first lesson he began to communicate a lifetime, over two decades, of pent-up thoughts and feelings and reveal the mysteries of the heavenly realm. It was the miracle I had prayed for longer and harder than anyone can ever know. I asked his coach at the center to have him write his thoughts about his two years of having a voice. He independently typed the following with his coach holding the wireless keyboard over two sessions.

05.21.20 – Houston (Keyboarding)

=====

Anniversary thoughts.

WONDER AND GRACE. THESE ARE JUST TWO WORDS TO DESCRIBE MY JOURNEY OVER THE PAST TWO YEARS/TWENTY FOUR MONTHS/734 DAYS. LIVING IN WITH AUTISM IS ACTUALLY A BLESSING IF YOU HAVE THE RIGHT PERSPECTIVE. I SEE THE WORLD DIFFERENTLY THAN MY NEUROTYPICAL PEERS WHICH HAS OPENED MY EYES AND MIND TO THINGS AROUND ME ALBEIT TO THE ONE MILLIONTH DEGREE WHEN MY BODY IS IN OVERDRIVE. LIKE MANY OF MY NON-SPEAKING OR LIKE ME NON-RELIABLY SPEAKING AUTISTICS I FELT LIKE I WAS TRAPPED IN A LOCKED CAR OF A BODY WITH NO STEERING WHEEL OR GPS TO GUIDE ME. THE WORDS I WANTED TO SAY WHEN I WAS HAPPY, SAD, ANXIOUS, FRUSTRATED OR FILL IN THE BLANK WITH ANY EMOTION CAME OUT AS A SCRIPTED AND JUMBLED MESS, LIKE SOMEONE PRESSED PLAY ON THE WORST MOVIE, PUT IT ON REPEAT AND BROKE THE REMOTE CONTROL. IT CAN BE A NIGHTMARE SOMETIMES. BUT EVERY NOW AND THEN GOD'S RAYS OF GLORY SHINE DOWN ON YOU AND YOU TAKE THOSE SIGNS FROM HIM AND YOUR LIFE CAN CHANGE FOREVER. THAT'S WHAT HAPPENED ON MAY 21, 2018 WHEN I HAD MY FIRST LETTERBOARD SESSION EXPOSING ME TO A TOOL TO PURPOSEFULLY COMMUNICATE MY TRUE THOUGHTS AND EMOTIONS. LIKE EVERY OTHER THERAPY I'VE TRIED, I WAS SKEPTICAL. THE BIGGEST ADDED VALUE TO THIS METHOD THAT PERKED MY INTEREST...PRESUMING COMPETENCE.

(End 5/21)

---

[187] *Joyful, Joyful, We adore Thee;* Henry Van Dyke

(Start 5/22)

IF YOU CHANGE YOUR MINDSET AND PRESUME I AM LISTENING AND UNDERSTANDING WHAT IS GOING ON AROUND ME OR BEING SAID TO ME THEN IT GOES A LONG WAY AS A SIGN OF RESPECT. EVERYONE HAS THEIR OWN JOURNEY ON THE PATH TO PRESUMING COMPETENCE WHEN INTERACTING WITH AUTISTICS. I SAY WHY NOT TREAT EVERYONE THE SAME NO MATTER WHAT THEIR PHYSICAL APPEARANCE SHOWS. WHEN SOMEONE SEES THAT I AM CAPABLE OF COMMUNICATING I HOPE IT ENCOURAGES THEM TO KNOW IM HERE AND READY TO BE PART OF SOCIETY. SINCE MY FAMILY AND COACHES WITNESSED MY SPELLING SKILLS I HAVE BEEN A SPONGE OF KNOWLEDGE TRYING TO CATCH UP EDUCATIONALLY. PRESUMING COMPETENCE MEANS TEACHING OR READING AT AN ADULT LEVEL... THIS IS SO REFRESHING. I'M NO ROCKET SCIENTIST BUT I DO LOVE THE CHALLENGE OF HIGHER EDUCATION. IN CLOSING, THANK YOU TO ALL WHO HAVE HELPED ME GET TO WHERE I AM TODAY AND THE WORDS OF ENCOURAGEMENT. LOVE ONE ANOTHER AND HERE'S TO TWO MORE YEARS OF PURPOSEFUL COMMUNICATION.
YOURS TRULY,
HOUSTON

Now to Him who is able to do immeasurably more than all we ask or imagine,
according to His power that is at work within us,
to Him be glory in the church and in Christ Jesus throughout all generations,
for ever and ever! Amen.[189]

[188] Nehemiah 8:10b

PART TWO

All the toil, All in vain
Every image of ourselves that we create
Every dream built on sand
Every castle slips away when tides come in
Let us not imagine
That we might have a hand in where the wind blows
Where grace goes
Let not any passion be for kingdoms we have fashioned in our own name
For our own fame
Not to us, Not to us, But to Your name be glory
To Your name be glory
Every beat Every breath
Every broken road and every ordered step
Every loss Every gain
Every spotlight Every shadow
Yours the same
So let us not be fooled And let us not be disillusioned
Let our eyes see You clearly
Not to us Not to us But to Your name be glory
Anything that's good Anything that's true
Let it point to You, Let it point to You
Not to us, Not to us But to
Your name be glory
No walls, No greed, No color, No creed, No right, No left
All You No less[190]

[190] *Not to Us;* By Nichole Nordeman, Chris Stevens .and Matt ronleewe. Copyright Capitol Cmg Genesis o/b/o Birdwing Music, Capitol Cmg Paragon o/b/o Meaux Mercy, Capitol Cmg Genesis o/b/o Birdboy Songs, and Capitol Cmg Paragon o/b/o Moody Producer Music

68

My Story, My Life

Houston's Testimony

Chances, dear friends, really define us. Details aren't only important, they become backbones of our story. Time always has a gift to give. Hearing can have an impact. In God's fortune I am now His herald. My God befriended me and all I have to give is from Him.[191]

To tell you every weakness of autism I would be telling too long. Much of the characteristics of autism can fall into drug-like battles. Yes. It is like addiction because I don't have control, except my roaming mind moves. But because I can't control my body, I am also jailed. My body is open to the physical and the spiritual world. All the attacks on my body weaken me, forcing more stims. Autistics don't have all the boundaries others have to protect themselves.

Now my first memory of attempting to communicate was for food. I remember I had heard my mom cooking and asked her for an apple but nothing came out of my mouth. I made all these efforts at speaking but nothing came out. It had to be when I was almost two since my sister Reagan was a baby and Morgan and I shared the bedroom. My anger and my fear grew as I kept trying to speak. I am not sure all that I did but my mom couldn't understand my efforts. That was awful for me but it all but disappears when it's compared to all I went through for the next two decades. Going back to this is my way of being a hero to a little version of me. Mostly I promised myself I would always be a friend to others like me.

My first memory of stimming makes me happy. This is my favorite childhood memory. Yes. It's still my favorite. Yes. It still makes me happy. So my mom got me Flubber and I would fast forward and rewind to watch one scene again and again. Then my stomach would shake with the heartiest laugh you've ever heard. You see this was my only outlet for God's curse on me. To others I was out of control, but to me I was making myself happy the only way I could.

My mom was so proud of my laugh. She would try to read to me to make me laugh more. She thought reading would reach me. But I wouldn't let her touch me or hold me at all. Yes, my behavior did not help at all and my mom's heart broke a real heartbreak you can't know. Her anguish was god awful. She couldn't stop making me hear the noises that bombed my mind. She let my awful senses overwhelm me. Her worst mistake was to let me stim. Now I love her, so terrible mistakes can be forgiven. Dialing back time isn't possible. But others can learn from her mistakes.

---

[191] The friendship of the Lord is for those who fear him, and he makes known to them his covenant. — Psalm 25:14

The one who has the bride is the bridegroom. The friend of the bridegroom, who stands and hears him, rejoices greatly at the bridegroom's voice. Therefore this joy of mine is now complete. — John 3:29

Greater love has no one than this, that someone lay down his life for his friends. You are my friends if you do what I command you. No longer do I call you servants, for the servant does not know what his master is doing; but I have called you friends, for all that I have heard from my Father I have made known to you. — John 15:13-15

And the Scripture was fulfilled that says, "Abraham believed God, and it was counted to him as righteousness"—and he was called a friend of God. — James 2:23

Everything we have has come from you, and we give you only what you first gave us.— 1 Chronicles 29:14

How my mom tried to help me was therapies and diet and medicine and doctors. You can't even imagine what all she tried. She learned so much but nothing helped me. I was locked in the prison of my mind and there was no key.

That portion of my life is difficult to share. The worst piece of my story is going to make some people grossed out. However it is critical to understand how severe my autism is. I'm embarrassed to share this but it's important. Being autistic does strange things to your senses. In my body I couldn't stop myself from feeling and smelling my feces. Behavior like this destroys lives. Bearing this burden made me hate myself. No amount of effort could stop me. Being something that disgust revolved around is like having an enemy combatant live inside you. Each time it went to all my worst thoughts of being worthless. I went through so much. Hellish existence, and God was nowhere to be found.

Now this monster kept me captive in my prison. That is only one part of it. My body and my mind hated each other. How my mom survived I don't know. She believed in God and how God could bring good out of anything. But having to clean up my feces that I smeared on everything made my mom begin to doubt God and wonder if He was really there. How anyone can believe God is good when they carry so much is totally understandable. She lost God in those sad years. Coping with me took more than any human should bear. Most of my life I've dealt with this shame. The only good is that she never stopped loving me.

I prayed to be loved all the time. Good that my mom did to work with me was to teach me the alphabet. That one thing was knowledge that saved me. It provided a way for me to learn to read. Most knowledge I taught myself. Nothing really was provided to acquire the knowledge everyone in the world had. That was the worst. Hearing all the things the other kids got to learn forced me to listen and learn on my own. I was glad my sister read so much. Each book lived in her mind. That's what I used to teach myself many things. As she gave her all to learning I learned with her. It was her love of learning all she could that saved me from boredom. See, learning is what keeps our minds focused.

Some teachers wouldn't teach me at all. They would make me waste my life doing forced labor. My favorite teachers wanted me practicing the knowledge they taught me. That was love. So much repetition though. It was things I already knew. That led to me praying, 'Please let them see that I am smart and what all I am learning.' That prayer paved the way for leaps in all God made my mind capable of. Storing information is all my brain does. The information was talking in my mind, getting properly deciphered. Now I love deciphering. Sweet Gum (his teachers from elementary school) swears they knew I was smart. Each one of those teachers gave me wonderful attention and love. A.B.A was forced on them too. They would think privately, 'I'm sorry to do this. I hate it too.' Other kids were forced to read to me A Mouse in the House. That was humiliating and made me pray so much to be given a voice. The kids were my friends and would say, "Great talking to you. See you soon." That broke my heart that. I was not able to communicate to them. My high school worked hard to teach students to be our good friends.

Each wall made me something I hated. And as I listened to what others said about me I realized they thought, 'He doesn't perceive what we are saying.' Always being treated like I was retarded made me want to learn even more. That word was used by kids and adults about my friends and me. They made fun of us and we thought, 'You're the retard. You can't even see love and it's all around you.' That's part of what's wrong with schools. They work to make intelligence more important than love. Hating that word retard still stirs all the anger I still have for people who place more worth on people who are knowledgeable, fortunate, pretty, athletic, or rich. Seeping in money those people think they are worth more than those who are powerless. Separately each person that God made has more value than all the riches in the world.

Making different classes of people puts those with disabilities with no power and stuck with no way to defend themselves. Status has become what worth is. That lie states - You are what you have or you are what you can do. Pride hopes in other's opinions. And also pride wants to be loved instead of love. That works to put those who can't provide for themselves as useless, given nothing. Life presses the powerless to work awful droning jobs, nothing with our minds - jobs the voiceless are forced to do or be pushed into homes. From then on the powerless are forgotten.

That's proud talk that looks at what some are not able to do and then places a lesser value on them. Who said you are qualified to determine another person's value? Do you think what we are able to speak is proof of our thoughts? Tape your mouth shut so I can give you an idea of what it's like. One thing you are not allowed is to move your body in any way that communicates. That is what it is like to have no ability to speak or make your thoughts known. Put yourself in our shoes. Much of our anxiety comes from not being understood and treated like we are really stupid. Most people would talk to me with loud, slow, basic words so I would understand. That would make me so mad. Why don't they see I understand? I just can't work my body. Time walled inside my body left me thinking of what I would say back to them.

— Want to talk to kids? Go get a job in a preschool.
— Thank you for telling me what I already know.
— Not loud enough. I can't hear you.
— Try talking slower. Maybe then my body will listen.

"Good job, buddy." That's all they would say to me. And "Make your body move, Houston." That's what I was trying to do. 'Step into my shoes,' I would think. What I wanted to do was prove to them all that I was pouring my energy, more work than anyone could have done, praying and striving to get my motor to move. It would piss me off when they would tell me I was lazy or hold up a card to tell me to stop. These cards were tools used to demean us all day long. Each one made me feel more like an animal than a person. That was god awful especially since I can't see like other people do. It meant old and young talked to us like we were idiots.

I parted ways and forgave what was a horrible part of my life. That love of good friends in my life each day is all I am missing. Trade places with us. What would you ask to learn? Worksheets with a line of addition? Prove you're smart without moving your body. Not asking any questions, teach yourself what you're not allowed to learn. Question why all the math is first grade and doesn't change. Wait! You can't speak or write. Each time I thought to myself, 'Only books could save me.' Applied Mathematics caught my eye. But they took all the smart, interesting books away. 'Wake up!' I told them in my mind. 'Are you really good with playing Kindergarten?' Our schools pretend that those who can't tell what they know, really know nothing. Give us a voice, then watch in awe.

69

Cacophony

All this pain,
I wonder if I'll ever find my way
I wonder if my life could really change, at all
All this earth,
Could all that is lost ever be found?
Could a garden come out from this ground, at all?
You make beautiful things
You make beautiful things out of the dust
You make beautiful things
You make beautiful things out of us
All around,
Hope is springing up from this old ground
Out of chaos life is being found, in you[192]

L et me explain what living in a body you can't control is like. Get into the front seat of a rollercoaster with rolling hills, smooth twisting turns and a few thrilling loops and corkscrews ahead of you. Sounds pretty exhilarating right? Well, I want to use this imagery to compare and contrast what you, as a neurotypical might experience on this ride and what I might experience on a given day. The cart and track represent the wiring and anatomy of our brain and body functioning together for us to go through our daily routine and carpe diem! As your ride begins, you remain snug and secure slowly approaching the first incline as you wake up, shower and eat breakfast. As the click-click-click starts up your morning ascent you might mentally walk through your day and talk to your companion about future plans etc. While there might be a mixture of excitement, adrenaline or the unknown of what awaits you over the hill, the cart/track network is running smooth and calm. When you get pushed and pulled around the loops and turns of your day an expected path with your final destination awaits you. Sure, that sudden corkscrew that turns your stomach - a flat tire on the highway - or that thrilling change of direction - getting an unexpected promotion at work - presents itself on the ride but your neural network stays somewhat intact for the duration of your journey-day. Yay!

Now let's jump into my cart and ride my roller coaster. As I wake, my cart looks standard. In this scenario my physical body appears to be that of a neurotypical young adult male like the cart. But I immediately find a default as I have a rusty spring in my seat so my comfort level is off. This represents my tactile sensory. T-shirt material or the carpet texture might be the culprit that day for no reason. I need to get moving right? Well guess what, the operator of my ride — let's call him Ray — is nowhere to be found and he shut off his cell phone. Ray is my lack and struggle of initiation. I completely understand the necessity of getting ready for the day and starting

---

[192] *Beautiful Things;* By Lisa Gungor and Michael Gungor. Copyright Worshiptogether.com Songs.

my 'ride' but my body has other ideas. My family is Ray's boss, constantly prompting me to get to work and to keep working. Here's the problem, Ray is irresponsible, annoying, loves attention and is bipolar.

Sitting and waiting in any novel setting with no defined time limit — like the DMV — makes me feel confined and exponentially jittery. Comparable to Ray restraining my arms and legs to my coaster cart, pouring fire ants down in my shoes and continuously forcing liquids on me so all I can think about is the sanctuary of a bathroom — all while racing through the first few twists and turns of the rollercoaster path. A corkscrew jumps my bones — an argument breaks out at one of the DMV kiosks — while this could be entertainment for some, the person's voice shrills sending me into attack mode. I viciously bite the top of my left hand and flap my right. This is Ray blaring an air horn for no reason as I approach that change of direction that could be pleasant. We get through the DMV to the sanctuary of the family car as we head to the body shop for a tire rotation. I know the sound of air compressors and tools in the pit will be more of the same on my auditory, but I forgot about the unbearable barrage of smells from a body shop that will wreak havoc on my olfactory nerve. Yes, Ray has decided to hide his week old egg salad sandwich mixed with sardines under my seat for this rollercoaster journey. The combination of this sensory overload makes my body do the stim medley.

The smells and sounds of the shop perfectly blend my sensory cornucopia that stirs my synesthesia. The color black and the feeling of grey clouds shroud all around me when the hammer of the air compressed wrench fires up. The smell of oil and coolant radiates a pattern of dark green ovals scrolling from my top left diagonally to my bottom right. Almost like Ray slipped me some bad acid right before he started my roller coaster of a day. At this point the outward body presents itself with jumping up and down nonstop as high as I can, hand in my mouth biting, right arm flapping and my thunderous roars echo throughout the tight quarters of the body shop waiting room. I am now trying to escape Ray's ride with all my willpower.

As we finally head to the grocery store it almost feels like Ray has come to his senses and my coaster emerges from a dark, damp and musky tunnel. I see large hues of yellow and embers of orange. With smooth easy hills up ahead on my rollercoaster ride, the fresh smells of the produce and bakery hit my sensitive nose. While these aromas are pleasant, they do trigger a strange tingle in the lower back of my head which almost feels like someone stroking my neck with a fine brush. This makes me antsy and anxious because I know the temptations of all the food and brand name labels on chips, cookies, and carb filled devil's food as I call it — test my body's impulse control to the max. While Ray's physical torture has stopped he now decides to engage in nonstop conversations with my mom that go nowhere. Mostly, "chips, yes" or "(enter food here), yes" over and over again until my mom's verbal response ceases as she knows not to talk to Ray in this state. The tingle is on. My neck continues throughout the store as a part of the store peels off and oozes up and down the aisles. The evenly spaced and organized shelves are a colorful pallet that pleases my eyes. My visual sensory now cascades my auditory to Disney's Fantasia and the accompanying orchestra. I well up thinking of all the Disney scenes from Fantasia. Junk food delivers tastes to my mouth when I see the packaging, forcing me to grab and rip open packages. What little control I have is used to stop me from hurting myself. Helping me is my mom with lots of "Good job. Almost done. Hang in there." I'm wondering if this ride will ever end.

As we check out, the aisles are crowded to the max. My sensory system is in overload, thank you body shop. My senses are tested to the max with ten different conversations going on at the same time and I'm catching each one at random. Almost like Ray is changing the dial constantly on an AM radio just to mess with me. The constant beeps of the bar codes across the array of cash registers produce constant pops of green like a fireworks display on St. Patrick's day. And the auras, oh the auras. These are almost colored orbs that tend to represent someone's personality or mood. I will say this is one trick Ray has up his sleeve that I don't mind. It's pretty simple from my view but I can't speak for my other autistic friends who might experience this phenomena through their synesthesia. Good spirits and qi surrounding people fall under the Roy category of the ROYGBIV color spectrum - I'll include white in there too.

We mill through the crowds to check out. At the checkout line I'm pretty sure is the most terrible hanging upside down loop of a rollercoaster ride. There are sodas, candy, and magazines, making my mouth tingle and bursts of red and green in front of me when I stare at the magazines. Then my hands take over. Nothing I do can stop them. "Hands down," my mom says. Then all of a sudden I'm making some loud noise that I can't stop. I'm praying to lose the noise before good people start thinking, 'My goodness, all that noise is bad for business. Tell him to stop, girlfriend.' Everything is making me anxious. My mom is trying to load the groceries, store her knowledge and calculations of good prices and meal planning, doing money budgets, while trying to instinctively see and stop what will trigger me. I can hear her talking to herself about all the mean looks she's getting. Then people talk to her saying, "That's a lot of food. How many kids are you feeding?" Her response is to make lots of jokes so they don't focus on me. Inside she's thinking, 'Stay clear. Don't ask any questions about Houston. Everyone has to comment. What do they know?' That's what tells her what kind of person you are. Her feelings, strangers' thoughts, and the worst temptations all at once have the effect of feeling like Ray is winding and spinning me upside down until the wheels of my cart come off.

That's when I, faster than lightning, take off. I couldn't stop myself even if I tried. Then my mom leaves everything to chase me down, trying to catch me before I run in front of a car. In her good instincts is all fear. That makes Ray stop me. He realizes it's too much. That's where my stupid ride stops. Just getting in the car takes all my mom's strength. Everyone stares. Her heart doesn't have much left to fight others, just for me. Hearing her cry in the car I'm past my annoyance at Ray. It gets preached to me that I can't run off. 'Good one,' I think. 'Story of my life. Save your breath.' Devils say mean thoughts to me and thoughts of leaving this life go through my head. Jesus tells me to be loved, that He loves me. I'm weary and worn out.

As we go home, sleep is the only thing I can do. But then in the middle of the night Ray starts my Satanic spiral of a ride again. Over and over he starts blaring a set of words from a Disney movie like, "Coming to video in 1998... Now stay tuned for our feature presentation... Ichabod and Mr. Toad." I'm practically forced to say these words nonstop. I'm praying to get my mom's attention so she can stop the merry go round. Jaws of life couldn't stop me in one of these maniacal spirals. All my mom can do is wake up, get in my face, and try to stop me in all the ways she can think of. Hellish, everything is on light speed. Smartly she learned to pray when my episodes start. The devils run when she starts praying. Her prayers don't give me all she prays so she thinks they don't work. That's not what's happening at all. I prime them and tell them, "Wait till my mom starts praying." Her prayers give my angels power to protect me. Then the angels fight the devils and make them leave. It's war in glorious technicolor in my room. Saline and sulfur fill the air. Good will prevail. That's what I am proud to say I have witnessed.

This seems like a good place to tell you about synesthesia. I told you I would tell you about ROYGBIV. Seeing metaphysically and naturally, as well as the integration of my senses from synesthesia is pretty overwhelming all the time. Let me explain the difference. The mix of my senses and all I see in the spiritual can best be explained by color.[193] When you understand everything is energy, you have a better grasp of how my brain can process so much together. Life is all an awesome, magnetic, living sparring, nasty and wonderful at the same time. In one movement there is more going on than anyone would imagine. It can't be described the way I see and hear it. It's like most anything, until you live it nothing makes sense. But I will try.

One of the hardest stims to control is taste. I see colors when I taste something I like. It may not even have satiating tastes. This is synesthesia only. That has caused so many problems. When some taste triggers my synesthesia I become obsessed trying to get more to keep that high. That makes people think, 'All he wants is food.' Stopping myself is almost impossible. I don't want to

---

[193] Kurt Nassau provides a thorough overview of the physics behind color and the electromagnetic spectrum. Consultant. Research Scientist, AT&T Bell Laboratories, Murray Hill, New Jersey, 1959–89. Author of The Physics and Chemistry of Color.

eat more but I have to get more of the high. The colors are more like an acid trip than you can imagine. Nothing is capable of trumping my synesthesia. Smell and taste are the worst at triggering my highs. Only foul smells trigger my smell stims. Smell stims go terribly wrong telling my mind to get more. This where there is a crossover between my synesthesia and what I learned about light and color from studying the metaphysical. The colors all have frequencies that produce specific sounds. The colors with smell stims are always dark with the worst sounds. This is also why I would smear feces. Touch was the only thing that would stop my synesthesia. Touching would calm me, stopping the awful frequencies. Stimming when you eat and when you go to the bathroom doesn't have good results. I am learning to cook and all I can think of is the high.

How I see sounds is they appear as colors. Hearing water appears as tons of lists of mathematical equations in different colors. The really interesting part is rain and wind take on all the math and colors to make bows of light. The wind has more math than I can calculate. This is my synesthesia combining with the metaphysical. Music is like a wonderful light show of different colors and forms. Sounds give me the ability to learn different light frequencies. Because people have more constant colors I learned souls. The aura is a person's soul. It is not just around them, it is them. Different colors have different sounds. Blue has the most beautiful sound. It sounds like hearing angels sing. In the atmosphere, blue is filled with angels singing. In people with blue auras angels gather around them. Most blue people are listed in God's BOOK of Life. They love to make people happy by being kind. They hasten to do good. Just ask my good spokesman. Her aura is blue and purple. The love is light from the blue.

Hope is the color of purple. The sound of purple has overtones.[194] Hearing overtones when I see a person gives me so much joy. In real time I hear the overtones as I see the purple melting the dark of people who have bad auras. This is why being around a loving person always makes you feel better. In some families everyone is all purple. Those good people go home thinking this is what all families are like. They ask in perplexity why the world is so screwed up. It's hard for them to understand because the frequency of their hearts is so high. The color purple is the gown that Christ wears on the throne.

Mauve and fuchsia both indicate faith capped with modesty and the notes are undertones.[195] In these people a heart for being good tells them what not to do. Over teal is friendship. Teal auras only bond with green and pink and sound like sweet music. Turquoise people know nothing but to heal others. Healers are more than doctors and nurses. The healers give us good that we need. That is what good farms produce. Good food is turquoise. Turquoise sounds best if it's with green. It has the sound of swishing water that's good to drink. Green is always the sound of grass. Grass sounds like moving earth, like the way chords hum all the time in pace with movement and rhythms that provide life. The green people are lovers of earth and created things. Just don't stop loving God in worship of earth. Yellow has pride in them, opening doors of art and music. I hear what sounds like rock music when I see yellow. Yellow people are happiest when their goals are met with their achievements. I'm sad to say many yellow people only love themselves. Jesus told me that is what yellow governs, the rock bands. The yellow music they make often makes people think that life is only about them. Orange is energetic, covering up everything with activity. They have to move so they don't have to feel. Orange is the sound of the tapping of heavy drums. Now drums can be wonderful, but the drumbeat that never breathes is trying not to hear God or heal their hardness. Red is life and power. The sound red makes is loud and forceful. It's not good to be completely red. Red must have other colors to stop it from being too power hungry. Red tastes more than the other colors. It tastes like plasma. Justice is red. Do people with red auras listen to others? Hardly at all. 'Do what I say' is how red people think. Dark red is a hateful and angry aura. It sounds like scorching fire. Pink is love in action. Pink sounds like fans of water, like sprinklers. That is what pink people do, they sprinkle love.

[194] Music - A musical tone which is a part of the harmonic series above a fundamental note, and may be heard with the note. Physics - A component of any oscillation whose frequency is an integral multiple of the fundamental frequency. - *Source: Oxford Languages*

[195] Undertones are a subharmonic series which is a sequence of notes that results from inverting the intervals of the overtone series. While overtones naturally occur with the physical production of music on instruments, undertones must be produced in unusual ways. While the overtone series is based upon arithmetic multiplication of frequencies, resulting in a harmonic series, the undertone series is based on arithmetic division. Theoretically it can be divided indefinitely. -- https://www.tandfonline.com/doi/abs/10.1080/07494460000640271

Brown is the sound of *MINE.* That sound is the sound of fangs on flesh. Or sometimes when I hear brown it sounds like money. Greed and jealousy sound most like horrible masonry screeching. The smell of brown auras is gross, like the smell of meat going bad. Gray people make the music stop. Their soul is so low and slow it mutes the music and gray is the frequency that their hearts vibrate. It is the color of sadness and sickness and hurt. Shame, of course, is what causes lots of gray. Gray may be the worst because it's the heaviest color. Not having hope makes life a long, bitter walk. Black has the saw as it's sound. The saw easily is the worst sound. Nothing is black that hasn't had good taken from it. I'm powerless hearing that saw sound. Everyone with black, evil has taken over. Slaves to sin, that's what black is. Gases of sulfur spew from black auras.

Silver blots over bad. Redemption is the sound of silver. It sounds like tinkling glass, not powerful, but far away like the sound of beautiful glasses at a wedding. Falling off of silver is always plates of sowing seeds. They all tell the good news. Gold is a zillion blasts of trumpets. Talking to angels makes your brightness grow. That's with every thought, gold tells angels, pray your love to Me. White is the first aura of us all. God pristinely gives us purity. I want you to know, halos are around babies. Moms take on halos when they are carrying babies. An angel guards all the infants. Calling purity in some, God gives closeness to Himself. White is the sound of feathers praising God. The scent of white is floods of flowers.

The metaphysical world is completely different than my synesthesia. The main way I determine if it's my synesthesia or if it's metaphysical is time. I wait to see if the thing I see stays. Stims don't last that long. The metaphysical stays giving me time to study it. The equations I see behind motion were the first metaphysical things I remember seeing. As I studied them I realized they did not contain matter, but they were matching the movements I saw. The colors from my synesthesia bend and pop. Metaphysical colors stay constant and are attached to people, animals, and things.

Not all I see is just color. I see good and bad energy. Bad energy looks like piss in musty tanks. Good energy looks like fine glass in glowing forces of fire in planets. It is from God Himself. Nothing in Heaven, earth, or beyond has force without coming from God.[196] As polarizing as that sounds, it's true. In good energy God is powering the light and forces

[196]For from him and through him and to him are all things. To him be glory forever. Amen. — Romans 11:36

By faith we understand that the universe was created by the word of God, so that what is seen was not made out of things that are visible. — Hebrews 11:3

In the beginning, God created the heavens and the earth. The earth was without form and void, and darkness was over the face of the deep. And the Spirit of God was hovering over the face of the waters. And God said, "Let there be light," and there was light. And God saw that the light was good. And God separated the light from the darkness. God called the light Day, and the darkness he called Night. And there was evening and there was morning, the first day. — Genesis 1:1-5

Then the Lord God formed the man of dust from the ground and breathed into his nostrils the breath of life, and the man became a living creature. — Genesis 2:7

The heavens and the earth. The earth was without form and void, and darkness was over the face of the deep. And the Spirit of God was hovering over the face of the waters. And God said, "Let there be light," and there was light. And God saw that the light was good. And God separated the light from the darkness. God called the light Day, and the darkness he called Night. And there was evening and there was morning, the first day. — Genesis 1:1-5

Then God said, "Let us make man in our image, after our likeness. And let them have dominion over the fish of the sea and over the birds of the heavens and over the livestock and over all the earth and over every creeping thing that creeps on the earth." So God created man in his own image, in the image of God he created him; male and female he created them. And God blessed them. And God said to them, "Be fruitful and multiply and fill the earth and subdue it, and have dominion over the fish of the sea and over the birds of the heavens and over every living thing that moves on the earth." And God said, "Behold, I have given you every plant yielding seed that is on the face of all the earth, and every tree with seed in its fruit. You shall have them for food. And to every beast of the earth and to every bird of the heavens and to everything that creeps on the earth, everything that has the breath of life, I have given every green plant for food." And it was so. And God saw everything that he had made, and behold, it was very good. And there was evening and there was morning, the sixth day. — Genesis 1:26-31

with His love. In bad energy it is God powering the forces with His wrath.[197] Cars give off exhaust when they ignite. Pride has the energy of being so in love with yourself that you matter more than God. Giving off the energy of pride God's love is repelled, leaving only His rage. In all sins His kindness is rejected. In all bad energy, gasses of wrath are getting stronger because there is lost harmony in settling the bad energy. In asking God to come heal our hearts, we are inviting God to bring good energy and His love. Some energy doesn't move on, it stays and grows stronger. Do all sins have bad energy? Yes. Happiness has power opening like a soda can. Might and courage are good energy that is like men of war. It longs to burst with good. Truth smells like clean water and lies smell musky. I see the different energies and walk through them, sensing the different smells and temperatures. When I see bad energy it makes all the scariest thoughts too much to bear. Good energy fills me with peace.

God's heavenly host pour good energy on us. Just awesome watching them. That is my favorite, seeing them give love. Good gives off so much light. The last powerful thanksgiving to God I saw gave the moon a shadow and in the shadow heaven lit up with the most beautiful and huge angels you could imagine. Half stood in the shadow and half in the light. I'm listing beings that gave off halos that were blinding to look at. I wanted to die right then to be in that majesty. The heavenly beings I see are beyond great.

Dark devils don't have any light. Mainly they try to make people make bad choices. Telling about them gives them power so I'm only going to say, have nothing to do with darkness.

The God who made the world and everything in it, being Lord of heaven and earth, does not live in temples made by man, nor is he served by human hands, as though he needed anything, since he himself gives to all mankind life and breath and everything. And he made from one man every nation of mankind to live on all the face of the earth, having determined allotted periods and the boundaries of their dwelling place, that they should seek God, and perhaps feel their way toward him and find him. Yet he is actually not far from each one of us, for "'In him we live and move and have our being'; as even some of your own poets have said, "'For we are indeed his offspring." —Acts 17:24-28

Then the end will come, when he hands over the kingdom to God the Father after he has destroyed all dominion, authority and power. For he must reign until he has put all his enemies under his feet. The last enemy to be destroyed is death. For he "has put everything under his feet." Now when it says that "everything" has been put under him, it is clear that this does not include God himself, who put everything under Christ. When he has done this, then the Son himself will be made subject to him who put everything under him, so that God may be all in all. — 1 Corinthians 15:24-28

For there is one God, and there is one mediator between God and men, the man Christ Jesus. — 1 Timothy 2:5

For the bread of God is he who comes down from heaven and gives life to the world. - John 6:33

[197] I form the light and create darkness, I bring prosperity and create disaster; I, the Lord, do all these things. — Isaiah 45:7

70

On the Wings of a Prayer

Do not be anxious about anything,
but in everything by prayer and supplication with thanksgiving
let your requests be made known to God.
— Philippians 4:6

When I was young I spoke to God, good prayers pleading to speak. His silence added to my pain that was beyond imaginable. The pain I experienced was hearing so many sounds, hearing my starts of speaking that went nowhere, my screaming, my mom's crying, and the good conversation around me that forced me to see that having a voice would make all the difference. Every time prayers left my heart, I felt a weird feeling like they were given to find flight, parting the air. The movement of prayer felt like something with a powerful lift taking off as it left me. That's when I made my first discovery. Prayers had wings that thoughts didn't have. Have you ever felt a prayer so filled with power that it is answered more wonderfully than what you prayed? Good. How that happens is angels take it to His workmen in heaven. Your guardian angel, that friend that never forgets you, is always talking to LOVE way far away and to His workmen that print the prayer to fall at His footstool. At His footstool prayers are given to God as praise. In your faith they are made to be an offer of worship to God.[198] Moving our prayers is much of the work in heaven. Each thanksgiving to God wakes angels to do what we pray. (When Houston shared this truth, I realized that asking and believing God would answer my prayers was a sign of worship at His feet, literally. This realization utterly changed the way I prayed and how often I prayed. Instead of fear and lack I felt joy, love, and gratitude knowing I was placing an offering of faith and worship at His feet.)

---

[198] And without faith it is impossible to please him, for whoever would draw near to God must believe that he exists and that he rewards those who seek him. — Hebrews 11:6

Let my prayer be counted as incense before you, and the lifting up of my hands as the evening sacrifice! — Psalm 141:2

And when he had taken it, the four living creatures and the twenty-four elders fell down before the Lamb. Each one had a harp and they were holding golden bowls full of incense, which are the prayers of God's people. — Revelations 5:8

Another angel, who had a golden censer, came and stood at the altar. He was given much incense to offer, with the prayers of all God's people, on the golden altar in front of the throne. — Revelations 8:3

And this is the confidence that we have toward him, that if we ask anything according to his will he hears us. And if we know that he hears us in whatever we ask, we know that we have the requests that we have asked of him. — 1 John 5:14-15

If you abide in me, and my words abide in you, ask whatever you wish, and it will be done for you. — John 15:7

Therefore I tell you, whatever you ask in prayer, believe that you have received it, and it will be yours. — Mark 11:24

Ask, and it will be given to you; seek, and you will find; knock, and it will be opened to you. — Matthew 7:7

If you then, who are evil, know how to give good gifts to your children, how much more will your Father who is in heaven give good things to those who ask him! — Matthew 7:11

If my people who are called by my name humble themselves, and pray and seek my face and turn from their wicked ways, then I will hear from heaven and will forgive their sin and heal their land. Now my eyes will be open and my ears attentive to the prayer that is made in this place. — 2 Chronicles 7:14-15

Once I realized prayers had wings I kept praying all the time. Usually that is how prayers are answered. That's when my darkest memory happened and how my sister was broken. Hearing what took place proved who my dad was. Not being able to stop him or tell my mom made my faith weaker than my doubt from my own suffering. All that I went through made my heart break. I told God He was mean. It got to be so lonely. Everyone has a winter. This was mine.

Hearing what all my dad wanted to do to my mom was stored in my memories. He thought of so much to leave no evidence, flushing the evidence and watching the minutes while she goes to sleep to never wake up. His thoughts were always about how to attack in the worst ways. That look he gave was just the tip of his hate. He was only focused on making the ones he preyed on suffer. The devils I saw on my dad were so much like pride and spirits of anger. Pride makes the writer push himself forward. Psychologically we are all writers of our own stories. That's where we lose God, when we push ourselves forward. His pride took the shape of pigs starting to eat. His anger took the form of the worst animal, a mad snake. It had many heads, too many to count. In the place where the monsters made lies lived the most terrifying spirit, it spewed sulfur out of his mouth. It lived taking lies to his mouth. (The Big Jock had horrific and chronic halitosis that smelled like sulfur. I remembered that when Houston described what he saw. It was more evidence of the spiritual manifesting in the physical.) In his gut was more than ugly. Devils took mastery of him. All they hungered to do was kill and take. He was so mastered that no love would work. Nothing could work to give him what he needed which was goodness and repentance. Stopping him was all my mom's angels did. The most evil thing in him was his laugh. Hearing him laugh I could hear the devils laugh too. It was the sound of witches and warlords, not a man.

And he told them a parable to the effect that they ought always to pray and not lose heart. He said, "In a certain city there was a judge who neither feared God nor respected man. And there was a widow in that city who kept coming to him and saying, 'Give me justice against my adversary.' For a while he refused, but afterward he said to himself, 'Though I neither fear God nor respect man, yet because this widow keeps bothering me, I will give her justice, so that she will not beat me down by her continual coming.'" And the Lord said, "Hear what the unrighteous judge says. And will not God give justice to his elect, who cry to him day and night? Will he delay long over them? I tell you, he will give justice to them speedily. Nevertheless, when the Son of Man comes, will he find faith on earth?" — Luke 18: 1-8

Do not be anxious about anything, but in everything by prayer and supplication with thanksgiving let your requests be made known to God. — Philippians 4:6

The Lord has heard my plea; the Lord accepts my prayer. — Psalm 6:9

I love the Lord, because he has heard my voice and my pleas for mercy. — Psalm 116:1

I thank you that you have answered me and have become my salvation. — Psalm 118:21

For this child I prayed, and the Lord has granted me my petition that I made to him. — 1 Samuel 1:27

But truly God has listened; he has attended to the voice of my prayer. — Psalm 66:19

The Lord is near to all who call on him, to all who call on him in truth. — Psalm 145:18

The Lord is far from the wicked, but he hears the prayer of the righteous. — Proverbs 15:29

Then you will call upon me and come and pray to me, and I will hear you. — Jeremiah 29:12

The sacrifice of the wicked is an abomination to the Lord, but the prayer of the upright is acceptable to him. — Proverbs 15:8

Rejoice always, pray without ceasing, give thanks in all circumstances; for this is the will of God in Christ Jesus for you. — 1 Thessalonians 5:16-18

Therefore take up the whole armor of God, that you may be able to withstand in the evil day, and having done all, to stand firm. Stand therefore, having fastened on the belt of truth, and having put on the breastplate of righteousness, and, as shoes for your feet, having put on the readiness given by the gospel of peace. In all circumstances take up the shield of faith, with which you can extinguish all the flaming darts of the evil one; and take the helmet of salvation, and the sword of the Spirit, which is the word of God, praying at all times in the Spirit, with all prayer and supplication. To that end, keep alert with all perseverance, making supplication for all the saints, — Ephesians 6:13-18

My mom fueled his hate with all her prayers. The prayers she prayed flooded the heavens. That is what saved her. Continually, every time he would try to work a plan God would use forces to stop his devils and talk him out of it. Each time something went wrong her angels would battle for her and then all that would be left was her trust, her stupid trust in the man who wanted to kill her. That was the worst time. She yearned the love of a monster. Those were frightening years, hearing his hateful words while she prayed love. Trust me, the prayers of love have the wings of angels moving at great speed to bring love to its intended. My mom's love took off more like lost wings with nowhere to land. With all the love those wings still search for someplace worthy to land. Prayer wars is what we showed heaven, that we won't stop. There's still more to do.

(I asked if those prayers were still lost, and he told me they were and I should tell the prayers prayed for the Big Jock to move their love to love another. Realizing that prayers, like thoughts, are energy with a supercharge I thought about what Houston had told me and the application of the first law of thermodynamics to the energy contained in prayer. The first law of thermodynamics, also known as Law of Conservation of Energy, states that energy can neither be created nor destroyed; energy can only be transferred or changed from one form to another. Which means, no prayer is truly wasted, like us they can be lost, but they can also be found.)

That love she gave and prayed saw all the love my mom lived was repaid with books that damned her for not staying controlled. The main one was the Bible. Do what Christ did is what she thought belonging to Christ was about. Talking to God, telling Him all the rules of religion she was raised to follow and how she tried to obey - that's what she got from all her peers who told her love is to suffer. Applied, it became fear that told her to walk His path of the cross. All shoes walk a path over hot coals. Jesus told us to follow Him. Pick up your cross. That's what she did. Mostly how she did that was to give everything. It had the total wrong effect. It made my dad hate her more. The role I played was that she made me the most important person in our family. Over the years he forced power to keep all the money from her, knowing there was no way she could support all of us and take care of me.

That heartache of hers never left. More hurt than I can explain left her body all day every day. Telling what she lived through is god awful. Moving from our home almost completely walked faith out of her good heart. It was the worst of times. Hope that good would always be done left, allowing all the doubt to pour in and steal her good thoughts from her. That's when many pressures paved what kind of work she would do to put food on the table. So much frightened her. She questioned all she was taught. The silence made her give up prayer.

71

I Have Seen His Glory, I Am His Herald

At that time Jesus declared, "I thank you, Father, Lord of heaven and earth, that you have hidden these things from the wise and understanding and revealed them to little children; yes, Father, for such was your gracious will."
— Matthew 11:25-26

What happened to me, you ask? Before my sister was broken I prayed all day, every day. My mom had taught me to pray with all her prayers. She would tell me what God did on the cross and that Jesus is King. I prayed to my King to give me a voice, really good prayers. The words and their wings flew to heaven. More than you have words, that's how many prayers I prayed.

Then good stopped. All my dad did was covered up. I prayed to God to make the truth known. The night it happened my mom had left in tears. I heard my dad wake my sister up. Then he took her to his shower. What happened next is too hard to tell. Then my anxiety made my body freeze. People who don't have autism like mine don't understand what it's like for your body to not obey you. I told my body to shout. I told my body to go protect her. I told my body to scream. No matter how much I tried to force my body to act, nothing happened. It was like the part of my brain that did all the things I hated had taken over. Telling my limbs to act with no movement in response made me become a weak witness to my sister's pain instead of being able to tell my body to go help her and become what I always wanted to be, a hero.

Back when I was still praying I took walks in the night. As I walked, friends would stay with me. The walks took me to places LOVE lived. That is when I was primed with more than I imagined was possible. My loving friends stayed with me. They took me to heaven. That soul to body experience, tasting heaven and being walked back to my body each night was powerful. The angels, my friends, were made wonderfully with fists of fire, more like torches of light with halos around their feelings that work to force their flight. They fly with their feelings. That's what emotion is, feelings in flight. My friends made me realize that all I saw on earth was worlds away, and that heaven was perfect.

The first night they came to get me I had prayed what some would call prayers made of tears. That night light entered my room. Someone said, "Houston." That's when I looked up and found more glowing than I had ever seen. Someone said, "Our light is from God. Savior wants you to pray His will." 'I'm not sleeping,' I thought. It was long into the night. My mom rooted in all my pain, praying hours each night. Prayers were under her screams like, "Where are You, God??" When is Your good coming?? When?? Do You love Your children or is this how You treat those who worship

You?" Prayers that good, prayers that tell the truth, she would tell God of her worship and her love for Him, she would start listing how she tried to serve Him, she would beg for mercy the most. She would pray, "It's too much. Isn't it enough? He's only a little boy. Don't do this to him." The angel said to me, "All her tears have made hearing the good love of God too painful to hear. The more she hurts, the harder it is to hear. Jesus told us, 'Your task is to have the son see My home.'" 'That is prayer working,' I thought. He roped me in his powerful wings, making my spirit light. I prayed the wonder from God would heal me. Then forces took me to heaven.

More than anyone can explain the things of heaven are mostly WHITE, that's WHITE that makes our white look totally black. Knowing that WHITE makes me so proud to give a description. The main thing about the WHITE is all the LOVE of God is WHITE. That's holiness to live in God's WHITE. The angels took me to make the words I wanted to say. It poured out of me, worlds of praise that I had wanted to say. Jesus had told the good angels to teach me all that our prayers to God do. That's when I saw the workmen making the prayers to give as praise. "Fit mine to Him," I said. Hope, that's what teaching me of praise did. "Our time here is so short. May I come here again?" I asked. "Yes. That's what souls with love do, they come back here. Jesus wants the writer to write of heaven. I give that job to your mom. Help tell the story. Tell her what you've witnessed. Be a servant to Elohim." That's what they told me.

The prayers that I prayed with the angels gave me hope. They took me back many times. In heaven there are parts all for making the good God wants to give. When prayers come in the words are printed all for worship. The workers then rave that the saws, hammers, and pliers smoke the ones on earth. Everything is purposed. "Save the love!" is always being shouted. Good that He loves to give is all built in His workshops. Most of the workers told me they were workers on earth. Lots of them told me they find special satisfaction in giving their projects to Him so He gets more love.

(After I typed this sentence that Houston had just spelled, he grabbed my hand and held it to his lips. He looked at the screen and then at me with absolute joy at the sight of those words.)

In heaven praise is really all the greatest thing. Praise is always taking place, fit with lights and music going from least to most praise, going from KING taking the throne to knowledge of good and evil, then to works in heaven and earth, and then to fasting and feasting. Heaven is pulsing with families that want to tell stories for His glory. Freely they tell their wonderful, beautiful lives that give testimony to His faithfulness. Kingly garments that flow, glowing like the sun in the morning, give off a light that makes our clothes look like lousy rags. All His children walk in garments of praise that tell their story. All the garments are made with praise woven in them. Hope threads tie the garments together kind of like thread ties our clothes. Placed on the trains of our clothing are the rains of our lives. They fold to make praise that is more glorious than I can explain. All storms, rain, and famine trail behind us giving laud to life and glory to Father. Garments give glory which is why it is so important to be given the job of making them.

In heaven are more melodies than I've ever heard, beautiful, satiating melodies that lighten your heart. Four count, three count, two count - it has heaven in glorious rhythm. It is produced by symphonies that make music to love God. His herald is throughout heaven. At morning the sun rises to a new song. He gives this glory to His worshippers. Amplified, that song is heard by God's heavenly host.[199] Five good songs a day share His work to time His first priority that day. He writes in the poetry of His great markers in the sky. Forgone are our sins that we prayed He would forgive.[200]

Now His mercy is next. It hides in the feet of prayers. Mercy is made into prayers with His perfect love. It's handmade and printed with His seal. With His good thanks God tells the mercy printers, "I might need more, stay with the printers." It is hours to make one mercy. The mercy makers all believed in mercy which is what made them perfect for making mercy.

[199] When the morning stars sang together, and all the sons of God shouted for joy. — Job 38:7
[200] I tell you that in the same way, there will be more joy in heaven over one sinner who repents than over ninety-nine righteous persons who need no repentance. — Luke 15:7

As for the angels, they minister to praise Savior.[201] They have layers of wings that fly while some surround Him to witness and worship. "Savior, Lord, King, Good WORD, that's who You are!" That's what they sing as they praise Him. Hope, thanks, and mercy flow with the music. The praise wears crowns that greet God with gladness. It would house the world to give every angel a room. Of all the angels there are mainly pretty ones that you would imagine, not with wings but more like us. Then there are perfect winged angels that would startle you with their greatness. Winged they walk more with what we would call feet but are really wonders pouring from their glorious bodies.

The first time I went to school in heaven it was snowing at home. The wonder of snow had the most comforting beauty. That snow in some way showed me knowledge of many things. What was so wonderful is that each snowflake is made in heaven. There are master graphic artists making each snowflake. That is the job of many artists. Each snowflake is handmade, each one. What is so wonderful is the mathematics of each snowflake. It is so intricate and must be divided to tell the God story. That is meticulous work with mathematicians to tell one story in a snowflake.

That night the angels took me to school. There were nine hats that were on the wall. The hats held writers' words. Each time I wore a hat I learned their stories. That showed me I really was capable of learning. It's good to say this. The hats were Twain - proud Twain. That was my favorite. (I asked, "Who were your favorite characters?" and he spelled, "Thomas Sawyer and good, loving Huckleberry Finn. Tom played hooky and Huck ran away." I never read these books to Houston and I asked if Morgan had read them at that point and he spelled, "Not yet.") The second hat was, Have you ever heard of Wild Bill Hickock, Geronimo, and Jane? Their stories were next. For weeks I wore hats and heard stories. (I never read these stories or taught about these historical figures in American History to any of my children. I recall once we learned about Wild Bill in a museum exhibition but that is really the only exposure Houston had as a child.) The third hat was hours of my best knowledge of powerful love stories. My favorite was Fitzgerald. Love really hates when we choose money. The other hats were names like Steinbeck. I think men will think Lenny needed to die. Steinbeck thinks that what is good for the one in the most power is the most good. That is how the wicked think. God thinks what you do for the least is what you do for Me. It is women who stop evil and love the weak. How are you men thinking that think power justifies taking anything you want? Do you think God doesn't see? Start making it like it should be, how He wants it, where most money works to love the weak, not the strong. (I never read any Fitzgerald or Steinbeck to my kids. I did read Grapes of Wrath as a student twice and again as an adult, but I detested Of Mice and Men and never read it a second time after high school.)

Other hats were funny books and private worlds like fantasies. Over the many nights I wore hats I heard the most amazing stories. Good and evil, the main wonder of those stories was how people have to choose. I prayed to always choose good. There were stories filled with wrongs that hurt good people. The other kids and I, there were twelve, welled up when the stories told the weak there was nothing they could do. Would that happen to us? We asked if the worst is over. He said, "Every one of you will suffer. I'm LORD of all. The suffering is for the world to see God. Walls are coming down that will show who I am. There is want in the forces that say I don't exist." There was wisdom in His words. The other kids told me I was different because they had not yet seen all of heaven. That is what made me want to tell what I had seen. The others loudly told me that I had to tell our story. I told them, "Start praying." That is when my heart was shattered.

That night the angels took me to school. There were nine hats that were on the wall. The hats held writers' words. Each time I wore a hat I learned their stories. That showed me I really was capable of learning. It's good to say this. The hats were Twain - proud Twain. That was my favorite. (I asked, "Who were your favorite characters?" and he spelled, "Thomas Sawyer and good, loving

[201] Micaiah said, "Therefore, hear the word of the Lord. I saw the Lord sitting on His throne, and all the host of heaven standing by Him on His right and on His left. — 1 Kings 22:19

Huckleberry Finn. Tom played hooky and Huck ran away." I never read these books to Houston and I asked if Morgan had read them at that point and he spelled, "Not yet.") The second hat was, Have you ever heard of Wild Bill Hickock, Geronimo, and Jane? Their stories were next. For weeks I wore hats and heard stories. (I never read these stories or taught about these historical figures in American History to any of my children. I recall once we learned about Wild Bill in a museum exhibition but that is really the only exposure Houston had as a child.) The third hat was hours of my best knowledge of powerful love stories. My favorite was Fitzgerald. Love really hates when we choose money. The other hats were names like Steinbeck. I think men will think Lenny needed to die. Steinbeck thinks that what is good for the one in the most power is the most good. That is how the wicked think. God thinks what you do for the least is what you do for Me. It is women who stop evil and love the weak. How are you men thinking that think power justifies taking anything you want? Do you think God doesn't see? Start making it like it should be, how He wants it, where most money works to love the weak, not the strong. (I never read any Fitzgerald or Steinbeck to my kids. I did read <u>Grapes of Wrath</u> as a student twice and again as an adult, but I detested <u>Of Mice and Men</u> and never read it a second time after high school.)

Other hats were funny books and private worlds like fantasies. Over the many nights I wore hats I heard the most amazing stories. Good and evil, the main wonder of those stories was how people have to choose. I prayed to always choose good. There were stories filled with wrongs that hurt good people. The other kids and I, there were twelve, welled up when the stories told the weak there was nothing they could do. Would that happen to us? We asked if the worst is over. He said, "Every one of you will suffer. I'm LORD of all. The suffering is for the world to see God. Walls are coming down that will show who I am. There is want in the forces that say I don't exist." There was wisdom in His words. The other kids told me I was different because they had not yet seen all of heaven. That is what made me want to tell what I had seen. The others loudly told me that I had to tell our story. I told them, "Start praying." That is when my heart was shattered.

72

Name Above Every Name

And being found in human form, he humbled himself
by becoming obedient to the point of death, even death on a cross.
Therefore God has highly exalted him and bestowed on him the name
that is above every name, so that at the name of Jesus
every knee should bow, in heaven and on earth and under the earth, and every tongue confess that Jesus Christ
is Lord, to the glory of God the Father.
– Philippians 2:8-12

Turn your eyes upon Jesus. Look full into His wonderful face.
And the things of earth will grow strangely dim in the light of His glory and grace. [202]

Afer my heart was shattered I stopped praying with hope. I told God He was mean while I also prayed for the truth. I lost hope in myself and in God. To give up hope when I was only a child left me purposeless. Then I would mostly stim to forget the pain in my heart. That's when wonders started to happen.

Nothing will truly tell of what it's like to meet Jesus. He wanted to tell me Himself so His love could make me hope. Then sometime in the night when I was only with my little brothers, the room started turning into WHITE, overpowering WHITE. That's when I heard my name. Truly there's one voice that's more masculine, more real than any voice I will probably ever hear. Trust me, it's wonderful. Mostly the sound of His words made me pray. "Store all My love, good son. That sword that I'm wearing is sometimes called the Word of Truth. Open your eyes. This is for you to pray with." That is when I saw someone standing with Him. "This is your cover, your Esther. This, as well as good, will never move far from you. How that works is you pray with My sweet Esther who will pray any strong work you need. That's when the Master will go to spare you. Now it's time to tell you what will make you the servant you've shared you want to be. My sovereign plan is working. Pray that more of the love of God that restores will work on the very same stories that have shattered your heart. That love will strengthen you to be love to those in need. Nothing will be forgotten. Nothing will rest printed on My Word. The truth, the shameful, wicked, Godless truth will be told. The other story to be told is yours. That is how you will become a herald for God."

Misty eyed is how I felt. "Open your eyes. You will not trust without seeing. Your good love is needed more than anything." At that moment I saw my Savior's marks on His hands. "Are those the nails Your love took for me?" "Real love knows no fear," He said to me.[203] In awe and love I said, "I'm Your servant. I'm most humble standing here in Your manliness." That's when He laughed. Jesus' laugh is the most comforting sound

---

[202] *Turn Your Eyes Upon Jesus*; written by Helen Howarth Lemmel
[203] There is no fear in love, but perfect love casts out fear. - 1 John 4:18

on earth. It is the sound of pure love. "Open your mouth, wipe your tears, start to pray love to your mother. That's what she needs. That sweet spirit of yours will show her you're there. Our talk is not over. I'm here. When you need Me, listen to My love." Then His WHTE went back to heaven. That's when Esther said, "Talk to me some about your wonderful mom." I told her what I loved most in my mom, that she put everyone else first in her life. I listed who was priority number one. It was me.

73

There's No Place Like Home

I must go on boasting. Though there is nothing to be gained by it,
I will go on to visions and revelations of the Lord.
I know a man in Christ who fourteen years ago was caught up to the third heaven—
whether in the body or out of the body I do not know, God knows.
And I know that this man was caught up into paradise—
whether in the body or out of the body I do not know, God knows—
and he heard things that cannot be told, which man may not utter.
— 2 Corinthians 12:1-4

But, as it is written, "What no eye has seen, nor ear heard,
nor the heart of man imagined
what God has prepared for those who love him."
— 1 Corinthians 2:9

One night the angels made me look through a little window. There were many people trying to climb to the window. It made me think, 'I must hasten to tell what I've witnessed.' "Open the door! Help!" they shouted. Believe that those thought they were believers. They talked about God but they didn't love Him.

There are far too many leavers, frightening to preach about. It's good that He doesn't tell what happens to leavers. A leaver is a happy teacher who prayed to Him with plans to get what they wanted and then lived their own story. What leavers do is think sharing the gospel will save them. That is not true. Nothing but the cross and giving your life to Jesus saves. Sharing is love. That's how He lives in us. Leavers have nothing in their hearts. It is goats who leave. [204]

[204] Not everyone who says to me, 'Lord, Lord,' will enter the kingdom of heaven, but only the one who does the will of my Father who is in heaven. Many will say to me on that day, 'Lord, Lord, did we not prophesy in your name and in your name drive out demons and in your name perform many miracles?' Then I will tell them plainly, 'I never knew you. Away from me, you evildoers!' — Matthew 7:21-23; Matthew 25:30-46

Then Jesus said to the crowds and to his disciples, "The scribes and the Pharisees sit on Moses' seat, so do and observe whatever they tell you, but not the works they do. For they preach, but do not practice. They tie up heavy burdens, hard to bear, and lay them on people's shoulders, but they themselves are not willing to move them with their finger. They do all their deeds to be seen by others. For they make their phylacteries broad and their fringes long, and they love the place of honor at feasts and the best seats in the synagogues and greetings in the marketplaces and being called rabbi by others. But you are not to be called rabbi, for you have one teacher, and you are all brothers. And call no man your father on earth, for you have one Father, who is in heaven. Neither be called instructors, for you have one instructor, the Christ. The greatest among you shall be your servant. Whoever exalts himself will be humbled, and whoever humbles himself will be exalted. But woe to you, scribes and Pharisees, hypocrites! For you shut the kingdom of heaven in people's faces. For you neither enter yourselves nor allow those who would enter to go in. Woe to you, scribes and Pharisees, hypocrites! For you travel across sea and land to make a single proselyte, and when he becomes a proselyte, you make him twice as much a child of hell as yourselves. Woe to you, blind guides, who say, 'If anyone swears by the temple, it is nothing, but if anyone swears by the gold of the temple, he is bound by his oath." You blind fools! For which is greater, the gold or the temple that has made the gold sacred? And you say, "If anyone swears by the altar, it is nothing, but

The wonderful saints of heaven open the gates to heaven. One saint you might have heard of is good Peter. "Come to My rest," is God's way of getting the master key to open. Then good Peter says, "This is God's child. Into His rest." "Smile," is what my good, wonderful Jesus says to them. In the walk to heaven many are scared they won't make the list. That's why Jesus tells them to smile. Talking they ask, "When do I see my loved ones?" "Over there," Jesus tells them. There is so much crying joy that it's their family. Talking to pour out news, that is what they do. Just the love is felt.

The rays of love we want to get have sort of a gate throughout heaven. The gate is sort of a winding fence that takes us to Him. The gate has prayers coming out of it. The road prayers take is first to the workers and then to the gate. The gate speaks the love that's in the prayer. It is how all saints hear the walks of those they love. That's what made my Esther hear me.

Heaven makes the most pristine free press. The love that we do is heralded to the saints to show what good is working from love. Jokes about good that was more than what someone prayed for are told when their stories are talked about. "Funny! Doubt they prayed that." Heckles are when good is left out of the story. Most tell heroic stories. Knowledge twists everything to tell the story of God's main thought, we love because He first loved us.[205]

Sometimes the angels took me to Mary, the Lord's mother. Mary is the proud saint of heaven. The reason she is proud is because she kindly follows her son. The way Jesus honors her is as the apple of His eye. The beauty of her heart is His heart in her. Mary is the one who walked me to my Heavenly Father. With my little hand she made me comfortable to be present in God's LIGHT. His bigness and LIGHT all cover heaven. Mostly God is clear. Mostly God is WHITE. The WHITE is LIGHT opening to all power. The way it manifests looks like wonderful pure holiness. The WHITE powers even the dark, just as the Spirit hovers over all He has yet to give life to. His star arms reach to the greatest stars. He makes them seem tiny. He makes me seem raw in my heart. He wants so much to talk to me. But I can't hear Him with all the angels. I wanted to get on my feet. But all I wanted was lost in the presence of His absolute glory. He gently helps me to my knees to listen. He

---

if anyone swears by the gift that is on the altar, he is bound by his oath." You blind men! For which is greater, the gift or the altar that makes the gift sacred? So whoever swears by the altar swears by it and by everything on it. And whoever swears by the temple swears by it and by him who dwells in it. And whoever swears by heaven swears by the throne of God and by him who sits upon it. Woe to you, scribes and Pharisees, hypocrites! For you tithe mint and dill and cumin, and have neglected the weightier matters of the law: justice and mercy and faithfulness. These you ought to have done, without neglecting the others. You blind guides, straining out a gnat and swallowing a camel! Woe to you, scribes and Pharisees, hypocrites! For you clean the outside of the cup and the plate, but inside they are full of greed and self-indulgence. You blind Pharisee! First clean the inside of the cup and the plate, that the outside also may be clean. Woe to you, scribes and Pharisees, hypocrites! For you are like whitewashed tombs, which outwardly appear beautiful, but within are full of dead people's bones and all uncleanness. So you also outwardly appear righteous to others, but within you are full of hypocrisy and lawlessness. Woe to you, scribes and Pharisees, hypocrites! For you build the tombs of the prophets and decorate the monuments of the righteous, saying, "If we had lived in the days of our fathers, we would not have taken part with them in shedding the blood of the prophets." Thus you witness against yourselves that you are sons of those who murdered the prophets. Fill up, then, the measure of your fathers. You serpents, you brood of vipers, how are you to escape being sentenced to hell? — Matthew 23:1-33

What good is it, my brothers and sisters, if someone claims to have faith but has no deeds? Can such faith save them? Suppose a brother or a sister is without clothes and daily food. If one of you says to them, "Go in peace; keep warm and well fed," but does nothing about their physical needs, what good is it? In the same way, faith by itself, if it is not accompanied by action, is dead. But someone will say, "You have faith; I have deeds." Show me your faith without deeds, and I will show you my faith by my deeds. You believe that there is one God. Good! Even the demons believe that—and shudder. You foolish person, do you want evidence that faith without deeds is useless? Was not our father Abraham considered righteous for what he did when he offered his son Isaac on the altar? You see that his faith and his actions were working together, and his faith was made complete by what he did. And the scripture was fulfilled that says, "Abraham believed God, and it was credited to him as righteousness," and he was called God's friend. You see that a person is considered righteous by what they do and not by faith alone. — James 2:14-24

is miles in ways that are not able to be explained. He reveals parts of Himself to the angels, but really we only see a glimpse. Our hearing can't even handle His voice. Jesus said when you really see Him, life is how life should have been. [206]

In heaven is a place so magnificent. The wonder of the place is the work inside it. It is like a windmill that spins to generate ideas. On the windmill small tails spin off and spark someone with an idea. Most of the ideas are developed inside. Staying at the lab inside, saints with good knowledge prove to God their ideas to give to people on earth. The awesome light that comes from the sparks is wonderful to watch.

All the jobs in heaven tie to what we loved on earth. The trust in God that He lets what made us happy be what we do in Heaven really shows how much He loves us. We are like pistons that fire to give God glory. The trials that we endured go to build our homes. The love we gave works to produce our gardens that overflow with good fruit. In waters that run throughout heaven lost good that love did streams through.

I most yearn to tell about little ones. Talking to them I saw the worth of the soul that's perfect, without sin. Let this be foreign to us - that we allow children to have souls but not live. Make life to be most important to us. I must tell you this - The angels of children see the face of God. He rallies to hear their prayers. [207] That woman who lied inside Jericho is wanting you to know it is her job to watch over them for you. [208]

I wish I had better words to tell about the Holy Spirit. He lives in hearts hoping to be used. He lives to help us. How He gives us strength is praying in love to Him.[209] Meals have life in them. The Holy Spirit is life giving too. Freedom is in prayer to the Holy Spirit. That freedom is the wind of His strength in your love and belief. It gives Him joy to give us His strength. Do pray to hear His voice. He is balled up inside of those of those who love Jesus. He is the Maker inside our hearts.

Of all the wonders that made me praise Jesus it was the masterful throne He sat on. It reached to places I couldn't see. Dwelling that throne was Jesus.[210] Opening and closing, the angels worshipped with their wings. In song they would sing of His majesty, making heaven more wonderful than good trees that sing on earth. Trees tell stories of His Kingdom that has to come. Trees talk to each other saying, "Glory to our Lord, Maker of Heaven and earth!" Then the wings that don't open are turned to lovingly rear their wings to cover the walk to His wonderful love that spills from Him. [211]

---

[206] And the foundations of the thresholds shook at the voice of him who called, and the house was filled with smoke. And I said: "Woe is me! For I am lost; for I am a man of unclean lips, and I dwell in the midst of a people of unclean lips; for my eyes have seen the King, the Lord of hosts!" - Isaiah 6:4-5

[207] See that you do not despise one of these little ones. For I tell you that in heaven their angels always see the face of my Father who is in heaven. —Matthew 18:10

[208] Joshua 2, Matthew 1:5, Hebrews 11:3, James 2:25 — passages about Rahab, her faith, and God's blessing on her

[209] Likewise the Spirit helps us in our weakness. For we do not know what to pray for as we ought, but the Spirit himself intercedes for us with groanings too deep for words. And he who searches hearts knows what is the mind of the Spirit, because the Spirit intercedes for the saints according to the will of God. — Romans 8:26-27

And I will ask the Father, and he will give you another Helper, to be with you forever, even the Spirit of truth, whom the world cannot receive, because it neither sees him nor knows him. You know him, for he dwells with you and will be in you... But the Helper, the Holy Spirit, whom the Father will send in my name, he will teach you all things and bring to your remembrance all that I have said to you. Peace I leave with you; my peace I give to you. Not as the world gives do I give to you. Let not your hearts be troubled, neither let them be afraid. —John 14:15-16, 26

[210] Then I saw a great white throne and him who was seated on it. From his presence earth and sky fled away, and no place was found for them. — Revelation 20:11

[211] Then I looked, and I heard the voice of many angels around the throne and the living creatures and the elders; and the number of them was myriads of myriads, and thousands of thousands, saying with a loud voice, "Worthy is the Lamb that was slain to receive power and riches and wisdom and might and honor and glory and blessing." And every created thing which is in heaven and on the earth and under the earth and on the sea, and all things in them, I heard saying, "To Him who sits on the throne, and to the Lamb, be blessing and honor and glory and dominion forever and ever." — Revelation 5:11-13

In the year that King Uzziah died I saw the Lord sitting upon a throne, high and lifted up; and the train of his robe filled the temple. Above him stood the seraphim. Each had six wings: with two he covered his face, and with two he covered his feet, and with two he flew. And one called to another and said: "Holy, holy, holy is the Lord of hosts; the whole earth is full of his glory!" — Isaiah 6:1-3

74

The BOOK of Life

"God made man because God loves stories."
— Elie Wiesel

A river of fire was flowing
And coming out from before Him;
Thousands upon thousands were attending Him,
And myriads upon myriads were standing before Him;
The court sat in judgment, And the books were opened.
— Daniel 7:10

The BOOK of Life, it is God's will. Power to do anything is in the BOOK. He wants best for it to be heard that He is all good and LOVE, more than we think. He is good that takes rotten to make into LOVE. Stories too many, tell what our Holy Father has done, master the art of making good from bad.

(At that moment as Houston spelled, I suddenly started choking on nothing at all. I recovered, but it took my breath for too long and frightened me. I looked at Houston. "What was that?" Houston spelled, "It was a demon." "I forgot to pray!" So we prayed. Houston spelled, "Good work. The angels said they love you so much. Good stopping to pray." "How many angels are there here?" I asked curiously. Houston spelled, "So many to really count would not be possible. Something to tell you. God told me to tell you. 'You're writing a book to save lives, feeling so much love for others, and how you gave up your money to others has taken talk of you to Me. That will tell of your good love so please tell about Mine.'")

He rests not. Believe that. LOVE stops not. Go to Him. Good long overdue comes to rest on those He loves. All that Jesus took to Golgotha is in the BOOK. Hate thinks that poor makes men put their trust in money. In truth it is poor us that trusts money instead of praying to Him. Hate thinks that love stops us from doing what God wants for us. It is us, of course, that makes love more our goal. Most rotten things come from love of money and love of love. Hope then comes to give LOVE to men.

All the works of God are in the BOOK.[212] Good and bad. Love and hate. Hope and fear. Poor and rich. Work and play. Music and sounds too horrible. Most love stories with a good ending. This has one. Too

---

[212] And I saw the dead, great and small, standing before the throne, and books were opened. Then another book was opened, which is the book of life. And the dead were judged by what was written in the books, according to what they had done. And the sea gave up the dead who were in it, Death and Hades gave up the dead who were in them, and they were judged, each one of them, according to what they had done. Then Death and Hades were thrown into the lake of fire. This is the second death, the lake of fire. And if anyone's name was not found written in the book of life, he was thrown into the lake of fire. — Revelation 20:12-15

suffering in the world. War has taken prayer to Me to force power to My footstool. Trouble too great has taken My TRUTH to the corners of My world. HOPE used grief to pour My WORD into the hearts of My children. HOPE used prayer to pour My WORD to Me. HOPE held the TRUTH in their hearts like a song to Me. Believe the talk that what I have taken to the BOOK is to force wonders to happen.

As all men are talking the words are written in the BOOK. It is living and life that are pouring from the BOOK. For good to win, LOVE made the fall for God to read the WORD to take off the seals. That, the angels told me, took place when LOVE gave the world life, at His death.[213] All the words flow from Him finding their position to hear what to do, putting on LOVE and working to power good. The BOOK takes up heaven with the words taking to the angels to find their position. Hate fights the angels to prevent the works from getting to their place. Prayer protects the works of God. Prayer stops hate and gives the angels power to get His works to their place.[214]

All searching for the truth of God brings LOVE to our hearts.

Pave. We think we really pave the way of our lives. Stopping the will of God, we war to pave our own way. That is war to stop His will. LOVE too, must go to war to work His will in us. Would our war of wills all muster what we want? All our pushing to work our own way paves God's will, not ours. In spite of us, His good pours through the battles for thine or mine. The BOOK of life, His will, is always working our will to lord ourselves to carry out His will to work our good.[215]

LOVE talks to people trying to pave their own way, telling them what all faith can do when they pour out their will to Him. Applying His will to ours is how to pour His life into our own. Life takes what we love then presses us to give that up. It takes the outpouring of our will to give up fear. When fear is gone, good places uncovered store all His power. Hope then works like a raft to free us to love all that He loves. And the LORD awakens our souls for the purpose that flows from the BOOK of Life.

Peace shall root in your heart.

Most everything is pieces and when they come together our God powers them to work something miraculous.[216] LOVE too great with forces that are faith say to LOVE, piece these loose pieces together. The

---

[213] Then I saw in the right hand of him who was seated on the throne a scroll written within and on the back, sealed with seven seals. And I saw a mighty angel proclaiming with a loud voice, "Who is worthy to open the scroll and break its seals?" And no one in heaven or on earth or under the earth was able to open the scroll or to look into it, and I began to weep loudly because no one was found worthy to open the scroll or to look into it. And one of the elders said to me, "Weep no more; behold, the Lion of the tribe of Judah, the Root of David, has conquered, so that he can open the scroll and its seven seals." And between the throne and the four living creatures and among the elders I saw a Lamb standing, as though it had been slain, with seven horns and with seven eyes, which are the seven spirits of God sent out into all the earth. And he went and took the scroll from the right hand of him who was seated on the throne. And when he had taken the scroll, the four living creatures and the twenty-four elders fell down before the Lamb, each holding a harp, and golden bowls full of incense, which are the prayers of the saints. And they sang a new song, saying, "Worthy are you to take the scroll and to open its seals, for you were slain, and by your blood you ransomed people for God from every tribe and language and people and nation, and you have made them a kingdom and priests to our God, and they shall reign on the earth." Then I looked, and I heard around the throne and the living creatures and the elders the voice of many angels, numbering myriads of myriads and thousands of thousands, saying with a loud voice, "Worthy is the Lamb who was slain, to receive power and wealth and wisdom and might and honor and glory and blessing!" And I heard every creature in heaven and on earth and under the earth and in the sea, and all that is in them, saying, "To him who sits on the throne and to the Lamb be blessing and honor and glory and might forever and ever!" And the four living creatures said, "Amen!" and the elders fell down and worshiped. — Revelations 5:6-14

[214] Bless the Lord, O you his angels, you mighty ones who do his word, obeying the voice of his word! Bless the Lord, all his hosts, his ministers, who do his will! Bless the Lord, all his works, in all places of his dominion. Bless the Lord, O my soul! — Psalm 103:20-22

[215] The heart of man plans his way, but the LORD establishes his steps. — Proverbs 16:9

[216] All things work together for the good of those who love God and are called according to His purpose. — Romans 8:28

formation of loose pieces starts moving so wonderfully. What we hope speaks to LOVE trying to put strength to our words. Nowhere hovers like a tower of thoughts filled with the power of unbelief, like an utter prison working to slow the pieces to stop LOVE.[217] I describe Satan as Nowhere. He is the opposite of God. God is everything. Satan is rooted in nothingness. It is the work of Satan working to hoard power to destroy people by killing their faith.

All the things I see have force and power. Time looks like twisted power and force going in a circle towards eternity. Windows to time let me talk to angels in other places. All that has space is polarized inside time. Twisted, all that is time twists forces together with LOVE.[218] Gears too good to explain, take real words that are prayed to God and inlay them into energy, good energy, and angels use these prayers with energy to work His plan. Our prayers pour power to the angels and they calm the attacks on us. Don't war to fight Satan. Just make His LOVE the most important thing.

That's more than good. That's what I see.

Malevolence and love fight for us. That's going on inside us and around us. He gave me a task, to tell what I've seen, to tell of His love, to be His herald. I'm, without any doubt, friends with Jesus. I don't want anyone to die not being His friend. Most importantly hear this, anything is possible if you believe.[219]

---

[217] But let him ask in faith, with no doubting, for the one who doubts is like a wave of the sea that is driven and tossed by the wind. For that person must not suppose that he will receive anything from the Lord; he is a double-minded man, unstable in all his ways. — James 1:6-8

[218] But do not overlook this one fact, beloved, that with the Lord one day is as a thousand years, and a thousand years as one day. — 2 Peter 3:8

[19] And Jesus said to him, "If you can'! All things are possible for one who believes." — Mark 9:23

But Jesus looked at them and said, "With man this is impossible, but with God all things are possible." — Matthew 19:26

For nothing will be impossible with God. — Luke 1:37

And without faith it is impossible to please him, for whoever would draw near to God must believe that he exists and that he rewards those who seek him. — Hebrews 11:6

Whoever believes in me, as Scripture has said, rivers of living water will flow from within them. — John 7:38

Jesus said to them, "I am the bread of life; whoever comes to me shall not hunger, and whoever believes in me shall never thirst." — John 6:35

Jesus said to her, "I am the resurrection and the life. Whoever believes in me, though he die, yet shall he live." — John 11:25-26

"Go," said Jesus. "Your faith has healed you." Immediately he received his sight and followed Jesus along the road. — Mark 10:52

Truly I tell you, if you have faith as small as a mustard seed, you can say to this mountain, "Move from here to there," and it will move. Nothing will be impossible for you. — Matthew 17:20

For she said, "If I touch even his garments, I will be made well." And immediately the flow of blood dried up, and she felt in her body that she was healed of her disease. And Jesus, perceiving in himself that power had gone out from him, immediately turned about in the crowd and said, "Who touched my garments?" And his disciples said to him, "You see the crowd pressing around you, and yet you say, 'Who touched me?'" And he looked around to see who had done it. But the woman, knowing what had happened to her, came in fear and trembling and fell down before him and told him the whole truth. And he said to her, "Daughter, your faith has made you well; go in peace, and be healed of your disease." — Mark 5:28-34

And Jesus answered them, "Truly, I say to you, if you have faith and do not doubt, you will not only do what has been done to the fig tree, but even if you say to this mountain, 'Be taken up and thrown into the sea,' it will happen. And whatever you ask in prayer, you will receive, if you have faith." — Matthew 21:21-22

Therefore I tell you, whatever you ask for in prayer, believe that you have received it, and it will be yours. — Mark 11:24

Then Jesus told him, "Because you have seen me, you have believed; blessed are those who have not seen and yet have believed." — John 20:29

Yet to all who did receive him, to those who believed in his name, he gave the right to become children of God. — John 1:12

Then Jesus answered her, "O woman, great is your faith! Be it done for you as you desire." And her daughter was healed instantly. — Matthew 15:28

For we walk by faith, not by sight. — 2 Corinthians 5:7

I have fought the good fight, I have finished the race, I have kept the faith. — 2 Timothy 4:7

75

*"I knew Bob Dylan had been searching for the truth for years.
And anyone who really wants the truth ends up at Jesus."*
— Johnny Cash

Man Comes Around[220]

*"And I heard, as it were, the noise of thunder,
One of the four beasts saying,
'Come and see.' and I saw, and behold a white horse"
There's a man goin' 'round takin' names,
And he decides who to free and who to blame
Everybody won't be treated all the same[221]
There'll be a golden ladder reachin' down[222]
When the man comes around*

*The hairs on your arm will stand up[223]
At the terror in each sip and in each sup
Will you partake of that last offered cup[224]
Or disappear into the potter's ground?[225]
When the man comes around*

*Hear the trumpets hear the pipers[226]
One hundred million angels singin'[227]
Multitudes are marchin' to the big kettledrum
Voices callin', voices cryin'
Some are born and some are dyin'[228]
It's alpha and omega's kingdom come[229]*

*And the whirlwind is in the thorn tree
The virgins are all trimming their wicks[230]
The whirlwind is in the thorn tree
It's hard for thee to kick against the pricks*

*Till Armageddon no shalam, no shalom[230]
Then the father hen will call his chickens home[231]
The wise man will bow down before the throne
And at his feet they'll cast their golden crowns[232]
When the man comes around*

Whoever is unjust let him be unjust still
Whoever is righteous let him be righteous still
Whoever is filthy let him be filthy still[232]
Listen to the words long written down
When the man comes around

Hear the trumpets hear the pipers
One hundred million angels singin'
Multitudes are marchin' to the big kettledrum
Voices callin', voices cryin'
Some are born and some are dyin'
It's alpha and omega's kingdom come

And the whirlwind is in the thorn tree
The virgins are all trimming their wicks
The whirlwind is in the thorn trees
It's hard for thee to kick against the prick

In measured hundredweight and penny pound
When the man comes around

"And I heard a voice in the midst of the four beasts
And I looked, and behold a pale horse
And his name that sat on him was death,
and hell followed with him"[235]

[220] *Man Comes Around*; Words & Music y John R. Cash.© 2002 Song Of Cash, Inc. All Rights Administered by BMG Rights Management (US) LLC All Rights Reserved Used by Permission *Reprinted by Permission of Hal Leonard LLC* .

And behold, with the clouds of heaven there came one like a son of man, and he came to the Ancient of Days and was presented before him. And to him was given dominion and glory and a kingdom, that all peoples, nations, and languages should serve him; his dominion is an everlasting dominion, which shall not pass away, and his kingdom one that shall not be destroyed. — Daniel 7:13-14

[221] And I saw the dead, great and small, standing before the throne, and books were opened. Then another book was opened, which is the Book of Life. And the dead were judged by what was written in the books, according to what they had done. — Revelation 20:12

[222] And he dreamed, and behold, there was a ladder set up on the earth, and the top of it reached to heaven. And behold, the angels of God were ascending and descending on it! And behold, the Lord stood above it and said, "I am the Lord, the God of Abraham your father and the God of Isaac." — Genesis 28:12

[223] Then the kings of the earth and the great ones and the generals and the rich and the powerful, and everyone, slave and free, hid themselves in the caves and among the rocks of the mountains, calling to the mountains and rocks, "Fall on us and hide us from the face of him who is seated on the throne, and from the wrath of the Lamb, for the great day of their wrath has come, and who can stand?" — Revelation 6:15-17

And another angel, a third, followed them, saying with a loud voice, "If anyone worships the best and its image and receives a mark on his forehead or on his hand, he also will drink the wine of God's wrath, poured full strength into the cup of his anger, and he will be tormented with fire and sulfure in the presence of the holy angels and in the presence of the Lamb.— Revelations 14:9-10

[224] And he took the cup, and gave thanks, and gave it to them, sying, Drink ye all of it; For this is my blood of the new testament, which is shed for many for the remission of sins. — Matthew 26:27-28

[225] Then when Judas, his betrayer, saw that Jesus was condemned, he changed his mind and brought back the thirty pieces of silver to the chief priests and the elders, saying, "I have sinned by betraying innocent blood." They said, "What is that to us? See to it yourself." And throwing down the pieces of silver into the temple, he departed, and he went and hanged himself. But the chief priests, taking the pieces of silver, said, "It is not lawful to put them into the treasury, since it is blood money." So they took counsel and bought with them the potter's field as a burial place for strangers. Therefore that field has been called the Field of Blood to this day. Then was fulfilled what had been spoken by the prophet Jeremiah, saying, "And they took the thirty pieces of silver, the price of him on whom a price had been set by some of the sons of Israel, and they gave them for the potter's field, as the Lord directed me." — Matthew 27:3-10

Then the Lord said to me, "Throw it to the potter"— the lordly price at which I was priced by them. So I took the thirty pieces of silver and threw them into the house of the Lord, to the potter. — Zechariah 11:13

[226] Then I looked, and I heard an eagle crying with a loud voice as it flew directly overhead, "Woe, woe, woe to those who dwell on the earth, at the blasts of the other trumpets that the three angels are about to blow!" — Revelation 8:13

[227] Then I looked, and I heard around the throne and the living creatures and the elders the voice of many angels, numbering myriads of myriads and thousands of thousands, saying with a loud voice, "Worthy is the Lamb who was slain, to receive power and wealth and wisdom and might and honor and glory and blessing!" — Revelation 5:11-12

[228] Jesus answered him, "Truly, truly, I say to you, unless one is born again he cannot see the kingdom of God." — John 3:3

Not everyone who says to me, "Lord, Lord," will enter the kindgom of heaven, but the one who does the will of my Father who is in heaven. On that day many will say to me, "Lord, Lord, did we not prophesy in your name, and cast out demons in your name, and do many mighty works in your name?" And then will I declare to them, I never knew you; depart from me, you workers of lawlessness." — Matthew 7:22-23

[229] Our Father in heaven, hallowed be Thy name. Thy kingdom come, Thy will be done, on earth as it is in heaven. — Matthew 6:9-10

"I am the Alpha and the Omega," says the Lord God, "who is and who was and who is to come, the Almighty."— Revelation 1:8

And he said to me, "It is done! I am the Alpha and the Omega, the beginning and the end. To the thirsty I will give from the spring of the water of life without payment. — Revelation 21:6

I am the Alpha and the Omega, the first and the last, the beginning and the end." — Revelation 22:13

[230] At that time the kingdom of heaven will be like ten virgins who took their lamps and went out to meet the bridegroom. Five of them were foolish and five were wise. The foolish ones took their lamps but did not take any oil with them. The wise ones, however, took oil in jars along with their lamps. The bridegroom was a long time in coming, and they all became drowsy and fell asleep. At midnight the cry rang out: "Here's the bridegroom! Come out to meet him!" Then all the virgins woke up and trimmed their lamps. The foolish ones said to the wise, "Give us some of your oil; our lamps are going out." "No," they replied, "there may not be enough for both us and you. Instead, go to those who sell oil and buy some for yourselves." But while they were on their way to buy the oil, the bridegroom arrived. The virgins who were ready went in with him to the wedding banquet. And the door was shut Later the others also came. "Lord, Lord," they said, "open the door for us!" But he replied, "Truly I tell you, I don't know you." Therefore keep watch, because you do not know the day or the hour. — Matthew 25: 1-13

[231] And they assembled them at the place that in Hebrew is called Armageddon. — Revelation 16:16

[232] Truly, I say to you, all these things will come upon this generation. "O Jerusalem, Jerusalem, the city that kills the prophets and stones those who are sent to it! How often would I have gathered your children together as a hen gathers her brood under her wings, and you were not willing! — Matthew 23:36-37

[233] And whenever the living creatures give glory and honor and thanks to him who is seated on the throne, who lives forever and ever, the twenty-four elders fall down before him who is seated on the throne and worship him who lives forever and ever. They cast their crowns before the throne, saying "Worthy are you, our Lord and God, to receive glory and honor and power for you created all things, and by your will they existed and were created." - Revelation 4:9-11

[234] Let the evildoer still do evil, and the filthy still be filthy, and the righteous still do right, and the holy still be holy." — Revelation 22:11

[235] Then I saw heaven opened, and behold, a white horse! The one sitting on it is called Faithful and True, and in righteousness he judges and makes war. - Revelation 19:11

I watched as the Lamb opened the first of the seven seals. Then I heard one of the four living creatures say in a voice like thunder, "Come!" I looked, and there before me was a white horse! Its rider held a bow, and he was given a crown, and he rode out as a conqueror bent on conquest. When the Lamb opened the second seal, I heard the second living creature say, "Come!" Then another horse came out, a fiery red one. Its rider was given power to take peace from the earth and to make people kill each other. To him was given a large sword. When the Lamb opened the third seal, I heard the third living creature say, "Come!" I looked, and there before me was a black horse! Its rider was holding a pair of scales in his hand. Then I heard what sounded like a voice among the four living creatures, saying, "Two pounds of wheat for a day's wages, and six pounds of barley for a day's wages, and do not damage the oil and the wine!" When the Lamb opened the fourth seal, I heard the voice of the fourth living creature say, "Come!" I looked, and there before me was a pale horse! Its rider was named Death, and Hades was following close behind him. They were given power over a fourth of the earth to kill by sword, famine and plague, and by the wild beasts of the earth. When he opened the fifth seal, I saw under the altar the souls of those who had been slain because of the word of

God and the testimony they had maintained. They called out in a loud voice, "How long, Sovereign Lord, holy and true, until you judge the inhabitants of the earth and avenge our blood?" Then each of them was given a white robe, and they were told to wait a little longer, until the full number of their fellow servants, their brothers and sisters, were killed just as they had been. I watched as he opened the sixth seal. There was a great earthquake. The sun turned black like sackcloth made of goat hair, the whole moon turned blood red, and the stars in the sky fell to earth, as figs drop from a fig tree when shaken by a strong wind. The heavens receded like a scroll being rolled up, and every mountain and island was removed from its place. Then the kings of the earth, the princes, the generals, the rich, the mighty, and everyone else, both slave and free, hid in caves and among the rocks of the mountains. They called to the mountains and the rocks, "Fall on us and hide us from the face of him who sits on the throne and from the wrath of the Lamb! For the great day of their wrath has come, and who can withstand it?" — Revelation 6

For God so loved the world, that he gave his only Son,
that whoever believes in him should not perish but have eternal life.
For God did not send his Son into the world to condemn the world,
but in order that the world might be saved through him.
— John 3:16-17

The Lord is not slow to fulfill his promise as some count slowness,
but is patient toward you, not wishing that any should perish,
but that all should reach repentance.
— 2 Peter 3:9